Principles of Distributed Database Systems

Second Edition

M. Tamer Özsu
University of Alberta
Edmonton, Canada

Patrick Valduriez
INRIA
Paris, France

Prentice Hall
Upper Saddle River, New Jersey   07458

Library of Congress Cataloging-in-Publication Data

Ozsu, M. Tamer
Principles of distributed database systems /
by M. Tamer Ozsu, Patrick Valduriez – 2nd ed.
    p. cm.
  Includes bibliographical references and index.
  ISBN 0-13-659707-6
  1. Distributed databases. I. Valduriez, Patrick. II. Title.
QA76.9.D3 0956   1999
005.758—dc21   98–11901
                                                  CIP

Publisher: *Alan Apt*
Development editor: *Sondra Chavez*
Editor-in-chief: *Marcia Horton*
Production editor: *Edward DeFilippis*
Managing editor: *Eileen Clark*
Manufacturing buyer: *Pat Brown*
Director of production and manufacturing: *David W. Riccardi*
Cover art director: *Jayne Conte*
Editorial Assistant: *Toni Holm*
Composition: *PreTEX, Inc.*

Printed in the United States of America

10 9 8 7 6

ISBN   0-13-659707-6

PRENTICE-HALL INTERNATIONAL (UK) LIMITED, *LONDON*
PRENTICE-HALL OF AUSTRALIA PTY. LIMITED, *SYDNEY*
PRENTICE-HALL CANADA INC., *TORONTO*
PRENTICE-HALL HISPANOAMERICANA, S.A., *MEXICO*
PRENTICE-HALL OF INDIA PRIVATE LIMITED, *NEW DELHI*
PRENTICE-HALL OF JAPAN, INC., *TOKYO*
PEARSON EDUCATION ASIA PTE. LTD., *SINGAPORE*
EDITORA PRENTICE-HALL DO BRASIL, LTDA., *RIO DE JANEIRO*

CONTENTS

PREFACE TO THE SECOND EDITION

Many things have changed since the publication of the first edition of this book in 1991. At the time, we reported projections that, by 1998, centralized database managers (DBMSs) would be an "antique curiosity" and most organizations would move towards distributed database managers. Distribution was slowly starting and "client/server" had just started to enter our daily jargon. These systems were generally multiple client/single server systems in which the distribution was mostly in terms of functionality, not data. If multiple servers were used, clients were responsible for managing the connections to these servers. Thus, transparency of access was not widely supported, and each client had to "know" the location of the required data. The distribution of data among multiple servers was very primitive; systems did not support fragmentation or replication of data. Systems of the time were "homogeneous" in that each system could manage only data that were stored in its own database, with no linkage to other repositories.

Things have changed dramatically since then. Many vendors are much closer to achieving true distribution in their development cycle. Client/server systems remain the preferred solution in many cases, but they are much more sophisticated. For example, today's client/server systems provide significant transparency in accessing data from multiple servers, support distributed transactions to facilitate transparency, and execute queries over (horizontally) fragmented data. Further, new systems implement both synchronous and asynchronous replication protocols, and many vendors have introduced gateways to access other databases. In addition, significant achievements have taken place in the development and deployment of parallel database servers. Object database managers have entered the marketplace and have found a niche market in some classes of applications which are inherently distributed.

In parallel with these developments in the database system front, there have been phenomenal changes in the computer networking infrastructure that supports these systems. The relatively slow (10Mbit/sec) Ethernet has been replaced as the de facto local area network standard by much faster networks (FDDI or switched Ethernet) operating at around 100Mbit/sec, and broadband networks (particularly the ATM technology) have been deployed for both local area and wide area networking. These networks, coupled with very low overhead networking protocols, such as SCI, reduce the differences between local area and wide area networks (other than latency considerations) and potentially eliminate the network as the major performance bottleneck. This, in turn, requires us to review our system development assumptions and performance tuning criteria. Use of the Internet—which is basically a heterogeneous network with links of varying capacities and capabilities—has exploded.

There is clearly a technology push/application pull in effect with respect to distributed DBMS development: new applications are requiring changes in DBMS capabilities, and new technological developments are making these changes possible. With these developments, it was time to prepare a revised second edition of the book. In the process, we have retained the fundamental characteristics and key features of the book as outlined in the Preface to the first edition. However, the material has been heavily edited. Every chapter has been revised—some in fundamental ways, others more superficially. The major changes are the following:

1. The query processing/optimization chapters (Chapters 7–9) have been revised to focus on the techniques employed in commercial systems. New algorithms, such as randomized search strategies, are now included.

2. The transaction management chapters (Chapters 10–12) now include material on advanced transaction models and workflows.

3. Chapter 13, which focused on the relationship of distributed DBMSs and distributed operating systems, has been dropped and some of the material is incorporated into the relevant chapters.

4. The first edition contained a chapter (Chapter 15) which discussed current issues at the time—parallel DBMSs, distributed knowledge-base systems (mainly deductive DBMSs), and distributed object DBMSs. In the intervening years, two of these topics have matured and become major forces in their own rights, while the third (deductive databases) has not achieved the same prominence. In this edition, we devote full chapters to parallel DBMSs (Chapter 13) and distributed object DBMSs (Chapter 14), and have dropped deductive DBMSs.

5. Following the same approach, we introduce a new chapter devoted to current issues (Chapter 16). This chapter now includes sections on data warehousing (from a distributed data management perspective), World Wide Web and databases, push-based technologies, and mobile DBMSs.

6. The chapter on multidatabase systems (Chapter 15 in the current edition) has been revised to include a discussion of general interoperability issues and distributed object platforms such as OMA/CORBA and DCOM/OLE.

We are quite satisfied with the result, which represents a compromise between our desire to address new and emerging issues, and maintain the main characteristic of the book in addressing the principles of distributed data management. Certain chapters, in particular Chapters 15 and 16, require further depth, but those will be topics of future editions.

The guide to reading the book, introduced in the Preface to the first edition, is still valid in general terms. However, we now discuss, in Chapter 3, the relationship between distributed DBMSs and the new networking technologies. Thus, this chapter no longer serves simply as background and should be read (at least the relevant sections) following Chapter 1.

We have set up a Web site to communicate with our readers. The site is at http://www.cs.ualberta.ca/~database/distdb.html. This site contains presentation slides that accompany the book as well as other information regarding the book's use as a textbook.

Many colleagues have helped with the revisions. Maggie Dunham and Nandid Soparkar provided detailed and early comments on the overall structure and content of the book. Maggie also provided input for the mobile database management section (Section 16.4). Ioannis Nikolaidis helped immensely with the revisions to Chapter 3—he made us rewrite that chapter three times. Jari Veijaleinen provided many exercises which have been incorporated into this edition. Esther Pacitti provided input for replication protocols. Peter Triantafillou provided material on this topic as well. Alexander Thomasian's input for performance evaluation work was invaluable, as was Elliot Moss's critical review of the nested transaction discussion in the transaction processing chapters. Mukesh Singhal advised us of the new advances in distributed deadlock management. Luc Bouganim contributed significantly to Chapter 13 on parallel DBMSs. Ken Barker and Kamalakar Karlapalem provided the material that formed the basis of distributed object database design in Chapter 14. Kaladhar Voruganti wrote the first draft of the architectural and system issues sections of Chapter 14. Randal Peters read Chapter 14 and forced us to revise many parts of it. The distributed garbage collection section of that chapter is based on a draft provided by Laurent Amsaleg and Michael Franklin. Amit Sheth provided input on the revised outline for Chapter 15. Asuman Dogac read the complete chapter and provided feedback. Mokrane Bouzeghoub and Eric Simon helped on the data warehouse section of Chapter 16. Dana Florescu, Alon Levy, Ioana Manolescu and Anthony Tomasic provided input for research prototypes in the section on Web and databases in Chapter 16. The material in push-based technologies section was reviewed (a number of times) by Stan Zdonik and Mike Franklin. Both of them also provided significant feedback about the characterization of data delivery alternatives. We are indebted to all of them, as well as to those who helped with the original edition of the book and whom we cite in the Preface to the First Edition. Many other colleagues have asked questions and provided suggestions over the years; unfortunately, we have not kept their names. Our thanks to everyone who has provided input. We look forward to receiving more suggestions on the second edition.

We have had very good luck with our editors at Prentice Hall. Our current editor, Alan Apt, and our development editor, Sondra Chavez, have been tremendously helpful in both pushing us forward and providing the necessary institutional support. Our production editors, Ed DeFelippis and Irwin Zucker, have managed the production process so that the production of earlier chapters could proceed in parallel with our writing of the later chapters. This allowed the revised edition to be ready within one year. Stephen Lee, as our copy editor, made the entire text significantly more readable. Anne Nield helped us in many ways—editing chapters, correcting the text and keeping us organized. Paul Iglinski wrote a number of scripts that helped immensely with cleaning up the bibliography. We thank them all.

M. Tamer Özsu (ozsu@cs.ualberta.ca)
Patrick Valduriez (Patrick.Valduriez@inria.fr)

PREFACE TO THE FIRST EDITION

Distributed database system technology is one of the major recent developments in the database systems area. There are claims that in the next ten years centralized database managers will be an "antique curiosity" and most organizations will move toward distributed database managers [Stonebraker, 1988, p. 189]. The intense interest in this subject in both the research community and the commercial marketplace certainly supports this claim. The extensive research activity in the last decade has generated results that now enable the introduction of commercial products into the marketplace. This book aims to introduce and explain the theory, algorithms, and methods that underly distributed database management systems (distributed DBMS). For the most part, our presentation emphasizes the principles that guide the design of such systems more than their use. However, the issues in designing a distributed database are also addressed.

With its emphasis on fundamentals, the book is meant to be used as a textbook for a one- or two-semester graduate-level course as well as a reference book. The material is currently being covered in a one-semester graduate course at the University of Alberta. If it is used in a two-semester course, the material can be complemented by current literature. The structure of the text also lends itself to be used as a companion text for undergraduate database courses. The key features of the text are as follows:

1. The book starts by placing the distributed database technology in its proper context vis-à-vis the distributed computing and database management technologies. The introductory chapters are also aimed at providing the necessary background in computer networks and in relational database systems that is necessary for following the subsequent material.

2. Coverage of each topic starts by an introductory overview that sets the framework and defines the problems that are addressed. The subsequent discussion elaborates these issues. In certain cases the introductory material is included within one chapter (e.g., Sections 5.1 and 5.2), whereas in others they are separated as independent chapters (e.g., Chapters 7 and 10). It is these parts

of the book, in addition to Chapter 1, that can be used to complement the
undergraduate courses in database systems.

3. In addition to covering matured technology, the book also discusses current
   research areas such as distributed data servers, distributed object-oriented
   databases, and distributed knowledge bases. Thus, it serves not only to describe the technology that has been developed during the past decade, but
   it also provides an introduction to the technology that the researchers will
   be working on during the next one. Furthermore, there is coverage of issues
   related to the integration of distributed database systems and distributed
   operating systems. These issues have to be topics of intense research and
   experimentation if distributed database managers are to provide the performance, functionality, and extensibility expected of them.

4. A database design of an engineering organization is used consistently throughout as an example. This consistency enables the development of topics in a
   systematic fashion. The only section where a different example is used is in
   the transaction management chapters (10 through 12), where we opt for an
   airline reservation system, which is a favorite example of the database community as well as being a major application domain for transaction-based
   systems.

5. The book is structured so that two different uses, as a textbook and as a reference material, can be accommodated. On the one hand, the topics (e.g., distributed database design, semantic data control, distributed query processing
   and distributed transaction management) are developed systematically with
   almost no forward referencing. The backward references are few and clearly
   marked. This enables its use as a textbook where issues can be developed
   one at a time based on one another. On the other hand, each topic is covered
   as a self-contained module to the extent that this is possible. Thus, readers
   who have the background can simply refer to the topics they are interested
   in. In this mode of use as a reference material, the only important backward
   references are to previous examples.

6. Exercises are at the end of most chapters. However, chapters that serve as
   an introduction to topics (Chapters 1 through 3, 7, and 10) or which cover
   discussion of issues (Chapters 4 and 13) do not contain exercises. Where
   available, the questions are classified with respect to their difficulty. The
   number of asterisks (*) in front of a question indicates their level of difficulty.

Organization of the Text

The organization of the book and the dependencies of the chapters are shown in the
following figure. The introductory chapter is followed by two chapters that provide
an overview of relational database technology and computer networks. If the reader
has the background, these chapters can be skipped without any effect on the rest

of the book. The only part of Chapter 2 that should be referenced is Example 2.1, which describes the engineering database example.

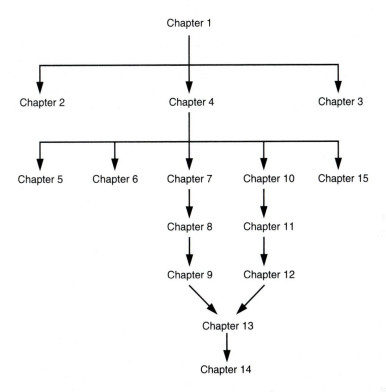

Figure 1. Organization of the Book

Chapter 4 covers the architectural issues, the types of transparencies that distributed DBMSs are supposed to provide and discusses the differences between what we consider distributed database systems and multidatabase systems. This separation is critical to the rest of the book; thus, this chapter should be covered. Most of the book addresses distributed database system issues; multidatabase issues are covered only in Chapter 14.

Chapter 5 describes the design of a distributed database. It is the only chapter of the book where we emphasize the use of a distributed DBMS rather than its development. A similar discussion relating to multidatabase systems is included in Chapter 14.

Chapter 6 covers a unique issue that is usually omitted from database textbooks—namely, semantic data control. Distributed semantic data control includes security aspects of distributed databases as well as integrity enforcement to ensure that the database is always consistent with respect to a set of semantic consistency rules.

Chapters 7 through 9 are devoted to a discussion of distributed query processing issues. The discussion starts with an introduction to the fundamental issues and the presentation of a methodology for carrying out this process. The following two chapters, on query decomposition and localization and distributed query optimization, discuss the steps of this methodology in more detail.

Chapters 10 through 12 are devoted to transaction management issues. The treatment is organized similar to query processing with an introductory chapter that defines the fundamental terms and presents the goals that transaction managers aim to achieve, and the subsequent chapters cover the two fundamental aspects of distributed transaction management: distributed concurrency control and the reliable execution of distributed transactions.

Chapter 13 is built on previous material, especially the distributed query processing and distributed transaction management issues, and the problems associated with implementing distributed DBMSs on top of distributed operating systems are discussed. This chapter also serves as a short introduction to operating systems issues for database researchers.

As we mentioned before, Chapter 14 is dedicated to a discussion of the issues related to multidatabase systems. They differ from what we call distributed database management environments in the high degree of autonomy that is associated with each data manager and their bottom-up design as opposed to the top-down approach utilized by distributed DBMSs. The treatment assumes knowledge of the related issued and solutions for distributed database systems.

Finally, Chapter 15 covers the current trends in distributed databases. Specifically, we address distributed data servers, distributed object-oriented databases, and distributed knowledge bases.

Acknowledgments

Sylvia Osborn read the entire manuscript and provided numerous suggestions. Her contributions to the text are invaluable. Janguk Kim reviewed the manuscript as well. A special thanks goes to both of them. Ahmed Kamal reviewed Chapter 3 and helped with the networking terminology. C. Mohan and Ahmed Elmagarmid provided critical comments on the transaction processing chapters. Ahmed, together with Amit Sheth, reviewed the multidatabase chapter and suggested many improvements. Ravi Krishnamurthy provided help on the query processing chapters, and Guy Lohman improved the precision of many aspects of the R* query optimizer. Eric Simon provided invaluable help on the semantic data control chapter.

The notes that form the basis of this book as well as the book's earlier versions were used in a graduate course on distributed database systems at the University of Alberta. The students who took this course in past years have tremendously helped its presentation. They debugged the text thoroughly and found subtle errors that could have otherwise gone unnoticed. We would like to extend to them our sincere appreciation for helping out as well as for putting up with the troubles of using a continuously changing set of notes as a textbook.

The graduate students in the Distributed Database Systems Group of the University of Alberta all made significant contributions to the text. The Ph.D. students, Ken Barker, Tse-Men Koon, Dave Straube and Randal Peters, all read parts of the manuscript and provided critical comments. The thesis of a former Ph.D. student, Abdel Farrag, provided important material for the transaction processing chapters. The works of M.Sc. students Christina Lau, Yan Li, David Meechan, and Mei-Fen Teo found their way into the book, especially in Chapter 13. Another M.Sc. student, Kok-Lung Wong, reviewed the distributed database design chapter and provided exercises for it. We thank them for all this effort over and above their own research.

The language of the text was edited by Suzanne Sauvé. If readers are not completely happy with some of the language in this edition, they should be grateful that they did not see the text before Suzanne went through it. The remaining errors are probably due to our stubbornness in not accepting some of her suggestions.

Throughout this effort, there was one person who maintained interest in the project perhaps even more than we did: our secretary Amanda Collins at the University of Alberta. She not only ably typed the text once, but then converted the full text to LaTeX. On top of all this, she kept pressing us to finish the writing so that she could start typing. We owe her a great deal for maintaining her enthusiasm and good nature even when things were not moving as smoothly as we all wanted.

M. Tamer Özsu would like to thank Lee White not only for creating an exciting environment within the Department of Computing Science at the University of Alberta during the period of writing this book, but also for the continuing friendship and many opportunities that he has provided over the years. Patrick Valduriez would like to thank Haran Boral and Georges Gardarin for their friendship and support as well as his colleagues of the System Architecture Group at MCC and the SABRE group at INRIA for the exceptional working environment.

We would like to thank our families. This project took valuable time away from them during the last four years. We appreciate their understanding and patience during this long period of time.

Another group who had to wait patiently during these years consists of our editors. We would like to thank Rick Williamson, for suggesting the project to us, and the editors at Prentice-Hall, Valerie Ashton, Marcia Horton and Thomas McElwee. They were all very patient and supportive. We would also like to acknowledge the professional help provided by our production editors, Christina Burghard and Jennifer Wenzel, during the production process.

To my family
and my parents
M.T.Ö.

To Esther, Sarah, Juliette,
and my parents
P.V.

Chapter 1

INTRODUCTION

Distributed database system (DDBS) technology is the union of what appear to be two diametrically opposed approaches to data processing: *database system* and *computer network* technologies. Database systems have taken us from a paradigm of data processing in which each application defined and maintained its own data (Figure 1.1) to one in which the data is defined and administered centrally (Figure 1.2). This new orientation results in *data independence*, whereby the application programs are immune to changes in the logical or physical organization of the data, and vice versa.

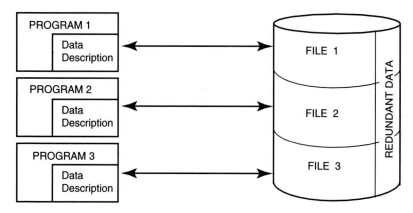

Figure 1.1. Traditional File Processing

One of the major motivations behind the use of database systems is the desire to integrate the operational data of an enterprise and to provide centralized, thus controlled access to that data. The technology of computer networks, on the other hand, promotes a mode of work that goes against all centralization efforts. At first glance it might be difficult to understand how these two contrasting approaches can possibly be synthesized to produce a technology that is more powerful and more promising than either one alone. The key to this understanding is the realization that the most important objective of the database technology is *integration*, not

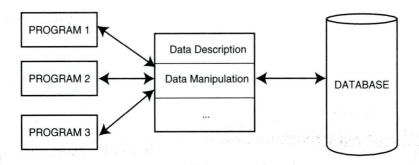

Figure 1.2. Database Processing

centralization. It is important to realize that either one of these terms does not necessarily imply the other. It is possible to achieve integration without centralization, and that is exactly what the distributed database technology attempts to achieve.

In this chapter we define the fundamental concepts and set the framework for discussing distributed databases. We start by examining distributed systems in general in order to clarify the role of database technology within distributed data processing, and then move on to topics that are more directly related to DDBS.

1.1 DISTRIBUTED DATA PROCESSING

The term *distributed processing* (or *distributed computing*) is probably the most abused term in computer science of the last couple of years. It has been used to refer to such diverse systems as multiprocessor systems, distributed data processing, and computer networks. This abuse has gone on to such an extent that the term *distributed processing* has sometimes been called "a concept in search of a definition and a name." Here are some of the other terms that have been used synonymously with *distributed processing*: distributed function, distributed computers or computing, networks, multiprocessors/multicomputers, satellite processing/satellite computers, backend processing, dedicated/special-purpose computers, time-shared systems, and functionally modular systems.

Obviously, some degree of distributed processing goes on in any computer system, even on single-processor computers. Starting with the second-generation computers, the central processing unit (CPU) and input/output (I/O) functions have been separated and overlapped. This separation and overlap can be considered as one form of distributed processing. However, it should be quite clear that what we would like to refer to as distributed processing, or distributed computing, has nothing to do with this form of distribution of functions in a single-processor computer system.

A term that has caused so much confusion is obviously quite difficult to define precisely. There have been numerous attempts to define what distributed processing is, and almost every researcher has come up with a definition. In this book we define distributed processing in such a way that it leads to a definition of what a distributed database system is. The working definition we use for a *distributed computing system* states that it is a number of autonomous processing elements (not necessarily homogeneous) that are interconnected by a computer network and that cooperate in performing their assigned tasks. The "processing element" referred to in this definition is a computing device that can execute a program on its own.

One fundamental question that needs to be asked is: What is being distributed? One of the things that might be distributed is the *processing logic*. In fact, the definition of a distributed computing system given above implicitly assumes that the processing logic or processing elements are distributed. Another possible distribution is according to *function*. Various functions of a computer system could be delegated to various pieces of hardware or software. A third possible mode of distribution is according to *data*. Data used by a number of applications may be distributed to a number of processing sites. Finally, *control* can be distributed. The control of the execution of various tasks might be distributed instead of being performed by one computer system. From the viewpoint of distributed database systems, these modes of distribution are all necessary and important. In the following sections we talk about these in more detail.

Distributed computing systems can be classified with respect to a number of criteria. Some of these criteria are as follows: degree of coupling, interconnection structure, interdependence of components, and synchronization between components [Bochmann, 1983]. *Degree of coupling* refers to a measure that determines how closely the processing elements are connected together. This can be measured as the ratio of the amount of data exchanged to the amount of local processing performed in executing a task. If the communication is done over a computer network, there exists *weak coupling* among the processing elements. However, if components are shared, we talk about *strong coupling*. Shared components can be both primary memory or secondary storage devices. As for the *interconnection structure*, one can talk about those cases that have a point-to-point interconnection between processing elements, as opposed to those which use a common interconnection channel. The processing elements might depend on each other quite strongly in the execution of a task, or this interdependence might be as minimal as passing messages at the beginning of execution and reporting results at the end. *Synchronization* between processing elements might be maintained by synchronous or by asynchronous means. Note that some of these criteria are not entirely independent. For example, if the synchronization between processing elements is synchronous, one would expect the processing elements to be strongly interdependent, and possibly to work in a strongly coupled fashion.

Another reasonable question to ask at this point is: Why do we distribute at all? The classical answers to this question indicate that distributed processing better corresponds to the organizational structure of today's widely distributed enterprises, and that such a system is more reliable and more responsive. More importantly, many of the current applications of computer technology are inherently distributed. Electronic commerce over the Internet, multimedia applications such as news-on-demand or medical imaging, manufacturing control systems are all examples of such applications.

From a more global perspective, however, it can be stated that the fundamental reason behind distributed processing is to be better able to solve the big and complicated problems that we face today, by using a variation of the well-known divide-and-conquer rule. If the necessary software support for distributed processing can be developed, it might be possible to solve these complicated problems simply by dividing them into smaller pieces and assigning them to different software groups, which work on different computers and produce a system that runs on multiple processing elements but can work efficiently toward the execution of a common task.

This approach has two fundamental advantages from an economics standpoint. First, distributed computing provides an economical method of harnessing more computing power by employing multiple processing elements optimally. This requires research in distributed processing as defined earlier, as well as in parallel processing, which is outside the scope of this book. The second economic reason is that by attacking these problems in smaller groups working more or less autonomously, it might be possible to discipline the cost of software development. Indeed, it is well known that the cost of software has been increasing in opposition to the cost trends of hardware.

Distributed database systems should also be viewed within this framework and treated as tools that could make distributed processing easier and more efficient. It is reasonable to draw an analogy between what distributed databases might offer to the data processing world and what the database technology has already provided. There is no doubt that the development of general-purpose, adaptable, efficient distributed database systems will aid greatly in the task of developing distributed software.

1.2 WHAT IS A DISTRIBUTED DATABASE SYSTEM?

We can define a *distributed database* as *a collection of multiple, logically interrelated databases distributed over a computer network*. A *distributed database management system* (distributed DBMS) is then defined as *the software system that permits the management of the DDBS and makes the distribution transparent to the users*. The two important terms in these definitions are "*logically interrelated*" and "*distributed over a computer network*." They help eliminate certain cases that have sometimes been accepted to represent a DDBS.

A DDBS is not a "collection of files" that can be individually stored at each node of a computer network. To form a DDBS, files should not only be logically related, but there should be structure among the files, and access should be via a common interface. We should note that there has been much recent activity in providing DBMS functionality over semi-structured data that are stored in files on the Internet (such as Web pages). In light of this activity, the above requirement may seem unnecessarily strict. However, providing "DBMS-like" access to data is different than a DDBS; in fact, we deal with issues such as these in Chapter 16, where we address Web and database issues.

It has sometimes been assumed that the physical distribution of data is not the most significant issue. The proponents of this view would therefore feel comfortable in labeling as a distributed database two (related) databases that reside in the same computer system. However, the physical distribution of data is very important. It creates problems that are not encountered when the databases reside in the same computer. These difficulties are discussed in Section 1.4. Note that physical distribution does not necessarily imply that the computer systems be geographically far apart; they could actually be in the same room. It simply implies that the communication between them is done over a network instead of through shared memory, with the network as the only shared resource.

This brings us to another point. The definition above also rules out multiprocessor systems as DDBSs. A multiprocessor system is generally considered to be a system where two or more processors share some form of memory, either primary memory, in which case the multiprocessor is called *shared memory* (also called *tightly coupled*) (Figure 1.3), or secondary memory, when it is called *shared disk* (also called *loosely coupled*) (Figure 1.4)[1].

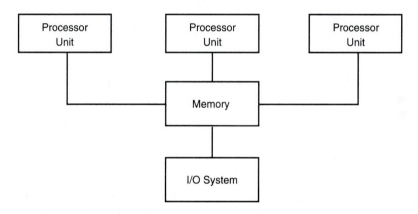

Figure 1.3. Shared Memory Multiprocessor

Another distinction that is commonly made in this context is between *shared-everything* and *shared-nothing* architectures. The former architectural model permits each processor to access everything (primary and secondary memories, and peripherals) in the system and covers the two models that we described above. Sharing memory enables the processors to communicate without exchanging mes-

---

[1]Note at this point that our definition of coupling modes is different from that of Bochmann discussed in the preceding section. We refer only to coupling in multiprocessors, not to distributed processing in general.

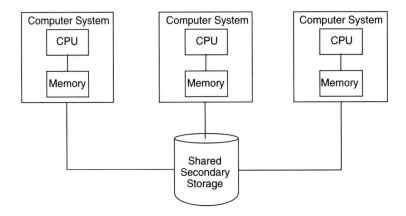

Figure 1.4. Shared Disk Multiprocessor

sages. The shared-nothing architecture (Figure 1.5) is one where each processor has its own primary and secondary memories as well as peripherals, and communicates with other processors over a very high speed interconnect (e.g., bus or a switch). In this sense the shared-nothing multiprocessors are quite similar to the distributed environment that we consider in this book. However, there are differences between the interactions in multiprocessor architectures and the rather loose interaction that is common in distributed computing environments. The fundamental difference is the mode of operation. A multiprocessor system design is rather symmetrical, consisting of a number of identical processor and memory components, and controlled

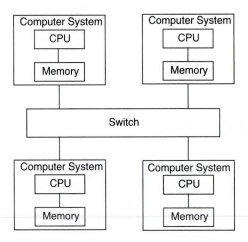

Figure 1.5. Shared Nothing Multiprocessor System

by one or more copies of the same operating system, which is responsible for a strict control of the task assignment to each processor. This is not true in distributed computing systems, where heterogeneity of the operating system as well as the hardware is quite common. We discuss these issues in much more detail in Chapter 13.

In addition, a DDBS is not a system where, despite the existence of a network, the database resides at only one node of the network (Figure 1.6). In this case, the problems of database management are no different from the problems encountered in a centralized database environment[2]. The database is centrally managed by one computer system (site 2 in Figure 1.6) and all the requests are routed to that site. The only additional consideration has to do with transmission delays. It is obvious that the existence of a computer network or a collection of "files" is not sufficient to form a distributed database system. What we are interested in is an environment where data is distributed among a number of sites (Figure 1.7).

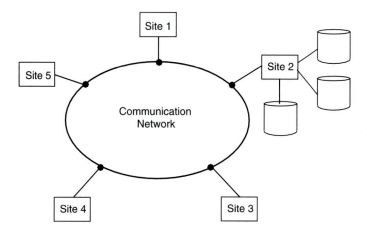

Figure 1.6. Central Database on a Network

1.3 PROMISES OF DDBSs

Many advantages of DDBSs have been cited in literature, ranging from sociological reasons for decentralization [D'Oliviera, 1977] to better economics. All of these can be distilled to four fundamentals which may also be viewed as promises of DDBS technology. In this section we discuss these promises and, in the process, introduce many of the concepts that we will study in subsequent chapters.

---

[2]In Chapter 4, we will discuss client/server systems which relax this requirement to a certain extent .

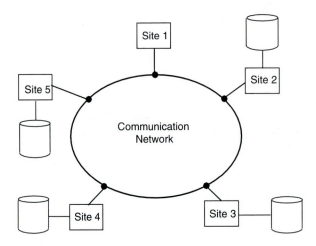

Figure 1.7. DDBS Environment

1.3.1 Transparent Management of Distributed and Replicated Data

Transparency refers to separation of the higher-level semantics of a system from lower-level implementation issues. In other words, a transparent system "hides" the implementation details from users. The advantage of a fully transparent DBMS is the high level of support that it provides for the development of complex applications. It is obvious that we would like to make all DBMSs (centralized or distributed) fully transparent.

Let us start our discussion with an example. Consider an engineering firm that has offices in Boston, Edmonton, Paris and San Francisco. They run projects at each of these sites and would like to maintain a database of their employees, the projects and other related data. Assuming that the database is relational, we can store this information in two relations: EMP(**ENO**, ENAME, TITLE)[3] and PROJ(**PNO**, PNAME, BUDGET). We also introduce a third relation to store salary information: PAY(**TITLE**, SAL) and a fourth relation ASG which indicates which employees have been assigned to which projects for what duration with what responsibility: ASG(**ENO, PNO**, DUR, RESP). If all of this data was stored in a centralized DBMS, and we wanted to find out the names and employees who worked on a project for more than 12 months, we would specify this using the following SQL query:

---

[3]We discuss relational systems in Chapter 2 where we develop this example further. For the time being, it is sufficient to note that this nomenclature indicates that we have just defined a relation with three attributes: ENO (which is the key), ENAME and TITLE.

```
SELECT    ENAME, SAL
FROM      EMP, ASG, PAY
WHERE     ASG.DUR > 12
AND       EMP.ENO = ASG.ENO
AND       PAY.TITLE = EMP.TITLE
```

However, given the distributed nature of this firm's business, it is preferable, under these circumstances, to localize each data such that data about the employees in Edmonton office are stored in Edmonton, those in the Boston office are stored in Boston, and so forth. The same applies to the project and salary information. Thus, what we are engaged in is a process where we partition each of the relations and store each partition at a different site. This is known as *fragmentation* and we discuss it further below and in detail in Chapter 5.

Furthermore, it may be preferable to duplicate some of this data at other sites for performance and reliability reasons. The result is a distributed database which is fragmented and replicated (Figure 1.8). Fully transparent access means that the users can still pose the query as specified above, without paying any attention to the fragmentation, location, or replication of data, and let the system worry about resolving these issues.

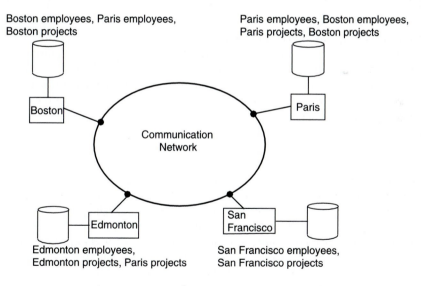

Figure 1.8. A Distributed Application

For a system to adequately deal with this type of query over a distributed, fragmented and replicated database, it needs to be able to deal with a number of different types of transparencies. We discuss these in this section.

Data Independence

Data independence is a fundamental form of transparency that we look for within a DBMS. It is also the only type that is important within the context of a centralized DBMS. It refers to the immunity of user applications to changes in the definition and organization of data, and vice versa.

As we will see later in Section 4.1, data definition can occur at two levels. At one level the logical structure of the data is specified, and at the other level the physical structure of the data is defined. The former is commonly known as the *schema definition*, whereas the latter is referred to as the *physical data description*. We can therefore talk about two types of data independence: logical data independence and physical data independence. *Logical data independence* refers to the immunity of user applications to changes in the logical structure of the database. In general, if a user application operates on a subset of the attributes of a relation, it should not be affected later when new attributes are added to the same relation. For example, let us consider the EMP relation discussed above. If a user application deals with only the address fields of this relation (it might be a simple mailing program), the later additions to the relation of say, skill, would not and should not affect the mailing application.

Physical data independence deals with hiding the details of the storage structure from user applications. When a user application is written, it should not be concerned with the details of physical data organization. The data might be organized on different disk types, parts of it might be organized differently (e.g., random versus indexed-sequential access) or might even be distributed across different storage hierarchies (e.g., disk storage and tape storage). The application should not be involved with these issues since, conceptually, there is no difference in the operations carried out against the data. Therefore, the user application should not need to be modified when data organizational changes occur with respect to these issues. Nevertheless, it is common knowledge that these changes may be necessary for performance considerations.

Network Transparency

In centralized database systems, the only available resource that needs to be shielded from the user is the data (i.e., the storage system). In a distributed database management environment, however, there is a second resource that needs to be managed in much the same manner: the network. Preferably, the user should be protected from the operational details of the network. Furthermore, it is desirable to hide even the existence of the network, if possible. Then there would be no difference between database applications that would run on a centralized database and those that would run on a distributed database. This type of transparency is referred to as *network transparency* or *distribution transparency*.

One can consider network transparency from the viewpoint of either the services provided or the data. From the former perspective, it is desirable to have uniform means by which services are accessed. From a DBMS perspective, distribution transparency requires that users do not have to specify where data is located.

Some have separated distribution transparency into two: location transparency and naming transparency. *Location transparency* refers to the fact that the command used to perform a task is independent of both the location of the data and the system on which an operation is carried out. *Naming transparency* means that a unique name is provided for each object in the database. In the absence of naming transparency, users are required to embed the location name (or an identifier) as part of the object name.

Replication Transparency

The issue of replicating data within a distributed database is discussed in quite some detail in Chapter 5. At this point, let us just mention that for performance, reliability, and availability reasons, it is usually desirable to be able to distribute data in a replicated fashion across the machines on a network. Such replication helps performance since diverse and conflicting user requirements can be more easily accommodated. For example, data that is commonly accessed by one user can be placed on that user's local machine as well as on the machine of another user with the same access requirements. This increases the locality of reference. Furthermore, if one of the machines fails, a copy of the data is still available on another machine on the network. Of course, this is a very simple-minded description of the situation. In fact, the decision as to whether to replicate or not, and how many copies of any database object to have, depends to a considerable degree on user applications. Note that replication causes problems in updating databases. Therefore, if the user applications are predominantly update-oriented, it may not be a good idea to have too many copies of the data. As this discussion is the subject matter of Chapter 5, we will not dwell further here on the pros and cons of replication.

Assuming that data is replicated, the issue related to transparency that needs to be addressed is whether the users should be aware of the existence of copies or whether the system should handle the management of copies and the user should act as if there is a single copy of the data (note that we are not referring to the placement of copies, only their existence). From a user's perspective the answer is obvious. It is preferable not to be involved with handling copies and having to specify the fact that a certain action can and/or should be taken on multiple copies. From a systems point of view, however, the answer is not that simple. As we will see in Chapter 11, when the responsibility of specifying that an action needs to be executed on multiple copies is delegated to the user, it makes transaction management simpler for distributed DBMSs. On the other hand, doing so inevitably results in the loss of some flexibility. It is not the system that decides whether or not to have copies and how many copies to have, but the user application. Any change in these decisions because of various considerations definitely affects the user application and therefore reduces data independence considerably. Given these considerations, it is desirable that replication transparency be provided as a standard feature of DBMSs. Remember that replication transparency refers only to the existence of replicas, not to their actual location. Note also that distributing these replicas across the network in a transparent manner is the domain of network transparency.

Fragmentation Transparency

The final form of transparency that needs to be addressed within the context of a distributed database system is that of fragmentation transparency. In Chapter 5 we discuss and justify the fact that it is commonly desirable to divide each database relation into smaller fragments and treat each fragment as a separate database object (i.e., another relation). This is commonly done for reasons of performance, availability, and reliability. Furthermore, fragmentation can reduce the negative effects of replication. Each replica is not the full relation but only a subset of it; thus less space is required and fewer data items need be managed.

There are two general types of fragmentation alternatives. In one case, called *horizontal fragmentation*, a relation is partitioned into a set of sub-relations each of which have a subset of the tuples (rows) of the original relation. The second alternative is *vertical fragmentation* where each sub-relation is defined on a subset of the attributes (columns) of the original relation.

When database objects are fragmented, we have to deal with the problem of handling user queries that were specified on entire relations but now have to be performed on subrelations. In other words, the issue is one of finding a query processing strategy based on the fragments rather than the relations, even though the queries are specified on the latter. Typically, this requires a translation from what is called a *global query* to several *fragment queries*. Since the fundamental issue of dealing with fragmentation transparency is one of query processing, we defer the discussion of techniques by which this translation can be performed until Chapter 8.

Who Should Provide Transparency?

In previous sections we discussed various possible forms of transparency within a distributed computing environment. Obviously, to provide easy and efficient access by novice users to the services of the DBMS, one would want to have full transparency, involving all the various types that we discussed. Nevertheless, the level of transparency is inevitably a compromise between ease of use and the difficulty and overhead cost of providing high levels of transparency.

What has not yet been discussed is who is responsible for providing these services. It is possible to identify three distinct layers at which the services of transparency can be provided. It is quite common to treat these as mutually exclusive means of providing the service, although it is more appropriate to view them as complementary.

We could leave the responsibility of providing transparent access to data resources to the access layer. The transparency features can be built into the user language, which then translates the requested services into required operations. In other words, the compiler or the interpreter takes over the task and no transparent service is provided to the implementer of the compiler or the interpreter.

The second layer at which transparency can be provided is the operating system level. State-of-the-art operating systems provide some level of transparency to system users. For example, the device drivers within the operating system handle the minute details of getting each piece of peripheral equipment to do what is requested. The typical computer user, or even an application programmer, does not normally write device drivers to interact with individual peripheral equipment; that operation is transparent to the user.

Providing transparent access to resources at the operating system level can obviously be extended to the distributed environment, where the management of the network resource is taken over by the distributed operating system. This is a good level at which to provide network transparency if it can be accomplished. The unfortunate aspect is that not all commercially available distributed operating systems provide a reasonable level of transparency in network management.

The third layer at which transparency can be supported is within the DBMS. The transparency and support for database functions provided to the DBMS designers by an underlying operating system is generally minimal and typically limited to very fundamental operations for performing certain tasks. It is the responsibility of the DBMS to make all the necessary translations from the operating system to the higher-level user interface. This mode of operation is the most common method today. There are, however, various problems associated with leaving the task of providing full transparency to the DBMS. These have to do with the interaction of the operating system with the distributed DBMS and are discussed throughout this book.

It is therefore quite important to realize that reasonable levels of transparency depend on different components within the data management environment. Network transparency can easily be handled by the distributed operating system as part of its responsibilities for providing replication and fragmentation transparencies (especially those aspects dealing with transaction management and recovery). The DBMS should be responsible for providing a high level of data independence together with replication and fragmentation transparencies. Finally, the user interface can support a higher level of transparency not only in terms of a uniform access method to the data resources from within a language, but also in terms of structure constructs that permit the user to deal with objects in his or her environment rather than focusing on the details of database description. Specifically, it should be noted that the interface to a distributed DBMS does not need to be a programming language but can be a graphical user interface, a natural language interface, and even a voice system.

A hierarchy of these transparencies is shown in Figure 1.9. It is not always easy to delineate clearly the levels of transparency, but such a figure serves an important instructional purpose even if it is not fully correct. To complete the picture we have added a "language transparency" layer, although it is not discussed in this chapter. With this generic layer, users have high-level access to the data (e.g., fourth-generation languages, graphical user interfaces, natural language access).

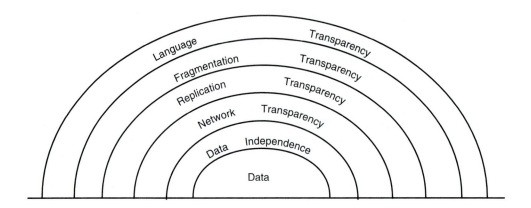

Figure 1.9. Layers of Transparency

How Do Existing Systems Fare?

Most of the commercial distributed DBMSs today have started to provide some level of transparency support. Typically the systems provide distribution transparency, support for horizontal fragmentation and some form of replication transparency.

This level of support is quite recent. Until recently, most commercial distributed DBMSs did not provide a sufficient level of transparency. Some (e.g., R* [Williams et al., 1982]) required users to embed the location names within the name of each database object. Furthermore, they required the user to specify the full name for access to the object. Obviously, one can set up aliases for these long names if the operating system provides such a facility. However, user-defined aliases are not real solutions to the problem in as much as they are attempts to avoid addressing them within the distributed DBMS. The system, not the user, should be responsible for assigning unique names to objects and for translating user-known names to these unique internal object names.

Besides these semantic considerations, there is also a very pragmatic problem associated with embedding location names within object names. Such an approach makes it very difficult to move objects across machines for performance optimization or other purposes. Every such move will require users to change their access names for the affected objects, which is clearly undesirable.

Other systems did not provide any support for the management of replicated data across multiple logical databases. Even those that did required that the user be physically "logged on" to one database at a given time (e.g., Oracle versions prior to V7).

At this point it is important to point out that full transparency is not a universally accepted objective. Gray argues that full transparency makes the management of distributed data very difficult and claims that "applications coded with transparent access to geographically distributed databases have: poor manageability, poor modularity, and poor message performance" [Gray, 1989]. He proposes a remote procedure call mechanism between the requestor users and the server DBMSs whereby the users would direct their queries to a specific DBMS. It is indeed true that the management of distributed data is more difficult if transparent access is provided to users, and that the client/server architecture (which we discuss in Chapter 4) with a remote procedure call-based communication between the clients and the servers is the right architectural approach. In fact, some commercial distributed DBMSs are organized in this fashion. However, the goal of fully transparent access to distributed and replicated data is an important one and it is up to the system vendors to resolve the system issues.

1.3.2 Reliability Through Distributed Transactions

Distributed DBMSs are intended to improve reliability since they have replicated components and, thereby eliminate single points of failure. The failure of a single site, or the failure of a communication link which makes one or more sites unreachable, is not sufficient to bring down the entire system. In the case of a distributed database, this means that some of the data may be unreachable, but with proper care, users may be permitted to access other parts of the distributed database. The "proper care" comes in the form of support for distributed transactions and application protocols.

We discuss transactions and transaction processing in detail in Chapters 10–12. A *transaction* is a basic unit of consistent and reliable computing, consisting of a sequence of database operations executed as an atomic action. It transforms a consistent database state to another consistent database state even when a number of such transactions are executed concurrently (sometimes called *concurrency transparency*), and even when failures occur (also called *failure atomicity*). Therefore, a DBMS that provides full transaction support guarantees that concurrent execution of user transactions will not violate database consistency in the face of system failures as long as each transaction is correct, i.e., obeys the integrity rules specified on the database.

Let us give an example of a transaction based on the engineering firm example that we discussed above. Assume that there is an application that updates the salaries of all the employees by 10%. It is desirable to encapsulate the query (or the program code) that accomplishes this task within transaction boundaries. For example, if a system failure occurs half-way through the execution of this program, we would like the DBMS to be able to determine, upon recovery, where it left off and continue with its operation (or start all over again). This is the topic of failure atomicity. Alternatively, if some other user runs a query calculating the average salaries of the employees in this firm while the original update action is going on, the calculated result will be in error. Therefore we would like the system to be able to synchronize the *concurrent* execution of these two programs. To encapsulate a query (or a program code) within transactional boundaries, it is sufficient to declare the begin of the transaction and its end:

Begin_transaction SALARY_UPDATE
begin
  EXEC SQL UPDATE   PAY
           SET   SAL = SAL*1.1
end.

Distributed transactions execute at a number of sites at which they access the local database. The above transaction, for example, will execute in Boston, Edmonton, Paris and San Francisco. With full support for distributed transactions, user applications can access a single logical image of the database and rely on the distributed DBMS to ensure that their requests will be executed correctly no matter what happens in the system. "Correctly" means that user applications do not need to be concerned with coordinating their accesses to individual local databases nor do they need to worry about the possibility of site or communication link failures during the execution of their transactions. This illustrates the link between distributed transactions and transparency, since both involve issues related to distributed naming and directory management, among other things.

Providing transaction support requires the implementation of distributed concurrency control (Chapter 11) and distributed reliability (Chapter 12) protocols — in particular, two-phase commit (2PC) and distributed recovery protocols — which are significantly more complicated than their centralized counterparts. Supporting replicas requires the implementation of replica control protocols that enforce a specified semantics of accessing them.

Commercial systems provide varying degrees of distributed transaction support. Some (e.g., Oracle V7 and V8) provide support for distributed transactions while earlier versions of Oracle required users to have one database open at a given time, thereby eliminating the need for distributed transactions, while others (e.g., Sybase) implement the basic primitives that are necessary for the 2PC protocol, but require the user applications to handle the coordination of the commit actions. In other words, the distributed DBMS does not enforce atomicity of distributed transactions, but provide the basic primitives by which user applications can enforce it.

1.3.3 Improved Performance

The case for the improved performance of distributed DBMSs is typically made based on two points:

1. A distributed DBMS fragments the conceptual database, enabling data to be stored in close proximity to its points of use (also called *data localization*). This has two potential advantages:

    - Since each site handles only a portion of the database, contention for CPU and I/O services is not as severe as for centralized databases, and

- Localization reduces remote access delays that are usually involved in wide area networks (for example, the minimum round-trip message propagation delay in satellite-based systems is about 1 second).

Most distributed DBMSs are structured to gain maximum benefit from data localization. Full benefits of reduced contention and reduced communication overhead can be obtained only by a proper fragmentation and distribution of the database.

2. The inherent parallelism of distributed systems may be exploited for inter-query and intra-query parallelism. Inter-query parallelism results from the ability to execute multiple queries at the same time while intra-query parallelism is achieved by breaking up a single query into a number of subqueries each of which is executed at a different site, accessing a different part of the distributed database.

The first point relates to the overhead of distributed computing if the data have to reside at remote sites and one has to access it by teleprocessing. The argument is that it is better, in these circumstances, to distribute the data management functionality to where the data is located rather than moving large amounts of data. This has lately become a topic of contention. Some argue that with the widespread use of high-speed, high-capacity networks, distributing data and data management functions no longer make sense and it may be much simpler to store data at a central site and access it (by downloading) over high-speed networks. This argument, while appealing, misses the point of distributed databases. First of all, in most of today's applications, data are distributed; what may be open for debate is how and where we process it. Second, and more important, is that this argument does not distinguish between bandwidth (the capacity of the computer links) and latency (how long it takes for data to be transmitted). Latency is inherent in the distributed environments and there are physical limits to how fast we can send data over computer networks. As indicated above, for example, satellite links take about half-a-second to transmit data between two ground stations. This is a function of the distance of the satellites from the earth and there is nothing that we can do to improve that performance. For some applications, this might constitute an unacceptable delay.

The parallelism argument is also important. If the user access to the distributed database consisted only of querying (i.e., read-only access), then provision of inter-query and intra-query parallelism would imply that as much of the database as possible should be replicated. However, since most database accesses are not read-only, the mixing of read and update operations requires the implementation of elaborate concurrency control and commit protocols.

In addition to optimizing the systems to deal with this issue, some existing commercial systems take a rather interesting approach to deal with the conflict between read-only performance and update performance. They multiplex the database by maintaining two copies. One copy is for ad hoc querying (called the *query database*[4]) and the other for updates by application programs (called the *production database*). At regular intervals, the production database is copied to the query database. This does not eliminate the need to implement concurrency control and reliability protocols for the production database since these are necessary to synchronize the write operations on the same data; however, it improves the performance of the queries since they can be executed without the overhead of transaction manipulation.

In addition to these, there is an administrative measure that some take to deal with the overhead of transaction management. Some installations open their databases only for queries (i.e., read-only access) during the regular operating hours while the updates are batched. The database is then closed to query activity during off-hours when the batched updates are run sequentially. This is time multiplexing between read activity and update activity.

In general, the performance characteristics of distributed database systems are not very well understood. There are not a sufficient number of true distributed database applications to provide a sound base to make practical judgments. In addition, the performance models of distributed database systems are not sufficiently developed. The database community has developed a number of benchmarks to test the performance of transaction processing applications, but it is not clear whether they can be used to measure the performance of distributed transaction management. The performance of the commercial DBMS products, even with respect to these benchmarks, are generally not openly published. NonStop SQL is one product for which performance figures, as well as the experimental setup that is used in obtaining them, has been published [Tandem, 1988].

1.3.4 Easier System Expansion

In a distributed environment, it is much easier to accommodate increasing database sizes. Major system overhauls are seldom necessary; expansion can usually be handled by adding processing and storage power to the network. Obviously, it may not be possible to obtain a linear increase in "power," since this also depends on the overhead of distribution. However, significant improvements are still possible.

An aspect of easier system expansion is economics. It normally costs much less to put together a system of smaller computers with the equivalent power of a single big machine. In the 1960s and early 1970s, it was commonly believed that it would be possible to purchase a fourfold powerful computer if one spent twice as much. This was known as Grosh's law. With the advent of minicomputers, and especially microcomputers, this law is considered invalid.

This should not be interpreted to mean that mainframes are dead. This is not the point that we are making here. There are many applications which are more suitably executed on mainframes. Indeed, in recent years, we have observed a resurgence in the world-wide sale of mainframes. The point is that for many applications, it is more economical to put together a distributed computer system with sufficient power.

---

[4]Data warehouses that have attracted much recent attention are of this type.

1.4 COMPLICATING FACTORS

The problems encountered in database systems take on additional complexity in a distributed environment, even though the basic underlying principles are the same. Furthermore, this additional complexity gives rise to new problems influenced mainly by three factors.

First, data may be replicated in a distributed environment. A distributed database can be designed so that the entire database, or portions of it, reside at different sites of a computer network. It is not essential that every site on the network contain the database; it is only essential that there be more than one site where the database resides. The possible duplication of data items is mainly due to reliability and efficiency considerations. Consequently, the distributed database system is responsible for (1) choosing one of the stored copies of the requested data for access in case of retrievals, and (2) making sure that the effect of an update is reflected on each and every copy of that data item.

Second, if some sites fail (e.g., by either hardware or software malfunction), or if some communication links fail (making some of the sites unreachable) while an update is being executed, the system must make sure that the effects will be reflected on the data residing at the failing or unreachable sites as soon as the system can recover from the failure.

The third point is that since each site cannot have instantaneous information on the actions currently being carried out at the other sites, the synchronization of transactions on multiple sites is considerably harder than for a centralized system.

These difficulties point to a number of potential problems with distributed DBMSs. These are discussed in the following.

Complexity. DDBS problems are inherently more complex than centralized database management ones, as they include not only the problems found in a centralized environment, but also a new set of unresolved problems. We discuss these new issues shortly.

Cost. Distributed systems require additional hardware (communication mechanisms, etc.), thus have increased hardware costs. However, the trend toward decreasing hardware costs does not make this a significant factor. A more important fraction of the cost lies in the fact that additional and more complex software and communication may be necessary to solve some of the technical problems. The development of software engineering techniques (distributed debuggers and the like) should help in this respect.

Perhaps the most important cost component is due to the replication of effort (manpower). When computer facilities are set up at different sites, it becomes necessary to employ people to maintain these facilities. This usually results in an increase in the personnel in the data processing operations. Therefore, the trade-off between increased profitability due to more efficient and timely use of information and the increased personnel costs has to be analyzed carefully.

Distribution of Control. This point was stated previously as an advantage of DDBSs. Unfortunately, distribution creates problems of synchronization and coordination (the reasons for this added complexity are studied in the next section). Distributed control can therefore easily become a liability if care is not taken to adopt adequate policies to deal with these issues.

Security.   One of the major benefits of centralized databases has been the control it provides over the access to data. Security can easily be controlled in one central location, with the DBMS enforcing the rules. However, in a distributed database system, a network is involved which is a medium that has its own security requirements. It is well known that there are serious problems in maintaining adequate security over computer networks. Thus the security problems in distributed database systems are by nature more complicated than in centralized ones.

1.5   PROBLEM AREAS

In Section 1.3, we discussed a number of technical problems that need to be resolved to realize the full potential of distributed DBMSs. In this section we discuss them in a more organized fashion as a prelude to our in-depth studies in the rest of the book.

1.5.1   Distributed Database Design

The question that is being addressed is how the database and the applications that run against it should be placed across the sites. There are two basic alternatives to placing data: *partitioned* (or *nonreplicated*) and *replicated*. In the partitioned scheme the database is divided into a number of disjoint partitions each of which is placed at a different site. Replicated designs can be either *fully replicated* (also called *fully duplicated*) where the entire database is stored at each site, or *partially replicated* (or *partially duplicated*) where each partition of the database is stored at more than one site, but not at all the sites. The two fundamental design issues are *fragmentation*, the separation of the database into partitions called *fragments*, and *distribution*, the optimum distribution of fragments.

The research in this area mostly involves mathematical programming in order to minimize the combined cost of storing the database, processing transactions against it, and communication. The general problem is NP-hard. Therefore, the proposed solutions are based on heuristics.

1.5.2   Distributed Query Processing

Query processing deals with designing algorithms that analyze queries and convert them into a series of data manipulation operations. The problem is how to decide on a strategy for executing each query over the network in the most cost-effective way, however cost is defined. The factors to be considered are the distribution of data, communication costs, and lack of sufficient locally-available information. The objective is to optimize where the inherent parallelism is used to improve the performance of executing the transaction, subject to the above-mentioned constraints. The problem is NP-hard in nature, and the approaches are usually heuristic.

1.5.3   Distributed Directory Management

A directory contains information (such as descriptions and locations) about data items in the database. Problems related to directory management are similar in nature to the database placement problem discussed in the preceding section. A directory may be global to the entire DDBS or local to each site; it can be centralized at one site or distributed over several sites; there can be a single copy or multiple copies.

1.5.4   Distributed Concurrency Control

Concurrency control involves the synchronization of accesses to the distributed database, such that the integrity of the database is maintained. It is, without any doubt, one of the most extensively studied problems in the DDBS field. The concurrency control problem in a distributed context is somewhat different than in a centralized framework. One not only has to worry about the integrity of a single database, but also about the consistency of multiple copies of the database. The condition that requires all the values of multiple copies of every data item to converge to the same value is called *mutual consistency*.

The alternative solutions are too numerous to discuss here, so we examine them in detail in Chapter 11. Let us only mention that the two general classes are *pessimistic*, synchronizing the execution of user requests before the execution starts, and *optimistic*, executing the requests and then checking if the execution compromised the consistency of the database. Two fundamental primitives that can be used with both approaches are *locking*, which is based on the mutual exclusion of accesses to data items, and *timestamping*, where the transactions are executed in some order. There are variations of these schemes as well as hybrid algorithms that attempt to combine the two basic mechanisms.

1.5.5   Distributed Deadlock Management

The deadlock problem in DDBSs is similar in nature to that encountered in operating systems. The competition among users for access to a set of resources (data, in this case) can result in a deadlock if the synchronization mechanism is based on locking. The well-known alternatives of prevention, avoidance, and detection/recovery also apply to DDBSs.

1.5.6   Reliability of Distributed DBMS

We mentioned earlier that one of the potential advantages of distributed systems is improved reliability and availability. This, however, is not a feature that comes automatically. It is important that mechanisms be provided to ensure the consistency of the database as well as to detect failures and recover from them. The implication for DDBSs is that when a failure occurs and various sites become either inoperable or inaccessible, the databases at the operational sites remain consistent and up to date. Furthermore, when the computer system or network recovers from the failure, the DDBSs should be able to recover and bring the databases at the failed sites up-to-date. This may be especially difficult in the case of network partitioning, where the sites are divided into two or more groups with no communication among them.

1.5.7 Operating System Support

The current implementation of distributed database systems on top of (or under) the conventional operating systems suffers from the performance bottleneck. The support provided by operating systems for database operations does not correspond properly to the requirements of the database management software. The major operating system-related problems in single-processor systems are memory management, file system and access methods, crash recovery, and process management. In distributed environments there is the additional problem of having to deal with multiple layers of network software. The work in this area is on finding solutions to the dichotomy of providing adequate and simple support for distributed database operations, as well as providing general operating system support for other applications.

1.5.8 Heterogeneous Databases

When there is no homogeneity among the databases at various sites either in terms of the way data is logically structured (data model) or in terms of the mechanisms provided for accessing it (data language), it becomes necessary to provide a translation mechanism between database systems. This translation mechanism usually involves a canonical form to facilitate data translation, as well as program templates for translating data manipulation instructions.

It turns out that heterogeneity is typically introduced if one is constructing a distributed DBMS from a number of autonomous, centralized DBMSs. In this setting the problems are more general than heterogeneity. In fact, such systems, which we call *multidatabase systems*, should be considered complementary to the distributed DBMSs as defined in this chapter. Thus, all the problems that we have discussed in the preceding sections have complementary specifications for multidatabase systems. We discuss these systems in Chapter 15.

1.5.9 Relationship among Problems

We should mention at this point that these problems are not isolated from one another. The reasons for studying them in isolation are that (1) problems are difficult enough to study by themselves, and would probably be impossible to present all together, and that (2) it might be possible to characterize the effect of one problem on another one, through the use of parameters and constraints. In fact, each problem is affected by the solutions found for the others, and in turn affects the set of feasible solutions for them. In this section we discuss how they are related.

The relationship among the components is shown in Figure 1.10. The design of distributed databases affects many areas. It affects directory management, because the definition of fragments and their placement determine the contents of the di-

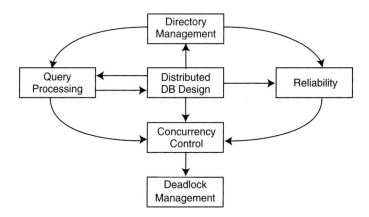

Figure 1.10. Relationship Among Research Issues

rectory (or directories) as well as the strategies that may be employed to manage them. The same information (i.e., fragment structure and placement) is used by the query processor to determine the query evaluation strategy. On the other hand, the access and usage patterns that are determined by the query processor are used as inputs to the data distribution and fragmentation algorithms. Similarly, directory placement and contents influence the processing of queries.

The replication of fragments when they are distributed affects the concurrency control strategies that might be employed. As we will study in Chapter 11, some concurrency control algorithms cannot be easily used with replicated databases. Similarly, usage and access patterns to the database will influence the concurrency control algorithms. If the environment is update intensive, the necessary precautions are quite different from those in a query-only environment.

There is a strong relationship among the concurrency control problem, the deadlock management problem, and reliability issues. This is to be expected, since together they are usually called the *transaction management* problem. The concurrency control algorithm that is employed will determine whether or not a separate deadlock management facility is required. If a locking-based algorithm is used, deadlocks will occur, whereas they will not if timestamping is the chosen alternative.

Reliability mechanisms are implemented on top of a concurrency control algorithm. Therefore, the relationship among them is self-explanatory. It should also be mentioned that the reliability mechanisms being considered have an effect on the choice of the concurrency control algorithm. Techniques to provide reliability also make use of data placement information since the existence of duplicate copies of the data serve as a safeguard to maintain reliable operation.

Two of the problems we discussed in the preceding sections—operating system issues and heterogeneous databases—are not illustrated in Figure 1.10. This is obviously not because they have no bearing on other issues; in fact, exactly the opposite is true. The type of operating system used and the features supported by that operating system greatly influence what solution strategies can be applied in any of the other problem areas. Similarly, the nature of all these problems change considerably when the environment is heterogeneous. The same issues have to be dealt with differently when the machine architecture, the operating systems, and the local database management software vary from site to site.

1.6 BIBLIOGRAPHIC NOTES

There are a few books on distributed DBMSs. Ceri and Pelagatti's book [Ceri and Pelagatti, 1983] is a classic in the area even though it is now dated. The book by Bell and Grimson [Bell and Grimson, 1992] also provides an overview of the topics addressed here. In addition, almost every database book now has a chapter on distributed DBMSs. A brief overview of the technology is provided in [Özsu and Valduriez, 1997]. Our papers [Özsu and Valduriez, 1994], [Özsu and Valduriez, 1991] provide discussions of the state-of-the-art at the time they were written.

Database design is discussed in an introductory manner in [Levin and Morgan, 1975] and more comprehensively in [Ceri et al., 1987]. A survey of the file distribution algorithms is given in [Dowdy and Foster, 1982]. Directory management has not been considered in detail in the research community, but general techniques can be found in [Chu and Nahouraii, 1975] and [Chu, 1976]. A survey of query processing techniques can be found in [Sacco and Yao, 1982]. Concurrency control algorithms are reviewed in [Bernstein and Goodman, 1981] and [Bernstein et al., 1987]. Deadlock management has also been the subject of extensive research; an introductory paper is [Isloor and Marsland, 1980] and a widely quoted paper is [Obermarck, 1982]. For deadlock detection, good surveys are [Knapp, 1987] and [Elmagarmid, 1986]. Reliability is one of the issues discussed in [Gray, 1979], which is one of the landmark papers in the field. Other important papers on this topic are [Verhofstadt, 1978] and [Härder and Reuter, 1983]. [Gray, 1979] is also the first paper discussing the issues of operating system support for distributed databases; the same topic is addressed in [Stonebraker, 1981]. Unfortunately, both papers emphasize centralized database systems. An excellent overview of heterogeneous and federated database systems is [Sheth and Larson, 1990].

Chapter 2

OVERVIEW OF
RELATIONAL DBMS

In this chapter we review fundamental relational database concepts. The aim of this chapter is to define the terminology and framework used in subsequent chapters, not to provide substantial background on database systems. Nevertheless, we try to be complete. The reasons for choosing the relational model of data as the underlying formalism are numerous: the mathematical foundation of the relational model makes it a good candidate for theoretical treatment; most of the problems discussed in future chapters are easier to formulate; the relational DBMS market has matured and is now sizable; and finally, most distributed database systems are also relational.

The relational model can be characterized by at least three powerful features [Codd, 1982]:

1. Its data structures are simple. They are relations that are two-dimensional tables whose elements are data items. This allows a high degree of independence from the physical data representation (e.g., files and indices).

2. The relational model provides a solid foundation to data consistency. Database design is aided by the normalization process that eliminates data anomalies. Also, consistent states of a database can be uniformly defined and maintained through integrity rules.

3. The relational model allows the set-oriented manipulation of relations. This feature has led to the development of powerful nonprocedural languages based either on set theory (relational algebra) or on logic (relational calculus).

The outline of this chapter is as follows. In Section 2.1 we define fundamental relational database concepts such as a relation, a tuple, a key, and so on. In Section 2.2 the concept of normalization is introduced and different normal forms are discussed. This is followed by a short discussion of integrity rules in Section 2.3.

Section 2.4 contains the details of relational data languages (relational algebra and relational calculus), and finally, Section 2.5 presents a short discussion of relational DBMSs. The latter section also serves as a preparation to the architecture discussions of Chapter 4.

2.1 RELATIONAL DATABASE CONCEPTS

A *database* is a structured collection of data related to some real-life phenomena that we are trying to model. A *relational database* is one where the database structure is in the form of tables. Formally, a relation R defined over n sets $D_1, D_2, \ldots, D_n$ (not necessarily distinct) is a set of *n-tuples* (or simply *tuples*) $< d_1, d_2, \ldots, d_n >$ such that $d_1 \in D_1, d_2 \in D_2, \ldots, d_n \in D_n$.

Example 2.1

> As an example we will use a database that models an engineering company. The entities to be modeled are the *employees* (EMP) and *projects* (PROJ). For each employee, we would like to keep track of the employee number (ENO), name (ENAME), title in the company (TITLE), salary (SAL), identification number of the project(s) the employee is working on (PNO), responsibility within the project (RESP), and duration of the assignment (DUR) in months. Similarly, for each project we would like to store the project number (PNO), the project name (JNAME), and the project budget (BUDGET).
>
> The *relation schemes* for this database can be defined as follows:
>
> EMP(ENO, ENAME, TITLE, SAL, PNO, RESP, DUR)
>
> PROJ(PNO, PNAME, BUDGET)
>
> In relation scheme EMP, there are seven *attributes*: ENO, ENAME, TITLE, SAL, PNO, RESP, DUR. The values of ENO come from the *domain* of all valid employee numbers, say D_1, the values of ENAME come from the domain of all valid names, say D_2, and so on. Note that each attribute of each relation does not have to come from a distinct domain. Various attributes within a relation or from a number of relations may be defined over the same domain.

The *key* of a relation scheme is the minimum nonempty subset of its attributes such that the values of the attributes comprising the key uniquely identify each tuple of the relation. The attributes that make up key are called *prime* attributes. The superset of a key is usually called a *superkey*. Thus in our example the key of PROJ is PNO, and that of EMP is the set (ENO, PNO). Each relation has at least one key. Sometimes, there may be more than one possibility for the key. In such cases, each alternative is considered a *candidate key*, and one of the candidate keys is chosen as the *primary key*. The number of attributes of a relation defines its *degree*, whereas the number of tuples of the relation defines its *cardinality*.

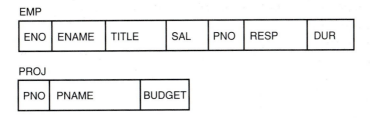

Figure 2.1. Sample Database Scheme

   In tabular form, the example database consists of two tables, as shown in Figure 2.1. The columns of the tables correspond to the attributes of the relations; if there were any information entered as the rows, they would correspond to the tuples. The empty table, showing the structure of the table, corresponds to the relation scheme; when the table is filled with rows, it corresponds to a *relation instance*. Since the information within a table varies over time, many instances can be generated from one relation scheme. Note that from now on, the term *relation* refers to a relation instance. In Figure 2.2 we depict instances of the relations that are defined in Figure 2.1.

   An attribute value may be undefined. This lack of definition may have various interpretations, the most common being unknown or not applicable. This special value of the attribute is generally referred to as the *null value*. The representation of a null value must be different from any other domain value, and special care should be given to differentiate it from zero. For example, value "0" for attribute DUR is *known information* (e.g., in the case of a newly hired employee), while value "null" for DUR means unknown in tuple E4 of Figure 2.2. Supporting null values is an important feature necessary to deal with *maybe* queries [Codd, 1979].

2.2 NORMALIZATION

"Normalization is a step-by-step reversible process of replacing a given collection of relations by successive collections in which relations have a progressively simpler and more regular structure" [Tsichritzis and Lochovsky, 1977]. The aim of normalization is to eliminate various anomalies (or undesirable aspects) of a relation in order to obtain "better" relations. The following four problems might exist in a relation scheme:

   1. *Repetition anomaly.* Certain information may be repeated unnecessarily. Consider, for example, the EMP relation in Figure 2.2. The name, title, and salary of an employee are repeated for each project on which this person serves. This is obviously a waste of storage and is contrary to the spirit of databases.

EMP

ENO	ENAME	TITLE	SAL	PNO	RESP	DUR
E1	J. Doe	Elect. Eng.	40000	P1	Manager	12
E2	M. Smith	Analyst	34000	P1	Analyst	24
E2	M. Smith	Analyst	34000	P2	Analyst	6
E3	A. Lee	Mech. Eng.	27000	P3	Consultant	10
E3	A. Lee	Mech. Eng.	27000	P4	Engineer	48
E4	J. Miller	Programmer	24000	P2	Programmer	18
E5	B. Casey	Syst. Anal.	34000	P2	Manager	24
E6	L. Chu	Elect. Eng.	40000	P4	Manager	48
E7	R. Davis	Mech. Eng.	27000	P3	Engineer	36
E8	J. Jones	Syst. Anal.	34000	P3	Manager	40

PROJ

PNO	PNAME	BUDGET
P1	Instrumentation	150000
P2	Database Develop.	135000
P3	CAD/CAM	250000
P4	Maintenance	310000

Figure 2.2. Sample Database Instance

2. *Update anomaly.* As a consequence of the repetition of data, performing updates may be troublesome. For example, if the salary of an employee changes, multiple tuples have to be updated to reflect this change.

3. *Insertion anomaly.* It may not be possible to add new information to the database. For example, when a new employee joins the company, we cannot add personal information (name, title, salary) to the EMP relation unless an appointment to a project is made. This is because the key of EMP includes the attribute PNO, and null values cannot be part of the key.

4. *Deletion anomaly.* This is the converse of the insertion anomaly. If an employee works on only one project, and that project is terminated, it is not possible to delete the project information from the EMP relation. To

do so would result in deleting the only tuple about the employee, thereby resulting in the loss of personal information we might want to retain.

Normalization transforms arbitrary relation schemes into ones without these problems. The most popular approach to normalizing a relational database scheme is the *decomposition* approach, where one starts with a single relation, called the *universal relation*, which contains all attributes (and probably anomalies) and iteratively reduces it. At each iteration, a relation is split into two or more relations of a higher *normal form*. A relation is said to be in a normal form if it satisfies the conditions associated with that normal form. Codd initially defined the *first*, *second*, and *third* normal forms (1NF, 2NF, and 3NF, respectively). Boyce and Codd [Codd, 1974] later defined a modified version of the third normal form, commonly known as the *Boyce-Codd normal form (BCNF)*. This was followed by the definition of the *fourth* (4NF) [Fagin, 1977] and *fifth* normal forms (5NF) [Fagin, 1979].

There is a hierarchical relationship among these normal forms. Every normalized relation is in 1NF; some of the relations in 1NF are also in 2NF, some of which are in 3NF, and so on. The higher normal forms have better properties than others with respect to the four anomalies discussed above.

One of the requirements of a normalization process is that the decomposition be lossless. This means that the replacement of a relation by several others should not result in loss of information. If it is possible to join the decomposed relations to obtain the original relation, the process is said to be a *lossless decomposition*.

The join operation is defined formally in Section 2.4.1. Intuitively, it is an operation that takes two relations and concatenates each tuple of the second relation with those tuples of the first relation that satisfy a specified condition. The condition is defined over the attributes of the two relations. For example, it might be specified that the value of an attribute of the first relation should be equal to the value of an attribute of the second relation.

Another requirement of the normalization process is *dependency preservation*. A decomposition is said to be dependency preserving if the union of the dependencies in the decomposed relations is equivalent to the closure (with respect to a set of inference rules) of the dependencies of the original relation.

2.2.1 Dependency Structures

The normal forms are based on certain dependency structures. BCNF and lower normal forms are based on *functional dependencies* (FDs), 4NF is based on *multivalued dependencies*, and 5NF is based on *projection-join dependencies*. In this section we define what we mean by dependence.

Let R be a relation defined over the set of attributes $A = \{A_1, A_2, \ldots, A_n\}$ and let $X \subset A$, $Y \subset A$. If for each value of X in R, there is only one associated Y value, we say that "X *functionally determines* Y" or that "Y is *functionally dependent* on X." Notationally, this is shown as $X \to Y$. The key of a relation functionally determines the nonkey attributes of the same relation.

Example 2.2

For example, in the PROJ relation of Figure 2.2, the valid FD is

$$\text{PNO} \rightarrow (\text{PNAME, BUDGET})$$

In the EMP relation we have

$$(\text{ENO, PNO}) \rightarrow (\text{ENAME,TITLE,SAL,RESP,DUR})$$

This last FD is not the only FD in EMP, however. If each employee is given unique employee numbers, we can write

$$\text{ENO} \rightarrow (\text{ENAME, TITLE, SAL})$$

$$(\text{ENO, PNO}) \rightarrow (\text{RESP, DUR})$$

It is also reasonable to state that the salary for a given position is fixed, which gives rise to the FD

$$\text{TITLE} \rightarrow \text{SAL}$$

Notice that some of the attributes on the right-hand side of the second FD are also dependent on a subset of the set of attributes at the left-hand side of the same FD. Such attributes (ENAME,TITLE,SAL) are said to be *partially functionally dependent* on (ENO,PNO), whereas the others (RESP, DUR) are said to be *fully functionally dependent*.

Let R be a relation defined over the set of attributes $A = \{A_1, A_2, \ldots, A_n\}$, and let $X \subset A$, $Y \subset A$, $Z \subset A$. If for each value of Z in R, there is only one value for the (X, Y) pair, and the value of Z depends only on the value of X, we say that "X *multidetermines* Z" or that "Z is *multidependent* on X." This type of dependency is called *multivalued dependency* (MVD) and is denoted as $X \rightarrow\rightarrow Z$.

Intuitively, a MVD represents a situation where the value of one attribute (or a set of attributes) determines a *set of values* of another attribute (or set of attributes). Note that every FD is also an MVD, but the reverse is not necessarily true.

Example 2.3

Going back to our example, let us assume that we want to maintain information on the set of employees and on the set of projects that the company is involved in, as well as the branch offices where this project may be carried out. This can be done by defining the relation

$$\text{SKILL(ENO, PNO, PLACE)}$$

SKILL

ENO	PNO	PLACE
E1	P1	Toronto
E1	P1	New York
E1	P1	London
E1	P1	Toronto
E1	P2	New York
E1	P2	London
E2	P1	Toronto
E2	P1	New York
E2	P1	London
E2	P2	Toronto
E2	P2	New York
E2	P2	London

Figure 2.3. Example of MVD

Let us assume (probably unrealistically) that (1) each employee can work on each project, that (2) each employee is willing to work at any of the branch offices, and that (3) each project can be carried out at any of the branch offices. A sample relation instance satisfying these conditions is illustrated in Figure 2.3.

Notice that there are no FDs in the SKILL relation; the relation consists solely of key attributes. The only dependencies are the two MVDs

$$ENO \twoheadrightarrow PNO$$

$$ENO \twoheadrightarrow PLACE$$

Let R be a relation defined over the set of attributes $A = \{A_1, A_2, \ldots, A_n\}$, and $X \subset A$, $Y \subset A$, $Z \subset A$. Then, if R is equal to the join of X, Y, and Z, (X, Y, Z) constitutes a *projection-join dependency* for R. Again, we have not yet defined the join operation formally, but the intuitive discussion that we gave before is sufficient.

There is a set of inference rules based on a set of axioms—known as *Armstrong's axioms* [Armstrong, 1974]—that permit the algebraic manipulation of dependencies. They enable the discovery of the minimal cover of a set of FDs that is the minimal set of FDs from which all others can be generated. Given the minimal cover of FDs and a set of attributes, an algorithm can be developed to generate a relational scheme in higher normal forms.

2.2.2 Normal Forms

The first normal form (1NF) states simply that the attributes of the relation contain atomic values only. In other words, the tables should be flat with no repeating groups. The relations EMP and PROJ in Figure 2.2 satisfy this condition, so they both are in 1NF.

Relations in 1NF still suffer from the anomalies discussed earlier. To eliminate some of these anomalies, they should be decomposed into relations in higher normal forms. We are not particularly interested in the second normal form. In fact, it is only of historical importance, since there are algorithms that take a 1NF relation and directly normalize it to third normal form (3NF) or higher.

A relation R is in 3NF if for each FD $X \rightarrow Y$ where Y is not in X, either X is a superkey of R or Y is a prime attribute. There are algorithms that provide a lossless and dependency-preserving decomposition of a 1NF relation into a 3NF relation.

Example 2.4

The PROJ relation in the example we are considering is in 3NF, but EMP is not because of FD:

$$TITLE \rightarrow SAL$$

This violates 3NF, because TITLE is not a superkey and SAL is not prime.

The problem with EMP is the following. If we want to insert the fact that a given position (title) earns a specific salary, we cannot do so unless there is at least one employee holding that title. (Similar arguments can be made for the update and deletion anomalies.) Thus we have to decompose EMP into the following two relations:

EMP(ENO, ENAME, TITLE, PNO, RESP, DUR)

PAY(TITLE, SAL)

A careful reader will notice that even though PAY is in 3NF, EMP is not due to the FD:

$$ENO \rightarrow (ENAME, TITLE)$$

ENO is not a superkey and ENAME and TITLE are not prime attributes. Therefore, EMP needs to be further decomposed into

EMP(ENO, ENAME, TITLE)

ASG(ENO, PNO, RESP, DUR)

both of which are in 3NF.

Boyce-Codd normal form (BCNF) is a stronger form of 3NF. The definitions are identical except for the last part. For a relation to be in BCNF, for every FD $X \rightarrow Y, X$ has to be a superkey. Notice that the clause "or Y is a prime attribute" is deleted from the definition. The final form of relation EMP, as well as the relations PAY, PROJ, and ASG, are in BCNF.

It is possible to decompose a 1NF relation directly into a set of relations in BCNF. These algorithms are guaranteed to generate lossless decompositions; however, they cannot be guaranteed to preserve dependencies.

A relation R is in fourth normal form (4NF) if for each MVD of the type $X \rightarrow\rightarrow Y$ in R, X also functionally determines all the attributes of R. Thus, if a relation is in BCNF, and all MVDs are also FDs, the relation is in 4NF. The point is that a 4NF relation either does not contain a real MVD (i.e., every MVD is actually a FD) or there is exactly one MVD represented in the attributes and nothing else.

Example 2.5

Note that the relations EMP, PAY, PROJ, and ASG are in 4NF since there is no MVD defined on them. However, the SKILL relation discussed previously is not in 4NF. To satisfy the requirements, it needs to be decomposed into two relations:

EP(ENO, PNO)

EL(ENO, PLACE)

The careful reader will notice that in all of the previous normal forms, decomposition was into two relations. Fifth normal form (5NF) deals with those situations where n-way decompositions ($n > 2$) may be necessary.

A relation R is in 5NF (also called *projection-join normal form---PJNF*) if every join dependency defined for the relation is implied by the candidate keys of R. For a join dependency to be implied by a candidate key of a relation, the subset (or projections) X, Y, and Z (see definition of join dependency) should be made according to a candidate key.

Example 2.6

For relation EMP we can define the join dependency

*((ENO, ENAME), (ENO, TITLE))

which is implied by the candidate key ENO (which also happens to be the primary key). It is quite easy to verify that the relations EMP, PAY, PROJ, and ASG are in 5NF. Thus the relation schemes that we end up with after the decompositions are as follows:

EMP

ENO	ENAME	TITLE
E1	J. Doe	Elect. Eng.
E2	M. Smith	Syst. Anal.
E3	A. Lee	Mech. Eng.
E4	J. Miller	Programmer
E5	B. Casey	Syst. Anal.
E6	L. Chu	Elect. Eng.
E7	R. Davis	Mech. Eng.
E8	J. Jones	Syst. Anal.

ASG

ENO	PNO	RESP	DUR
E1	P1	Manager	12
E2	P1	Analyst	24
E2	P2	Analyst	6
E3	P3	Consultant	10
E3	P4	Engineer	48
E4	P2	Programmer	18
E5	P2	Manager	24
E6	P4	Manager	48
E7	P3	Engineer	36
E8	P3	Manager	40

PROJ

PNO	PNAME	BUDGET
P1	Instrumentation	150000
P2	Database Develop.	135000
P3	CAD/CAM	250000
P4	Maintenance	310000

PAY

TITLE	SAL
Elect. Eng.	40000
Syst. Anal.	34000
Mech. Eng.	27000
Programmer	24000

Figure 2.4. Normalized Relations

EMP(ENO, ENAME, TITLE)

PAY(TITLE, SAL)

PROJ(PNO, PNAME, BUDGET)

ASG(ENO, PNO, RESP, DUR)

The normalized instances of these relations are shown in Figure 2.4.

All NFs presented above are lossless. An important result [Fagin, 1977] is that a 5NF relation cannot be further decomposed without loss of information.

2.3 INTEGRITY RULES

Integrity rules are constraints that define consistent states of the database. They are usually expressed as assertions. Integrity constraints can be *structural* or *behavioral*. Structural constraints are inherent to the data model in the sense that they capture information on data relationships that cannot be modeled directly. Behavioral constraints permit the capturing of the semantics of the applications. The dependencies discussed in the preceding section are behavioral constraints. Maintaining integrity constraints is generally expensive in terms of system resources. Ideally, they should be verified at each database update since updates can lead to inconsistent database states. The problem of maintaining distributed integrity constraints is covered in Chapter 6.

According to [Codd, 1982], the two minimal structural constraints of the relational model are the *entity rule* and the *referential integrity rule*. By definition, any relation has a primary key. The entity rule dictates that each attribute of the key is nonnull. In Example 2.1, attribute PNO of relation PROJ and attributes (ENO, PNO) of relation EMP cannot have null values. This constraint is necessary to enforce the fact that keys are unique.

Referential integrity [Date, 1983] is useful for capturing relationships between objects that the relational model cannot represent. We make use of referential integrity in Chapter 5 during our discussion of distributed database design. Other data models, such as the hierarchical model [Tsichritzis and Lochovsky, 1976] or the entity/relationship model [Chen, 1976], can capture this type of information directly. Referential integrity involves two relations and imposes the constraint that a group of attributes in one relation is the key of another relation. In Example 2.1 there can be a referential integrity constraint between relations PROJ and EMP on attribute PNO. This rule prescribes that each employee belong to at least one existing project. In other words, the set of PNO values in relation EMP is included in relation PROJ. Thus there cannot be employees that belong to projects not in relation PROJ.

2.4 RELATIONAL DATA LANGUAGES

Data manipulation languages developed for the relational model (commonly called *query languages*) fall into two fundamental groups: *relational algebra*-based languages and *relational calculus*-based languages. The difference between them is based on how the user query is formulated. The relational algebra is procedural in that the user is expected to specify, using certain high-level operators, how the result is to be obtained. The relational calculus, on the other hand, is nonprocedural; the user only specifies the relationships that should hold in the result. Both of these languages were originally proposed by Codd [Codd, 1970], who also proved that they were equivalent in terms of expressive power [Codd, 1972].

Relational algebra is used more than relational calculus in the study of distributed database issues, because it is of lower level and corresponds more directly to the programs exchanged on a network. However, for the sake of completeness, we discuss them both here. Essentially, relational calculus can be translated into relational algebra.

2.4.1 Relational Algebra

Relational algebra consists of a set of operators that operate on relations. It is derived from set theory (relations corresponding to sets). Each operator takes one or two relations as operands and produces a result relation, which, in turn, may be an operand to another operator. These operations permit the querying and updating of a relational database.

Algebra operations.

There are five fundamental relational algebra operators and five others that can be defined in terms of these. The fundamental operators are *selection, projection, union, set difference*, and *Cartesian product*. The first two of these operators are unary operators, and the last three are binary operators. The additional operators that can be defined in terms of these fundamental operators are *intersection, θ-join, natural join, semijoin* and *quotient*. In practice, relational algebra is extended with operators for grouping or sorting the results, and for performing arithmetic and aggregate functions. Other operators, such as *outer join* and *transitive closure*, are sometimes used as well to provide additional functionality. However, they are not discussed here.

The operands of some of the binary relations should be *union compatible*. Two relations R and S are union compatible if and only if they are of the same degree and the ith attribute of each is defined over the same domain. The second part of the definition holds, obviously, only when the attributes of a relation are identified by their relative positions within the relation and not by their names. If relative ordering of attributes is not important, it is necessary to replace the second part of the definition by the phrase "the corresponding attributes of the two relations should be defined over the same domain." The correspondence is defined rather loosely here.

Selection.　　Selection produces a horizontal subset of a given relation. The subset consists of all the tuples that satisfy a formula (condition). The selection from a relation R is

$$\sigma_F(R)$$

where R is the relation and F is a formula.

Since we refer to formulas repeatedly in this chapter, let us define precisely what we mean at this point. We define a formula within the context of first-order predicate calculus ([Stoll, 1963] and [Enderton, 1972]) (since we use that formalism later), and follow the notation of [Gallaire et al., 1984]. First-order predicate calculus is based on a *symbol alphabet* that consists of (1) variables, constants, functions, and predicate symbols; (2) parentheses; (3) the logical connectors $\wedge$ (and), $\vee$ (or), $\neg$ (not), $\rightarrow$ (implication), and $\leftrightarrow$ (equivalence); and (4) quantifiers $\forall$ (for all) and $\exists$ (there exists). A *term* is either a constant or a variable. Recursively, if f is an $n$ary function and $t_1, \ldots, t_n$ are terms, $f(t_1, \ldots, t_n)$ is also a term. An *atomic formula* is of the form $P(t_1, \ldots, t_n)$, where P is an $n$ary predicate symbol and the t_i's are terms. A *well-formed formula* (*wff*) can be defined recursively as follows: If w_i and w_j are wffs, then $(w_i), \neg(w_i), (w_i) \wedge (w_j), (w_i) \vee (w_j), (w_i) \rightarrow (w_j)$, and $(w_i) \leftrightarrow (w_j)$ are all wffs. Variables in a wff may be *free* or they may be *bound* by one of the two quantifiers.

The formula in the selection operation is called a *selection predicate* and is an atomic formula whose terms are of the form $A\theta c$, where A is an attribute of R and θ is one of the arithmetic comparison operators $<, >, =, \neq, \leq$, and $\geq$. The terms can be connected by the logical connectors $\wedge, \vee$, and $\neg$. Furthermore, the selection predicate does not contain any quantifiers.

Example 2.7

Consider the relation EMP shown in Figure 2.4. The result of selecting those tuples for electrical engineers is shown in Figure 2.5.

$\sigma_{\text{TITLE="Elect. Eng."}}(\text{EMP})$

ENO	ENAME	TITLE
E1	J. Doe	Elect. Eng
E6	L. Chu	Elect. Eng.

Figure 2.5. Result of Selection

Projection.   Projection produces a vertical subset of a relation. The result relation contains only those attributes of the original relation over which projection is performed. Thus the degree of the result is less than or equal to the degree of the original relation.

The projection of relation R over attributes A and B is denoted as

$$\Pi_{A,B}(R)$$

Note that the result of a projection might contain tuples which are identical. In that case the duplicate tuples may be deleted from the result relation. It is possible to specify projection with or without duplicate elimination.

Example 2.8

The projection of relation PROJ shown in Figure 2.4 over attributes PNO and BUDGET is depicted in Figure 2.6.

$\Pi_{\text{PNO,BUDGET}}(\text{PROJ})$

PNO	BUDGET
P1	150000
P2	135000
P3	250000
P4	310000

Figure 2.6. Result of Projection

Union.   The union of two relations R and S (denoted as $R \cup S$) is the set of all tuples that are in R, or in S, or in both. We should note that R and S should be union compatible. As in the case of projection, the duplicate tuples are normally eliminated. Union may be used to insert new tuples into an existing relation, where these tuples form one of the operand relations.

Set Difference.   The set difference of two relations R and S $(R - S)$ is the set of all tuples that are in R but not in S. In this case, not only should R and S be union compatible, but the operation is also asymmetric (i.e., $R - S \neq S - R$). This operation allows the deletion of tuples from a relation. Together with the union operation, we can perform modification of tuples by deletion followed by insertion.

Cartesian Product.   The Cartesian product of two relations R of degree k_1 and S of degree k_2 is the set of $(k_1 + k_2)$-tuples, where each result tuple is a concatenation of one tuple of R with one tuple of S, for all tuples of R and S. The Cartesian product of R and S is denoted as $R \times S$.

It is possible that the two relations might have attributes with the same name. In this case the attribute names are prefixed with the relation name so as to maintain the uniqueness of the attribute names within a relation.

Example 2.9

Consider relations EMP and PAY in Figure 2.4. EMP $\times$ PAY is shown in Figure 2.7. Note that the attribute TITLE, which is common to both relations, appears twice, prefixed with the relation name.

Intersection.   Intersection of two relations R and S $(R \cap S)$ consists of the set of all tuples that are in both R and S. In terms of the basic operators, it can be specified as follows:

$$R \cap S = R - (R - S)$$

θ-Join.   Join is a derivative of Cartesian product. There are various forms of join, the most general of which is the θ-join, commonly called the join. The θ-join of two relations R and S is denoted as

$$R \bowtie_F S$$

where F is a formula specifying the *join predicate*. A join predicate is specified similar to a selection predicate, except that the terms are of the form $R.A\theta S.B$, where A and B are attributes of R and S, respectively.

The join of two relations is equivalent to performing a selection, using the join predicate as the selection formula, over the Cartesian product of the two operand relations. Thus

$$R \bowtie_F S = \sigma_F(R \times S)$$

EMP x PAY

ENO	ENAME	E.TITLE	PAY.TITLE	SAL
E1	J. Doe	Elect. Eng.	Elect. Eng.	40000
E1	J. Doe	Elect. Eng.	Syst. Anal.	34000
E1	J. Doe	Elect. Eng.	Mech. Eng.	27000
E1	J. Doe	Elect. Eng.	Programmer	24000
E2	M. Smith	Syst. Anal.	Elect. Eng.	40000
E2	M. Smith	Syst. Anal.	Syst. Anal.	34000
E2	M. Smith	Syst. Anal.	Mech. Eng.	27000
E2	M. Smith	Syst. Anal.	Programmer	24000
E3	A. Lee	Mech. Eng.	Elect. Eng.	40000
E3	A. Lee	Mech. Eng.	Syst. Anal.	34000
E3	A. Lee	Mech. Eng.	Mech. Eng.	27000
E3	A. Lee	Mech. Eng.	Programmer	24000
E8	J. Jones	Syst. Anal.	Elect. Eng.	40000
E8	J. Jones	Syst. Anal.	Syst. Anal.	34000
E8	J. Jones	Syst. Anal.	Mech. Eng.	27000
E8	J. Jones	Syst. Anal.	Programmer	24000

Figure 2.7. Partial Result of Cartesian Product

In the equivalence above, we should note that if F involves attributes of the two relations that are common to both of them, a projection is necessary to make sure that those attributes do not appear twice in the result.

Example 2.10

Figure 2.8 shows the θ-join of relations EMP and PAY in Figure 2.4 over the join predicate EMP.TITLE=PAY.TITLE. The same result could have been obtained as

$$\text{EMP}\bowtie_{\text{EMP.TITLE=PAY.TITLE}}\text{PAY} =$$
$$\Pi_{\text{ENO, ENAME, TITLE, SAL}}(\sigma_{\text{EMP.TITLE =PAY.TITLE}}(\text{EMP} \times \text{PAY}))$$

This example demonstrates a special case of θ-join which is called the *equi-join*. This is a case where the formula F only contains equality (=) as the arithmetic operator. It should be noted, however, that an equi-join does not have to be specified over a common attribute as the example above might suggest.

EMP ⋈ EMP.TITLE=PAY.TITLE PAY

ENO	ENAME	TITLE	SAL
E1	J. Doe	Elect. Eng.	40000
E2	M. Smith	Analyst	34000
E3	A. Lee	Mech. Eng.	27000
E4	J. Miller	Programmer	24000
E5	B. Casey	Syst. Anal.	34000
E6	L. Chu	Elect. Eng.	40000
E7	R. Davis	Mech. Eng.	27000
E8	J. Jones	Syst. Anal.	34000

Figure 2.8. The Result of Join

Natural Join. A natural join is an equi-join of two relations over a specified attribute, more specifically, over attributes with the same domain. There is a difference, however, in that usually the attributes over which the natural join is performed appear only once in the result. A natural join is denoted as the join without the formula

$$R \bowtie_A S$$

where A is the attribute common to both R and S. We should note here that the natural join attribute may have different names in the two relations; what is required is that they come from the same domain. In this case the join is denoted as

$$R_A \bowtie_B S$$

where B is the corresponding join attribute of S.

Example 2.11

The join of EMP and PAY in Example 2.10 is actually a natural join.

Semijoin. The semijoin of relation R, defined over the set of attributes A, by relation S, defined over the set of attributes B, is the subset of the tuples of R that participate in the join of R with S. It is denoted as $R \ltimes_F S$ (where F is a predicate as defined before) and can be obtained as follows:

$$R \ltimes_F S = \Pi_A(R \bowtie_F S) = \Pi_A(R) \bowtie_F \Pi_{A \cap B}(S)$$

$$= R \bowtie_F \Pi_{A \cap B}(S)$$

The advantage of semijoin is that it decreases the number of tuples that need to be handled to form the join. In centralized database systems, this is important because it usually results in a decreased number of secondary storage accesses by making better use of the memory. It is even more important in distributed databases since it usually reduces the amount of data that needs to be transmitted between sites in order to evaluate a query. We talk about this in more detail in Chapters 5 and 9. At this point note that the operation is asymmetric (i.e., $R \ltimes_F S \neq S \ltimes_F R$).

Example 2.12

To demonstrate the difference between join and semijoin, let us consider the semijoin of EMP with PAY over the predicate EMP.TITLE = PAY.TITLE, that is,

$$\text{EMP} \ltimes_{\text{EMP.TITLE = PAY.TITLE}} \text{PAY}$$

The result of the operation is shown in Figure 2.9. We would like to encourage the reader to compare Figures 2.8 and 2.9 to see the difference between the join and the semijoin operations. Note that the resultant relation does not have the PAY attribute and is therefore smaller.

$$\text{EMP} \ltimes_{\text{EMP.TITLE=PAY.TITLE}} \text{PAY}$$

ENO	ENAME	TITLE
E1	J. Doe	Elect. Eng.
E2	M. Smith	Analyst
E3	A. Lee	Mech. Eng.
E4	J. Miller	Programmer
E5	B. Casey	Syst. Anal.
E6	L. Chu	Elect. Eng.
E7	R. Davis	Mech. Eng.
E8	J. Jones	Syst. Anal.

Figure 2.9. The Result of Semijoin

(Division) Quotient. The division of relation R of degree r with relation S of degree s (where $r > s$ and $s \neq 0$) is the set of $(r - s)$-tuples t such that for all s-tuples u in S, the tuple tu is in R. The division operation is denoted as $R \div S$ and can be specified in terms of the fundamental operators as follows:

$$R \div S = \Pi_{\bar{A}}(R) - \Pi_{\bar{A}}((\Pi_{\bar{A}}(R) \times S) - R)$$

where $\bar{A}$ is the set of attributes of R that are not in S [i.e., the $(r - s)$-tuples].

Example 2.13

Assume that we have a modified version of the ASG relation (call it ASG′) depicted in Figure 2.10a and defined as follows:

$$\text{ASG}' = \Pi_{\text{ENO,PNO}} \text{ (ASG)} \bowtie_{\text{PNO}} \text{PROJ}$$

If one wants to find the employee numbers of those employees who are assigned to all the projects that have a budget greater than \$200,000, it is necessary to divide ASG′ with a restricted version of PROJ, called PROJ′ (see Figure 2.10b). The result of division $(G' \div J')$ is shown in Figure 2.10c.

The keyword in the query above is "*all.*" This rules out the possibility of doing a selection on ASG′ to find the necessary tuples, since that would only give those which correspond to employees working on *some* project with a budget greater than \$200,000, not those who work on all projects. Note that the result contains only the tuple <E3> since the tuples <E3, P3, CAD/CAM, 250000> and <E3, P4, Maintenance, 310000> both exist in ASG′. On the other hand, for example, <E7> is not in the result, since even though the tuple <E7, P3, CAD/CAM, 250000> is in ASG′, the tuple <E7, P4, Maintenance, 310000> is not.

Relational algebra programs.

Since all operations take relations as input and produce relations as outputs, we can nest operations using a parenthesized notation and represent relational algebra programs. The parentheses indicate the order of execution. The following are a few examples that demonstrate the issue.

Example 2.14

Consider the relations of Figure 2.4. The retrieval query

"Find the names of employees working on the CAD/CAM project"

can be answered by the relational algebra program

$$\Pi_{\text{ENAME}}(((\sigma_{\text{PNAME}} = \text{"CAD/CAM"} \text{ PROJ}) \bowtie_{\text{PNO}} \text{ASG}) \bowtie_{\text{ENO}} \text{EMP})$$

The order of execution is: the selection on PROJ, followed by the join with ASG, followed by the join with EMP, and finally the project on ENAME.

An equivalent program where the size of the intermediate relations is smaller is

$$\Pi_{\text{ENAME}} \text{ (EMP} \bowtie_{\text{ENO}} (\Pi_{\text{ENO}} \text{ (ASG} \bowtie_{\text{PNO}} (\sigma_{\text{PNAME}= \text{"CAD/CAM"}} \text{PROJ}))))$$

ASG'

ENO	PNO	PNAME	BUDGET
E1	P1	Instrumentation	150000
E2	P1	Instrumentation	150000
E2	P2	Database Develop.	135000
E3	P3	CAD/CAM	250000
E3	P4	Maintenance	310000
E4	P2	Database Develop.	135000
E5	P2	Database Develop.	135000
E6	P4	Maintenance	310000
E7	P3	CAD/CAM	250000
E8	P3	CAD/CAM	250000

(a)

PROJ'

PNO	PNAME	BUDGET
P3	CAD/CAM	250000
P4	Maintenance	310000

(b)

(ASG' ÷ PROJ')

ENO
E3

(c)

Figure 2.10. The Result of Division

Example 2.15

The update query

"Replace the salary of programmers by \$25,000"

can be computed by

$$(\text{PAY} - (\sigma_{\text{TITLE} = \text{``Programmer''}} \text{PAY})) \cup (<\text{Programmer}, 25000>)$$

2.4.2   Relational Calculus

In relational calculus-based languages, instead of specifying *how* to obtain the result, one specifies *what* the result is by stating the relationship that is supposed to hold for the result. Relational calculus languages fall into two groups: *tuple rela-*

tional calculus and *domain relational calculus*. The difference between the two is in terms of the primitive variable used in specifying the queries. We briefly review these two types of languages.

Relational calculus languages have a solid theoretical foundation since they are based on first-order predicate logic as we discussed before. Semantics is given to formulas by interpreting them as assertions on the database. A relational database can be viewed as a collection of tuples or a collection of domains. Tuple relational calculus interprets a variable in a formula as a tuple of a relation, whereas domain relational calculus interprets a variable as the value of a domain.

Tuple relational calculus.

The primitive variable used in tuple relational calculus is a *tuple variable* which specifies a tuple of a relation. In other words, it ranges over the tuples of a relation. Tuple calculus is the original relational calculus developed by Codd [Codd, 1970].

In tuple relational calculus queries are specified as

$$\{t|F(t)\}$$

where t is a tuple variable and F is a well-formed formula. The atomic formulas are of two forms:

1. *Tuple-variable membership expressions.* If t is a tuple variable ranging over the tuples of relation R (predicate symbol), the expression "tuple t belongs to relation R" is an atomic formula, which is usually specified as $R.t$ or $R(t)$.

2. *Conditions.* These can be defined as follows:

   (a) $s[A]\theta t[B]$, where s and t are tuple variables and A and B are components of s and t, respectively. θ is one of the arithmetic comparison operators $<$, $>$, $=$, $\neq$, $\leq$, and $\geq$. This condition specifies that component A of s stands in relation θ to the B component of t: for example, $s[\text{SAL}] > t[\text{SAL}]$.

   (b) $s[A]\theta c$, where s, A, and θ are as defined above and c is a constant. For example, $s[\text{ENAME}] = $ "Smith".

Note that A is defined as a component of the tuple variable s. Since the range of s is a relation instance, say S, it is obvious that component A of s corresponds to attribute A of relation S. The same thing is obviously true for B.

There are many languages that are based on relational tuple calculus, the most popular ones being SQL[1] [Date, 1987] and QUEL [Stonebraker et al., 1976]. SQL is now an international standard (actually, the only one) with standard versions

---

[1]Sometimes SQL is cited as lying somewhere between relational algebra and relational calculus. Its originators called it a "mapping language." However, it follows the tuple calculus definition quite closely; hence we classify it as such.

released in 1986 (known as SQL1), 1989 (modifications to SQL1) and 1992 (known as SQL2). A new version, including object-oriented language extensions, is in the works. This version, known as SQL3, will be released in parts starting in 1998.

SQL provides a uniform approach to data manipulation (retrieval, update), data definition (schema manipulation), and control (authorization, integrity, etc.). We limit ourselves to the expression, in SQL, of the queries in Examples 2.14 and 2.15.

Example 2.16

The query from Example 2.14,

"Find the names of employees working on the CAD/CAM project"

can be expressed as follows:

```
SELECT    EMP.ENAME
FROM      EMP,ASG,PROJ
WHERE     EMP.ENO = ASG.ENO
AND       ASG.PNO = PROJ.PNO
AND       PROJ.PNAME = "CAD/CAM"
```

Note that a retrieval query generates a new relation similar to the relational algebra operations.

Example 2.17

The update query of Example 2.15,

"Replace the salary of programmers by $25,000"

is expressed as

```
UPDATE    PAY
SET       SAL = 25000
WHERE     PAY.TITLE = "Programmer"
```

Domain relational calculus.

The domain relational calculus was first proposed by [Lacroix and Pirotte, 1977]. The fundamental difference between a tuple relational language and a domain relational language is the use of a *domain variable* in the latter. A domain variable ranges over the values in a domain and specifies a component of a tuple. In other words, the range of a domain variable consists of the domains over which the relation is defined. The wffs are formulated accordingly. The queries are specified in the following form:

$$x_1, x_2, ..., x_n | F(x_1, x_2, ..., x_n)$$

where F is a wff in which $x_1, \ldots, x_n$ are the free variables.

EMP	ENO	ENAME	TITLE
	E2	P.	

ASG	ENO	PNO	RESP	DUR
	E2	P3		

PROJ	PNO	PNAME	BUDGET
	P3	CAD/CAM	

Figure 2.11. Retrieval Query in QBE

The success of domain relational calculus languages is due mainly to QBE [Zloof, 1977], which is a visual application of domain calculus. QBE, designed only for interactive use from a visual terminal, is user friendly. The basic concept is an *example*: the user formulates queries by providing a possible example of the answer. Typing relation names triggers the printing, on screen, of their schemes. Then, by supplying keywords into the columns (domains), the user specifies the query. For instance, the attributes of the project relation are given by P, which stands for "Print."

By default, all queries are retrieval. An update query requires the specification of U under the name of the updated relation or in the updated column. The retrieval query corresponding to Example 2.16 is given in Figure 2.11 and the update query of Example 2.17 is given in Figure 2.12. To distinguish examples from constants, examples are underlined.

PAY	TITLE	SAL
	Programmer	U.25000

Figure 2.12. Update Query in QBE

2.4.3 Interface with Programming Languages

Relational data languages are insufficient to write complex application programs. Therefore, interfacing a relational data language to a programming language in which the application is written is usually necessary. We can distinguish between two main approaches in providing this service: the *tightly coupled* and *loosely coupled* approaches. The tightly coupled approach consists of extending some programming language with data manipulation commands. The loosely coupled approach consists of integrating the data language with a programming language using database calls.

Tightly coupled approach.

In this approach the programming language and the database language are merged in a single language. A typical example of this approach is Pascal/R [Schmidt, 1977], in which the language Pascal is extended with a new variable type *relation* that contains several (possibly many) instances of tuples (implemented via Pascal records) and with commands to manipulate relations (e.g., for each tuple in relation).

Another typical example of this approach is that of *fourth-generation languages* (4GL) [Martin, 1985]. They are well known because of their commercial success. Fourth-generation languages are high-level languages that combine relational algebra operators with programming constructs. The possibility of using temporary variables and powerful programming constructs (e.g., loops) makes them "database-oriented programming languages" in which application development is facilitated.

Example 2.18

To illustrate this type of language, let us consider the following simple application program (based on relation ASG in Figure 2.4):

"For the tuples in relation ASG where DUR > 40, perform a complex subprogram on attribute DUR, and produce a report that uses ENO and the result of the subprogram"

Assuming a generic 4GL, this program can be written as

```
for each ASG where DUR > 40
do
    perform subprogram X on DUR giving RESULT
    produce Report on ENO, RESULT
end
```

where RES is the results of the subprogram and Report is a predefined query to a report generator (often part of a 4GL).

Loosely coupled approach.

In this approach the programming language is a high-level language such as COBOL or PL/I which does not know about the database concepts. The programming language is simply extended with special commands that call the database system.

These commands are database language constructs simply preceded by a key character (e.g., $) to distinguish them from the constructs of the programming language.

The database languages used with these types of programming languages are
usually based on the tuple relational calculus and are set oriented. The programming language, on the other hand, is procedural. The conversion from the set-
oriented mode to the procedural mode required by the programming language is
generally simple; it is based on the use of a cursor on a set. A cursor can be explicit,
as in embedded SQL, or implicit, as in EQUEL (Embedded QUEL).

Two execution modes of such extended languages are possible: interpretation
of database calls at run time or precompilation of database calls. The latter mode
is more efficient.

Example 2.19

We illustrate this approach by considering the same application program as
in Example 2.18, but this time writing it in SQL embedded in PL/I, as shown
in Figure 2.13. The $ indicates a database command.

```
                          .
                          .
                          .
        $DCL VARDUR INT;
        $DCL VARENO INT;
                          .
                          .
                          .
        $LET C BE { cursor definition }
              SELECT    ASG.ENO: VARENO,ASG.DUR: VARDUR
              FROM      ASG
              WHERE     ASG.DUR>40
                          .
                          .
                          .
        $OPEN C
        DO WHILE "not end C"
        BEGIN
            $FETCH C;
            perform subprogram X on DUR giving RESULT;
            produce Report on ENO, RESULT
        END;
```

Figure 2.13. Example PL/I Program

2.5 RELATIONAL DBMS

A relational DBMS is a software component supporting the relational model and a relational language. A DBMS is a reentrant program shared by multiple alive entities, called *transactions*, that run database programs. When running on a general purpose computer, a DBMS is interfaced with two other components: the communication subsystem and the operating system. The generic architecture of a (centralized) DBMS is depicted in Figure 2.14. The communication subsystem permits interfacing the DBMS with other subsystems in order to communicate with applications. For example, the terminal monitor needs to communicate with the DBMS to run interactive transactions. The operating system provides the interface between the DBMS and computer resources (processor, memory, disk drives, etc.).

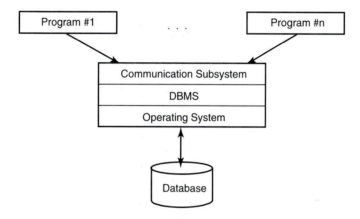

Figure 2.14. Generic Architecture of a Centralized DBMS

The functions performed by a relational DBMS can be layered as in Figure 2.15, where the arrows indicate the direction of the data and the control flow. Taking a top-down approach, the layers are the interface, control, compilation, execution, data access, and consistency management.

The *interface layer* manages the interface to the applications. There can be several interfaces such as SQL embedded in COBOL and QBE (query by example). Database application programs are executed against external *views* of the database. For an application, a view is useful in representing its particular perception of the database (shared by many applications). A relational view is a virtual relation derived from base relations by applying relational algebra operations.[2] View management consists of translating the user query from external data to conceptual

---

[2]Note that this does not mean that the real-world views are, or should be, specified in relational algebra. On the contrary, they are specified by some high-level data language such as SQL. The translation from one of these languages to relational algebra is now well understood, and the effects of the view definition can be specified in terms of relational algebra operations.

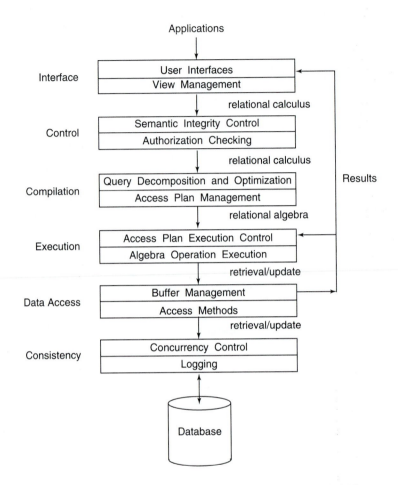

Figure 2.15. Functional Layers of a Relational DBMS

data (base relations). If the user query is expressed in relational calculus, the query applied to conceptual data is still in the same form.

The *control layer* controls the query by adding semantic integrity predicates and authorization predicates. Semantic integrity constraints and authorizations are specified in relational calculus, as discussed in Chapter 6. The output of this layer is an enriched query in relational calculus.

The *query processing* layer maps the query into an optimized sequence of lower-level operations. This layer is concerned with performance. It decomposes the query into a tree of relational algebra operations and tries to find the "optimal" ordering of the operations. The result is stored in an access plan. The output of this layer is a query expressed in relational algebra (or in lower-level code).

The *execution layer* directs the execution of the access plans, including transaction management (commit, restart) and synchronization of relational algebra operations. It interprets the relational operations by calling the data access layer through the retrieval and update requests.

The *data access layer* manages the data structures that implement the relations (files, indices). It also manages the buffers by caching the most frequently accessed data. Careful use of this layer minimizes the access to disks to get or write data.

Finally, the *consistency layer* manages concurrency control and logging for update requests. This layer allows transaction, system, and media recovery after failure.

2.6 BIBLIOGRAPHIC NOTES

This chapter covered the basic issues related to relational database systems. We chose to go into these concepts in some detail since the discussion in the remainder of the book is based on this data model. For those readers who may need additional coverage of these topics, we refer to a number of excellent database books, such as [Gardarin and Valduriez, 1989], [Ullman, 1982], [Ullman, 1988], [Elmasri and Navathe, 1994], [Korth and Silberschatz, 1986], and [Date, 1986]. A good source for additional information about other data models is [Tsichritzis and Lochovsky, 1981].

Chapter 3

REVIEW OF COMPUTER NETWORKS

In this chapter we discuss the issues related to computer networks and concentrate on the concepts and issues that are important for distributed database systems. We therefore omit most of the details of the technological and technical issues in favor of these conceptual presentations.

We define a *computer network* as an *interconnected collection of autonomous computers that are capable of exchanging information among them* (Figure 3.1). The keywords in this definition are *interconnected* and *autonomous*. We want the computers to be autonomous so that each computer can execute programs on its own. We also want the computers to be interconnected so that they are capable

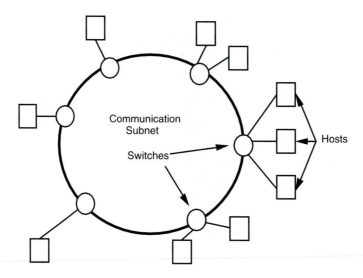

Figure 3.1. Computer Network

of exchanging information. Computers on a network are commonly referred to as *nodes*, *hosts*, or *sites*. They form one of the fundamental hardware components of a network. The other fundamental component is the communication path that interconnects the nodes among them. Note that sometimes the terms *host* and *node* are used to refer simply to the equipment, whereas *site* is reserved for the equipment as well as the software that runs on it.

A computer network is a special case of distributed computing environment where computers are the equipment connected to the data communication channel. In a general distributed environment, though, some of this equipment may be terminals or other specialized devices (such as banking machines). The fundamental data communication concepts discussed in Section 3.1 hold in these environments as well. However, our main interest in this book lies in computer networks since they provide the basic support for distributed database systems.

3.1 DATA COMMUNICATION CONCEPTS

Let us first define a few fundamental terms. To quote [Stallings, 1988]: "... *data* [are defined] as entities that convey meaning. *Signals* are electric or electromagnetic encoding of data. *Signaling* is the act of propagating the signal along some suitable medium. Finally, *transmission* is the communication of data by the propagation and processing of signals."

Equipment in a data communication environment is connected by *links* each of which can carry one or more *channels*. Link is a physical entity whereas channel is a logical one. Communication links can carry signals either in digital form or in analog form. Telephone lines, for example, can carry data in analog form, even though such links are being replaced by ones more suitable to digital transmission. Each communication channel has a *capacity*, which can be defined as the amount of data that can be transmitted over the channel in a given time unit. This capacity is commonly referred to as the *bandwidth* of the channel. In analog transmission channels, the bandwidth is defined as the difference (in hertz) between the lowest and highest frequencies that can be transmitted over the channel per second. In digital links, *bandwidth* refers (less formally) to the number of bits that can be transmitted per second (bps). Three ranges of communication links can be identified according to their bandwidth:

1. *Analog telephone channels*: can carry up to 33 Kbps with suitable modulation techniques

2. *Digital telephone circuits*: can carry 56 or 64 Kbps (referred to as ISDN rates)

3. *Broadband channels*: can carry 1.5 Mbps and above; these form the trunks of digital phone circuits

If data is transmitted over analog transmission links, it needs to be *modulated*. This means that the digital data is encoded onto an analog carrier signal by changing one or more of its basic characteristics (amplitude, frequency and phase). The modulated carrier signal propagates to the receiving end, where it is again converted into digital form. The advantage of using higher-bandwidth links is that the data being transmitted can be *multiplexed*, thereby allowing more than one signal to be transmitted over the same line simultaneously. Two types of multiplexing are possible to simultaneously transmit multiple logical channels over a single physical link. One alternative is to divide the link bandwidth such that each signal is transmitted at a different frequency. This form of multiplexing is known as *frequency-division multiplexing* (FDM). An alternative to this is to divide the unit transmission time into slots and assign the entire channel (i.e., the entire frequency band) to the transmission of one signal. This form of multiplexing is called *time-division multiplexing* (TDM) and is used more commonly in data communications.

We should mention that multiplexing for data transmission may be somewhat different. Depending on the characteristics of the link (i.e., whether the link is working as a digital transmission medium or an analog transmission medium), different forms of modulation and multiplexing may be necessary. However, these topics are beyond the scope of our discussion in this chapter. The fundamental point here is that the high-bandwidth links provide the ability to multiplex many signals onto the same physical line. On the other hand, the higher-bandwidth links are considerably costlier than their lower-bandwidth counterparts.

Another characteristic of a communication link from the perspective of distributed database systems is its mode of operation. A communication link may operate in a *simplex*, *half-duplex*, or *full-duplex* mode. A link that operates in simplex mode can transmit signals and data in only one direction. Typical application areas of such lines include connection to printers and card readers and real-time control applications where they are used to transmit signals from sensors to a central computer. Such links are considerably cheap, but they provide no flexibility of use whatsoever. Half-duplex links can transmit data in both directions, but they cannot do so simultaneously. The transmission has to proceed first in one direction, then the link has to be "turned around" and the transmission in the reverse direction can begin. The classic example is the very popular simple Ethernet where a station cannot receive and transmit at the same time. Thus, the Ethernet can be assumed to operate on half-duplex links without loss of functionality. Half-duplex links obviously provide more flexibility than simplex links, with an added cost. However, there is a delay in turning the link around that may be significant in distributed applications. Full-duplex links can transmit signals and data in both directions simultaneously. They are the most flexible transmission media and also the most costly. Leased lines generally operate in full-duplex mode. Full duplex operation on the analog telephone lines can also be implemented using FDM.

With respect to delays or to getting the user's work done, the bandwidth and the operating mode of a transmission channel are significant factors, but they are not necessarily the only ones that affect how long it takes to transfer data back and forth on a computer network. The other factor in the transmission time is the software employed. There are usually overhead costs involved in data transmission due to the redundancies within the message itself, necessary for error detection and correction. Furthermore, the network software adds headers and trailers to any message, for example, to specify the destination or to check for errors in the entire message. All of these activities contribute to delays in transmitting data. The actual rate at which data is transmitted across the network is known as the *data transfer rate* and this rate is usually less than the actual bandwidth of the transmission channel.

In computer-to-computer communication, data is usually transmitted in *frames*. Usually, upper limits on frame sizes are established for each network and each contains data as well as some control information, such as the destination and source addresses, block error check codes, and so on (Figure 3.2). If a message that is to be sent from a source node to a destination node cannot fit one frame, it is split over a number of frames. This will be discussed further in Section 3.3.

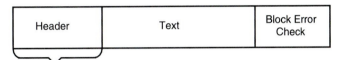

- Source address
- Destination address
- Message number
- Packet number
- Acknowledgment
- Control information

Figure 3.2. Typical Frame Format

Later in this chapter we will talk about "packets" and "packet switching". The terms "packet" and "frame" are sometimes used interchangeably, but this is not precisely correct even though they refer to similar concepts. In terms of communication protocols, they refer to entities at different layers. Specifically, in the ISO/OSI nomenclature that we discuss in Section 3.3, the term packet refers to a unit of transmission at the network layer while frame refers to a unit of transmission at the data link layer. From a practical perspective, the difference between the two often has to do with their formats. A packet format contains in its header network layer information, i.e., information about routing, while a frame includes only information related to the reliability mechanism of the data link layer.

3.2 TYPES OF NETWORKS

There are various criteria by which computer networks can be classified. One criterion is the *interconnection structure* of computers (also called *topology*), another is the mode of transmission, and a third is the geographic distribution (also called *scale* [Tanenbaum, 1997]).

3.2.1　Topology

As the name indicates, interconnection structure or topology refers to the way computers on a network are interconnected. Some of the more common alternatives are star, ring, bus, meshed, and irregular.

In *star* networks (Figure 3.3), all the computers are connected to a central computer that coordinates the transmission on the network. Thus if two computers want to communicate, they have to go through the central computer. Since there is a separate link between the central computer and each of the others, there is a negotiation between the "satellite" computers and the central computer when they wish to communicate.

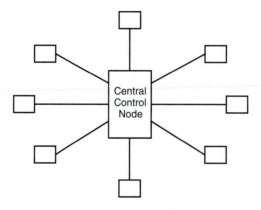

Figure 3.3. Star Network

This type of network is commonly used in organizations that are spread over a large geographical area with a central computer either at headquarters or at the regional centers. In this case local processing is performed at each node and data is eventually transmitted to the central computer. One disadvantage of star-type networks is their unreliability. Since the communication between any two computers depends on the availability of the central computer, a failure at this node will cause transmission over the network to cease completely. Another disadvantage is the excessive load on the central computer; since it has to coordinate the communication that goes on over the network, it has a heavier load to bear than do the other sites. Thus it is common to find a central site that is much more powerful than the satellite computers. Because of these disadvantages, star-type networks are commonly used only where the amount of data transmission between satellite computers is not excessive.

In ring networks (Figure 3.4), the computers are connected to the transmission medium, which is in the form of a loop. Data transmission around the ring is usually unidirectional, with each station (actually the interface to which each station is connected) serving as an active repeater which receives a message, checks the address, copies the message if it is addressed to that station, and retransmits it.

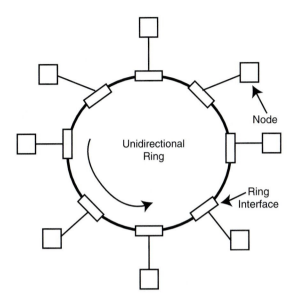

Figure 3.4. Ring Network

Control of communication in ring type networks is generally controlled by means of a *control token*. In the simplest type of token ring networks, a token, which has one bit pattern to indicate that the network is free and a different bit pattern to indicate that it is in use, is circulated around the network. Any site wanting to transmit a message waits for the token. When it arrives, the site checks the token's bit pattern to see if the network is free or in use. If it is free, the site changes the bit pattern to indicate that the network is in use and then places the messages on the ring. The message circulates around the ring and returns to the sender which changes the bit pattern to free and sends the token to the next computer down the line.

Networks that have a single ring-type transmission medium can be unreliable simply because breakage in the link at any point, or the failure of one of the stations, may disable the network. To provide more reliability, a double-loop topology may be employed [Wolf et al., 1979]. In such a network, the failure of one tap does not necessarily make the remaining portions of the network inaccessible since the damaged station can be bypassed by routing the transmission over the second ring.

An alternative mode of providing reliability is to use a central switch. The connections between the stations are made via a switching center even though the operation of the network can be in the form of a ring. If a station fails, or if a link breakage occurs, that portion of the network can very easily be bypassed within the central switch. This architecture was developed at the IBM Zurich Laboratory [Bux et al., 1983] and is implemented in the IBM token ring LAN.

Another popular topology is the bus (Figure 3.5), where a common channel used to transmit data is tapped by computers and terminals. In this type of network, the link control is performed in two fundamental ways. One scheme is called *carrier sense multiple access* (CSMA), and the other, *carrier sense multiple access with collision detection* (CSMA/CD). In addition to these two fundamental link control mechanisms, the bus can also be controlled by the use of a token, thus avoiding collisions. If this scheme is used, the bus is assumed to form a logical ring.

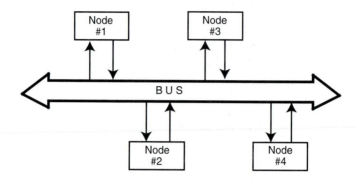

Figure 3.5. Bus Network

The CSMA/CD bus control mechanism, on the other hand, can best be described as a "listen while you transmit" scheme. The *basic CSMA/CD* operates in the following fashion: The sites function as in the CSMA scheme, except that they keep listening to the bus even after they transmit their message. The purpose of listening during transmission is to detect if collisions occur. There is a collision when two sites transmit messages concurrently (a site starts transmission while another is transmitting). In such a case, and when the collision is detected, the sites abort the transmission, wait a random amount of time, and then retransmit the message. The basic CSMA/CD scheme is used in the Ethernet local area network.

Another interconnection scheme is a *complete (meshed)* interconnection, where each node is interconnected to every other node (Figure 3.6). Such an interconnection structure obviously provides more reliability and the possibility of better performance than that of the structures noted previously. However, it is also the costliest.

A complete (meshed) interconnection scheme is not very realistic. Even if the number of computers on the network is small, the number of connections that are required are prohibitively large. For example, a complete connection of 10,000 computers would require approximately $(10,000)^2$ links.[1]

Communication networks frequently consist of irregularly placed communication links. That is, the links may be neither symmetrical nor follow a regular connectiv-

---

[1] The general form of the equation is $n(n-1)/2$, where n is the number of nodes on the network.

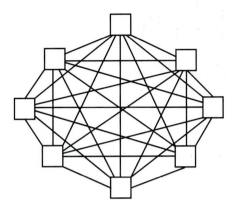

Figure 3.6. Meshed Network

ity pattern. It is possible to find a node that is connected to only one other node, as well as nodes that have connections to a number of nodes. Connections among the computers on the Internet, for example, are irregular.

3.2.2 Communication Schemes

In terms of the physical communication schemes employed, networks can be either *point-to-point* (also called *unicast*) networks, or *broadcast* (sometimes also called *multi-point*) networks.

In point-to-point networks, there are one or more links between each pair of nodes. There may not be a direct link between each pair, but there are usually a number of indirect links with intermediate connections. The communication is always between two nodes and the receiver and sender are identified by their addresses that are included in the frame header. Data transmission from the sender to the receiver follows one of the possibly many links between them, some of which may involve visiting other intermediate nodes. The intermediate nodes check the destination address in the frame header and if it is not addressed to them, pass it along to the next intermediate node. This is called *switching*. The selection of the links via which frames are sent is determined by usually elaborate protocols which are beyond our scope.

The fundamental transmission media for point-to-point networks are coaxial or fiber optic cables. The telephone network connection to customer equipment traditionally uses twisted pair copper wires. Thus it has limited potential for fast data communication. Instead, the cable TV network uses a coaxial-to-the-home infrastructure that facilitates high speed data networking. Similarly, many existing local area networks are coaxial based. However, these are now being converted to fiber optic cables which provide higher capacity and speed.

In broadcast networks, there is a common communication channel that is utilized by all the nodes in the network. Frames are transmitted over this common channel and received by all the nodes. Each node checks the receiver address within the header and if the frame is not addressed to it, ignores it.

A special case of broadcasting is *multicasting* where the message is sent to a subset of the nodes in the network. The receiver address in the frame header is somehow encoded to indicate which nodes are the recipients.

Broadcast networks are generally radio or satellite-based. In case of satellite transmission, each site beams its transmission to a satellite which then beams it back at a different frequency (Figure 3.7). Every site on the network listens to the receiving frequency and has to disregard the message if it is not addressed to that site. A network that uses this technique is the SATNET network [Jacobs et al., 1978].

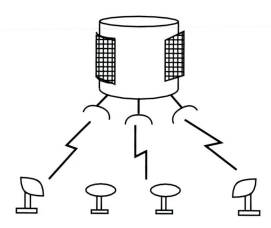

Figure 3.7. Satellite-Based Network

Microwave transmission is another very popular mode of data communication and it can be over satellite or terrestrial. Terrestrial microwave links already form a major portion of most countries' telephone networks. In addition to the public carriers, many companies are making extensive use of private terrestrial microwave links. In fact, major metropolitan cities face the problem of microwave interference among privately owned and public carrier links. An example of a network using satellite microwave transmission as its data communication medium is ALOHA [Abramson, 1973].

A final word on broadcasting topologies is that they have the advantage that it is easier to check for errors and to send messages to more than one site than to do so in point-to-point topologies. On the other hand, since everybody listens in, broadcast networks are not as secure as point-to-point networks.

3.2.3 Scale

In terms of geographic distribution, networks are classified as wide area networks, metropolitan area networks and local area networks. The distinctions among these are somewhat blurred, but in the following, we give some general guidelines that identify each of these networks. It should be pointed out that the primary distinction among the various types of networks are probably the protocols that are used in managing them. In the next section, we briefly discuss the more common wide area and local area network protocols.

A wide area network (WAN) is one where the link distance between any two nodes is greater than approximately 20 kilometers (km) and can go as high as thousands of kilometers. Use of routers and /or switches allow the aggregation of communication over wider areas such as this, but the increase in scale is achieved at the expense of a performance penalty resulting from the delays due to several routers/switches being involved between the two end points of communication. WANs can be constructed using either broadcast or point-to-point topologies, even though point-to-point is more common. Probably the most common form of point-to-point wide area networks is one with an irregular connection topology, even though others can be found as well.

There are various possible forms of switching that can occur in point-to-point networks. It is possible to establish a connection such that a dedicated channel exists between the sender and the receiver. This is called *circuit switching* and is commonly used in telephone connections. When a subscriber dials the number of another subscriber, a circuit is established between the two phones by means of various switches. The circuit is maintained during the period of conversation and is broken when one side hangs up.

Another form of switching used in computer communication is *packet switching*, where a message is broken up into packets and each packet transmitted individually. Packets for the same message may travel independently of each other and may, in fact, take different routes. The result of routing packets along possibly different links in the network is that they may arrive at the destination out-of-order. Thus the software at the destination site should be able to sort them into their original order to reconstruct the message.

The advantages of packet switching are many. First, packet-switching networks provide higher link utilization since each link is not dedicated to a pair of communicating equipment and can be shared by many. This is especially useful in computer communication due to its bursty nature. Typically, a terminal user will type in a command, wait for it to be executed and responded to, and then will spend some time thinking before typing in the next request. In such an environment, data transmission over the network is not continuous, but rather, bursty. The link can be used by others when the user is waiting for an answer or is thinking. Another reason is that packetizing may permit the parallel transmission of data. There is usually no requirement that various packets belonging to the same message travel the same route through the network. In such a case, they may be sent in parallel via different routes to improve the total data transmission time. As mentioned above, the result of routing frames this way is that their in-order delivery cannot be guaranteed.

On the other hand, circuit switching provides a dedicated channel between the receiver and the sender. If there is a sizable amount of data to be transmitted between the two, then the dedicated channel facilitates this significantly. Therefore, schemes similar to circuit switching (i.e., reservation-based schemes) gained favor in the broadband networks that support applications such as multimedia with very high data transmission loads.

Local area networks (LANs) are typically packet communication networks that are limited in geographic scope (usually less than 2 km). They provide high-bandwidth communication over inexpensive transmission media. The most common topologies are the bus and the ring and their variants such as the switched bus or switched ring. The types of transmission media employed in local area networks are usually coaxial cables, twisted-wire pairs, or optical fibers. A comparison of local area and wide area networks reveals the following differences:

1. In wide area networks, the cost of communication is quite high, whereas in local area networks, it is relatively low. There are various reasons for this difference, an obvious one being that the transmission distance is considerably shorter in local area networks than in wide area networks.

2. Traditional wide area networks usually have a limited bandwidth of less than a few megabits-per-second (Mbps), whereas local area networks have a larger bandwidth, typically about 10 -100 Mbps. We should note that broadband networks that we discuss later blur this difference.

3. Owing to the distances that need to be traveled, long delays are involved in wide area data transmission. For example, via satellite, there is a minimum delay of half a second for data to be transmitted from the source to the destination and acknowledged. This is because the speed with which signals can be transmitted is limited to the speed of light, and the distances that need to be spanned are great (19,200 miles from an earth station to a satellite). In contrast, the delays in local area networks are very short.

4. Owing to the heterogeneity of the transmission media, the computers, and the user community involved, as well as the low noise quality of the links being used, elaborate protocols are required in wide area networks to guarantee reliable data transmission. In local area networks the links have much less noise and interference, the heterogeneity among the computers that are connected is easier to manage, and a common transmission medium is used. Therefore, simpler protocols are generally sufficient.

5. Local area networks are owned and used by a single organization. However, wide area networks are rarely owned by their users. Thus, LAN users purchase a product while WAN users purchase a service.

LANs also provide additional opportunities, such as office automation applications, distributed process control applications, and central file servers, which could possibly decrease the cost of secondary storage on the system. Furthermore, local area networks are commonly broadcast type and therefore enjoy their associated advantages.

Metropolitan area networks (MANs) are in between LANs and WANs in scale and cover a city or a portion of it. The distances between nodes is typically on the order of 10 km. MANs have significant similarities with LANs and, in one sense, can be thought of as their larger versions. However, in MANs, the larger user population creates the need to solve new issues, such as the access and performance fairness for all users despite their physical location. Hence, although in principle some of the LAN protocols can be "scaled up" for MAN use, a separate set of protocols and design concerns are frequently involved. An example of a specific MAN protocol is DQDB.

3.3   PROTOCOL STANDARDS

Establishing a physical connection between two computers is not sufficient for them to communicate. Error-free, reliable and efficient communication between computers requires the implementation of elaborate software systems that are generally called *protocols*. The complexity of these protocols differ between wide area, local area and metropolitan networks.

Wide area networks commonly have to accommodate equipment that has been manufactured by different companies. This requires that the transmission media be able to handle the *heterogeneity* of equipment and connection. There might be differences in equipment in terms of speed, word length, coding scheme used to represent information, or any other criteria. Therefore, WANs have created a more urgent need for protocols. Thus, we start our discussion with WAN protocols and then move on to LANs. Until recently, the most extensively known WAN protocol is based on the open systems interconnection architecture of the International Standards Organization (commonly referred to as the *ISO/OSI architecture*) [ISO, 1983].

The ISO/OSI architecture specifies that the network is to be built in a layered fashion (thus the term *protocol stack*). Between layers at a given node, *interfaces* that facilitate the passing of information between the layers of software and hardware need to be clearly defined. Between the corresponding layers at different sites, *protocols* are defined to specify how the two nodes, more specifically, the same layers at different nodes present messages to each other. The ISO/OSI architecture, whose structure is shown in Figure 3.8, consists of seven layers. Starting from the lowest layer, these are the physical layer, the data link layer, the network layer, the transport layer, the session layer, the presentation layer, and the application layer. The lowest three layers, the physical, data link, and network layers, are together known as the *communication subnet*. The communication subnet is fundamentally responsible for providing a reliable physical communication between two sites. We do not discuss the details of these layers in detail. Interested readers can consult [Tanenbaum, 1997] or one of the many computer network books.

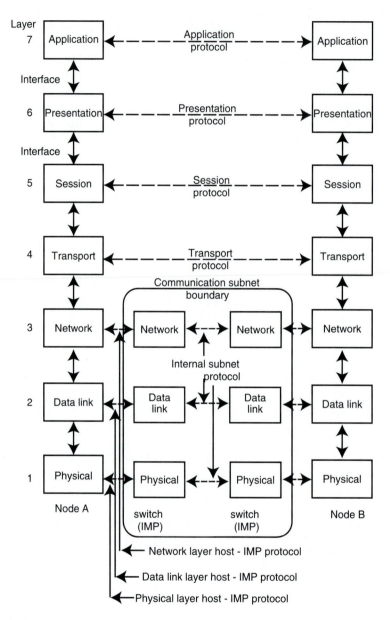

Figure 3.8. ISO/OSI Architecture (From: A.S. Tanenbaum, COMPUTER NET-WORKS 3/E, ©1997, p. 29. Reprinted by permission of Prentice-Hall, Inc., Englewood Cliffs, NJ.)

Another popular WAN protocol stack is the TCP/IP. The general idea is the same as ISO/OSI but the number of layers is five instead of seven. The protocol stack has "emerged" rather than developed as a consistent model. The relationship of the ISO/OSI and TCP/IP protocols is depicted in Figure 3.9. One significant difference between the two protocol stacks is that all layers of ISO/OSI are well-defined but the host-to-network layer of TCP/IP is not specified at all.

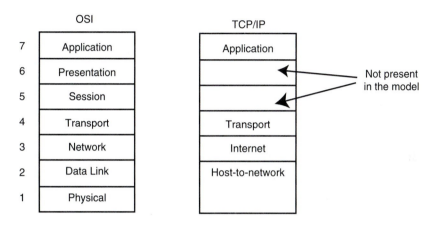

Figure 3.9. TCP/IP and ISO/OSI Comparison (From: A.S. Tanenbaum, COMPUTER NETWORKS 3/E, ©1997, p. 36. Reprinted by permission of Prentice-Hall, Inc., Englewood Cliffs, NJ.)

Achieving connectivity in the local area network is seemingly simpler than the same task over WANs because we are frequently interested with only the three lower layers of the protocol stack and in LANs the network equipment is more likely to be homogeneous in the first place. However, as we shall see, even LAN communication involves the interoperation at all the network layers and is also frequently accomplished using the IP and TCP/IP protocols.

The standardization in this area is spearheaded by the Institute of Electrical and Electronics Engineers (IEEE), specifically their Committee No. 802. This committee has established a standard that has two or three layers. The number of layers depends somewhat on how each layer is viewed. The fundamental requirements that were specified for this standard, known as the IEEE 802 Standard, are as follows. LANs are designed for commercial and light industrial applications, and to support reasonable reliability. The networks can transmit up to 2 km at a data rate of 1 to 10 Mbps. These specifications indicate that networks developed according to the standard are not to be used in heavy industrial applications for

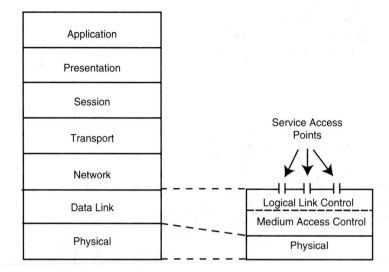

Figure 3.10. ISO/OSI–IEEE 802 Relationship (From: LOCAL AREA & MUL-TIPLE ACCESS NETWORKS, by William Stallings, edited by Raymond L. Pick-holtz. Copyright ©1986 by Computer Science Press. Reprinted by permission of W.H. Freeman and Company.)

example, in real-time control. The IEEE 802 standard IEEE 802 Standard requires that the protocols allow peer-to-peer communication. The latter specification elim-inates star-type networks where a central node monitors and controls access to the transmission channel. The three layers of the IEEE 802 local area network standard are the physical layer, the medium access control layer, and the logical link control layer. Their structure and their relationship to the ISO standard appear in Figure 3.10. TCP/IP is also used quite commonly in LANs, in which case the TCP/IP layers (Internet and transport) run on top of the IEEE 802 layers discussed below.

To enable it to cover a variety of the products on the market, the 802 local area network standard is actually a number of standards rather than a single one. Originally, it was specified to support three mechanisms at the medium access control level: the CSMA/CD mechanism, token ring, and token access mechanism for bus networks. The underlying wiring technology for these were twisted-pair or coaxial cables to support speeds in the range of 1 Mbps to 10 Mbps. Current LANs, however, operate at much higher speeds than that specified in the IEEE 802 protocol. Fiber optic-based FDDI networks as well as switched Ethernet operate at 100 Mbps. Thus, the 802 protocol has now accommodated FDDI as well as the metropolitan area network protocol DQDB. There are proposals to support broadband local area network standards such as ATM (see next section). The resulting protocol architecture is depicted in Figure 3.11. It should also be noted that most current LANs also support the TCP/IP protocol.

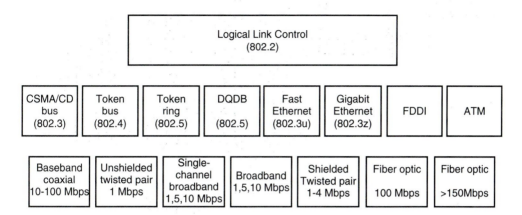

Figure 3.11. IEEE 802 Standard

3.4 BROADBAND NETWORKS

Up to this point, we have concentrated on "data networks," or networks that are specifically configured to carry digital data in either digital form or in modulated analog form. Thus, the data networks are, at least logically, separate from the voice (telephone) networks. However, many of the new applications that use computer networks (e.g., multimedia information systems) require capabilities to transmit other forms of data in addition to digital data, such as video and audio streams with real-time delivery requirements and still images with large bandwidth requirements (a 1024x1024 digital X-ray image with 8 bits/pixel requires 10 Mbps in uncompressed form). Broadband networks are designed to address these requirements in a single network environment. Their identifying characteristics are their high capacity (greater than 150 Mbps), ability to carry multiple data streams with varying characteristics, the possibility of negotiating for a level of quality of service (QoS) and reserving network resources sufficient to fulfill this level of QoS.

The most popular broadband network technology is the Asynchronous Transfer Mode (ATM) networks [ATM, 1996]. ATM networks have been developed for both WAN and LAN applications. At the user level, ATM supports five classes of service [Garrett, 1996]:

1. **CBR service**: This is the constant bit rate service where the network transmits data at an agreed upon bit rate. This service is provided for video and audio transmission (real time traffic) where the source offers

traffic constantly at the agreed rate. It does not involve any interactive services, so it is more suitable for applications such as video-on-demand.

2. **UBR service**: This is the unspecified bit rate service which is appropriate for applications that are interested in sending data in units rather than at a fixed rate. Most computer communications are this way; there are no real-time constraints and data is bursty. UBR service makes a "best effort" to deliver data, but does not provide any guarantees.

3. **rt-VBR service**: This service is also for real time traffic, but the source rate is allowed to vary. The variation allows optimizations since sources with varying bit rates can be multiplexed resulting in more efficient bandwidth use. It also accommodates interactive real time applications.

4. **nrt-VBR service**: The non-real time variable bit rate service category is for unit-oriented transmission similar to UBR. However, it improves UBR loss and delay characteristics by introducing QoS parameters such as peak and sustainable rates and the loss rate.

5. **ABR service**: Available bit rate service assigns whatever bit rate is currently available on the network to the requesting application. The emphasis is on minimizing the loss of frames and on adjusting the source reservations based on the variable traffic demand.

ATM is a packet switched network with special purpose switches that are connected by fiber optic links. The packets, which are called *cells* in ATM terminology, are 53 bytes in length (48 data, 5 header bytes). ATM technology fits the physical layer of ISO/OSI and TCP/IP protocol stacks (Figure 3.12) and requires an ATM adaptation layer (AAL) to compensate for the differences between ATM technology and the more traditional network technology developed for the upper protocol layers. AAL is responsible for handling lost and misdelivered cells, timing recovery,

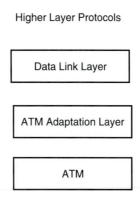

Figure 3.12. ATM Networks

splitting frames from upper protocol layers into ATM cells at the source and their reassembly at the destination. The cell routing and multiplexing/demultiplexing tasks are accomplished by the ATM layer using the ATM switches.

Current broadband networks operate around 155 Mbps. There are many trial WAN ATM systems in operation and many more ATM LANs have been deployed. The ability to carry multiple types of data at very high speeds and the opportunity to internetwork with other technology have hightened interest in this technology.

3.5 WIRELESS NETWORKS

Mobility and mobile computing are emerging as major forces. Wireless telephony is now widespread in many parts of the world. The earlier systems were analog and based on frequency modulation. Most of these wireless networks are now being converted to digital which increases the opportunity for mobile computing.

The term "wireless" is used somewhat carelessly. Satellite and microwave-based communications have existed for some time and they are indeed wireless. The current "wireless" networks in support of mobile computing are in fact "cellular" networks. These networks consist of a "wireline" backbone network on which a number of control stations are located. Each control station coordinates the communication from a mobile computers in their respective cell to another mobile computer in the same cell or in another cell or to a stationary computer on the wireline network (Figure 3.13).

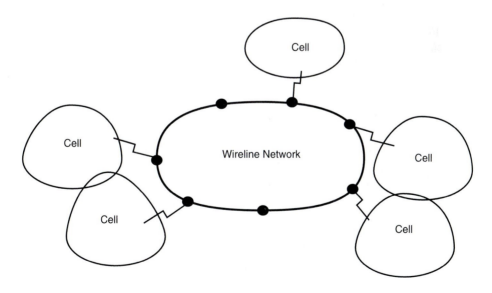

Figure 3.13. Cellular Networks

In cellular networks, each cell is (logically) organized as a star topology with the control station serving as the central node. Establishment of communication between two mobile stations in the same cell is straightforward. Establishment of communication between stations in different cells involves the coordination of multiple control stations. Since the mobile stations can move, they can cross the boundaries of a number of cells. This requires a "hand-over" process where one control station hands over the mobile station to another control station. Keeping track of this mobility requires some sort of directory management.

There can be a number of different types of mobile stations. One type involves fairly simple computers with limited capabilities. In this case, data are located in computers on the wireline network with the mobile stations "downloading" data as they need them. This scenario is realistic for some applications. However, in this case, the distributed data management problem is not significantly affected by mobility because data resides primarily on wireline computers. More interesting is the environment in which the mobile stations are more powerful and store native data that may need to be shared by others — the so-called "walkstation" case [Imielinski and Badrinath, 1994]. This approach causes significant difficulties for data management due to the communication, mobility, and portability characteristics of the mobile environment [Forman and Zahorjan, 1994].

Communication is over wireless networks which are prone to disconnection, noise, echo, and low bandwidth. Mobility of some of the equipment on the network causes static data in stationary networks to become dynamic and volatile in wireless networks. Mobility raises issues such as address migration, maintenance of directories and difficulty in locating stations. Finally, portability places restrictions on the type of equipment that can be used in these environments. For example, easy portability and the desire for long operation between battery recharges usually restrict the type and size of storage that can be used.

3.6 INTERNET

Internet is the term used to refer to the world-wide network of computers. In fact, it is a heterogeneous federation of networks, each with its own characteristics and protocols. The connections to Internet are voluntary and in most cases ad hoc in the sense that there is no controlling entity that enforces policies and guidelines for the communication of these networks. There is an Internet Engineering Task Force (IETF) but its effect has so far been minor.

The number of nodes on the Internet is growing very fast with more than 100 million connected computers expected by 2000. Perhaps the primary impetus for the fast growth of Internet has been the adoption of TCP/IP as the primary protocol. TCP/IP is now bundled with virtually all the operating systems, making it easier to connect to the Internet which can accommodate a variety of protocols (Figure 3.14).

Internet poses significant challenges, in particular due to the heterogeneity of the equipment and the networks. These are not issues that we will go into in

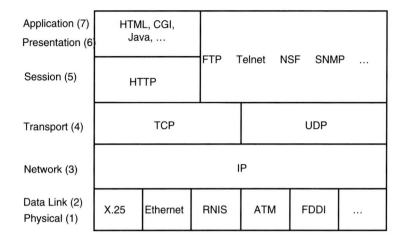

Figure 3.14. Internet Protocols

this chapter. However, the data management problems that it introduces will be discussed in the next section.

The identifying characteristics of Internet are the decentralized management structure (some even say that there is no management), the lack of security, and the many distributed services offered by the users and enterprises connected to the Internet. The main characteristic of Internet, however, is that all the computers connected to it support the same protocol (Internet Protocol - IP) at the network layer and the TCP/IP protocol is now provided with almost all of the operating systems.

3.7   CONCLUDING REMARKS

Even though computer networks are perhaps the fundamental infrastructure on which distributed DBMSs are built, it cannot be said that we have a good handle on the role of the network architectures and protocols in the performance of distributed DBMSs. Almost all the performance studies that we know assume a very simple network cost model, sometimes as unrealistic as using a fixed communication delay that is independent of all network characteristics such as the load, message size, network size and so on. The inappropriateness of these models can be demonstrated easily. Consider, for example, a distributed DBMS that runs on an Ethernet-type local area network. Message delays in Ethernet increase as the network load increases, and, in general, cannot be bounded. Therefore, realistic performance models of an Ethernet-based distributed DBMS cannot realistically use a constant network delay or even a delay function which does not consider network load.

As will be evident in future chapters, the cost models adopted for various distributed data management functions are overly simple. In general, the performance of the proposed algorithm and protocols in different local area network architectures is not well understood, let alone their comparative behavior in moving from local area networks to wide area networks. The proper way to deal with scalability issues is to develop general and sufficiently powerful performance models, measurement tools and methodologies. Such work for centralized DBMSs has been going on for some time, but has not yet been sufficiently extended to distributed DBMSs.

This does not mean that we do not have some understanding of the trade-offs. In fact, certain trade-offs have long been recognized and even the earlier systems have considered them in their design. For example, in traditional WANs, the network speeds are far lower than I/O speeds and these have been taken into account in building systems. However, these trade-offs can mostly be spelled out only in qualitative terms; their quantification requires more research on performance models.

The effect of networks has to be more realistically taken into account in the design of distributed DBMSs; that has motivated us to include significant details on the network infrastructure. Furthermore, the newer networks, such as broadband and wireless networks, raise additional data management concerns.

Broadband networks force us to rethink many of the assumptions of distributed database system design. In this approach, the network is no longer the bottleneck, as network speeds can exceed I/O speeds. This has led to the claim, as presented in Chapter 1, that the emergence of broadband networks threatens distributed databases because they make access to a remote centralized database feasible. Although we do not believe this to be a realistic outcome, there is no question that important architectural re-evaluation is necessary. For example, the tradeoffs of accessing data from a "neighbor's" cache rather than retrieving it from its own disk are under investigation[Franklin et al., 1992b], [Dahlin et al., 1994], [Freeley et al., 1995].

Mobile networks and their mobility, portability and communication characteristics also raise many issues. Here are some aspects that need consideration:

- **Architectural issues.** The nature of the portable equipment, their connection to a backbone wireline network and the capabilities of such a network (from the perspective of distributed data management) are important issues to study. If one assumes the existence of walkstations, as discussed above, then an important problem is the "optimum" distribution of data across the nodes of the backbone stationary network as well as the data that can reside on the walkstations. This is a difficult problem in stationary networks and becomes more difficult in mobile environments due to the mobility of the walkstations (which moves resident data), as well as the other access stations. The typical optimality measures take into account who is trying to access data from where and attempt to place some or all of that data in close proximity to the access points. These measures and the related design arguments need to be revisited in mobile environments. Another important issue may be the incorporation of global positioning systems (GPS) for proper location identification [Rappaport et al., 1996]. This has effects not only on directory management, but also on the types of queries the system can allow. Specifically, one can now ask position-dependent queries using real-world coordinates such as "Show me all the gas stations within 50 km of my current location."

- **Query processing and optimization.** As discussed in Chapter 1, query optimization takes into account cost measures such as local processing cost and communication cost. The mobility of access stations makes it difficult to determine communication costs between the accessing station and the station where the data resides. Furthermore, if the requested data is stored on one of the walkstations, then both network nodes may be in motion. The low bandwidth and, more importantly, the variability of the bandwidth between the wireless part and the backbone, further complicate the picture.

- **Concurrent sharing and reliability.** Transactions are the accepted primitives for providing concurrent access to shared data. Typical transaction management techniques rely on "locking" the shared data during access by one transaction in order to enforce mutual exclusion. Since wireless networks are more failure-prone than their stationary counterparts, locking may not be a good solution. Locks on data items at a failed station may be held for a long time, blocking the termination of that transaction. If that transaction holds locks at other sites, this would reduce the availability of data. It is necessary to consider different consistency criteria as well as algorithms and techniques to enforce them.

This is not an exhaustive list, but a representative sample. A more detailed discussion of mobile data management issues can be found in [Imielinski and Badrinath, 1994].

To complicate matters, these two technologies are proliferating simultaneously so the networks of tomorrow will likely be broadband backbones connected to wireless networks. Some of the broadband backbone may even be wireless, going over satellite channels. Additional difficulties will arise from the fact that bandwidth availability is offset by communication latency between earth stations and satellites. For example, query processing will have to take quality of service into account.

Internet poses its own database management problems simply due to the diversity of repositories it introduces. Many of these repositories are not full-fledged DBMSs, but "documents" of various types. In recent years, most of these repositories have been made available over the World Wide Web (WWW or Web) whose growth has been, at least partially, fostered by the availability of Internet connections. Most of these WWW repositories can now be accessed by interfaces that support navigation and browsing with very limited querying capabilities. These could be accessed as part of a distributed database infrastructure, but this raises many issues such as the lack of a schema, the heterogeneity of repositories, etc.

3.8 BIBLIOGRAPHIC NOTES

Details on data communication issues can be found in many books such as [Sherman, 1985], [Stallings, 1988], and [Halsall, 1988]. The classical text on the topic is [Tanenbaum, 1997]. Local networking issues are discussed in detail in [Stallings, 1984].

An excellent tutorial on ATM technology is [Boudec, 1992] although it is somewhat dated and written prior to finalization of many design decisions. The application of ATM technology to local area networks is discussed in [Newman, 1994].

Wireless networks are treated in depth in [Holtzman and Goodman, 1993]. An earlier tutorial paper is [Goodman, 1991]. [Forman and Zahorjan, 1994] is an excellent introduction to this topic and to the issues that it raises. The data management issues in mobile wireless networks is discussed in [Imielinski and Badrinath, 1994] and [Imielinski and Korth, 1996].

There have been many things written about the Internet. Perhaps the most cited reference on the World Wide Web is [Berners-Lee et al., 1994].

Chapter 4

DISTRIBUTED DBMS ARCHITECTURE

The architecture of a system defines its structure. This means that the components of the system are identified, the function of each component is specified, and the interrelationships and interactions among these components are defined. This general framework also holds true for computer systems in general and software systems in particular. The specification of the architecture of a software system requires identification of the various modules, with their interfaces and interrelationships, in terms of the data and control flow through the system. From a software engineering perspective, the task of developing individual modules is called *programming-in-the-small*, whereas the task of integrating them into a complete system is referred to as *programming-in-the-large*.

Since we are treating distributed DBMSs as large-scale software systems, we can define their architecture in a similar manner. In this chapter we develop three "reference" architectures for a distributed DBMS: client/server systems, peer-to-peer distributed DBMS, and multidatabase systems. These are "idealized" views of a DBMS in that many of the commercially available systems may deviate from them; however, the architectures will serve as a reasonable framework within which the issues related to distributed DBMS can be discussed. A reference architecture is commonly created by standards developers since it clearly defines the interfaces that need to be standardized. For example, the ISO/OSI model discussed in Chapter 3 is a reference architecture for wide area computer networks.

We started discussing the architectural features of relational DBMSs in Chapter 2. In this chapter we extend the discussion by studying generic architectures. The primary objective of the architecture definition is to structure the distributed DBMS such that it provides the functionality identified in Section 1.3. In particular, the transparency levels identified in that section are important, because the structure of a system should match the level of transparency one wants to provide. We start by looking at the DBMS standardization efforts (Section 4.1) and present a well-known reference architecture for centralized DBMSs. This is followed (Section 4.2) by a study of the design space for distributed DBMS implementation. We identify the alternatives and give examples. The reference architecture for distributed DBMSs that is used in the remainder of this book is introduced in Section 4.3. Finally, in Section 4.4, global directory issues are dealt with.

4.1 DBMS STANDARDIZATION

In this section we discuss the standardization efforts related to DBMSs because of the close relationship between the architecture of a system and the reference model of that system, which is developed as a precursor to any standardization activity. For all practical purposes, the reference model can be thought of as an idealized architectural model of the system. It is defined as "a conceptual framework whose purpose is to divide standardization work into manageable pieces, and to show at a general level how these pieces are related with each other" [DAFTG, 1986]. A reference model (and therefore a system architecture) can be described according to three different approaches [Kangassalo, 1983]:

1. Based on *components*. The components of the system are defined together with the interrelationships between components. Thus a DBMS consists of a number of components, each of which provides some functionality. Their orderly and well-defined interaction provides total system functionality. This is a desirable approach if the ultimate objective is to design and implement the system under consideration. On the other hand, it is difficult to determine the functionality of a system by examining its components. The DBMS standard proposals prepared by the Computer Corporation of America for the National Bureau of Standards ([CCA, 1980], [CCA, 1982]) fall within this category.

2. Based on *functions*. The different classes of users are identified and the functions that the system will perform for each class are defined. The system specifications within this category typically specify a hierarchical structure for user classes. This results in a hierarchical system architecture with well-defined interfaces between the functionalities of different layers. The ISO/OSI architecture discussed in Chapter 3 [ISO, 1983] fall in this category. The advantage of the functional approach is the clarity with which the objectives of the system are specified. However, it gives very little insight into how these objectives will be attained or the level of complexity of the system.

3. Based on *data*. The different types of data are identified, and an architectural framework is specified which defines the functional units that will realize or use data according to these different views. Since data is the central resource that a DBMS manages, this approach (also referred as the *datalogical* approach) is claimed to be the preferable choice for standardization activities [DAFTG, 1986]. The advantage of the data

approach is the central importance it associates with the data resource. This is significant from the DBMS viewpoint since the fundamental resource that a DBMS manages is data. On the other hand, it is impossible to specify an architectural model fully unless the functional modules are also described. The ANSI/SPARC architecture [Tsichritzis and Klug, 1978] discussed in the next section belongs in this category.

Even though three distinct approaches are identified, one should never lose sight of the interplay among them. As indicated in a report of the Database Architecture Framework Task Group of ANSI [DAFTG, 1986], all three approaches need to be used together to define an architectural model, with each point of view serving to focus our attention on different aspects of an architectural model.

A more important issue is the orthogonality of the foregoing classification schemes and the DBMS objectives (e.g., functionality, performance, etc.). Regardless of how we choose to view a DBMS, these objectives have to be taken into account. For example, in the functional approach, the objectives have to be addressed within each functional unit (e.g., query processor, transaction manager, etc.). In the remainder of this section we concentrate on a reference architecture that has generated considerable interest and is the basis of our reference model, described in Section 4.3.

In late 1972, the Computer and Information Processing Committee (X3) of the American National Standards Institute (ANSI) established a Study Group on Database Management Systems under the auspices of its Standards Planning and Requirements Committee (SPARC). The mission of the study group was to study the *feasibility* of setting up standards in this area, as well as determining which aspects should be standardized if it was feasible. The study group issued its interim report in 1975 [SPARC, 1975], and its final report in 1977 [Tsichritzis and Klug, 1978]. The architectural framework proposed in these reports came to be known as the "ANSI/SPARC architecture," its full title being "ANSI/X3/SPARC DBMS Framework." The study group proposed that the interfaces be standardized, and defined an architectural framework that contained 43 interfaces, 14 of which would deal with the physical storage subsystem of the computer and therefore not be considered essential parts of the DBMS architecture.

With respect to our earlier discussion on alternative approaches to standardization, the ANSI/SPARC architecture is claimed to be based on the data organization. It recognizes three views of data: the *external view*, which is that of the user, who might be a programmer; the *internal view*, that of the system or machine; and the *conceptual view*, that of the enterprise. For each of these views, an appropriate schema definition is required. Figure 4.1 depicts the ANSI/SPARC architecture from the data organization perspective.

At the lowest level of the architecture is the internal view, which deals with the physical definition and organization of data. The location of data on different storage devices and the access mechanisms used to reach and manipulate data are the issues dealt with at this level. At the other extreme is the external view, which is concerned with how users view the database. An individual user's view represents

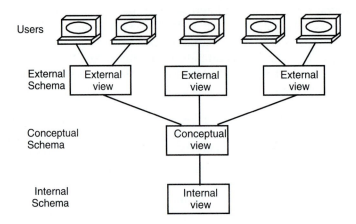

Figure 4.1. The ANSI/SPARC Architecture

the portion of the database that will be accessed by that user as well as the relationships that the user would like to see among the data. A view can be shared among a number of users, with the collection of user views making up the external schema. In between these two ends is the conceptual schema, which is an abstract definition of the database. It is the "real world" view of the enterprise being modeled in the database [Yormark, 1977]. As such, it is supposed to represent the data and the relationships among data without considering the requirements of individual applications or the restrictions of the physical storage media. In reality, however, it is not possible to ignore these requirements completely, due to performance reasons. The transformation between these three levels is accomplished by mappings that specify how a definition at one level can be obtained from a definition at another level.

Example 4.1

Let us consider the engineering database example we have been using and indicate how it can be described using a fictitious DBMS that conforms to the ANSI/SPARC architecture. Remember that we have four relations: EMP, PROJ, ASG, and PAY. The conceptual schema should describe each relation with respect to its attributes and its key. The description might look like the following:[1]

---

[1]Two points to note here. First, we are using the relational representation for the conceptual schema, but by no means do we suggest that the relational model is the only suitable formalism at the conceptual level. Second, the syntax of the description does not conform to any programming language.

```
RELATION EMP [
   KEY = {ENO}
   ATTRIBUTES = {
           ENO         : CHARACTER(9)
           ENAME       : CHARACTER(15)
           TITLE       : CHARACTER(10)
           }    ]
RELATION PAY[
   KEY = {TITLE}
   ATTRIBUTES = {
           TITLE       : CHARACTER(10)
           SAL         : NUMERIC(6)
           }    ]
RELATION PROJ [
   KEY = {PNO}
   ATTRIBUTES = {
           PNO         : CHARACTER(7)
           PNAME       : CHARACTER(20)
           BUDGET      : NUMERIC(7)
           }    ]
RELATION ASG [
   KEY = {ENO,PNO}
   ATTRIBUTES = {
           ENO         : CHARACTER(9)
           PNO         : CHARACTER(7)
           RESP        : CHARACTER(10)
           DUR         : NUMERIC(3)
           }    ]
```

At the internal level, the storage details of these relations are described. Let us assume that the EMP relation is stored in an indexed file, where the index is defined on the key attribute (i.e., the ENO) called EMINX.[2] Let us also assume that we associate a HEADER field which might contain flags (delete, update, etc.) and other control information. Then the internal schema definition of the relation may be as follows:

```
INTERNAL_REL EMPL [
   INDEX ON E# CALL EMINX
   FIELD = {
           HEADER      : BYTE(1)
           E#          : BYTE(9)
           E:NAME      : BYTE(15)
           TIT         : BYTE(10)
           }
   ]
```

---

[2]To keep the presentation simple, we will not concern ourselves with the details of indexing. Consider EMINX to be a primary index.

We have used similar syntaxes for both the conceptual and the internal descriptions. This is done for convenience only and does not imply the true nature of languages for these functions.

Finally, let us consider the external views, which we will describe using SQL notation. We consider two applications: one that calculates the payroll payments for engineers, and a second that produces a report on the budget of each project.[3] Notice that for the first application, we need attributes from both the EMP and the PAY relations. In other words, the view consists of a join, which can be defined as

```
CREATE    VIEW    PAYROLL(ENO, ENAME, SAL)
AS        SELECT  EMP.ENO,
                  EMP.ENAME,
                  PAY.SAL
          FROM    EMP, PAY
          WHERE   EMP.TITLE=PAY.TITLE
```

The second application is simply a projection of the PROJ relation, which can be specified as

```
CREATE    VIEW    BUDGET(PNAME, BUD)
AS        SELECT  PNAME, BUDGET
          FROM    PROJ
```

The investigation of the ANSI/SPARC architecture with respect to its functions results in a considerably more complicated view, as depicted in Figure 4.2.[4] The square boxes represent processing functions, whereas the hexagons are administrative roles. The arrows indicate data, command, program, and description flow, whereas the "I"-shaped bars on them represent interfaces.

The major component that permits mapping between different data organizational views is the data dictionary/directory (depicted as a triangle), which is a meta-database. It should at least contain schema and mapping definitions. It may also contain usage statistics, access control information, and the like. It is clearly seen that the data dictionary/directory serves as the central component in both processing different schemas and in providing mappings among them.

We also see in Figure 4.2 a number of administrator roles, which might help to define a functional interpretation of the ANSI/SPARC architecture . The three roles are the database administrator, the enterprise administrator, and the application administrator. The database administrator is responsible for defining the internal schema definition. The enterprise administrator's role is to prepare the conceptual schema definition. The person in this role is the focal point of the use of information within an enterprise. Finally, the application administrator is responsible for preparing the external schema for applications. Note that these are roles

---

[3]For simplicity, we will ignore semantic data control aspects of external view generation. These issues are discussed in Chapter 6.

[4]This is only a part of the system schematic that is provided in [Tsichritzis and Klug, 1978].

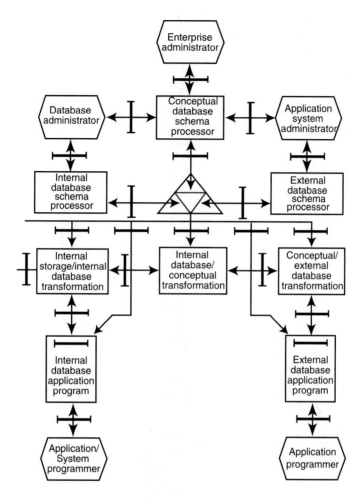

Figure 4.2. Partial Schematic of the ANSI/SPARC Architectural Model (Adapted from [Tsichritzis and Klug, 1978])

that might be fulfilled by one particular person or by several people. Hopefully, the system will provide sufficient support for these roles.

In addition to these three classes of administrative user defined by the roles, there are two more, the application programmer and the system programmer. Two more user classes can be defined, namely casual users and novice end users. Casual users occasionally access the database to retrieve and possibly to update information. Such users are aided by the definition of external schemas and by an easy-to-use query language. Novice users typically have no knowledge of databases and access information by means of predefined menus and transactions (e.g., banking machines).

4.2 ARCHITECTURAL MODELS FOR DISTRIBUTED DBMSs

Let us consider the possible ways in which multiple databases may be put together for sharing by multiple DBMSs. We use a classification (Figure 4.3) that organizes the systems as characterized with respect to (1) the autonomy of local systems, (2) their distribution, and (3) their heterogeneity.

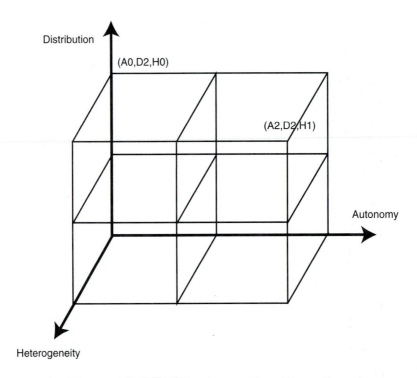

Figure 4.3. DBMS Implementation Alternatives

4.2.1 Autonomy

Autonomy refers to the distribution of control, not of data. It indicates the degree to which individual DBMSs can operate independently. Autonomy is a function of a number of factors such as whether the component systems exchange information, whether they can independently execute transactions, and whether one is allowed to modify them. Requirements of an autonomous system have been specified in a variety of ways. For example, [Gligor and Popescu–Zeletin, 1986] lists these requirements as follows:

1. The local operations of the individual DBMSs are not affected by their participation in the multidatabase system.

2. The manner in which the individual DBMSs process queries and optimize them should not be affected by the execution of global queries that access multiple databases.

3. System consistency or operation should not be compromised when individual DBMSs join or leave the multidatabase confederation.

On the other hand, [Du and Elmagarmid, 1989] specifies the dimensions of autonomy as:

1. Design autonomy: Individual DBMSs are free to use the data models and transaction management techniques that they prefer.

2. Communication autonomy: Each of the individual DBMSs is free to make its own decision as to what type of information it wants to provide to the other DBMSs or to the software that controls their global execution.

3. Execution autonomy: Each DBMS can execute the transactions that are submitted to it in any way that it wants to.

In the taxonomy that we consider in the book, we will use a classification that covers the important aspects of these features. One alternative is *tight integration*, where a single-image of the entire database is available to any user who wants to share the information, which may reside in multiple databases. From the users' perspective, the data is logically centralized in one database. In these tightly-integrated systems, the data managers are implemented so that one of them is in control of the processing of each user request even if that request is serviced by more than one data manager. The data managers do not typically operate as independent DBMSs even though they usually have the functionality to do so.

Next we identify *semiautonomous* systems that consist of DBMSs that can (and usually do) operate independently, but have decided to participate in a federation to make their local data sharable. Each of these DBMSs determine what parts of their own database they will make accessible to users of other DBMSs. They are not fully autonomous systems because they need to be modified to enable them to exchange information with one another.

The last alternative that we consider is *total isolation*, where the individual systems are stand-alone DBMSs, which know neither of the existence of other DBMSs nor how to communicate with them. In such systems, the processing of user transactions that access multiple databases is especially difficult since there is no global control over the execution of individual DBMSs.

It is important to note at this point that the three alternatives that we consider for autonomous systems are not the only possibilities. We simply highlight the three most popular ones.

4.2.2 Distribution

Whereas autonomy refers to the distribution of control, the distribution dimension of the taxonomy deals with data. Of course, we are considering the physical distribution of data over multiple sites; as we discussed in Chapter 1, the user sees the data as one logical pool. There are a number of ways DBMSs have been distributed. We abstract these alternatives into two classes: *client/server* distribution and *peer-to-peer* distribution (or *full* distribution). Together with the non-distributed option, the taxonomy identifies three alternative architectures.

The client/server distribution, which has become quite popular in the last number of years, concentrates data management duties at servers while the clients focus on providing the application environment including the user interface. The communication duties are shared between the client machines and servers. Client/server DBMSs represent the first attempt at distributing functionality. There are a variety of ways of structuring them, each providing a different level of distribution. With respect to the framework, we abstract these differences and leave that discussion to Section 4.1, which we devote to client/server DBMS architectures. What is important at this point is that the sites on a network are distinguished as "clients" and "servers" and their functionality is different.

In *peer-to-peer systems*, there is no distinction of client machines versus servers. Each machine has full DBMS functionality and can communicate with other machines to execute queries and transactions. These systems, which are also called *fully distributed*, are our main focus in this book, even though many of the techniques carry over to client/server systems as well.

4.2.3 Heterogeneity

Heterogeneity may occur in various forms in distributed systems, ranging from hardware heterogeneity and differences in networking protocols to variations in data managers. The important ones from the perspective of this book relate to data models, query languages, and transaction management protocols. Representing data with different modeling tools creates heterogeneity because of the inherent expressive powers and limitations of individual data models. Heterogeneity in query languages not only involves the use of completely different data access paradigms in different data models (set-at-a-time access in relational systems versus record-at-a-time access in network and hierarchical systems), but also covers differences in languages even when the individual systems use the same data model. Different query languages that use the same data model often select very different methods for expressing identical requests (e.g., DB2 uses SQL, while INGRES uses QUEL).[5]

4.2.4 Architectural Alternatives

Let us consider the architectural alternatives starting at the origin in Figure 4.3 and moving along the autonomy dimension. For identification, we use a notation based on the alternatives along the three dimensions. The dimensions are identified as A

---

[5]For completeness, note that INGRES also supports SQL.

(autonomy), D (distribution) and H (heterogeneity). The alternatives along each dimension are identified by numbers as 0, 1 or 2. These numbers, of course, have different meanings along each of the dimensions. Along the autonomy dimension, 0 represents tight integration, 1 represents semiautonomous systems and 2 represents total isolation. Along distribution, 0 is for no distribution, 1 is for client/server systems, and 2 is for peer-to-peer distribution. Finally, along the heterogeneity dimension, 0 identifies homogeneous systems while 1 stands for heterogeneous systems. In Figure 4.3, we have identified two alternative architectures that are the focus of this book: (A0, D2, H0) which is a (peer-to-peer) distributed homogeneous DBMS and (A2, D2, H1) which represents a (peer-to-peer) distributed, heterogeneous multidatabase system. We should note that not all the architectural alternatives that are identified by this design space are meaningful. We will, nevertheless, discuss each and indicate the unrealistic architectures where appropriate.

(A0, D0, H0): The first class of systems are those which are logically integrated. Such systems can be given the generic name *composite systems* [Heimbigner and McLeod, 1985]. If there is no distribution or heterogeneity, the system is a set of multiple DBMSs that are logically integrated. There are not many examples of such systems, but they may be suitable for shared-everything multiprocessor systems.

(A0, D0, H1): If heterogeneity is introduced, one has multiple data managers that are heterogeneous but provide an integrated view to the user. In the past, some work was done in this class where systems were designed to provide integrated access to network, hierarchical, and relational databases residing on a single machine (see, e.g., [Dogac and Ozkarahan, 1980]).

(A0, D1, H0): The more interesting case is where the database is distributed even though an integrated view of the data is provided to users. This alternative represents client/server distribution that we mentioned earlier and will discuss further in Section 4.3.1.

(A0, D2, H0): This point in the design space represents a scenario where the same type of transparency is provided to the user in a fully distributed environment. There is no distinction among clients and servers, each site providing identical functionality. We discuss this design point in more detail in Section 4.3.2 and this alternative remains our main focus in this book.

Recall from Chapter 1 that the last two cases exactly match the definition of what we have called a *distributed DBMS* but without any heterogneity. The following cases will introduce various degrees of heterogeneity to the system.

(A1, D0, H0): The next point in the autonomy dimension are semiautonomous systems, which are commonly termed *federated DBMS* [Heimbigner and McLeod, 1985]. As specified before, the component systems in a federated environment have significant autonomy in their execution, but their participation in a federation indicate that they are willing to cooperate with others in executing user requests that access multiple databases. At this point of the design space, the component systems do not have to be distributed or heterogeneous. An example may be multiple installations (on the same machine) of an "open" DBMS. Here open means that the DBMS knows how to participate in a federation. In such a set-up, each DBMS is devoted to a particular function yet a layer of software on top of them provides the user the capability to access all of them in an integrated manner. This is not a very realistic design alternative, but it establishes the framework for the next two architectures.

(A1, D0, H1): These are systems that introduce heterogeneity as well as autonomy, what we might call a *heterogeneous federated DBMS*. Examples of these are easy to find in everyday use. Assume, for example, that there is a relational DBMS that manages structured data, an image DBMS that handles still images and a video server.[6] If we wish to provide an integrated view to the users, then it is necessary to "hide" the autonomy and heterogeneity of the component systems and establish a common interface. Systems of this type are the focus of Chapter 15.

(A1, D1, H1): Systems of this type introduce distribution by placing component systems on different machines. They may be referred to as *distributed, heterogeneous federated DBMS*. It is fair to state that the distribution aspects of these systems are less important than their autonomy and heterogeneity. Distribution introduces some new problems, but generally the techniques developed for homogeneous and non-autonomous distributed DBMSs (i.e., alternatives (A0, D1, H0) and (A0, D2, H0)) can be applied to deal with those issues.

(A2, D0, H0): If we move to full autonomy, we get what we call the class of *multidatabase system* (MDBS) architectures. The identifying characteristic of these systems is that the components have no concept of cooperation and they do not even know how to "talk to each other". Without heterogeneity or distribution, an MDBS is an interconnected collection of autonomous databases. A multidatabase management system (multi-DBMS) is the software that provides for the management of this collection of autonomous databases and transparent access to it. This is not a very realistic alternative either since it assumes no heterogeneity among component systems. This can happen in only two cases: either we have multiple installations of the same DBMS or we have a set of DBMSs with identical functionality and interface. Neither of these circumstances are likely to occur.

(A2, D0, H1): This case is realistic, maybe even more so than (A1, D0, H1), in that we always want to build applications which access data from multiple

---

[6]We are assuming, at the moment, that these systems have sacrificed some of their autonomy by agreeing to join a federation. What this sacrifice means is not , as we will discuss in Chapter 15.

storage systems with different characteristics. Some of these storage systems may not even be DBMSs and they certainly have not been designed and developed with a view to interoperating with any other software. The example that we give for (A1, D0, H1) applies to this case as well if we assume that the component systems have no concept of entering a federation.

(A2, D1, H1) and (A2, D2, H1): We consider these two cases together simply because of the similarity of the problems. They both represent the case where component databases that make up the MDBS are distributed over a number of sites – we call this the *distributed MDBS*. As indicated above, the solutions to distribution issues for the two cases are similar and the general approach to dealing with interoperability does not differ too much. Perhaps the major difference is that in the case of client/server distribution (A2, D1, H1), most of the interoperability concerns are delegated to *middleware* systems resulting in a *three layer architecture*.

The organization of a distributed MDBS as well as its management is quite different from that of a distributed DBMS. We discuss this issue in more detail in the upcoming sections. At this point it suffices to point out that the fundamental difference is one of the level of autonomy of the local data managers. Centralized or distributed multidatabase systems can be homogeneous or heterogeneous.

The fundamental point of the foregoing discussion is that the distribution of databases, their possible heterogeneity, and their autonomy are orthogonal issues. Since our concern in this book is on distributed systems, it is more important to note the orthogonality between autonomy and heterogeneity. Thus it is possible to have autonomous distributed databases that are not heterogeneous. In that sense, the more important issue is the autonomy of the databases rather than their heterogeneity. In other words, if the issues related to the design of a distributed multidatabase are resolved, introducing heterogeneity may not involve significant additional difficulty. This, of course, is true only from the perspective of database management; there may still be significant heterogeneity problems from the perspective of the operating system and the underlying hardware.

It is fair to claim that the fundamental issues related to multidatabase systems can be investigated without reference to their distribution. The additional considerations that distribution brings, in this case, are no different from those of logically integrated distributed database systems. Therefore, in this chapter we consider architectural models of logically integrated distributed DBMSs and multidatabase systems.

4.3 DISTRIBUTED DBMS ARCHITECTURE

In this section we consider, in detail, three of the system architectures from among the thirty that we identified in the previous section. The three are client/server systems (where we discount the heterogeneity and autonomy issues – i.e., (Ax, D1,

Hy)), distributed databases, corresponding to (A0, D2, H0), and multidatabase systems, corresponding to (A2, Dx, Hy). These represent extremes that help focus the discussion on the most important issues.

4.3.1 Client/Server Systems

Client/server DBMSs entered the computing scene at the beginning of 1990's and have made a significant impact on both the DBMS technology and the way we do computing. The general idea is very simple and elegant: distinguish the functionality that needs to be provided and divide these functions into two classes: server functions and client functions. This provides a *two-level architecture* which makes it easier to manage the complexity of modern DBMSs and the complexity of distribution.

As with any highly popular term, client/server has been much abused and has come to mean different things. If one takes a process-centric view, then any process that requests the services of another process is its client and vice versa. In this sense, client/server computing is not new. However, it is important to note that "client/server computing" and "client/server DBMS," as it is used in its more modern context, do not refer to processes, but to actual machines. Thus, we focus on what software should run on the client machines and what software should run on the server machine.

Put this way, the issue is clearer and we can begin to study the differences in client and server functionality. The first thing to note is that the server does most of the data management work. This means that all of query processing and optimization, transaction management and storage management is done at the server. The client, in addition to the application and the user interface, has a *DBMS client* module that is responsible for managing the data that is cached to the client and (sometimes) managing the transaction locks that may have been cached as well. It is also possible to place consistency checking of user queries at the client side, but this is not common since it requires the replication of the system catalog at the client machines. Of course, there is operating system and communication software that runs on both the client and the server, but we only focus on the DBMS related functionality. This architecture, depicted in Figure 4.4, is quite common in relational systems where the communication between the clients and the server(s) is at the level of SQL statements. In other words, the client passes SQL queries to the server without trying to understand or optimize them. The server does most of the work and returns the result relation to the client.

There are a number of different types of client/server architecture. The simplest is the case where there is only one server which is accessed by multiple clients. We call this *multiple client-single server*. From a data management perspective, this is not much different from centralized databases since the database is stored on only one machine (the server) which also hosts the software to manage it. However, there are some (important) differences from centralized systems in the way transactions are executed and caches are managed. We do not consider such issues at this point. A more sophisticated client/server architecture is one where there are multiple

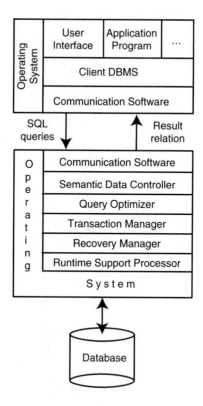

Figure 4.4. Client/Server Reference Architecture

servers in the system (the so-called *multiple client-multiple server* approach). In this case, two alternative management strategies are possible: either each client manages its own connection to the appropriate server or each client knows of only its "home server" which then communicates with other servers as required. The former approach simplifies server code, but loads the client machines with additional responsibilities. This leads to what has been called "heavy client" systems. The latter approach, on the other hand, concentrates the data management functionality at the servers. Thus, the transparency of data access is provided at the server interface, leading to "light clients."

From a datalogical perspective, client/server DBMSs provide the same view of data as do peer-to-peer systems that we discuss next. That is, they give the user the appearance of a logically single database, while at the physical level data **may** be distributed. Thus the primary distinction between client/server systems and peer-to-peer ones is not in the level of transparency that is provided to the users and applications, but in the architectural paradigm that is used to realize this level of transparency.

4.3.2   Peer-to-Peer Distributed Systems

Let us start the description of the architecture by looking at the data organizational view. We first note that the physical data organization on each machine may be, and probably is, different. This means that there needs to be an individual internal schema definition at each site, which we call the *local internal schema* (LIS). The enterprise view of the data is described by the *global conceptual schema* (GCS), which is global because it describes the logical structure of the data at all the sites.

As we discussed briefly in Chapter 1, data in a distributed database is usually fragmented and replicated. To handle this phenomenon of fragmentation and replication, the logical organization of data at each site needs to be described. Therefore, there needs to be a third layer in the architecture, the *local conceptual schema* (LCS). In the architectural model we have chosen, then, the global conceptual schema is the union of the local conceptual schemas. Finally, user applications and user access to the database is supported by *external schemas* (ESs), defined as being above the global conceptual schema.

This architecture model, depicted in Figure 4.5, provides the levels of transparency discussed in Section 4.1. Data independence is supported since the model is an extension of ANSI/SPARC, which provides such independence naturally. Location and replication transparencies are supported by the definition of the local and global conceptual schemas and the mapping in between. Network transparency, on the other hand, is supported by the definition of the global conceptual schema. The user queries data irrespective of its location or of which local component of the distributed database system will service it. As mentioned before, the distributed DBMS translates global queries into a group of local queries, which are executed by distributed DBMS components at different sites that communicate with one another.

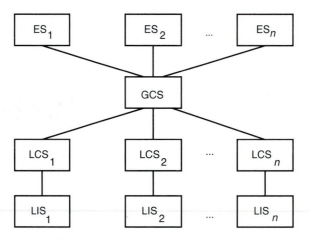

Figure 4.5. Distributed Database Reference Architecture

In terms of the detailed functional description of our model, the ANSI/SPARC model is extended by the addition of a *global directory/dictionary* (GD/D)[7] that permits the required global mappings. The local mappings are still performed by a *local directory/dictionary* (LD/D). Thus the local database management components are integrated by means of global DBMS functions (Figure 4.6).

As we can see in Figure 4.6, the local conceptual schemas are mappings of the global schema onto each site. Furthermore, such databases are typically designed in a top-down fashion, and therefore, all external view definitions are made globally. We have also depicted, in Figure 4.6, a local database administrator at each site. The existence of such a role may be controversial. However, remember that one of the primary motivations of distributed processing is the desire to have local control over the administration of data.

The detailed components of a distributed DBMS are shown in Figure 4.7. One component handles the interaction with users, and another deals with the storage. The first major component, which we call the *user processor*, consists of four elements:

1. The *user interface handler* is responsible for interpreting user commands as they come in, and formatting the result data as it is sent to the user.

2. The *semantic data controller* uses the integrity constraints and authorizations that are defined as part of the global conceptual schema to check if the user query can be processed. This component, which is studied in detail in Chapter 6, is also responsible for authorization and other functions.

3. The *global query optimizer and decomposer* determines an execution strategy to minimize a cost function, and translates the global queries into local ones using the global and local conceptual schemas as well as the global directory. The global query optimizer is responsible, among other things, for generating the best strategy to execute distributed join operations. These issues are discussed in Chapters 7 through 9.

4. The *distributed execution monitor* coordinates the distributed execution of the user request. The execution monitor is also called the *distributed transaction manager*. In executing queries in a distributed fashion, the execution monitors at various sites may, and usually do, communicate with one another.

The second major component of a distributed DBMS is the *data processor* and consists of three elements:

---

[7]In the remainder, we will simply refer to this as the *global directory*.

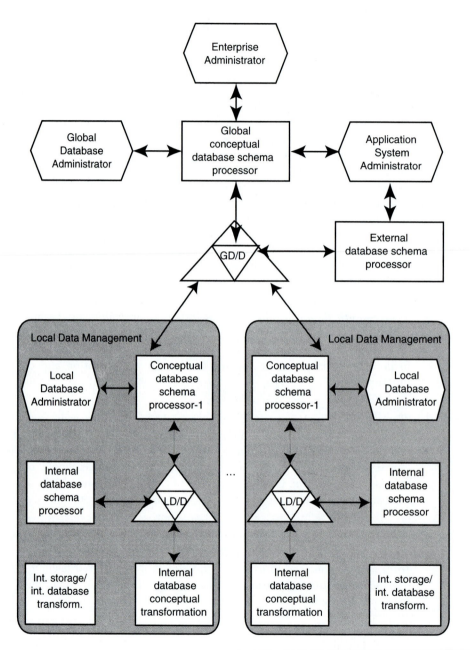

Figure 4.6. Functional Schematic of an Integrated Distributed DBMS

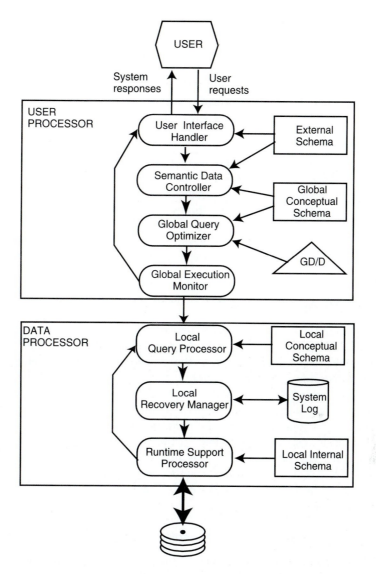

Figure 4.7. Components of a Distributed DBMS

1. The *local query optimizer*, which actually acts as the *access path selector*, is responsible for choosing the best access path[8] to access any data item (touched upon briefly in Chapter 9).

---

[8]The term *access path* refers to the data structures and the algorithms that are used to access the data. A typical access path, for example, is an index on one or more attributes of a relation.

2. The *local recovery manager* is responsible for making sure that the local database remains consistent even when failures occur (Chapter 12).

3. The *run-time support processor* physically accesses the database according to the physical commands in the schedule generated by the query optimizer. The run-time support processor is the interface to the operating system and contains the *database buffer* (or *cache*) *manager*, which is responsible for maintaining the main memory buffers and managing the data accesses.

It is important to note, at this point, that our use of the terms "user processor" and "data processor" does not imply a functional division similar to client/server systems. These divisions are merely organizational and there is no suggestion that they should be placed on different machines. In peer-to-peer systems, one expects to find both the user processor modules and the data processor modules on each machine. However, there have been suggestions to separate "query-only sites" in a system from full-functionality ones. In this case, the former sites would only need to have the user processor.

4.3.3 MDBS Architecture

The differences in the level of autonomy between the distributed multi-DBMSs and distributed DBMSs are also reflected in their architectural models. The fundamental difference relates to the definition of the global conceptual schema. In the case of logically integrated distributed DBMSs, the global conceptual schema defines the conceptual view of the *entire* database, while in the case of distributed multi-DBMSs, it represents only the collection of *some* of the local databases that each local DBMS wants to share. Thus the definition of a *global database* is different in MDBSs than in distributed DBMSs. In the latter, the global database is equal to the union of local databases, whereas in the former it is only a subset of the same union. There are even arguments as to whether the global conceptual schema should even exist in multidatabase systems. This question forms the basis of our architectural discussions in this section.

Models Using a Global Conceptual Schema

In a MDBS, the GCS is defined by integrating either the external schemas of local autonomous databases or parts of their local conceptual schemas (Figure 4.8). Furthermore, users of a local DBMS define their own views on the local database and do not need to change their applications if they do not want to access data from another database. This is again an issue of autonomy.

Designing the global conceptual schema in multidatabase systems involves the integration of either the local conceptual schemas or the local external schemas. A major difference between the design of the GCS in multi-DBMSs and in logically integrated distributed DBMSs is that in the former the mapping is from local conceptual schemas to a global schema. In the latter, however, mapping is in the reverse direction. As we discuss in Chapter 5, this is because the design in the

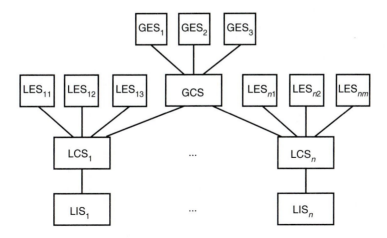

Figure 4.8. MDBS Architecture with a GCS

former is usually a bottom-up process, whereas in the latter it is usually a top-down procedure. Furthermore, if heterogeneity exists in the multidatabase system, a canonical data model has to be found to define the GCS.

Once the GCS has been designed, views over the global schema can be defined for users who require global access. It is not necessary for the GES and GCS to be defined using the same data model and language; whether they do or not determines whether the system is homogeneous or heterogeneous.

If heterogeneity exists in the system, then two implementation alternatives exist: unilingual and multilingual. A *unilingual* multi-DBMS requires the users to utilize possibly different data models and languages when both a local database and the global database are accessed. The identifying characteristic of unilingual systems is that any application that accesses data from multiple databases must do so by means of an external view that is defined on the global conceptual schema. This means that the user of the global database is effectively a different user than those who access only a local database, utilizing a different data model and a different data language. Thus, one application may have a *local external schema* (LES) defined on the local conceptual schema as well as a *global external schema* (GES) defined on the global conceptual schema. The different external view definitions may require the use of different access languages. Figure 4.8 actually depicts the datalogical model of a unilingual database system that integrates the local conceptual schemas (or parts of them) into a global conceptual schema. Examples of such an architecture are the MULTIBASE system ([Landers and Rosenberg, 1982], [Smith et al., 1981]) Mermaid [Templeton et al., 1987] and DDTS [Dwyer et al., 1986].

An alternative is *multilingual* architecture, where the basic philosophy is to permit each user to access the global database (i.e., data from other databases) by means of an external schema, defined using the language of the user's local

DBMS. The GCS definition is quite similar in the multilingual architecture and the unilingual approach, the major difference being the definition of the external schemas, which are described in the language of the external schemas of the local database. Assuming that the definition is purely local, a query issued according to a particular schema is handled exactly as any query in the centralized DBMSs. Queries against the global database are made using the language of the local DBMS, but they generally require some processing to be mapped to the global conceptual schema.

The multilingual approach obviously makes querying the databases easier from the user's perspective. However, it is more complicated because we must deal with translation of queries at run time. The multilingual approach is used in Sirius-Delta [Ferrier and Stangret, 1982] and in the HD-DBMS project [Cardenas, 1987].

Models Without a Global Conceptual Schema

The existence of a global conceptual schema in a multidatabase system is a controversial issue. There are researchers who even define a multidatabase management system as one that manages "several databases without a global schema" [Litwin, 1988]. It is argued that the absence of a GCS is a significant advantage of multidatabase systems over distributed database systems. One prototype system that has used this architectural model is the MRDSM project ([Litwin and Abdellatif, 1987], [Litwin and Abdellatif, 1986]). The architecture depicted in Figure 4.9, identifies two layers: the local system layer and the multidatabase layer on top of it. The local system layer consists of a number of DBMSs, which present to the multidatabase layer the part of their local database they are willing to share with users of other databases. This shared data is presented either as the actual local conceptual schema or as a local external schema definition. (Figure 4.9 shows this layer as a collection of local conceptual schemas.) If heterogeneity is involved, each of these schemas, LCS_i, may use a different data model.

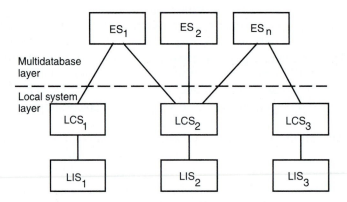

Figure 4.9. MDBS Architecture Without a GCS (From [Litwin, 1988])

Above this layer, external views are constructed where each view may be defined on one local conceptual schema or on multiple conceptual schemas. Thus the responsibility of providing access to multiple (and maybe heterogeneous) databases is delegated to the mapping between the external schemas and the local conceptual schemas. This is fundamentally different from architectural models that use a global conceptual schema, where this responsibility is taken over by the mapping between the global conceptual schema and the local ones. This shift in responsibility has a practical consequence. Access to multiple databases is provided by means of a powerful language in which user applications are written [Siegel, 1987].

Federated database architectures, which we discussed briefly, do not use a global conceptual schema either. In the specific system described in [Heimbigner and McLeod, 1985], each local DBMS defines an *export schema*, which describes the data it is willing to share with others. In the terminology that we have been using, the global database is the union of all the export schemas. Each application that accesses the global database does so by the definition of an *import schema*, which is simply a global external view.

The component-based architectural model of a multi-DBMS is significantly different from a distributed DBMS. The fundamental difference is the existence of full-fledged DBMSs, each of which manages a different database. The MDBS provides a layer of software that runs on top of these individual DBMSs and provides users with the facilities of accessing various databases (Figure 4.10). Depending on the existence (or lack) of the global conceptual schema or the existence of heterogeneity (or lack of it), the contents of this layer of software would change significantly. Note that Figure 4.10 represents a nondistributed multi-DBMS. If the system is distributed, we would need to replicate the multidatabase layer to each site where there is a local DBMS that participates in the system. Also note that as far as the individual DBMSs are concerned, the MDBS layer is simply another application that submits requests and receives answers.

The domain of federated database and multidatabase systems is complicated by the proliferation of terminology and different architectural models. We bring some order to the field in this section, but the architectural approaches that we summarize are not unique. In Chapter 15, we discuss another architectural specification that is widely cited, due to [Sheth and Larson, 1990].

4.4   GLOBAL DIRECTORY ISSUES

The discussion of the global directory issues is relevant only if one talks about a distributed DBMS or a multi-DBMS that uses a global conceptual schema. Otherwise, there is no concept of a global directory. If it exists, the global directory is an extension of the dictionary as described in the ANSI/SPARC report. It includes information about the location of the fragments as well as the makeup of the fragments.

As stated earlier, the directory is itself a database that contains *meta-data* about the actual data stored in the database. Therefore, the techniques we discuss in Chapter 5 with respect to distributed database design also apply to directory

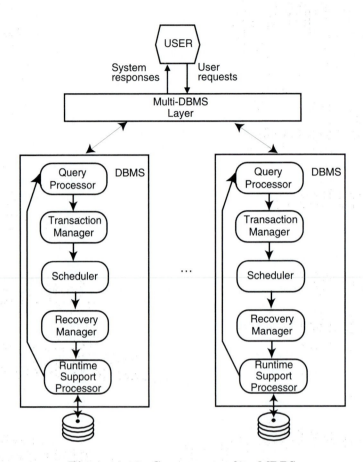

Figure 4.10. Components of an MDBS

management. Briefly, a directory may be either *global* to the entire database or *local* to each site. In other words, there might be a single directory containing information about all the data in the database, or a number of directories, each containing the information stored at one site. In the latter case, we might either build hierarchies of directories to facilitate searches, or implement a distributed search strategy that involves considerable communication among the sites holding the directories.

The second issue has to do with location. The directory may be maintained *centrally* at one site, or in a *distributed* fashion by distributing it over a number of sites. Keeping the directory at one site might increase the load at that site, thereby causing a bottleneck as well as increasing message traffic around that site. Distributing it over a number of sites, on the other hand, increases the complexity of managing directories. In the case of multi-DBMSs, the choice is dependent on whether or not the system is distributed. If it is, the directory is always distributed; otherwise of course, it is maintained centrally.

The final issue is replication. There may be a *single* copy of the directory or *multiple* copies. Multiple copies would provide more reliability, since the probability of reaching one copy of the directory would be higher. Furthermore, the delays in accessing the directory would be lower, due to less contention and the relative proximity of the directory copies. On the other hand, keeping the directory up to date would be considerably more difficult, since multiple copies would need to be updated. Therefore, the choice should depend on the environment in which the system operates and should be made by balancing such factors as the response-time requirements, the size of the directory, the machine capacities at the sites, the reliability requirements, and the volatility of the directory (i.e., the amount of change experienced by the database, which would cause a change to the directory). Of course, these choices are valid only in the case of a distributed DBMS. A nondistributed multi-DBMS always maintains a single copy of the directory, while a distributed one typically maintains multiple copies, one at each site.

These three dimensions are orthogonal to one another (Figure 4.11). Even though some combinations may not be realistic, a large number of them are. In Figure 4.11 we have designated the unrealistic combinations by a question mark. Note that the choice of an appropriate directory management scheme should also depend on the query processing and the transaction management techniques that will be used in subsequent chapters. We will come back to this issue again.

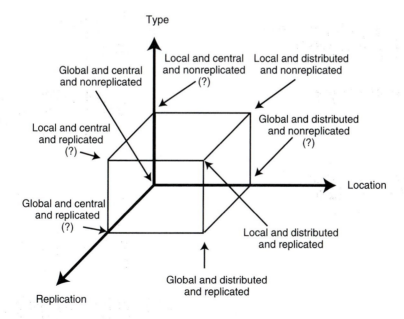

Figure 4.11. Alternative Directory Management Strategies

4.5 CONCLUSION

In this chapter we have considered the architectural issues in designing distributed database systems. Specifically, we considered two alternative design approaches which can be differentiated according to the degree of local autonomy that they provide for the management of local databases. The purposes of discussing the generic reference architectures are twofold: (1) to present the issues that need to be addressed in designing a distributed DBMS or a distributed multi-DBMS, and (2) to present a framework within which the design and implementation issues of such systems can be discussed. We should note that these are only abstract architectural models that we use in this book. There may not be (and probably is not) any distributed DBMS that adopts exactly this organization of components. Nevertheless, these models provide a pedagogically useful framework within which we can discuss the issues covered in the book.

We should indicate at this point that most of this book is devoted to a discussion of the issues related to logically integrated distributed database rather than mutidatabase systems. The reason for this emphasis is simple. Most research results obtained to date emphasize distributed DBMSs; research in multidatabase systems is relatively new and has not yet generated general-purpose solutions. For example, there is no transaction management theory for multidatabase systems, which in most cases prevents global updates of local databases. The material is simply not available to provide an in-depth and detailed analysis of solutions to problems. The notable exception is schema integration; most of this research has started with interest in heterogeneous database systems and several methodologies have been developed to design the global conceptual schema by integrating local conceptual schemas. Therefore, we devote Chapter 15 to a discussion of the issues in designing multi-DBMSs.

The standardization activity on database systems is an ongoing activity. Numerous other architectural proposals have been reported in the literature, but these are outside the scope of this book.

4.6 BIBLIOGRAPHIC NOTES

In addition to the early CODASYL reports and the ANSI/SPARC proposal, each of which defined new architectural models, recent activity has included reports by the Relational Database Task Group [Brodie and Schmidt, 1982] and the report of the Database Architecture Framework Task Group [DAFTG, 1986] of the ANSI/X3/SPARC Database System Study Group. International DBMS standardization activity as of 1982 is described in detail in [Locke, 1982], [Steel, 1982].

The intuitive and logical nature of the ANSI/SPARC architecture has prompted many researchers to investigate ways of extending it to the distributed environment. The proposals range from simple extensions, such as that described by [Mohan and Yeh, 1978], to very complicated ones, such as Shreiber's model [Schreiber, 1977], and anything in between [Adiba et al., 1978]. In this book we use a simple extension of the ANSI/SPARC architecture.

Among other architectural frameworks, the following are the most interesting. Schreiber [Schreiber, 1977] describes a quite detailed extension of the ANSI/SPARC framework which attempts to accommodate heterogeneity of the data models. The proposal by Mohan and Yeh [Mohan and Yeh, 1978] is quite similar to ours. The detailed component-wise system architecture given in Figure 4.7 also derives from [Rahimi, 1987]. An alternative to the classification that we provide in Figure 4.3 can be found in [Sheth and Larson, 1990].

Most of the discussion on architectural models for multi-DBMSs is from [Barker and Özsu, 1988] and [Özsu and Barker, 1990]. Other architectural discussions on multi-DBMSs are given in [Gligor and Luckenbaugh, 1984], [Litwin, 1988], and [Sheth and Larson, 1990]. All of these papers provide overview discussions of various prototype and commercial systems.

Chapter 5

DISTRIBUTED DATABASE DESIGN

The design of a distributed computer system involves making decisions on the placement of *data* and *programs* across the sites of a computer network, as well as possibly designing the network itself. In the case of distributed DBMSs, the distribution of applications involves two things: the distribution of the distributed DBMS software and the distribution of the application programs that run on it. The former is not a significant problem, since we assume that a copy of the distributed DBMS software exists at each site where data are stored. In this chapter we do not concern ourselves with application program placement either. Furthermore, we assume that the network has already been designed, or will be designed at a later stage, according to the decisions related to the distributed database design. We concentrate on distribution of data. It has been suggested that the organization of distributed systems can be investigated along three orthogonal dimensions [Levin and Morgan, 1975]:

1. Level of sharing

2. Behavior of access patterns

3. Level of knowledge on access pattern behavior

Figure 5.1 depicts the alternatives along these dimensions. In terms of the level of sharing, there are three possibilities. First, there is *no sharing*: each application and its data execute at one site, and there is no communication with any other program or access to any data file at other sites. This characterizes the very early days of networking and is probably not very common today. We then find the level of *data sharing*; all the programs are replicated at all the sites, but data files are not. Accordingly, user requests are handled at the site where they originate and the necessary data files are moved around the network. Finally, in *data-plus-program sharing*, both data and programs may be shared, meaning that a program at a given site can request a service from another program at a second site, which, in turn, may have to access a data file located at a third site.

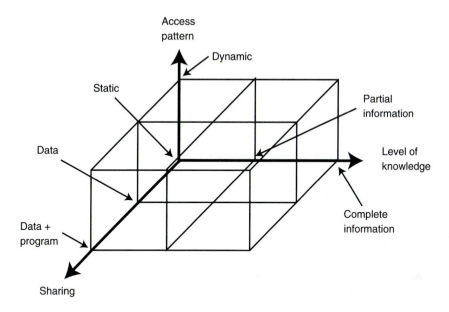

Figure 5.1. Framework of Distribution

Levin and Morgan draw a distinction between data sharing and data-plus-program sharing to illustrate the differences between homogeneous and heterogeneous distributed computer systems. They indicate, correctly, that in a heterogeneous environment it is usually very difficult, and sometimes impossible, to execute a given program on different hardware under a different operating system. It might, however, be possible to move data around relatively easily.

Along the second dimension of access pattern behavior, it is possible to identify two alternatives. The access patterns of user requests may be *static*, so that they do not change over time, or *dynamic*. It is obviously considerably easier to plan for and manage the static environments than would be the case for dynamic distributed systems. Unfortunately, it is difficult to find many real-life distributed applications that would be classified as static. The significant question, then, is not whether a system is static or dynamic, but how dynamic it is. Incidentally, it is along this dimension that the relationship between the distributed database design and query processing is established (refer to Figure 1.10).

The third dimension of classification is the level of knowledge about the access pattern behavior. One possibility, of course, is that the designers do not have any information about how users will access the database. This is a theoretical possibility, but it is very difficult, if not impossible, to design a distributed DBMS that can effectively cope with this situation. The more practical alternatives are that the designers have *complete information*, where the access patterns can reasonably be predicted and do not deviate significantly from these predictions, and *partial information*, where there are deviations from the predictions.

The distributed database design problem should be considered within this general framework. In all the cases discussed, except in the no-sharing alternative, new problems are introduced in the distributed environment which are not relevant in a centralized setting. In this chapter it is our objective to focus on these unique problems. The outline of this chapter is as follows. In Section 5.1 we discuss briefly two approaches to distributed database design: the top-down and the bottom-up design strategies. The details of the top-down approach are given in Sections 5.3 and 5.4, while the details of the bottom-up approach are postponed to another chapter (Chapter 15). Prior to the discussion of these alternatives, in Section 5.2 we present the issues in distribution design.

5.1 ALTERNATIVE DESIGN STRATEGIES

Two major strategies that have been identified [Ceri et al., 1987] for designing distributed databases are the *top-down approach* and the *bottom-up approach*. As the names indicate, they constitute very different approaches to the design process. But as any software designer knows, real applications are rarely simple enough to fit nicely in either of these alternatives. It is therefore important to keep in mind that in most database designs, the two approaches may need to be applied to complement one another.

We should also indicate that the issue addressed here is one of designing a database system using a distributed DBMS within the framework discussed in Section 4.3. This activity is a joint function of the database, enterprise, and application system administrators (or of the administrator performing all three roles).

5.1.1 Top-Down Design Process

A framework for this process is shown in Figure 5.2. The activity begins with a requirements analysis that defines the environment of the system and "elicits both the data and processing needs of all potential database users" [Yao et al., 1982a]. The requirements study also specifies where the final system is expected to stand with respect to the objectives of a distributed DBMS as identified in Section 1.3. To reiterate, these objectives are defined with respect to performance, reliability and availability, economics, and expandability (flexibility).

The requirements document is input to two parallel activities: view design and conceptual design. The *view design* activity deals with defining the interfaces for end users. The *conceptual design*, on the other hand, is the process by which the enterprise is examined to determine entity types and relationships among these entities. One can possibly divide this process into two related activity groups [Davenport, 1981]: entity analysis and functional analysis. *Entity analysis* is concerned with determining the entities, their attributes, and the relationships among them. *Functional analysis*, on the other hand, is concerned with determining the fundamental functions with which the modeled enterprise is involved. The results of these two steps need to be cross-referenced to get a better understanding of which functions deal with which entities.

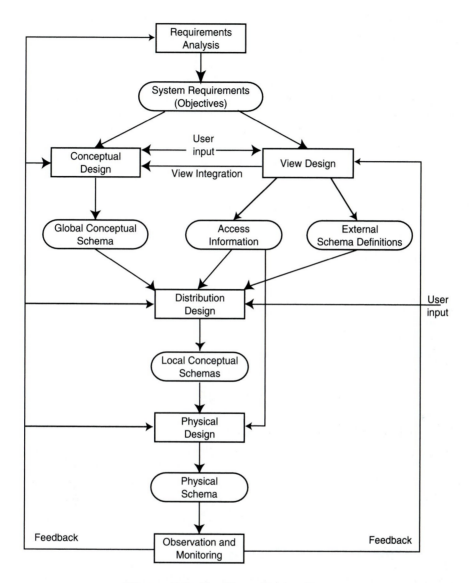

Figure 5.2. Top-Down Design Process

There is a relationship between the conceptual design and the view design. In one sense, the conceptual design can be interpreted as being an integration of user views. Even though this *view integration* activity is very important, the conceptual model should support not only the existing applications, but also future applications. view integration should be used to ensure that entity and relationship requirements for all the views are covered in the conceptual schema.

In conceptual design and view design activities the user needs to specify the data entities and must determine the applications that will run on the database as well as statistical information about these applications. Statistical information includes the specification of the frequency of user applications, the volume of various information, and the like. Note that from the conceptual design step comes the definition of global conceptual schema discussed in Section 4.3. We have not yet considered the implications of the distributed environment; in fact, up to this point, the process is identical to that in a centralized database design.

The global conceptual schema (GCS) and access pattern information collected as a result of view design are inputs to the *distribution design* step. The objective at this stage, which is the focus of this chapter, is to design the local conceptual schemas (LCSs) by distributing the entities over the sites of the distributed system. It is possible, of course, to treat each entity as a unit of distribution. Given that we use the relational model as the basis of discussion in this book, the entities correspond to relations.

Rather than distributing relations, it is quite common to divide them into subrelations, called *fragments*, which are then distributed. Thus the distribution design activity consists of two steps: *fragmentation* and *allocation*. The reason for separating the distribution design into two steps is to better deal with the complexity of the problem. However, as we discuss at the end of the chapter, this raises other concerns. These are the major issues that are treated in this chapter, so we delay discussing them until later sections.

The last step in the design process is the physical design, which maps the local conceptual schemas to the physical storage devices available at the corresponding sites. The inputs to this process are the local conceptual schema and access pattern information about the fragments in these.

It is well known that design and development activity of any kind is an ongoing process requiring constant monitoring and periodic adjustment and tuning. We have therefore included observation and monitoring as a major activity in this process. Note that one does not monitor only the behavior of the database implementation but also the suitability of user views. The result is some form of feedback, which may result in backing up to one of the earlier steps in the design.

5.1.2 Bottom-Up Design Process

Top-down design is a suitable approach when a database system is being designed from scratch. Commonly, however, a number of databases already exist, and the design task involves integrating them into one database. The bottom-up approach is suitable for this type of environment. The starting point of bottom-up design is the individual local conceptual schemas. The process consists of integrating local schemas into the global conceptual schema.

This type of environment exists primarily in the context of heterogeneous databases. Significant research has been conducted within this context as well. We will, therefore, defer the discussion of the bottom-up design process until Chapter 15. The rest of this chapter concentrates on the two fundamental issues in top-down design: fragmentation and allocation.

5.2 DISTRIBUTION DESIGN ISSUES

In the preceding section we indicated that the relations in a database schema are usually decomposed into smaller fragments, but we did not offer any justification or details for this process. The objective of this section is to fill in these details.

The following set of interrelated questions covers the entire issue. We will therefore seek to answer them in the remainder of this section.

- Why fragment at all?
- How should we fragment?
- How much should we fragment?
- Is there any way to test the correctness of decomposition?
- How should we allocate?
- What is the necessary information for fragmentation and allocation?

5.2.1 Reasons for Fragmentation

From a data distribution viewpoint, there is really no reason to fragment data. After all, in distributed file systems, the distribution is performed on the basis of entire files. In fact, the earlier work dealt specifically with the allocation of files to nodes on a computer network. We consider earlier models in Section 5.4.

With respect to fragmentation, the important issue is the appropriate unit of distribution. A relation is not a suitable unit, for a number of reasons. First, application views are usually subsets of relations. Therefore, the locality of accesses of applications is defined not on entire relations but on their subsets. Hence it is only natural to consider subsets of relations as distribution units.

Second, if the applications that have views defined on a given relation reside at different sites, two alternatives can be followed, with the entire relation being the unit of distribution. Either the relation is not replicated and is stored at only one site, or it is replicated at all or some of the sites where the applications reside. The former results in an unnecessarily high volume of remote data accesses. The latter, on the other hand, has unnecessary replication, which causes problems in executing updates (to be discussed later) and may not be desirable if storage is limited.

Finally, the decomposition of a relation into fragments, each being treated as a unit, permits a number of transactions to execute concurrently. In addition, the fragmentation of relations typically results in the parallel execution of a single query by dividing it into a set of subqueries that operate on fragments. Thus fragmentation typically increases the level of concurrency and therefore the system throughput. This form of concurrency, which we choose to refer to as *intraquery concurrency*, is dealt with mainly in Chapters 8 and 9, under query processing.

For the sake of completeness, we should also indicate the disadvantages of fragmentation. If the applications have conflicting requirements which prevent decomposition of the relation into mutually exclusive fragments, those applications whose views are defined on more than one fragment may suffer performance degradation.

It might, for example, be necessary to retrieve data from two fragments and then take either their union or their join, which is costly. Avoiding this is a fundamental fragmentation issue.

The second problem is related to semantic data control, specifically to integrity checking. As a result of fragmentation, attributes participating in a dependency may be decomposed into different fragments which might be allocated to different sites. In this case, even the simpler task of checking for dependencies would result in chasing after data in a number of sites. In Chapter 6 we return to the issue of semantic data control.

5.2.2 Fragmentation Alternatives

Relation instances are essentially tables, so the issue is one of finding alternative ways of dividing a table into smaller ones. There are clearly two alternatives for this: dividing it *horizontally* or dividing it *vertically*.

Example 5.1

In this chapter we use a modified version of the relational database scheme developed in Chapter 2. We have added to the PROJ relation a new attribute (LOC) that indicates the place of each project. Figure 5.3 depicts

EMP

ENO	ENAME	TITLE
E1	J. Doe	Elect. Eng
E2	M. Smith	Syst. Anal.
E3	A. Lee	Mech. Eng.
E4	J. Miller	Programmer
E5	B. Casey	Syst. Anal.
E6	L. Chu	Elect. Eng.
E7	R. Davis	Mech. Eng.
E8	J. Jones	Syst. Anal.

ASG

ENO	PNO	RESP	DUR
E1	P1	Manager	12
E2	P1	Analyst	24
E2	P2	Analyst	6
E3	P3	Consultant	10
E3	P4	Engineer	48
E4	P2	Programmer	18
E5	P2	Manager	24
E6	P4	Manager	48
E7	P3	Engineer	36
E8	P3	Manager	40

PROJ

PNO	PNAME	BUDGET	LOC
P1	Instrumentation	150000	Montreal
P2	Database Develop.	135000	New York
P3	CAD/CAM	250000	New York
P4	Maintenance	310000	Paris

PAY

TITLE	SAL
Elect. Eng.	40000
Syst. Anal.	34000
Mech. Eng.	27000
Programmer	24000

Figure 5.3. Modified Example Database

PROJ$_1$

PNO	PNAME	BUDGET	LOC
P1	Instrumentation	150000	Montreal
P2	Database Develop.	135000	New York

PROJ$_2$

PNO	PNAME	BUDGET	LOC
P3	CAD/CAM	255000	New York
P4	Maintenance	310000	Paris

Figure 5.4. Example of Horizontal Partitioning

the database schema instance we will use. Figure 5.4 shows the PROJ relation of Figure 5.3 divided horizontally into two relations. Subrelation PROJ$_1$
contains information about projects whose budgets are less than \$200,000,
whereas PROJ$_2$ stores information about projects with larger budgets.

Example 5.2

Figure 5.5 shows the PROJ relation of Figure 5.3 partitioned vertically into
two subrelations, PROJ$_1$ and PROJ$_2$. PROJ$_1$ contains only the information
about project budgets, whereas PROJ$_2$ contains project names and locations.
It is important to notice that the primary key to the relation (PNO) is included
in both fragments.

PROJ$_1$

PNO	BUDGET
P1	150000
P2	135000
P3	250000
P4	310000

PROJ$_2$

PNO	PNAME	LOC
P1	Instrumentation	Montreal
P2	Database Develop.	New York
P3	CAD/CAM	New York
P4	Maintenance	Paris

Figure 5.5. Example of Vertical Partitioning

The fragmentation may, of course, be nested. If the nestings are of different types, one gets *hybrid fragmentation* . Even though we do not treat hybrid fragmentation as a primitive type of fragmentation strategies, it is quite obvious that many real-life partitionings may be hybrid.

5.2.3 Degree of Fragmentation

The extent to which the database should be fragmented is an important decision that affects the performance of query execution. In fact, the issues in Section 5.2.1 concerning the reasons for fragmentation constitute a subset of the answers to the question we are addressing here. The degree of fragmentation goes from one extreme, that is, not to fragment at all, to the other extreme, to fragment to the level of individual tuples (in the case of horizontal fragmentation) or to the level of individual attributes (in the case of vertical fragmentation).

We have already addressed the adverse effects of very large and very small units of fragmentation. What we need, then, is to find a suitable level of fragmentation which is a compromise between the two extremes. Such a level can only be defined with respect to the applications that will run on the database. The issue is, how? In general, the applications need to be characterized with respect to a number of parameters. According to the values of these parameters, individual fragments can be identified. In Section 5.3 we describe how this characterization can be carried out for alternative fragmentations.

5.2.4 Correctness Rules of Fragmentation

When we looked at normalization in Chapter 2, we mentioned a number of rules to ensure the consistency of the database. It is important to note the similarity between the fragmentation of data for distribution (specifically, vertical fragmentation) and the normalization of relations. Thus fragmentation rules similar to the normalization principles can be defined.

We will enforce the following three rules during fragmentation, which, together, ensure that the database does not undergo semantic change during fragmentation.

1. *Completeness*. If a relation instance R is decomposed into fragments $R_1, R_2, \ldots, R_n$, each data item that can be found in R can also be found in one or more of R_i's. This property, which is identical to the *lossless decomposition* property of normalization (Chapter 2), is also important in fragmentation since it ensures that the data in a global relation is mapped into fragments without any loss [Grant, 1984]. Note that in the case of horizontal fragmentation, the "item" typically refers to a tuple, while in the case of vertical fragmentation, it refers to an attribute.

2. *Reconstruction*. If a relation R is decomposed into fragments $R_1, R_2, \ldots, R_n$, it should be possible to define a relational operator $\triangledown$ such that

$$R = \triangledown R_i, \quad \forall R_i \in F_R$$

The operator $\triangledown$ will be different for the different forms of fragmentation; it is important, however, that it can be identified. The reconstructability of the relation from its fragments ensures that constraints defined on the data in the form of dependencies are preserved.

3. *Disjointness.* If a relation R is horizontally decomposed into fragments $R_1, R_2, \ldots, R_n$ and data item d_i is in R_j, it is not in any other fragment R_k $(k \neq j)$. This criterion ensures that the horizontal fragments are disjoint. If relation R is vertically decomposed, its primary key attributes are typically repeated in all its fragments. Therefore, in case of vertical partitioning, disjointness is defined only on the nonprimary key attributes of a relation.

5.2.5   Allocation Alternatives

Assuming that the database is fragmented properly, one has to decide on the allocation of the fragments to various sites on the network. When data is allocated, it may either be replicated or maintained as a single copy. The reasons for replication are reliability and efficiency of read-only queries. If there are multiple copies of a data item, there is a good chance that some copy of the data will be accessible somewhere even when system failures occur. Furthermore, read-only queries that access the same data items can be executed in parallel since copies exist on multiple sites. On the other hand, the execution of update queries cause trouble since the system has to ensure that all the copies of the data are updated properly. Hence the decision regarding replication is a trade-off which depends on the ratio of the read-only queries to the update queries. This decision affects almost all of the distributed DBMS algorithms and control functions.

A nonreplicated database (commonly called a *partitioned* database) contains fragments that are allocated to sites, and there is only one copy of any fragment on the network. In case of replication, either the database exists in its entirety at each site (*fully replicated* database), or fragments are distributed to the sites in such a way that copies of a fragment may reside in multiple sites (*partially replicated* database). In the latter the number of copies of a fragment may be an input to the allocation algorithm or a decision variable whose value is determined by the algorithm. Figure 5.6 compares these three replication alternatives with respect to various distributed DBMS functions.

5.2.6   Information Requirements

One aspect of distribution design is that too many factors contribute to an optimal design. The logical organization of the database, the location of the applications, the access characteristics of the applications to the database, and the properties of the computer systems at each site all have an influence on distribution decisions. This makes it very complicated to formulate a distribution problem.

The information needed for distribution design can be divided into four categories: database information, application information, communication network

	Full replication	Partial replication	Partitioning
QUERY PROCESSING	Easy	←———— Same	difficulty ————→
DIRECTORY MANAGEMENT	Easy or nonexistent	←———— Same	difficulty ————→
CONCURRENCY CONTROL	Moderate	Difficult	Easy
RELIABILITY	Very high	High	Low
REALITY	Possible application	Realistic	Possible application

Figure 5.6. Comparison of Replication Alternatives

information, and computer system information. The latter two categories are completely quantitative in nature and are used in allocation models rather than in fragmentation algorithms. We do not consider them in detail here. Instead, the detailed information requirements of the fragmentation and allocation algorithms are discussed in their respective sections.

5.3 FRAGMENTATION

In this section we present the various fragmentation strategies and algorithms. As mentioned previously, there are two fundamental fragmentation strategies: horizontal and vertical. Furthermore, there is a possibility of nesting fragments in a hybrid fashion.

5.3.1 Horizontal Fragmentation

As we explained earlier, horizontal fragmentation partitions a relation along its tuples. Thus each fragment has a subset of the tuples of the relation. There are two versions of horizontal partitioning: primary and derived. *Primary horizontal fragmentation* of a relation is performed using predicates that are defined on that relation. *Derived horizontal fragmentation*, on the other hand, is the partitioning of a relation that results from predicates being defined on another relation.

Later in this section we consider an algorithm for performing both of these fragmentations. However, first we investigate the information needed to carry out horizontal fragmentation activity.

Information Requirements of Horizontal Fragmentation

Database Information. The database information concerns the global conceptual schema. In this context it is important to note how the database relations are connected to one another, especially with joins. In the relational model, these relationships are also depicted as relations. However, in other data models, such as the entity-relationship (E–R) model [Chen, 1976], these relationships between database objects are depicted explicitly. In [Ceri et al., 1983] the relationship is also modeled explicitly, within the relational framework, for purposes of the distribution design. In the latter notation, directed *links* are drawn between relations that are related to each other by an equijoin operation.

Example 5.3

Figure 5.7 shows the expression of links among the database relations given in Figure 2.4. Note that the direction of the link shows a one-to-many relationship. For example, for each title there are multiple employees with that title; thus there is a link between the PAY and EMP relations. Along the same lines, the many-to-many relationship between the EMP and PROJ relations is expressed with two links to the ASG relation.

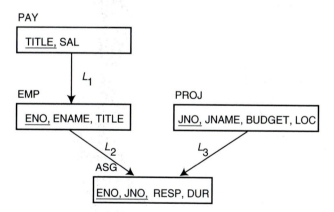

Figure 5.7. Expression of Relationships Among Relations Using Links

The links between database objects (i.e., relations in our case) should be quite familiar to those who have dealt with network models of data. In the relational model they are introduced as join graphs, which we discuss in detail in subsequent chapters on query processing. We introduce them here because they help to simplify the presentation of the distribution models we discuss later.

The relation at the tail of a link is called the *owner* of the link and the relation at the head is called the *member* [Ceri et al., 1983]. More commonly used terms, within the relational framework, are *source* relation for owner and *target* relation for member. Let us define two functions: *owner* and *member*, both of which provide mappings from the set of links to the set of relations. Therefore, given a link, they return the member or owner relations of the link, respectively.

Example 5.4

Given link L_1 of Figure 5.7, the *owner* and *member* functions have the following values:

$$
\begin{aligned}
owner(L_1) &= \text{PAY} \\
member(L_1) &= \text{EMP}
\end{aligned}
$$

The quantitative information required about the database is the cardinality of each relation R, denoted $card(R)$.

Application Information.   As indicated previously in relation to Figure 5.2, both qualitative and quantitative information is required about applications. The qualitative information guides the fragmentation activity, whereas the quantitative information is incorporated primarily into the allocation models.

The fundamental qualitative information consists of the predicates used in user queries. If it is not possible to analyze all of the user applications to determine these predicates, one should at least investigate the most "important" ones. It has been suggested that as a rule of thumb, the most active 20% of user queries account for 80% of the total data accesses [Wiederhold, 1982]. This "80/20 rule" may be used as a guideline in carrying out this analysis.

At this point we are interested in determining *simple predicates*. Given a relation $R(A_1, A_2, \ldots, A_n)$, where A_i is an attribute defined over domain D_i, a simple predicate p_j defined on R has the form

$$p_j : A_i \ \theta \ Value$$

where $\theta \in \{=, <, \neq, \leq, >, \geq\}$ and *Value* is chosen from the domain of A_i ($Value \in D_i$). We use Pr_i to denote the set of all simple predicates defined on a relation R_i. The members of Pr_i are denoted by p_{ij}.

Example 5.5

Given the relation instance PROJ of Figure 5.3,

$$\text{PNAME} = \text{``Maintenance''}$$

is a simple predicate, as well as

$$\text{BUDGET} \leq 200000$$

Even though simple predicates are quite elegant to deal with, user queries quite often include more complicated predicates, which are Boolean combinations of simple predicates. One combination that we are particularly interested in, called a *minterm predicate*, is the conjunction of simple predicates. Since it is always possible to transform a Boolean expression into conjunctive normal form, the use of minterm predicates in the design algorithms does not cause any loss of generality.

Given a set $Pr_i = \{p_{i1}, p_{i2}, \ldots, p_{im}\}$ of simple predicates for relation R_i, the set of minterm predicates $M_i = \{m_{i1}, m_{i2}, \ldots, m_{iz}\}$ is defined as

$$M_i = \{m_{ij} | m_{ij} = \bigwedge_{p_{ik} \in Pr_i} p_{ik}^*\}, \ 1 \le k \le m, \ 1 \le j \le z$$

where $p_{ik}^* = p_{ik}$ or $p_{ik}^* = \neg p_{ik}$. So each simple predicate can occur in a minterm predicate either in its natural form or its negated form.

It is important to note one point here. The reference to the negation of a predicate is meaningful for equality predicates of the form

$$Attribute = Value$$

For inequality predicates, the negation should be treated as the complement. For example, the negation of the simple predicate

$$Attribute \le Value$$

is

$$Attribute > Value$$

Besides theoretical problems of complementation in infinite sets, there is also the practical problem that the complement may be difficult to define. For example, if two simple predicates of the form

$$Lower\_bound \ \le \ Attribute\_1$$

$$Attribute\_1 \ \le \ Upper\_bound$$

are defined, their complements are

$$\neg(Lower\_bound \le Attribute\_1)$$

and

$$\neg(Attribute\_1 \le Upper\_bound)$$

However, the original two simple predicates can be written as

$$Lower\_bound \le Attribute\_1 \le Upper\_bound$$

with a complement,

$$\neg(Lower\_bound \le Attribute\_1 \le Upper\_bound)$$

that may not be easy to define. Therefore, the research in this area typically considers only simple equality predicates ([Ceri et al., 1982a], [Ceri and Pelagatti, 1984]).

Example 5.6

Consider relation PAY of Figure 5.3. The following are some of the possible simple predicates that can be defined on PAY.

$$p_1: \quad \text{TITLE} = \text{``Elect. Eng.''}$$
$$p_2: \quad \text{TITLE} = \text{``Syst. Anal.''}$$
$$p_3: \quad \text{TITLE} = \text{``Mech. Eng.''}$$
$$p_4: \quad \text{TITLE} = \text{``Programmer''}$$
$$p_5: \quad \text{SAL} \leq 30000$$
$$p_6: \quad \text{SAL} > 30000$$

The following are *some* of the minterm predicates that can be defined based on these simple predicates.

$$m_1: \quad \text{TITLE} = \text{``Elect. Eng.''} \land \text{SAL} \leq 30000$$
$$m_2: \quad \text{TITLE} = \text{``Elect. Eng.''} \land \text{SAL} > 30000$$
$$m_3: \quad \neg(\text{TITLE} = \text{``Elect. Eng.''}) \land \text{SAL} \leq 30000$$
$$m_4: \quad \neg(\text{TITLE} = \text{``Elect. Eng.''}) \land \text{SAL} > 30000$$
$$m_5: \quad \text{TITLE} = \text{``Programmer''} \land \text{SAL} \leq 30000$$
$$m_6: \quad \text{TITLE} = \text{``Programmer''} \land \text{SAL} > 30000$$

There are two points to mention here. First, these are not all the minterm predicates that can be defined; we are presenting only a representative sample. Second, some of these may be meaningless given the semantics of relation PAY. We are not addressing that issue here either. In addition, note that m_3 can also be rewritten as

$$m_3: \quad \text{TITLE} \neq \text{``Elect. Eng.''} \land \text{SAL} \leq 30000$$

In terms of quantitative information about user applications, we need to have two sets of data.

1. *Minterm selectivity*: number of tuples of the relation that would be accessed by a user query specified according to a given minterm predicate. For example, the selectivity of m_1 of Example 5.6 is 0 since there are no tuples in PAY that satisfy the minterm predicate. The selectivity of m_2, on the other hand, is 1. We denote the selectivity of a minterm m_i as $sel(m_i)$.

2. *Access frequency*: frequency with which user applications access data. If $Q = \{q_1, q_2, \ldots, q_q\}$ is a set of user queries, $acc(q_i)$ indicates the access frequency of query q_i in a given period.

Note that minterm access frequencies can be determined from the query frequencies. We refer to the access frequency of a minterm m_i as $acc(m_i)$.

Primary Horizontal Fragmentation

Before we present a formal algorithm for horizontal fragmentation, we should intuitively discuss the process for both primary and derived horizontal fragmentation. A *primary horizontal fragmentation* is defined by a selection operation on the owner relations of a database schema. Therefore, given relation R, its horizontal fragments are given by

$$R_i = \sigma_{F_i}(R), \ 1 \leq i \leq w$$

where F_i is the selection formula used to obtain fragment R_i. Note that if F_i is in conjunctive normal form, it is a minterm predicate (m_i). The algorithm we discuss will, in fact, insist that F_i be a minterm predicate.

Example 5.7

The decomposition of relation PROJ into horizontal fragments $PROJ_1$ and $PROJ_2$ in Example 5.1 is defined as follows:[1]

$$
\begin{aligned}
PROJ_1 &= \sigma_{BUDGET \leq 200000}(PROJ) \\
PROJ_2 &= \sigma_{BUDGET > 200000}(PROJ)
\end{aligned}
$$

Example 5.7 demonstrates one of the problems of horizontal partitioning. If the domain of the attributes participating in the selection formulas are continuous and infinite, as in Example 5.7, it is quite difficult to define the set of formulas $F = \{F_1, F_2, \ldots, F_n\}$ that would fragment the relation properly. One possible course of action is to define ranges as we have done in Example 5.7. However, there is always the problem of handling the two endpoints. For example, if a new tuple with a BUDGET value of, say, \$600,000 were to be inserted into PROJ, one would have had to review the fragmentation to decide if the new tuple is to go into $PROJ_2$ or if the fragments need to be revised and a new fragment needs to be defined as

$$
\begin{aligned}
PROJ_2 &= \sigma_{200000 < BUDGET \leq 400000}(PROJ) \\
PROJ_3 &= \sigma_{BUDGET > 400000}(PROJ)
\end{aligned}
$$

---

[1]We assume that the nonnegativity of the BUDGET values is a feature of the relation that is enforced by an integrity constraint. Otherwise, a simple predicate of the form $0 \leq BUDGET$ also needs to be included in Pr. We assume this to be true in all our examples and discussions in this chapter.

This issue can obviously be resolved in practice by limiting the domain of the attribute(s) according to the requirements of the application.

Example 5.8

Consider relation PROJ of Figure 5.3. We can define the following horizontal fragments based on the project location. The resulting fragments are shown in Figure 5.8.

$$\mathrm{PROJ}_1 = \sigma_{\mathrm{LOC}=\text{"Montreal"}}(\mathrm{PROJ})$$
$$\mathrm{PROJ}_2 = \sigma_{\mathrm{LOC}=\text{"New York"}}(\mathrm{PROJ})$$
$$\mathrm{PROJ}_3 = \sigma_{\mathrm{LOC}=\text{"Paris"}}(\mathrm{PROJ})$$

PROJ$_1$

PNO	PNAME	BUDGET	LOC
P1	Instrumentation	150000	Montreal

PROJ$_2$

PNO	PNAME	BUDGET	LOC
P2	Database Develop.	135000	New York
P3	CAD/CAM	250000	New York

PROJ$_3$

PNO	PNAME	BUDGET	LOC
P4	Maintenance	310000	Paris

Figure 5.8. Primary Horizontal Fragmentation of Relation PROJ

Now we can define a horizontal fragment more carefully. A horizontal fragment R_i of relation R consists of all the tuples of R that satisfy a minterm predicate m_i. Hence, given a set of minterm predicates M, there are as many horizontal fragments of relation R as there are minterm predicates. This set of horizontal fragments is also commonly referred to as the set of *minterm fragments*.

From the foregoing discussion it is obvious that the definition of the horizontal fragments depends on minterm predicates. Therefore, the first step of any fragmentation algorithm is to determine a set of simple predicates that will form the minterm predicates.

An important aspect of simple predicates is their *completeness*; another is their *minimality*. A set of simple predicates Pr is said to be *complete* if and only if there is an equal probability of access by every application to any tuple belonging to any minterm fragment that is defined according to Pr.[2]

Example 5.9

> Consider the fragmentation of relation PROJ given in Example 5.8. If the only application that accesses PROJ wants to access the tuples according to the location, the set is complete since each tuple of each fragment PROJ$_i$ (Example 5.8) has the same probability of being accessed. If, however, there is a second application which accesses only those project tuples where the budget is less than \$200,000, then Pr is not complete. Some of the tuples within each PROJ$_i$ have a higher probability of being accessed due to this second application. To make the set of predicates complete, we need to add (BUDGET $\leq$ 200000, BUDGET $>$ 200000) to Pr:
>
> $$Pr \quad = \quad \{\text{LOC=``Montreal'',LOC=``New York'',LOC=``Paris''},$$
> $$\text{BUDGET} \leq 200000, \text{BUDGET} \geq 200000\}$$

The reason completeness is a desirable property is because fragments obtained according to a complete set of predicates are logically uniform since they all satisfy the minterm predicate. They are also statistically homogeneous in the way applications access them. Therefore, we will use a complete set of predicates as the basis of primary horizontal fragmentation.

It is possible to define completeness more formally so that a complete set of predicates can be obtained automatically. However, this would require the designer to specify the access probabilities for *each* tuple of a relation for *each* application under consideration. This is considerably more work than appealing to the common sense and experience of the designer to come up with a complete set. Shortly, we will present an algorithmic way of obtaining this set.

The second desirable property of the set of predicates, according to which minterm predicates and, in turn, fragments are to be defined, is minimality, which is very intuitive. It simply states that if a predicate influences how fragmentation is performed (i.e., causes a fragment f to be further fragmented into, say, f_i and f_j), there should be at least one application that accesses f_i and f_j differently. In other words, the simple predicate should be *relevant* in determining a fragmentation. If all the predicates of a set Pr are relevant, Pr is *minimal*.

A formal definition of relevance can be given as follows [Ceri et al., 1982a]. Let m_i and m_j be two minterm predicates that are identical in their definition, except

---

[2]It is clear that the definition of completeness of a set of simple predicates is different from the completeness rule of fragmentation given in Section 5.2.4.

that m_i contains the simple predicate p_i in its natural form while m_j contains $\neg p_i$. Also, let f_i and f_j be two fragments defined according to m_i and m_j, respectively. Then p_i is *relevant* if and only if

$$\frac{acc(m_i)}{card(f_i)} \neq \frac{acc(m_j)}{card(f_j)}$$

Once again, we appeal to the intuition and expertise of the designer rather than employing the formal definition.

Example 5.10

> The set Pr defined in Example 5.9 is complete and minimal. If, however, we were to add the predicate

$$\text{PNAME} = \text{``Instrumentation''}$$

> to Pr, the resulting set would not be minimal since the new predicate is not relevant with respect to Pr. There is no application that would access the resulting fragments any differently.

We can now present an iterative algorithm that would generate a complete and minimal set of predicates Pr' given a set of simple predicates Pr. This algorithm, called COM_MIN, is given in Algorithm 5.1. To avoid lengthy wording, we have adopted the following notation:

Rule 1: fundamental rule of completeness and minimality, which states that a relation or fragment is partitioned "into at least two parts which are accessed differently by at least one application."

f_i *of* Pr': fragment f_i defined according to a minterm predicate defined over the predicates of Pr'.

Algorithm 5.1   *COM_MIN*
    input: R: relation; Pr: set of simple predicates
    output: Pr': set of simple predicates
    declare
        F: set of minterm fragments
    begin
        find a $p_i \in Pr$ such that p_i partitions R according to *Rule 1*
        $Pr' \leftarrow p_i$
        $Pr \leftarrow Pr - p_i$
        $F \leftarrow f_i$ $\{f_i$ is the minterm fragment according to $p_i\}$
        do

begin
    find a $p_j \in Pr$ such that p_j partitions some f_k of Pr' according
        to *Rule 1*
    $Pr' \leftarrow Pr' \cup p_j$
    $Pr \leftarrow Pr - p_j$
    $F \leftarrow F \cup f_j$
    if $\exists p_k \in Pr'$ which is nonrelevant **then**
    begin
        $Pr' \leftarrow Pr' - p_k$
        $F \leftarrow F - f_k$
    end-if
  end-begin
until Pr' is complete
end. {COM_MIN}

The algorithm begins by finding a predicate that is relevant and that partitions the input relation. The **do-until** loop iteratively adds predicates to this set, ensuring minimality at each step. Therefore, at the end the set Pr' is both minimal and complete.

The second step in the primary horizontal design process is to derive the set of minterm predicates that can be defined on the predicates in set Pr'. These minterm predicates determine the fragments that are used as candidates in the allocation step. Determination of individual minterm predicates is trivial; the difficulty is that the set of minterm predicates may be quite large (in fact, exponential on the number of simple predicates). In the next step we look at ways of reducing the number of minterm predicates that need to be considered in fragmentation.

The third step of the design process is the elimination of some of the minterm fragments that may be meaningless. This elimination is performed by identifying those minterms that might be contradictory to a set of implications I. For example, if $Pr' = \{p_1, p_2\}$, where

$$p_1 : \quad att = value\_1$$
$$p_2 : \quad att = value\_2$$

and the domain of att is $\{value\_1, value\_2\}$, it is obvious that I contains two implications, which state

$$i_1 : \quad (att = value\_1) \Rightarrow \neg(att = value\_2)$$
$$i_2 : \quad \neg(att = value_1) \Rightarrow (att = value\_2)$$

The following four minterm predicates are defined according to Pr':

$$m_1 : \quad (att = value\_1) \wedge (att = value\_2)$$
$$m_2 : \quad (att = value\_1) \wedge \neg(att = value\_2)$$
$$m_3 : \quad \neg(att = value\_1) \wedge (att = value\_2)$$
$$m_4 : \quad \neg(att = value\_1) \wedge \neg(att = value\_2)$$

In this case the minterm predicates m_1 and m_4 are contradictory to the implications I and can therefore be eliminated from M.

The algorithm for primary horizontal fragmentation is given in Algorithm 5.2. The input to the algorithm PHORIZONTAL is a relation R that is subject to primary horizontal fragmentation, and Pr, which is the set of simple predicates that have been determined according to applications defined on relation R.

Algorithm 5.2   *PHORIZONTAL*
    input: R: relation; Pr: set of simple predicates
    output: M: set of minterm fragments
    begin
        $Pr' \leftarrow \text{COM\_MIN}(R, Pr)$
        determine the set M of minterm predicates
        determine the set I of implications among $p_i \in Pr'$
        for each $m_i \in M$ **do**
            if m_i is contradictory according to I **then**
                $M \leftarrow M - m_i$
            end-if
        end-for
    end. {PHORIZONTAL}

Example 5.11

We now consider the design of the database scheme given in Figure 5.7. The first thing to note is that there are two relations that are the subject of primary horizontal fragmentation: PAY and PROJ relations.

Suppose that there is only one application that accesses PAY. That application checks the salary information and determines a raise accordingly. Assume that employee records are managed in two places, one handling the records of those with salaries less than or equal to $30,000, and the other handling the records of those who earn more than $30,000. Therefore, the query is issued at two sites.

The simple predicates that would be used to partition relation PAY are

$$p_1: \quad \text{SAL} \leq 30000$$
$$p_2: \quad \text{SAL} > 30000$$

thus giving the initial set of simple predicates $Pr = \{p_1, p_2\}$. Applying the COM_MIN algorithm with $i = 1$ as initial value results in $Pr' = \{p_1\}$. This is complete and minimal since p_2 would not partition f_1 (which is the minterm fragment formed with respect to p_1) according to Rule 1. We can form the following minterm predicates as members of M:

$$m_1: \quad (\text{SAL} < 30000)$$
$$m_2: \quad \neg(\text{SAL} \leq 30000) = \text{SAL} > 30000$$

PAY$_1$

TITLE	SAL
Mech. Eng.	27000
Programmer	24000

PAY$_2$

TITLE	SAL
Elect. Eng.	40000
Syst. Anal.	34000

Figure 5.9. Horizontal Fragmentation of Relation PAY

Therefore, we define two fragments $F_s = \{S_1, S_2\}$ according to M (Figure 5.9).

Let us next consider relation PROJ. Assume that there are two applications. The first is issued at three sites and finds the names and budgets of projects given their location. In SQL notation, the query is

```
SELECT    PNAME, BUDGET
FROM      PROJ
WHERE     PNO=Value
```

For this application, the simple predicates that would be used are the following:

$$p_1: \quad \text{LOC} = \text{``Montreal''}$$
$$p_2: \quad \text{LOC} = \text{``New York''}$$
$$p_3: \quad \text{LOC} = \text{``Paris''}$$

The second application is issued at two sites and has to do with the management of the projects. Those projects that have a budget of less than $200,000 are managed at one site, whereas those with larger budgets are managed at a second site. Thus the simple predicates that should be used to fragment according to the second application are

$$p_4: \quad \text{BUDGET} \leq 200000$$
$$p_5: \quad \text{BUDGET} > 200000$$

If the algorithm COM_MIN is followed, the set $Pr' = \{p_1, p_2, p_3, p_4, p_5\}$ is obviously complete and minimal.

Based on Pr', the following six minterm predicates that form M can be defined:

$$
\begin{array}{ll}
m_1: & (\text{LOC} = \text{``Montreal''}) \wedge (\text{BUDGET} \leq 200000) \\
m_2: & (\text{LOC} = \text{``Montreal''}) \wedge (\text{BUDGET} > 200000) \\
m_3: & (\text{LOC} = \text{``New York''}) \wedge (\text{BUDGET} \leq 200000) \\
m_4: & (\text{LOC} = \text{``New York''}) \wedge (\text{BUDGET} > 200000) \\
m_5: & (\text{LOC} = \text{``Paris''}) \wedge (\text{BUDGET} \leq 200000) \\
m_6: & (\text{LOC} = \text{``Paris''}) \wedge (\text{BUDGET} > 200000)
\end{array}
$$

These are not the only minterm predicates that can be generated. It is, for example, possible to specify predicates of the form

$$p_1 \wedge p_2 \wedge p_3 \wedge p_4 \wedge p_5$$

However, the obvious implications

$$
\begin{array}{ll}
i_1: & p_1 \Rightarrow \neg p_2 \wedge \neg p_3 \\
i_2: & p_2 \Rightarrow \neg p_1 \wedge \neg p_3 \\
i_3: & p_3 \Rightarrow \neg p_1 \wedge \neg p_2 \\
i_4: & p_4 \Rightarrow \neg p_5 \\
i_5: & p_5 \Rightarrow \neg p_4 \\
i_6: & \neg p_4 \Rightarrow p_5 \\
i_7: & \neg p_5 \Rightarrow p_4
\end{array}
$$

eliminate these minterm predicates and we are left with m_1 to m_6.

Looking at the database instance in Figure 5.3, one may be tempted to claim that the following implications hold:

$$
\begin{array}{ll}
i_8: & \text{LOC} = \text{``Montreal''} \Rightarrow \neg (\text{BUDGET} > 200000) \\
i_9: & \text{LOC} = \text{``Paris''} \Rightarrow \neg (\text{BUDGET} \leq 200000) \\
i_{10}: & \neg (\text{LOC} = \text{``Montreal''}) \Rightarrow \text{BUDGET} \leq 200000 \\
i_{11}: & \neg (\text{LOC} = \text{``Paris''}) \Rightarrow \text{BUDGET} > 200000
\end{array}
$$

However, remember that implications should be defined according to the semantics of the database, not according to the current values. Some of the fragments defined according to $M = \{m_1, \ldots, m_6\}$ may be empty, but they are, nevertheless, fragments. There is nothing in the database semantics that suggest that the implications i_8 through i_{11} hold.

The result of the primary horizontal fragmentation of PROJ is to form six fragments $F_{PROJ} = \{\text{PROJ}_1, \text{PROJ}_2, \text{PROJ}_3, \text{PROJ}_4, \text{PROJ}_5, \text{PROJ}_6\}$ of relation PROJ according to the minterm predicates M (Figure 5.10). We should also note that some of these fragments are empty (PROJ$_2$, PROJ$_5$) and therefore are not depicted in Figure 5.10.

PROJ$_1$

PNO	PNAME	BUDGET	LOC
P1	Instrumentation	150000	Montreal

PROJ$_3$

PNO	PNAME	BUDGET	LOC
P2	Database Develop.	135000	New York

PROJ$_4$

PNO	PNAME	BUDGET	LOC
P3	CAD/CAM	250000	New York

PROJ$_6$

PNO	PNAME	BUDGET	LOC
P4	Maintenance	310000	Paris

Figure 5.10. Horizontal Partitioning of Relation PROJ

Derived Horizontal Fragmentation

A derived horizontal fragmentation is defined on a member relation of a link according to a selection operation specified on its owner. It is important to remember two points. First, the link between the owner and the member relations is defined as an equi-join. Second, an equi-join can be implemented by means of semijoins. This second point is especially important for our purposes, since we want to partition a member relation according to the fragmentation of its owner, but we also want the resulting fragment to be defined *only* on the attributes of the member relation.

Accordingly, given a link L where $owner(L) = S$ and $member(L) = R$, the derived horizontal fragments of R are defined as

$$R_i = R \ltimes S_i, 1 \leq i \leq w$$

where w is the maximum number of fragments that will be defined on R, and $S_i = \sigma_{F_i}(S)$, where F_i is the formula according to which the primary horizontal fragment S_i is defined.

Example 5.12

Consider link L_1 in Figure 5.7, where $owner(L_1) = $ PAY and $member(L_1) = $ EMP. Then we can group engineers into two groups according to their salary: those making less than or equal to \$30,000, and those making more than \$30,000. The two fragments EMP$_1$ and EMP$_2$ are defined as follows:

$$\begin{aligned} EMP_1 &= EMP \ltimes PAY_1 \\ EMP_2 &= EMP \ltimes PAY_2 \end{aligned}$$

EMP$_1$

ENO	ENAME	TITLE
E3	A. Lee	Mech. Eng.
E4	J. Miller	Programmer
E7	R. Davis	Mech. Eng.

EMP$_2$

ENO	ENAME	TITLE
E1	J. Doe	Elect. Eng.
E2	M. Smith	Syst. Anal.
E5	B. Casey	Syst. Anal.
E6	L. Chu	Elect. Eng.
E8	J. Jones	Syst. Anal.

Figure 5.11. Derived Horizontal Fragmentation of Relation EMP

where

$$PAY_1 = \sigma_{SAL \leq 30000}(PAY)$$
$$PAY_2 = \sigma_{SAL > 30000}(PAY)$$

The result of this fragmentation is depicted in Figure 5.11.

To carry out a derived horizontal fragmentation, three inputs are needed: the set of partitions of the owner relation (e.g., PAY_1 and PAY_2 in Example 5.12), the member relation, and the set of semijoin predicates between the owner and the member (e.g., EMP.TITLE = PAY.TITLE in Example 5.12). The fragmentation algorithm, then, is quite trivial, so we will not present it in any detail.

There is one potential complication that deserves some attention. In a database schema, it is common that there are more than two links into a relation R (e.g., in Figure 5.7, ASG has two incoming links). In this case there is more than one possible derived horizontal fragmentation of R. The decision as to which candidate fragmentation to choose is based on two criteria:

1. The fragmentation with better join characteristics

2. The fragmentation used in more applications

Let us discuss the second criterion first. This is quite straightforward if we take into consideration the frequency with which applications access some data. If possible, one should try to facilitate the accesses of the "heavy" users so that their total impact on system performance is minimized.

Applying the first criterion, however, is not that straightforward. Consider, for example, the fragmentation we discussed in Example 5.12. The effect (and the objective) of this fragmentation is that the join of the EMP and PAY relations to answer the query is assisted (1) by performing it on smaller relations (i.e., fragments), and (2) by potentially performing joins in a distributed fashion.

The first point is obvious. The fragments of EMP are smaller than EMP itself. Therefore, it will be faster to join any fragment of PAY with any fragment of

EMP than to work with the relations themselves. The second point, however, is more important and is at the heart of distributed databases. If, besides executing a number of queries at different sites, we can execute one query in parallel, the response time or throughput of the system can be expected to improve. In the case of joins, this is possible under certain circumstances. Consider, for example, the join graph (i.e., the links) between the fragments of EMP and PAY derived in Example 5.10 (Figure 5.12). There is only one link coming in or going out of a fragment. Such a join graph is called a *simple* graph. The advantage of a design where the join relationship between fragments is simple is that the member and owner of a link can be allocated to one site and the joins between different pairs of fragments can proceed independently and in parallel.

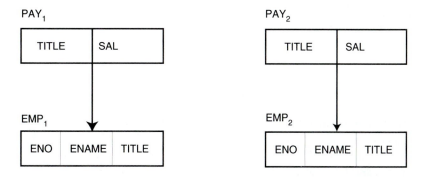

Figure 5.12. Join Graph Between Fragments

Unfortunately, obtaining simple join graphs may not always be possible. In that case, the next desirable alternative is to have a design that results in a *partitioned* join graph. A partitioned graph consists of two or more subgraphs with no links between them. fragments so obtained may not be distributed for parallel execution as easily as those obtained via simple join graphs, but the allocation is still possible.

Example 5.13

Let us continue with the distribution design of the database we started in Example 5.11. We already decided on the fragmentation of relation EMP according to the fragmentation of PAY (Example 5.12). Let us now consider ASG. Assume that there are the following two applications:

  1. The first application finds the names of engineers who work at certain places. It runs on all three sites and accesses the information about the engineers who work on local projects with higher probability than those of projects at other locations.

2. At each administrative site where employee records are managed, users would like to access the projects that these employees work on and learn how long they will work on those projects.

The first application results in a fragmentation of ASG according to the fragments $PROJ_1$, $PROJ_3$, $PROJ_4$ and $PROJ_6$ of PROJ obtained in Example 5.11. Remember that

$$PROJ_1: \quad \sigma_{LOC=\text{"Montreal"} \wedge BUDGET \leq 200000} (PROJ)$$
$$PROJ_3: \quad \sigma_{LOC=\text{"New York"} \wedge BUDGET \leq 200000} (PROJ)$$
$$PROJ_4: \quad \sigma_{LOC=\text{"New York"} \wedge BUDGET > 200000} (PROJ)$$
$$PROJ_6: \quad \sigma_{LOC=\text{"Paris"} \wedge BUDGET > 200000} (PROJ)$$

Therefore, the derived fragmentation of ASG according to $\{PROJ_1, PROJ_2, PROJ_3\}$ is defined as follows:

$$ASG_1 = ASG \ltimes PROJ_1$$
$$ASG_2 = ASG \ltimes PROJ_3$$
$$ASG_3 = ASG \ltimes PROJ_4$$
$$ASG_4 = ASG \ltimes PROJ_6$$

These fragment instances are shown in Figure 5.13.

The second query can be specified in SQL as

```
SELECT    RESP, DUR
FROM      ASG, EMP i
WHERE     ASG.ENO = EMPi.ENO
```

ASG_1

ENO	PNO	RESP	DUR
E1	P1	Manager	12
E2	P1	Analyst	24

ASG_3

ENO	PNO	RESP	DUR
E3	P3	Consultant	10
E6	P3	Engineer	36
E7	P3	Manager	40

ASG_2

ENO	PNO	RESP	DUR
E2	P2	Analyst	6
E4	P2	Programmer	18
E5	P2	Manager	24

ASG_4

ENO	PNO	RESP	DUR
E3	P4	Engineer	48
E6	P4	Manager	48

Figure 5.13. Derived Fragmentation of ASG with respect to PROJ

ASG₁

ENO	PNO	RESP	DUR
E3	P3	Consultant	10
E3	P4	Engineer	48
E4	P2	Programmer	18
E7	P3	Engineer	36

ASG₂

ENO	PNO	RESP	DUR
E1	P1	Manager	12
E2	P1	Analyst	24
E3	P2	Analyst	6
E4	P2	Manager	24
E5	P4	Manager	48
E6	P3	Manager	40

Figure 5.14. Derived Fragmentation of ASG with respect to EMP

where $i = 1$ or $i = 2$, depending on which site the query is issued at. The derived fragmentation of ASG according to the fragmentation of EMP is defined below and depicted in Figure 5.14.

$$\text{ASG}_1 = \text{ASG} \ltimes \text{EMP}_1$$
$$\text{ASG}_2 = \text{ASG} \ltimes \text{EMP}_2$$

This example demonstrates two things:

1. Derived fragmentation may follow a chain where one relation is fragmented as a result of another one's design and it, in turn, causes the fragmentation of another relation (e.g., the chain PAY–EMP–ASG).

2. Typically, there will be more than one candidate fragmentation for a relation (e.g., relation ASG). The final choice of the fragmentation scheme may be a decision problem addressed during allocation.

Checking for Correctness

We should now check the fragmentation algorithms discussed so far with respect to the three correctness criteria presented in Section 5.2.4.

Completeness. The completeness of a primary horizontal fragmentation is based on the selection predicates used. As long as the selection predicates are complete, the resulting fragmentation is guaranteed to be complete as well. Since the basis of the fragmentation algorithm is a set of *complete* and *minimal* predicates, Pr', completeness is guaranteed as long as no mistakes are made in defining Pr'.

The completeness of a derived horizontal fragmentation is somewhat more difficult to define. The difficulty is due to the fact that the predicate determining the fragmentation involves two relations. Let us first define the completeness rule formally and then look at an example.

Let R be the member relation of a link whose owner is relation S, which is fragmented as $F_S = \{S_1, S_2, \ldots, S_w\}$. Furthermore, let A be the join attribute between R and S. Then for each tuple t of R, there should be a tuple t' of S such that

$$t[A] = t'[A].$$

For example, there should be no ASG tuple which has a project number that is not also contained in PROJ. Similarly, there should be no EMP tuples with TITLE values where the same TITLE value does not appear in PAY as well. This rule is known as *referential integrity* and ensures that the tuples of any fragment of the member relation are also in the owner relation.

Reconstruction. Reconstruction of a global relation from its fragments is performed by the union operator in both the primary and the derived horizontal fragmentation. Thus, for a relation R with fragmentation $F_R = \{R_1, R_2, \ldots, R_w\}$,

$$R = \bigcup R_i, \quad \forall R_i \in F_R$$

Disjointness. It is easier to establish disjointness of fragmentation for primary than for derived horizontal fragmentation. In the former case, disjointness is guaranteed as long as the minterm predicates determining the fragmentation are mutually exclusive.

In derived fragmentation, however, there is a semijoin involved that adds considerable complexity. Disjointness can be guaranteed if the join graph is simple. If it is not simple, it is necessary to investigate actual tuple values. In general, we do not want a tuple of a member relation to join with two or more tuples of the owner relation when these tuples are in different fragments of the owner. This may not be very easy to establish, and illustrates why derived fragmentation schemes that generate a simple join graph are always desirable.

Example 5.14

In fragmenting relation PAY (Example 5.11), the minterm predicates $M = \{m_1, m_2\}$ were

$$
\begin{aligned}
m_1 &: \quad \text{SAL} \leq 30000 \\
m_2 &: \quad \text{SAL} > 30000
\end{aligned}
$$

Since m_1 and m_2 are mutually exclusive, the fragmentation of PAY is disjoint. For relation EMP, however, we require that

1. Each engineer have a single title.

2. Each title have a single salary value associated with it.

Since these two rules follow from the semantics of the database, the fragmentation of EMP with respect to PAY is also disjoint.

5.3.2 Vertical Fragmentation

Remember that a vertical fragmentation of a relation R produces fragments $R_1, R_2,$ $\ldots, R_r$, each of which contains a subset of R's attributes as well as the primary key of R. The objective of vertical fragmentation is to partition a relation into a set of smaller relations so that many of the user applications will run on only one fragment. In this context, an "optimal" fragmentation is one that produces a fragmentation scheme which minimizes the execution time of user applications that run on these fragments.

Vertical fragmentation has been investigated within the context of centralized database systems as well as distributed ones. Its motivation within the centralized context is as a design tool, which allows the user queries to deal with smaller relations, thus causing a smaller number of page accesses [Navathe et al., 1984]. It has also been suggested that the most "active" subrelations can be identified and placed in a faster memory subsystem in those cases where memory hierarchies are supported [Eisner and Severance, 1976].

Vertical partitioning is inherently more complicated than horizontal partitioning. This is due to the total number of alternatives that are available. For example, in horizontal partitioning, if the total number of simple predicates in Pr is n, there are 2^n possible minterm predicates that can be defined on it. In addition, we know that some of these will contradict the existing implications, further reducing the candidate fragments that need to be considered. In the case of vertical partitioning, however, if a relation has m nonprimary key attributes, the number of possible fragments is equal to $B(m)$, which is the mth Bell number [Niamir, 1978]. For large values of $m, B(m) \approx m^m$; for example, for $m=10$, $B(m) \approx 115,000$, for $m=15$, $B(m) \approx 10^9$, for $m=30$, $B(m) = 10^{23}$ ([Hammer and Niamir, 1979], [Navathe et al., 1984]).

These values indicate that it is futile to attempt to obtain optimal solutions to the vertical partitioning problem; one has to resort to heuristics. Two types of heuristic approaches exist for the vertical fragmentation of global relations:

1. *Grouping:* starts by assigning each attribute to one fragment, and at each step, joins some of the fragments until some criteria is satisfied. Grouping was first suggested in [Hammer and Niamir, 1979] for centralized databases, and was used later in [Sacca and Wiederhold, 1985] for distributed databases.

2. *Splitting:* starts with a relation and decides on beneficial partitionings based on the access behavior of applications to the attributes. The technique was first discussed for centralized database design in [Hoffer and Severance, 1975]. It was then extended to the distributed environment in [Navathe et al., 1984].

In what follows we discuss only the splitting technique, since it fits more naturally within the top-down design methodology, and as stated in [Navathe et al., 1984], since the "optimal" solution is probably closer to the full relation than to a set of fragments each of which consists of a single attribute. Furthermore, splitting generates nonoverlapping fragments whereas grouping typically results in overlapping fragments. Within the context of distributed database systems, we are concerned with nonoverlapping fragments, for obvious reasons. Of course, nonoverlapping refers only to nonprimary key attributes.

Before we proceed, let us clarify an issue that we only mentioned in Example 5.2, namely, the replication of the global relation's key in the fragments. This is a characteristic of vertical fragmentation that allows the reconstruction of the global relation. Therefore, splitting is considered only for those attributes that do not participate in the primary key.

There is a strong advantage to replicating the key attributes despite the obvious problems it causes. This advantage has to do with semantic integrity enforcement, to be discussed in Chapter 6. Note that every dependency presented in Chapter 2 is, in fact, a constraint that has to hold among the attribute values of the respective relations at all times. Remember also that most of these dependencies involve the key attributes of a relation. If we now design the database so that the key attributes are part of one fragment that is allocated to one site, and the implied attributes are part of another fragment that is allocated to a second site, every update request that causes an integrity check will necessitate communication among sites. Replication of the key attributes at each fragment reduces the chances of this occurring but does not eliminate it completely, since such communication may be necessary due to integrity constraints that do not involve the primary key, as well as due to concurrency control.

One alternative to the replication of the key attributes is the use of *tuple identifiers* (TIDs), which are system-assigned unique values to the tuples of a relation. Since TIDs are maintained by the system, the fragments are disjoint as far as the user is concerned.

Information Requirements of Vertical Fragmentation

The major information required for vertical fragmentation is related to applications. The following discussion, therefore, is exclusively on what needs to be determined about applications that will run against the distributed database. Since vertical partitioning places in one fragment those attributes usually accessed together, there is a need for some measure that would define more precisely the notion of "togetherness." This measure is the *affinity* of attributes, which indicates how closely related the attributes are. Unfortunately, it is not realistic to expect the designer or the users to be able to easily specify these values. We now present one way by which they can be obtained from more primitive data.

The major data requirement related to applications is their access frequencies. Let $Q = \{q_1, q_2, \ldots, q_q\}$ be the set of user queries (applications) that will run on relation $R(A_1, A_2, \ldots, A_n)$. Then, for each query q_i and each attribute A_j, we associate an *attribute usage value*, denoted as $use(q_i, A_j)$, and defined as follows:

$$use(q_i, A_j) = \begin{cases} 1 & \text{if attribute } A_j \text{ is referenced by query } q_i \\ 0 & \text{otherwise} \end{cases}$$

The $use(q_i, \bullet)$ vectors for each application are easy to define if the designer knows the applications that will run on the database. Again, remember that the 80-20 rule discussed in Section 5.3.1 should be helpful in this task.

Example 5.15

Consider relation PROJ of Figure 5.3. Assume that the following applications are defined to run on this relation. In each case we also give the SQL specification.

q_1: Find the budget of a project, given its identification number.

```
SELECT    BUDGET
FROM      PROJ
WHERE     PNO=Value
```

q_2: Find the names and budgets of all projects.

```
SELECT    PNAME, BUDGET
FROM      PROJ
```

q_3: Find the names of projects located at a given city.

```
SELECT    PNAME
FROM      PROJ
WHERE     LOC=Value
```

q_4: Find the total project budgets for each city.

```
SELECT    SUM(BUDGET)
FROM      PROJ
WHERE     LOC=Value
```

According to these four applications, the attribute usage values can be defined. As a notational convenience, we let $A_1 = $ PNO, $A_2 = $ PNAME, $A_3 = $ BUDGET, and $A_4 = $ LOC. The usage values are defined in matrix form (Figure 5.15), where entry (i, j) denotes $use(q_i, A_j)$.

$$\begin{array}{cccc} & A_1 & A_2 & A_3 & A_4 \\ q_1 & \begin{bmatrix} 1 & 0 & 1 & 1 \\ q_2 & 0 & 1 & 1 & 0 \\ q_3 & 0 & 1 & 0 & 1 \\ q_4 & 0 & 0 & 1 & 1 \end{bmatrix} \end{array}$$

Figure 5.15. Example Attribute Usage Matrix

Attribute usage values are not sufficiently general to form the basis of attribute splitting and fragmentation. This is because these values do not represent the weight of application frequencies. The frequency measure can be included in the definition of the attribute affinity measure $aff(A_i, A_j)$, which measures the bond between two attributes of a relation according to how they are accessed by applications.

The attribute affinity measure between two attributes A_i and A_j of a relation $R(A_1, A_2, \ldots, A_n)$ with respect to the set of applications $Q = \{q_1, q_2, \ldots, q_q\}$ is defined as

$$aff(A_i, A_j) = \sum_{k | use(q_k, A_i) = 1 \wedge use(q_k, A_j) = 1} \sum_{\forall PAY_l} ref_l(q_k) acc_l(q_k)$$

where $ref_l(q_k)$ is the number of accesses to attributes (A_i, A_j) for each execution of application q_k at site S_l and $acc_l(q_k)$ is the application access frequency measure previously defined and modified to include frequencies at different sites.

The result of this computation is an $n \times n$ matrix, each element of which is one of the measures defined above. We call this matrix the *attribute affinity matrix* (AA).

Example 5.16

Let us continue with the case that we examined in Example 5.15. For simplicity, let us assume that $ref_l(q_k) = 1$ for all q_k and S_l. If the application frequencies are

$$\begin{array}{lll} acc_1(q_1) = 15 & acc_2(q_1) = 20 & acc_3(q_1) = 10 \\ acc_1(q_2) = 5 & acc_2(q_2) = 0 & acc_3(q_2) = 0 \\ acc_1(q_3) = 25 & acc_2(q_3) = 25 & acc_3(q_3) = 25 \\ acc_1(q_4) = 3 & acc_2(q_4) = 0 & acc_3(q_4) = 0 \end{array}$$

then the affinity measure between attributes A_1 and A_3 can be measured as

$$aff(A_1, A_3) = \sum_{k=1}^{1} \sum_{l=1}^{3} acc_l(q_k) = acc_1(q_1) + acc_2(q_1) + acc_3(q_1) = 45$$

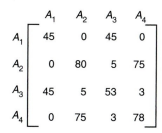

Figure 5.16. Attribute Affinity Matrix

since the only application that accesses both of the attributes is q_1. The complete attribute affinity matrix is shown in Figure 5.16. Note that for completeness the diagonal values are also computed even though they are meaningless.

The attribute affinity matrix will be used in the rest of this chapter to guide the fragmentation effort. The process involves first clustering together the attributes with high affinity for each other, and then splitting the relation accordingly.

Clustering Algorithm

The fundamental task in designing a vertical fragmentation algorithm is to find some means of grouping the attributes of a relation based on the attribute affinity values in AA. It has been suggested by [Hoffer and Severance, 1975] and [Navathe et al., 1984] that the bond energy algorithm (BEA) [McCormick et al., 1972] should be used for this purpose. It is considered appropriate for the following reasons [Hoffer and Severance, 1975]:

1. It is designed specifically to determine groups of similar items as opposed to, say, a linear ordering of the items (i.e., it clusters the attributes with larger affinity values together, and the ones with smaller values together).

2. The final groupings are insensitive to the order in which items are presented to the algorithm.

3. The computation time of the algorithm is reasonable $[O(n^2)$, where n is the number of attributes].

4. Secondary interrelationships between clustered attribute groups are identifiable.

The bond energy algorithm takes as input the attribute affinity matrix, permutes its rows and columns, and generates a *clustered affinity matrix* (CA). The permutation is done in such a way as to *maximize* the following *global affinity measure (AM)*:

$$AM = \sum_{i=1}^{n} \sum_{j=1}^{n} aff(A_i, A_j)[aff(A_i, A_{j-1}) + aff(A_i, A_{j+1})$$

$$+ \quad aff(A_{i-1}, A_j) + aff(A_{i+1}, A_j)]$$

where

$$aff(A_0, A_j) = aff(A_i, A_0) = aff(A_{n+1}, A_j) = aff(A_i, A_{n+1}) = 0$$

The last set of conditions takes care of the cases where an attribute is being placed in CA to the left of the leftmost attribute or to the right of the rightmost attribute during column permutations, and prior to the topmost row and following the last row during row permutations. In these cases, we take 0 to be the *aff* values between the attribute being considered for placement and its left or right (top or bottom) neighbors, which do not exist in CA.

The maximization function considers the nearest neighbors only, thereby resulting in the grouping of large values with large ones, and small values with small ones. Also, the attribute affinity matrix (AA) is symmetric, which reduces the objective function of the formulation above to

$$AM = \sum_{i=1}^{n} \sum_{j=1}^{n} aff(A_i, A_j)[aff(A_i, A_{j-1}) + aff(A_i, A_{j+1})]$$

The details of the bond energy algorithm are given in Algorithm 5.3. Generation of the clustered affinity matrix (CA) is done in three steps:

1. *Initialization.* Place and fix one of the columns of AA arbitrarily into CA. Column 1 was chosen in the algorithm.

2. *Iteration.* Pick each of the remaining $n-i$ columns (where i is the number of columns already placed in CA) and try to place them in the remaining $i+1$ positions in the CA matrix. Choose the placement that makes the greatest contribution to the global affinity measure described above. Continue this step until no more columns remain to be placed.

3. *Row ordering.* Once the column ordering is determined, the placement of the rows should also be changed so that their relative positions match the relative positions of the columns.[3]

---

[3]From now on, we may refer to elements of the AA and CA matrices as $AA(i,j)$ and $CA(i,j)$, respectively. This is done for notational convenience only. The mapping to the affinity measures is $AA(i,j) = aff(A_i, A_j)$ and $CA(i,j) = aff$(attribute placed at column i in CA, attribute placed at column j in CA). Even though AA and CA matrices are identical except for the ordering of attributes, since the algorithm orders all the CA columns before it orders the rows, the affinity measure of CA is specified with respect to columns. Note that the endpoint condition for the calculation of the affinity measure (AM) can be specified, using this notation, as $CA(0,j) = CA(i,0) = CA(n+1,j) = CA(i,n+1) = 0$.

Algorithm 5.3   *BEA*

    input: *AA*: attribute affinity matrix
    output: *CA*: clustered affinity matrix
    begin
        {initialize; remember that *AA* is an $n \times n$ matrix}
        $CA(\bullet, 1) \leftarrow AA(\bullet, 1)$
        $CA(\bullet, 2) \leftarrow AA(\bullet, 2)$
        $index \leftarrow 3$
        while $index \leq n$ **do** {choose the "best" location for attribute AA_{index}}
        begin
            for i **from** 1 **to** $index - 1$ **by** 1 **do**
                calculate $cont(A_{i-1}, A_{index}, A_i)$
            end-for
            calculate $cont(A_{index-1}, A_{index}, A_{index+1})$ {boundary condition}
            $loc \leftarrow$ placement given by maximum $cont$ value
            for j **from** $index$ **to** loc **by** -1 **do**   {shuffle the two matrices}
                $CA(\bullet, j) \leftarrow CA(\bullet, j - 1)$
            end-for
            $CA(\bullet, loc) \leftarrow AA(\bullet, index)$
            $index \leftarrow index + 1$
        end-while
        order the rows according to the relative ordering of columns
    end. {BEA}

For the second step of the algorithm to work, we need to define what is meant by the contribution of an attribute to the affinity measure. This contribution can be derived as follows. Recall that the global affinity measure *AM* was previously defined as

$$AM = \sum_{i=1}^{n} \sum_{j=1}^{n} aff(A_i, A_j)[aff(A_i, A_{j-1}) + aff(A_i, A_{j+1})]$$

which can be rewritten as

$$AM = \sum_{i=1}^{n} \sum_{j=1}^{n} [aff(A_i, A_j)aff(A_i, A_{j-1}) + aff(A_i, A_j)aff(A_i, A_{j+1})]$$

$$= \sum_{j=1}^{n} \left[\sum_{i=1}^{n} aff(A_i, A_j)aff(A_i, A_{j-1}) + \sum_{i=1}^{n} aff(A_i, A_j)aff(A_i, A_{j+1}) \right]$$

Let us define the *bond* between two attributes A_x and A_y as

$$bond(A_x, A_y) = \sum_{z=1}^{n} aff(A_z, A_x)aff(A_z, A_y)$$

Then AM can be written as

$$AM = \sum_{j=1}^{n} [bond(A_j, A_{j-1}) + bond(A_j, A_{j+1})]$$

Now consider the following n attributes

$$\underbrace{A_1 \; A_2 \; \cdots \; A_{i-1}}_{AM'} \; A_i \; A_j \; \underbrace{A_{j+1} \; \cdots \; A_n}_{AM''}$$

The global affinity measure for these attributes can be written as

$$
\begin{aligned}
AM_{old} \; = \; & AM' + AM'' \\
& + bond(A_{i-1}, A_i) + bond(A_i, A_j) + bond(A_j, A_i) + bond(A_j, A_{j+1}) \\
= \; & \sum_{l=1}^{n} [bond(A_l, A_{l-1}) + bond(A_l, A_{l+1})] \\
& + \sum_{l=i+2}^{n} [bond(A_l, A_{l-1}) + bond(A_l, A_{l+1})] \\
& + 2bond(A_i, A_j)
\end{aligned}
$$

Now consider placing a new attribute A_k between attributes A_i and A_j in the clustered affinity matrix. The new global affinity measure can be similarly written as

$$
\begin{aligned}
AM_{new} \; = \; & AM' + AM'' + bond(A_i, A_k) + bond(A_k, A_i) \\
& + bond(A_k, A_j) + bond(A_j, A_k) \\
= \; & AM' + AM'' + 2bond(A_i, A_k) + 2bond(A_k, A_j)
\end{aligned}
$$

Thus, the net *contribution*[4] to the global affinity measure of placing attribute A_k between A_i and A_j is

$$
\begin{aligned}
cont(A_i, A_k, A_j) \; = \; & AM_{new} - AM_{old} \\
= \; & 2bond(A_i, A_k) + 2bond(A_k, A_j) - 2bond(A_i, A_j)
\end{aligned}
$$

---

[4]In literature [Hoffer and Severance, 1975] this measure is specified as $bond(A_i, A_k) + bond(A_k, A_j) - 2bond(A_i, A_j)$. However, this is a pessimistic measure which does not follow from the definition of AM.

Example 5.17

Let us consider the AA matrix given in Figure 5.16 and study the contribution of moving attribute A_4 between attributes A_1 and A_2, given by the formula

$$cont(A_1, A_4, A_2) = 2bond(A_1, A_4) + 2bond(A_4, A_2) - 2bond(A_1, A_2)$$

Computing each term, we get

$$
\begin{aligned}
bond(A_1, A_4) &= 45*0 + 0*75 + 45*3 + 0*78 = 135 \\
bond(A_4, A_2) &= 11865 \\
bond(A_1, A_2) &= 225
\end{aligned}
$$

Therefore,

$$cont(A_1, A_4, A_2) = 2*135 + 2*11865 - 2*225 = 23550$$

Note that the calculation of the bond between two attributes requires the multiplication of the respective elements of the two columns representing these attributes and taking the row-wise sum.

The algorithm and our discussion so far have both concentrated on the columns of the attribute affinity matrix. We can make the same arguments and redesign the algorithm to operate on the rows as well. Since the AA matrix is symmetric, both of these approaches will generate the same result.

Another point about Algorithm 5.3 is that to improve the efficiency, the second column is also fixed and placed next to the first one during the initialization step. This is acceptable since, according to the algorithm, A_2 can be placed either to the left of A_1 or to its right. The bond between the two, however, is independent of their positions relative to one another.

Finally, we should indicate the problem of computing $cont$ at the endpoints. If an attribute A_i is being considered for placement to the left of the leftmost attribute, one of the bond equations to be calculated is between a nonexistent left element and A_k [i.e., $bond(A_0, A_k)$]. Thus we need to refer to the conditions imposed on the definition of the global affinity measure AM, where $CA(0, k) = 0$. The other extreme is if A_j is the rightmost attribute that is already placed in the CA matrix and we are checking for the contribution of placing attribute A_k to the right of A_j. In this case the $bond(k, k + 1)$ needs to be calculated. However, since no attribute is yet placed in column $k + 1$ of CA, the affinity measure is not defined. Therefore, according to the endpoint conditions, this $bond$ value is also 0.

Example 5.18

We consider the clustering of the PROJ relation attributes and use the attribute affinity matrix AA of Figure 5.16.

$$
\begin{array}{c}
\begin{array}{cc} A_1 & A_2 \end{array} \\
\begin{array}{c} A_1 \\ A_2 \\ A_3 \\ A_4 \end{array}
\left[
\begin{array}{cc}
45 & 0 \\
0 & 80 \\
45 & 5 \\
0 & 75
\end{array}
\right]
\end{array}
\qquad
\begin{array}{c}
\begin{array}{ccc} A_1 & A_3 & A_2 \end{array} \\
\begin{array}{c} A_1 \\ A_2 \\ A_3 \\ A_4 \end{array}
\left[
\begin{array}{ccc}
45 & 45 & 0 \\
0 & 5 & 80 \\
45 & 53 & 5 \\
0 & 3 & 75
\end{array}
\right]
\end{array}
$$

(a)   (b)

$$
\begin{array}{c}
\begin{array}{cccc} A_1 & A_3 & A_2 & A_4 \end{array} \\
\begin{array}{c} A_1 \\ A_2 \\ A_3 \\ A_4 \end{array}
\left[
\begin{array}{cccc}
45 & 45 & 0 & 0 \\
0 & 5 & 80 & 75 \\
45 & 53 & 5 & 3 \\
0 & 3 & 75 & 78
\end{array}
\right]
\end{array}
\qquad
\begin{array}{c}
\begin{array}{cccc} A_1 & A_3 & A_2 & A_4 \end{array} \\
\begin{array}{c} A_1 \\ A_3 \\ A_2 \\ A_4 \end{array}
\left[
\begin{array}{cccc}
45 & 45 & 0 & 0 \\
45 & 53 & 5 & 3 \\
0 & 5 & 80 & 75 \\
0 & 3 & 75 & 78
\end{array}
\right]
\end{array}
$$

(c)   (d)

Figure 5.17. Calculation of the Clustered Affinity (CA) Matrix

According to the initialization step, we copy columns 1 and 2 of the AA matrix to the CA matrix (Figure 5.17a) and start with column 3 (i.e., attribute A_3). There are three alternative places where column 3 can be placed: to the left of column 1, resulting in the ordering (3-1-2), in between columns 1 and 2, giving (1-3-2), and to the right of 2, resulting in (1-2-3). Note that to compute the contribution of the last ordering we have to compute $cont(A_2, A_3, A_4)$ rather than $cont(A_1, A_2, A_3)$. Furthermore, in this context A_4 refers to the fourth index position in the CA matrix, which is empty (Figure 5.17b), not to the attribute column A_4 of the AA matrix. Let us calculate the contribution to the global affinity measure of each alternative.

Ordering (0-3-1):

$$
cont(A_0, A_3, A_1) = 2bond(A_0, A_3) + 2bond(A_3, A_1) - 2bond(A_0, A_1)
$$

We know that

$$
\begin{aligned}
bond(A_0, A_1) &= bond(A_0, A_3) = 0 \\
bond(A_3, A_1) &= 45 * 45 + 5 * 0 + 53 * 45 + 3 * 0 = 4410
\end{aligned}
$$

Thus

$$
cont(A_0, A_3, A_1) = 8820
$$

Ordering (1-3-2):

$$cont(A_1, A_3, A_2) = 2bond(A_1, A_3) + 2bond(A_3, A_2) - 2bond(A_1, A_2)$$
$$bond(A_1, A_3) = bond(A_3, A_1) = 4410$$
$$bond(A_3, A_2) = 890$$
$$bond(A_1, A_2) = 225$$

Thus

$$cont(A_1, A_3, A_2) = 10150$$

Ordering (2-3-4):

$$cont(A_2, A_3, A_4) = 2bond(A_2, A_3) + 2bond(A_3, A_4) - 2bond(A_2, A_4)$$
$$bond(A_2, A_3) = 890$$
$$bond(A_3, A_4) = 0$$
$$bond(A_2, A_4) = 0$$

Thus

$$cont(A_2, A_3, A_4) = 1780$$

Since the contribution of the ordering (1-3-2) is the largest, we select to place A_3 to the right of A_1 (Figure 5.17b). Similar calculations for A_4 indicate that it should be placed to the right of A_2 (Figure 5.17c).

Finally, the rows are organized in the same order as the columns and the result is shown in Figure 5.17d.

In Figure 5.17d we see the creation of two clusters: one is in the upper left corner and contains the smaller affinity values and the other is in the lower right corner and contains the larger affinity values. This clustering indicates how the attributes of relation PROJ should be split. However, in general the border for this split is not this clear-cut. When the CA matrix is big, usually more than two clusters are formed and there are more than one candidate partitionings. Thus there is a need to approach this problem more systematically.

Partitioning Algorithm

The objective of the splitting activity is to find sets of attributes that are accessed solely, or for the most part, by distinct sets of applications. For example, if it is possible to identify two attributes, A_1 and A_2, which are accessed only by applica-

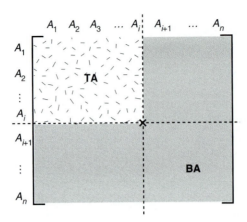

Figure 5.18. Locating a Splitting Point

tion q_1, and attributes A_3 and A_4, which are accessed by, say, two applications q_2 and q_3, it would be quite straightforward to decide on the fragments. The task lies in finding an algorithmic method of identifying these groups.

Consider the clustered attribute matrix of Figure 5.18. If a point along the diagonal is fixed, two sets of attributes are identified. One set $\{A_1, A_2, \ldots, A_i\}$ is at the upper left-hand corner and the second set $\{A_{i+1}, \ldots, A_n\}$ is to the right and to the bottom of this point. We call the former set *top* and the latter set *bottom* and denote the attribute sets as TA and BA, respectively.

We now turn to the set of applications $Q = \{q_1, q_2, \ldots, q_q\}$ and define the set of applications that access only TA, only BA, or both. These sets are defined as follows:

$$AQ(q_i) = \{A_j | use(q_i, A_j) = 1\}$$
$$TQ = \{q_i | AQ(q_i) \subseteq TA\}$$
$$BQ = \{q_i | AQ(q_i) \subseteq BA\}$$
$$OQ = Q - \{TQ \cup BQ\}$$

The first of these equations defines the set of attributes accessed by application q_i; TQ and BQ are the sets of applications that only access TA or BA, respectively, and OQ is the set of applications that access both.

There is an optimization problem here. If there are n attributes of a relation, there are $n - 1$ possible positions where the dividing point can be placed along the diagonal of the clustered attribute matrix for that relation. The best position for division is one which produces the sets TQ and BQ such that the total accesses to *only one* fragment are maximized while the total accesses to *both* fragments are minimized. We therefore define the following cost equations:

$$CQ = \sum_{q_i \in Q} \sum_{\forall S_j} ref_j(q_i)acc_j(q_i)$$

$$CTQ = \sum_{q_i \in TQ} \sum_{\forall S_j} ref_j(q_i)acc_j(q_i)$$

$$CBQ = \sum_{q_i \in BQ} \sum_{\forall S_j} ref_j(q_i)acc_j(q_i)$$

$$COQ = \sum_{q_i \in OQ} \sum_{\forall S_j} ref_j(q_i)acc_j(q_i)$$

Each of the equations above counts the total number of accesses to attributes by applications in their respective classes. Based on these measures, the optimization problem is defined as finding the point x ($1 \leq x \leq n$) such that the expression

$$z = CTQ * CBQ - COQ^2$$

is maximized [Navathe et al., 1984]. The important feature of this expression is that it defines two fragments such that the values of CTQ and CBQ are as nearly equal as possible. This enables the balancing of processing loads when the fragments are distributed to various sites. It is clear that the partitioning algorithm has linear complexity in terms of the number of attributes of the relation, that is, $O(n)$.

There are two complications that need to be addressed. The first is with respect to the splitting. The procedure splits the set of attributes two-way. For larger sets of attributes, it is quite likely that m-way partitioning may be necessary.

Designing an m-way partitioning is possible but computationally expensive. Along the diagonal of the CA matrix, it is necessary to try 1, 2, ..., $m-1$ split points, and for each of these, it is necessary to check which place maximizes z. Thus the complexity of such an algorithm is $O(2^m)$. Of course, the definition of z has to be modified for those cases where there are multiple split points. The alternative solution is to recursively apply the binary partitioning algorithm to each of the fragments obtained during the previous iteration. One would compute TQ, BQ, and OQ, as well as the associated access measures for each of the fragments, and partition them further.

The second complication relates to the location of the block of attributes that should form one fragment. Our discussion so far assumed that the split point is unique and single and divides the CA matrix into an upper left-hand partition and a second partition formed by the rest of the attributes. The partition, however, may also be formed in the middle of the matrix. In this case we need to modify the algorithm slightly. The leftmost column of the CA matrix is shifted to become the rightmost column and the topmost row is shifted to the bottom. The shift operation is followed by checking the $n-1$ diagonal positions to find the maximum z. The idea behind shifting is to move the block of attributes that should form a cluster to the topmost left corner of the matrix, where it can easily be identified. With the addition of the shift operation, the complexity of the partitioning algorithm increases by a factor of n and becomes $O(n^2)$.

Assuming that a shift procedure, called SHIFT, has already been implemented, the partitioning algorithm is given in Algorithm 5.4. The input of the PARTITION is the clustered affinity matrix CA, the relation R to be fragmented, and the attribute usage and access frequency matrices. The output is a set of fragments $F_R = \{R_1, R_2\}$, where $R_i \subseteq \{A_1, A_2 \ldots, A_n\}$ and $R_1 \cap R_2 = $ the key attributes of relation R. Note that for n-way partitioning, this routine should either be invoked iteratively, or implemented as a recursive procedure that iterates itself.

Algorithm 5.4 *PARTITION*

> **input:** CA: clustered affinity matrix; R: relation; ref: attribute usage matrix; acc: access frequency matrix
> **output:** F: set of fragments
> **begin**
>   {determine the z value for the first column}
>   {the subscripts in the cost equations indicate the split point}
>   calculate CTQ_{n-1}
>   calculate CBQ_{n-1}
>   calculate COQ_{n-1}
> $best \leftarrow CTQ_{n-1} * CBQ_{n-1} - (COQ_{n-1})^2$
>   **do**   {determine the best partitioning}
>   **begin**
>   **for** i **from** $n-2$ **to** 1 **by** -1 **do**
>   **begin**
>   calculate CTQ_i
>   calculate CBQ_i
>   calculate COQ_i
> $z \leftarrow CTQ * CBQ_i - COQ_i^2$
>   **if** $z > best$ **then**
>   **begin**
> $best \leftarrow z$
>   record the split point within shift
>   **end-if**
>   **end-for**
>   call SHIFT(CA)
>   **end-begin**
>   **until** no more SHIFT is possible
>   reconstruct the matrix according to the shift position
> $R_1 \leftarrow \Pi_{TA}(R) \cup K$ {K is the set of primary key attributes of R}
> $R_2 \leftarrow \Pi_{BA}(R) \cup K$
> $F \leftarrow \{R_1, R_2\}$
> **end.** {PARTITION}

Example 5.19

When the PARTITION algorithm is applied to the CA matrix obtained for relation PROJ (Example 5.18), the result is the definition of fragments F_{PROJ} = {PROJ$_1$,PROJ$_2$}, where PROJ$_1$ = $\{A_1, A_3\}$ and PROJ$_2$ = $\{A_1, A_2, A_4\}$. Thus

$$
\begin{aligned}
\text{PROJ}_1 &= \{\text{PNO, BUDGET}\} \\
\text{PROJ}_2 &= \{\text{PNO, PNAME, LOC}\}
\end{aligned}
$$

Note that in this exercise we performed the fragmentation over the entire set of attributes rather than only on the nonkey ones. The reason for this is the simplicity of the example. For that reason, we included PNO, which is the key of PROJ in PROJ$_2$ as well as in PROJ$_1$.

Checking for Correctness

We follow arguments similar to those of horizontal partitioning to prove that the PARTITION algorithm yields a correct vertical fragmentation.

Completeness.   Completeness is guaranteed by the PARTITION algorithm since each attribute of the global relation is assigned to one of the fragments. As long as the set of attributes A over which the relation R is defined consists of

$$ A = \cup R_i $$

completeness of vertical fragmentation is ensured.

Reconstruction.   We have already mentioned that the reconstruction of the original global relation is made possible by the join operation. Thus, for a relation R with vertical fragmentation $F_R = \{R_1, R_2, \ldots, R_r\}$ and key attribute(s) K,

$$ R = \bowtie_K R_i, \forall R_i \in F_R $$

Therefore, as long as each R_i is complete, the join operation will properly reconstruct R. Another important point is that either each R_i should contain the key attribute(s) of R, or it should contain the system assigned tuple IDs (TIDs).

Disjointness.   As we indicated before, the disjointness of fragments is not as important in vertical fragmentation as it is in horizontal fragmentation. There are two cases here:

1.   TIDs are used, in which case the fragments are disjoint since the TIDs that are replicated in each fragment are system assigned and managed entities, totally invisible to the users.

2. The key attributes are replicated in each fragment, in which case one cannot claim that they are disjoint in the strict sense of the term. However, it is important to realize that this duplication of the key attributes is known and managed by the system and does not have the same implications as tuple duplication in horizontally partitioned fragments. In other words, as long as the fragments are disjoint except for the key attributes, we can be satisfied and call them disjoint.

5.3.3 Hybrid Fragmentation

In most cases a simple horizontal or vertical fragmentation of a database schema will not be sufficient to satisfy the requirements of user applications. In this case a vertical fragmentation may be followed by a horizontal one, or vice versa, producing a tree-structured partitioning (Figure 5.19). Since the two types of partitioning strategies are applied one after the other, this alternative is called *hybrid* fragmentation. It has also been named *mixed* fragmentation or *nested* fragmentation.

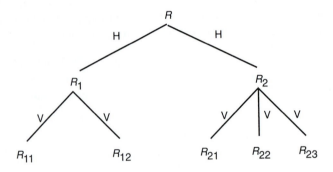

Figure 5.19. Hybrid Fragmentation

A good example for the necessity of hybrid fragmentation is relation PROJ, which we have been working with. In Example 5.11 we partitioned it into six horizontal fragments based on two applications. In Example 5.19 we partitioned the same relation vertically into two. What we have, therefore, is a set of horizontal fragments, each of which is further partitioned into two vertical fragments.

The number of levels of nesting can be large, but it is certainly finite. In the case of horizontal fragmentation, one has to stop when each fragment consists of only one tuple, whereas the termination point for vertical fragmentation is one attribute per fragment. These limits are quite academic, however, since the levels of nesting in most practical applications do not exceed 2. This is due to the fact that normalized global relations already have small degrees and one cannot perform too many vertical fragmentations before the cost of joins becomes very high.

We will not discuss in detail the correctness rules and conditions for hybrid fragmentation, since they follow naturally from those for vertical and horizontal

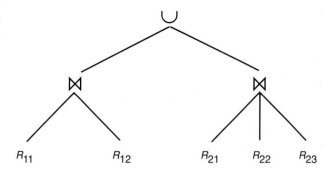

Figure 5.20. Reconstruction of Hybrid Fragmentation

fragmentations. For example, to reconstruct the original global relation in case of hybrid fragmentation, one starts at the leaves of the partitioning tree and moves upward by performing joins and unions (Figure 5.20). The fragmentation is complete if the intermediate and leaf fragments are complete. Similarly, disjointness is guaranteed if intermediate and leaf fragments are disjoint.

5.4 ALLOCATION

The allocation of resources across the nodes of a computer network is an old problem that has been studied extensively. Most of this work, however, does not address the problem of distributed database design, but rather that of placing individual files on a computer network. We will examine the differences between the two shortly. We first need to define the allocation problem more precisely.

5.4.1 Allocation Problem

Assume that there are a set of fragments $F = \{F_1, F_2, \ldots, F_n\}$ and a network consisting of sites $S = \{S_1, S_2, \ldots, S_m\}$ on which a set of applications $Q = \{q_1, q_2, \ldots, q_q\}$ is running. The allocation problem involves finding the "optimal" distribution of F to S.

One of the important issues that needs to be discussed is the definition of optimality. The optimality can be defined with respect to two measures [Dowdy and Foster, 1982]:

1. *Minimal cost.* The cost function consists of the cost of storing each F_i at a site S_j, the cost of querying F_i at site S_j, the cost of updating F_i at all sites where it is stored, and the cost of data communication. The allocation problem, then, attempts to find an allocation scheme that minimizes a combined cost function.

2. *Performance.* The allocation strategy is designed to maintain a performance metric. Two well-known ones are to minimize the response time and to maximize the system throughput at each site.

Most of the models that have been proposed to date make this distinction of optimality. However, if one really examines the problem in depth, it is apparent that the "optimality" measure should include both the performance and the cost factors. In other words, one should be looking for an allocation scheme that, for example, answers user queries in minimal time while keeping the cost of processing minimal. A similar statement can be made for throughput maximization. One can then ask why such models have not been developed. The answer is quite simple: complexity.

Let us consider a *very* simple formulation of the problem. Let F and S be defined as before. For the time being, we consider only a single fragment, F_k. We make a number of assumptions and definitions that will enable us to model the allocation problem.

1. Assume that Q can be modified so that it is possible to identify the update and the retrieval-only queries, and to define the following for a *single* fragment F_k:

$$T = \{t_1, t_2, \ldots, t_m\}$$

where t_i is the read-only traffic generated at site S_i for F_k, and

$$U = \{u_1, u_2, \ldots, u_m\}$$

where u_i is the update traffic generated at site S_i for F_k.

2. Assume that the communication cost between any two pair of sites S_i and S_j is fixed for a unit of transmission. Furthermore, assume that it is different for updates and retrievals in order that the following can be defined:

$$C(T) = \{c_{12}, c_{13}, \ldots, c_{1m}, \ldots, c_{m-1,m}\}$$
$$C'(U) = \{c'_{12}, c'_{13}, \ldots, c'_{1m}, \ldots, c'_{m-1,m}\}$$

where c_{ij} is the unit communication cost for retrieval requests between sites S_i and S_j, and c'_{ij} is the unit communication cost for update requests between sites S_i and S_j.

3. Let the cost of storing the fragment at site S_i be d_i. Thus we can define $D = \{d_1, d_2, \ldots, d_m\}$ for the storage cost of fragment F_k at all the sites.

4. Assume that there are no capacity constraints for either the sites or the communication links.

Then the allocation problem can be specified as a cost-minimization problem where we are trying to find the set $I \subseteq S$ that specifies where the copies of the fragment will be stored. In the following, x_j denotes the decision variable for the placement such that

$$x_j = \begin{cases} 1 & \text{if the fragment } F_k \text{ is assigned to site } S_j \\ 0 & \text{otherwise} \end{cases}$$

The precise specification is as follows:

$$\min \left[\sum_{i=1}^{m} \left(\sum_{j|S_j \in I} x_j u_j c'_{ij} + t_j \min_{j|S_j \in I} c_{ij} \right) + \sum_{j|S_j \in I} x_j d_j \right]$$

subject to

$$x_j = 0 \ or \ 1$$

The second term of the objective function calculates the total cost of storing all the duplicate copies of the fragment. The first term, on the other hand, corresponds to the cost of transmitting the updates to all the sites that hold the replicas of the fragment, and to the cost of executing the retrieval-only requests at the site, which will result in minimal data transmission cost.

This is a very simplistic formulation that is not suitable for distributed database design. But even if it were, there is another problem. This formulation, which comes from [Casey, 1972], has been proven to be NP-complete [Eswaran, 1974]. Various different formulations of the problem have been proven to be just as hard over the years (e.g., [Sacca and Wiederhold, 1985] and [Lam and Yu, 1980]). The implication is, of course, that for large problems (i.e., large number of fragments and sites), obtaining optimal solutions is probably not computationally feasible. Considerable research has therefore been devoted to finding good heuristics that provide suboptimal solutions.

There are a number of reasons why simplistic formulations such as the one we have discussed are not suitable for distributed database design. These are inherent in all the early file allocation models for computer networks.

1. One cannot treat fragments as individual files that can be allocated one at a time, in isolation. The placement of one fragment usually has an impact on the placement decisions about the other fragments which are accessed together since the access costs to the the remaining fragments may change (e.g., due to distributed join). Therefore, the relationship between fragments should be taken into account.

2. The access to data by applications is modeled very simply. A user request is issued at one site and all the data to answer it is transferred to that site. In distributed database systems, access to data is more complicated than this simple "remote file access" model suggests. Therefore, the relationship between the allocation and query processing should be properly modeled.

3. These models do not take into consideration the cost of integrity enforcement, yet locating two fragments involved in the same integrity constraint at two different sites can be costly.

4. Similarly, the cost of enforcing concurrency control mechanisms should be considered [Rothnie and Goodman, 1977].

In summary, let us remember the interrelationship between the distributed database problems as depicted in Figure 1.8. Since the allocation is so central, its relationship with algorithms that are implemented for other problem areas needs to be represented in the allocation model. However, this is exactly what makes it quite difficult to solve these models. To separate the traditional problem of file allocation from the fragment allocation in distributed database design, we refer to the former as the *file allocation problem* (FAP) and to the latter as the *database allocation problem* (DAP).

There are no general heuristic models that take as input a set of fragments and produce a near-optimal allocation subject to the types of constraints discussed here. The models developed to date make a number of simplifying assumptions and are applicable to certain specific formulations. Therefore, instead of presenting one or more of these allocation algorithms, we present a relatively general model and then discuss a number of possible heuristics that might be employed to solve it.

5.4.2 Information Requirements

It is at the allocation stage that we need the quantitative data about the database, the applications that run on it, the communication network, the processing capabilities, and storage limitations of each site on the network. We will discuss each of these in detail.

Database Information

To perform horizontal fragmentation, we defined the selectivity of minterms. We now need to extend that definition to fragments, and define the selectivity of a fragment F_j with respect to query q_i. This is the number of tuples of F_j that need to be accessed in order to process q_i. This value will be denoted as $sel_i(F_j)$.

Another piece of necessary information on the database fragments is their size. The size of a fragment F_j is given by

$$size(F_j) = card(F_j) * length(F_j)$$

where $length(F_j)$ is the length (in bytes) of a tuple of fragment F_j.

Application Information

Most of the application-related information is already compiled during the fragmentation activity, but a few more are required by the allocation model. The two important measures are the number of read accesses that a query q_i makes to a fragment F_j during its execution (denoted as RR_{ij}), and its counterpart for the update accesses (UR_{ij}). These may, for example, count the number of block accesses required by the query.

We also need to define two matrices UM and RM, with elements u_{ij} and r_{ij}, respectively, which are specified as follows:

$$u_{ij} = \begin{cases} 1 & \text{if query } q_i \text{ updates fragment } F_j \\ 0 & \text{otherwise} \end{cases}$$

$$r_{ij} = \begin{cases} 1 & \text{if query } q_i \text{ retrieves from fragment } F_j \\ 0 & \text{otherwise} \end{cases}$$

A vector O of values $o(i)$ is also defined, where $o(i)$ specifies the originating site of query q_i. Finally, to define the response-time constraint, the maximum allowable response time of each application should be specified.

Site Information

For each computer site, we need to know about its storage and processing capacity. Obviously, these values can be computed by means of elaborate functions or by simple estimates. The unit cost of storing data at site S_k will be denoted as USC_k. There is also a need to specify a cost measure LPC_k as the cost of processing one unit of work at site S_k. The work unit should be identical to that of the RR and UR measures.

Network Information

In our model we assume the existence of a simple network where the cost of communication is defined in terms of one frame of data. Thus g_{ij} denotes the communication cost per frame between sites S_i and S_j. To enable the calculation of the number of messages, we use $fsize$ as the size (in bytes) of one frame. There is no question that there are more elaborate network models which take into consideration the channel capacities, distances between sites, protocol overhead, and so on. However, the derivation of those equations is beyond the scope of this chapter.

5.4.3   Allocation Model

We discuss an allocation model that attempts to minimize the total cost of processing and storage while trying to meet certain response time restrictions. The model we use has the following form:

$$\min(\text{Total Cost})$$

subject to

response-time constraint storage constraint processing constraint

In the remainder of this section we expand the components of this model based on the information requirements discussed in Section 5.4.2. The decision variable is x_{ij}, which is defined as

$$x_{ij} = \begin{cases} 1 & \text{if the fragment } F_i \text{ is stored at site } S_j \\ 0 & \text{otherwise} \end{cases}$$

Total Cost

The total cost function has two components: query processing and storage. Thus it can be expressed as

$$TOC = \sum_{\forall q_i \in Q} QPC_i + \sum_{\forall S_k \in S} \sum_{\forall F_j \in F} STC_{jk}$$

where QPC_i is the query processing cost of application q_i, and STC_{jk} is the cost of storing fragment F_j at site S_k.

Let us consider the storage cost first. It is simply given by

$$STC_{jk} = USC_k * size(F_j) * x_{jk}$$

and the two summations find the total storage costs at all the sites for all the fragments.

The query processing cost is more difficult to specify. Most models of the file allocation problem (FAP) separate it into two components: the retrieval-only processing cost, and the update processing cost. We choose a different approach in our model of the database allocation problem (DAP) and specify it as consisting of the processing cost (PC) and the transmission cost (TC). Thus the query processing cost (QPC) for application q_i is

$$QPC_i = PC_i + TC_i$$

According to the guidelines presented in Section 5.4.1, the processing component, PC, consists of three cost factors, the access cost (AC), the integrity enforcement cost (IE), and the concurrency control cost (CC):

$$PC_i = AC_i + IE_i + CC_i$$

The detailed specification of each of these cost factors depends on the algorithms used to accomplish these tasks. However, to demonstrate the point, we specify AC in some detail.

$$AC_i = \sum_{\forall S_k \in S} \sum_{\forall F_j \in F} (u_{ij} * UR_{ij} + r_{ij} * RR_{ij}) * x_{jk} * LPC_k$$

The first two terms in the formula above calculate the number of accesses of user query q_i to fragment F_j. Note that $(UR_{ij} + RR_{ij})$ gives the total number of update and retrieval accesses. We assume that the local costs of processing them are identical. The summation gives the total number of accesses for all the fragments referenced by q_i. Multiplication by LPC_k gives the cost of this access at site S_k. We again use x_{jk} to select only those cost values for the sites where fragments are stored.

A very important issue needs to be pointed out here. The access cost function assumes that processing a query involves decomposing it into a set of subqueries, each of which works on a fragment stored at the site, followed by transmitting the results back to the site where the query has originated. As we discussed earlier, this is a very simplistic view which does not take into consideration the complexities of database processing. For example, the cost function does not take into account the cost of performing joins (if necessary), which may be executed in a number of ways, studied in Chapter 9. In a model that is more realistic than the generic model we are considering, these issues should not be omitted.

The integrity enforcement cost factor can be specified much like the processing component, except that the unit local processing cost would probably change to reflect the true cost of integrity enforcement. Since the integrity checking and concurrency control methods are discussed later in the book, we do not need to study these cost components further here. The reader should refer back to this section after reading Chapters 6 and 11 to be convinced that the cost functions can indeed be derived.

The transmission cost function can be formulated along the lines of the access cost function. However, the data transmission overhead for update and that for retrieval requests are quite different. In update queries it is necessary to inform all the sites where replicas exist, while in retrieval queries, it is sufficient to access only one of the copies. In addition, at the end of an update request, there is no data transmission back to the originating site other than a confirmation message, whereas the retrieval-only queries may result in significant data transmission.

The update component of the transmission function is

$$TCU_i = \sum_{\forall S_k \in S} \sum_{\forall F_j \in F} u_{ij} * x_{jk} * g_{o(i),k} + \sum_{\forall S_k \in S} \sum_{\forall F_j \in F} u_{ij} * x_{jk} * g_{k,o(i)}$$

The first term is for sending the update message from the originating site $o(i)$ of q_i to all the fragment replicas that need to be updated. The second term is for the confirmation.

The retrieval cost can be specified as

$$TCR_i = \sum_{\forall F_j \in F} \min_{S_k \in S} \left(u_{ij} * x_{jk} * g_{o(i),k} + r_{ij} * x_{jk} * \frac{sel_i(F_j) * length(F_j)}{fsize} * g_{k,o(i)} \right)$$

The first term in TCR represents the cost of transmitting the retrieval request to those sites which have copies of fragments that need to be accessed. The second term accounts for the transmission of the results from these sites to the originating site. The equation states that among all the sites with copies of the same fragment, only the site that yields the minimum total transmission cost should be selected for the execution of the operation.

Now the transmission cost function for query q_i can be specified as

$$TC_i = TCU_i + TCR_i$$

which fully specifies the total cost function.

Constraints

The constraint functions can be specified in similar detail. However, instead of describing these functions in depth, we will simply indicate what they should look like. The response-time constraint should be specified as

$$\text{execution time of } q_i \leq \text{ maximum response time of } q_i, \forall q_i \in Q$$

Preferably, the cost measure in the objective function should be specified in terms of time, as it makes the specification of the execution-time constraint relatively straightforward.

The storage constraint is

$$\sum_{\forall F_j \in F} STC_{jk} \leq \text{storage capacity at site } S_k, \forall S_k \in S$$

whereas the processing constraint is

$$\sum_{\forall q_i \in Q} \text{processing load of } q_i \text{ at site } S_k \leq \text{ processing capacity of } S_k, \forall S_k \in S$$

This completes our development of the allocation model. Even though we have not developed it entirely, the precision in some of the terms indicates how one goes about formulating such a problem. In addition to this aspect, we have indicated the important issues that need to be addressed in allocation models.

5.4.4 Solution Methods

In the preceding section we developed a generic allocation model which is considerably more complex than the FAP model presented in Section 5.4.1. Since the FAP model is NP-complete, one would expect the solution of this formulation of the database allocation problem (DAP) also to be NP-complete. Even though we will not prove this conjecture, it is indeed true. Thus one has to look for heuristic methods that yield suboptimal solutions. The test of "goodness" in this case is, obviously, how close the results of the heuristic algorithm are to the optimal allocation.

A number of different heuristics have been applied to the solution of FAP and DAP models. It was observed early on that there is a correspondence between FAP and the plant location problem that has been studied in operations research. In fact, the isomorphism of the simple FAP and the single commodity warehouse location problem has been shown [Ramamoorthy and Wah, 1983]. Thus heuristics developed by operations researchers have commonly been adopted to solve the FAP and DAP problems. Examples are the knapsack problem solution [Ceri et al., 1982b], branch-and-bound techniques [Fisher and Hochbaum, 1980], and network flow algorithms [Chang and Liu, 1982].

There have been other attempts to reduce the complexity of the problem. One strategy has been to assume that all the candidate partitionings have been determined together with their associated costs and benefits in terms of query processing. The problem, then, is modeled so as to choose the optimal partitioning and placement for each relation [Ceri et al., 1983]. Another simplification frequently employed is to ignore replication at first and find an optimal nonreplicated solution. Replication is handled at the second step by applying a greedy algorithm which starts with the nonreplicated solution as the initial feasible solution, and tries to improve upon it ([Ceri et al., 1983] and [Ceri and Pernici, 1985]). For these heuristics, however, there is not enough data to determine how close the results are to the optimal.

5.5 CONCLUSION

In this chapter we presented the techniques that can be used for distributed database design with special emphasis on the fragmentation and allocation issues. There are a number of lines of research that have been followed in distributed database design. For example, Chang has independently developed a theory of fragmentation [Chang and Cheng, 1980], and allocation [Chang and Liu, 1982]. However, for its maturity of development, we have chosen to develop this chapter along the track developed by Ceri, Pelagatti, Navathe, and Wiederhold. Our references to the literature by these authors reflect this quite clearly.

There is a considerable body of literature on the allocation problem, focusing mostly on the simpler file allocation issue. We still do not have sufficiently general models that take into consideration all the aspects of data distribution. The model presented in Section 5.4 highlights the types of issues that need to be taken into account. Within this context, it might be worthwhile to take a somewhat different approach to the solution of the distributed allocation problem. One might develop a set of heuristic rules that might accompany the mathematical formulation and reduce the solution space, thus making the solution feasible.

In this chapter we have discussed, in detail, the algorithms that one can use to fragment a relational schema in various ways. These algorithms have been developed quite independently and there is no underlying design methodology that combines the horizontal and vertical partitioning techniques. If one starts with a global relation, there are algorithms to decompose it horizontally as well as algorithms to decompose it vertically into a set of fragment relations. However, there are no algorithms that fragment a global relation into a set of fragment relations some of which are decomposed horizontally and others vertically. It is always pointed out that most real-life fragmentations would be mixed, i.e., would involve both horizontal and vertical partitioning of a relation, but the methodology research to accomplish this is lacking. What is needed is a distribution design methodology which encompasses the horizontal and vertical fragmentation algorithms and uses them as part of a more general strategy. Such a methodology should take a global relation together with a set of design criteria and come up with a set of fragments some of which are obtained via horizontal and others obtained via vertical fragmentation.

The second part of distribution design, namely allocation, is typically treated independently of fragmentation. The process is, therefore, linear when the output of fragmentation is input to allocation. At first sight, the isolation of the fragmentation and the allocation steps appears to simplify the formulation of the problem by reducing the decision space. However, closer examination reveals that isolating the two steps actually contributes to the complexity of the allocation models. Both steps have similar inputs, differing only in that fragmentation works on global relations whereas allocation considers fragment relations. They both require information about the user applications (e.g., how often they access data, what the relationship of individual data objects to one another is, etc.), but ignore how each other makes use of these inputs. The end result is that the fragmentation algorithms decide how to partition a relation based partially on how applications access it, but the allocation models ignore the part that this input plays in fragmentation. Therefore, the allocation models have to include all over again detailed specification of the relationship among the fragment relations and how user applications access them. What would be more promising is to formulate a methodology that more properly reflects the interdependence of the fragmentation and the allocation decisions. This requires extensions to existing distribution design strategies. We recognize that integrated methodologies such as the one we propose here may be considerably complex. However, there may be synergistic effects of combining these two steps enabling the development of quite acceptable heuristic solution methods. There are some early studies that give us hope that such integrated methodologies and proper solution mechanisms can be developed (e.g., [Muro et al., 1983], [Muro et al., 1985], [Yoshida et al., 1985]). These methodologies build a simulation model of the distributed DBMS, taking as input a specific database design, and measure its effectiveness. Development of tools based on such methodologies, which aid the human designer rather than attempt to replace him, is probably the more appropriate approach to the design problem.

Another aspect of the work described in this chapter is that it assumes a static environment where design is conducted only once and this design can persist. Reality, of course, is quite different. Both physical (e.g., network characteristics, available storage at various sites) and logical (e.g., migration of applications from one site to another, access pattern modifications) changes occur necessitating redesign of the database. In recent years this problem has been studied by Navathe and Karlapalem. In a dynamic environment, the process becomes one of design-redesign-materialization of the redesign. The design step follows techniques that have been described in this chapter. Redesign can either be limited in that only parts of the database are affected, or total, requiring a complete redistribution [Wilson and Navathe, 1986]. Materialization refers to the reorganization of the distributed database to reflect the changes required by the redesign step. Limited redesign, in particular, the materialization issue is studied in [Rivera-Vega et al., 1990], [Varadarajan et al., 1989]. Complete redesign and materialization issues have been studied in [Karlapalem et al., 1996b], [Karlapalem and Navathe, 1994], [Kazerouni and Karlapalem, 1997]. In particular, [Kazerouni and Karlapalem, 1997] describes a stepwise redesign methodology which involves a split phase where fragments are further subdivided based on the changed application requirements until no further subdivision is profitable based on a cost function. At this point, the merging phase starts where fragments that are accessed together by a set of applications are merged into one fragment.

5.6   BIBLIOGRAPHIC NOTES

Most of the known results about fragmentation have been covered in this chapter. Work on fragmentation in distributed databases initially concentrated on horizontal fragmentation. Most of the literature on this has been cited in the appropriate section. The topic of vertical fragmentation for distribution design has been addressed in several recent papers ([Navathe et al., 1984] and [Sacca and Wiederhold, 1985]. The original work on vertical fragmentation goes back to Hoffer's dissertation [Hoffer, 1975] and to Hammer and Niamir's work ([Niamir, 1978] and [Hammer and Niamir, 1979]). Parts of Hoffer's dissertation were reported in [Hoffer and Severance, 1975].

It is not possible to be as exhaustive when discussing allocation as we have been for fragmentation, given there is no limit to the literature on the subject. The investigation of FAP on wide area networks goes back to [Chu, 1969] and [Chu, 1973]. Most of the early work on FAP has been covered in the excellent survey by [Dowdy and Foster, 1982]. Some theoretical results about FAP are reported in [Grapa and Belford, 1977] and in [Kollias and Hatzopoulos, 1981].

The DAP work dates back to the mid-1970s to the works of [Eswaran, 1974] and others. In their earlier work, Levin and Morgan [1975] concentrated on data allocation, but later they considered program and data allocation together [Morgan and Levin, 1977]. The DAP has been studied in many specialized settings as well. Work has been done to determine the placement of computers and data in a wide area network design [Gavish and Pirkul, 1986]. Channel capacities have been examined along with data placement [Mahmoud and Riordon, 1976] and data allocation on supercomputer systems [Irani and Khabbaz, 1982] as well as on a cluster of processors [Sacca and Wiederhold, 1985]. An interesting work is the one by Apers, where the relations are optimally placed on the nodes of a virtual network, and then the best matching between the virtual network nodes and the physical network are found [Apers, 1981].

Some of the allocation work has also touched upon physical design. The assignment of files to various levels of a memory hierarchy has been studied in [Foster and Browne, 1976] and in [Navathe et al., 1984]. These are outside the scope of this chapter, as are those that deal with general resource and task allocation in distributed systems (e.g., [Bucci and Golinelli, 1977], [Ceri and Pelagatti, 1982], and [Haessig and Jenny, 1980]).

We should finally point out that some effort was spent to develop a general methodology for distributed database design along the lines that we presented (Figure 5.2). Ours is similar to the DATAID-D methodology discussed in [Ceri and Navathe, 1983] and [Ceri et al., 1987]. Other attempts to develop a methodology are reported in [Fisher et al., 1980], [Dawson, 1980], [Hevner and Schneider, 1980] and [Mohan, 1979].

5.7 EXERCISES

*5.1 Given relation EMP as in Figure 5.3, let p_1: TITLE < "Programmer" and p_2: TITLE > "Programmer" be two simple predicates. Assume that character strings have an order among them, based on the alphabetical order.

(a) Perform a horizontal fragmentation of relation EMP with respect to $\{p_1, p_2\}$.

(b) Explain why the resulting fragmentation (EMP$_1$, EMP$_2$) does not fulfill the correctness rules of fragmentation.

(c) Modify the predicates p_1 and p_2 so that they partition EMP obeying the correctness rules of fragmentaion. To do this, modify the predicates, compose all minterm predicates and deduce the corresponding implications, and then perform a horizontal fragmentation of EMP based on these minterm predicates. Finally, show that the result has completeness, reconstruction and disjointness properties.

*5.2 Consider relation ASG in Figure 5.3. Suppose there are two applications that access ASG. The first is issued at five sites and attempts to find the duration of assignment of employees given their numbers. Assume that managers, consultants, engineers, and programmers are located at four different sites. The second application is issued at two sites where the employees with an assignment duration of less than 20 months are managed at one site, whereas those with longer duration are managed at a second site. Derive the primary horizontal fragmentation of ASG using the foregoing information.

5.4 Consider relations EMP and PAY in Figure 5.3. EMP and PAY are horizontally fragmented as follows:

$$
\begin{aligned}
\text{EMP}_1 &= \sigma_{\text{TITLE= "Elect.Eng."}}(\text{EMP}) \\
\text{EMP}_2 &= \sigma_{\text{TITLE="Syst.Anal."}}(\text{EMP}) \\
\text{EMP}_3 &= \sigma_{\text{TITLE="Mech.Eng."}}(\text{EMP}) \\
\text{EMP}_4 &= \sigma_{\text{TITLE="Programmer"}}(\text{EMP}) \\
\text{PAY}_1 &= \sigma_{\text{SAL} \geq 30000}(\text{PAY}) \\
\text{PAY}_2 &= \sigma_{\text{SAL} < 30000}(\text{PAY})
\end{aligned}
$$

Draw the join graph of EMP $\bowtie_{\text{TITLE}}$ S. Is the graph simple or partitioned? If it is partitioned, modify the fragmentation of either EMP or PAY so that the join graph of EMP $\bowtie_{\text{TITLE}}$ PAY is simple.

5.5 Give an example of a CA matrix where the split point is not unique and the partition is in the middle of the matrix. Show the number of shift operations required to obtain a single, unique split point.

**5.5 Given relation PAY as in Figure 5.3, let p_1: SAL < 30000 and p_2: SAL ≥ 3000 be two simple predicates. Perform a horizontal fragmentation of PAY with respect to these predicates to obtain PAY$_1$, and PAY$_2$. Using the fragmentation of PAY, perform further derived horizontal fragmentation for EMP. Show completeness, reconstruction, and disjointness of the fragmentation of EMP.

**5.6 Let $Q = \{q_1, q_2, q_3, q_4, q_5\}$ be a set of queries, $A = \{A_1, A_2, A_3, A_4, A_5\}$ be a set of attributes, and $S = \{S_1, S_2, S_3\}$ be a set of sites. The matrix of Figure 5.21a describes the attribute usage values and the matrix of Figure 5.21b gives the application access frequencies. Assume that $ref_i(q_k) = 1$ for all q_k and S_i and that A_1 is the key attribute. Use the bond energy and vertical partitioning algorithms to obtain a vertical fragmentation of the set of attributes in A.

	A_1	A_2	A_3	A_4	A_5
q_1	0	1	1	0	1
q_2	1	1	1	0	1
q_3	1	0	0	1	1
q_4	0	0	1	0	0
q_5	1	1	1	0	0

	S_1	S_2	S_3
q_1	10	20	0
q_2	5	0	10
q_3	0	35	5
q_4	0	10	0
q_5	0	15	0

(a)   (b)

Figure 5.21. Attribute Usage Values and Application Access Frequencies in Exercise 5.6

**5.7 Write an algorithm for derived horizontal fragmentation.

**5.8 Assume the following view definition

```
CREATE   VIEW     EMPVIEW(ENO, ENAME, PNO, RESP)
AS       SELECT   EMP.ENO, EMP.ENAME, ASG.PNO, ASG.RESP
         FROM     EMP, ASG
         WHERE    EMP.ENO=ASG.ENO
         AND      DUR=24
```

is accessed by application q_1, located at sites 1 and 2, with frequencies 10 and 20, respectively. Let us further assume that there is another query q_2 defined as

```
SELECT   ENO, DUR
FROM     ASG
```

which is run at sites 2 and 3 with frequencies 20 and 10, respectively. Based on the above information, construct the $use(q_i, A_j)$ matrix for the attributes of both relations EMP and ASG. Also construc tthe affinity matrix containing all attributes of EMP and ASG. Finally, transform the affinity matrix so that it could be used to split the relation into two vertical fragments using heuristics or BEA.

**5.9 Formally define the three correctness criteria for derived horizontal fragmentation.

*5.10 Show that the bond energy algorithm generates the same results using either row or column operation.

**5.11 Modify algorithm PARTITION to allow n-way partitioning, and compute the complexity of the resulting algorithm.

**5.12 Formally define the three correctness criteria for hybrid fragmentation.

5.13 Discuss how the order in which the two basic fragmentation schemas are applied in hybrid fragmentation affects the final fragmentation.

**5.14 Describe how the following can be properly modeled in the database allocation problem.

(a) Relationships among fragments

(b) Query processing

(c) Integrity enforcement

(d) Concurrency control mechanisms

**5.15 Consider the various heuristic algorithms for the database allocation problem.

(a) What are some of the reasonable criteria for comparing these heuristics? Discuss.

(b) Compare the heuristic algorithms with respect to these criteria.

*5.16 Pick one of the heuristic algorithms used to solve the DAP, and write a program for it.

**5.17 Assume the environment of Exercise 5.8. Also assume that 60% of the accesses of query q_1 are updates to PNO adn RESP of view EMPVIEW and that ASG.DUR is not updated through EMPVIEW. In addition, assume that the data transfer rate between site 1 and site 2 is half of that between site 2 and site 3. Based on the above information, find a reasonable fragmentation of ASG and EMP and an optimal replication and placement for the fragments, assuming that storage costs do not matter here, but copies are kept consistent.

Hint: Consider horizontal fragmentation for ASG based on DUR=24 predicate and the corresponding derived horizontal fragmentation for EMP. Also look at the affinity matrix obtained in Example 5.8 for EMP and ASG together, and consider whether it would make sense to perform a vertical fragmentation for ASG.

Chapter 6

SEMANTIC DATA CONTROL

An important requirement of a centralized or a distributed DBMS is the ability to support semantic data control. Semantic data control typically includes view management, security control, and semantic integrity control. Informally, these functions must ensure that *authorized* users perform *correct* operations on the database, contributing to the maintenance of database integrity. The functions necessary for maintaining the physical integrity of the database in the presence of concurrent accesses and failures are studied separately in Chapters 10 through 12. In the relational framework, semantic data control can be achieved in a uniform fashion. Views, security constraints, and semantic integrity constraints can be defined as rules that the system automatically enforces. The violation of some such rule by a user program (a set of database operations) generally implies the rejection of the effects of that program.

The definition of the rules for controlling data manipulation is part of the administration of the database, a function generally performed by a database administrator (DBA). This person is also in charge of applying the organizational policies. Well-known solutions for semantic data control have been proposed for centralized DBMSs. In this chapter we briefly review the centralized solution to semantic data control, and present the problems incurred in a distributed environment and solutions to these problems. The cost of enforcing semantic data control, which is high in terms of resource utilization in a centralized DBMS, can be prohibitive in a distributed environment.

Since the rules for semantic data control must be stored in a catalog, the management of a distributed directory (also called a catalog) is also relevant in this chapter. We discussed directories in Chapter 4. Remember that the directory of a distributed DBMS is itself a distributed database. There are several ways to store semantic data control definitions, according to the way the directory is managed. Directory information can be stored differently according to its type; in other words, some information might be fully duplicated whereas other information might be distributed. For example, information that is useful at compile time, such as security control information, could be duplicated. In this chapter we emphasize the impact of directory management on the performance of semantic data control mechanisms.

This chapter is organized as follows. View management is the subject of Section 6.1. Security control is presented in Section 6.2. Finally, semantic integrity control is treated in Section 6.3. For each section we first outline the solution in a centralized DBMS and then give the distributed solution, which is often an extension of the centralized one, although more difficult.

6.1 VIEW MANAGEMENT

One of the main advantages of the relational model is that it provides full logical data independence. As introduced in Chapter 4, external schemas enable user groups to have their particular *view* of the database. In a relational system, a view is a *virtual relation*, defined as the result of a query on *base relations* (or real relations), but not materialized like a base relation, which is stored in the database. A view is a dynamic window in the sense that it reflects all updates to the database. An external schema can be defined as a set of views and/or base relations. Besides their use in external schemas, views are useful for ensuring data security in a simple way. By selecting a subset of the database, views *hide* some data. If users may only access the database through views, they cannot see or manipulate the hidden data, which are therefore secure.

In the remainder of this section we look at view management in centralized and distributed systems as well as the problems of updating views. Note that in a distributed DBMS, a view can be derived from distributed relations, and the access to a view requires the execution of the distributed query corresponding to the view definition. An important issue in a distributed DBMS is to make view materialization efficient. We will see how the concept of snapshots helps to solve this problem, but first let us concentrate on centralized DBMSs.

6.1.1 Views in Centralized DBMSs

Most relational DBMSs use a view mechanism similar to those of INGRES [Stonebraker, 1975] and System R [Chamberlin et al., 1975]. In this context a view is a relation derived from base relations as the result of a relational query. It is defined by associating the name of the view with the retrieval query that specifies it.

Example 6.1

The view of system analysts (SYSAN) derived from relation EMP (ENO,ENAME,TITLE), can be defined by the following SQL query:

```
CREATE    VIEW      SYSAN(ENO, ENAME)
AS        SELECT    ENO, ENAME
          FROM      EMP
          WHERE     TITLE = ''Syst. Anal.''
```

The single effect of this statement is the storage of the view definition in the catalog. No other information needs to be recorded. Therefore, the result to the

SYSAN

ENO	ENAME
E2	M.Smith
E5	B.Casey
E8	J.Jones

Figure 6.1. Relation Corresponding to the View SYSAN

query defining the view (i.e., a relation having the attributes ENO and ENAME for the system analysts as shown in Figure 6.1) is *not* produced. However, the view SYSAN can be manipulated as a base relation.

Example 6.2

The query

"Find the names of all the system analysts with their project number and responsibility(ies)"

involving the view SYSAN and relation ASG(ENO,PNO,RESP,DUR) can be expressed as

```
SELECT    ENAME, PNO, RESP
FROM      SYSAN, ASG
WHERE     SYSAN.ENO = ASG.ENO
```

Mapping a query expressed on views into a query expressed on base relations can be done by *query modification* [Stonebraker, 1975]. With this technique the variables are changed to range on base relations and the query qualification is merged (ANDed) with the view qualification.

Example 6.3

The preceding query can be modified to

```
SELECT    ENAME, PNO, RESP
FROM      EMP, ASG
WHERE     EMP.ENO = ASG.ENO
AND       TITLE = ''Syst. Anal.''
```

The result of this query is illustrated in Figure 6.2.

ENAME	PNO	RESP
M.Smith	P1	Analyst
M.Smith	P2	Analyst
B.Casey	P3	Manager
J.Jones	P4	Manager

Figure 6.2. Result of Query involving View SYSAN

The modified query is expressed on base relations and can therefore be processed by the query processor. It is important to note that view processing can be done at compile time. The view mechanism can also be used for refining the access controls to include subsets of objects. To specify any user from whom one wants to hide data, the key word USER generally refers to the logged-on user identifier.

Example 6.4

The view ESAME restricts the access by any user to those employees having the same title:

```
CREATE    VIEW      ESAME
AS        SELECT    *
          FROM      EMP E1, EMP E2
          WHERE     E1.TITLE = E2.TITLE
          AND       E1.ENO = USER
```

In the view definition above, * stands for "all attributes" and the two tuple variables (E1 and E2) ranging over relation EMP are required to express the join of one tuple of EMP (the one corresponding to the logged-on user) with all tuples of EMP based on the same title. For example, the following query issued by the user PROJ. Doe,

```
SELECT    *
FROM      ESAME
```

returns the relation of Figure 6.3. Note that the user PROJ. Doe also appears in the result. If the user who creates ESAME is an electrical engineer, as in this case, the view represents the set of all electrical engineers.

6.1.2 Updates through Views

Views can be defined using arbitrarily complex relational queries involving selection, projection, join, aggregate functions, and so on. All views can be interrogated as

ENO	ENAME	TITLE
E1	J. Doe	Elect. Eng
E2	L. Chu	Elect. Eng

Figure 6.3. Result of Query on View ESAME

base relations, but not all views can be manipulated as such. Updates through views can be handled automatically only if they can be propagated correctly to the base relations. We can classify views as being updatable and not updatable. A view is updatable only if the updates to the view can be propagated to the base relations without ambiguity. The view SYSAN above is updatable; the insertion, for example, of a new system analyst <201, Smith> will be mapped into the insertion of a new employee <201, Smith, Syst. Anal.>. If attributes other than TITLE were hidden by the view, they would be assigned *null values*. The following view, however, is not updatable:

```
CREATE    VIEW      EG(ENAME, RESP)
AS        SELECT    ENAME, RESP
          FROM      EMP, ASG
          WHERE     EMP.ENO = ASG.ENO
```

The deletion, for example, of the tuple <Smith, Analyst> cannot be propagated, since it is ambiguous. Deletions of Smith in relation EMP or analyst in relation ASG are both meaningful, but the system does not know which is correct.

Current systems are very restrictive about supporting updates through views. Views can be updated only if they are derived from a single relation by selection and projection. This precludes views defined by joins, aggregates, and so on. However, it is theoretically possible to automatically support updates of a larger class of views ([Bancilhon and Spyratos, 1981], [Dayal and Bernstein, 1978], [Keller, 1982]). It is interesting to note that views derived by join are updatable if they include the keys of the base relations.

6.1.3 Views in Distributed DBMSs

The definition of a view is similar in a distributed DBMS and in centralized systems. However, a view in a distributed system may be derived from fragmented relations stored at different sites. When a view is defined, its name and its retrieval query are stored in the catalog.

Since views may be used as base relations by application programs, their definition should be stored in the directory in the same way as the base relation descriptions. Depending on the degree of site autonomy offered by the system [Williams
et al., 1982], view definitions can be centralized at one site, partially duplicated,
or fully duplicated. In any case, the information associating a view name to its
definition site should be duplicated. If the view definition is not present at the site
where the query is issued, remote access to the view definition site is necessary.

The mapping of a query expressed on views into a query expressed on base
relations (which can potentially be fragmented) can also be done in the same way
as in centralized systems, that is, through query modification. With this technique,
the qualification defining the view is found in the distributed database catalog
and then merged with the query to provide a query on base relations. Such a
modified query is a *distributed query*, which can be processed by the distributed
query processor (see Chapter 7). The query processor maps the distributed query
into a query on physical fragments.

In Chapter 5 we presented alternative ways of fragmenting base relations. The
definition of fragmentation is, in fact, very similar to the definition of particular
views. In [Adiba, 1981], a unified mechanism for managing views and fragments
is proposed. It is based on the observation that views in a distributed DBMS can
be defined with rules similar to fragment definition rules. Furthermore, replicated
data can be handled in the same way. The value of such a unified mechanism
is to facilitate distributed database administration. The objects manipulated by
the database administrator can be seen as a hierarchy where the leaves are the
fragments from which relations and views can be derived. Therefore, the DBA may
increase locality of reference by making views in one-to-one correspondence with
fragments. For example, it is possible to implement the view SYSAN illustrated in
Example 6.1 by a fragment at a given site, provided that most users accessing the
view SYSAN are at the same site.

Views derived from distributed relations may be costly to evaluate. Since in a
given organization it is likely that many users access the same views, some proposals
have been made to optimize view derivation. We saw in Section 6.1.1 that view
derivation is done by merging the view qualification with the query qualification.
An alternative solution proposed in [Adiba and Lindsay, 1980] is to avoid view
derivation by maintaining actual versions of the views, called *snapshots*. A snapshot
represents a particular state of the database and is therefore *static*, meaning that it
does not reflect updates to base relations. Snapshots are useful when users are not
particularly interested in seeing the most recent version of the database. They are
managed as temporary relations in the sense that they do not have access methods
other than sequential scanning. Therefore, a query expressed on a snapshot will
not exploit indices available on the base relations from which it is derived. Access
through snapshots seems more adequate for queries that have bad selectivity and
scan the entire snapshot. In this case a snapshot behaves more like a predefined
answer to a query. It is necessary to recalculate snapshots periodically. However,
this can be done when the system is idle. In addition, for snapshots derived by
selection and projection, only the difference needs to be calculated [Blakeley et al.,
1986].

6.2   DATA SECURITY

Data security is an important function of a database system that protects data against unauthorized access. Data security includes two aspects: *data protection* and *authorization control*.

Data protection is required to prevent unauthorized users from understanding the physical content of data. This function is typically provided by file systems in the context of centralized and distributed operating systems. The main data protection approach is data encryption [Fernandez et al., 1981], which is useful both for information stored on disk and for information exchanged on a network. Encrypted (encoded) data can be decrypted (decoded) only by authorized users who "know" the code. The two main schemes are the Data Encryption Standard [NBS, 1977] and the public-key encryption schemes ([Diffie and Hellman, 1976] and [Rivest et al., 1978]). In this section we concentrate on the second aspect of data security, which is more specific to database systems. A complete presentation of protection techniques can be found in [Fernandez et al., 1981].

Authorization control must guarantee that only authorized users perform operations they are allowed to perform on the database. Many different users may have access to a large collection of data under the control of a single centralized or distributed system. The centralized or distributed DBMS must thus be able to restrict the access of a subset of the database to a subset of the users. Authorization control has long been provided by operating systems, and more recently, by distributed operating systems [Tanenbaum and van Renesse, 1985] as services of the file system. In this context, a centralized control is offered. Indeed, the central controller creates objects, and this person may allow particular users to perform particular operations (read, write, execute) on these objects. Also, objects are identified by their external names.

Authorization control in database systems differs in several aspects from that in traditional file systems. Authorizations must be refined so that different users have different rights on the same database objects. This requirement implies the ability to specify subsets of objects more precisely than by name and to distinguish between groups of users. In addition, the decentralized control of authorizations is of particular importance in a distributed context. In relational systems, authorizations can be uniformly controlled by database administrators using high-level constructs. For example, controlled objects can be specified by predicates in the same way as is a query qualification.

From solutions to authorization control in centralized systems, we derive those for distributed DBMSs. However, there is the additional complexity which stems from the fact that objects and users can be distributed. In what follows we first present authorization control in centralized systems and then the additional problems and their solutions in distributed systems.

6.2.1   Centralized Authorization Control

Three main actors are involved in authorization control: the *users*, who trigger the execution of application programs; the *operations*, which are embedded in application programs; and the *database objects*, on which the operations are performed [Hoffman, 1977]. Authorization control consists of checking whether a given triple (user, operation, object) can be allowed to proceed (i.e., the user can execute the operation on the object). An authorization can be viewed as a triple (user, operation type, object definition) which specifies that the user has the right to perform an operation of operation type on a object. To control authorizations properly, the DBMS requires users, objects, and rights to be defined.

The introduction of a user (a person or a group of persons) in the system is typically done by a pair (user name, password). The user name uniquely *identifies* the users of that name in the system, while the password, known only to the users of that name, *authenticates* the users. Both user name and password must be supplied in order to log in the system. This prevents people who do not know the password from entering the system with only the user name.

The objects to protect are subsets of the database. Relational systems provide finer and more general protection granularity than do earlier systems. In a file system, the protection granule is the file, while in the network or hierarchical DBMS ([Taylor and Frank, 1976] and [Tsichritzis and Lochovsky, 1976]), it is the object type (e.g., record, file). In a relational system, objects can be defined by their type (view, relation, tuple, attribute) as well as by their content using selection predicates. Furthermore, the view mechanism as introduced in Section 6.1 permits the protection of objects simply by hiding subsets of relations (attributes or tuples) to unauthorized users.

A right expresses a relationship between a user and an object for a particular set of operations. In an SQL-based relational DBMS, an operation is a high-level statement such as SELECT, INSERT, UPDATE, or DELETE, and rights are defined (granted or revoked) using the following statements:

> GRANT <operation type(s)> ON <object> TO <user(s)>
> REVOKE <operation type(s)> FROM <object> TO <user(s)>

The keyword *public* can be used to mean all users. Authorization control can be characterized based on who (the grantors) can grant the rights. In its simplest form, the control is centralized: a single user or user class, the database administrators, has all privileges on the database objects and is the only one allowed to use the GRANT and REVOKE statements.

A more flexible but complex form of control is decentralized [Griffiths and Wade, 1976]: the creator of an object becomes its owner and is granted all privileges on it. In particular, there is the additional operation type GRANT. Granting the GRANT privilege means that all the rights of the grantor performing the statement are given to the specified users. Therefore, the person receiving the right (the grantee) may subsequently grant privileges on that object. The main difficulty with this approach is that the revoking process must be recursive. For example, if A, who granted B who granted C the GRANT privilege on object O, wants to revoke all the privileges of B on O, all the privileges of C on O must also be revoked. To perform revocation, the system must maintain a hierarchy of grants per object where the creator of the

	EMP	ENAME	ASG
Casey	UPDATE	UPDATE	UPDATE
Jones	SELECT	SELECT	SELECT WHERE RESP ≠ "Manager"
Smith	NONE	SELECT	NONE

Figure 6.4. Example of Authorization Matrix

object is the root. A complete scheme for handling revocation is proposed in [Fagin, 1978].

The privileges of the subjects over objects are recorded in the catalog (directory) as authorization rules. There are several ways to store the authorizations. The most convenient approach is to consider all the privileges as an *authorization matrix*, in which a row defines a subject, a column an object, and a matrix entry (for a pair <subject, object>), the authorized operations. The authorized operations are specified by their operation type (e.g., SELECT, UPDATE). It is also customary to associate with the operation type a predicate that further restricts the access to the object. The latter option is provided when the objects must be base relations and cannot be views. For example, one authorized operation for the pair <Jones, relation EMP> could be

```
SELECT WHERE TITLE = ''Syst. Anal.''
```

which authorizes Jones to access only the employee tuples for system analysts. Figure 6.4 gives an example of an authorization matrix where objects are either relations (EMP and ASG) or attributes (ENAME).

The authorization matrix can be stored in three ways: by row, by column, or by element. When the matrix is stored by *row*, each subject is associated with the list of objects that may be accessed together with the related access rights. This approach makes the enforcement of authorizations efficient, since all the rights of the logged-on user are together (in the user profile). However, the manipulation of access rights per object (e.g., making an object public) is not efficient since all subject profiles must be accessed. When the matrix is stored by *column*, each object is associated with the list of subjects who may access it with the corresponding access rights. The advantages and disadvantages of this approach are the disadvantages and advantages of the previous approach.

The respective advantages of the two approaches can be combined in the third approach, in which the matrix is stored by *element*, that is, by relation (subject, object, right). This relation can have indices on both subject and object, thereby providing fast-access right manipulation per subject and per object.

6.2.2   Distributed Authorization Control

The additional problems of authorization control in a distributed environment stem from the fact that objects and subjects are distributed. These problems are: remote user authentication, management of distributed authorization rules, as well as handling of views and of user groups.

Remote user authentication is necessary since any site of a distributed DBMS may accept programs initiated, and authorized, at remote sites. To prevent remote access by unauthorized users (e.g., from a site that is not part of the distributed DBMS), users must also be identified and authenticated at the accessed site. Two solutions are possible:

1. The information for authenticating users (user name and password) is replicated at all sites in the catalog. Local programs, initiated at a remote site, must also indicate the user name and password.

2. All sites of the distributed DBMS identify and authenticate themselves similarly to the way users do. Intersite communication is thus protected by the use of the site password. Once the initiating site has been authenticated, there is no need for authenticating their remote users.

The first solution is more costly in terms of directory management given that the introduction of a new user is a distributed operation. However, users can access the distributed database from any site. The second solution is necessary if user information is not replicated. Nevertheless, it can also be used if there is replication of the user information. In this case it makes remote authentication more efficient. If user names and passwords are not replicated, they should be stored at the sites where the users accessed the system (i.e., the home site). The latter solution is based on the realistic assumption that users are more static, or at least they always access the distributed database from the same site.

Distributed authorization rules are expressed in the same way as centralized ones. Like view definitions, they must be stored in the catalog. They can be either fully replicated at each site or stored at the sites of the referenced objects. In the latter case the rules are duplicated only at the sites where the referenced objects are distributed. The main advantage of the fully replicated approach is that authorization can be processed by query modification [Stonebraker, 1975] at compile time. However, directory management is more costly because of data duplication. The second solution is better if locality of reference is very high. However, distributed authorization cannot be controlled at compile time.

Views may be considered to be objects by the authorization mechanism. Views are composite objects, that is, composed of other underlying objects. Therefore, granting access to a view translates into granting access to underlying objects. If view definition and authorization rules for all objects are fully replicated (as in many systems), this translation is rather simple and can be done locally. The translation is harder when the view definition and its underlying objects are all stored separately [Wilms and Lindsay, 1981], as is the case with site autonomy assumption. In this situation, the translation is a totally distributed operation. The authorizations granted on views depend on the access rights of the view creator on the underlying objects. A solution is to record the association information at the site of each underlying object.

Handling user groups for the purpose of authorization simplifies distributed database administration. In a centralized DBMS, "all users" can be referred to as *public*. In a distributed DBMS, the same notion is useful, the public denoting all the users of the system. However an intermediate level is often introduced to specify the public at a particular site, denoted by public@site_s, in [Wilms and Lindsay, 1981]. The public is a particular user group. More precise groups can be defined by the command

```
DEFINE GROUP <group_id> AS <list of subject ids>
```

The management of groups in a distributed environment poses some problems since the subjects of a group can be located at various sites and access to an object may be granted to several groups, which are themselves distributed. If group information as well as authorization rules are fully replicated at all sites, the enforcement of access rights is similar to that of a centralized system. However, maintaining this replication is quite expensive. The problem is more difficult if site autonomy (with decentralized control) must be maintained. Several solutions to this problem are identified in [Wilms and Lindsay, 1981]. One solution enforces access rights by performing a remote query to the nodes holding the group definition. Another solution replicates a group definition at each node containing an object that may be accessed by subjects of that group. These solutions tend to decrease the degree of site autonomy.

In conclusion, full replication of authorization information has two strong advantages: authorization control is much simpler and can be done at compile time. However, the overhead cost incurred for managing the distributed catalog can be significant if there are many sites in the system.

6.3 SEMANTIC INTEGRITY CONTROL

Another important and difficult problem for a database system is how to guarantee *database consistency*. A database state is said to be consistent if the database satisfies a set of constraints, called *semantic integrity constraints*. Maintaining a consistent database requires various mechanisms such as concurrency control, reliability, protection, and semantic integrity control. Semantic integrity control ensures database consistency by rejecting update programs which lead to inconsistent database states, or by activating specific actions on the database state, which compensate for the effects of the update programs. Note that the updated database must satisfy the set of integrity constraints.

In general, semantic integrity constraints are rules that represent the *knowledge* about the properties of an application. They define static or dynamic application properties which cannot be directly captured by the object and operation concepts of a data model. Thus the concept of an integrity rule is strongly connected with that of a data model in the sense that more semantic information about the application can be captured by means of these rules.

Two main types of integrity constraints can be distinguished: structural constraints and behavioral constraints. *Structural constraints* express basic semantic properties inherent to a model. Examples of such constraints are unique key constraints in the relational model, or one-to-many associations between objects in the network model. *Behavioral constraints*, on the other hand, regulate the application behavior. Thus they are essential in the database design process. They can express associations between objects, such as inclusion dependency in the relational model, or describe object properties and structures. The increasing variety of database applications and the recent development of database design aid tools call for powerful integrity constraints which can enrich the data model.

Integrity control appeared with data processing and evolved from procedural methods (in which the controls were embedded in application programs) to declarative methods. Declarative methods have emerged with the relational model to alleviate the problems of program/data dependency, code redundancy, and poor performance of the procedural methods. The idea, formerly suggested in [Florentin, 1974], is to express integrity constraints using assertions of predicate calculus. Thus a set of semantic integrity assertions defines database consistency. This approach allows one to easily declare and modify complex integrity assertions.

The main problem in supporting automatic semantic integrity control is that the cost of checking assertions can be prohibitive. Enforcing integrity assertions is costly because it generally requires access to a large amount of data which is not involved in the database updates. The problem is more difficult when assertions are defined over a distributed database.

Various solutions have been investigated to design an integrity subsystem by combining optimization strategies. Their purpose is to (1) limit the number of assertions that need to be enforced, (2) decrease the number of data accesses to enforce a given assertion in the presence of an update program, (3) define a preventive strategy that detects inconsistencies in a way that avoids undoing updates, (4) perform as much integrity control as possible at compile time. A few of these solutions have been implemented, but they suffer from a lack of generality. Either they are restricted to a small set of assertions (more general constraints would have a prohibitive checking cost) or they only support restricted programs (e.g., single-tuple updates).

In this section we present the solutions for semantic integrity control first in centralized systems and then in distributed systems. Since our context is the relational model, we consider only declarative methods. The content of this section is strongly based on the work on semantic integrity control for centralized systems reported in [Simon and Valduriez, 1984] and [Simon and Valduriez, 1987] and for distributed systems [Simon and Valduriez, 1986]. In addition, the relational integrity subsystem proposed in [Simon and Valduriez, 1987] offers a rich functionality, by supporting a large subset of multivariable, multirelation assertions with aggregates, and general database programs.

6.3.1 Centralized Semantic Integrity Control

A semantic integrity subsystem has two main components: a language for expressing and manipulating integrity assertions, and an enforcement mechanism that
performs specific actions to enforce database integrity at updates.

Specification of Integrity Constraints

Integrity constraints should be manipulated by the database administrator using a
high level language. In this section we illustrate a declarative language for specifying
integrity constraints, defined in [Simon and Valduriez, 1987]. This language is much
in the spirit of the standard SQL language, but with more generality. It allows one
to specify, read, or drop integrity constraints. These constraints can be defined
either at relation creation time, or at any time, even if the relation already contains
tuples. In both cases, however, the syntax is almost the same.

In relational database systems, integrity constraints are defined as assertions.
An assertion is a particular expression of tuple relational calculus (see Chapter 2), in
which each variable is either universally ($\forall$) or existentially ($\exists$) quantified. Thus an
assertion can be seen as a query qualification that is either true or false for each tuple
in the Cartesian product of the relations determined by the tuple variables. We can
distinguish between three types of integrity constraints: predefined, precompiled,
or general constraints.

Examples of integrity constraints will be given on the following database:

  EMP(ENO, ENAME, TITLE)

  PROJ(PNO, PNAME, BUDGET)

  ASG(ENO, PNO, RESP, DUR)

Predefined constraints are based on simple keywords. Through them, it is possible to express concisely the more common constraints of the relational model, such
as nonnull attribute, unique key, foreign key, or functional dependency [Fagin and
Vardi, 1984]. Examples 6.5 through 6.8 demonstrate predefined constraints.

Example 6.5 *Nonnull Attribute*

Employee number in relation EMP cannot be null.

```
ENO NOT NULL IN EMP
```

Example 6.6 *Unique Key*

The pair (ENO, PNO) is the unique key in relation ASG.

```
(ENO, PNO) UNIQUE IN ASG
```

Example 6.7 *Foreign Key*

The project number PNO in relation ASG is a foreign key matching the primary key PNO of relation PROJ. In other words, a project referred to in relation ASG must exist in relation PROJ.

```
PNO IN ASG REFERENCES PNO IN PROJ
```

Example 6.8 *Functional Dependency*

The employee number functionally determines the employee name.

```
ENO IN EMP DETERMINES ENAME
```

Precompiled constraints express preconditions that must be satisfied by all tuples in a relation for a given update type. The update type, which might be INSERT, DELETE, or MODIFY, permits restricting the integrity control. To identify in the constraint definition the tuples that are subject to update, two variables, NEW and OLD, are implicitly defined. They range over new tuples (to be inserted) and old tuples (to be deleted), respectively [Astrahan et al., 1979]. Precompiled constraints can be expressed with the SQL CHECK statement enriched with the ability to specify the update type. The syntax of the CHECK statement is

```
CHECK ON   < relation name > WHEN < update type >
           ( < qualification over relation name >)
```

Examples of precompiled constraints are the following:

Example 6.9 *Domain Constraint*

The budget of a project is between 500K and 1000K.

```
CHECK ON PROJ (BUDGET ≥ 500000 AND BUDGET ≤ 1000000)
```

Example 6.10 *Domain Constraint on Deletion*

Only the tuples whose budget is 0 may be deleted.

```
CHECK ON PROJ WHEN DELETE (BUDGET = 0)
```

Example 6.11 *Transition Constraint*

The budget of a project can only increase.

```
CHECK ON PROJ (NEW.BUDGET > OLD.BUDGET
AND NEW.PNO = OLD.PNO)
```

General constraints are formulas of tuple relational calculus where all variables are quantified. The database system must ensure that those formulas are always true. General constraints are more concise than precompiled constraints since the former may involve more than one relation. For instance, at least three precompiled constraints are necessary to express a general constraint on three relations. A general constraint may be expressed with the following syntax:

```
CHECK ON list of <variable name>:<relation name>, (<qualification>)
```

Examples of general constraints are given below.

Example 6.12   *Functional Dependency*

The constraint of Example 6.8 may also be expressed as

```
CHECK ON e1:EMP, e2:EMP
       (e1.ENAME = e2.ENAME IF e1.ENO = e2.ENO)
```

Example 6.13   *Constraint with Aggregate Function*

The total duration for all employees in the CAD project is less than 100.

```
CHECK ON g:ASG, j:PROJ (SUM(g.DUR WHERE g.PNO=j.PNO)<100
       IF j.PNAME=''CAD/CAM'')
```

Integrity Enforcement

Enforcing semantic integrity consists of rejecting update programs that violate some integrity constraints. A constraint is violated when it becomes false in the new database state produced by the update. A major difficulty in designing an integrity subsystem is finding efficient enforcement algorithms. Two basic methods permit the rejection of inconsistent updates. The first one is based on the *detection* of inconsistencies. The update u is executed, causing a change of the database state D to D_u. The enforcement algorithm verifies, by applying tests derived from these constraints, that all relevant constraints hold in state D_u. If state D_u is inconsistent, the DBMS can try either to reach another consistent state, D'_u, by modifying D_u with compensation actions, or to restore state D by undoing u. Since these tests are applied *after* having changed the database state, they are generally called *posttests*. This approach may be inefficient if a large amount of work (the update of D) must be undone in the case of an integrity failure.

The second method is based on the *prevention* of inconsistencies. An update is executed only if it changes the database state to a consistent state. The tuples subject to the update are either directly available (in the case of insert) or must be retrieved from the database (in the case of deletion or modification). The enforcement algorithm verifies that all relevant constraints will hold after updating those tuples. This is generally done by applying to those tuples tests that are derived from the integrity constraints. Given that these tests are applied *before* the database state is changed, they are generally called *pretests*. The preventive approach is more efficient than the detection approach since updates never need to be undone because of integrity violation.

The query modification algorithm [Stonebraker, 1975] is an example of a preventive method that is particularly efficient at enforcing domain constraints. It adds the assertion qualification to the query qualification by an AND operator so that the modified query can enforce integrity.

Example 6.14

The query for increasing the budget of the CAD/CAM project by 10%, which would be specified as

```
UPDATE    PROJ
SET       BUDGET = BUDGET*1.1
WHERE     PNAME= ''CAD/CAM''
```

will be transformed into the following query in order to enforce the domain constraint discussed in Example 6.9.

```
UPDATE    PROJ
SET       BUDGET = BUDGET * 1.1
WHERE     PNAME= ''CAD/CAM''
AND       NEW.BUDGET ≥ 500000
AND       NEW.BUDGET ≤ 1000000
```

The query modification algorithm, which is well known for its elegance, produces pretests at run time by ANDing the assertion predicates with the update predicates of each instruction of the transaction. However, the algorithm only applies to tuple calculus formulas and can be specified as follows. Consider the assertion $(\forall x \in R)F(x)$, where F is a tuple calculus expression in which x is the only free variable. An update of R can be written as $(\forall x \in R)(Q(x) \Rightarrow update(x))$, where Q is a tuple calculus expression whose only free variable is x. Roughly speaking, the query modification consists in generating the update $(\forall x \in R)((Q(x)$ and $F(x)) \Rightarrow update(x))$. Thus x needs to be universally quantified.

Example 6.15

The foreign key assertion of Example 6.7 that can be rewritten as

$$\forall\, g \in \text{ASG},\, \exists\, j \in \text{PROJ} : g.\text{PNO} = j.\text{PNO}$$

could not be processed by query modification because the variable j is not universally quantified.

To handle more general assertions, pretests can be generated at assertion definition time, and enforced at run time when updates occur ([Bernstein et al., 1980a], [Bernstein and Blaustein, 1982], [Blaustein, 1981], [Nicolas, 1982]). The method described in [Nicolas, 1982] is restricted to updates that insert or delete a *single* tuple of a single relation. The algorithm proposed in [Bernstein et al., 1980a] and [Blaustein, 1981] is an improvement over the one in [Nicolas, 1982]. Updates are also single tuple. The algorithm builds a pretest at assertion definition time for each assertion and each update type (insert, delete). These pretests are enforced at run time. This method accepts multirelation, monovariable assertions, possibly with aggregates. The principle is the substitution of the tuple variables in the assertion by constants from an updated tuple. Despite its important contribution to research, the method is hardly usable in a real environment because of the restriction on updates.

In the rest of this section, we present the method reported in [Simon and Valduriez, 1986] and [Simon and Valduriez, 1987], which combines the generality of updates supported in [Stonebraker, 1975] with at least the generality of assertions for which pretests can be produced in [Blaustein, 1981]. This method is based on the production, at assertion definition time, of *compiled assertions* which are used subsequently to prevent the introduction of inconsistencies in the database. This is a general preventive method that handles the entire set of assertions introduced in the preceding section. It significantly reduces the proportion of the database that must be checked when enforcing assertions in the presence of updates.

The definition of compiled assertions is based on the notion of differential relations. Let u be an update of relation R. R^+ and R^- are *differential relations* of R by u, where R^+ contains the tuples inserted by u into R, and R^- contains the tuples of R deleted by u. If u is an insertion, R^- is empty. If u is a deletion, R^+ is empty. Finally, if u is a modification, relation R after modification is equal to $R^+ \cup (R - R^-)$.

A *compiled assertion* is a triple (R, T, C) in which R is a relation, T is an update type, and C is an assertion ranging over the differential relation(s) involved in an update of type T. When an integrity constraint I is defined, a set of compiled assertions may be produced for the relations used by I. Whenever a relation involved in I is updated by a program u, the compiled assertions that must be checked to enforce I are only those defined on I for the update type of u. The performance advantage of this approach is twofold. First, the number of assertions to enforce is minimized since only the compiled assertions of type u need be checked. Second, the cost of enforcing a compiled assertion is less than that of enforcing I since differential relations are, in general, much smaller than the base relations.

Compiled assertions may be obtained by applying transformation rules to the original assertion. These rules are based on a syntactic analysis of the assertion and quantifier permutations. They permit the substitution of differential relations for base relation. Since the compiled assertions are simpler than the original ones, the process that generates them is called *simplification*.

Example 6.16

Consider the modified expression of the foreign key constraint in Example 6.15. The compiled assertions associated with this constraint are

(ASG, **INSERT**, C_1), (PROJ, **DELETE**, C_2) and (PROJ, **MODIFY**, C_3)

where C_1 is

$$\forall \ \textbf{NEW} \in ASG^+, \exists j \in PROJ: \textbf{NEW}.PNO = j.PNO$$

C_2 is

$$\forall g \in ASG, \forall \textbf{OLD} \in PROJ^- : g.PNO \neq \textbf{OLD}.PNO$$

and C_3 is

$$\forall g \in ASG, \forall \textbf{OLD} \in PROJ^-, \exists \ \textbf{NEW} \in PROJ^+ :$$
$$g.PNO \neq \textbf{OLD}.PNO \ OR \ \textbf{OLD}.PNO = \textbf{NEW}.PNO$$

The advantage provided by such compiled assertions is obvious. For instance, a deletion on relation ASG does not incur any assertion checking.

The enforcement algorithm described in [Simon and Valduriez, 1984] makes use of compiled assertions and is specialized according to the class of the assertions. Three classes of assertions are distinguished: the single-relation and multirelation assertions, and assertions involving aggregate functions.

Let us now summarize the enforcement algorithm. We recall that an update program updates all tuples of relation R that satisfy some qualification. The algorithm acts in two steps. The first step generates the differential relations R^+ and R^- from R. The second step simply consists of retrieving the tuples of R^+ and R^-, which do not satisfy the compiled assertions. If no tuples are retrieved, the assertion is valid.

Example 6.17

Suppose there is a deletion on PROJ. Enforcing (PROJ, **DELETE**, C_2) consists in generating the following statement:

$$result \leftarrow \text{retrieve all tuples of } PROJ^- \text{ where } \neg(C_2)$$

Then, if the result is empty, the assertion is verified by the update.

6.3.2 Distributed Semantic Integrity Control

In this section we present algorithms for ensuring the semantic integrity of distributed databases. They are extensions of the simplification method discussed previously. In what follows we assume site autonomy, meaning that each site processes local queries and performs data control as a centralized DBMS. This assumption simplifies the description of the method. However, the method obviously works with replicated directories. The two main problems of designing an integrity subsystem for a distributed DBMS are the definition and storage of assertions, and the enforcement of these assertions.

Definition of Distributed Integrity Assertions

An integrity assertion is supposed to be expressed in tuple relational calculus. Each assertion is seen as a query qualification which is either true or false for each tuple in the Cartesian product of the relations determined by tuple variables. Since assertions can involve data stored at different sites, their storage must be decided so as to minimize the cost of integrity checking. There is a strategy based on a taxonomy of integrity assertions that distinguishes three classes of assertions:

1. *Individual assertions*: single-relation single-variable assertions. They refer only to tuples to be updated independently of the rest of the database. For instance, domain constraint of Example 6.9 is an individual assertion.

2. *Set-oriented assertions*: include single-relation multivariable constraints such as functional dependency (Example 6.8) and multirelation multivariable constraints such as foreign key constraints (Example 6.7).

3. *Assertions involving aggregates*: require special processing because of the cost of evaluating the aggregates. The assertion in Example 6.13 is representative of an assertion of this class.

The definition of a new integrity assertion can be started at one of the sites that store the relations involved in the assertion. Remember that the relations can be fragmented. A fragmentation predicate is a particular case of assertion of class 1. Different fragments of the same relation can be located at different sites. Thus, defining an integrity assertion becomes a distributed operation, which is done in two steps. The first step is to transform the high-level assertions into compiled assertions, using the techniques discussed in the preceding section. The next step is to store compiled assertions according to the class of assertion. Assertions of class 3 are treated like those of class 1 or 2, depending on whether they are individual or set-oriented.

Individual assertions. The assertion definition is sent to all other sites that contain fragments of the relation involved in the assertion. The assertion must be compatible with the relation data at each site. Compatibility can be checked at two levels: predicate and data. First, predicate compatibility is verified by comparing the assertion predicate with the fragment predicate. An assertion C is not compatible with a fragment predicate p if "C is true" implies that "p is false," and is compatible with p otherwise. If noncompatibility is found at one of the sites, the assertion definition is globally rejected because tuples of that fragment do not satisfy the integrity constraints. Second, if predicate compatibility has been found, the assertion is tested against the instance of the fragment. If it is not satisfied by that instance, the assertion is also globally rejected. If compatibility is found, the assertion is stored at each site. Note that the compatibility checks are performed only for compiled assertions whose update type is "insert" (the tuples in the fragments are considered "inserted").

Example 6.18

Consider relation EMP, horizontally fragmented across three sites using the predicates

$$p_1 : \quad 0 \leq \text{ENO} < \text{"E3"}$$
$$p_2 : \quad \text{"E3"} \leq \text{ENO} \leq \text{"E6"}$$
$$p_3 : \quad \text{ENO} > \text{"E6"}$$

and the domain assertion C: ENO < "E4". Assertion C is compatible with p_1 (if C is true, p_1 is true) and p_2 (if C is true, p_2 is not necessarily false), but is not with p_3 (if C is true, then p_3 is false). Therefore, assertion C should be globally rejected because the tuples at site 3 cannot satisfy C, and thus relation EMP does not satisfy C.

Set-oriented assertions. Set-oriented assertions are multivariable; that is, they involve join predicates. Although the assertion predicate may be multirelation, a compiled assertion is associated with a single relation. Therefore, the assertion definition can be sent to all the sites that store a fragment referenced by these variables. Compatibility checking also involves fragments of the relation used in the join predicate. Predicate compatibility is useless here because it is impossible to infer that a fragment predicate p is false, if the assertion C (based on a join predicate) is true. Therefore C must be checked for compatibility against the data. This compatibility check basically requires joining each fragment of the relation, say R, with all fragments of the other relation, say S, involved in the assertion predicate. This operation may be expensive and, as any join, should be optimized by the distributed query processor. Three cases, given in increasing cost of checking, can occur:

1. The fragmentation of R is derived (see Chapter 5) from that of S based on a semijoin on the attribute used in the assertion join predicate.

2. S is fragmented on join attribute.

3. S is not fragmented on join attribute.

   In the first case, compatibility checking is cheap since the tuple of S matching with a tuple of R is at the same site. In the second case, each tuple of R must be compared with at most one fragment of S, because the join attribute value of the tuple of R can be used to find the site of the corresponding fragment of S. In the third case, each tuple of R must be compared with all fragments of S. If compatibility is found for all tuples of R, the assertion is stored at each site.

Example 6.19

   Consider the set-oriented compiled assertion (ASG, **INSERT**, C_1) defined in Example 6.16, where C_1 is

$$\forall \textbf{NEW} \in \text{ASG}^+, \exists j \in \text{PROJ} : \textbf{NEW}.\text{PNO} = j.\text{PNO}$$

   Let us consider the three following cases:

   1. ASG is fragmented using the predicate

$$\text{ASG} \bowtie_{\text{PNO}} \text{PROJ}_i$$

   where PROJ_i is a fragment of relation PROJ. In this case each tuple **NEW** of ASG has been placed at the same site as tuple j such that **NEW**.PNO $= j$.PNO. Since the fragmentation predicate is identical to that of C_1, compatibility checking does not incur communication.

   2. PROJ is horizontally fragmented based on the two predicates

$$p_1 : \quad \text{PNO} < \text{``J3''}$$
$$p_2 : \quad \text{PNO} \geq \text{``J3''}$$

   In this case each tuple **NEW** of ASG is compared with either fragment PROJ_1, if **NEW**.PNO $<$ "J3", or fragment PROJ_2 if **NEW**.PNO $\geq$ "J3".

   3. PROJ is horizontally fragmented based on the two predicates

$$p_1 : \quad \text{PNAME} = \text{``CAD/CAM''}$$
$$p_2 : \quad \text{PNAME} \neq \text{``CAD/CAM''}$$

   In this case each tuple of ASG must be compared with both fragments PROJ_1 and PROJ_2.

Enforcement of Distributed Integrity Assertions

Enforcing distributed integrity assertions is more complex than needed in centralized DBMSs. The main problem is to decide where (at which site) to enforce the integrity assertions. The choice depends on the class of the assertion, the type of update, and the nature of the site where the update is issued (called the *query master site*). This site may, or may not, store the updated relation or some of the relations involved in the integrity assertions. The critical parameter we consider is the cost of transferring data, including messages, from one site to another. We now discuss the different types of strategies according to these criteria.

Individual assertions.   Two cases are considered. If the update is an insert statement, all the tuples to be inserted are explicitly provided by the user. In this case, all individual assertions can be enforced at the site where the update is submitted. If the update is a qualified update (delete or modify statements), it is sent to the sites storing the relation that will be updated. The query processor executes the update qualification for each fragment. The resulting tuples at each site are combined into one temporary relation in the case of a delete statement, or two, in the case of a modify statement (i.e., R^+ and R^-). Each site involved in the distributed update enforces the assertions relevant at that site (e.g., domain constraints when it is a delete).

Set-oriented assertions.   We first study single-relation constraints by means of an example. Consider the functional dependency of Example 6.8. The compiled assertion associated with update type INSERT is

$$(\text{EMP}, \textbf{INSERT}, C)$$

where C is

$$(\forall e \in \text{EMP})(\forall \textbf{NEW1} \in \text{EMP})(\forall \textbf{NEW2} \in \text{EMP}) \tag{1}$$

$$(\textbf{NEW1}.\text{ENO} = e.\text{ENO} \Rightarrow \textbf{NEW1}.\text{ENAME} = e.\text{ENAME}) \wedge \tag{2}$$

$$(\textbf{NEW1}.\text{ENO} = \textbf{NEW2}.\text{ENO} \Rightarrow \textbf{NEW1}.\text{ENAME} = \textbf{NEW2}.\text{ENAME}) \tag{3}$$

The second line in the definition of C checks the constraint between the inserted tuples (NEW1) and the existing ones (e), while the third checks it between the inserted tuples themselves. That is why two variables (NEW1 and NEW2) are declared in the first line.

Consider now an update of EMP. First, the update qualification is executed by the query processor and returns one or two temporary relations, as in the case of individual assertions. These temporary relations are then sent to all sites storing EMP. Assume that the update is an INSERT statement. Then each site storing a fragment of EMP will enforce assertion C described above. Because e in C is universally quantified, C must be satisfied by the local data of each site. This is due to the fact that $\forall x \in \{a_1, \ldots, a_n\} f(x)$ is equivalent to $[f(a_1) \wedge f(a_2) \wedge \cdots \wedge f(a_n)]$.

Thus the site where the update is submitted must receive for each site a message indicating that this assertion is satisfied and that it is a condition for all sites. If the assertion is not true for one site, this site sends an error message indicating that the assertion has been violated. The update is then invalid, and it is the responsibility of the integrity subsystem to decide if the entire program must be rejected.

Let us now consider multirelation assertions. For the sake of clarity, we assume that the integrity assertions do not have more than one tuple variable ranging over the same relation. Note that this is likely to be the most frequent case. As with single-relation assertions, the update is computed at the site where it was submitted. The enforcement is done at the query master site, using the ENFORCE algorithm given in Algorithm 6.1.

Algorithm 6.1 *ENFORCE*
    input: T: update type; R: relation
    begin
       retrieve all compiled assertions (R, T, C_i)
       inconsistency ← **false**
       for each compiled assertion do
       begin
          result ← retrieve all new (respectively old), tuples of R where $\neg(C_i)$
          if *card(result)* $\neq$ 0 **then**
          begin
             inconsistency ← **true**
             exit
          end-if
       end-for
       if not *(inconsistency)* **then**
          send the tuples to update to all the sites storing fragments of R
       else reject the update
       end-if
    end. {ENFORCE}

Example 6.20

We illustrate this algorithm through an example based on the foreign key assertion of Example 6.7. Let u be an insertion of a new tuple into ASG. The previous algorithm uses the compiled assertion (ASG, **INSERT**, C), where C is

$$\forall \textbf{NEW} \in \text{ASG}^+, \exists j \in \text{PROJ} : \textbf{NEW}.\text{PNO} = j.\text{PNO}$$

For this assertion, the retrieval statement is to retrieve all new tuples in ASG$^+$ where C is not true.

This statement can be expressed in SQL as

```
SELECT    NEW.*
FROM      ASG⁺ NEW, PROJ
WHERE     COUNT(PROJ.PNO WHERE NEW.PNO = PROJ.PNO)=0
```

Note that **NEW**.* denotes all the attributes of ASG$^+$.

Thus the strategy is to send new tuples to sites storing relation PROJ in order to perform the joins, and then to centralize all results at the query master site. For each site storing a fragment of PROJ, the site joins the fragment with ASG$^+$ and sends the result to the query master site, which performs the union of all results. If the union is empty, the database is consistent. Otherwise, the update leads to an inconsistent state. The rejection of the program depends on the strategy chosen by the program manager of the distributed DBMS.

Assertions involving aggregates. These assertions are among the most costly to test because they require the calculation of the aggregate functions. The aggregate functions generally manipulated are MIN, MAX, SUM, and COUNT. Each aggregate function contains a projection part and a selection part. To enforce these assertions efficiently, it is possible to produce compiled assertions that isolate redundant data which can be stored at each site storing the associated relation [Bernstein and Blaustein, 1982]. This data is called *concrete views*.

Summary of Distributed Integrity Control

The main problem of distributed integrity control is that the communication and processing costs of enforcing distributed assertions can be prohibitive. The two main issues in designing a distributed integrity subsystem are the definition of the distributed assertions and of the enforcement algorithms, which minimize the cost of distributed integrity checking. We have shown that distributed integrity control can be completely achieved, by extending a preventive method based on the compilation of semantic integrity assertions. The method is general since all types of assertions expressed in first-order predicate logic can be handled. It is compatible with fragment definition and minimizes intersite communication. A better performance of distributed integrity enforcement can be obtained if fragments are defined carefully. Therefore, the specification of distributed integrity constraints is an important aspect of the distributed database design process.

6.4 CONCLUSION

Semantic data control includes view management, security control, and semantic integrity control. In the relational framework, these functions can be uniformly achieved by enforcing rules that specify data manipulation control. Well known solutions exist for handling these functions in centralized systems. However, few solutions exist for distributed systems. The main reason is that semantic data control is costly in centralized systems and can be prohibitive in distributed systems. The two main issues for efficiently performing data control are the definition and storage of the rules (site selection) and the design of enforcement algorithms which minimize communication costs. The problem is difficult since increased functionality (and generality) tends to increase site communication. Solutions for distributed semantic data control are extensions of centralized solutions. The problem is simplified if control rules are fully replicated at all sites and harder if site autonomy is to be preserved. In addition, specific optimizations can be done to minimize the cost of data control but with extra overhead such as managing snapshots or redundant data. Thus the specification of distributed data control must be included in the distributed database design so that the cost of control for update programs is also considered.

6.5 BIBLIOGRAPHIC NOTES

A few papers deal with semantic data control in distributed databases. Generally, the problems of view management, authorization control, and semantic integrity control are treated separately in a distributed context. However, more references are available for centralized systems [Gardarin and Valduriez, 1989].

The two basic papers on centralized view management are [Chamberlin et al., 1975] and [Stonebraker, 1975]. The first reference presents an integrated solution for view and authorization management in System R. The second reference describes INGRES's query modification technique for uniformly handling views, authorizations, and semantic integrity control. This method was presented in Section 6.1.

Theoretical solutions to the problem of view updates are given in [Bancilhon and Spyratos, 1981], [Dayal and Bernstein, 1978], and [Keller, 1982]. Semantic information about the base relations is particularly useful for finding unique propagation of updates. The current commercial systems are very restrictive in supporting updates through views.

The notion of snapshot for optimizing view derivation in distributed database systems is due to [Adiba and Lindsay, 1980]. [Adiba, 1981] generalizes the notion of snapshot by that of derived relation in a distributed context. He also proposes a unified mechanism for managing views, and snapshots, as well as fragmented and replicated data.

[Fernandez et al., 1981] deals with security and integrity in database systems, mainly in a centralized context. Authorization and protection are extensively treated, while only physical integrity (not semantic integrity) is described. [Hoffman, 1977] describes security and protection in computer systems in general. The authorization mechanism of System R is presented in [Griffiths and Wade, 1976] in a more complete way than in [Chamberlin et al., 1975]. In [Wilms and Lindsay, 1981] the authorization mechanism of System R is extended to handle groups of users and to run in a distributed environment.

The content of Section 6.3 comes largely from the work on semantic integrity control described in [Simon and Valduriez, 1984], [Simon and Valduriez, 1986] and [Simon and Valduriez, 1987]. In particular, [Simon and Valduriez, 1986] extends a preventive strategy for centralized integrity control based on compiled assertions to run in a distributed environment. The initial idea of declarative methods, that is, to use assertions of predicate logic to specify integrity constraints, is due to [Florentin, 1974]. The most important declarative methods are in [Bernstein et al., 1980a], [Blaustein, 1981], [Nicolas, 1982], [Simon and Valduriez, 1984], and [Stonebraker, 1975]. The notion of concrete views for storing redundant data is described in [Bernstein and Blaustein, 1982]. Note that concrete views are useful in optimizing the enforcement of assertions involving aggregates. [Civelek et al., 1988], [Sheth et al., 1988b] and [Sheth et al., 1988a] describe systems and tools for semantic data control, particularly view management.

6.6 EXERCISES

6.1 Define in SQL-like syntax a view of the engineering database V(ENO, - ENAME, PNO, RESP), where the duration is 24. Is view V updatable? Assume that relations EMP and ASG are horizontally fragmented based on access frequencies as follows:

Site 1	Site 2	Site 3
EMP_1	EMP_2	
	ASG_1	ASG_2

where

$$
\begin{aligned}
EMP_1 &= \sigma_{TITLE \neq \text{``Engineer''}}(EMP) \\
EMP_2 &= \sigma_{TITLE = \text{``Engineer''}}(EMP) \\
ASG_1 &= \sigma_{0 < DUR < 36}(ASG) \\
ASG_2 &= \sigma_{DUR \geq 36}(ASG)
\end{aligned}
$$

At which site(s) should the definition of V be stored without being fully replicated, to increase locality of reference?

6.2 Express the following query: names of employees in view V who work on the CAD project.

*6.3 Assume that relation PROJ is horizontally fragmented as

$$
\begin{aligned}
PROJ_1 &= \sigma_{PNAME = \text{``CAD''}}(PROJ) \\
PROJ_2 &= \sigma_{PNAME \neq \text{``CAD''}}(PROJ)
\end{aligned}
$$

Modify the query obtained in Exercise 6.2 to a query expressed on fragments.

**6.4 Propose an algorithm to efficiently update a snapshot derived by projection from horizontally fragmented relations.

6.5 Propose a relation schema for storing the access rights associated with user groups in a distributed database catalog, and give a fragmentation scheme for that relation, assuming that all members of a group are at the same site.

**6.6   Give an algorithm for executing the REVOKE statement in a distributed DBMS, assuming that the GRANT privilege can be granted only to a group of users where all its members are at the same site.

6.7   Using the assertion specification language of this chapter, express an integrity constraint which states that the duration spent in a project cannot exceed 48 months.

*6.8   Define the compiled assertions associated with integrity constraints covered in Examples 6.5 to 6.8.

6.9   Assume the following vertical fragmentation of relations EMP, ASG and PROJ:

Site 1	Site 2	Site 3	Site 4
EMP_1	EMP_2		
	$PROJ_1$	$PROJ_2$	
		ASG_1	ASG_2

where

$$
\begin{aligned}
EMP_1 &= \Pi_{ENO,\ ENAME}(EMP) \\
EMP_2 &= \Pi_{ENO,\ TITLE}(EMP) \\
PROJ_1 &= \Pi_{PNO,\ PNAME}(PROJ) \\
PROJ_2 &= \Pi_{PNO,\ BUDGET}(PROJ) \\
ASG_1 &= \Pi_{ENO,\ PNO,\ RESP}(ASG) \\
ASG_2 &= \Pi_{ENO,\ PNO,\ DUR}(ASG)
\end{aligned}
$$

Where should the compiled assertions obtained in Exercise 6.8 be stored assuming site autonomy?

**6.10   Apply algorithm ENFORCE for distributed integrity assertions for the compiled assertions derived from assertion (b).

Chapter 7

OVERVIEW OF QUERY
PROCESSING

The success of relational database technology in data processing is due, in part, to the availability of nonprocedural languages (i.e., SQL), which can significantly improve application development and end-user productivity. By hiding the low-level details about the physical organization of the data, relational database languages allow the expression of complex queries in a concise and simple fashion. In particular, to construct the answer to the query, the user does not precisely specify the procedure to follow. This procedure is actually devised by a DBMS module, usually called a *query processor*. This relieves the user from query optimization, a time-consuming task that is best handled by the query processor, since it can exploit a large amount of useful information about the data.

Because it is a critical performance issue, query processing has received (and is still receiving) considerable attention in the context of both centralized and distributed DBMSs. However, the query processing problem is much more difficult in distributed environments than in centralized ones, because a larger number of parameters affect the performance of distributed queries. In particular, the relations involved in a distributed query may be fragmented and/or replicated, thereby inducing communication overhead costs. Furthermore, with many sites to access, query response time may become very high.

In this chapter we give an overview of query processing in distributed DBMSs, leaving the details of the important aspects of distributed query processing to the next two chapters. The context chosen is that of relational calculus and relational algebra, because of their generality and wide use in distributed DBMSs. As we saw in Chapter 5, distributed relations are implemented by fragments. Distributed database design is of major importance for query processing since the definition of fragments is based on the objective of increasing reference locality, and sometimes parallel execution for the most important queries. The role of a distributed query processor is to map a high-level query (assumed to be expressed in relational calculus) on a distributed database (i.e., a set of global relations) into a sequence of database operations (of relational algebra) on relation fragments. Several important functions characterize this mapping. First, the *calculus query* must be *decomposed* into a sequence of relational operations called an *algebraic query*. Second, the data accessed by the query must be *localized* so that the operations on relations are translated to bear on local data (fragments). Finally, the algebraic query on fragments must be extended with communication operations and *optimized* with respect to a cost function to be minimized. This cost function typically refers to computing resources such as disk I/Os, CPUs, and communication networks.

The chapter is organized as follows. In Section 7.1 we illustrate the query processing problem. In Section 7.2 we define precisely the objectives of query processing algorithms. The complexity of relational algebra operations, which affect mainly the performance of query processing, is given in Section 7.3. In Section 7.4 we provide a characterization of query processors based on their implementation choices. Finally, in Section 7.5 we introduce the different layers of query processing starting from a distributed query down to the execution of operations on local sites and communication between sites. The layers introduced in Section 7.5 are described in detail in the next two chapters.

7.1 QUERY PROCESSING PROBLEM

The main function of a relational query processor is to transform a high-level query (typically, in relational calculus) into an equivalent lower-level query (typically, in some variation of relational algebra). The low-level query actually implements the execution strategy for the query. The transformation must achieve both correctness and efficiency. It is correct if the low-level query has the same semantics as the original query, that is, if both queries produce the same result. The well-defined mapping from relational calculus to relational algebra (see Chapter 2) makes the correctness issue easy. But producing an efficient execution strategy is more involved. A relational calculus query may have many equivalent and correct transformations into relational algebra. Since each equivalent execution strategy can lead to very different consumptions of computer resources, the main difficulty is to select the execution strategy that minimizes resource consumption.

Example 7.1

We consider the following subset of the engineering database scheme given in Figure 2.4:

    EMP(ENO, ENAME, TITLE)
    ASG(ENO, PNO, RESP, DUR)

and the following simple user query:

"Find the names of employees who are managing a project"

The expression of the query in relational calculus using the SQL syntax is

```
SELECT  ENAME
FROM    EMP,ASG
WHERE   EMP.ENO = ASG.ENO
AND     RESP = ''Manager''
```

Two equivalent relational algebra queries that are correct transformations of the query above are

$$\Pi_{\text{ENAME}}(\sigma_{\text{RESP="Manager"} \wedge \text{EMP.ENO=ASG.ENO}} (\text{EMP} \times \text{ASG}))$$

and

$$\Pi_{\text{ENAME}}(\text{EMP} \bowtie_{\text{ENO}} (\sigma_{\text{RESP="Manager"}} (\text{ASG})))$$

It is intuitively obvious that the second query, which avoids the Cartesian product of EMP and ASG, consumes much less computing resource than the first and thus should be retained.

In a centralized context, query execution strategies can be well expressed in an extension of relational algebra. The main role of a centralized query processor is to choose, for a given query, the best relational algebra query among all equivalent ones. Since the problem is computationally intractable with a large number of relations [Ibaraki and Kameda, 1984], it is generally reduced to choosing a solution close to the optimum.

In a distributed system, relational algebra is not enough to express execution strategies. It must be supplemented with operations for exchanging data between sites. Besides the choice of ordering relational algebra operations, the distributed query processor must also select the best sites to process data, and possibly the way data should be transformed. This increases the solution space from which to choose the distributed execution strategy, making distributed query processing significantly more difficult.

Example 7.2

This example illustrates the importance of site selection and communication for a chosen relational algebra query against a fragmented database. We consider the following query of Example 7.1:

$$\Pi_{\text{ENAME}} (\text{EMP} \bowtie_{\text{ENO}} (\sigma_{\text{RESP="Manager"}} (\text{ASG})))$$

We assume that relations EMP and ASG are horizontally fragmented as follows:

$$
\begin{aligned}
\text{EMP}_1 &= \sigma_{\text{ENO} \leq \text{"E3"}} (\text{EMP}) \\
\text{EMP}_2 &= \sigma_{\text{ENO} > \text{"E3"}} (\text{EMP}) \\
\text{ASG}_1 &= \sigma_{\text{ENO} \leq \text{"E3"}} (\text{ASG}) \\
\text{ASG}_2 &= \sigma_{\text{ENO} > \text{"E3"}} (\text{ASG})
\end{aligned}
$$

Fragments ASG_1, ASG_2, EMP_1, and EMP_2 are stored at sites 1, 2, 3, and 4, respectively, and the result is expected at site 5.

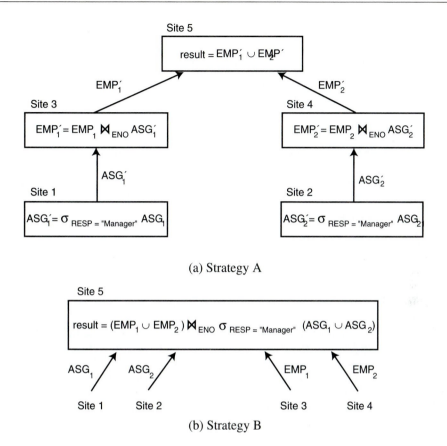

Figure 7.1. Equivalent Distributed Execution Strategies

For the sake of pedagogical simplicity, we ignore the project operation in the following. Two equivalent distributed execution strategies for the above query are shown in Figure 7.1. An arrow from site i to site j labeled with R indicates that relation R is transferred from site i to site j. Strategy A exploits the fact that relations EMP and ASG are fragmented the same way in order to perform the select and join operation in parallel. Strategy B centralizes all the operand data at the result site before processing the query.

To evaluate the resource consumption of these two strategies, we use a simple cost model. We assume that a tuple access, denoted *tupacc*, is 1 unit (which we leave unspecified) and a tuple transfer, denoted *tuptrans*, is 10 units. We assume that relations EMP and ASG have 400 and 1000 tuples, respectively, and that there are 20 managers in relation ASG. We also assume that data is uniformly distributed among sites. Finally, we assume that relations ASG and EMP are locally clustered on attributes RESP and ENO, respectively. Therefore, there is direct access to tuples of ASG (respectively, EMP) based on the value of attribute RESP (respectively, ENO).

The total cost of strategy A can be derived as follows:

1. Produce ASG′ by selecting ASG requires $(10 + 10) * tupacc$ =   20
2. Transfer ASG′ to the sites of EMP requires $(10 + 10) * tuptrans$ =   200
3. Produce EMP′ by joining ASG′ and EMP requires $(10 + 10) * tupacc * 2$ =   40
4. Transfer EMP′ to result site requires $(10 + 10) * tuptrans$ =   200

  The total cost is   460

The cost of strategy B can be derived as follows:

1. Transfer EMP to site 5 requires $400 * tuptrans$ =   4,000
2. Transfer ASG to site 5 requires $1000 * tuptrans$ =   10,000
3. Produce ASG′ by selecting ASG requires $1000 * tupacc$ =   1,000
4. Join EMP and ASG′ requires $400 * 20 * tupacc$ =   8,000

  The total cost is   23,000

In strategy B we assumed that the access methods to relations EMP and ASG based on attributes RESP and ENO are lost because of data transfer. This is a reasonable assumption in practice. Strategy A is better by a factor of 50, which is quite significant. Furthermore, it provides better distribution of work among sites. The difference would be even higher if we assumed slower communication and/or higher degree of fragmentation.

7.2 OBJECTIVES OF QUERY PROCESSING

As stated before, the objective of query processing in a distributed context is to transform a high-level query on a distributed database, which is seen as a single database by the users, into an efficient execution strategy expressed in a low-level language on local databases. We assume that the high-level language is relational calculus, while the low-level language is an extension of relational algebra with communication operations. The different layers involved in the query transformation are detailed in Section 7.5. An important aspect of query processing is query optimization. Because many execution strategies are correct transformations of the same high-level query, the one that optimizes (minimizes) resource consumption should be retained.

A good measure of resource consumption is the *total cost* that will be incurred in processing the query [Sacco and Yao, 1982]. Total cost is the sum of all times incurred in processing the operations of the query at various sites and in intersite communication. Another good measure is the *response time* of the query [Epstein et al., 1978], which is the time elapsed for executing the query. Since operations can be executed in parallel at different sites, the response time of a query may be significantly less than its total cost.

In a distributed database system, the total cost to be minimized includes CPU, I/O, and communication costs. The CPU cost is incurred when performing operations on data in main memory. The I/O cost is the time necessary for disk input/output operations. This cost can be minimized by reducing the number of I/O operations through fast access methods to the data and efficient use of main memory (buffer management). The communication cost is the time needed for exchanging data between sites participating in the execution of the query. This cost is incurred in processing the messages (formatting/deformatting), and in transmitting the data on the communication network.

The first two cost components (I/O and CPU cost) are the only factors considered by centralized DBMSs. The communication cost component is probably the most important factor considered in distributed databases. Most of the early proposals for distributed query optimization assume that the communication cost largely dominates local processing cost (I/O and CPU cost), and thus ignore the latter. This assumption is based on very slow communication networks (e.g., wide area networks with a bandwidth of a few kilobytes per second) rather than on networks with disk bandwidths. Therefore, the aim of distributed query optimization reduces to the problem of minimizing communication costs generally at the expense of local processing. The advantage is that local optimization can be done independently using the known methods for centralized systems. However, modern distributed processing environments have much faster communication networks, as discussed in Chapter 3, whose bandwidth is comparable to that of disks. Therefore, more recent research efforts consider a weighted combination of these three cost components since they all contribute significantly to the total cost of evaluating a query[1] [Page and Popek, 1985]. Nevertheless, in distributed environments with high bandwidths, the overhead cost incurred for communication between sites (e.g., software protocols) makes communication cost still an important factor—as important as I/O cost [Valduriez and Gardarin, 1984]. For completeness, let us consider the methods that minimize all cost components.

7.3 COMPLEXITY OF RELATIONAL ALGEBRA OPERATIONS

In this chapter we consider relational algebra as a basis to express the output of query processing. Therefore, the complexity of relational algebra operations, which directly affects their execution time, dictates some principles useful to a query processor. These principles can help in choosing the final execution strategy.

The simplest way of defining complexity is in terms of relation cardinalities independent of physical implementation details such as fragmentation and storage structures. Figure 7.2 shows the complexity of unary and binary operations in the order of increasing complexity, and thus of increasing execution time. Complexity is $O(n)$ for unary operations, where n denotes the relation cardinality, if the resulting tuples may be obtained independently of each other. Complexity is $O(n * \log n)$ for binary operations if each tuple of one relation must be compared with each tuple

---

[1] There are some recent studies that investigate the feasibility of retrieving data from a neighboring nodes main memory cache rather than accessing them from a local disk[Franklin et al., 1992b], [Dahlin et al., 1994], [Freeley et al., 1995]. These approaches would have a significant impact on query optimization, but they are not implemented in any system at this time.

Operation	Complexity
Select Project (without duplicate elimination)	$O(n)$
Project (with duplicate elimination) Group	$O(n*\log n)$
Join Semijoin Division Set Operators	$O(n*\log n)$
Cartesian Product	$O(n^2)$

Figure 7.2. Complexity of Relational Algebra Operations

of the other on the basis of the equality of selected attributes. This complexity assumes that tuples of each relation must be sorted on the comparison attributes. Projects with duplicate elimination and group operations require that each tuple of the relation be compared with each other tuple, and thus have $O(n * \log n)$ complexity. Finally, complexity is $O(n^2)$ for the Cartesian product of two relations because each tuple of one relation must be combined with each tuple of the other.

This simple look at operation complexity suggests two principles. First, because complexity is relative to relation cardinalities, the most selective operations that reduce cardinalities (e.g., selection) should be performed first. Second, operations should be ordered by increasing complexity so that Cartesian products can be avoided or delayed.

7.4 CHARACTERIZATION OF QUERY PROCESSORS

It is quite difficult to evaluate and compare query processors in the context of both centralized systems [Jarke and Koch, 1984] and distributed systems ([Sacco and Yao, 1982], [Apers et al., 1983]) because they may differ in many aspects. In what follows, we list important characteristics of query processors that can be used as a basis for comparison. The first four characteristics hold for both centralized and distributed query processors, while the next four characteristics are particular to distributed query processors. This characterization is used in Chapter 9 to compare various algorithms.

7.4.1 Languages

Initially, most work on query processing was done in the context of relational DBMSs because their high-level languages give the system many opportunities for optimization. The input language to the query processor can be based on relational calculus or relational algebra. With object DBMSs (Chapter 14), the language is based on object calculus which is merely an extension of relational calculus. Thus, decomposition in object algebra is also needed.

The former requires an additional phase to decompose a query expressed in relational calculus into relational algebra. In a distributed context, the output language is generally some internal form of relational algebra augmented with communication primitives. The operations of the output language are implemented directly in the system. Query processing must perform efficient mapping from the input language to the output language.

7.4.2 Types of Optimization

Conceptually, query optimization aims at choosing the best point in the solution space of all possible execution strategies. An immediate method for query optimization is to search the solution space, exhaustively predict the cost of each strategy, and select the strategy with minimum cost. Although this method is effective in selecting the best strategy, it may incur a significant processing cost for the optimization itself. The problem is that the solution space can be large; that is, there may be many equivalent strategies, even with a small number of relations. The problem becomes worse as the number of relations or fragments increases (e.g., becomes greater than 5 or 6). Having high optimization cost is not necessarily bad, particularly if query optimization is done once for many subsequent executions of the query. Therefore, an "exhaustive" search approach is often used whereby (almost) all possible execution strategies are considered [Selinger et al., 1979].

To avoid the high cost of exhaustive search, *randomized* strategies, such as Iterative Improvement [Swami, 1989] and Simulated Annealing [Ioannidis and Wong, 1987] have been proposed. They try to find a very good solution, not necessarily the best one, but avoid the high cost of optimization, in terms of memory and time consumption.

Another popular way of reducing the cost of exhaustive search is the use of heuristics, whose effect is to restrict the solution space so that only a few strategies are considered. In both centralized and distributed systems, a common heuristic is to minimize the size of intermediate relations. This can be done by performing unary operations first, and ordering the binary operations by the increasing sizes of their intermediate relations. An important heuristic in distributed systems is to replace join operations by combinations of semijoins to minimize data communication.

7.4.3   Optimization Timing

A query may be optimized at different times relative to the actual time of query execution. Optimization can be done *statically* before executing the query or *dynamically* as the query is executed. Static query optimization is done at query compilation time. Thus the cost of optimization may be amortized over multiple query executions. Therefore, this timing is appropriate for use with the exhaustive search method. Since the sizes of the intermediate relations of a strategy are not known until run time, they must be estimated using database statistics. Errors in these estimates can lead to the choice of suboptimal strategies.

Dynamic query optimization proceeds at query execution time. At any point of execution, the choice of the best next operation can be based on accurate knowledge of the results of the operations executed previously. Therefore, database statistics are not needed to estimate the size of intermediate results. However, they may still be useful in choosing the first operations. The main advantage over static query optimization is that the actual sizes of intermediate relations are available to the query processor, thereby minimizing the probability of a bad choice. The main shortcoming is that query optimization, an expensive task, must be repeated for each execution of the query. Therefore, this approach is best for ad-hoc queries.

Hybrid query optimization attempts to provide the advantages of static query optimization while avoiding the issues generated by inaccurate estimates. The approach is basically static, but dynamic query optimization may take place at run time when a high difference between predicted sizes and actual size of intermediate relations is detected.

7.4.4   Statistics

The effectiveness of query optimization relies on *statistics* on the database. Dynamic query optimization requires statistics in order to choose which operations should be done first. Static query optimization is even more demanding since the size of intermediate relations must also be estimated based on statistical information. In a distributed database, statistics for query optimization typically bear on fragments, and include fragment cardinality and size as well as the size and number of distinct values of each attribute. To minimize the probability of error, more detailed statistics such as histograms of attribute values are sometimes used at the expense of higher management cost. The accuracy of statistics is achieved by periodic updating. With static optimization, significant changes in statistics used to optimize a query might result in query reoptimization.

7.4.5   Decision Sites

When static optimization is used, either a single site or several sites may participate in the selection of the strategy to be applied for answering the query. Most systems use the centralized decision approach, in which a single site generates the strategy. However, the decision process could be distributed among various sites participating in the elaboration of the best strategy. The centralized approach is simpler but requires knowledge of the entire distributed database, while the distributed approach requires only local information. Hybrid approaches where one site makes the major decisions and other sites can make local decisions are also frequent. For example, System R* [Williams et al., 1982] uses a hybrid approach.

7.4.6 Exploitation of the Network Topology

The network topology is generally exploited by the distributed query processor. With wide area networks, the cost function to be minimized can be restricted to the data communication cost, which is considered to be the dominant factor. This assumption greatly simplifies distributed query optimization, which can be divided into two separate problems: selection of the global execution strategy, based on intersite communication, and selection of each local execution strategy, based on a centralized query processing algorithm.

With local area networks, communication costs are comparable to I/O costs. Therefore, it is reasonable for the distributed query processor to increase parallel execution at the expense of communication cost. The broadcasting capability of some local area networks can be exploited successfully to optimize the processing of join operations ([Özsoyoglu and Zhou, 1987], [Wah and Lien, 1985]). Other algorithms specialized to take advantage of the network topology are presented in [Kerschberg et al., 1982] for star networks and in [LaChimia, 1984] for satellite networks.

In a client-server environment, the power of the client workstation can be exploited to perform database operations using *data shipping* [Franklin et al., 1996]. The optimization problem becomes to decide which part of the query should be performed on the client and which part on the server using query shipping.

7.4.7 Exploitation of Replicated Fragments

A distributed relation is usually divided into relation fragments as described in Chapter 5. Distributed queries expressed on global relations are mapped into queries on physical fragments of relations by translating relations into fragments. We call this process *localization* because its main function is to localize the data involved in the query. For reliability purposes it is useful to have fragments replicated at different sites. Most optimization algorithms consider the localization process independently of optimization. However, some algorithms exploit the existence of replicated fragments at run time in order to minimize communication times. The optimization algorithm is then more complex because there are a larger number of possible strategies.

7.4.8 Use of Semijoins

The semijoin operation has the important property of reducing the size of the operand relation. When the main cost component considered by the query processor is communication, a semijoin is particularly useful for improving the processing of distributed join operations as it reduces the size of data exchanged between sites. However, using semijoins may result in an increase in the number of messages and in the local processing time. The early distributed DBMSs, such as SDD-1 [Bernstein et al., 1981], which were designed for slow wide area networks, make extensive use of semijoins. Some later systems, such as R* [Williams et al., 1982], assume faster networks and do not employ semijoins. Rather, they perform joins directly since using joins leads to lower local processing costs. Nevertheless, semijoins are still beneficial in the context of fast networks when they induce a strong reduction of the

join operand. Therefore, some recent query processing algorithms aim at selecting
an optimal combination of joins and semijoins ([Özsoyoglu and Zhou, 1987], [Wah
and Lien, 1985]).

7.5 LAYERS OF QUERY PROCESSING

In Chapter 4 we have seen where query processing fits within the distributed DBMS
architecture. The problem of query processing can itself be decomposed into several subproblems, corresponding to various layers. In Figure 7.3 a generic layering
scheme for query processing is shown where each layer solves a well-defined sub-

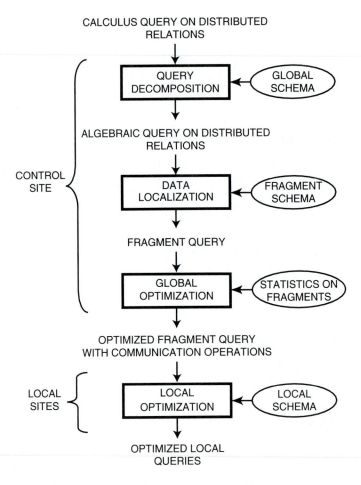

Figure 7.3. Generic Layering Scheme for Distributed Query Processing

problem. To simplify the discussion, let us assume a static and semicentralized query processor that does not exploit replicated fragments. The input is a query on distributed data expressed in relational calculus. This distributed query is posed on global (distributed) relations, meaning that data distribution is hidden. Four main layers are involved to map the distributed query into an optimized sequence of local operations, each acting on a local database. These layers perform the functions of *query decomposition, data localization, global query optimization*, and *local query optimization*. Query decomposition and data localization correspond to query rewriting. The first three layers are performed by a central site and use global information; the fourth is done by the local sites. The first two layers are treated extensively in Chapter 8, while the two last layers are detailed in Chapter 9. In the remainder of this chapter we present an overview of the layers.

7.5.1 Query Decomposition

The first layer decomposes the distributed calculus query into an algebraic query on global relations. The information needed for this transformation is found in the global conceptual schema describing the global relations. However, the information about data distribution is not used here but in the next layer. Thus the techniques used by this layer are those of a centralized DBMS.

Query decomposition can be viewed as four successive steps. First, the calculus query is rewritten in a *normalized* form that is suitable for subsequent manipulation. Normalization of a query generally involves the manipulation of the query quantifiers and of the query qualification by applying logical operator priority.

Second, the normalized query is *analyzed* semantically so that incorrect queries are detected and rejected as early as possible. Techniques to detect incorrect queries exist only for a subset of relational calculus. Typically, they use some sort of graph that captures the semantics of the query.

Third, the correct query (still expressed in relational calculus) is *simplified*. One way to simplify a query is to eliminate redundant predicates. Note that redundant queries are likely to arise when a query is the result of system transformations applied to the user query. As seen in Chapter 6, such transformations are used for performing semantic data control (views, protection, and semantic integrity control).

Fourth, the calculus query is *restructured* as an algebraic query. Recall from Section 7.1 that several algebraic queries can be derived from the same calculus query, and that some algebraic queries are "better" than others. The quality of an algebraic query is defined in terms of expected performance. The traditional way to do this transformation toward a "better" algebraic specification is to start with an initial algebraic query and transform it in order to find a "good" one. The initial algebraic query is derived immediately from the calculus query by translating the predicates and the target statement into relational operations as they appear in the query. This directly translated algebra query is then restructured through transformation rules. The algebraic query generated by this layer is good in the sense that the worse executions are avoided. For instance, a relation will be accessed only once, even if there are several select predicates. However, this query is generally far from providing an optimal execution, since information about data distribution and local fragments is not used at this layer.

7.5.2 Data Localization

The input to the second layer is an algebraic query on distributed relations. The main role of the second layer is to localize the query's data using data distribution information. In Chapter 5 we saw that relations are fragmented and stored in disjoint subsets, called fragments, each being stored at a different site. This layer determines which fragments are involved in the query and transforms the distributed query into a fragment query. Fragmentation is defined through fragmentation rules which can be expressed as relational operations. A distributed relation can be reconstructed by applying the fragmentation rules, and then deriving a program, called a *localization program*, of relational algebra operations which then acts on fragments. Generating a fragment query is done in two steps. First, the distributed query is mapped into a fragment query by substituting each distributed relation by its reconstruction program (also called *materialization program*), discussed in Chapter 5. Second, the fragment query is simplified and restructured to produce another "good" query. Simplification and restructuring may be done according to the same rules used in the decomposition layer. As in the decomposition layer, the final fragment query is generally far from optimal because information regarding fragments is not utilized.

7.5.3 Global Query Optimization

The input to the third layer is a fragment query, that is, an algebraic query on fragments. The goal of query optimization is to find an execution strategy for the query which is close to optimal. Remember that finding the optimal solution is computationally intractable. An execution strategy for a distributed query can be described with relational algebra operations and *communication primitives* (send/receive operations) for transferring data between sites. The previous layers have already optimized the query, for example, by eliminating redundant expressions. However, this optimization is independent of fragment characteristics such as cardinalities. In addition, communication operations are not yet specified. By permuting the ordering of operations within one fragment query, many equivalent queries may be found.

Query optimization consists of finding the "best" ordering of operations in the fragment query, including communication operations which minimize a cost function. The cost function, often defined in terms of time units, refers to computing resources such as disk space, disk I/Os, buffer space, CPU cost, communication cost, and so on. Generally, it is a weighted combination of I/O, CPU, and communication costs. Nevertheless, a typical simplification made by distributed DBMSs, as we mentioned before, is to consider communication cost as the most significant factor. This is valid for wide area networks, where the limited bandwidth makes communication much more costly than local processing. To select the ordering of operations it is necessary to predict execution costs of alternative candidate orderings. Determining execution costs before query execution (i.e., static optimization) is based on fragment statistics and the formulas for estimating the cardinalities of results of relational operations. Thus the optimization decisions depend on the available statistics on fragments.

An important aspect of query optimization is *join ordering*, since permutations of the joins within the query may lead to improvements of orders of magnitude.

One basic technique for optimizing a sequence of distributed join operations is through the semijoin operator. The main value of the semijoin in a distributed system is to reduce the size of the join operands and then the communication cost. However, more recent techniques, which consider local processing costs as well as communication costs, do not use semijoins because they might increase local processing costs. The output of the query optimization layer is an optimized algebraic query with communication operations included on fragments.

7.5.4 Local Query Optimization

The last layer is performed by all the sites having fragments involved in the query. Each subquery executing at one site, called a *local query*, is then optimized using the local schema of the site. At this time, the algorithms to perform the relational operations may be chosen. Local optimization uses the algorithms of centralized systems (see Chapter 9).

7.6 CONCLUSION

In this chapter we provided an overview of query processing in distributed DBMSs. We first introduced the function and objectives of query processing. The main assumption is that the distributed query is expressed in relational calculus since that is the case with most current distributed DBMS. The complexity of the problem is proportional to the expressive power and the abstraction capability of the query language. For instance, the problem is even harder with logic-based languages for deductive databases ([Gallaire et al., 1984], [Valduriez and Boral, 1986]).

The goal of distributed query processing may be summarized as follows: given a calculus query on a distributed database, find a corresponding execution strategy that minimizes a system cost function that includes I/O, CPU, and communication costs. An execution strategy is specified in terms of relational algebra operations and communication primitives (send/receive) applied to the local databases (i.e., the relation fragments). Therefore, the complexity of relational operations that affect the performance of query execution is of major importance in the design of a query processor.

We gave a characterization of query processors based on their implementation choices. Query processors may differ in various aspects such as type of algorithm, optimization granularity, optimization timing, use of statistics, choice of decision site(s), exploitation of the network topology, exploitation of replicated fragments, and use of semijoins. This characterization is useful for comparing alternative query processor designs and to understand the trade-offs between efficiency and complexity.

The query processing problem is very difficult to understand in distributed environments because many elements are involved. However, the problem may be divided into several subproblems which are easier to solve individually. Therefore, we have proposed a generic layering scheme for describing distributed query processing. Four main functions have been isolated: query decomposition, data localization, global query optimization, and local query optimization. These functions successively refine the query by adding more details about the processing environment. Query decomposition and data localization are treated in detail in Chapter 8. Distributed and local query optimization is the topic of Chapter 9.

7.7 BIBLIOGRAPHIC NOTES

[Kim et al., 1985] provides a comprehensive set of papers presenting the results of research and development in query processing within the context of the relational model. After a survey of the state of the art in query processing, the book treats most of the important topics in the area. In particular, there are three papers on distributed query processing. [Gardarin and Valduriez, 1989] includes a chapter on query processing in centralized DBMSs.

[Ceri and Pelagatti, 1984] deals extensively with distributed query processing by treating the problem of localization and optimization separately in two chapters. The main assumption is that the query is expressed in relational algebra, so the decomposition phase that maps a calculus query into an algebraic query is ignored.

There are several survey papers on query processing and query optimization in the context of the relational model. A detailed survey is available in [Graefe, 1993]. An earlier survey is [Jarke and Koch, 1984]. Both of these mainly deal with centralized query processing. The initial solutions to distributed query processing are extensively compiled in [Sacco and Yao, 1982], [Yu and Chang, 1984]. Many of the more recent query processing techniques are compiled in the book [Freytag et al., 1994].

In [Ibaraki and Kameda, 1984] it is formally shown that finding the optimal execution strategy for a query is computationally intractable. Assuming a simplified cost function including the number of page accesses, it is proven that the minimization of this cost function for a multiple-join query is NP-complete.

A recent Ph.D. thesis [Pongpinigpinyo, 1996] investigates the use of a randomized search strategy, namely simulated annealing, for distributed query processing.

Chapter 8

QUERY DECOMPOSITION AND DATA LOCALIZATION

In Chapter 7 we discussed a generic layering scheme for distributed query processing in which the first two layers are responsible for query decomposition and data localization. These two functions are applied successively to transform a calculus query specified on distributed relations (i.e., global relations) into an algebraic query defined on relation fragments. In this chapter we present the techniques for query decomposition and data localization.

Query decomposition maps a distributed calculus query into an algebraic query on global relations. The techniques used at this layer are those of the centralized DBMS since relation distribution is not yet considered at this point. The resultant algebraic query is "good" in the sense that even if the subsequent layers apply a straightforward algorithm, the worst executions will be avoided. However, the subsequent layers usually perform important optimizations, as they add to the query increasing detail about the processing environment.

Data localization takes as input the decomposed query on global relations and applies data distribution information to the query in order to localize its data. In Chapter 5 we have seen that to increase the locality of reference and/or parallel execution, relations are fragmented and then stored in disjoint subsets, called fragments, each being placed at a different site. Data localization determines which fragments are involved in the query and thereby transforms the distributed query into a fragment query. Similar to the decomposition layer, the final fragment query is generally far from optimal because quantitative information regarding fragments is not exploited at this point. Quantitative information is used by the query optimization layer that will be presented in Chapter 9.

This chapter is organized as follows. In Section 8.1 we present the four successive phases of query decomposition: normalization, semantic analysis, simplification, and restructuring of the query. In Section 8.2 we describe data localization, with emphasis on reduction and simplification techniques for the four following types of fragmentation: horizontal, vertical, derived, and hybrid.

8.1 QUERY DECOMPOSITION

Query decomposition (see Figure 7.3 is the first phase of query processing that transforms a relational calculus query into a relational algebra query. Both input and output queries refer to global relations, without knowledge of the distribution of data. Therefore, query decomposition is the same for centralized and distributed systems [Gardarin and Valduriez, 1989]. In this section the input query is assumed to be syntactically correct. When this phase is completed successfully the output query is semantically correct and good in the sense that redundant work is avoided. The successive steps of query decomposition are (1) normalization, (2) analysis, (3) elimination of redundancy, and (4) rewriting. Steps 1, 3, and 4 rely on the fact that various transformations are equivalent for a given query, and some can have better performance than others. We present the first three steps in the context of tuple relational calculus (e.g., SQL). Only the last step rewrites the query into relational algebra.

8.1.1 Normalization

The input query may be arbitrarily complex, depending on the facilities provided by the language. It is the goal of normalization to transform the query to a normalized form to facilitate further processing. With relational languages such as SQL, the most important transformation is that of the query qualification (the WHERE clause), which may be an arbitrarily complex, quantifier-free predicate, preceded by all necessary quantifiers ($\forall$ or $\exists$). There are two possible normal forms for the predicate, one giving precedence to the AND ($\land$) and the other to the OR ($\lor$). The *conjunctive normal form* is a conjunction ($\land$ predicate) of disjunctions ($\lor$ predicates) as follows:

$$(p_{11} \lor p_{12} \lor \cdots \lor p_{1n}) \land \cdots \land (p_{m1} \lor p_{m2} \lor \cdots \lor p_{mn})$$

where p_{ij} is a simple predicate. A qualification in *disjunctive normal form*, on the other hand, is as follows:

$$(p_{11} \land p_{12} \land \cdots \land p_{1n}) \lor \cdots \lor (p_{m1} \land p_{m2} \land \cdots \land p_{mn})$$

The transformation of the quantifier-free predicate is straightforward using the well-known equivalence rules for logical operations ($\land$, $\lor$, and $\neg$):

1. $p_1 \land p_2 \Leftrightarrow p_2 \land p_1$
2. $p_1 \lor p_2 \Leftrightarrow p_2 \lor p_1$
3. $p_1 \land (p_2 \land p_3) \Leftrightarrow (p_1 \land p_2) \land p_3$
4. $p_1 \lor (p_2 \lor p_3) \Leftrightarrow (p_1 \lor p_2) \lor p_3$
5. $p_1 \land (p_2 \lor p_3) \Leftrightarrow (p_1 \land p_2) \lor (p_1 \land p_3)$
6. $p_1 \lor (p_2 \land p_3) \Leftrightarrow (p_1 \lor p_2) \land (p_1 \lor p_3)$
7. $\neg(p_1 \land p_2) \Leftrightarrow \neg p_1 \lor \neg p_2$
8. $\neg(p_1 \lor p_2) \Leftrightarrow \neg p_1 \land \neg p_2$
9. $\neg(\neg p) \Leftrightarrow p$

In the disjunctive normal form, the query can be processed as independent conjunctive subqueries linked by unions (corresponding to the disjunctions). However, this form may lead to replicated join and select predicates, as shown in the following example. The reason is that predicates are very often linked with the other predicates by AND. The use of rule 5 mentioned above, with p_1 as a join or select predicate, would result in replicating p_1. The conjunctive normal form is more practical since query qualifications typically include more AND than OR predicates. However, it leads to predicate replication for queries involving many disjunctions and few conjunctions, a rare case.

Example 8.1

Let us consider the following query on the engineering database that we have been referring to:

"Find the names of employees who have been working on project P1 for 12 or 24 months"

The query expressed in SQL is

```
SELECT     ENAME
FROM       EMP, ASG
WHERE      EMP.ENO = ASG.ENO
AND        ASG.PNO = ''P1''
AND        DUR = 12 OR DUR = 24
```

The qualification in conjunctive normal form is

$$\text{EMP.ENO} = \text{ASG.ENO} \land \text{ASG.PNO} = \text{``P1''} \land (\text{DUR} = 12 \lor \text{DUR} = 24)$$

while the qualification in disjunctive normal form is

$$(\text{EMP.ENO} = \text{ASG.ENO} \land \text{ASG.PNO} = \text{``P1''} \land \text{DUR} = 12) \lor$$
$$(\text{EMP.ENO} = \text{ASG.ENO} \land \text{ASG.PNO} = \text{``P1''} \land \text{DUR} = 24)$$

In the latter form, treating the two conjunctions independently may lead to redundant work if common subexpressions are not eliminated.

8.1.2 Analysis

Query analysis enables rejection of normalized queries for which further processing is either impossible or unnecessary. The main reasons for rejection are that the query is *type incorrect* or *semantically incorrect*. When one of these cases is detected, the query is simply returned to the user with an explanation. Otherwise, query processing is continued. Below we present techniques to detect these incorrect queries.

A query is type incorrect if any of its attribute or relation names are not defined in the global schema, or if operations are being applied to attributes of the wrong type. The technique used to detect type incorrect queries is similar to type checking for programming languages. However, the type declarations are part of the global schema rather than of the query, since a relational query does not produce new types.

Example 8.2

The following SQL query on the engineering database

```
SELECT   E#
FROM     EMP
WHERE    ENAME > 200
```

is type incorrect for two reasons. First, attribute E# is not declared in the schema. Second, the operation ">200" is incompatible with the type string of ENAME.

A query is semantically incorrect if components of it do not contribute in any way to the generation of the result. In the context of relational calculus, it is not possible to determine the semantic correctness of general queries. However, it is possible to do so for a large class of relational queries, those which do not contain disjunction and negation [Rosenkrantz and Hunt, 1980]. This is based on the representation of the query as a graph, called a *query graph* or *connection graph* [Ullman, 1982]. We define this graph for the most useful kinds of queries involving select, project, and join operators. In a query graph, one node indicates the result relation, and any other node indicates an operand relation. An edge between two nodes that are not results represents a join, whereas an edge whose destination node is the result represents a project. Furthermore, a nonresult node may be labeled by a select or a self-join (join of the relation with itself) predicate. An important subgraph of the relation connection graph is the *join graph*, in which only the joins are considered. The join graph is particularly useful in the query optimization phase.

Example 8.3

Let us consider the following query:

"Find the names and responsibilities of programmers who have been working on the CAD/CAM project for more than 3 years, and their manager's name"

The query expressed in SQL is

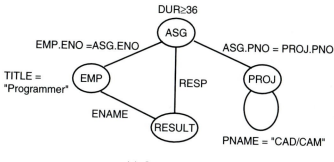

(a) Query graph

(b) Corresponding join graph

Figure 8.1. Relation Graphs

```
SELECT   ENAME, RESP
FROM     EMP, ASG, PROJ
WHERE    EMP.ENO = ASG.ENO
AND      ASG.PNO = PROJ.PNO
AND      PNAME = ''CAD/CAM''
AND      DUR ≥ 36
AND      TITLE = ''Programmer''
```

The query graph for the query above is shown in Figure 8.1a. Figure 8.1b shows the join graph for the graph in Figure 8.1a.

The query graph is useful to determine the semantic correctness of a conjunctive multivariable query without negation. Such a query is semantically incorrect if its query graph is not connected. In this case one or more subgraphs (corresponding to subqueries) are disconnected from the graph that contains the result relation. The query could be considered correct (which some systems do) by considering the missing connection as a Cartesian product. But, in general, the problem is that join predicates are missing and the query should be rejected.

Example 8.4

Let us consider the following SQL query:

```
SELECT   ENAME, RESP
FROM     EMP, ASG, PROJ
WHERE    EMP.ENO = ASG.ENO
AND      PNAME = ''CAD/CAM''
AND      DUR ≥ 36
AND      TITLE = ''Programmer''
```

Its query graph, shown in Figure 8.2, is disconnected, which tells us that the query is semantically incorrect. There are basically three solutions to the problem: (1) reject the query, (2) assume that there is an implicit Cartesian product between relations ASG and PROJ, or (3) infer (using the schema) the missing join predicate ASG.PNO = PROJ.PNO which transforms the query into that of Example 8.3.

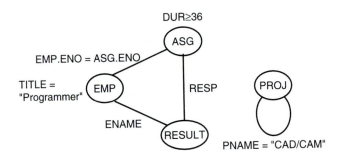

Figure 8.2. Disconnected Query Graph

8.1.3 Elimination of Redundancy

As we saw in Chapter 6, relational languages can be used uniformly for semantic data control. In particular, a user query typically expressed on a view may be enriched with several predicates to achieve view-relation correspondence, and ensure semantic integrity and security. The enriched query qualification may then contain redundant predicates. A naive evaluation of a qualification with redundancy can well lead to duplicated work. Such redundancy and thus redundant work may be eliminated by simplifying the qualification with the following well-known idempotency rules:

1. $p \wedge p \Leftrightarrow p$

2. $p \vee p \Leftrightarrow p$

3. $p \wedge true \Leftrightarrow p$

4. $p \vee false \Leftrightarrow p$

5. $p \wedge false \Leftrightarrow false$

6. $p \vee true \Leftrightarrow true$

7. $p \wedge \neg p \Leftrightarrow false$

8. $p \vee \neg p \Leftrightarrow true$

9. $p_1 \wedge (p_1 \vee p_2) \Leftrightarrow p_1$

10. $p_1 \vee (p_1 \wedge p_2) \Leftrightarrow p_1$

Example 8.5

The SQL query

```
SELECT   TITLE
FROM     EMP
WHERE    (NOT (TITLE = ''Programmer'')
AND      (TITLE = ''Programmer''
OR       TITLE = ''Elect. Eng.'')
AND      NOT (TITLE = ''Elect. Eng.''))
OR       ENAME = ''J. Doe''
```

can be simplified using the previous rules to become

```
SELECT   TITLE
FROM     EMP
WHERE    ENAME = ''J. Doe''
```

The simplification proceeds as follows. Let p_1 be $<\text{TITLE} = \text{``Programmer''}>$, $p_2$ be $<\text{TITLE} = \text{``Elect. Eng.''}>$, and p_3 be $<\text{ENAME} = \text{``J. Doe''}>$. The query qualification is

$$(\neg p_1 \wedge (p_1 \vee p_2) \wedge \neg p_2) \vee p_3$$

The disjunctive normal form for this qualification is obtained by applying rule 5 defined in Section 8.1.1, which yields

$$(\neg p_1 \wedge ((p_1 \wedge \neg p_2) \vee (p_2 \wedge \neg p_2))) \vee p_3$$

and then rule 3 defined in Section 8.1.1, which yields

$$(\neg p_1 \wedge p_1 \wedge \neg p_2) \vee (\neg p_1 \wedge p_2 \wedge \neg p_2) \vee p_3$$

By applying rule 7 defined above, we obtain

$$(false \wedge \neg p_2) \vee (\neg p_1 \wedge false) \vee p_3$$

By applying the same rule, we get

$$false \lor false \lor p_3$$

which is equivalent to p_3 by rule 4 above.

8.1.4 Rewriting

The last step of query decomposition rewrites the query in relational algebra. This is typically divided into the following two substeps: (1) straightforward transformation of the query from relational calculus into relational algebra, and (2) restructuring of the relational algebra query to improve performance. For the sake of clarity it is customary to represent the relational algebra query graphically by an *operator tree*. An operator tree is a tree in which a leaf node is a relation stored in the database, and a nonleaf node is an intermediate relation produced by a relational algebra operator. The sequence of operations is directed from the leaves to the root, which represents the answer to the query.

The transformation of a tuple relational calculus query into an operator tree can easily be achieved as follows. First, a different leaf is created for each different tuple variable (corresponding to a relation). In SQL, the leaves are immediately available in the FROM clause. Second, the root node is created as a project operation involving the result attributes. These are found in the SELECT clause in SQL. Third, the qualification (SQL WHERE clause) is translated into the appropriate sequence of relational operations (select, join, union, etc.) going from the leaves to the root. The sequence can be given directly by the order of appearance of the predicates and operators.

Example 8.6

The query

"Find the names of employees other than J. Doe who worked on the CAD/CAM project for either one or two years" whose SQL expression is

```
SELECT   ENAME
FROM     PROJ, ASG, EMP
WHERE    ASG.ENO = EMP.ENO
AND      ASG.PNO = PROJ.PNO
AND      ENAME ≠ ''J. Doe''
AND      PROJ.PNAME = ''CAD/CAM''
AND      (DUR = 12 OR DUR = 24)
```

can be mapped in a straightforward way in the tree in Figure 8.3. The predicates have been transformed in order of appearance as join and then select operations.

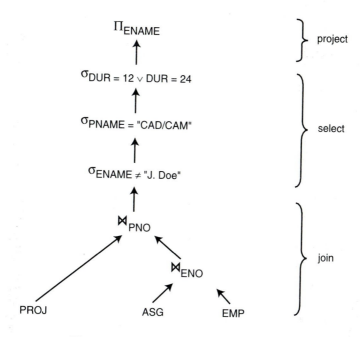

Figure 8.3. Example of Operator Tree

By applying *transformation rules*, many different trees may be found equivalent to the one produced by the method described above [Smith and Chang, 1975]. The six most useful equivalence rules, which concern the basic relational algebra operators, are now presented. The correctness of these rules is given in [Ullman, 1982].

In the remainder of this section, R, S, and T are relations where R is defined over attributes $A = \{A_1, A_2, \ldots, A_n\}$ and S is defined over $B = \{B_1, B_2, \ldots, B_n\}$.

1. **Commutativity of binary operators.** The Cartesian product of two relations R and S is commutative:

$$R \times S \Leftrightarrow S \times R$$

Similarly, the join of two relations is commutative:

$$R \bowtie S \Leftrightarrow S \bowtie R$$

This rule also applies to union but not to set difference or semijoin.

2. **Associativity of binary operators.** The Cartesian product and the join are associative operators:

$$(R \times S) \times T \Leftrightarrow R \times (S \times T)$$
$$(R \bowtie S) \bowtie T \Leftrightarrow R \bowtie (S \bowtie T)$$

3. **Idempotence of unary operators.** Several subsequent projections on the same relation may be grouped. Conversely, a single projection on several attributes may be separated into several subsequent projections. If R is defined over the attribute set A, and $A' \subseteq A, A'' \subseteq A$, and $A' \subseteq A''$, then

$$\Pi_{A'}(\Pi_{A''}(R)) \Leftrightarrow \Pi_{A'}(R)$$

Several subsequent selections $\sigma_{p_i(A_i)}$ on the same relation, where p_i is a predicate applied to attribute A_i, may be grouped as follows:

$$\sigma_{p_1(A_1)}(\sigma_{p_2(A_2)}(R)) = \sigma_{p_1(A_1) \wedge p_2(A_2)}(R)$$

Conversely, a single selection with a conjunction of predicates may be separated into several subsequent selections.

4. **Commuting selection with projection.** Selection and projection on the same relation can be commuted as follows:

$$\Pi_{A_1,\ldots,A_n}(\sigma_{p(A_p)}(R)) \Leftrightarrow \Pi_{A_1,\ldots,A_n}(\sigma_{p(A_p)}(\Pi_{A_1,\ldots,A_n,A_p}(R)))$$

Note that if A_p is already a member of $\{A_1, \ldots, A_n\}$, the last projection on $[A_1, \ldots, A_n]$ on the right-hand side of the equality is useless.

5. **Commuting selection with binary operators.** Selection and Cartesian product can be commuted using the following rule (remember that attribute A_i belongs to relation R):

$$\sigma_{p(A_i)}(R \times S) \Leftrightarrow (\sigma_{p(A_i)}(R)) \times S$$

Selection and join can be commuted:

$$\sigma_{p(A_i)}(R \bowtie_{p(A_j,B_k)} S) \Leftrightarrow \sigma_{p(A_i)}(R) \bowtie_{p(A_j,B_k)} S$$

Selection and union can be commuted if R and T are union compatible (have the same schema):

$$\sigma_{p(A_i)}(R \cup T) \Leftrightarrow \sigma_{p(A_i)}(R) \cup \sigma_{p(A_i)}(T)$$

Selection and difference can be commuted in a similar fashion.

6. **Commuting projection with binary operators.** Projection and Cartesian product can be commuted. If $C = A' \cup B'$, where $A' \subseteq A$, $B' \subseteq B$, and A and B are the sets of attributes over which relations R and S, respectively, are defined, we have

$$\Pi_C(R \times S) \Leftrightarrow \Pi_{A'}(R) \times \Pi_{B'}(S)$$

Projection and join can also be commuted.

$$\Pi_C(R \bowtie_{p(A_i, B_j)} S) \Leftrightarrow \Pi_{A'}(R) \bowtie_{p(A_i, B_j)} \Pi_{B'}(S)$$

For the join on the right-hand side of the implication to hold we need to have $A_i \in A'$ and $B_j \in B'$. Since $C = A' \cup B'$, A_i and B_j are in C and therefore we don't need a projection over C once the projections over A' and B' are performed. Projection and union can be commuted as follows:

$$\Pi_C(R \cup S) \Leftrightarrow \Pi_C(R) \cup \Pi_C(S)$$

Projection and difference can be commuted similarly.

The application of these six rules enables the generation of many equivalent trees. For instance, the tree in Figure 8.4 is equivalent to the one in Figure 8.3. However, the one in Figure 8.4 requires a Cartesian product of relations EMP and PROJ, and may lead to a higher execution cost than the original tree. In the optimization phase, one can imagine comparing all possible trees based on their predicted cost. However, the excessively large number of possible trees makes this approach unrealistic. The rules presented above can be used to restructure the tree in a systematic way so that the "bad" operator trees are eliminated. These rules can be used in four different ways. First, they allow the separation of the unary operations, simplifying the query expression. Second, unary operations on the same relation may be grouped so that access to a relation for performing unary operations can be done only once. Third, unary operations can be commuted with binary operations so that some operations (e.g., selection) may be done first. Fourth, the binary operations can be ordered. This last rule is used extensively in query optimization. A simple restructuring algorithm, presented in [Ullman, 1982], uses a single heuristic that consists of applying unary operations (select/project) as soon as possible to reduce the size of intermediate relations.

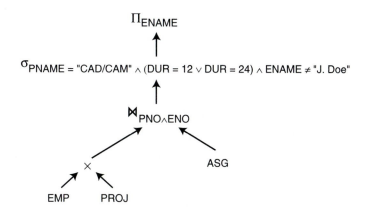

Figure 8.4. Equivalent Operator Tree

Example 8.7

The restructuring of the tree in Figure 8.3 leads to the tree in Figure 8.5. The resulting tree is good in the sense that repeated access to the same relation (as in Figure 8.3) is avoided and that the most selective operations are done first. However, this tree is far from optimal. For example, the select operation on EMP is not very useful before the join because it does not greatly reduce the size of the operand relation.

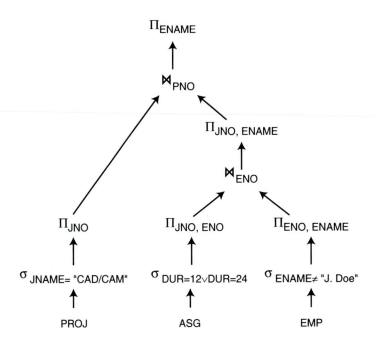

Figure 8.5. Rewritten Operator Tree

8.2 LOCALIZATION OF DISTRIBUTED DATA

In Section 8.1 we presented general techniques for decomposing and restructuring queries expressed in relational calculus. These global techniques apply to both centralized and distributed DBMSs and do not take into account the distribution of data. This is the role of the localization layer. As shown in the generic layering scheme of query processing described in Chapter 7, the localization layer translates an algebraic query on global relations into an algebraic query expressed on physical fragments. Localization uses information stored in the fragment schema.

Fragmentation is defined through fragmentation rules, which can be expressed as relational queries. As we discussed in Chapter 5, a global relation can be reconstructed by applying the reconstruction (or reverse fragmentation) rules and deriving a relational algebra program whose operands are the fragments. We call this a *localization program*. To simplify this section, we do not consider the fact that data fragments may be replicated, although this can improve performance. Replication is considered in Chapter 9.

A naive way to localize a distributed query is to generate a query where each global relation is substituted by its localization program. This can be viewed as replacing the leaves of the operator tree of the distributed query with subtrees corresponding to the localization programs. We call the query obtained this way the *generic query*. In general, this approach is inefficient because important restructurings and simplifications of the generic query can still be made ([Ceri and Pelagatti, 1983], [Ceri et al., 1986]). In the remainder of this section, for each type of fragmentation we present *reduction techniques* that generate simpler and optimized queries. We use the transformation rules and the heuristics, such as pushing unary operations down the tree, that were introduced in Section 8.1.4.

8.2.1 Reduction for Primary Horizontal Fragmentation

The horizontal fragmentation function distributes a relation based on selection predicates. The following example is used in subsequent discussions.

Example 8.8

Relation EMP(ENO, ENAME, TITLE) of Figure 2.4 can be split into three horizontal fragments EMP_1, EMP_2, and EMP_3, defined as follows:

$$
\begin{aligned}
EMP_1 &= \sigma_{\text{ENO} \leq \text{``E3''}}(EMP) \\
EMP_2 &= \sigma_{\text{``E3''} < \text{ENO} \leq \text{``E6''}}(EMP) \\
EMP_3 &= \sigma_{\text{ENO} > \text{``E6''}}(EMP)
\end{aligned}
$$

Note that this fragmentation of the EMP relation is different from the one discussed in Example 5.12.

The localization program for an horizontally fragmented relation is the union of the fragments. In our example we have

$$EMP = EMP_1 \cup EMP_2 \cup EMP_3$$

Thus the generic form of any query specified on EMP is obtained by replacing it by $(EMP_1 \cup EMP_2 \cup EMP_3)$.

The reduction of queries on horizontally fragmented relations consists primarily of determining, after restructuring the subtrees, those that will produce empty relations, and removing them. Horizontal fragmentation can be exploited to simplify both selection and join operations.

Reduction with Selection

Selections on fragments that have a qualification contradicting the qualification of the fragmentation rule generate empty relations. Given a relation R that has been horizontally fragmented as R_1, R_2, ..., R_w, where $R_j = \sigma_{p_j}(R)$, the rule can be stated formally as follows:

Rule 1:
$$\sigma_{p_i}(R_j) = \phi \text{ if } \forall x \text{ in } R : \neg(p_i(x) \wedge p_j(x))$$

where p_i and p_j are selection predicates, x denotes a tuple, and $p(x)$ denotes "predicate p holds for x."

For example, the selection predicate ENO="E1" conflicts with the predicates of fragments EMP_2 and EMP_3 of Example 8.8 (i.e., no tuple in EMP_2 and EMP_3 can satisfy this predicate). Determining the contradicting predicates requires theorem-proving techniques if the predicates are quite general [Hunt and Rosenkrantz, 1979]. However, DBMSs generally simplify predicate comparison by supporting only simple predicates for defining fragmentation rules (by the database administrator).

Example 8.9

We now illustrate reduction by horizontal fragmentation using the following example query:

```
SELECT   *
FROM     EMP
WHERE    ENO = ''E5''
```

Applying the naive approach to localize EMP from EMP_1, EMP_2, and EMP_3 gives the generic query of Figure 8.6a. By commuting the selection with the union operation, it is easy to detect that the selection predicate contradicts the predicates of EMP_1 and EMP_3, thereby producing empty relations. The reduced query is simply applied to EMP_2 as shown in Figure 8.6b.

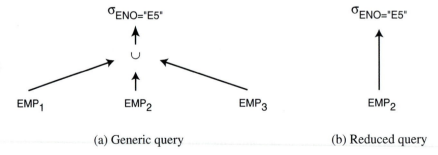

(a) Generic query   (b) Reduced query

Figure 8.6. Reduction for Horizontal Fragmentation (with Selection)

Reduction with Join

Joins on horizontally fragmented relations can be simplified when the joined relations are fragmented according to the join attribute. The simplification consists of distributing joins over unions and eliminating useless joins. The distribution of join over union can be stated as

$$(R_1 \cup R_2) \bowtie S = (R_1 \bowtie S) \cup (R_2 \bowtie S)$$

where R_i are fragments of R and S is a relation.

With this transformation, unions can be moved up in the operator tree so that all possible joins of fragments are exhibited. Useless joins of fragments can be determined when the qualifications of the joined fragments are contradicting. Assuming that fragments R_i and R_j are defined, respectively, according to predicates p_i and p_j on the same attribute, the simplification rule can be stated as follows:

Rule 2:

$$R_i \bowtie R_j = \phi \text{ if } \forall x \text{ in } R_i, \forall y \text{ in } R_j : \neg(p_i(x) \wedge p_j(y))$$

The determination of useless joins can thus be performed by looking only at the fragment predicates. The application of this rule permits the join of two relations to be implemented as parallel partial joins of fragments [Ceri et al., 1986]. It is not always the case that the reduced query is better (i.e., simpler) than the generic query. The generic query is better when there are a large number of partial joins in the reduced query. This case arises when there are few contradicting fragmentation predicates. The worst case occurs when each fragment of one relation must be joined with each fragment of the other relation. This is tantamount to the Cartesian product of the two sets of fragments, with each set corresponding to one relation. The reduced query is better when the number of partial joins is small. For example, if both relations are fragmented using the same predicates, the number of partial joins is equal to the number of fragments of each relation. One advantage of the reduced query is that the partial joins can be done in parallel, and thus increase response time.

Example 8.10

Assume that relation EMP is fragmented between EMP_1, EMP_2, and EMP_3, as above, and that relation ASG is fragmented as

$$ASG_1 = \sigma_{ENO \leq \text{``E3''}}(ASG)$$
$$ASG_2 = \sigma_{ENO > \text{``E3''}}(ASG)$$

EMP_1 and ASG_1 are defined by the same predicate. Furthermore, the predicate defining ASG_2 is the union of the predicates defining EMP_2 and EMP_3. Now consider the join query

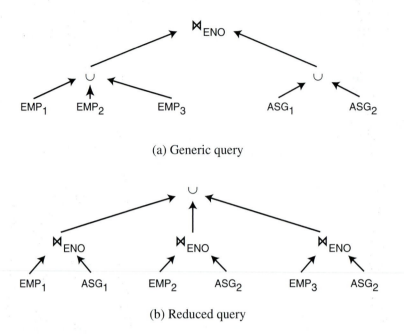

(a) Generic query

(b) Reduced query

Figure 8.7. Reduction by Horizontal Fragmentation (with Join)

```
SELECT   *
FROM     EMP, ASG
WHERE    EMP.ENO = ASG.ENO
```

The equivalent generic query is given in Figure 8.7a. The query reduced by distributing joins over unions and applying rule 2 can be implemented as a union of three partial joins that can be done in parallel (Figure 8.7b).

8.2.2   Reduction for Vertical Fragmentation

The vertical fragmentation function distributes a relation based on projection attributes. Since the reconstruction operator for vertical fragmentation is the join, the localization program for a vertically fragmented relation consists of the join of the fragments on the common attribute. For vertical fragmentation, we use the following example.

Example 8.11

Relation EMP can be divided into two vertical fragments where the key attribute ENO is duplicated:

$$EMP_1 = \Pi_{ENO,ENAME}(EMP)$$
$$EMP_2 = \Pi_{ENO,TITLE}(EMP)$$

The localization program is

$$EMP = EMP_1 \bowtie_{ENO} EMP_2$$

Similar to horizontal fragmentation, queries on vertical fragments can be reduced by determining the useless intermediate relations and removing the subtrees that produce them. Projections on a vertical fragment that has no attributes in common with the projection attributes (except the key of the relation) produce useless, though not empty relations. Given a relation R, defined over attributes $A = \{A_1, \ldots, A_n\}$, which is vertically fragmented as $R_i = \Pi_{A'}(R)$, where $A' \subseteq A$, the rule can be formally stated as follows:

Rule 3: $\Pi_{D,K}(R_i)$ is useless if the set of projection attributes D is not in A'.

Example 8.12

Let us illustrate the application of this rule using the following example query in SQL:

```
SELECT    ENAME
FROM      EMP
```

The equivalent generic query on EMP_1 and EMP_2 (as obtained in Example 8.10) is given in Figure 8.8a. By commuting the projection with the join (i.e., projecting on ENO, ENAME), we can see that the projection on EMP_2 is useless because ENAME is not in EMP_2. Therefore, the projection needs to apply only to EMP_1, as shown in Figure 8.8b.

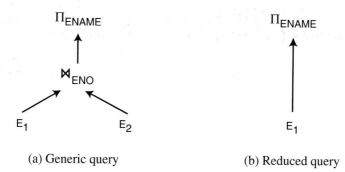

(a) Generic query   (b) Reduced query

Figure 8.8. Reduction for Vertical Fragmentation

8.2.3   Reduction for Derived Fragmentation

As we saw in previous sections, the join operation, which is probably the most important operation because it is both frequent and expensive, can be optimized using primary horizontal fragmentation when the joined relations are fragmented according to the join attributes. In this case the join of two relations is implemented as a union of partial joins. However, this method precludes one of the relations from being fragmented on a different attribute used for selection. Derived horizontal fragmentation is another way of distributing two relations so that the joint processing of select and join is improved. Typically, if relation R is subject to derived horizontal fragmentation due to relation S, the fragments of R and S that have the same join attribute values are located at the same site. In addition, S can be fragmented according to a selection predicate.

Since tuples of R are placed according to the tuples of S, derived fragmentation should be used only for one-to-many (hierarchical) relationships of the form $S \rightarrow R$, where a tuple of S can match with n tuples of R, but a tuple of R matches with exactly one tuple of S. Note that derived fragmentation could be used for many-to-many relationships provided that tuples of S (that match with n tuples of R) are replicated. Such replication is difficult to maintain consistently. For simplicity, we assume and advise that derived fragmentation be used only for hierarchical relationships.

Example 8.13

> Given a one-to-many relationship from EMP to ASG, relation ASG(ENO, PNO, RESP, DUR) can be indirectly fragmented according to the following rules:

$$\text{ASG}_1 \quad = \quad \text{ASG} \ltimes_{\text{ENO}} \text{EMP}_1$$
$$\text{ASG}_2 \quad = \quad \text{ASG} \ltimes_{\text{ENO}} \text{EMP}_2$$

> Recall from Chapter 5 that the predicate on

$$\text{EMP}_1 \quad = \quad \sigma_{\text{TITLE}=\text{“Programmer”}}(\text{EMP})$$
$$\text{EMP}_2 \quad = \quad \sigma_{\text{TITLE}\neq\text{“Programmer”}}(\text{EMP})$$

> The localization program for a horizontally fragmented relation is the union of the fragments. In our example, we have

$$\text{ASG} = \text{ASG}_1 \cup \text{ASG}_2$$

Queries on derived fragments can also be reduced. Since this type of fragmentation is useful for optimizing join queries, a useful transformation is to distribute joins over unions (used in the localization programs) and to apply rule 2 introduced earlier. Because the fragmentation rules indicate what the matching tuples are, certain joins will produce empty relations if the fragmentation predicates conflict. For example, the predicates of ASG_1 and EMP_2 conflict; thus we have

$$\text{ASG}_1 \bowtie \text{EMP}_2 = \phi$$

Contrary to the reduction with join discussed previously, the reduced query is always preferable to the generic query because the number of partial joins usually equals the number of fragments of R.

Example 8.14

The reduction by derived fragmentation is illustrated by applying it to the following SQL query, which retrieves all attributes of tuples from EMP and ASG that have the same value of ENO and the title "Mech. Eng.":

```
SELECT   *
FROM     EMP, ASG
WHERE    ASG.ENO = EMP.ENO
AND      TITLE = ''Mech. Eng.''
```

The generic query on fragments EMP_1, EMP_2, ASG_1, and ASG_2, defined previously is given in Figure 8.9a. By pushing selection down to fragments EMP_1 and EMP_2, the query reduces to that of Figure 8.9b. This is because the selection predicate conflicts with that of EMP_1, and thus EMP_1 can be removed. In order to discover conflicting join predicates, we distribute joins over unions. This produces the tree of Figure 8.9c. The left subtree joins two fragments, ASG_1 and EMP_2, whose qualifications conflict because of predicates TITLE = "Programmer" in ASG_1, and TITLE $\neq$ "Programmer" in EMP_2. Therefore the left subtree which produces an empty relation can be removed, and the reduced query of Figure 8.9d is obtained. This example illustrates the value of fragmentation in improving the execution performance of distributed queries.

8.2.4 Reduction for Hybrid Fragmentation

Hybrid fragmentation is obtained by combining the fragmentation functions discussed above. The goal of hybrid fragmentation is to support, efficiently, queries involving projection, selection, and join. Note that the optimization of an operation or of a combination of operations is always done at the expense of other operations. For example, hybrid fragmentation based on selection-projection will make selection only, or projection only, less efficient than with horizontal fragmentation (or vertical fragmentation). The localization program for a hybrid fragmented relation uses unions and joins of fragments.

Example 8.15

Here is an example of hybrid fragmentation of relation EMP:

$$\begin{aligned}
EMP_1 &= \sigma_{ENO \leq \text{"E4"}}(\Pi_{ENO, ENAME}(EMP)) \\
EMP_2 &= \sigma_{ENO > \text{"E4"}}(\Pi_{ENO, ENAME}(EMP)) \\
EMP_3 &= \Pi_{ENO, TITLE}(EMP)
\end{aligned}$$

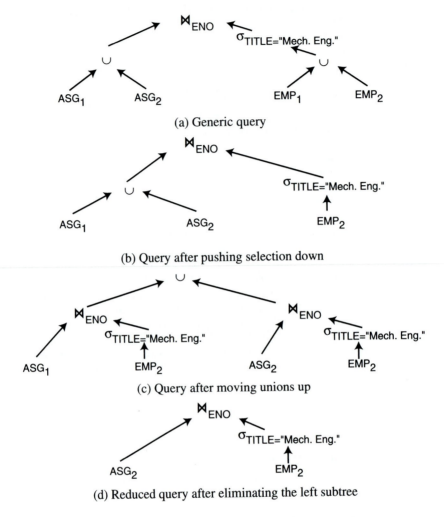

(a) Generic query

(b) Query after pushing selection down

(c) Query after moving unions up

(d) Reduced query after eliminating the left subtree

Figure 8.9. Reduction for Indirect Fragmentation

In our example, the localization program is

$$EMP = (EMP_1 \cup EMP_2) \Join_{ENO} EMP_3$$

Queries on hybrid fragments can be reduced by combining the rules used, respectively, in primary horizontal, vertical, and derived horizontal fragmentation. These rules can be summarized as follows:

1. Remove empty relations generated by contradicting selections on horizontal fragments.

2. Remove useless relations generated by projections on vertical fragments.

3. Distribute joins over unions in order to isolate and remove useless joins.

Example 8.16

The following example query in SQL illustrates the application of rules (1) and (2) to the horizontal-vertical fragmentation of relation EMP into EMP_1, EMP_2 and EMP_3 given above:

```
SELECT    ENAME
FROM      EMP
WHERE     ENO=''E5''
```

The generic query of Figure 8.10a can be reduced by first pushing selection down, eliminating fragment EMP_1, and then pushing projection down, eliminating fragment EMP_3. The reduced query is given in Figure 8.10b.

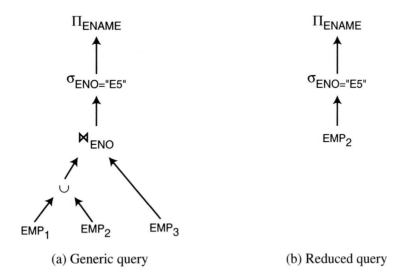

(a) Generic query   (b) Reduced query

Figure 8.10. Reduction for Hybrid Fragmentation

8.3 CONCLUSION

In this chapter we focused on the techniques for query decomposition and data localization layers of the generic query processing scheme that was introduced in Chapter 7. Query decomposition and data localization are the two successive functions that map a calculus query, expressed on distributed relations, into an algebraic query (query decomposition), expressed on relation fragments (data localization).

These two layers can produce a generic query corresponding to the input query in a naive way. Query decomposition can generate an algebraic query simply by translating into relational operations the predicates and the target statement as they appear. Data localization can, in turn, express this algebraic query on relation fragments, by substituting for each distributed relation an algebraic query corresponding to its fragmentation rules.

Many algebraic queries may be equivalent to the same input query. The queries produced with the naive approach are inefficient in general, since important simplifications and optimizations have been missed. Therefore, a generic query expression is restructured using a few transformation rules and heuristics. The rules enable separation of unary operations, grouping of unary operations on the same relation, commuting of unary operations with binary operations, and permutation of the binary operations. Examples of heuristics are to push selections down the tree and do projection as early as possible. In addition to the transformation rules, data localization uses reduction rules to simplify the query further, and therefore optimize it. Two main types of rules may be used. The first one avoids the production of empty relations which are generated by contradicting predicates on the same relation(s). The second type of rule determines which fragments yield useless attributes.

The query produced by the query decomposition and data localization layers is good in the sense that the worse executions are avoided. However, the subsequent layers usually perform important optimizations, as they add to the query increasing detail about the processing environment. In particular, quantitative information regarding fragments has not yet been exploited. This information will be used by the query optimization layer for selecting an "optimal" strategy to execute the query. Query optimization is the subject of Chapter 9.

8.4 BIBLIOGRAPHIC NOTES

Traditional techniques for query decomposition are surveyed in [Jarke and Koch, 1984], [Gardarin and Valduriez, 1989]. Techniques for semantic analysis and simplification of queries have their origins in citerh80. The notion of query graph or connection graph is introduced in [Ullman, 1982]. The notion of query tree, which we called operator tree in this chapter, and the transformation rules to manipulate algebraic expressions have been introduced in [Smith and Chang, 1975] and developed in [Ullman, 1982]. Proofs of completeness and correctness of the rules are given in the latter reference.

Data localization is treated in detail in [Ceri and Pelagatti, 1983] for horizontally partitioned relations which are referred to as multirelations. In particular, an algebra of qualified relations is defined as an extension of relation algebra, where a qualified relation is a relation name and the qualification of the fragment. Proofs of correctness and completeness of equivalence transformations between expressions of algebra of qualified relations are also given. The formal properties of horizontal and vertical fragmentation are used in [Ceri et al., 1986] to characterize distributed joins over fragmented relations.

8.5 EXERCISES

8.1 Simplify the following query, expressed in SQL, on our example database using idempotency rules:

```
SELECT    ENO
FROM      ASG
WHERE     RESP = ''Analyst''
AND       NOT(PNO=''P2'' OR DUR=12)
AND       PNO ≠ ''P2''
AND       DUR=12
```

8.2 Give the query graph of the following query, expressed in SQL, on our example database:

```
SELECT    ENAME, PNAME
FROM      EMP, ASG, PROJ
WHERE     DUR > 12
AND       EMP.ENO = ASG.ENO
```

and map it into an operator tree.

*8.3 Simplify the following query:

```
SELECT    ENAME, PNAME
FROM      EMP, ASG, PROJ
WHERE     DUR > 12
AND       EMP.ENO = ASG.ENO
AND       (TITLE = ''Elect. Eng.''
OR        ASG.PNO < ''P3'')
AND       ASG.PNO = PROJ.PNO
```

and transform it into an optimized operator tree using the restructuring algorithm.

*8.4 Transform the operator tree of Figure 8.5 back to the tree of Figure 8.3 using the restructuring algorithm. Describe each intermediate tree and show which rule the transformation is based on.

**8.5 Consider the following query on our Engineering database:

```
SELECT   ENAME,SAL
FROM     EMP,PROJ,ASG,PAY
WHERE    EMP.ENO = ASG.ENO
AND      EMP.TITLE = PAY.TITLE
AND      (BUDGET>200000 OR DUR>24)
AND      ASG.PNO = PROJ.PNO
```

Compose the selection predicate corresponding to the WHERE-clause and transform it, using the idempotency rules, into the simplest equivalent form. Furthermore, compose an operator tree corresponding to the query and transform it, using relational algebra transformation rules, to a form that is optimal with respect to total execution time, by considering only the selectivity factors of operations.

8.6 Assume that relation PROJ of the sample database is horizontally fragmented in

$$PROJ_1 \quad = \quad \sigma_{PNO \leq \text{``P2''}}(PROJ)$$
$$PROJ_2 \quad = \quad \sigma_{PNO > \text{``P2''}}(PROJ)$$

Transform the following query into a reduced query on fragments:

```
SELECT   BUDGET
FROM     PROJ,ASG
WHERE    PROJ.PNO = ASG.PNO
AND      ASG.PNO = ''P4''
```

*8.7 Assume that relation PROJ is horizontally fragmented as in Exercise 8.6, and that relation ASG is horizontally fragmented as

$$ASG_1 \quad = \quad \sigma_{PNO \leq \text{``P2''}}(ASG)$$
$$ASG_2 \quad = \quad \sigma_{\text{``P2''} < PNO \leq \text{``P3''}}(ASG)$$
$$ASG_3 \quad = \quad \sigma_{PNO > \text{``P3''}}(ASG)$$

Transform the following query into a reduced query on fragments, and determine whether it is better than the generic query:

```
SELECT   RESP, BUDGET
FROM     ASG, PROJ
WHERE    ASG.PNO = PROJ.PNO
AND      PNAME = ''CAD/CAM''
```

**8.8   Assume that relation PROJ is fragmented as in Exercise 8.6. Furthermore, relation ASG is indirectly fragmented as

$$ASG_1 \quad = \quad ASG \ltimes_{PNO} PROJ_1$$
$$ASG_2 \quad = \quad ASG \ltimes_{PNO} PROJ_2$$

and relation EMP is vertically fragmented as

$$EMP_1 \quad = \quad \Pi_{ENO,ENAME}(EMP)$$
$$EMP_2 \quad = \quad \Pi_{ENO,TITLE}(EMP)$$

Transform the following query into a reduced query on fragments:

```
SELECT   ENAME
FROM     EMP,ASG,PROJ
WHERE    PROJ.PNO = ASG.PNO
AND      PNAME = ''Instrumentation ''
AND      EMP.ENO = ASG.ENO
```

Chapter 9

OPTIMIZATION OF DISTRIBUTED QUERIES

Chapter 8 shows how a calculus query expressed on distributed relations can be mapped into a query on relation fragments by decomposition and data localization. This mapping uses the fragment schema. During this process, the application of transformation rules permits the simplification of the query by eliminating common subexpressions and useless expressions. This type of optimization is independent of fragment characteristics such as cardinalities. The query resulting from decomposition and localization can be executed in that form simply by adding communication primitives in a systematic way. However, the permutation of the ordering of operations within the query can provide many equivalent strategies to execute it. Finding an "optimal" ordering of operations for a given query is the main role of the query optimization layer, or *optimizer* for short.

Selecting the optimal execution strategy for a query is NP-hard in the number of relations [Ibaraki and Kameda, 1984]. For complex queries with many relations, this can incur a prohibitive optimization cost. Therefore, the actual objective of the optimizer is to find a strategy close to optimal and, perhaps more important, to avoid bad strategies. In this chapter we refer to the strategy (or operation ordering) produced by the optimizer as the *optimal strategy* (or *optimal ordering*). The output of the optimizer is an optimized *query execution plan* consisting of the algebraic query specified on fragments and the communication operations to support the execution of the query over the fragment sites.

The selection of the optimal strategy generally requires the prediction of execution costs of the alternative candidate orderings prior to actually executing the query. The execution cost is expressed as a weighted combination of I/O, CPU, and communication costs. A typical simplification of the earlier distributed query optimizers was to ignore local processing cost (I/O and CPU costs) by assuming that the communication cost is dominant. Important inputs to the optimizer for estimating execution costs are fragment statistics and formulas for estimating the cardinalities of results of relational operations. In this chapter we focus mostly on the ordering of join operations for two reasons; it is a well-understood problem, and queries involving joins, selections, and projections are usually considered to be the most frequent type. Furthermore, it is easier to generalize the basic algorithm for other binary operations, such as unions. We also discuss how semijoin operations can help to process a join efficiently.

This chapter is organized as follows. In Section 9.1 we introduce the main components of query optimization, including the search space, the search strategy and the cost model. Centralized query optimization is described in Section 9.2 as a prerequisite to understand distributed query optimization, which is more complex. In Section 9.3 we discuss the major optimization issue, which deals with the join ordering in fragment queries. We also examine alternative join strategies based on semijoin. In Section 9.4 we illustrate the use of the techniques and concepts in three basic distributed query optimization algorithms.

9.1 QUERY OPTIMIZATION

This section introduces query optimization in general, i.e., independent of whether the environment is centralized or distributed. The input query is supposed to be expressed in relational algebra on database relations (which can obviously be fragments) after query rewriting from a calculus expression.

Query optimization refers to the process of producing a query execution plan (QEP) which represents an execution strategy for the query. The selected plan minimizes an objective cost function. A query optimizer, the software module that performs query optimization, is usually seen as three components: a search space, a cost model, and a search strategy (see Figure 9.1). The *search space* is the set of alternative execution plans to represent the input query. These plans are equivalent, in the sense that they yield the same result but they differ on the execution order of operations and the way these operations are implemented, and therefore on performance. The search space is obtained by applying transformation rules, such as those for relational algebra described in Section 8.1.4. The *cost model* predicts the cost of a given execution plan. To be accurate, the cost model must have good knowledge about the distributed execution environment. The *search strategy* explores the search space and selects the best plan, using the cost model. It defines which plans are examined and in which order. The details of the environment (centralized versus distributed) are captured by the search space and the cost model.

9.1.1 Search Space

Query execution plans are typically abstracted by means of operator trees (see Section 8.1.4), which define the order in which the operations are executed. They are enriched with additional information, such as the best algorithm chosen for each operation. For a given query, the search space can thus be defined as the set of equivalent operator trees that can be produced using transformation rules. To characterize query optimizers, it is useful to concentrate on *join trees*, operator trees whose operators are join or Cartesian product. This is because permutations of the join order have the most important effect on performance of relational queries.

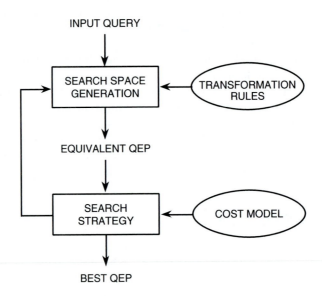

Figure 9.1. Query Optimization Process

Example 9.1

Consider the following query:

```
SELECT   ENAME, RESP
FROM     EMP, ASG, PROJ
WHERE    EMP.ENO=ASG.ENO
AND      ASG.PNO=PROJ.PNO
```

Figure 9.2 illustrates three equivalent join trees for that query, which are obtained by exploiting the associativity of binary operators. Each of these join trees can be assigned a cost based on the estimated cost of each operator. Join tree (c) which starts with a Cartesian product may have a much higher cost than the other join trees.

For a complex query (involving many relations and many operators), the number of equivalent operator trees can be very high. For instance, the number of alternative join trees that can be produced by applying the commutativity and associativity rules is $O(N!)$ for N relations. Investigating a large search space may make optimization time prohibitive, sometimes much more expensive than the ac-

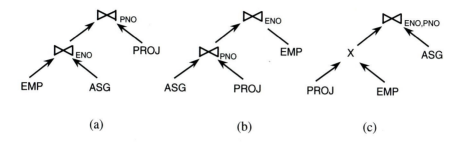

Figure 9.2. Equivalent Join Trees

tual execution time. Therefore, query optimizers typically restrict the size of the search space they consider. The first restriction is to use heuristics. The most common heuristic is to perform selection and projection when accessing base relations. Another common heuristic is to avoid Cartesian products that are not required by the query. For instance, in Figure 9.2, operator tree (c) would not be part of the search space considered by the optimizer.

Another important restriction is with respect to the shape of the join tree. Two kinds of join trees are usually distinguished: linear versus bushy trees (see Figure 9.3). A *linear tree* is a tree such that at least one operand of each operator node is a base relation. A *bushy tree* is more general and may have operators with no base relations as operands (i.e., both operands are intermediate relations). By considering only linear trees, the size of the search space is reduced to $O(2^N)$. However, in a distributed environment, bushy trees are useful in exhibiting parallelism.

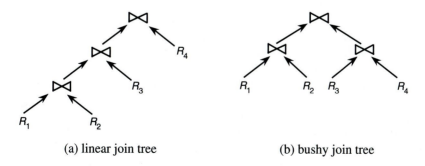

(a) linear join tree   (b) bushy join tree

Figure 9.3. The Two Major Shapes of Join Trees

9.1.2 Search Strategy

The most popular search strategy used by query optimizers is *dynamic programming*, which is *deterministic*. Deterministic strategies proceed by *building* plans, starting from base relations, joining one more relation at each step until complete plans are obtained, as in Figure 9.4. Dynamic programming builds all possible plans, breadth-first, before it chooses the "best" plan. To reduce the optimization cost, partial plans that are not likely to lead to the optimal plan are *pruned* (i.e., discarded) as soon as possible. By contrast, another deterministic strategy, the greedy algorithm, builds only one plan, depth-first.

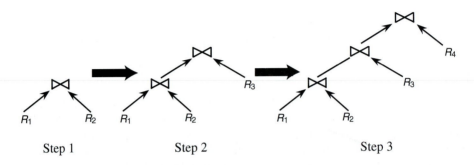

Figure 9.4. Optimizer Actions in a Deterministic Strategy

Dynamic programming is almost exhaustive and assures that the "best" of all plans is found. It incurs an acceptable optimization cost (in terms of time and space) when the number of relations in the query is small. However, this approach becomes too expensive when the number of relations is greater than 5 or 6. For this reason, there has been recent interest in *randomized* strategies, which reduce the optimization complexity but do not guarantee the best of all plans. Unlike deterministic strategies, *randomized* strategies allow the optimizer to trade optimization time for execution time [Lanzelotte et al., 1993].

Randomized strategies, such as Iterative Improvement [Swami, 1989] and Simulated Annealing [Ioannidis and Wong, 1987] concentrate on searching the optimal solution around some particular points. They do not guarantee that the best solution is obtained, but avoid the high cost of optimization, in terms of memory and time consumption. First, one or more *start* plans are built by a greedy strategy. Then, the algorithm tries to improve the start plan by visiting its *neighbors*. A neighbor is obtained by applying a random *transformation* to a plan. An example of a typical transformation consists in exchanging two randomly chosen operand relations of the plan, as in Figure 9.5. In [Lanzelotte et al., 1993], it is shown experimentally that randomized strategies provide better performance than deterministic strategies as soon as the query involves more than several relations.

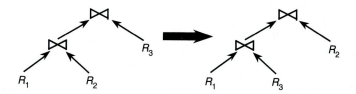

Figure 9.5. Optimizer Action in a Randomized Strategy

9.1.3   Distributed Cost Model

An optimizer's cost model includes cost functions to predict the cost of operators, statistics and base data and formulas to evaluate the sizes of intermediate results.

Cost Functions

The cost of a distributed execution strategy can be expressed with respect to either the total time or the response time. The total time is the sum of all time (also referred to as cost) components, while the response time is the elapsed time from the initiation to the completion of the query. A general formula for determining the total time can be specified as follows [Lohman et al., 1985]:

$$Total\_time = T_{CPU} * \#insts + T_{I/O} * \#I/Os + T_{MSG} * \#msgs + T_{TR} * \#bytes$$

The two first components measure the local processing time, where T_{CPU} is the time of a CPU instruction and $T_{I/O}$ is the time of a disk I/O. The communication time is depicted by the two last components. T_{MSG} is the fixed time of initiating and receiving a message, while T_{TR} is the time it takes to transmit a data unit from one site to another. The data unit is given here in terms of bytes (*#bytes* is the sum of the sizes of all messages), but could be in different units (e.g., packets). A typical assumption is that T_{TR} is constant. This might not be true for wide area networks, where some sites are farther away than others. However, this assumption greatly simplifies query optimization. Thus the communication time of transferring *#bytes* of data from one site to another is assumed to be a linear function of *#bytes*:

$$CT(\#bytes) = T_{MSG} + T_{TR} * \#bytes$$

Costs are generally expressed in terms of time units, which in turn, can be translated into other units (e.g., dollars).

The relative values of the cost coefficients characterize the distributed database environment. The topology of the network greatly influences the ratio between these components. In a wide area network such as the Internet, the communication time is generally the dominant factor. In local area networks, however, there is more of a balance among the components. Earlier studies cite ratios of communication time to I/O time for one page to be on the order of 20:1 for wide area networks [Selinger and Adiba, 1980] while it is 1:1.6 for a typical (10Mbps) Ethernet [Page and Popek, 1985]. Thus, most early distributed DBMSs designed for wide area networks have ignored the local processing cost and concentrate on minimizing the communication cost. Distributed DBMSs designed for local area networks, on the other hand, consider all three cost components. The new faster networks, both at the wide area network and at the local area network levels, have improved the above ratios in favor of communication cost when all things are equal. However, communication is still the dominant time factor in wide area networks such as the Internet because of the longer distances that data is retrieved from (or shipped to).

When the response time of the query is the objective function of the optimizer, parallel local processing and parallel communications must also be considered [Khoshafian and Valduriez, 1987]. A general formula for response time is

$$Response\_time = T_{CPU} * seq\_\#insts + T_{I/O} * seq\_\#I/Os$$
$$+ \ T_{MSG} * seq\_\#msgs + T_{TR} * seq\_\#bytes$$

where $seq\_\#x$, in which x can be instructions ($insts$), I/O, messages ($msgs$) or $bytes$, is the maximum number of x which must be done sequentially for the execution of the query. Thus any processing and communication done in parallel is ignored.

Example 9.2

Let us illustrate the difference between total cost and response time using the example of Figure 9.6, which computes the answer to a query at site 3 with data from sites 1 and 2. For simplicity, we assume that only communication cost is considered.

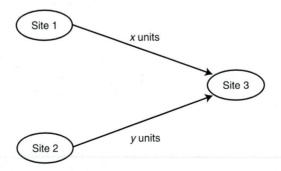

Figure 9.6. Example of Data Transfers for a Query

Assume that T_{MSG} and T_{TR} are expressed in time units. The total cost of transferring x data units from site 1 to site 3 and y data units from site 2 to site 3 is

$$Total\_time = 2\,T_{MSG} + T_{TR} * (x + y)$$

The response time of the same query can be approximated as

$$Response\_time = max\{T_{MSG} + T_{TR} * x, T_{MSG} + T_{TR} * y\}$$

since the transfers can be done in parallel.

Minimizing response time is achieved by increasing the degree of parallel execution. This does not, however, imply that the total time is also minimized. On the contrary, it can increase the total time, for example, by having more parallel local processing and transmissions. Minimizing the total time implies that the utilization of the resources improves, thus increasing the system throughput. In practice, a compromise between the two is desired. In Section 9.4 we present algorithms that can optimize a combination of total time and response time, with more weight on one of them.

Database Statistics

The main factor affecting the performance of an execution strategy is the size of the intermediate relations that are produced during the execution. When a subsequent operation is located at a different site, the intermediate relation must be transmitted over the network. Therefore, it is of prime interest to estimate the size of the intermediate results of relational algebra operations in order to minimize the size of data transfers. This estimation is based on statistical information about the base relations and formulas to predict the cardinalities of the results of the relational operations. There is a direct trade-off between the precision of the statistics and the cost of managing them, the more precise statistics being the more costly [Piatetsky and Connell, 1984]. For a relation R defined over the attributes $A = \{A_1,\ A_2,\ \dots,\ A_n\}$ and fragmented as $R_1,\ R_2,\ \dots,\ R_r$, the statistical data typically are the following:

1. For each attribute A_i, its length (in number of bytes), denoted by $length(A_i)$, and for each attribute A_i of each fragment R_j, the number of distinct values of A_i, with the cardinality of the projection of fragment R_j on A_i, denoted by $card(\Pi_{A_i}(R_j))$.

2. For the domain of each attribute A_i, which is defined on a set of values that can be ordered (e.g., integers or reals), the minimum and maximum possible values, denoted by $min(A_i)$ and $max(A_i)$.

3. For the domain of each attribute A_i, the cardinality of the domain of A_i, denoted by $card(dom[A_i])$. This value gives the number of unique values in the $dom[A_i]$.

4. The number of tuples in each fragment R_j, denoted by $card(R_j)$.

Sometimes, the statistical data also include the join selectivity factor for some pairs of relations, that is the proportion of tuples participating in the join. The *join selectivity factor*, denoted SF_J, of relations R and S is a real value between 0 and 1:

$$SF_J(R, S) = \frac{card(R \bowtie S)}{card(R) * card(S)}$$

For example, a join selectivity factor of 0.5 corresponds to a very large joined relation, while 0.001 corresponds to a small one. We say that the join has bad selectivity in the former case and good selectivity in the latter case.

These statistics are useful to predict the size of intermediate relations. Remember that in Chapter 5 we defined the size of an intermediate relation R as follows:

$$size(R) = card(R) * length(R)$$

where $length(R)$ is the length (in bytes) of a tuple of R, computed from the lengths of its attributes. The estimation of $card(R)$, the number of tuples in R, requires the use of the formulas given in the following section.

Cardinalities of Intermediate Results

Database statistics are useful in evaluating the cardinalities of the intermediate results of queries. Two simplifying assumptions are commonly made about the database. The distribution of attribute values in a relation is supposed to be uniform, and all attributes are independent, meaning that the value of an attribute does not affect the value of any other attribute. These two assumptions are often wrong in practice, but they make the problem tractable. In what follows we give the formulas for estimating the cardinalities of the results of the basic relational algebra operations (selection, projection, Cartesian product, join, semijoin, union, and difference). The operand relations are denoted by R and S. The *selectivity factor* of an operation, that is, the proportion of tuples of an operand relation that participate in the result of that operation, is denoted SF_{OP}, where OP denotes the operation.

Selection.   The cardinality of selection is

$$card(\sigma_F(R)) = SF_S(F) * card(R)$$

where $SF_S(F)$ is dependent on the selection formula and can be computed as follows [Selinger et al., 1979], where $p(A_i)$ and $p(A_j)$ indicate predicates over attributes A_i and A_j, respectively:

$$SF_S(A = value) \ = \ \frac{1}{card(\Pi_A(R))}$$

$$SF_S(A > value) \ = \ \frac{max(A) - value}{max(A) - min(A)}$$

$$SF_S(A < value) \ = \ \frac{value - min(A)}{max(A) - min(A)}$$

$$SF_S(p(A_i) \wedge p(A_j)) \ = \ SF_S(p(A_i)) * SF_S(p(A_j))$$

$$SF_S(p(A_i) \vee p(A_j)) \ = \ SF_S(p(A_i)) + SF_S(p(A_j)) - (SF_S(p(A_i)) * SF_S(p(A_j)))$$

$$SF_S(A \in \{values\}) \ = \ SF_S(A = value) * card(\{values\})$$

Projection.   As indicated in Chapter 2, projection can be with or without duplicate elimination. We consider projection with duplicate elimination. An arbitrary projection is difficult to evaluate precisely because the correlations between projected attributes are usually unknown [Gelenbe and Gardy, 1982]. However, there are two particularly useful cases where it is trivial. If the projection of relation R is based on a single attribute A, the cardinality is simply the number of tuples when the projection is performed. If one of the projected attributes is a key of R, then

$$card(\Pi_A(R)) = card(R)$$

Cartesian product.   The cardinality of the Cartesian product of R and S is simply

$$card(R \times S) = card(R) * card(S)$$

Join.   There is no general way to estimate the cardinality of a join without additional information. The upper bound of the join cardinality is the cardinality of the Cartesian product. Some systems, such as Distributed INGRES [Epstein et al., 1978], use this upper bound, which is quite pessimistic. R* [Selinger and Adiba, 1980] uses this upper bound divided by a constant to reflect the fact that the join result is smaller than that of the Cartesian product. However, there is a case, which occurs frequently, where the estimation is simple. If relation R is equijoined with S over attribute A from R, and B from S, where A is a key of relation R, and B is a foreign key of relation S, the cardinality of the result can be approximated as

$$card(R \bowtie_{A=B} S) = card(S)$$

because each tuple of S matches with at most one tuple of R. Obviously, the same thing is true if B is a key of S and A is a foreign key of R. However, this estimation is an upper bound since it assumes that each tuple of R participates in the join. For other important joins, it is worthwhile to maintain their join selectivity factor SF_J as part of statistical information. In that case the result cardinality is simply

$$card(R \bowtie S) = SF_J * card(R) * card(S)$$

Semijoin.   The selectivity factor of the semijoin of R by S gives the fraction (percentage) of tuples of R that join with tuples of S. An approximation for the semijoin selectivity factor is given in [Hevner and Yao, 1979] as

$$SF_{SJ}(R \ltimes_A S) = \frac{card(\Pi_A(S))}{card(dom[A])}$$

This formula depends only on attribute A of S. Thus it is often called the selectivity factor of attribute A of S, denoted $SF_{SJ}(S.A)$, and is the selectivity factor of $S.A$ on any other joinable attribute. Therefore, the cardinality of the semijoin is given by

$$card(R \ltimes_A S) = SF_{SJ}(S.A) * card(R)$$

This approximation can be verified on a very frequent case, that of $R.A$ being a foreign key of S ($S.A$ is a primary key). In this case, the semijoin selectivity factor is 1 since $\Pi_A(S)) = card(dom[A])$ yielding that the cardinality of the semijoin is $card(R)$.

Union.   It is quite difficult to estimate the cardinality of the union of R and S because the duplicates between R and S are removed by the union. We give only the simple formulas for the upper and lower bounds, which are, respectively,

$$card(R) + card(S)$$
$$max\{card(R), card(S)\}$$

Note that these formulas assume that R and S do not contain duplicate tuples.

Difference.   Like the union, we give only the upper and lower bounds. The upper bound of $card(R - S)$ is $card(R)$, whereas the lower bound is 0.

9.2 CENTRALIZED QUERY OPTIMIZATION

In this section we present two of the most popular query optimization techniques for centralized systems. This presentation is a prerequisite to understanding distributed query optimization for three reasons. First, a distributed query is translated into local queries, each of which is processed in a centralized way. Second, distributed query optimization techniques are often extensions of the techniques for centralized systems. Finally, centralized query optimization is a simpler problem; the minimization of communication costs makes distributed query optimization more complex. Since we discussed in Chapter 8 some common techniques for query decomposition, we will concentrate on the optimization aspects used by two popular relational database systems: INGRES [Stonebraker et al., 1976] and System R [Astrahan et al., 1979]. Furthermore, both systems have distributed versions (see Section 9.4) whose optimization algorithms are extensions of the centralized version.

The optimization techniques of these systems differ significantly (see [Gardarin and Valduriez, 1989] for more details). INGRES employs a dynamic optimization algorithm and System R uses a static optimization algorithm based on exhaustive search using statistics about the database. We note that most commercial relational DBMSs (see [Valduriez and Gardarin, 1989] for a survey) implement variants of the exhaustive search approach for its efficiency and compatibility with query compilation.

9.2.1 INGRES Algorithm

INGRES uses a dynamic query optimization algorithm [Wong and Youssefi, 1976] that recursively breaks up a calculus query into smaller pieces. It combines the two phases of calculus-algebra decomposition and optimization. A query is first decomposed into a sequence of queries having a unique relation (more precisely a unique tuple variable) in common. Then each monorelation query is processed by a "one-variable query processor" (OVQP). The OVQP optimizes the access to a single relation by selecting, based on the predicate, the best access method to that relation (e.g., index, sequential scan). For example, if the predicate is of the form $< A = value >$, an index available on attribute A would be used. However, if the predicate is of the form $< A \neq value >$, an index on A would not help, and sequential scan should be used.

We concentrate our presentation on the main query type, which is the "retrieve" command of the QUEL language [Stonebraker et al., 1976], which is used by INGRES and is similar to the "select" command of SQL. However, to maintain uniformity throughout the book, we use SQL to express our examples. The algorithm executes first the unary (monorelation) operations and tries to minimize the sizes of intermediate results in ordering binary (multirelation) operations.

Let us denote by $q_{i-1} \rightarrow q_i$ a query q decomposed into two subqueries, q_{i-1} and q_i, where q_{i-1} is executed first and its result is consumed by q_i. Given an n-relation query q, the INGRES query processor decomposes q into n subqueries $q_1 \rightarrow q_2 \rightarrow \cdots \rightarrow q_n$. This decomposition uses two basic techniques: *detachment* and *substitution*. These techniques are presented and illustrated in the rest of this section.

Detachment is the first technique employed by the query processor. It breaks a query q into $q' \rightarrow q''$, based on a common relation that is the result of q'. If the query q expressed in SQL is of the form

```
SELECT    R_2.A_2, R_3.A_3, ..., R_n.A_n
FROM      R_1, R_2, ..., R_n
WHERE     P_1(R_1.A'_1)
AND       P_2(R_1.A_1, R_2.A_2, ..., R_n.A_n)
```

where A_i and A'_i are lists of attributes of relation R_i, P_1 is a predicate involving attributes from relation R_1, and P_2 is a multirelation predicate involving attributes of relations $R_1, R_2, \ldots, R_n$. Such a query may be decomposed into two subqueries, q' followed by q'', by detachment of the common relation R_1:

```
q' :  SELECT    R_1.A_1 INTO R'_1
      FROM      R_1
      WHERE     P_1(R_1.A'_1)
```

where R'_1 is a temporary relation containing the information necessary for the continuation of the query:

```
q'' :  SELECT    R_2.A_2, ..., R_n.A_n
       FROM      R'_1, R_2, ..., R_n
       WHERE     P_2(V_1.A_1, ..., V_n.A_n)
```

This step has the effect of reducing the size of the relation on which the query q'' is defined. Furthermore, the created relation R'_1 may be stored in a particular structure to speed up the following subqueries. For example, the storage of R'_1 in a hashed file on the join attributes of q'' will make processing the join more efficient. Detachment extracts the select operations, which are usually the most selective ones. Therefore, detachment is systematically done whenever possible. Note that this can have adverse effects on performance if the selection has bad selectivity.

Example 9.3

To illustrate the detachment technique, we apply it to the following query:

"Names of employees working on the CAD/CAM project"

This query can be expressed in SQL by the following query q_1 on the engineering database of Chapter 2:

```
q₁:   SELECT   EMP.ENAME
      FROM     EMP, ASG, PROJ
      WHERE    EMP.ENO=ASG.ENO
      AND      ASG.PNO=PROJ.PNO
      AND      PNAME=''CAD/CAM''
```

After detachment of the selections, query q_1 is replaced by q_{11} followed by q', where JVAR is an intermediate relation.

```
q₁₁:  SELECT   PROJ.PNO INTO JVAR
      FROM     PROJ
      WHERE    PNAME=''CAD/CAM''

q':   SELECT   EMP.ENAME
      FROM     EMP, ASG, JVAR
      WHERE    EMP.ENO=ASG.ENO
      AND      ASG.PNO=JVAR.PNO
```

The successive detachments of q' may generate

```
q₁₂:  SELECT   ASG.ENO INTO GVAR
      FROM     ASG, JVAR
      WHERE    ASG.PNO=JVAR.PNO

q₁₃:  SELECT   EMP.ENAME
      FROM     EMP, GVAR
      WHERE    EMP.ENO=GVAR.ENO
```

Note that other subqueries are also possible.

Thus query q_1 has been reduced to the subsequent queries $q_{11} \rightarrow q_{12} \rightarrow q_{13}$. Query q_{11} is monorelation and can be performed by the OVQP. However, q_{12} and q_{13} are not monorelation and cannot be reduced by detachment.

Multirelation queries, which cannot be further detached (e.g., q_{12} and q_{13}), are *irreducible*. A query is irreducible if and only if its query graph is a chain with two nodes or a cycle with k nodes where $k > 2$. Irreducible queries are converted into monorelation queries by tuple substitution. Given an n-relation query q, the tuples of one variable are substituted by their values, thereby producing a set of $(n-1)$-variable queries. Tuple substitution proceeds as follows. First, one relation in q is chosen for tuple substitution. Let R_1 be that relation. Then for each tuple

t_{1i} in R_1, the attributes referred to by in q are replaced by their actual values in t_{1i}, thereby generating a query q' with $n-1$ relations. Therefore, the total number of queries q' produced by tuple substitution is $card(R_1)$. Tuple substitution can be summarized as follows:

$$q(R_1, R_2, \ldots, R_n) \text{ is replaced by } \{q'(t_{1i}, R_2, R_3, \ldots, R_n), t_{1i} \in R_1\}$$

For each tuple thus obtained, the subquery is recursively processed by substitution if it is not yet irreducible.

Example 9.4

Let us consider the query q_{13}:

```
SELECT     EMP.ENAME
FROM       EMP, GVAR
WHERE      EMP.ENO=GVAR.ENO
```

The relation defined by the variable GVAR is over a single attribute (ENO). Assume that it contains only two tuples: <E1> and <E2>. The substitution of GVAR generates two one-relation subqueries:

```
q131:   SELECT     EMP.ENAME
        FROM       EMP
        WHERE      EMP.ENO=''E1''

q132:   SELECT     EMP.ENAME
        FROM       EMP
        WHERE      EMP.ENO=''E2''
```

These queries may then be processed by the OVQP.

The query optimization algorithm of INGRES (called INGRES-QOA) is depicted in Algorithm 9.1. The algorithm works recursively until there remain no more monorelation queries to be processed. It consists of applying the selections and projections as soon as possible by detachment. The results of the monorelation queries are stored in data structures that are capable of optimizing the later queries (such as joins) and will be used by the OVQP. The irreducible queries that remain after detachment must be processed by tuple substitution. For the irreducible query, denoted by MRQ', the smallest relation whose cardinality is known from the result of the preceding query is chosen for substitution. This simple method enables one to generate the smallest number of subqueries. Monorelation queries generated by the reduction algorithm are processed by the OVQP that chooses the best existing access path to the relation, according to the query qualification.

Algorithm 9.1 *INGRES-QOA*

    input: *MRQ*:   multirelation query with n relations
    output: *output*:   result of execution
    begin
      output $\leftarrow \phi$
      if $n = 1$ **then**
         output $\leftarrow run(MRQ)$ {execute the one relation query}
      else begin
         {detach *MRQ* into m one-relation queries and one multirelation query}
         $OVQ_1, \ldots, OVQ_m, MRQ' \leftarrow MRQ$
         for $i \leftarrow 1$ **to** m **do**
         begin
            output' $\leftarrow run(OVQ_i)$ {execute OVQ_i}
            output $\leftarrow output \cup output'$ {merge all results}
         end-for
         $V \leftarrow$ CHOOSE_VARIABLE(MRQ') {R chosen for tuple substitution}
         for each tuple $t \in R$ **do**
         begin
            $MRQ'' \leftarrow$ substitute values for t in MRQ'
            output' $\leftarrow$ INGRES-QOA(MRQ'') {recursive call}
            output $\leftarrow output \cup output'$ {merge all results}
         end-for
      end-if
    end. { INGRES-QOA }

9.2.2 System R Algorithm

System R performs static query optimization based on the exhaustive search of the solution space [Selinger et al., 1979]. The input to the optimizer of System R is a relational algebra tree resulting from the decomposition of an SQL query. The output is an execution plan that implements the "optimal" relational algebra tree.

    Instead of systematically executing the select operations before the joins as in INGRES, System R does so only if this leads to a better strategy. The optimizer assigns a cost (in terms of time) to every candidate tree and retains the one with the smallest cost. The candidate trees are obtained by a permutation of the join orders of the n relations of the query using the commutativity and associativity rules. To limit the overhead of optimization, the number of alternative trees is reduced using dynamic programming. The set of alternative strategies is constructed dynamically so that, when two joins are equivalent by commutativity, only the cheapest one is kept. Furthermore, the strategies that include Cartesian products are eliminated whenever possible.

The cost of a candidate strategy is a weighted combination of I/O and CPU costs (times). The estimation of such costs (at compile time) is based on a cost model that provides a cost formula for each low-level operation (e.g., select using a B-tree index with a range predicate). For most operations (except exact match select), these cost formulas are based on the cardinalities of the operands. The cardinality information for the relations stored in the database is found in the database statistics, automatically managed by System R. The cardinality of the intermediate results is estimated based on the operation selectivity factors (see Section 9.1.3).

The optimization algorithm consists of two major steps. First, the best access method to each individual relation based on a select predicate is predicted (this is the one with least cost). Second, for each relation R, the best join ordering is estimated, where R is first accessed using its best single-relation access method. The cheapest ordering becomes the basis for the best execution plan.

In considering the joins, there are two algorithms available, with one of them being optimal in a given context. For the join of two relations, the relation whose tuples are read first is called the *external*, while the other, whose tuples are found according to the values obtained from the external relation, is called the *internal relation*. An important decision with either join method is to determine the cheapest access path to the internal relation.

The first method, called *nested loops*, composes the product of the two relations. For each tuple of the external relation, the tuples of the internal relation that satisfy the join predicate are retrieved one by one to form the resulting relation. An index on the join attribute is a very efficient access path for the internal relation. In the absence of an index, for relations of n_1 and n_2 pages, respectively, this algorithm has a cost proportional to $n_1 * n_2$, which may be prohibitive if n_1 and n_2 are high.

The second method, called *merge join*, consists of merging two sorted relations on the join attribute. Indices on the join attribute may be used as access paths. If the join criterion is equality, the cost of joining two relations of n_1 and n_2 pages, respectively, is proportional to $n_1 + n_2$. Therefore, this method is always chosen when there is an equijoin, and when the relations are previously sorted. If only one or neither of the relations are sorted, the cost of the nested loop algorithm is to be compared with the combined cost of the merge join and of the sorting. The cost of sorting n pages is proportional to $n \log n$. In general, it is useful to sort and apply the merge join algorithm when large relations are considered.

The simplified version of the System R optimization algorithm, for a select-project-join query, is shown in Algorithm 9.2. It consists of two loops, the first of which selects the best single-relation access method to each relation in the query, while the second examines all possible permutations of join orders (there are $n!$ permutations with n relations) and selects the best access strategy for the query. The permutations are produced by the dynamic construction of a tree of alternative strategies. First, the join of each relation with every other relation is considered, followed by joins of three relations. This continues until joins of n relations are optimized. Actually, the algorithm does not generate all possible permutations since some of them are useless. As we discussed earlier, permutations involving

Cartesian products are eliminated, as are the commutatively equivalent strategies with the highest cost. With these two heuristics, the number of strategies examined has an upper bound of 2^n rather than $n!$.

Algorithm 9.2   *R-QOA*

> **input:** QT: query tree with n relations
> **output:** *output: the result of execution*
> **begin**
>   **for each** relation $R_i \in QT$ **do**
>   **begin**
>   **for each** access path AP_{ij} to R_i **do**
>   determine $\text{cost}(AP_{ij})$
>   **end-for**
>   *best_AP$_i$* $\leftarrow$ AP_{ij} with minimum cost
>   **end-for**
>   **for each** order $(R_{i1}, R_{i2}, \cdots, R_{in})$ with $i{=}1, \cdots, n!$ **do**
>   **begin**
>   build strategy $(\ldots((\text{ best } AP_{i1} \bowtie R_{i2}) \bowtie R_{i3}) \bowtie \ldots \bowtie R_{in})$
>   compute the cost of strategy
>   **end-for**
>   *output* $\leftarrow$ strategy with minimum cost
> **end.** { R-QOA }

Example 9.5

Let us illustrate this algorithm with the query q_1 (see Example 9.3) on the engineering database. The join graph of q_1 is given in Figure 9.7. For short, the label ENO on edge EMP–ASG stands for the predicate EMP.ENO=ASG.ENO and the label PNO on edge ASG–PROJ stands for the predicate ASG.PNO=PROJ.PNO. We assume the following indices:

> EMP has an index on ENO
> ASG has an index on PNO
> PROJ has an index on PNO and an index on PNAME

We assume that the first loop of the algorithm selects the following best single-relation access paths:

> EMP: sequential scan (because there is no selection on EMP)
> ASG: sequential scan (because there is no selection on ASG)
> PROJ: index on PNAME (because there is a selection on PROJ based on PNAME)

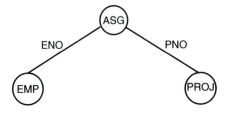

Figure 9.7. Join Graph of Query q_1

The dynamic construction of the tree of alternative strategies is illustrated in Figure 9.8. Note that the maximum number of join orders is 3!; dynamic search considers fewer alternatives, as depicted in Figure 9.8. The operations marked "pruned" are dynamically eliminated. The first level of the tree indicates the best single-relation access method. The second level indicates, for each of these, the best join method with any other relation. Strategies (EMP × PROJ) and (PROJ × EMP) are pruned because they are Cartesian products that can be avoided (by other strategies). We assume that (EMP ⋈ ASG) and (ASG ⋈ PROJ) have a cost higher than (ASG ⋈ EMP) and (PROJ ⋈ ASG), respectively. Thus they can be pruned because there are better join orders equivalent by commutativity. The two remaining possibilities are given at the third level of the tree. The best total join order is the least costly of ((ASG ⋈ EMP) ⋈ PROJ) and ((PROJ ⋈ ASG) ⋈ EMP). The latter is the only one that has a useful index on the select attribute and direct access to the joining tuples of ASG and EMP. Therefore, it is chosen with the following access methods:

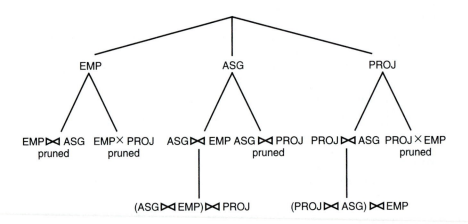

Figure 9.8. Alternative Join Orders

Select PROJ using index on PNAME

Then join with ASG using index on PNO

Then join with EMP using index on ENO

The performance measurement of System R [Mackert and Lohman, 1986] substantiates the important contribution of the CPU time to the total time of the query. The accuracy of the optimizer's estimations is generally good when the relations can be contained in the main memory buffers, but degrades as the relations increase in size and are written to disk. An important performance parameter that should also be considered for better predictions is buffer utilization.

9.3 JOIN ORDERING IN FRAGMENT QUERIES

As we have seen in Section 9.2, ordering joins is an important aspect of centralized query optimization. Join ordering in a distributed context is even more important since joins between fragments may increase the communication time. Two basic approaches exist to order joins in fragment queries. One tries to optimize the ordering of joins directly, whereas the other replaces joins by combinations of semijoins in order to minimize communication costs.

9.3.1 Join Ordering

Some algorithms optimize the ordering of joins directly without using semijoins. Distributed INGRES and R* algorithms are representative of algorithms that use joins rather than semijoins. The purpose of this section is to stress the difficulty that join ordering presents and to motivate the subsequent section, which deals with the use of semijoins to optimize join queries.

A number of assumptions are necessary to concentrate on the main issues. Since the query is localized and expressed on fragments, we do not need to distinguish between fragments of the same relation and fragments of different relations. To simplify notation, we use the term *relation* to designate a fragment stored at a particular site. Also, to concentrate on join ordering, we ignore local processing time, assuming that reducers (selection, projection) are executed locally either before or during the join (remember that doing selection first is not always efficient). Therefore, we consider only join queries whose operand relations are stored at different sites. We assume that relation transfers are done in a set-at-a-time mode rather than in a tuple-at-a-time mode. Finally, we ignore the transfer time for producing the data at a result site.

Let us first concentrate on the simpler problem of operand transfer in a single join. The query is $R \bowtie S$, where R and S are relations stored at different sites. The obvious choice of the relation to transfer is to send the smaller relation to

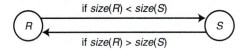

Figure 9.9. Transfer of Operands in Binary Operation

the site of the larger one, which gives rise to two possibilities, as shown in Figure 9.9. To make this choice we need to evaluate the size of R and of S. We now consider the case where there are more than two relations to join. As in the case of a single join, the objective of the join-ordering algorithm is to transmit smaller operands. The difficulty stems from the fact that the join operations may reduce or increase the size of the intermediate results. Thus, estimating the size of join results is mandatory, but also difficult. A solution is to estimate the communication costs of all alternative strategies and to choose the best one. However, the number of strategies grows rapidly with the number of relations. This approach, used by System R*, makes optimization costly, although this overhead is amortized rapidly if the query is executed frequently.

Example 9.6

Consider the following query expressed in relational algebra:

$$\text{PROJ} \bowtie_{\text{PNO}} \text{EMP} \bowtie_{\text{ENO}} \text{ASG}$$

whose join graph is given in Figure 9.10. Note that we have made certain assumptions about the locations of the three relations. This query can be executed in at least five different ways. We describe these strategies by the following programs, where (R → site j) stands for "relation R is transferred to site j."

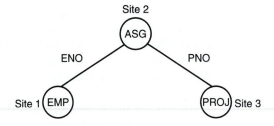

Figure 9.10. Join Graph of Distributed Query

1. EMP → site 2 Site 2 computes EMP′ = EMP ⋈ ASG EMP′ → site 3 Site 3 computes EMP′ ⋈ PROJ

2. ASG → site 1 Site 1 computes EMP′ = EMP ⋈ ASG EMP′ → site 3 Site 3 computes EMP′ ⋈ PROJ

3. ASG → site 3 Site 3 computes ASG′ = ASG ⋈ PROJ ASG′ → site 1 Site 1 computes ASG′ ⋈ EMP

4. PROJ → site 2 Site 2 computes PROJ′ = PROJ ⋈ ASG PROJ′ → site 1 Site 1 computes PROJ′ ⋈ EMP

5. EMP → site 2 PROJ → site 2 Site 2 computes EMP ⋈ PROJ ⋈ ASG

To select one of these programs, the following sizes must be known or predicted: $size$(EMP), $size$(ASG), $size$(PROJ), $size$(EMP ⋈ ASG), and $size$(ASG ⋈ PROJ). Furthermore, if it is the response time that is being considered, the optimization must take into account the fact that transfers can be done in parallel with strategy 5. An alternative to enumerating all the solutions is to use heuristics that consider only the sizes of the operand relations by assuming, for example, that the cardinality of the resulting join is the product of cardinalities. In this case, relations are ordered by increasing sizes and the order of execution is given by this ordering and the join graph. For instance, the order (EMP, ASG, PROJ) could use strategy 1, while the order (PROJ, ASG, EMP) could use strategy 4.

9.3.2 Semijoin Based Algorithms

In this section we show how the semijoin operation can be used to decrease the total time of join queries. The theory of semijoins is defined in [Bernstein and Chiu, 1981]. We are making the same assumptions as in Section 9.3.1. The main shortcoming of the join approach described in the preceding section is that entire operand relations must be transferred between sites. The semijoin acts as a size reducer for a relation much as a selection does.

The join of two relations R and S over attribute A, stored at sites 1 and 2, respectively, can be computed by replacing one or both operand relations by a semijoin with the other relation, using the following rules:

$$R \bowtie_A S \Leftrightarrow (R \ltimes_A S) \bowtie_A S$$
$$\Leftrightarrow R \bowtie_A (S \ltimes_A R)$$
$$\Leftrightarrow (R \ltimes_A S) \bowtie_A (S \ltimes_A R)$$

The choice between one of the three semijoin strategies requires estimating their respective costs.

The use of the semijoin is beneficial if the cost to produce and send it to the other site is less than the cost of sending the whole operand relation and of doing the actual join. To illustrate the potential benefit of the semijoin, let us compare the costs of the two alternatives: $R \bowtie_A S$ versus $(R \ltimes_A S) \bowtie_A S$, assuming that $size(R) < size(S)$.

The following program, using the notation of Section 9.3.1, uses the semijoin operation:

1. $\Pi_A(S) \rightarrow$ site 1

2. Site 1 computes $R' = R \ltimes_A S$

3. $R' \rightarrow$ site 2

4. Site 2 computes $R' \bowtie_A S$

For the sake of simplicity, let us ignore the constant T_{MSG} in the communication time assuming that the term $T_{TR} * size(R)$ is much larger. We can then compare the two alternatives in terms of the amount of transmitted data. The cost of the join-based algorithm is that of transferring relation R to site 2. The cost of the semijoin-based algorithm is the cost of steps 1 and 3 above. Therefore, the semijoin approach is better if

$$size(\Pi_A(S)) + size(R \ltimes_A S) < size(R)$$

The semijoin approach is better if the semijoin acts as a sufficient reducer, that is, if a few tuples of R participate in the join. The join approach is better if almost all tuples of R participate in the join, because the semijoin approach requires an additional transfer of a projection on the join attribute. The cost of the projection step can be minimized by encoding the result of the projection in bit arrays [Valduriez, 1982], thereby reducing the cost of transferring the joined attribute values. It is important to note that neither approach is systematically the best; they should be considered as complementary.

More generally, the semijoin can be useful in reducing the size of the operand relations involved in multiple join queries. However, query optimization becomes more complex in these cases. Consider again the join graph of relations EMP, ASG, and PROJ given in Figure 9.10. We can apply the previous join algorithm using semijoins to each individual join. Thus an example of a program to compute EMP ⋈ ASG ⋈ PROJ is EMP' ⋈ ASG' ⋈ PROJ, where EMP' = EMP ⋉ ASG and ASG' = ASG ⋉ PROJ.

However, we may further reduce the size of an operand relation by using more than one semijoin. For example, EMP' can be replaced in the preceding program by EMP'' derived as

$$EMP'' = EMP \ltimes (ASG \ltimes PROJ)$$

since if $size(\text{ASG} \ltimes \text{PROJ}) \leq size(\text{ASG})$, we have $size(\text{EMP}'') \leq size(\text{EMP}')$. In this way, EMP can be reduced by the sequence of semijoins: EMP $\ltimes$ (ASG $\ltimes$ PROJ). Such a sequence of semijoins is called a *semijoin program* for EMP. Similarly, semijoin programs can be found for any relation in a query. For example, PROJ could be reduced by the semijoin program PROJ $\ltimes$ (ASG $\ltimes$ EMP). However, not all of the relations involved in a query need to be reduced; in particular, we can ignore those relations that are not involved in the final joins.

For a given relation, there exist several potential semijoin programs. The number of possibilities is in fact exponential in the number of relations. But there is one optimal semijoin program, called the *full reducer*, which for each relation R reduces R more than the others [Chiu and Ho, 1980]. The problem is to find the full reducer. A simple method is to evaluate the size reduction of all possible semijoin programs and to select the best one. The problems with the enumerative method are twofold:

1. There is a class of queries, called *cyclic queries*, that have cycles in their join graph and for which full reducers cannot be found.

2. For other queries, called *tree queries*, full reducers exist, but the number of candidate semijoin programs is exponential in the number of relations, which makes the enumerative approach NP-hard.

In what follows we discuss solutions to these problems.

Example 9.7

Consider the following relations, where attribute CITY has been added to relations EMP (renamed ET) and PROJ (renamed PT) of the engineering database:

    ET(ENO, ENAME, TITLE, CITY)
    ASG(ENO, PNO, RESP, DUR)
    PT(PNO, PNAME, BUDGET, CITY)

The following SQL query retrieves the names of all employees living in the city in which their project is located.

```
SELECT   ET.ENAME
FROM     ET, ASG, PT
WHERE    ET.ENO = ASG.ENO
AND      ASG.ENO = PT.ENO
AND      ET.CITY = PT.CITY
```

As illustrated in Figure 9.11a, this query is cyclic.

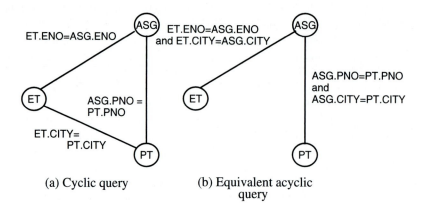

Figure 9.11. Transformation of Cyclic Query

No full reducer exists for the query in Example 9.7. In fact, it is possible to derive semijoin programs for reducing it, but the number of operations is multiplied by the number of tuples in each relation, making the approach inefficient. One solution consists of transforming the cyclic graph into a tree by removing one arc of the graph and by adding appropriate predicates to the other arcs such that the removed predicate is preserved by transitivity [Kambayashi et al., 1982].

In the example of Figure 9.11b, where the arc (ET, PT) is removed, the additional predicate ET.CITY = ASG.CITY and ASG.CITY = PT.CITY imply ET.CITY = PT.CITY by transitivity. Thus the acyclic query is equivalent to the cyclic query. The addition of these predicates implies the addition of attribute CITY in relation ASG. Hence, the values for attribute CITY must be sent from either ET or ASG.

Although full reducers for tree queries exist, the problem of finding them is NP-hard. However, there is an important class of queries, called *chained queries*, for which a polynomial algorithm exists ([Chiu and Ho, 1980] and [Ullman, 1982]). A chained query has a join graph where relations can be ordered, and each relation joins only with the next relation in the order. Furthermore, the result of the query is at the end of the chain. For instance, the query in Figure 9.10 is a chain query. Because of the difficulty of implementing an algorithm with full reducers, most systems use single semijoins to reduce the relation size.

9.3.3 Join versus Semijoin

Compared with the join, the semijoin induces more operations but possibly on smaller operands. Figure 9.12 illustrates these differences with an equivalent pair of join and semijoin strategies for the query whose join graph is given in Figure 9.10. The join of two relations, EMP ⋈ ASG in Figure 9.10, is done by sending one relation, ASG, to the site of the other one, EMP, to complete the join locally. When a semijoin is used, however, the transfer of relation ASG is avoided. Instead, it is replaced by the transfer of the join attribute values of relation EMP to the site of relation ASG, followed by the transfer of the matching tuples of relation ASG to the site of relation EMP, where the join is completed. If the join attribute length is smaller than the length of an entire tuple and the semijoin has good selectivity, then the semijoin approach can result in significant savings in communication time. Using semijoins may well increase the local processing time, since one of the two joined relations must be accessed twice. For example, relations EMP and PROJ are accessed twice in Figure 9.12. Furthermore, the join of two intermediate relations produced by semijoins cannot exploit the indices that were available on the base relations. Therefore, using semijoins might not be a good idea if the communication time is not the dominant factor, as is the case with local area networks [Lu and Carey, 1985].

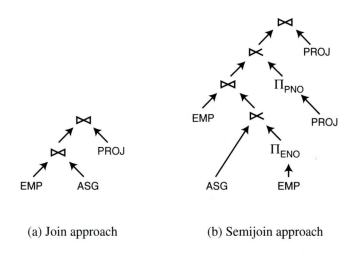

(a) Join approach   (b) Semijoin approach

Figure 9.12. Join versus Semijoin Approaches

Semijoins can still be beneficial with fast networks if they have very good selectivity and are implemented with bit arrays [Valduriez, 1982]. A bit array $BA[1:n]$ is useful in encoding the join attribute values present in one relation. Let us consider the semijoin $R \ltimes S$. Then $BA[i]$ is set to 1 if there exists a join attribute value $A = val$ in relation S such that $h(val) = i$, where h is a hash function. Otherwise, $BA[i]$ is set to 0. Such a bit array is much smaller than a list of join attribute values. Therefore, transferring the bit array instead of the join attribute values to the site of relation R saves communication time. The semijoin can be completed as follows. Each tuple of relation R, whose join attribute value is val, belongs to the semijoin if $BA[h(val)] = 1$.

9.4 DISTRIBUTED QUERY OPTIMIZATION ALGORITHMS

In this section we illustrate the use of the techniques presented previously in three basic query optimization algorithms: the reduction algorithm of Distributed IN-GRES [Epstein et al., 1978], System R* algorithm [Selinger et al., 1979], and SDD-1 algorithm [Bernstein et al., 1981]. We describe them because they are representative of different classes of algorithms and are therefore often used as paradigms. The differences among them can be specified in terms of the features introduced in Chapter 7 (specifically, Section 7.4:

1. The optimization timing is dynamic for distributed INGRES, while it is static for the others.

2. The objective function of SDD-1 and R* is to minimize total time, while distributed INGRES aims at decreasing a combination of response time and total time.

3. The optimization factors of the cost function are the message size for SDD-1. System R*, which takes into account local processing time, uses message size, number of messages, I/O, and CPU costs. Distributed INGRES considers both message size and local processing time (I/O + CPU time).

4. The network topology is assumed to be a wide area point-to-point network by SDD-1. The algorithms of distributed INGRES and R* can work in both local and wide area networks.

5. The use of semijoins as a query optimization technique is employed by SDD-1. Distributed INGRES and R* perform joins in a fashion similar to that of the centralized query optimization algorithms of their counterparts: INGRES and System R.

6. Each algorithm assumes statistical information about the data. As shown in Figure 9.13, semijoin algorithms typically use more information.

7. INGRES can handle fragments.

The differences between these three algorithms are summarized in Figure 9.13. In the rest of this section we detail each of these algorithms.

9.4.1 Distributed INGRES Algorithm

The query optimization algorithm of Distributed INGRES [Epstein et al., 1978] is derived from the algorithm used in centralized INGRES (see Section 9.2.1). There-

Algorithms	Optm. Timing	Objective Function	Optm. Factors	Network Topology	Semi Joins	Stats[†]	Fragments
Dist. INGRES	Dynamic	Response time or total cost	Msg size, proc. cost	General or broadcast	No	1	Horizontal
R *	Static	Total cost	#Msg, Msg size, IO, CPU	General or local	No	1, 2	No
SDD–1	Static	Total Cost	Msg size,	General	Yes	1, 3, 4, 5	No

Figure 9.13. Comparison of Query Optimization Algorithms[†] 1 = relation cardinality, 2 = number of unique values per attribute, 3 = join selectivity factor, 4 = size of projection on each join attribute, 5 = attribute size and tuple size.

fore, it consists of dynamically optimizing the processing strategy of a given query. The objective function of the algorithm is to minimize a combination of both the communication time and the response time. However, these two objectives may be conflicting. For instance, increasing communication time (by means of parallelism) may well decrease response time. Thus, the function can give a greater weight to one or the other. Note that this query optimization algorithm ignores the cost of transmitting the data to the result site. The algorithm also takes advantage of fragmentation, but only horizontal fragmentation is handled for simplicity.

Since both general and broadcast networks are considered, the query processing algorithm takes into account the network topology. In broadcast networks, the same data unit can be transmitted from one site to all the other sites in a single transfer, and the algorithm explicitly takes advantage of this capability. For example, broadcasting is used to replicate fragments and then to maximize the degree of parallelism.

The input to the query processing algorithm is a query expressed in tuple relational calculus (in conjunctive normal form) and schema information (the network type, as well as the location and size of each fragment). As in the centralized version, we describe the distributed query optimization algorithm for the case of a retrieval query. This algorithm is executed by the site, called the *master site*, where the query is initiated. The algorithm, which we call D-INGRES-QOA, is given in Algorithm 9.3.

Algorithm 9.3   *D-INGRES-QOA*

> **input:** MRQ: multirelation query
> **output:** result of the last multirelation query
> **begin**
>> **for** each detachable OVQ_i in MRQ **do** {run all one-relation queries}
>>> run(OVQ_i);   (1)
>>
>> **end-for**
>> $MVQ'\_list \leftarrow$ REDUCE(MRQ)   {replace MRQ by a list of n
>>   irreducible queries}   (2)
>> **while** $n \neq 0$ **do**   {n is the number of irreducible queries} (3)
>> **begin**
>>> {choose next irreducible query involving the smallest fragments}
>>> $MRQ' \leftarrow$ SELECT_QUERY(MRQ'_list)   (3.1)
>>> {determine fragments to transfer and processing site for MRQ'}
>>> Fragment-site-list $\leftarrow$ SELECT_STRATEGY(MRQ')   (3.2)
>>> {move the selected fragments to the selected sites}
>>> **for** each pair (F, S) in Fragment-site-list **do**   (3.3)
>>>> move fragment F to site S
>>>
>>> **end-for**
>>> run(MRQ')   (3.4)
>>> $n \leftarrow n - 1$
>>
>> **end-while** {output of the algorithm is the result of the last MRQ'}
> **end.**{ D-INGRES-QOA }

All monorelation queries (e.g., selection and projection) that can be detached are first processed locally [Step (1)]. Then the reduction algorithm [Wong and Youssefi, 1976] is applied to the original query [Step (2)]. Reduction is a technique that isolates all irreducible subqueries and monorelation subqueries by detachment (see Section 9.2.1). Monorelation subqueries are ignored because they have already been processed in step (1). Thus the REDUCE procedure produces a sequence of irreducible subqueries $q_1 \rightarrow q_2 \rightarrow \cdots \rightarrow q_n$, with at most one relation in common between two consecutive subqueries. In [Wong and Youssefi, 1976], it is shown that such a sequence is unique. Example 9.3 (in Section 9.2.1), which illustrated the detachment technique, also illustrates what the REDUCE procedure would produce.

Based on the list of irreducible queries isolated in step (2) and the size of each fragment, the next subquery, MVQ', which has at least two variables, is chosen at step (3.1) and steps (3.2), (3.3), and (3.4) are applied to it. Steps (3.1) and (3.2) are discussed below. Step (3.2) selects the best strategy to process the query MRQ'. This strategy is described by a list of pairs (F, S), in which F is a fragment to transfer to the processing site S. Step (3.3) transfers all the fragments to their processing sites. Finally, step (3.4) executes the query MRQ'. If there are remaining subqueries, the algorithm goes back to step (3) and performs the next iteration. Otherwise, the algorithm terminates.

Optimization occurs in steps (3.1) and (3.2). The algorithm has produced subqueries with several components and their dependency order (similar to the one given by a relational algebra tree). At step (3.1) a simple choice for the next subquery is to take the next one having no predecessor and involving the smaller fragments. This minimizes the size of the intermediate results. For example, if a query q has the subqueries q_1, q_2, and q_3, with dependencies $q_1 \rightarrow q_3, q_2 \rightarrow q_3$, and if the fragments referred to by q_1 are smaller than those referred to by q_2, then q_1 is selected. Depending on the network, this choice can also be affected by the number of sites having relevant fragments. [Epstein et al., 1978] provides more details about this choice.

The subquery selected must then be executed. Since the relation involved in a subquery may be stored at different sites and even fragmented, the subquery may nevertheless be further subdivided.

Example 9.8

Assume that relations EMP, ASG, and PROJ of the query of Example 9.3 are stored as follows, where relation EMP is fragmented.

Site 1	Site 2
EMP$_1$	EMP$_2$
ASG	PROJ

There are several possible strategies, including the following:

1. Execute the entire query (EMP $\bowtie$ ASG $\bowtie$ PROJ) by moving EMP$_1$ and ASG to site 2.

2. Execute (EMP $\bowtie$ ASG) $\bowtie$ PROJ by moving (EMP$_1$ $\bowtie$ ASG) and ASG to site 2, and so on.

The choice between the possible strategies requires an estimate of the size of the intermediate results. For example, if $size(\text{EMP}_1 \bowtie \text{ASG}) > size\ (\text{EMP}_1)$, strategy 1 is preferred to strategy 2. Therefore, an estimate of the size of joins is required.

At step (3.2), the next optimization problem is to determine how to execute the subquery by selecting the fragments that will be moved and the sites where the processing will take place. For an n-relation subquery, fragments from $n - 1$ relations must be moved to the site(s) of fragments of the remaining relation, say R_p, and then replicated there. Also, the remaining relation may be further partitioned into k "equalized" fragments in order to increase parallelism. This method is called *fragment-and-replicate* and performs a substitution of fragments rather than of tuples as in centralized INGRES. The selection of the remaining relation and of the number of processing sites k on which it should be partitioned is based on the objective function and the topology of the network. Remember that replication is cheaper in broadcast networks than in point-to-point networks. Furthermore, the choice of the number of processing sites involves a trade-off between response time and total time. A larger number of sites decreases response time (by parallel processing) but increases total time, in particular increasing communication costs.

In [Epstein et al., 1978], formulas are given to minimize either communication time or processing time. These formulas use as input the location of fragments, their size, and the network type. They can minimize both costs but with a priority to one. To illustrate these formulas, we give the rules for minimizing communication time. The rule for minimizing response time is even more complex. We use the following assumptions. There are n relations $R_1, R_2, \ldots, R_n$ involved in the query. R_i^j denotes the fragment of R_i stored at site j. There are m sites in the network. Finally, $CT_k(\#bytes)$ denotes the communication time of transferring $\#bytes$ to k sites, with $1 \le k \le m$.

The rule for minimizing communication time considers the types of networks separately. Let us first concentrate on a broadcast network. In this case we have

$$CT_k(\#bytes) = CT_1(\#bytes)$$

The rule can be stated as

if $\max_{j=1,m}(\sum_{i=1}^n size(R_i^j)) > \max_{i=1,n}(size(R_i))$
then
   the processing site is the j that has the largest amount of data
else
   R_p is the largest relation and site of R_p is the processing site

If the inequality predicate is satisfied, one site contains an amount of data useful to the query larger than the size of the largest relation. Therefore, this site should be the processing site. If the predicate is not satisfied, one relation is larger than the maximum useful amount of data at one site. Therefore, this relation should be the R_p, and the processing sites are those which have its fragments.

Let us now consider the case of the point-to-point networks. In this case we have

$$CT_k(\#bytes) = k * CT_1(\#bytes)$$

The choice of R_p that minimizes communication is obviously the largest relation. Assuming that the sites are arranged by decreasing order of amounts of useful data for the query, that is,

$$\sum_{i=1}^n size(R_i^j) > \sum_{i=1}^n size(R_i^{j+1})$$

the choice of k, the number of sites at which processing needs to be done, is given as

if $\sum_{i\neq p}(size(R_i) - size(R_i^1)) > size(R_p^1)$
then
   $k = 1$
else
   k is the largest j such that $\sum_{i\neq p}(size(R_i) - size(R_i^j)) \leq size(R_p^j)$

This rule chooses a site as the processing site only if the amount of data it must receive is smaller than the additional amount of data it would have to send if it were not a processing site. Obviously, the then-part of the rule assumes that site 1 stores a fragment of R_p.

Example 9.9

Let us consider the query PROJ ⋈ ASG, where PROJ and ASG are fragmented. Assume that the allocation of fragments and their sizes are as follows (in kilobytes):

	Site 1	Site 2	Site 3	Site 4
PROJ	1000	1000	1000	1000
ASG			2000	

With a point–to–point network, the best strategy is to send each $PROJ_i$ to site 3, which requires a transfer of 3000 kbytes, versus 6000 kbytes if ASG is sent to sites 1, 2, and 4. However, with a broadcast network, the best strategy is to send ASG (in a single transfer) to sites 1, 2, and 4, which incurs a transfer of 2000 kbytes. The latter strategy is faster and maximizes response time because the joins can be done in parallel.

The algorithm of Distributed INGRES is characterized by a limited search of the solution space, where an optimization decision is taken for each step without concerning itself with the consequences of that decision on global optimization. However, the algorithm is able to correct a local decision that proves to be incorrect. An alternative to the limited search is the exhaustive search approach (used by R*), where all possible strategies are evaluated to find the best one. In [Epstein and Stonebraker, 1980], the two approaches are simulated and compared on the basis of the size of data transfers. An important conclusion of this study is that exhaustive search significantly outperforms limited search as soon as the query accesses more than three relations. Another conclusion is that dynamic optimization is beneficial because the exact sizes of the intermediate results are known.

9.4.2 R* Algorithm

The distributed query optimization algorithm of R* ([Selinger and Adiba, 1980], [Lohman et al., 1985]) is a substantial extension of the techniques developed for System R's optimizer (see Section 9.2.2). Therefore, it uses a compilation approach where an exhaustive search of all alternative strategies is performed in order to choose the one with the least cost. Although predicting and enumerating these strategies is costly, the overhead of exhaustive search is rapidly amortized if the query is executed frequently. Although the algorithm described in [Selinger and Adiba, 1980] deals with fragmentation, the implemented version of R* supports neither fragmentation nor replication. Therefore, the R* query processing algorithm deals only with relations as basic units. Query compilation is a distributed task in R*, coordinated by a *master site*, where the query is initiated. The optimizer of the master site makes all intersite decisions, such as the selection of the execution sites and the fragments as well as the method for transferring data. The *apprentice sites*, which are the other sites that have relations involved in the query, make the remaining local decisions (such as the ordering of joins at a site) and generate local access plans for the query. The objective function of the System R*'s optimizer is the general total time function, including local processing and communications costs (see Section 9.1.1).

We now summarize the query optimization algorithm of R*. The input to the algorithm is a localized query expressed as a relational algebra tree (the query tree), the location of relations, and their statistics. The algorithm is described by the procedure R*-QOA in Algorithm 9.4.

Algorithm 9.4   *R*-QOA*

> **input:** QT: query tree
> **output:** *strat*: minimum cost strategy
> **begin**
>> **for** each relation $R_i \in QT$ **do**
>> **begin**
>>> **for each** access path AP_{ij} to R_i **do**
>>>> determine $cost(AP_{ij})$
>>> **end-for**
>>> $best\_AP_i \leftarrow AP_{ij}$ with minimum cost
>> **end**
>> **for** each order $(R_{i1}, R_{i2}, \cdots, R_{in})$ with $i = 1, \cdots, n!$ **do**
>> **begin**
>>> build strategy $(\ldots((\text{ best } AP_{i1} \bowtie R_{i2}) \bowtie R_{i3}) \bowtie \ldots \bowtie R_{in})$
>>> compute the cost of strategy
>> **end-for**
>> $strat \leftarrow$ strategy with minimum cost
>> **for** each site k storing a relation involved in QT **do**
>> **begin**
>>> $LS_k \leftarrow$ local strategy (strategy, k)
>>> send $(LS_k,$ site $k)$ {each local strategy is optimized at site k}
>> **end-for**
> **end.** { R*-QOA }

As in the centralized case, the optimizer must select the join ordering, the join algorithm (nested loop or merge join), and the access path for each fragment (e.g., clustered index, sequential scan, etc.). These decisions are based on statistics and formulas used to estimate the size of intermediate results and access path information. In addition, the optimizer must select the sites of join results and the method of transferring data between sites. To join two relations, there are three candidate sites: the site of the first relation, the site of the second relation, or a third site (e.g., the site of a third relation to be joined with). In R*, two methods are supported for intersite data transfers.

1. *Ship-whole.* The entire relation is shipped to the join site and stored in a temporary relation before being joined. If the join algorithm is merge join, the relation does not need to be stored, and the join site can process incoming tuples in a pipeline mode, as they arrive.

2. *Fetch-as-needed.* The external relation is sequentially scanned, and for each tuple the join value is sent to the site of the internal relation, which selects the internal tuples matching the value and sends the selected tuples to the site of the external relation. This method is equivalent to the semijoin of the internal relation with each external tuple.

The trade-off between these two methods is obvious. Ship-whole generates a larger data transfer but fewer messages than fetch-as-needed. It is intuitively better to ship whole relations when they are small. On the contrary, if the relation is large and the join has good selectivity (only a few matching tuples), the relevant tuples should be fetched as needed. R* does not consider all possible combinations of join methods with transfer methods since some of them are not worthwhile. For example, it would be useless to transfer the external relation using fetch-as-needed in the nested-loop join algorithm, because all the outer tuples must be processed anyway and therefore should be transferred as a whole.

Given the join of an external relation R with an internal relation S on attribute A, there are four join strategies. In what follows we describe each strategy in detail and provide a simplified cost formula for each, where LT denotes local processing time (I/O + CPU time) and CT denotes communication time. For simplicity, we ignore the cost of producing the result. For convenience, we denote by s the average number of tuples of S that match one tuple of R:

$$s = \frac{card(S \bowtie_A R)}{card(R)}$$

Strategy 1. *Ship the entire external relation to the site of the internal relation.* In this case the external tuples can be joined with S as they arrive. Thus we have

$$Total\_cost = LT(\text{retrieve } card(R) \text{ tuples from } R)$$
$$+ CT(size(R))$$
$$+ LT(\text{retrieve } s \text{ tuples from } S) * card(R)$$

Strategy 2. *Ship the entire internal relation to the site of the external relation.* In this case, the internal tuples cannot be joined as they arrive, and they need to be stored in a temporary relation T. Thus we have

$$Total\_cost = LT(\text{retrieve } card(S) \text{ tuples from } S)$$
$$+ \ CT(size(S))$$
$$+ \ LT(\text{store } card(S) \text{ tuples in } T)$$
$$+ \ LT(\text{retrieve } card(R) \text{ tuples from } R)$$
$$+ \ LT(\text{retrieve } s \text{ tuples from } T) * card(R)$$

Strategy 3. *Fetch tuples of the internal relation as needed for each tuple of the external relation.* In this case, for each tuple in R, the join attribute value is sent to the site of S. Then the s tuples of S which match that value are retrieved and sent to the site of R to be joined as they arrive. Thus we have

$$Total\_cost = LT(\text{retrieve } card(R) \text{ tuples from } R)$$
$$+ \ CT(length(A)) * card(R)$$
$$+ \ LT(\text{retrieve } s \text{ tuples from } S) * card(R)$$
$$+ \ CT(s * length(S)) * card(R)$$

Strategy 4. *Move both relations to a third site and compute the join there.* In this case the internal relation is first moved to a third site and stored in a temporary relation T. Then the external relation is moved to the third site and its tuples are joined with T as they arrive. Thus we have

$$Total\_cost = LT(\text{retrieve } card(S) \text{ tuples from } S)$$
$$+ \ CT(size(S))$$
$$+ \ LT(\text{store } card(S) \text{ tuples in } T)$$
$$+ \ LT(\text{retrieve } card(R) \text{ tuples from } R)$$
$$+ \ CT(size(R))$$
$$+ \ LT(\text{retrieve } s \text{ tuples from } T) * card(R)$$

Example 9.10

Let us consider a query that consists of the join of relations PROJ, the external relation, and ASG, the internal relation, on attribute PNO. We assume that PROJ and ASG are stored at two different sites and that there is an index on attribute PNO for relation ASG. The possible execution strategies for the query are as follows:

1. Ship whole PROJ to site of ASG.

2. Ship whole ASG to site of PROJ.

3. Fetch ASG tuples as needed for each tuple of PROJ.

4. Move ASG and PROJ to a third site.

The R* algorithm predicts the total time of each strategy and selects the cheapest. Given that there is no operation following the join PROJ ⋈ ASG, strategy 4 obviously incurs the highest cost since both relations must be transferred. If $size$(PROJ) is much larger than $size$(ASG), strategy 2 minimizes the communication time and is likely to be the best if local processing time is not too high compared to strategies 1 and 3. Note that the local processing time of strategies 1 and 3 is probably much better than that of strategy 2 since they exploit the index on the join attribute.

If strategy 2 is not the best, the choice is between strategies 1 and 3. Local processing costs in both of these alternatives are identical. If PROJ is large and only a few tuples of ASG match, strategy 3 probably incurs the least communication time and is the best. Otherwise, that is, if PROJ is small or many tuples of ASG match, strategy 1 should be the best.

Conceptually, the algorithm can be viewed as an exhaustive search among all alternatives that are defined by the permutation of the relation join order, join methods (including the selection of the join algorithm), result site, access path to the internal relation, and intersite transfer mode. Such an algorithm has a combinatorial complexity in the number of relations involved. Actually, the R* algorithm significantly reduces the number of alternatives by using dynamic programming and the heuristics, as does the System R's optimizer (see Section 9.2.2). With dynamic programming, the tree of alternatives is dynamically constructed and pruned by eliminating the inefficient choices.

In [Lohman and Mackert, 1986] and [Mackert and Lohman, 1986], an instructive performance evaluation of the R* optimizer is described in the context of both high-speed networks (similar to local networks) and medium-speed wide area networks. The tests confirm the significant contribution of local processing costs, even for wide area networks. It is shown in particular that for the distributed join, transferring the entire internal relation outperforms the fetch-as-needed method.

9.4.3 SDD-1 Algorithm

The query optimization algorithm of SDD-1 [Bernstein et al., 1981] is derived from an earlier method called the "hill-climbing" algorithm [Wong, 1977], which has the distinction of being the first distributed query processing algorithm. In this algorithm, refinements of an initial feasible solution are recursively computed until no more cost improvements can be made. The algorithm does not use semijoins, nor does it assume data replication and fragmentation. It is devised for wide area point-to-point networks. The cost of transferring the result to the final site is ignored. This algorithm is quite general in that it can minimize an arbitrary objective function, including the total time and response time.

The hill-climbing algorithm proceeds as follows. The input to the algorithm includes the query graph, location of relations, and relation statistics. Following the completion of initial local processing, an initial feasible solution is selected which is a global execution schedule that includes all intersite communication. It is obtained by computing the cost of all the execution strategies that transfer all the required relations to a single candidate result site, and then choosing the least costly strategy. Let us denote this initial strategy as ES_0. Then the optimizer splits ES_0 into two strategies, ES_1 followed by ES_2, where ES_1 consists of sending one of the relations involved in the join to the site of the other relation. The two relations are joined locally and the resulting relation is transmitted to the chosen result site (specified as schedule ES_2). If the cost of executing strategies ES_1 and ES_2, plus the cost of local join processing, is less than that of ES_0, then ES_0 is replaced in the schedule by ES_1 and ES_2. The process is then applied recursively to ES_1 and ES_2 until no more benefit can be gained. Notice that if n-way joins are involved, ES_0 will be divided into n subschedules instead of just two.

The hill-climbing algorithm is in the class of greedy algorithms, which start with an initial feasible solution and iteratively improve it. The main problem is that strategies with higher initial cost, which could nevertheless produce better overall benefits, are ignored. Furthermore, the algorithm may get stuck at a local minimum cost solution and fail to reach the global minimum.

Example 9.11

Let us illustrate the hill-climbing algorithm using the following query involving relations EMP, PAY, PROJ, and ASG of the engineering database:

"Find the salaries of engineers who work on the CAD/CAM project"

The query in relational algebra is

$$\Pi_{\text{SAL}} \left(\text{PAY} \bowtie_{\text{TITLE}} \left(\text{EMP} \bowtie_{\text{ENO}} \left(\text{ASG} \bowtie_{\text{PNO}} (\sigma_{\text{PNAME = "CAD/CAM"}} (\text{PROJ})) \right) \right) \right)$$

We assume that $T_{MSG} = 0$ and $T_{TR} = 1$. Furthermore, we ignore the local processing, following which the database is

Relation	Size	Site
EMP	8	1
PAY	4	2
PROJ	1	3
ASG	10	4

To simplify this example, we assume that the length of a tuple (of every relation) is 1, which means that the size of a relation is equal to its cardinality. Furthermore, the placement of the relation is arbitrary. Based on join selectivities, we know that $size(\text{EMP} \bowtie \text{PAY}) = size(\text{EMP})$, $size(\text{PROJ} \bowtie \text{ASG}) = 2 * size(\text{PROJ})$, and $size(\text{ASG} \bowtie \text{EMP}) = size(\text{ASG})$.

Considering only data transfers, the initial feasible solution is to choose site 4 as the result site, producing the schedule

$$
\begin{aligned}
ES_0 : \quad & \text{EMP} \rightarrow \text{site 4} \\
& \text{PAY} \rightarrow \text{site 4} \\
& \text{PROJ} \rightarrow \text{site 4} \\
& Total\_cost(ES_0) = 4 + 8 + 1 = 13
\end{aligned}
$$

This is true because the cost of any other solution is greater than the foregoing alternative. For example, if one chooses site 2 as the result site and transmits all the relations to that site, the total cost will be

$$
\begin{aligned}
Total\_cost \quad = \quad & cost(\text{EMP} \rightarrow \text{site 2}) \; + cost(\text{ASG} \rightarrow \text{site 2}) \\
+ \quad & cost(\text{PROJ} \rightarrow \text{site 2}) \\
= \quad & 19
\end{aligned}
$$

Similarly, the total cost of choosing either site 1 or site 3 as the result site is 15 and 22, respectively.

One way of splitting this schedule (call it ES') is the following:

$$
\begin{aligned}
ES_1 : \quad & \text{EMP} \rightarrow \text{site 2} \\
ES_2 : \quad & (\text{EMP} \bowtie \text{PAY}) \rightarrow \text{site 4} \\
ES_3 : \quad & \text{PROJ} \rightarrow \text{site 4} \\
& Total\_cost(ES') = 8 + 8 + 1 = 17
\end{aligned}
$$

A second splitting alternative (ES'') is as follows:

$$
\begin{aligned}
ES_1 : \quad & \text{PAY} \rightarrow \text{site 1} \\
ES_2 : \quad & (\text{PAY} \bowtie \text{EMP}) \rightarrow \text{site 4} \\
ES_3 : \quad & \text{PROJ} \rightarrow \text{site 4} \\
& Total\_cost(ES'') = 4 + 8 + 1 = 13
\end{aligned}
$$

Since the cost of either of the alternatives is greater than or equal to the cost of ES_0, ES_0 is kept as the final solution. A better solution (ignored by the algorithm) is

$$
\begin{aligned}
B : \quad & \text{PROJ} \rightarrow \text{site 4} \\
& \text{ASG}' = (\text{PROJ} \bowtie \text{ASG}) \rightarrow \text{site 1} \\
& (\text{ASG}' \bowtie \text{EMP}) \rightarrow \text{site 2} \\
& Total\_cost(B) = 1 + 2 + 2 = 5
\end{aligned}
$$

The hill-climbing algorithm has been substantially improved in SDD-1 [Bernstein et al., 1981] in a number of ways. The improved version makes extensive use of semijoins. The objective function is expressed in terms of total communication time (local time and response time are not considered). Finally, the algorithm uses statistics on the database, called *database profiles*, where a profile is associated with a relation. The improved version also selects an initial feasible solution that is iteratively refined. Furthermore, a postoptimization step is added to improve the total time of the solution selected. The main step of the algorithm consists of determining and ordering beneficial semijoins, that is semijoins whose cost is less than their benefit.

The cost of a semijoin is that of transferring the semijoin attributes A,

$$Cost(R \ltimes_A S) = T_{MSG} + T_{TR} * size(\Pi_A(S))$$

while its benefit is the cost of transferring irrelevant tuples of R (which is avoided by the semijoin):

$$Benefit(R \ltimes_A S) = (1 - SF_{SJ}(S.A)) * size(R) * T_{TR}$$

The SDD-1 algorithm proceeds in four phases: initialization, selection of beneficial semijoins, assembly site selection, and postoptimization. The output of the algorithm is a global strategy for executing the query. The algorithm is detailed in Algorithm 9.5 by the procedure SDD-1-QOA.

Algorithm 9.5   *SDD-1-QOA*

> **input**: QG: query graph with n relations; statistics for each relation
> **output**: ES: execution strategy
> **begin**
>   ES ← local-operations (QG);
>   modify statistics to reflect the effect of local processing
>   BS ← ϕ {set of beneficial semijoins}
>   **for each** semijoin SJ in QG **do**
>   **if** $cost(SJ) < benefit(SJ)$ **then**
> $BS \leftarrow BS \cup SJ$
>   **end-if**
>   **end-for**
>   **while** $BS \neq \phi$ **do**   {selection of beneficial semijoins}
>   **begin**
> $SJ \leftarrow most\_beneficial(BS)$ {SJ: semijoin with $max(benefit - cost)$}
> $BS \leftarrow BS - SJ$ {remove SJ from BS}
> $ES \leftarrow ES + SJ$ {append SJ to execution strategy}
>   modify statistics to reflect the effect of incorporating SJ
> $BS \leftarrow BS-$ nonbeneficial semijoins
> $BS \leftarrow BS\cup$ new beneficial semijoins
>   **end-while**

{assembly site selection}
$AS(ES) \leftarrow$ select site i such that i stores the largest amount
    of data after all local operations
$ES \leftarrow ES \cup$ transfers of intermediate relations to $AS(ES)$
{postoptimization}
for each relation R_i at $AS(ES)$ **do**
    for each semijoin SJ of R_i by R_j **do**
        if $cost(ES) > cost(ES - SJ)$ **then**
            $ES \leftarrow ES - SJ$
        end-if
    end-for
  end-for
end. { SDD-1-QOA }

The initialization phase generates a set of beneficial semijoins, $BS = \{SJ_1, SJ_2, \ldots, SJ_k\}$, and an execution strategy ES that includes only local processing. The next phase selects the beneficial semijoins from BS by iteratively choosing the most beneficial semijoin, SJ_i, and modifying the database statistics and BS accordingly. The modification affects the statistics of relation R involved in SJ_i and the remaining semijoins in BS that use relation R. The iterative phase terminates when all semijoins in BS have been appended to the execution strategy. The order in which semijoins are appended to ES will be the execution order of the semijoins.

The next phase selects the assembly site by evaluating, for each candidate site, the cost of transferring to it all the required data and taking the one with the least cost. Finally, a postoptimization phase permits the removal from the execution strategy of those semijoins that affect only relations stored at the assembly site. This phase is necessary because the assembly site is chosen after all the semijoins have been ordered. The SDD-1 optimizer is based on the assumption that relations can be transmitted to another site. This is true for all relations except those stored at the assembly site, which is selected after beneficial semijoins are considered. Therefore, some semijoins may incorrectly be considered beneficial. It is the role of postoptimization to remove them from the execution strategy.

Example 9.12

Let us consider the following query:

    SELECT $R_3.C$
    FROM R_1, R_2, R_3
    WHERE $R_1.A = R_2.A$
    AND $R_2.B = R_3.B$

Figure 9.14 gives the join graph of the query and of relation statistics. We assume that $T_{MSG} = 0$ and $T_{TR} = 1$. The initial set of beneficial semijoins will contain the following two:

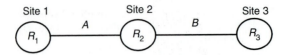

relation	card	tuple size	relation size
R_1	30	50	1500
R_2	100	30	3000
R_3	50	40	2000

attribute	SF_{SJ}	$size(\Pi_{attribute})$
$R_1.A$	0.3	36
$R_2.A$	0.8	320
$R_3.B$	1.0	400
$R_4.B$	0.4	80

Figure 9.14. Example Query and Statistics

SJ_1: $R_2 \ltimes R_1$, whose benefit is $2100 = (1 - 0.3) * 3000$ and cost is 36
SJ_2: $R_2 \ltimes R_3$, whose benefit is $1800 = (1 - 0.4) * 3000$ and cost is 80

Furthermore there are two nonbeneficial semijoins:

SJ_3: $R_1 \ltimes R_2$, whose benefit is $300 = (1 - 0.8) * 1500$ and cost is 320
SJ_4: $R_3 \ltimes R_2$, whose benefit is 0 and cost is 400.

At the first iteration of the selection of beneficial semijoins, SJ_1 is appended to the execution strategy ES. One effect on the statistics is to change the size of R_2 to $900 = 3000 * 0.3$. Furthermore, the semijoin selectivity factor of attribute $R_2.A$ is reduced because $card(\Pi_A(R_2))$ is reduced. We approximate $SF_{SJ}(R_2.A)$ by $0.8 * 0.3 = 0.24$. Finally, size of $\Pi_{R_2.A}$ is also reduced to $96 = 320 * 0.3$.

At the second iteration, there are two beneficial semijoins:

SJ_2 : $R_2' \ltimes R_3$, whose benefit is $540 = 900 * (1 - 0.4)$ and cost is 200
   (here $R_2' = R_2 \ltimes R_1$, which is obtained by SJ_1)
SJ_3: $R_1 \ltimes R_2'$, whose benefit is $1140 = (1 - 0.24) * 1500$ and cost is 96

The most beneficial semijoin is SJ_3 and is appended to ES. One effect on the statistics of relation R_1 is to change the size of R_1 to $360 = (1500 * 0.24)$. Another effect is to change the selectivity of R_1 and size of $\Pi_{R_1.A}$.

At the third iteration, the only remaining beneficial semijoin, SJ_2, is appended to ES. Its effect is to reduce the size of relation R_2 to $360 = 900 * 0.4$. Again, the statistics of relation R_2 may also change.

After reduction, the amount of data stored is 360 at site 1, 360 at site 2, and 2000 at site 3. Site 3 is therefore chosen as the assembly site. The postoptimization does not remove any semijoin since they all remain beneficial. The strategy selected is to send $(R_2 \ltimes R_1) \ltimes R_3$ and $R_1 \ltimes R_2$ to site 3, where the final result is computed.

Like its predecessor hill-climbing algorithm, the SDD-1 algorithm selects locally optimal strategies. Therefore, it ignores the higher-cost semijoins which would result in increasing the benefits and decreasing the costs of other semijoins. Thus this algorithm may not be able to select the global minimum cost solution.

9.5   CONCLUSION

In this chapter we have presented the basic concepts and techniques for distributed query optimization. We have reviewed their application in the basic query optimization algorithms of Distributed INGRES, R*, and SDD-1. Earlier distributed DBMSs employ an objective function that considers transmission costs only in terms of the message size. With the availability of faster communication networks (e.g., local area networks), more recent distributed DBMSs consider local processing costs as well. Performance evaluation of R* ([Lohman and Mackert, 1986], [Mackert and Lohman, 1986]) has shown significant contributions of local costs, even for general networks, which have become faster.

Important inputs to the query optimization problem are the database statistics and the formulas used to estimate the size of intermediate results. There is a direct trade-off between performance and the accuracy (and maintenance cost) of statistics. The critical operation is generally the join of distributed relations. For most frequent joins that are not on foreign keys, join selectivity factors should be of great benefit [Mackert and Lohman, 1986]. The use of statistics can be avoided by applying a simple algorithm based on heuristics to transform a query. However, it has been recognized in [Epstein and Stonebraker, 1980] that exhaustive search of the solution space, based on statistics, significantly outperforms the heuristic approaches. When done statically (at compile time), the overhead incurred by exhaustive search is rapidly amortized if the query becomes complex or is executed frequently.

As a prerequisite to understanding distributed query optimization, we have introduced centralized query optimization. The two most popular algorithms used by INGRES and System R were presented. These algorithms form the basis of a distributed optimization algorithm for distributed INGRES and R*, respectively.

We have seen two approaches to solve distributed join queries, which are usually considered the most important type of queries. The first, illustrated by Distributed INGRES and R*, considers join ordering. The second, exemplified by SDD-1, computes joins with semijoins. Semijoins are beneficial only when a join has good selectivity, in which case the semijoins act as powerful size reducers. The first systems that make extensive use of semijoins assumed a slow wide area network and therefore concentrated on minimizing only the communication time at the expense of local processing time. However, with fast local area networks, the local processing time is as important as the communication time and sometimes even more important. Therefore, semijoins should be employed carefully and not systematically since they tend to increase the local processing time. Join and semijoin techniques should both be employed as shown in [Valduriez and Gardarin, 1984], because each technique is better than the other, depending on database-dependent parameters. Semijoins implemented by hashed bit arrays [Valduriez, 1982] are shown in [Mackert and Lohman, 1986] to be very beneficial.

Another promising approach to solving join queries is through the use of auxiliary and small data structures, called join indices [Valduriez, 1987], which have the potential of minimizing both local processing time and communication time. The performance analyses reported in [Valduriez and Boral, 1986] and [Valduriez et al., 1986] already exhibit the value of join indices in a centralized context for optimizing both complex relational queries and recursive queries [Valduriez, 1986]. Join indices can be useful in a distributed context as well.

In this chapter we focused mostly on join queries for two reasons: join queries are the most frequent queries in the relational framework and they have been studied extensively. Furthermore, the number of joins involved in queries expressed in languages of higher expressive power than relational calculus (e.g., Horn clause logic) can be extremely large, making the join ordering more crucial [Krishnamurthy et al., 1986]. However, the optimization of general queries containing joins, unions, and aggregate functions is a harder problem [Selinger and Adiba, 1980]. Distributing unions over joins is a simple and good approach since the query can be reduced as a union of join subqueries, which are optimized individually. Note also that the unions are more frequent in distributed DBMSs than in centralized DBMSs because they permit the localization of horizontally fragmented relations.

The concepts and solutions presented in this chapter have been illustrated by their use in three query processing algorithms, chosen for their generality and practical interest (all of which were implemented). However, other methods can be derived from these concepts (see [Sacco and Yao, 1982] and [Yu and Chang, 1984] for excellent surveys). Apers, Hevner, and Yao [Apers et al., 1983] have proposed a family of interesting algorithms using semijoins to minimize either the response time or the total time. The method decomposes the query in a set of simple queries that can be optimally solved and integrates them in a unique execution strategy. Another approach is to specialize the optimization algorithm to take advantage of the network topology, such as star networks [Kerschberg et al., 1982], satellite networks [LaChimia, 1984], and broadcast networks ([Özsoyoglu and Zhou, 1987] and [Wah and Lien, 1985]). Assuming that relations are fragmented by a hash function, Shasha and Wang [Shasha and Wang, 1991] propose optimal solutions for processing multijoin queries which closed chain queries and heuristics to process the harder kinds of queries (start, tree and general graph queries).

9.6 BIBLIOGRAPHIC NOTES

A good, recent survey of query optimization is provided in [Ioannidis, 1996].

The two basic algorithms for query optimization in centralized systems are those of INGRES [Wong and Youssefi, 1976] and System R [Selinger et al., 1979]. They are described in more detail in [Gardarin and Valduriez, 1989] and [Valduriez and Gardarin, 1989]. INGRES uses a dynamic optimization algorithm, while System R uses a static exhaustive search of the best solution. A general and simple data structure called a join index is defined in [Valduriez, 1986] to optimize join queries in both centralized and parallel environments.

The theory of semijoins and their value for distributed query processing has been covered in [Bernstein and Chiu, 1981], [Chiu and Ho, 1980], and [Kambayashi et al., 1982]. Algorithms for improving the processing of semijoins in distributed systems are proposed in [Valduriez, 1982]. The value of semijoins for multiprocessor database machines having fast communication networks is also shown in [Valduriez and Gardarin, 1984]. Parallel execution strategies for horizontally fragmented databases is treated in [Ceri and Pelagatti, 1983] and [Khoshafian and Valduriez, 1987]. The solutions in [Shasha and Wang, 1991] are also applicable to parallel systems.

The query processing algorithm of Distributed INGRES is defined in [Epstein et al., 1978] as an extension of the reduction algorithm of INGRES, based on a heuristic approach. The algorithm takes advantage of the network topology (general or broadcast networks). Improvements on this method based on the enumeration of all possible solutions are given and analyzed in [Epstein and Stonebraker, 1980].

The query optimization algorithm of R* is presented in [Selinger and Adiba, 1980] as an extension of the algorithm of System R. It is one of the first papers to recognize the significance of local processing on the performance of distributed queries. Measurements on the R* prototype [Lohman and Mackert, 1986] have confirmed this important statement.

The first algorithm for SDD-1 [Wong, 1977], based on the hill-climbing strategy, is the first paper on distributed query processing. The improved implementation of this algorithm [Bernstein et al., 1981] is based on semijoins.

The AHY algorithms ([Hevner and Yao, 1979] and [Apers et al., 1983]) have optimal solutions for simple distributed queries and general (but not optimal) algorithms based on these optimal solutions. Algorithms for query optimization in local area networks are proposed in [Kerschberg et al., 1982], [Özsoyoglu and Zhou, 1987], [Page and Popek, 1985], and [Wah and Lien, 1985].

9.7 EXERCISES

*9.1 Apply the algorithm of INGRES to the query of Exercise 8.3, and illustrate the successive detachments and substitutions by giving the monorelation subqueries generated.

9.2 Consider the join graph of Figure 9.10 and the following information: $size(\text{EMP}) = 100$, $size(\text{ASG}) = 200$, $size(\text{PROJ}) = 300$, $size(\text{EMP} \bowtie \text{ASG}) = 300$, and $size(\text{ASG} \bowtie \text{PROJ}) = 200$. Describe an optimal join program based on the objective function of total transmission time.

9.3 Consider the join graph of Figure 9.10 and the same assumptions as in Exercise 9.2. Describe an optimal join program that minimizes response time (consider only communication).

9.4 Consider the join graph of Figure 9.10, and give a program (possibly not optimal) that reduces each relation fully by semijoins.

*9.5 Consider the join graph of Figure 9.10 and the fragmentation depicted in Figure 9.15. Also assume that $size(\text{EMP} \bowtie \text{ASG}) = 2000$ and $size(\text{ASG} \bowtie \text{PROJ}) = 1000$. Apply the algorithm of distributed INGRES in two cases, general network and broadcast network, so that communication time is minimized.

Rel.	Site 1	Site 2	Site 3
EMP	1000	1000	1000
ASG		2000	
PROJ	1000		

Figure 9.15. Fragmentation

9.6 Consider the join graph of Figure 9.16 and the statistics given in Figure 9.17. Apply the SDD-1 algorithm with $T_{MSG} = 20$ and $T_{TR} = 1$.

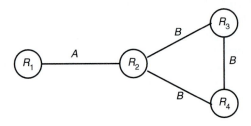

Figure 9.16. Join Graph

**9.7 Consider the query in Exercise 8.5. Assume that relations EMP, ASG, PROJ and PAY have been stored at sites 1,2 and 3 according to the table in Figure 9.18. Assume also that the transfer rate between any two sites is

relation	size
R_1	1000
R_2	1000
R_3	2000
R_3	1000

attribute	size	SF_{SJ}
$R_1.A$	200	0.5
$R_2.A$	100	0.1
$R_2.A$	100	0.2
$R_3.B$	300	0.9
$R_4.B$	150	0.4

(a)   (b)

Figure 9.17. Relation Statistics

equal and that data transfer is 100 times slower than data processing performed by any site. Finally, assume that $size(R \bowtie S) = \max(size(R), size(S))$
for any two relations R and S, and the selectivity factor of the disjunctive
selection of the query in Exercise 8.5 is 0.5. Compose a distributed program,
using a technique of your choice, which computes the answer to the query
and minimizes total time.

Rel.	Site 1	Site 2	Site 3
EMP	2000		
ASG		3000	
PROJ			1000
PAY			500

Figure 9.18. Fragmentation Statistics

Chapter 10

INTRODUCTION TO TRANSACTION MANAGEMENT

Up to this point the basic access primitive that we have considered has been a query. In Chapters 7 to 9 we discussed how queries are processed and optimized. However, we never considered what happens if, for example, two queries attempt to update the same data item, or if a system failure occurs during execution of a query. For retrieve-only queries, neither of these conditions is a problem. One can have two queries reading the value of the same data item concurrently. Similarly, a read-only query can simply be restarted after a system failure is handled. On the other hand, it is not difficult to see that for update queries, these conditions can have disastrous effects on the database. We cannot, for example, simply restart the execution of an update query following a system failure since certain data item values may already have been updated prior to the failure and should not be updated again when the query is restarted. Otherwise, the database would contain incorrect data.

The fundamental point here is that there is no notion of "consistent execution" or "reliable computation" associated with the concept of a query. The concept of a *transaction* is used within the database domain as a basic unit of consistent and reliable computing. Thus queries are executed as transactions once their execution strategies are determined and they are translated into primitive database operations.

In the discussion above, we used the terms *consistent* and *reliable* quite informally. Due to their importance in our discussion, we need to define them more precisely. We should first point out that we differentiate between *database consistency* and *transaction consistency*.

A database is in a *consistent state* if it obeys all of the consistency (integrity) constraints defined over it (see Chapter 6). State changes occur due to modifications, insertions, and deletions (together called *updates*). Of course, we want to ensure that the database never enters an inconsistent state. Note that the database can be (and usually is) temporarily inconsistent during the execution of a transaction. The important point is that the database should be consistent when the transaction terminates (Figure 10.1).

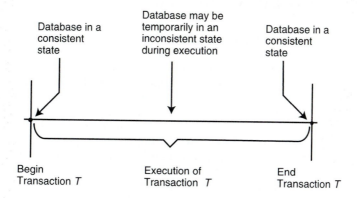

Figure 10.1. A Transaction Model

Transaction consistency, on the other hand, refers to the actions of concurrent transactions. We would like the database to remain in a consistent state even if there are a number of user requests that are concurrently accessing (reading or updating) the database. A complication arises when replicated databases are considered. A replicated replicated databasedatabase is in a *mutually consistent state* if all the copies of every data item in it have identical values. This is referred to as *one-copy equivalence* since all replica copies are forced to assume the same state at the end of a transaction's execution. There are more relaxed notions of replica consistency that allow replica values to diverge. These will be discussed later in the text.

Reliability refers to both the *resiliency* of a system to various types of failures and its capability to *recover* from them. A resilient system is tolerant of system failures and can continue to provide services even when failures occur. A recoverable DBMS is one that can get to a consistent state (by moving back to a previous consistent state or forward to a new consistent state) following various types of failures.

Transaction management deals with the problems of always keeping the database in a consistent state even when concurrent accesses and failures occur. In the upcoming two chapters, we investigate the issues related to managing transactions. The purpose of the current chapter is to define the fundamental terms and to provide the framework within which these issues can be discussed. It also serves as a concise introduction to the problem and the related issues. We will therefore discuss the concepts at a high level of abstraction and will not present any management techniques.

The organization of this chapter is as follows. In the next section we formally and intuitively define the concept of a transaction. In Section 10.2 we discuss the properties of transactions and what the implications of each of these properties are in terms of transaction management. In Section 10.3 we present various types of transactions. In Section 10.4 we revisit the architectural model defined in Chapter 4 and indicate the modifications that are necessary to support transaction management.

10.1 DEFINITION OF A TRANSACTION

In [Gray, 1981] the author indicates that the transaction concept has its roots in contract law. He states, "In making a contract, two or more parties negotiate for a while and then make a deal. The deal is made binding by the joint signature of a document or by some other act (as simple as a handshake or a nod). If the parties are rather suspicious of one another or just want to be safe, they appoint an intermediary (usually called an escrow officer) to coordinate the commitment of the transaction." The nice aspect of this historical perspective is that the description above does indeed encompass *some* of the fundamental properties of a transaction (atomicity and durability) as the term is used in database systems. It also serves to indicate the differences between a transaction and a query.

As indicated before, a transaction is a unit of consistent and reliable computation. Thus, intuitively, a transaction takes a database, performs an action on it, and generates a new version of the database, causing a state transition. This is similar to what a query does, except that if the database was consistent before the execution of the transaction, we can now guarantee that it will be consistent at the end of its execution regardless of the fact that (1) the transaction may have been executed concurrently with others, and (2) failures may have occurred during its execution.

In general, a transaction is considered to be made up of a sequence of read and write operations on the database, together with computation steps. In that sense, a transaction may be thought of as a program with embedded database access queries [Papadimitriou, 1986]. Another definition of a transaction is that it is a single execution of a program [Ullman, 1988]. A single query can also be thought of as a program that can be posed as a transaction.

Example 10.1

Consider the following SQL query for increasing by 10% the budget of the CAD/CAM project that we discussed (in Example 6.14):

```
UPDATE    PROJ
SET       BUDGET = BUDGET*1.1
WHERE     PNAME= ''CAD/CAM''
```

This query can be specified, using the embedded SQL notation, as a transaction by giving it a name (e.g., BUDGET_UPDATE) and declaring it as follows:

Begin_transaction BUDGET_UPDATE
begin
   EXEC SQL   UPDATE   PROJ
         SET   BUDGET = BUDGET*1.1
         WHERE   PNAME= "CAD/CAM"
end.

The **Begin_transaction** and **end** statements delimit a transaction. Note that the use of delimiters is not enforced in every DBMS. For example, if delimiters are not specified, DB2 would simply treat as a transaction the entire program that performs a database access.

Example 10.2

In our discussion of transaction management concepts, we will use an airline reservation system example instead of the one used in the first nine chapters. The real-life implementation of this application almost always makes use of the transaction concept. Let us assume that there is a FLIGHT relation that records the data about each flight, a CUST relation for the customers who book flights, and an FC relation indicating which customers are on what flights. Let us also assume that the relation definitions are as follows (where the underlined attributes constitute the keys):

> FLIGHT(<u>FNO,DATE</u>,SRC,DEST,STSOLD,CAP)
> CUST(<u>CNAME</u>,ADDR,BAL)
> FC(<u>FNO,DATE,CNAME</u>,SPECIAL)

The definition of the attributes in this database schema are as follows: FNO is the flight number, DATE denotes the flight date, SRC and DEST indicate the source and destination for the flight, STSOLD indicates the number of seats that have been sold on that flight, CAP denotes the passenger capacity on the flight, CNAME indicates the customer name whose address is stored in ADDR and whose account balance is in BAL, and SPECIAL corresponds to any special requests that the customer may have for a booking.

Let us consider a simplified version of a typical reservation application, where a travel agent enters the flight number, the date, and a customer name, and asks for a reservation. The transaction to perform this function can be implemented as follows, where database accesses are specified in embedded SQL notation:

> **Begin_transaction** Reservation
> **begin**
>   **input**(flight_no, date, customer_name);   (1)
>   EXEC SQL UPDATE FLIGHT   (2)
>   SET   STSOLD = STSOLD + 1
>   WHERE   FNO = flight_no
>   AND   DATE = date;
>   EXEC SQL INSERT   (3)
>   INTO   FC(FNO,DATE,CNAME,SPECIAL)
>   VALUES (flight_no,date,customer_name, *null*);
>   **output**("reservation completed")   (4)
> **end**.

Let us explain this example. First a point about notation. Even though we use embedded SQL, we do not follow its syntax very strictly. The lowercase terms are the program variables; the uppercase terms denote database relations and attributes as well as the SQL statements. Numeric constants are used as they are, whereas character constants are enclosed in quotes. Keywords of the host language are written in boldface, and *null* is a keyword for the null string.

The first thing that the transaction does [line (1)], is to input the flight number, the date, and the customer name. Line (2) updates the number of sold seats on the requested flight by one. Line (3) inserts a tuple into the FC relation. Here we assume that the customer is an old one, so it is not necessary to have an insertion into the CUST relation, creating a record for the client. The keyword *null* in line (3) indicates that the customer has no special requests on this flight. Finally, line (4) reports the result of the transaction to the agent's terminal.

10.1.1 Termination Conditions of Transactions

The reservation transaction of Example 10.2 has an implicit assumption about its termination. It assumes that there will always be a free seat and does not take into consideration the fact that the transaction may fail due to lack of seats. This is an unrealistic assumption that brings up the issue of termination possibilities of transactions.

A transaction always terminates, even when there are failures as we will see in Chapter 12. If the transaction can complete its task successfully, we say that the transaction *commits*. If, on the other hand, a transaction stops without completing its task, we say that it *aborts*. Transactions may abort for a number of reasons, which are discussed in the upcoming chapters. In our example, a transaction aborts itself because of a condition that would prevent it from completing its task successfully. Additionally, the DBMS may abort a transaction due to, for example, deadlocks or other conditions. When a transaction is aborted, its execution is stopped and all of its already executed actions are *undone* by returning the database to the state before their execution. This is also known as *rollback*.

The importance of commit is twofold. The commit command signals to the DBMS that the effects of that transaction should now be reflected in the database, thereby making it visible to other transactions which may access the same data items. Second, the point at which a transaction is committed is a "point of no return." The results of the committed transaction are now *permanently* stored in the database and cannot be undone. The specific implementation of the commit command is the topic of Chapter 12.

Example 10.3

Let us return to our reservation system example. One thing we did not consider is that there may not be any free seats available on the desired flight. To cover this possibility, the reservation transaction needs to be revised as follows:

Begin_transaction Reservation
begin
    input(flight_no, date, customer_name);
    EXEC SQL   SELECT   STSOLD,CAP
                INTO   temp1,temp2
                FROM   FLIGHT
                WHERE   FNO = flight_no
                AND   DATE = date;
   if temp1 = temp2 **then**
   begin
     output("no free seats");
     Abort
   end
   else begin
      EXEC SQL   UPDATE   FLIGHT
                 SET   STSOLD = STSOLD + 1
                 WHERE   FNO = flight_no
                 AND   DATE = date;
      EXEC SQL   INSERT
                 INTO   FC(FNO,DATE,CNAME,SPECIAL)
                 VALUES   (flight_no, date, customer_name, *null*);
     Commit;
     output("reservation completed")
    end
   end-if
 end.

In this version the first SQL statement gets the STSOLD and CAP into the two variables temp1 and temp2. These two values are then compared to determine if any seats are available. The transaction either aborts if there are no free seats, or updates the STSOLD value and inserts a new tuple into the FC relation to represent the seat that was sold.

Several things are important in this example. One is, obviously, the fact that if no free seats are available, the transaction is aborted.[1] The second is the ordering of the output to the user with respect to the abort and commit commands. Note that if the transaction is aborted, the user can be notified before the DBMS is instructed to abort it. However, in case of commit, the user notification has to follow the successful servicing (by the DBMS) of the commit command, for reliability reasons. This is discussed further in Section 10.2.4 and in Chapter 12.

---

[1] We will be kind to the airlines and assume that they never overbook. Thus our reservation transaction does not need to check for that condition.

10.1.2 Characterization of Transactions

Observe in the preceding examples that transactions read and write some data. This has been used as the basis for characterizing a transaction. The data items that a transaction reads are said to constitute its *read set* (RS). Similarly, the data items that a transaction writes are said to constitute its *write set* (WS). Note that the read set and write set of a transaction need not be mutually exclusive. Finally, the union of the read set and write set of a transaction constitutes its *base set* ($BS = RS \cup WS$).

Example 10.4

Considering the reservation transaction as specified in Example 10.3 and the insert to be a number of write operations, the above-mentioned sets are defined as follows:

$$
\begin{aligned}
RS[\text{Reservation}] \;&=\; \{\text{FLIGHT.STSOLD, FLIGHT.CAP}\} \\
WS[\text{Reservation}] \;&=\; \{\text{FLIGHT.STSOLD, FC.FNO, FC.DATE,} \\
&\qquad \text{FC.CNAME, FC.SPECIAL}\} \\
BS[\text{Reservation}] \;&=\; \{\text{FLIGHT.STSOLD, FLIGHT.CAP,} \\
&\qquad \text{FC.FNO, FC.DATE, FC.CNAME, FC.SPECIAL}\}
\end{aligned}
$$

Note that it may be appropriate to include FLIGHT.FNO and FLIGHT.DATE in the read set of Reservation since they are accessed during execution of the SQL query. We omit them to simplify the example.

We have characterized transactions only on the basis of their read and write operations, without considering the insertion and deletion operations. We therefore base our discussion of transaction management concepts on *static* databases that do not grow or shrink. This simplification is made in the interest of simplicity. Dynamic databases have to deal with the problem of *phantoms*, which can be explained using the following example. Consider that transaction T_1, during its execution, searches the FC table for the names of customers who have ordered a special meal. It gets a set of CNAME for customers who satisfy the search criteria. While T_1 is executing, transaction T_2 inserts new tuples into FC with the special meal request, and commits. If T_1 were to re-issue the same search query later in its execution, it will get back a set of CNAME which is different than the original set it had retrieved. Thus, "phantom" tuples have appeared in the database. We do not discuss phantoms any further in this book. Interested readers should refer to [Eswaran et al., 1976], [Bernstein et al., 1987].

We should also point out that the read and write operations to which we refer are abstract operations that do not have one-to-one correspondence to physical I/O primitives. One read in our characterization may translate into a number of primitive read operations to access the index structures and the physical data pages. The reader should treat each read and write as a language primitive rather than as an operating system primitive.

10.1.3 Formalization of the Transaction Concept

By now, the meaning of a transaction should be intuitively clear. To reason about transactions and about the correctness of the management algorithms, it is necessary to define the concept formally. We denote by $O_{ij}(x)$ some *operation* O_j of transaction T_i that operates on a database entity x. Following the conventions adopted in the preceding section, $O_{ij} \in \{\text{read, write}\}$. Operations are assumed to be *atomic* (i.e., each is executed as an indivisible unit). We let OS_i denote the set of all operations in T_i (i.e., $OS_i = \bigcup_j O_{ij}$). We denote by N_i the termination condition for T_i, where $N_i \in \{\text{abort, commit}\}$.[2]

With this terminology we can define a transaction T_i as a partial ordering over its operations and the termination condition. A partial order $P = \{\Sigma, \prec\}$ defines an ordering among the elements of Σ (called the *domain*) according to an irreflexive and transitive binary relation $\prec$ defined over Σ. In our case Σ consists of the operations and termination condition of a transaction, whereas $\prec$ indicates the execution order of these operations (which we will read as "precedes in execution order"). Formally, then, a transaction T_i is a partial order $T_i = \{\Sigma_i, \prec_i\}$, where

1. $\Sigma_i = OS_i \cup \{N_i\}$.

2. For any two operations $O_{ij}, O_{ik} \in OS_i$, if $O_{ij} = \{R(x) \text{ or } W(x)\}$ and $O_{ik} = W(x)$ for any data item x, then either $O_{ij} \prec_i O_{ik}$ or $O_{ik} \prec_i O_{ij}$.

3. $\forall O_{ij} \in OS_i, O_{ij} \prec_i N_i$.

The first condition formally defines the domain as the set of read and write operations that make up the transaction, plus the termination condition, which may be either commit or abort. The second condition specifies the ordering relation between the conflicting read and write operations of the transaction, while the final condition indicates that the termination condition always follows all other operations.

There are two important points about this definition. First, the ordering relation $\prec$ is given and the definition does not attempt to construct it. The ordering relation is actually application dependent. Second, condition two indicates that the ordering between conflicting operations has to exist within $\prec$. Two operations, $O_i(x)$ and $O_j(x)$, are said to be in *conflict* if $O_i = \text{Write}$ or $O_j = \text{Write}$ (i.e., at least one of them is a Write and they access the same data item).

Example 10.5

Consider a simple transaction T that consists of the following steps:

$$\text{Read}(x)$$
$$\text{Read}(y)$$
$$x \leftarrow x + y$$
$$\text{Write}(x)$$
$$\text{Commit}$$

---

[2]From now on we use the abbreviations R, W, A and C for the Read, Write, Abort, and Commit operations, respectively.

The specification of this transaction according to the formal notation that we have introduced is as follows:

$$\Sigma \;=\; \{R(x), R(y), W(x), C\}$$
$$\prec \;=\; \{(R(x), W(x)), (R(y), W(x)), (W(x), C), (R(x), C), (R(y), C)\}$$

where (O_i, O_j) as an element of the $\prec$ relation indicates that $O_i \prec O_j$.

Notice that the ordering relation specifies the relative ordering of all operations with respect to the termination condition. This is due to the third condition of transaction definition. Also note that we do not specify the ordering between every pair of operations. That is why it is a *partial* order.

Example 10.6

The reservation transaction developed in Example 10.3 is more complex. Notice that there are two possible termination conditions, depending on the availability of seats. It might first seem that this is a contradiction of the definition of a transaction, which indicates that there can be only one termination condition. However, remember that a transaction is the execution of a program. It is clear that in any execution, only one of the two termination conditions can occur. Therefore, what exists is one transaction that aborts and another one that commits. Using this formal notation, the former can be specified as follows:

$$\Sigma \;=\; \{R(\text{STSOLD}), R(\text{CAP}), A\}$$
$$\prec \;=\; \{(O_1, A), (O_2, A)\}$$

and the latter can be specified as

$$\Sigma \;=\; \{R(\text{STSOLD}), R(\text{CAP}), W(\text{STSOLD}),$$
$$W(\text{FNO}), W(\text{DATE}), W(\text{CNAME}), W(\text{SPECIAL}), C\}$$
$$\prec \;=\; \{(O_1, O_3), (O_2, O_3), (O_1, O_4), (O_1, O_5), (O_1, O_6), (O_1, O_7), (O_2, O_4),$$
$$(O_2, O_5), (O_2, O_6), (O_2, O_7), (O_1, C), (O_2, C), (O_3, C), (O_4, C),$$
$$(O_5, C), (O_6, C), (O_7, C)\}$$

where $O_1 = R(\text{STSOLD})$, $O_2 = R(\text{CAP})$, $O_3 = W(\text{STSOLD})$, $O_4 = W(\text{FNO})$, $O_5 = W(\text{DATE})$, $O_6 = W(\text{CNAME})$, and $O_7 = W(\text{SPECIAL})$.

One advantage of defining a transaction as a partial order is its correspondence to a directed acyclic graph (DAG). Thus a transaction can be specified as a DAG whose vertices are the operations of a transaction and whose arcs indicate the ordering relationship between a given pair of operations. This will be useful in discussing the concurrent execution of a number of transactions (Chapter 11) and in arguing about their correctness by means of graph-theoretic tools.

Example 10.7

The transaction discussed in Example 10.5 can be drawn as a DAG, as shown in Figure 10.2. Note that we do not draw the arcs that are implied by transitivity even though we indicate them as elements of $\prec$.

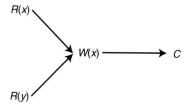

Figure 10.2. DAG Representation of a Transaction

In most cases we do not need to refer to the domain of the partial order separately from the ordering relation. Therefore, it is common to drop Σ from the transaction definition and use the name of the partial order to refer to both the domain and the name of the partial order. This is convenient since it allows us to specify the ordering of the operations of a transaction in a more straightforward manner by making use of their relative ordering in the transaction definition. For example, we can define the transaction of Example 10.5 as follows:

$$T = \{R(x), R(y), W(x), C\}$$

instead of the longer specification given before. We will therefore use the modified definition in this and subsequent chapters.

10.2 PROPERTIES OF TRANSACTIONS

The previous discussion clarifies the concept of a transaction. However, we have not yet provided any justification of our earlier claim that it is a unit of consistent and reliable computation. We do that in this section. The consistency and reliability aspects of transactions are due to four properties: (1) atomicity, (2) consistency, (3) isolation, and (4) durability. Together, these are commonly referred to as the "ACIDity" of transactions. These properties are not entirely independent of each other; usually there are dependencies among them as we will indicate below. We discuss each of these properties in the following sections. Note that this discussion sets the framework for Chapters 11 and 12.

10.2.1 Atomicity

Atomicity refers to the fact that a transaction is treated as a unit of operation. Therefore, either all the transaction's actions are completed, or none of them are.

This is also known as the "all-or-nothing property." Notice that we have just extended the concept of atomicity from individual operations to the entire transaction. Atomicity requires that if the execution of a transaction is interrupted by any sort of failure, the DBMS will be responsible for determining what to do with the transaction upon recovery from the failure. There are, of course, two possible courses of action: it can either be terminated by completing the remaining actions, or it can be terminated by undoing all the actions that have already been executed.

One can generally talk about two types of failures. A transaction itself may fail due to input data errors, deadlocks, or other factors. In these cases either the transaction aborts itself, as we have seen in Example 10.2, or the DBMS may abort it while handling deadlocks, for example. Maintaining transaction atomicity in the presence of this type of failure is commonly called the *transaction recovery*. The second type of failure is caused by system crashes, such as media failures, processor failures, communication link breakages, power outages, and so on. Ensuring transaction atomicity in the presence of system crashes is called *crash recovery*. An important difference between the two types of failures is that during some types of system crashes, the information in volatile storage may be lost or inaccessible. Both types of recovery are parts of the reliability issue, which we discuss in considerable detail in Chapter 12.

10.2.2 Consistency

The *consistency* of a transaction is simply its correctness. In other words, a transaction is a correct program that maps one consistent database state to another. Verifying that transactions are consistent is the concern of semantic data control, covered in Chapter 6. Ensuring transaction consistency as defined at the beginning of this chapter, on the other hand, is the objective of concurrency control mechanisms, which we discuss in Chapter 11.

There is an interesting classification of consistency that parallels our discussion above and is equally important. This classification groups databases into four levels of consistency [Gray et al., 1976]. In the following definition (which is taken verbatim from the original paper), *dirty* data refers to data values that have been updated by a transaction prior to its commitment. Then, based on the concept of dirty data, the four levels are defined as follows:

"Degree 3: Transaction T sees *degree 3 consistency* if:

1. T does not overwrite dirty data of other transactions.
2. T does not commit any writes until it completes all its writes [i.e., until the end of transaction (EOT)].
3. T does not read dirty data from other transactions.
4. Other transactions do not dirty any data read by T before T completes.

Degree 2: Transaction T sees *degree 2 consistency* if:

1. T does not overwrite dirty data of other transactions.
2. T does not commit any writes before EOT.
3. T does not read dirty data from other transactions.

Degree 1: Transaction T sees *degree 1 consistency* if:

1. T does not overwrite dirty data of other transactions.

2. T does not commit any writes before EOT.

Degree 0: Transaction T sees *degree 0 consistency* if:

1. T does not overwrite dirty data of other transactions."

Of course, it is true that a higher degree of consistency encompasses all the lower degrees. The point in defining multiple levels of consistency is to provide application programmers the flexibility to define transactions that operate at different levels. Consequently, while some transactions operate at Degree 3 consistency level, others may operate at lower levels and may see, for example, dirty data.

10.2.3 Isolation

Isolation is the property of transactions which requires each transaction to see a consistent database at all times. In other words, an executing transaction cannot reveal its results to other concurrent transactions before its commitment.

There are a number of reasons for insisting on isolation. One has to do with maintaining the interconsistency of transactions. If two concurrent transactions access a data item that is being updated by one of them, it is not possible to guarantee that the second will read the correct value.

Example 10.8

Consider the following two concurrent transactions (T_1 and T_2), both of which access data item x. Assume that the value of x before they start executing is 50.

$$
\begin{array}{llll}
T_1: & \text{Read}(x) & T_2: & \text{Read}(x) \\
     & x \leftarrow x + 1 & & x \leftarrow x + 1 \\
     & \text{Write}(x) & & \text{Write}(x) \\
     & \text{Commit} & & \text{Commit}
\end{array}
$$

The following is one possible sequence of execution of the actions of these transactions:

$$
\begin{array}{ll}
T_1: & \text{Read}(x) \\
T_1: & x \leftarrow x + 1 \\
T_1: & \text{Write}(x) \\
T_1: & \text{Commit} \\
T_2: & \text{Read}(x) \\
T_2: & x \leftarrow x + 1 \\
T_2: & \text{Write}(x) \\
T_2: & \text{Commit}
\end{array}
$$

In this case there are no problems; transactions T_1 and T_2 are executed one after the other and transaction T_2 reads 51 as the value of x. Note that if, instead, T_2 executes before T_1, T_2 reads 51 as the value of x. So, if T_1 and T_2 are executed one after the other (regardless of the order), the second transaction will read 51 as the value of x and x will have 52 as its value at the end of execution of these two transactions. However, since transactions are executing concurrently, the following execution sequence is also possible:

$$
\begin{array}{ll}
T_1: & \text{Read}(x) \\
T_1: & x \leftarrow x + 1 \\
T_2: & \text{Read}(x) \\
T_1: & \text{Write}(x) \\
T_2: & x \leftarrow x + 1 \\
T_2: & \text{Write}(x) \\
T_1: & \text{Commit} \\
T_2: & \text{Commit}
\end{array}
$$

In this case, transaction T_2 reads 50 as the value of x. This is incorrect since T_2 reads x while its value is being changed from 50 to 51. Furthermore, the value of x is 51 at the end of execution of T_1 and T_2 since T_2's Write will overwrite T_1's Write.

Ensuring isolation by not permitting incomplete results to be seen by other transactions, as the previous example shows, solves the *lost updates* problem. This type of isolation has been called *cursor stability*. In the example above, the second execution sequence resulted in the effects of T_1 being lost.[3]   A second reason for isolation is *cascading aborts*. If a transaction permits others to see its incomplete results before committing and then decides to abort, any transaction that has read its incomplete values will have to abort as well. This chain can easily grow and impose considerable overhead on the DBMS.

It is possible to treat consistency levels discussed in the preceding section from the perspective of the isolation property (thus demonstrating the dependence between isolation and consistency). As we move up the hierarchy of consistency levels, there is more isolation among transactions. Degree 0 provides very little isolation other than preventing lost updates. However, since transactions commit before they complete all their writes, if an abort occurs later it will require undoing the updates to data items that have been committed and are currently being accessed by other transactions. Degree 2 consistency avoids cascading aborts. Degree 3 provides full isolation which forces one of the conflicting transactions to wait until the other one

---

[3] A more dramatic example may be to consider x to be your bank account and T_1 a transaction that executes as a result of your *depositing* money into your account. Assume that T_2 is a transaction that is executing as a result of your spouse *withdrawing* money from the account at another branch. If the same problem as described in Example 10.8 occurs and the results of T_1 are lost, you will be terribly unhappy. If, on the other hand, the results of T_2 are lost, the bank will be furious. A similar argument can be made for the reservation transaction example we have been considering.

terminates. Such execution sequences are called *strict* and will be discussed further in the next chapter. It is obvious that the issue of isolation is directly related to database consistency and is therefore the topic of concurrency control.

ANSI, as part of the SQL2 (also known as SQL-92) standard specification, has defined a set of isolation levels [ANSI, 1992]. SQL isolation levels are defined on the basis of what ANSI call *phenomena* which are situations that can occur if proper isolation is not maintained. Three phenomena are specified:

Dirty Read: As defined earlier, dirty data refer to data items whose values have been modified by a transaction that has not yet committed. Consider the case where transaction T_1 modifies a data item value, which is then read by another transaction T_2 before T_1 performs a Commit or Abort. In case T_1 aborts, T_2 has read a value which never exists in the database.

A precise specification[4] of this phenomenon is as follows (where subscripts indicate the transaction identifiers)

$$\ldots, W_1(x), \ldots, R_2(x), \ldots, C_1(\text{or} A_1), \ldots, C_2(\text{or} A_2)$$

or

$$\ldots, W_1(x), \ldots, R_2(x), \ldots, C_2(\text{or} A_2), \ldots, C_1(\text{or} A_1)$$

Non-repeatable or Fuzzy Read: Transaction T_1 reads a data item value. Another transaction T_2 then modifies or deletes that data item and commits. If T_1 then attempts to reread the data item, it either reads a different value or it can't find the data item at all; thus two reads within the same transaction T_1 return different results.

A precise specification of this phenomenon is as follows:

$$\ldots, R_1(x), \ldots, W_2(x), \ldots, C_1(\text{or} A_1), \ldots, C_2(\text{or} A_2)$$

or

$$\ldots, R_1(x), \ldots, W_2(x), \ldots, C_2(\text{or} A_2), \ldots, C_1(\text{or} A_1)$$

Phantom: The phantom condition that was defined earlier occurs when T_1 does a search with a predicate and T_2 inserts new tuples that satisfy the predicate. Again, the precise specification of this phenomenon is (where P is the search predicate)

$$\ldots, R_1(P), \ldots, W_2(y \text{in} P), \ldots, C_1(\text{or} A_1), \ldots, C_2(\text{or} A_2)$$

or

$$\ldots, R_1(P), \ldots, W_2(y \text{in} P), \ldots, C_2(\text{or} A_2), \ldots, C_1(\text{or} A_1)$$

Based on these phenomena, the isolation levels are defined as follows. The objective of defining multiple isolation levels is the same as defining multiple consistency levels.

---

[4]The precise specifications of these phenomena are taken from [Berenson et al., 1995] and correspond to their *loose interpretations* which they indicate are the more appropriate interpretations.

Read Uncommitted: For transactions operating at this level all three phenomena are possible.

Read Committed: Fuzzy reads and phantoms are possible, but dirty reads are not.

Repeatable Read: Only phantoms are possible.

Anomaly Serializable: None of the phenomena are possible.

ANSI SQL standard uses the term "serializable" rather than "anomaly Serializable." However, as noted in [Berenson et al., 1995], a serializable isolation level, as precisely defined in the next chapter, cannot be defined solely in terms of the three phenomena identified above. Therefore, we follow [Berenson et al., 1995] in naming this isolation level as "Anomaly Serializable." The relationship between SQL isolation levels and the four levels of consistency defined in the previous section are also discussed in [Berenson et al., 1995].

10.2.4 Durability

Durability refers to that property of transactions which ensures that once a transaction commits, its results are permanent and cannot be erased from the database. Therefore, the DBMS ensures that the results of a transaction will survive subsequent system failures. This is exactly why in Example 10.2 we insisted that the transaction commit before it informs the user of its successful completion. The durability property brings forth the issue of *database recovery*, that is, how to recover the database to a consistent state where all the committed actions are reflected. This issue is discussed further in Chapter 12.

10.3 TYPES OF TRANSACTIONS

A number of transaction models have been proposed in literature, each being appropriate for a class of applications. The fundamental problem of providing "ACID"ity usually remains, but the algorithms and techniques that are used to address them may be considerably different. In some cases, various aspects of ACID requirements are relaxed, removing some problems and adding new ones. In this section we provide an overview of some of the transaction models that have been proposed and then identify our focus in Chapters 11 and 12.

Transactions have been classified according to a number of criteria. One criterion is the duration of transactions. Accordingly, transactions may be classified as *on-line* or *batch* [Gray, 1987]. More common names for these two classes are *short-life* and *long-life* transactions, respectively. On-line transactions are characterized by very short execution/response times (typically, on the order of a couple of seconds) and by access to a relatively small portion of the database. This class of transactions probably covers a large majority of current transaction applications. Examples include banking transactions and airline reservation transactions.

Batch transactions, on the other hand, take longer to execute (response time being measured in minutes, hours, or even days) and access a larger portion of the database. Typical applications that might require batch transactions are

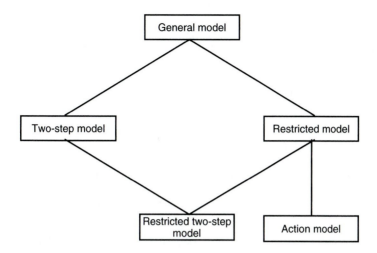

Figure 10.3. Various Transaction Models (From: C.H. Papadimitriou and P.C. Kanellakis, ON CONCURRENCY CONTROL BY MULTIPLE VERSIONS. ACM Trans. Database Sys.; December 1984; 9(1): 89–99.)

CAD/CAM databases, statistical applications, report generation, complex queries, and image processing. Along this dimension, one can also define a *conversational* transaction, which is executed by interacting with the user issuing it.

Another classification that has been proposed is with respect to the organization of the read and write actions. The examples that we have considered so far intermix their read and write actions without any specific ordering. We call this type of transactions *general*. If the transactions are restricted so that all the read actions are performed before any write action, the transaction is called a *two-step* transaction [Papadimitriou, 1979]. Similarly, if the transaction is restricted so that a data item has to be read before it can be updated (written), the corresponding class is called *restricted* (or *read-before-write*) [Stearns et al., 1976]. If a transaction is both two-step and restricted, it is called a *restricted two-step* transaction. Finally, there is the *action* model of transactions [Kung and Papadimitriou, 1979], which consists of the restricted class with the further restriction that each <read, write> pair be executed atomically. This classification is shown in Figure 10.3, where the generality increases upward.

Example 10.9

The following are some examples of the above-mentioned models. We omit the declaration and commit commands.

General:

$$T_1 : \{R(x), R(y), W(y), R(z), W(x), W(z), W(w), C\}$$

Two-step:

$$T_2 : \{R(x), R(y), R(z), W(x), W(z), W(y), W(w), C\}$$

Restricted:

$$T_3 : \{R(x), R(y), W(y), R(z), W(x), W(z), R(w), W(w), C\}$$

Note that T_3 has to read w before writing.
Two-step restricted:

$$T_4 : \{R(x), R(y), R(z), R(w), W(x), W(z), W(y), W(w), C\}$$

Action:

$$T_5 : \{[R(x), W(x)], [R(y), W(y)], [R(z), W(z)], [R(w), W(w)], C\}$$

Note that each pair of actions within square brackets is executed atomically.

Transactions can also be classified according to their structure. We distinguish four broad categories in increasing complexity: *flat transactions, closed nested transactions* as in [Moss, 1985], and *open nested transactions* such as sagas [Garcia-Molina and Salem, 1987], and *workflow models* which, in some cases, are combinations of various nested forms. This classification is arguably the most dominant one and we will discuss it at some length.

10.3.1 Flat Transactions

Flat transactions have a single start point (**Begin_transaction**) and a single termination point (**End_transaction**). All our examples in this section are of this type. Most of the transaction management work in databases has concentrated on flat transactions (see, for example [Bernstein et al., 1987] and [Gray and Reuter, 1993]). This model will also be our main focus in this book, even though we discuss management techniques for other transaction types, where appropriate.

10.3.2 Nested Transactions

An alternative transaction model is to permit a transaction to include other transactions with their own begin and commit points. Such transactions are called *nested transactions*. These transactions that are embedded in another one are usually called *subtransactions*.

Example 10.10

Let us extend the reservation transaction of Example 10.2. Most travel agents will make reservations for hotels and car rentals in addition to the flights. If one chooses to specify all of this as one transaction, the reservation transaction would have the following structure:

Begin_transaction Reservation
begin
    Begin_transaction Airline

       . . .

    end. {Airline}
    Begin_transaction Hotel

       . . .

    end. {Hotel}
    Begin_transaction Car

       . . .

    end. {Car}
end.

Nested transactions have received considerable interest as a more generalized transaction concept. The level of nesting is generally open, allowing subtransactions themselves to have nested transactions. This generality is necessary to support application areas where transactions are more complex than in traditional data processing.

In this taxonomy, we differentiate between *closed* and *open* nesting because of their termination characteristics. Closed nested transactions [Moss, 1985] commit in a bottom-up fashion through the root. Thus, a nested subtransaction begins *after* its parent and finishes *before* it, and the commitment of the subtransactions is conditional upon the commitment of the parent. The semantics of these transactions enforce atomicity at the top-most level. Open nesting relaxes the top-level atomicity restriction of closed nested transactions. Therefore, an open nested transaction allows its partial results to be observed outside the transaction. Sagas [Garcia-Molina and Salem, 1987], [Garcia-Molina et al., 1990] and split transactions [Pu, 1988] are examples of open nesting.

A saga is a "sequence of transactions that can be interleaved with other transactions" [Garcia-Molina and Salem, 1987]. The DBMS guarantees that either all the transactions in a saga are successfully completed or *compensating transactions* [Garcia-Molina, 1983], [Korth et al., 1990] are run to recover from a partial execution. A compensating transaction effectively does the inverse of the transaction that it is associated with. For example, if the transaction adds $100 to a bank account, its compensating transaction deducts $100 from the same bank account. If a transaction is viewed as a function, f, that maps the old database state to a new database state, its compensating transaction is the inverse function, f'.

Two properties of sagas are: (1) only two levels of nesting are allowed, and (2) at the outer level, the system does not support full atomicity. Therefore, a saga differs from a closed nested transaction in that its level structure is more restricted (only 2) and that it is open (the partial results of component transactions or sub-sagas are visible to the outside). Furthermore, the transactions that make up a saga have to be executed sequentially.

The saga concept is extended in [Garcia-Molina et al., 1990] and placed within a more general model that deals with long-lived transactions and with activities which consist of multiple steps. The fundamental concept of the model is that of a module which captures code segments that accomplish a given task and access a database in the process. The modules are modeled (at some level) as sub-sagas which communicate with each other via messages over ports. The transactions that make up a saga can be executed in parallel. The model is multi-layer where each subsequent layer adds a level of abstraction.

The advantages of nested transactions are the following. First, they provide a higher-level of concurrency among transactions. Since a transaction consists of a number of other transactions, more concurrency is possible within a single transaction. For example, if the reservation transaction of Example 10.10 is implemented as a flat transaction, it may not be possible to access records about a specific flight concurrently. In other words, if one travel agent issues the reservation transaction for a given flight, any concurrent transaction that wishes to access the same flight data will have to wait until the termination of the first, which includes the hotel and car reservation activities in addition to flight reservation. However, a nested implementation will permit the second transaction to access the flight data as soon as the Airline subtransaction of the first reservation transaction is completed. In other words, it may be possible to perform a finer level of synchronization among concurrent transactions.

A second argument in favor of nested transactions is related to recovery. It is possible to recover independently from failures of each subtransaction. This limits the damage to a smaller part of the transaction, making it less costly to recover. In a flat transaction, if any operation fails, the entire transaction has to be aborted and restarted, whereas in a nested transaction, if an operation fails, only the subtransaction containing that operation needs to be aborted and restarted.

Finally, it is possible to create new transactions from existing ones simply by inserting the old one inside the new one as a subtransaction.

10.3.3 Workflows

Flat transactions model relatively simple and short activities very well. However, they are less appropriate for modeling longer and more elaborate activities.That is the reason for the development of the various nested transaction models discussed above. It has been argued that these extensions are not sufficiently powerful to model business activities: "after several decades of data processing, we have learned that we have not won the battle of modeling and automating complex enterprises" [Medina-Mora et al., 1993]. To meet these needs, more complex transaction models which are combinations of open and nested transactions have been proposed. There are well-justified arguments for not calling these transactions, since they hardly follow any of the ACID properties; a more appropriate name that has been proposed is a *workflow* [Dogac et al., 1998a], [Georgakopoulos et al., 1995].

The term "workflow," unfortunately, does not have a clear and uniformly accepted meaning. A working definition is that a workflow is "a collection of *tasks* organized to accomplish some business process." [Georgakopoulos et al., 1995]. This definition, however, leaves a lot undefined. This is perhaps unavoidable given the very different contexts where this term is used. In [Georgakopoulos et al., 1995], three types of workflows are identified:

1. *Human-oriented workflows*, which involve humans in performing the tasks. The system support is provided to facilitate collaboration and coordination among humans, but it is the humans themselves who are ultimately responsible for the consistency of the actions.

2. *System-oriented workflows* are those which consist of computation-intensive and specialized tasks that can be executed by a computer. The system support in this case is substantial and involves concurrency control and recovery, automatic task execution, notification, etc.

3. *Transactional workflows* range in between human-oriented and system-oriented workflows and borrow characteristics from both. They involve "coordinated execution of multiple tasks that (a) may involve humans, (b) require access to HAD [heterogeneous, autonomous, and/or distributed] systems, and (c) support selective use of tranactional properties [i.e., ACID properties] for individual tasks or entire workflows." [Georgakopoulos et al., 1995].

   Among the features of transactional workflows, the selective use of transactional properties is particularly important as it characterizes possible relaxations of ACID properties.

In this book, our primary interest is with transactional workflows. There have been many transactional workflow proposals ([Elmagarmid, 1990], [Nodine and Zdonik, 1990], [Buchmann et al., 1992], [Dayal et al., 1991], [Hsu, 1993]) which differ in a number of ways. The common point among them is that a workflow is defined as an *activity* consisting of a set of tasks with well-defined precedence relationship among them.

Example 10.11

Let us further extend the reservation transaction of Example 10.11. The entire reservation activity consists of the following taks and involves the following data

- Customer request is obtained (task T_1) and Customer Database is accessed to obtain customer information, preferences, etc.;
- Airline reservation is performed (T_2) by accessing the Flight Database;
- Hotel reservation is performed (T_3), which may involve sending a message to the hotel involved;
- Auto reservation is performed (T_4), which may also involve communication with the car rental company;
- Bill is generated (T_5) and the billing info is recorded in the billing database.

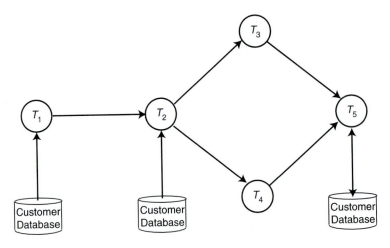

Figure 10.4. Example Workflow

Figure 10.4 depicts this workflow where there is a serial dependency of T_2 on T_1, and T_3, T_4 on T_2; however, T_3 and T_4 (hotel and car reservations) are performed in parallel and T_5 waits until their completion.

A number of workflow models go beyond this basic model by both defining more precisely what tasks can be and by allocating different relationships among the tasks. In the following, we define one model which is similar to the models of [Buchmann et al., 1992], [Dayal et al., 1991].

A workflow is modeled as an *activity* which has open nesting semantics in that it permits partial results to be visible outside the activity boundaries. Thus, tasks which make up the activity are allowed to commit individually. Tasks may be other activities (with the same open transaction semantics) or closed nested transactions that make their results visible to the entire system when they commit. Even though an activity can have both other activities and closed nested transactions as its component, a closed nested transaction task can only be composed of other closed nested transactions (i.e., once closed nesting semantics begins, it is maintained for all components).

An activity commits when its components are ready to commit. However, the components commit individually, without waiting for the root activity to commit. This raises problems in dealing with aborts since when an activity aborts, all of its components should be aborted. The problem is dealing with the components that have already committed. Therefore, compensating transactions are defined for the components of an activity. Thus, if a component has already committed when an activity aborts, the corresponding compensating transaction is executed to "undo" its effects.

Some components of an activity may be marked as *vital*. When a vital component aborts, its parent must also abort. If a non-vital component of a workflow model aborts, it may continue executing. A workflow, on the other hand, always aborts when one of its components aborts. For example, in the reservation workflow of Example 10.11, T_2 (airline reservation) and T_3 (hotel reservation) may be declared as vital so that if an airline reservation or a hotel reservation cannot be made, the workflow aborts and the entire trip is canceled. However, if a car reservation cannot be committed, the workflow can still successfully terminate.

It is possible to define *contingency tasks* which are invoked if their counterparts fail. For example, in the Reservation example presented earlier, one can specify that the contingency to making a reservation at Hilton is to make a reservation at Sheraton. Thus, if the hotel reservation component for Hilton fails, the Sheraton alternative is tried rather than aborting the task and the entire workflow.

10.4 ARCHITECTURE REVISITED

With the introduction of the transaction concept, we need to revisit the architectural model introduced in Chapter 4. We do not need to revise the model but simply need to expand the role of the distributed execution monitor.

The distributed execution monitor consists of two modules: a *transaction manager* (TM) and a *scheduler* (SC). The transaction manager is responsible for coordinating the execution of the database operations on behalf of an application. The scheduler, on the other hand, is responsible for the implementation of a specific concurrency control algorithm for synchronizing access to the database.

A third component that participates in the management of distributed transactions is the local recovery managers that exist at each site. Their function is to implement the local procedures by which the local database can be recovered to a consistent state following a failure.

Each transaction originates at one site, which we will call its *originating site*. The execution of the database operations of a transaction is coordinated by the TM at that transaction's originating site.

The transaction managers implement an interface for the application programs which consists of five commands: begin_transaction, read, write, commit, and abort. The processing of each of these commands in a replicated distributed DBMS is discussed below at an abstract level. For simplicity, we ignore the scheduling of concurrent transactions as well as the details of how data is physically retrieved by the data processor. These assumptions permit us to concentrate on the interface to the TM. The details are presented in the Chapters 11 and 12.

1. *Begin_transaction*. This is an indicator to the TM that a new transaction is starting. The TM does some bookkeeping, such as recording the transaction's name, the originating application, and so on.

2. *Read*. If the data item x is stored locally, its value is read and returned to the transaction. Otherwise, the TM selects one copy of x and requests its copy to be returned.

3. *Write.* The TM coordinates the updating of x's value at each site where it resides.

4. *Commit.* The TM coordinates the physical updating of all databases that contain copies of each data item for which a previous write was issued.

5. *Abort.* The TM makes sure that no effects of the transaction are reflected in the database.

In providing these services, a TM can communicate with SCs and data processors at the same or at different sites. This arrangement is depicted in Figure 10.5.

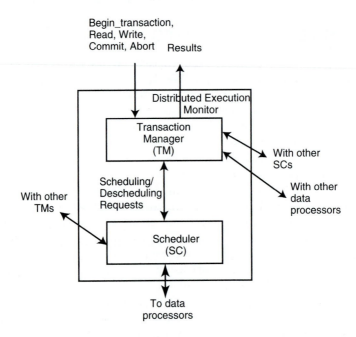

Figure 10.5. Detailed Model of the Distributed Execution Monitor

As we indicated in Chapter 4, the architectural model that we have described is only an abstraction that serves a pedagogical purpose. It enables the separation of many of the transaction management issues and their independent and isolated discussion. In Chapter 11 we focus on the interface between a TM and an SC and between an SC and a data processor, in addition to the scheduling algorithms. In Chapter 12 we consider the execution strategies for the commit and abort commands in a distributed environment, in addition to the recovery algorithms that need to be implemented for the recovery manager. We should point out that the computational model that we described here is not unique. Other models have been proposed based on dividing a transaction into subtransactions each of which is executed at a site, or on the use of private workspaces for each transaction.

10.5 CONCLUSION

In this chapter we introduced the concept of a transaction as a unit of consistent and reliable access to the database. The properties of transactions indicate that they are larger atomic units of execution which transform one consistent database to another consistent database. The properties of transactions also indicate what the requirements for managing them are, which is the topic of the next two chapters. Consistency requires a definition of integrity enforcement (which we did in Chapter 6), as well as concurrency control algorithms (which is the topic of Chapter 11). Concurrency control also deals with the issue of isolation. Durability and atomicity properties of transactions require a discussion of reliability, which we cover in Chapter 12. Specifically, durability is supported by various commit protocols and commit management, whereas atomicity requires the development of appropriate recovery protocols.

10.6 BIBLIOGRAPHIC NOTES

Transaction management has been the topic of considerable study since DBMSs have become a significant research area. There are a number of very good books on the subject. [Bernstein et al., 1987] is a very good, algorithmic introduction to the topic while [Papadimitriou, 1986] treats the issue mainly from the perspective of complexity theory and concentrates almost exclusively on concurrency control. For building a transaction management system, the ultimate book that one has to have is [Gray and Reuter, 1993]. An excellent companion to this one is [Bernstein and Newcomer, 1997] which provides an in-depth discussion of transaction processing principles. The latter one should be read first. It also gives a view of transaction processing and transaction monitors which is more general than the database-centric view that we provide in this book. A good collection of papers that focus on the concurrency control and reliability aspects of distributed systems is [Bhargava, 1987]. Two recent books focus on the performance of concurrency control mechanisms with a focus on centralized systems [Kumar, 1996], [Thomasian, 1996]. Distributed concurrency control is the topic of [Cellary et al., 1988].

Advanced transaction models are discussed and various examples are given in [Elmagarmid, 1992]. Nested transactions are also covered in [Lynch et al., 1993]. A good introduction to workflow systems is [Georgakopoulos et al., 1995]. The same topic is covered in detail in [Dogac et al., 1998a].

A very important work is a set of notes on database operating systems by Jim Gray [Gray, 1979]. These notes contain valuable information on transaction management, among other things.

The discussion concerning transaction classification in Section 10.3 comes from a number of sources. Part of it is from [Farrag, 1986]. The structure discussion is from [Özsu, 1994], [Buchmann et al., 1992], where the authors combine transaction structure with the structure of the objects that these transactions operate upon to develop a more complete classification.

There are numerous papers dealing with various transaction management issues. The ones referred to in this chapter are those that deal with the concept of a transaction. More detailed references on their management are left to Chapters 11 and 12.

Chapter 11

DISTRIBUTED CONCURRENCY CONTROL

As we discussed in Chapter 10, concurrency control deals with the isolation and consistency properties of transactions. The distributed concurrency control mechanism of a distributed DBMS ensures that the consistency of the database, as defined in Section 10.2.2, is maintained in a multiuser distributed environment. If transactions are internally consistent (i.e., do not violate any consistency constraints), the simplest way of achieving this objective is to execute each transaction alone, one after another. It is obvious that such an alternative is only of theoretical interest and cannot be implemented in any practical system, since it minimizes the system throughput. The level of concurrency (i.e., the number of concurrent transactions) is probably the most important parameter in distributed systems [Balter et al., 1982]. Therefore, the concurrency control mechanism attempts to find a suitable trade-off between maintaining the consistency of the database and maintaining a high level of concurrency.

In this chapter we make one major assumption: the distributed system is fully reliable and does not experience any failures (of hardware or software). Even though this is an entirely unrealistic assumption, there is a reason for making it. It permits us to delineate the issues related to the management of concurrency from those related to the operation of a reliable distributed system. In Chapter 12, we discuss how the algorithms that are presented in this chapter need to be revised to operate in an unreliable environment. We start our discussion of concurrency control with a presentation of serializability theory in Section 11.1. Serializability is the most widely accepted correctness criterion for concurrency control algorithms. In Section 11.2 we present a taxonomy of algorithms that will form the basis for most of the discussion in the remainder of the chapter. Sections 11.3 and 11.4 cover the two major classes of algorithms: locking-based and timestamp ordering-based. Both locking and timestamp ordering classes cover what is called pessimistic algorithms; optimistic concurrency control is discussed in Section 11.5. Any locking-based algorithm may result in deadlocks, requiring special management methods.

Various deadlock management techniques are therefore the topic of Section 11.6. In Section 11.7, we discuss "relaxed" concurrency control approaches. These are mechanisms which use weaker correctness criteria than serializability, or relax the isolation property of transactions.

11.1 SERIALIZABILITY THEORY

In Section 10.1.3 we discussed the issue of isolating transactions from one another in terms of their effects on the database. We also pointed out that if the concurrent execution of transactions leaves the database in a state that can be achieved by their serial execution in some order, problems such as lost updates will be resolved. This is exactly the point of the serializability argument. The remainder of this section addresses serializability issues more formally.

A *schedule* S (also called a *history*) is defined over a set of transactions $T = \{T_1, T_2, \ldots, T_n\}$ and specifies an interleaved order of execution of these transactions' operations. Based on the definition of a transaction introduced in Section 10.1, the schedule can be specified as a partial order over T. We need a few preliminaries, though, before we present the formal definition.

Recall the definition of conflicting operations that we gave in Chapter 10. Two operations $O_{ij}(x)$ and $O_{kl}(x)$ (i and k not necessarily distinct) accessing the same database entity x are said to be in *conflict* if at least one of them is a write. Note two things in this definition. First, read operations do not conflict with each other. We can, therefore, talk about two types of conflicts: *read-write* (or *write-read*), and *write-write*. Second, the two operations can belong to the same transaction or to two different transactions. In the latter case, the two transactions are said to be *conflicting*. Intuitively, the existence of a conflict between two operations indicate that their order of execution is important. The ordering of two read operations is insignificant.

We first define a *complete schedule*, which defines the execution order of all operations in its domain. We will then define a schedule as a prefix of a complete schedule. Formally, a complete schedule S_T^c defined over a set of transactions $T = \{T_1, T_2, \ldots, T_n\}$ is a partial order $S_T^c = \{\Sigma_T, \prec_T\}$ where

1. $\Sigma_T = \bigcup_{i=1}^{n} \Sigma_i$.

2. $\prec_T \supseteq \bigcup_{i=1}^{n} \prec_i$.

3. For any two conflicting operations $O_{ij}, O_{kl} \in \Sigma_T$, either $O_{ij} \prec_T O_{kl}$, or $O_{kl} \prec_T O_{ij}$.

The first condition simply states that the domain of the schedule is the union of the domains of individual transactions. The second condition defines the ordering relation as a superset of the ordering relations of individual transactions. This maintains the ordering of operations within each transaction. The final condition simply defines the execution order among conflicting operations.

Example 11.1

Consider the two transactions from Example 10.8. They were specified as

$$
\begin{array}{ll}
T_1: & \text{Read}(x) \qquad\qquad T_2: \quad \text{Read}(x) \\
     & x \leftarrow x + 1 \qquad\qquad\qquad\quad x \leftarrow x + 1 \\
     & \text{Write}(x) \qquad\qquad\qquad\quad \text{Write}(x) \\
     & \text{Commit} \qquad\qquad\qquad\quad\ \text{Commit}
\end{array}
$$

A possible complete schedule S_T^c over $T = \{T_1, T_2\}$ can be written as the following partial order (where the subscripts indicate the transactions):

$$
S_T^c = \{\Sigma_T, \prec_T\}
$$

where

$$
\begin{aligned}
\Sigma_1 &= \{R_1(x), W_1(x), C_1\} \\
\Sigma_2 &= \{R_2(x), W_2(x), C_2\}
\end{aligned}
$$

Thus

$$
\Sigma_T = \Sigma_1 \cup \Sigma_2 = \{R_1(x), W_1(x), C_1, R_2(x), W_2(x), C_2\}
$$

and

$$
\begin{aligned}
\prec_T = \ & \{(R_1, R_2), (R_1, W_1), (R_1, C_1), (R_1, W_2), (R_1, C_2), (R_2, W_1), \\
& (R_2, C_1), (R_2, W_2), (R_2, C_2), (W_1, C_1), (W_1, W_2), (W_1, C_2), \\
& (C_1, W_2), (C_1, C_2), (W_2, C_2)\}
\end{aligned}
$$

which can be specified as a DAG as depicted in Figure 11.1. Note that consistent with our earlier adopted convention (see Example 10.7), we do not draw the arcs that are implied by transitivity [e.g., (R_1, C_1)]. Also note that we omit the data items that these operations operate on since this is obvious from the context.

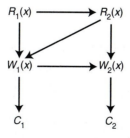

Figure 11.1. DAG Representation of a Complete Schedule

At this point we should mention a convention that is commonly employed to simplify the notation of a schedule. It is often specified as a listing of the operations in Σ_T, where their execution order is relative to their order in this list. Thus S_T^c can be specified as

$$S_T^c = \{R_1(x), R_2(x), W_1(x), C_1, W_2(x), C_2\}$$

Because of its simplicity, we use the latter notation in the remainder of this chapter.

A schedule is defined as a prefix of a complete schedule. A prefix of a partial order can be defined as follows. Given a partial order $P = \{\Sigma, \prec \}, P' = \{\Sigma', \prec' \}$ is a *prefix* of P if

1. $\Sigma' \subseteq \Sigma$;

2. $\forall e_i \in \Sigma', e_1 \prec' e_2$ if and only if $e_1 \prec e_2$; and

3. $\forall e_i \in \Sigma'$, if $\exists e_j \in \Sigma$ and $e_j \prec e_i$, then $e_j \in \Sigma'$.

The first two conditions define P' as a *restriction* of P on domain Σ', whereby the ordering relations in P are maintained in P'. The last condition indicates that for any element of Σ', all its predecessors in Σ have to be included in Σ' as well.

The real question that needs to be asked is: What does this definition of a schedule as a prefix of a partial order provide for us? The answer is simply that we can now deal with incomplete schedules. This is useful for a number of reasons. From the perspective of the serializability theory, we deal only with those operations of transactions that conflict rather than with all operations. Furthermore, and perhaps more important, when we introduce failures, we need to be able to deal with incomplete schedules, which is what a prefix enables us to do.

The schedule discussed in Example 11.1 is special in that it is complete. It needs to be complete in order to talk about the execution order of these two transactions' operations. The following example demonstrates a schedule that is not complete.

Example 11.2

Consider the following three transactions:

T_1: Read(x) T_2: Write(x) T_3: Read(x)
      Write(x)   Write(y)   Read(y)
      Commit   Read(z)   Read(z)
               Commit   Commit

A complete schedule S^c for these transactions is given in Figure 11.2, and a schedule S (as a prefix of S^c) is depicted in Figure 11.3.

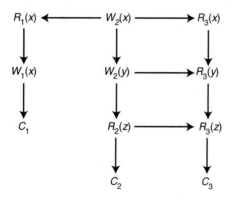

Figure 11.2. A Complete Schedule

If in a schedule S, the operations of various transactions are not interleaved (i.e., the operations of each transaction occur consecutively), the schedule is said to be *serial*. As we indicated before, the serial execution of a set of transactions maintains the consistency of the database. This follows naturally from the consistency property of transactions: each transaction, when executed alone on a consistent database, will produce a consistent database.

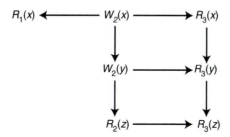

Figure 11.3. Prefix of Complete Schedule in Figure 11.2

Example 11.3

Consider the three transactions of Example 11.2. The following schedule,

$$S = \{W_2(x), W_2(y), R_2(z), C_2, R_1(x), W_1(x), C_1, R_3(x), R_3(y), R_3(z), C_3\}$$

is serial since all the operations of T_2 are executed before all the operations of T_1 and all operations of T_1 are executed before all operations of T_3. One common way to denote this precedence relationship between transaction executions is $T_2 \prec_S T_1 \prec_S T_3$ or $T_2 \rightarrow T_1 \rightarrow T_3$.

Based on the precedence relationship introduced by the partial order, it is possible to discuss the equivalence of schedules with respect to their effects on the database. Intuitively, two schedules S_1 and S_2, defined over the same set of transactions T, are *equivalent* if they have the same effect on the database. More formally, two schedules, S_1 and S_2, defined over the same set of transactions T, are said to be *equivalent* if for each pair of conflicting operations O_{ij} and O_{kl} ($i \neq k$), whenever $O_{ij} \prec_1 O_{kl}$, then $O_{ij} \prec_2 O_{kl}$. This is called *conflict equivalence* since it defines equivalence of two schedules in terms of the relative order of execution of the conflicting operations in those schedules. In the definition above, for the sake of simplicity, we assume that T does not include any aborted transaction. Otherwise, the definition needs to be modified to specify only those conflicting operations that belong to unaborted transactions.[1]

Example 11.4

Again consider the three transactions of Example 11.2. The following schedule S' defined over them is conflict equivalent to S given in Example 11.3:

$$S' = \{W_2(x), R_1(x), W_1(x), C_1, R_3(x), W_2(y), R_3(y), R_2(z), C_2, R_3(z), C_3\}$$

We are now ready to define serializability more formally. A schedule S is said to be *serializable* if and only if it is conflict equivalent to a serial schedule. Note that serializability roughly corresponds to degree 3 consistency, which we defined in Section 10.2.2. Serializability so defined is also known as *conflict-based serializability* since it is defined according to conflict equivalence.

Example 11.5

Schedule S' in Example 11.4 is serializable since it is equivalent to the serial schedule S of Example 11.3. Also note that the problem with the uncontrolled execution of transactions T_1 and T_2 in Example 10.8 was that they could generate an unserializable schedule.

Now that we have formally defined serializability, we can indicate that the primary function of a concurrency controller is to generate a serializable schedule for

---

[1] For the sake of completeness, we should also point out that there is another form of equivalence, called *view equivalence*. The concept of serializability can also be defined based on view equivalence. We will not dwell on this point further since conflict equivalence is a more useful concept to work with in concurrency control.

the execution of pending transactions. The issue, then, is to devise algorithms that are guaranteed to generate only serializable schedules.

Serializability theory extends in a straightforward manner to the nonreplicated (or partitioned) distributed databases. The schedule of transaction execution at each site is called a *local schedule*. If the database is not replicated and each local schedule is serializable, their union (called the *global schedule*) is also serializable as long as local serialization orders are identical. In a replicated distributed database, however, the extension of the serializability theory requires more care. It is possible that the local schedules are serializable, but the mutual consistency of the database is still compromised.

Example 11.6

We will give a very simple example to demonstrate the point. Consider two sites and one data item (x) that is duplicated in both sites. Further consider the following two transactions:

$$T_1: \quad \text{Read}(x) \qquad\qquad T_2: \quad \text{Read}(x)$$
$$x \leftarrow x + 5 \qquad\qquad\qquad x \leftarrow x * 10$$
$$\text{Write}(x) \qquad\qquad\qquad \text{Write}(x)$$
$$\text{Commit} \qquad\qquad\qquad \text{Commit}$$

Obviously, both of these transactions need to run at both sites. Consider the following two schedules that may be generated locally at the two sites:

$$S_1 \;=\; \{R_1(x), W_1(x), C_1, R_2(x), W_2(x), C_2\}$$
$$S_2 \;=\; \{R_2(x), W_2(x), C_2, R_1(x), W_1(x), C_1\}$$

Note that both of these schedules are serializable; indeed, they are serial. Therefore, each represents a correct execution order. However, observe that they serialize T_1 and T_2 in reverse order. Assume that the value of x prior to the execution of these transactions was 1. At the end of the execution of these schedules, the value of x is 60 at site 1 while it is 15 at site 2. This violates the mutual consistency of the two local databases.

Mutual consistency requires that all the values of all replicated data items be identical. Schedules that can maintain mutual consistency are called *one-copy serializable* [Bernstein and Goodman, 1985]. Intuitively, a one-copy serializable global schedule has to meet the following conditions:

1. Each local schedule should be serializable.

2. Two conflicting operations should be in the same relative order in all of the local schedules where they appear together.

The second condition simply ensures that the serialization order be the same at all the sites where the conflicting transactions execute together. Recall that concurrency control algorithms ensure serializability by synchronizing conflicting accesses to the database. In replicated databases, the additional task of ensuring one-copy serializability is usually the responsibility of the *replica control protocol*.

Let us assume the existence of a data item x with copies $x_1, x_2, \ldots, x_n$. We will refer to x as the *logical data* item and to its copies as *physical data* items. If replication transparency is to be provided, user transactions will issue read and write operations on the logical data item x. The replica control protocol is responsible for mapping each read on the logical data item x [Read(x)] to a read on one of the physical data item copies x_j [Read(x_j)]. Each write on the logical data item x, on the other hand, is mapped to a set of writes on a (possibly proper) subset of the physical data item copies of x. Whether this mapping is to the full set of physical data item copies or to a subset is the basis of classifying replica control algorithms. In this chapter, and for the most part in this book, we consider replica control protocols that map a read on a logical data item to only *one* copy of the data item, but map a write on a logical data item to a set of writes on *all* physical data item copies. Such a protocol is commonly known as the *read-once/write-all* (ROWA) protocol.

The common complaint about the ROWA protocol is that it reduces the availability of the database in case of failures since the transaction may not complete unless it reflects the effects of the write operation on all the copies (more on this in Chapter 12). Therefore, there have been a number of algorithms that have attempted to maintain mutual consistency without employing the ROWA protocol. They are all based on the premise that one can continue processing an operation as long as the operation can be scheduled at a subset of the sites which correspond to a majority of the sites where copies are stored [Thomas, 1979] or to all sites that can be reached (i.e., available) [Bernstein and Goodman, 1984] and [Goodman et al., 1983]. There are still other protocols that perform the updates on an identified master copy of the replicated data item and then propagate these updates to other replica copies *lazily*.

11.2   TAXONOMY OF CONCURRENCY CONTROL MECHANISMS

There are a number of ways that the concurrency control approaches can be classified. One obvious classification criterion is the mode of database distribution. Some algorithms that have been proposed require a fully replicated database, while others can operate on partially replicated or partitioned databases. The concurrency control algorithms may also be classified according to network topology, such as those requiring a communication subnet with broadcasting capability or those working in a star-type network or a circularly connected network.

The most common classification criterion, however, is the synchronization primitive. The corresponding breakdown of the concurrency control algorithms results in two classes: those algorithms that are based on mutually exclusive access to shared data (locking), and those that attempt to order the execution of the transactions according to a set of rules (protocols). However, these primitives may be used in algorithms with two different viewpoints: the pessimistic view that many transactions will conflict with each other, or the optimistic view that not too many transactions will conflict with one another.

We will thus group the concurrency control mechanisms into two broad classes: pessimistic concurrency control methods and optimistic concurrency control methods. *Pessimistic* algorithms synchronize the concurrent execution of transactions early in their execution life cycle, whereas *optimistic* algorithms delay the synchronization of transactions until their termination. The pessimistic group consists of *locking-based* algorithms, *ordering* (or *transaction ordering*) *based* algorithms, and *hybrid* algorithms. The optimistic group can, similarly, be classified as locking-based or timestamp ordering-based. This classification is depicted in Figure 11.4.

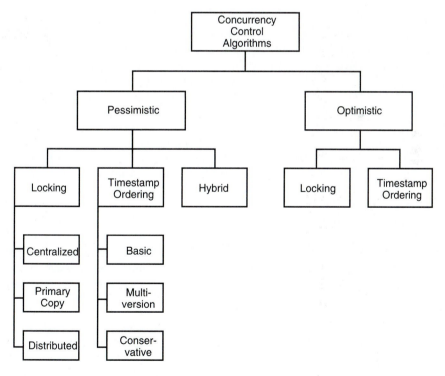

Figure 11.4. Classification of Concurrency Control Algorithms

In the *locking-based* approach, the synchronization of transactions is achieved by employing physical or logical locks on some portion or granule of the database. The size of these portions (usually called *locking granularity*) is an important issue. However, for the time being, we will ignore it and refer to the chosen granule as a *lock unit*. This class is subdivided further according to where the lock management activities are performed:

1. In *centralized locking*, one of the sites in the network is designated as the primary site where the lock tables for the entire database are stored and is charged with the responsibility of granting locks to transactions.

2. In *primary copy locking*, on the other hand, one of the copies (if there are multiple copies) of each lock unit is designated as the primary copy, and it is this copy that has to be locked for the purpose of accessing that particular unit. For example, if lock unit x is replicated at sites 1, 2, and 3, one of these sites (say, 1) is selected as the primary site for x. All transactions desiring access to x obtain their lock at site 1 before they can access a copy of x. If the database is not replicated (i.e., there is only one copy of each lock unit), the primary copy locking mechanisms distribute the lock management responsibility among a number of sites.

3. In *decentralized locking*, the lock management duty is shared by all the sites of a network. In this case, the execution of a transaction involves the participation and coordination of schedulers at more than one site. Each local scheduler is responsible for the lock units local to that site. Using the same example as above, entities accessing x must obtain locks at all three sites.

The *timestamp ordering* (TO) class involves organizing the execution order of transactions so that they maintain mutual and interconsistency. This ordering is maintained by assigning timestamps to both the transactions and the data items that are stored in the database. These algorithms can be *basic TO*, *multiversion TO*, or *conservative TO*.

We should indicate that in some locking-based algorithms, timestamps are also used. This is done primarily to improve efficiency and the level of concurrency. We call this class the *hybrid* algorithm. We will not discuss these algorithms in this chapter since they have not been implemented in any commercial or research prototype distributed DBMS. The rules for integrating locking and timestamp ordering protocols are given in [Bernstein and Goodman, 1981].

11.3 LOCKING-BASED CONCURRENCY CONTROL ALGORITHMS

The main idea of locking-based concurrency control is to ensure that the data that is shared by conflicting operations is accessed by one operation at a time. This is accomplished by associating a "lock" with each lock unit. This lock is set by a transaction before it is accessed and is reset at the end of its use. Obviously a lock unit cannot be accessed by an operation if it is already locked by another. Thus a lock request by a transaction is granted only if the associated lock is not being held by any other transaction.

Since we are concerned with synchronizing the conflicting operations of conflicting transactions, there are two types of locks (commonly called *lock modes*) associated with each lock unit: *read lock* (rl) and *write lock* (wl). A transaction T_i that wants to read a data item contained in lock unit x obtains a read lock on x [denoted $rl_i(x)$]. The same happens for write operations. It is common to talk about the *compatibility* of lock modes. Two lock modes are compatible if two transactions which access the same data item can obtain these locks on that data item at the same time. As Figure 11.5 shows, read locks are compatible, whereas read-write or write-write locks are not. Therefore, it is possible, for example, for two transactions to read the same data item concurrently.

	$rl_j(x)$	$wl_j(x)$
$rl_i(x)$	compatible	not compatible
$wl_i(x)$	not compatible	not compatible

Figure 11.5. Compatibility Matrix of Lock Modes

The distributed DBMS not only manages locks but also handles the lock management responsibilities on behalf of the transactions. In other words, the users do not need to specify when data needs to be locked; the distributed DBMS takes care of that every time the transaction issues a read or write operation.

In locking-based systems, the scheduler (see Figure 10.4) is a *lock manager* (LM). The transaction manager passes to the lock manager the database operation (read or write) and associated information (such as the item that is accessed and the identifier of the transaction that issues the database operation). The lock manager then checks if the lock unit that contains the data item is already locked. If so, and if the existing lock mode is incompatible with that of the current transaction, the current operation is delayed. Otherwise, the lock is set in the desired mode and the database operation is passed on to the data processor for actual database access. The transaction manager is then informed of the results of the operation. The termination of a transaction results in the release of its locks and the initiation of another transaction that might be waiting for access to the same data item.

The basic locking algorithm is given in Algorithm 11.1. In Figure 11.6 we give the type declarations and the procedure definitions that we use in the algorithms of this chapter. Note that the definitions in Figure 11.6 are at a high level of abstraction. Also, in Algorithm 11.1, we do not yet pay any attention to how the commit and abort operations of transactions are serviced. Those complications are not added until Chapter 12.

declare-type

> *Operation*: one of Begin_Transaction, Read, Write, Abort, or Commit
>
> *DataItem*: a data item in the distributed database
>
> *TransactionId*: a unique identifier assigned to each transaction
>
> *DataVal*: a primitive data-type value (i.e., integer, real, etc.)
>
> *SiteId*: a unique site identifier
>
> *Dbop*: a 3-tuple of {a database operation from the application program}
>> *opn* : *Operation*
>>
>> *data* : *DataItem*
>>
>> *tid* : *TransactionId*
>
> *Dpmsg*: a 3-tuple of   {a message from the data processor}
>> *opn* : *Operation*
>>
>> *tid* : *TransactionId*
>>
>> *res* : *DataVal*
>
> *Scmsg*: a 3-tuple of   {a message from the scheduler}
>> *opn* : *Operation*
>>
>> *tid* : *TransactionId*
>>
>> *res* : *DataVal*
>
> *Transaction* ← a 2-tuple of
>> *tid* : *TransactionId*
>>
>> *body* : a transaction body as defined in Chapter 10
>
> *Message* ← a string of characters that are to be transmitted
>
> *OpSet*: a set of *DbOp*'s
>
> *SiteSet*: a set of *SiteId*'s
>
> WAIT(*msg* : *Message*)

begin

> {wait until a message arrives}

end

Figure 11.6. Preliminary Definitions for the Upcoming Algorithms

Algorithm 11.1 *Basic LM*

> **declare-var**
>> *msg* : *Message*
>>
>> *dop* : *Dbop*
>>
>> *Op* : *Operation*
>>
>> *x* : *DataItem*
>>
>> *T* : *TransactionId*
>>
>> *pm* : *Dpmsg*
>>
>> *res* : *DataVal*
>>
>> *SOP* : *OpSet*
>
> **begin**
>> **repeat**
>>> WAIT(*msg*)
>>>
>>> **case of** *msg*

Dbop :
begin
$\quad Op \leftarrow dop.opn$
$\quad x \leftarrow dop.data$
$\quad T \leftarrow dop.tid$
case of Op
Begin_transaction:
begin
$\quad$ send *dop* to the data processor
end
Read **or** Write: {requires locking}
begin
$\quad$ find the lock unit *lu* such that $x \subseteq lu$
$\quad$ **if** *lu* is unlocked **or** lock mode of *lu* is compatible with Op **then**
$\quad$ **begin**
$\qquad$ set lock on *lu* in appropriate mode
$\qquad$ send *dop* to the data processor
$\quad$ **end**
$\quad$ **else** put *dop* on a queue for *lu*
$\quad$ **end-if**
end
Abort **or** Commit:
begin
$\quad$ send *dop* to the data processor
end
end-case
Dpmsg :   {acknowledgment from the data processor}
begin   {requires unlocking}
$\quad Op \leftarrow pm.opn$
$\quad res \leftarrow pm.result$
$\quad T \leftarrow pm.tid$
$\quad$ find lock unit *lu* such that $x \subseteq lu$ release lock on *lu* held by T
$\quad$ **if** there are no more locks on *lu* **and**
$\qquad$ there are operations waiting in queue to lock *lu* **then**
$\quad$ **begin**
$\qquad SOP \leftarrow$ first operation from the queue
$\qquad SOP \leftarrow SOP \cup \{O | O$ is a operation on queue that can lock *lu*
$\qquad\quad$ in a compatible mode with the current operations in SOP$\}$
$\qquad$ set the locks on *lu* on behalf of operations in SOP
$\qquad$ **for all** the operations in SOP **do**
$\qquad\quad$ send each operation to the data processor
$\qquad$ **end-for**
$\quad$ **end-if**
end
end-case
until *forever*
end. {Basic LM}

The locking algorithm that is given in Algorithm 11.1 will not, unfortunately, properly synchronize transaction executions. This is because to generate serializable schedules, the locking and releasing operations of transactions also need to be coordinated. We demonstrate this by an example.

Example 11.7

Consider the following two transactions:

$$T_1: \quad \text{Read}(x) \qquad T_2: \quad \text{Read}(x)$$
$$x \leftarrow x + 1 \qquad\qquad x \leftarrow x * 2$$
$$\text{Write}(x) \qquad\qquad \text{Write}(x)$$
$$\text{Read}(y) \qquad\qquad \text{Read}(y)$$
$$y \leftarrow y - 1 \qquad\qquad y \leftarrow y * 2$$
$$\text{Write}(y) \qquad\qquad \text{Write}(y)$$
$$\text{Commit} \qquad\qquad \text{Commit}$$

The following is a valid schedule that a lock manager employing the algorithm of Algorithm 11.1 may generate:

$$S \quad = \quad \{wl_1(x), R_1(x), W_1(x), lr_1(x), wl_2(x), R_2(x), w_2(x), lr_2(x), wl_2(y),$$
$$R_2(y), W_2(y), lr_2(y), C_2, wl_1(y), R_1(y), W_1(y), lr_1(y), C_1\}$$

Here, $lr_i(z)$ indicates the release of the lock on z that transaction T_i holds.

Note that S is not a serializable schedule. For example, if prior to the execution of these transactions, the values of x and y are 50 and 20, respectively, one would expect their values following execution to be, respectively, either 102 and 38 if T_1 executes before T_2, or 101 and 39 if T_2 executes before T_1. However, the result of executing S would give x and y the values 102 and 39. Obviously, S is not serializable.

The problem with schedule S in Example 11.7 is the following. The locking algorithm releases the locks that are held by a transaction (say, T_i) as soon as the associated database command (read or write) is executed, and that lock unit (say x) no longer needs to be accessed. However, the transaction itself is locking other items (say, y), after it releases its lock on x. Even though this may seem to be advantageous from the viewpoint of increased concurrency, it permits transactions to interfere with one another, resulting in the loss of total isolation and atomicity. Hence the argument for *two-phase locking* (2PL).

The two-phase locking rule simply states that no transaction should request a lock after it releases one of its locks. Alternatively, a transaction should not release a lock until it is certain that it will not request another lock. 2PL algorithms execute transactions in two phases. Each transaction has a *growing phase*, where it obtains locks and accesses data items, and a *shrinking phase*, during which it releases locks (Figure 11.7). The *lock point* is the moment when the transaction has achieved all its locks but has not yet started to release any of them. Thus the lock point determines the end of the growing phase and the beginning of the shrinking phase of a transaction. It is a well-known theorem [Eswaran et al., 1976] that any schedule generated by a concurrency control algorithm that obeys the 2PL rule is serializable.

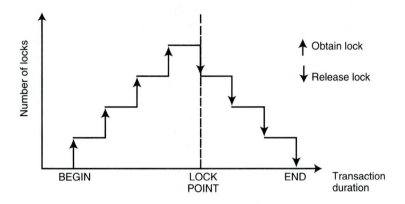

Figure 11.7. 2PL Lock Graph

Figure 11.7 indicates that the lock manager releases locks as soon as access to that data item has been completed. This permits other transactions awaiting access to go ahead and lock it, thereby increasing the degree of concurrency. However, this is difficult to implement since the lock manager has to know that the transaction has obtained all its locks and will not need to lock another data item. The lock manager also needs to know that the transaction no longer needs to access the data item in question, so that the lock can be released. Finally, if the transaction aborts after it releases a lock, it may cause other transactions that may have accessed the unlocked data item to abort as well. This is known as *cascading aborts*. Because of these difficulties, most 2PL schedulers implement what is called *strict two-phase locking*, which releases all the locks together when the transaction terminates (commits or aborts). Thus the lock graph is as shown in Figure 11.8.

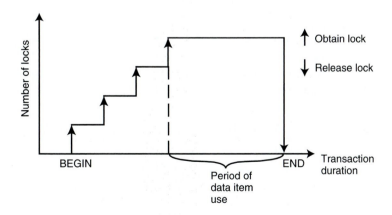

Figure 11.8. Strict 2PL Lock Graph

The strict 2PL lock manager requires minimal modification of the algorithm of Algorithm 11.1. In fact, the only modification that is necessary is to change the section that handles the responses from the data processor. This is necessary to ensure that the locks are released only if the operation is a commit or abort. For completeness, we present the strict 2PL algorithm in its entirety in Algorithm 11.2. The transaction manager algorithm for 2PL scheduling is given in Algorithm 11.3.

Algorithm 11.2 *S2PL-LM*
    declare-var
        $msg : Message$
        $dop : Dbop$
        $Op : Operation$
        $x : DataItem$
        $T : TransactionId$
        $pm : Dpmsg$
        $res : DataVal$
        $SOP : OpSet$
    begin
      repeat
        WAIT(msg)
        case of msg
          $Dbop$:
          begin
            $Op \leftarrow dop.opn$
            $x \leftarrow dop.data$
            $T \leftarrow dop.tid$
            case of Op
              Begin_transaction:
              begin
                send dop to the data processor
              end
              Read **or** Write: {requires locking}
              begin
                find the lock unit lu such that $x \subseteq lu$
                if lu is unlocked **or** lock mode of lu is compatible with Op **then**
                begin
                  set lock on lu in appropriate mode
                  send dop to the data processor
                end

           else

                put *dop* on a queue for *lu*

           end-if

        end

        Abort **or** Commit:

        begin

           send *dop* to the data processor

        end

      end-case

    Dpmsg :

    begin

      $Op \leftarrow pm.opn$

      $res \leftarrow pm.result$

      $T \leftarrow pm.tid$

      if $Op=$Abort **or** $Op=$Commit **then**

      begin

        for each lock unit *lu* locked by T **do**

        begin

          release lock on *lu* held by T

          if there are no more locks on *lu* **and**

            there are operations waiting in queue for *lu* **then**

          begin

            $SOP \leftarrow$ first operation from the queue

            $SOP \leftarrow SOP \cup \{O|O$ is an operation on queue that

                      can lock *lu* in a compatible mode with

                      the current operations in $SOP\}$

           set the locks on *lu* on behalf of operations in SOP

           for all the operations in SOP **do**

             send each operation to the data processor

          end-for

         end-if

        end-for

       end-if

      end

     end-case

    until *forever*

  end. {S2PL-LM}

Algorithm 11.3 *2PL-TM*
  declare-var
    msg : *Message*
    Op : *Operation*
    x : *DataItem*
    T : *TransactionId*
    O : *Dbop*
    sm : *Scmsg*
    res : *DataVal*
    SOP : *OpSet*
  begin
    repeat
      WAIT(*msg*)
      case of *msg*
        Dbop :
        begin
          send *O* to the lock manager
        end
        Scmsg :   {acknowledgment from the lock manager}
        begin
          Op ← *sm.opn*
          res ← *sm.result*
          T ← *sm.tid*
          case of *Op*
            Read:
            begin
              return *res* to the user application (i.e., the transaction)
            end
            Write:
            begin
              inform user application of completion of the write
              return res to the user application
            end
            Commit:
            begin
              destroy *T*'s workspace
              inform user application of successful completion of transaction
            end
            Abort:
            begin
              inform user application of completion of the abort of *T*
            end
          end-case
        end
      end-case
    until *forever*
  end. {2PL-TM}

We should note that even though a 2PL algorithm enforces conflict serializability, it does not allow all schedules that are conflict serializable. Consider the following schedule taken from [Agrawal and El-Abbadi, 1990]:

$$S = w_1(x)r_2(x)r_3(y)w_1(y)$$

S is not allowed by 2PL algorithm since T_1 would need to obtain a write lock on y after it releases its write lock on x. However, this history is serializable in the order $T_3 \rightarrow T_1 \rightarrow T_2$ [Agrawal and El-Abbadi, 1990]. The order of locking can be exploited to design locking algorithms that allow schedules such as these [Agrawal and El-Abbadi, 1990].

The main idea is to observe that in serializability theory, the order of serialization of conflicting operations is as important as detecting the conflict in the first place and this can be exploited in defining locking modes. Consequently, in addition to read (shared) and write (exclusive) locks, a third lock mode is defined: *ordered shared*. Ordered shared locking of an object x by transactions T_i and T_j has the following meaning: Given a schedule S that allows ordered shared locks between operations $o \in T_i$ and $p \in T_j$, if T_i acquires o-lock before T_j acquires p-lock, then o is executed before p. Consider the compatibility table between read and write locks given in Figure 11.5. If the ordered shared mode is added, there are eight variants of this table. Figure 11.5 depicts one of them and two more are shown in Figure 11.9. In Figure 11.9(a), for example, there is an ordered shared relationship between $rl_j(x)$ and $wl_i(x)$ [denoted as $rl_j(x) \Rightarrow wl_i(x)$] indicating that T_i can acquire a write lock on x while T_j holds a read lock on x as long as the ordered shared relationship from $rl_j(x)$ to $wl_i(x)$ is observed. The eight compatibility tables can be compared with respect to their permissiveness (i.e., with respect to the histories that can be produced using them) to generate a lattice of tables such that the one in Fig. 11.5 is the most restrictive and the one in Fig. 11.9(b) is the most liberal.

	$rl_i(x)$	$wl_i(x)$		$rl_i(x)$	$wl_i(x)$
$rl_j(x)$	compatible	not compatible	$rl_j(x)$	compatible	ordered shared
$wl_j(x)$	ordered shared	not compatible	$wl_j(x)$	ordered shared	ordered shared
	(a)			(b)	

Figure 11.9. Commutativity Table with Ordered Shared Lock Mode

In the above example, the write lock on behalf of T_i is said to be *on hold* since it was acquired after T_k acquired its read lock on x. The locking protocol that enforces a compatibility matrix involving ordered shared lock modes is identical to 2PL, except that a transaction may not release any locks as long as any of its locks are on hold. Otherwise circular serialization orders can exist.

11.3.1 Centralized 2PL

The 2PL algorithm discussed in the preceding section can easily be extended to the (replicated or partitioned) distributed DBMS environment. One way of doing this is to delegate lock management responsibility to a single site only. This means that only one of the sites has a lock manager; the transaction managers at the other sites communicate with it rather than with their own lock managers. This approach is also known as the *primary site* 2PL algorithm [Alsberg and Day, 1976].

The communication between the cooperating sites in executing a transaction according to a centralized 2PL (C2PL) algorithm is depicted in Figure 11.10. This communication is between the transaction manager at the site where the transaction is initiated (called the *coordinating* TM), the lock manager at the central site, and the data processors (DP) at the other participating sites. The participating sites are those at which the operation is to be carried out. The order of messages is denoted in the figure.

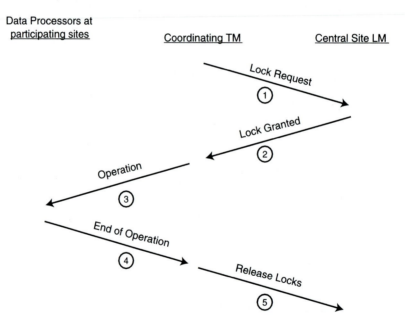

Figure 11.10. Communication Structure of Centralized 2PL

An important difference between the centralized TM algorithm and the TM algorithm of Algorithm 11.3 is that the distributed TM has to implement the replica control protocol if the database is replicated. The C2PL-LM algorithm also differs from the strict 2PL lock manager in one major way. The central lock manager does not send the operations to the respective data processors; that is done by the coordinating TM.

The centralized 2PL transaction management algorithm (C2PL-TM) that incorporates these changes is given in Algorithm 11.4, while the centralized 2PL lock management algorithm (C2PL-LM) is shown in Algorithm 11.5.

Algorithm 11.4 *C2PL-TM*
    declare-var
        $T : Transaction$
        $Op : Operation$
        $x : DataItem$
        $msg : Message$
        $O : Dbop$
        $pm : Dpmsg$
        $res : DataVal$
        $S : SiteSet$
    begin
      repeat
        WAIT(msg)
        case of msg
          $Dbop$:
          begin
            $Op \leftarrow O.opn$
            $x \leftarrow O.data$
            $T \leftarrow O.tid$
            case of Op
              Begin_Transaction:
              begin
                $S \leftarrow \emptyset$
              end
              Read:
              begin
                $S \leftarrow S \cup$ {the site that stores x and has the lowest
                          access cost to it}
                send O to the central lock manager
              end
              Write:
              begin
                $S \leftarrow S \cup \{S_i | x$ is stored at site $S_i\}$
                send O to the central lock manager
              end
              Abort or Commit:
              begin
                send O to the central lock manager
              end
            end-case
          end

Scmsg :   {lock request granted on locks released}
begin
   if lock request granted **then**
      send O to the data processors in S
   else
      inform user about the termination of transaction
   end-if
end
Dpmsg :
begin
  $Op \leftarrow pm.opn$
  $res \leftarrow pm.result$
  $T \leftarrow pm.tid$
  case of Op
    Read:
    begin
      return res to the user application (i.e., the transaction)
    end
    Write:
    begin
      inform user application of completion of the write
    end
    Commit:
    begin
      if commit msg has been received from all participants **then**
      begin
        inform user application of successful completion of
          transaction
        send pm to the central lock manager
      else   {wait until commit msg comes from all}
        record the arrival of the commit message
      end-if
    end
    Abort:
    begin
      inform user application of completion of the abort of T
      send pm to the central lock manager
    end
    end-case
  end
  end-case
 until *forever*
end. {C2PL-TM}

Algorithm 11.5 *C2PL-LM*
    declare-var
        msg : *Message*
        dop : *SingleOp*
        Op : *Operation*
        x : *DataItem*
        T : *TransactionId*
        SOP : *OpSet*
    begin
      repeat
        WAIT(msg)   {The only msg that can arrive is from coordinating TM }
        $Op \leftarrow dop.opn$
        $x \leftarrow dop.data$
        $T \leftarrow dop.tid$
        case of Op
          Read **or** Write:
          begin
            find the lock unit lu such that $x \subseteq lu$
            if lu is unlocked **or** lock mode of lu is compatible with Op **then**
            begin
              set lock on lu in appropriate mode
              $msg \leftarrow$ "Lock granted for operation dop"
              send msg to the coordinating TM of T
            end
            else
              put Op on a queue for lu
            end-if
          end
          Commit **or** Abort:
          begin
            for each lock unit lu locked by T **do**
            begin
              release lock on lu held by T
              if there are operations waiting in queue for lu **then**
              begin
                $SOP \leftarrow$ first operation (call O) from the queue
                $SOP \leftarrow SOP \cup \{O|O$ is a operation on queue that can lock lu
                  in a compatible mode with the current operations in $SOP\}$
                set the locks on lu on behalf of operations in SOP
                for all the operations O in SOP **do**

> **begin**
> $msg \leftarrow$ "Lock granted for operation O"
>   send msg to all the coordinating TM's
> **end-for**
> **end-if**
> **end-for**
> $msg \leftarrow$ "Locks of T released"
> send msg to the coordinating TM of T
> **end**
> **end-case**
> **until** $forever$
> **end**. {C2PL-LM}

One common criticism of C2PL algorithms is that a bottleneck may quickly form around the central site. Furthermore, the system may be less reliable since the failure or inaccessibility of the central site would cause major system failures. There are studies that indicate that the bottleneck will indeed form as the transaction rate increases, but is insignificant at low transaction rates ([Özsu, 1985a], [Koon and Özsu, 1986]). Furthermore, sharp performance degradation at high loads is observed in other locking-based algorithms as well.

11.3.2 Primary Copy 2PL

Primary copy 2PL (PC2PL) is a straightforward extension of centralized 2PL in an attempt to counter the latter's potential performance problems, discussed above. Basically, it implements lock managers at a number of sites and makes each lock manager responsible for managing the locks for a given set of lock units. The transaction managers then send their lock and unlock requests to the lock managers that are responsible for that specific lock unit. Thus the algorithm treats one copy of each data item as its primary copy.

We do not give the detailed primary copy 2PL algorithm since the changes from centralized 2PL are minimal. Basically, the only change is that the primary copy locations have to be determined for each data item prior to sending a lock or unlock request to the lock manager at that site. This is a directory design and management issue that we discussed in Chapter 4.

Primary copy 2PL was proposed for the prototype distributed version of IN-GRES [Stonebraker and Neuhold, 1977]. Even though it demands a more sophisticated directory at each site, it also reduces the load of the central site without causing a large amount of communication among the transaction managers and lock managers. In one sense it is an intermediate step between the centralized 2PL that we discussed in the preceding section and the distributed 2PL that we will cover next.

11.3.3 Distributed 2PL

Distributed 2PL (D2PL) expects the availability of lock managers at each site. If the database is not replicated, distributed 2PL degenerates into the primary copy

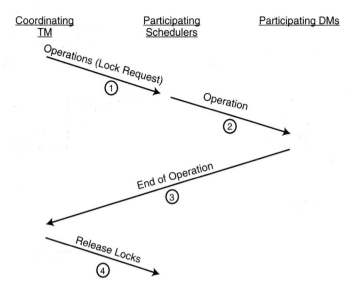

Figure 11.11. Communication Structure of Distributed 2PL

2PL algorithm. If data is replicated, the transaction implements the ROWA replica control protocol.

The communication between cooperating sites that execute a transaction according to the distributed 2PL protocol is depicted in Figure 11.11. Notice that Figure 11.11 does not show application of the ROWA rule.

The distributed 2PL transaction management algorithm is similar to the C2PL-TM, with two major modifications. The messages that are sent to the central site lock manager in C2PL-TM are sent to the lock managers at all participating sites in D2PL-TM. The second difference is that the operations are not passed to the data processors by the coordinating transaction manager, but by the participating lock managers. This means that the coordinating transaction manager does not wait for a "lock request granted" message. Another point about Figure 11.11 is the following. The participating data processors send the "end of operation" message to the coordinating TM. The alternative is for each DP to send it to its own lock manager who can then release the locks and inform the coordinating TM. We have chosen to describe the former since it uses an LM algorithm identical to the strict 2PL lock manager that we have already discussed and it makes the discussion of the commit protocols simpler (see Chapter 12). Owing to these similarities, we do not give the distributed TM and LM algorithms here. Distributed 2PL algorithms are used in System R* [Mohan et al., 1986] and in NonStop SQL ([Tandem, 1987], [Tandem, 1988] and [Borr, 1988]).

11.4　TIMESTAMP-BASED CONCURRENCY CONTROL ALGORITHMS

Unlike the locking-based algorithms, timestamp-based concurrency control algorithms do not attempt to maintain serializability by mutual exclusion. Instead, they select, a priori, a serialization order and execute transactions accordingly. To establish this ordering, the transaction manager assigns each transaction T_i a unique *timestamp*, $ts(T_i)$, at its initiation.

A timestamp is a simple identifier that serves to identify each transaction uniquely and to permit ordering. *Uniqueness* is only one of the properties of timestamp generation. The second property is *monotonicity*. Two timestamps generated by the same transaction manager should be monotonically increasing. Thus timestamps are values derived from a totally ordered domain. It is this second property that differentiates a timestamp from a transaction identifier.

There are a number of ways that timestamps can be assigned. One method is to use a global (systemwide) monotonically increasing counter. However, the maintenance of global counters is a problem in distributed systems. Therefore, it is preferable that each site autonomously assign timestamps based on its local counter. To maintain uniqueness, each site appends its own identifier to the counter value. Thus the timestamp is a two-tuple of the form <local counter value, site identifier>. Note that the site identifier is appended in the least significant position. Hence it serves only to order the timestamps of two transactions that might have been assigned the same local counter value. If each system can access its own system clock, it is possible to use system clock values instead of counter values.

With this information, it is simple to order the execution of the transactions' operations according to their timestamps. Formally, the timestamp ordering (TO) rule can be specified as follows:

TO Rule. Given two conflicting operations O_{ij} and O_{kl} belonging, respectively, to transactions T_i and T_k, O_{ij} is executed before O_{kl} if and only if $ts(T_i) < ts(T_k)$. In this case T_i is said to be the *older* transaction and T_k is said to be the *younger* one.

A scheduler that enforces the TO rule checks each new operation against conflicting operations that have already been scheduled. If the new operation belongs to a transaction that is younger than all the conflicting ones that have already been scheduled, the operation is accepted; otherwise, it is rejected, causing the entire transaction to restart with a *new* timestamp.

A timestamp ordering scheduler that operates in this fashion is guaranteed to generate serializable schedules. However, this comparison between the transaction timestamps can be performed only if the scheduler has received all the operations to be scheduled. If operations come to the scheduler one at a time (which is the realistic case), it is necessary to be able to detect if an operation has arrived out of sequence. To facilitate this check, each data item x is assigned two timestamps: a *read timestamp* $[rts(x)]$, which is the largest of the timestamps of the transactions that have read x, and a *write timestamp* $[wts(x)]$, which is the largest of the timestamps of the transactions that have written (updated) x. It is now sufficient to compare the timestamp of an operation with the read and write timestamps of the data item that it wants to access to determine if any transaction with a larger timestamp has already accessed the same data item.

Architecturally (see Figure 10.5), the transaction manager is responsible for assigning a timestamp to each new transaction and attaching this timestamp to each database operation that it passes on to the scheduler. The latter component is responsible for keeping track of read and write timestamps as well as performing the serializability check.

11.4.1 Basic TO Algorithm

The basic TO algorithm is a straightforward implementation of the TO rule. The coordinating transaction manager assigns the timestamp to each transaction, determines the sites where each data item is stored, and sends the relevant operations to these sites. The basic TO transaction manager algorithm (BTO-TM) is depicted in Algorithm 11.6. The schedulers at each site simply enforce the TO rule. The scheduler algorithm is given in Algorithm 11.7.

Algorithm 11.6 *BTO-TM*

> **declare-var**
>> $T : Transaction$
>> $Op : Operation$
>> $x : DataItem$
>> $msg : Message$
>> $O : Dbop$
>> $pm : Dpmsg$
>> $res : DataVal$
>> $S : SiteSet$
> **begin**
>> **repeat**
>>> WAIT(msg)
>>> **case of** msg
>>>> $Dbop$:   {database operation from the application program}
>>>> **begin**
>>>>> $Op \leftarrow O.opn$
>>>>> $x \leftarrow O.data$
>>>>> $T \leftarrow O.tid$
>>>>> **case of** Op
>>>>>> Begin_Transaction:
>>>>>> **begin**
>>>>>>> $S \leftarrow \phi$
>>>>>>> assign a timestamp to T $[ts(T)]$
>>>>>> **end**

Read:
begin
    $S \leftarrow S \cup$ {the site that stores x and has the lowest access cost to it}
    send O and $ts(T)$ to the scheduler at S
end
Write:
begin
    $S \leftarrow S \cup \{S_i \mid x \text{ is stored at site } S_i\}$
    send O and $ts(T)$ to the schedulers at S
end
Abort or Commit:
begin
    send O to the schedulers in S
end
end-case
$Scmsg$:   {the operation must have been rejected by a scheduler}
begin
    $msg \leftarrow$ "Abort T"
    send msg to schedulers in S
    restart T {will assign a new timestamp}
end
$Dpmsg$:
begin
    $Op \leftarrow pm.opn$ $res \leftarrow pm.result$ $T \leftarrow pm.tid$
    case of Op
        Read:
        begin
            return res to the user application (i.e., the transaction)
        end
        Write:
        begin
            inform user application of completion of the write
        end
        Commit:
        begin
            inform user application of successful completion of transaction
        end
        Abort:
        begin
            inform user application of completion of the abort of T
        end
           end-case
        end
      end-case
    until *forever*
end. {BTO-TM}

Algorithm 11.7 *BTO-SC*
   declare-var
     msg : *Message*
     dop : *SingleOp*
     Op : *Operation*
     x : *DataItem*
     T : *TransactionId*
     SOP : *OpSet*
   begin
    repeat
      WAIT(*msg*)
      case of *msg*
        Dbop :   {database operation passed from the transaction manager}
        begin
          $Op \leftarrow dop.opn$
          $x \leftarrow dop.data$
          $T \leftarrow dop.tid$
          save initial $rts(x)$ and $wts(x)$
          case of *Op*
            Read:
            begin
              if $ts(T) > rts(x)$ **then**
              begin
                send *dop* to the data processor
                $rts(x) \leftarrow ts(T)$
              end
              else begin
                $msg \leftarrow$ "Reject T"
                send *msg* to the coordinating *TM*
              end
              end-if
            end {of Read case}
            Write:
            begin
              if $ts(T) > rts(x)$ **and** $ts(T) > wts(x)$ **then**
              begin
                send *dop* to the data processor
                $rts(x) \leftarrow ts(T)$
                $wts(x) \leftarrow ts(T)$
              end
              else begin
                $msg \leftarrow$ "Reject T"
                send *msg* to the coordinating TM
              end
              end-if
            end {of Write case}

```
                        Commit:
                        begin
                            send dop to the data processor
                        end {of Commit case}
                        Abort:
                        begin
                            for all x that has been accessed by T do
                                reset rts(x) and wts(x) to their initial values
                            end-for
                            send dop to the data processor
                        end {of Abort case}
                    end-case
                end
            end-case
        until forever
    end. {BTO-SC}
```

As indicated before, a transaction which contains an operation that is rejected by a scheduler is restarted by the transaction manager with a new timestamp. This ensures that the transaction has a chance to execute in its next try. Since the transactions never wait while they hold access rights to data items, the basic TO algorithm never causes deadlocks. However, the penalty of deadlock freedom is potential restart of a transaction numerous times. There is an alternative to the basic TO algorithm that reduces the number of restarts, which we consider in the next section.

Another detail that needs to be considered relates to the communication between the scheduler and the data processor. When an accepted operation is passed on to the data processor, the scheduler needs to refrain from sending another incompatible, but acceptable operation to the data processor until the first is processed and acknowledged. This is a requirement to ensure that the data processor executes the operations in the order in which the scheduler passes them on. Otherwise, the read and write timestamp values for the accessed data item would not be accurate.

Example 11.8

Assume that the TO scheduler first receives $W_i(x)$ and then receives $W_j(x)$, where $ts(T_i) < ts(T_j)$. The scheduler would accept both operations and pass them on to the data processor. The result of these two operations is that $wts(x) = ts(T_j)$, and we then expect the effect of $W_j(x)$ to be represented in the database. However, if the data processor does not execute them in that order, the effects on the database will be wrong.

The scheduler can enforce the ordering by maintaining a queue for each data item that is used to delay the transfer of the accepted operation until an acknowledgment is received from the data processor regarding the previous operation on the same data item. This detail is not shown in Algorithm 11.7.

Such a complication does not arise in 2PL-based algorithms because the lock manager effectively orders the operations by releasing the locks only after the operation is executed. In one sense the queue that the TO scheduler maintains may be thought of as a lock. However, this does not imply that the schedule generated by a TO scheduler and a 2PL scheduler would always be equivalent. There are some schedules that a TO scheduler would generate that would not be admissible by a 2PL schedule.

Remember that in the case of strict 2PL algorithms, the releasing of locks is delayed further, until the commit or abort of a transaction. It is possible to develop a strict TO algorithm by using a similar scheme. For example, if $W_i(x)$ is accepted and released to the data processor, the scheduler delays all $R_j(x)$ and $W_j(x)$ operations (for all T_j) until T_i terminates (commits or aborts).

11.4.2 Conservative TO Algorithm

We indicated in the preceding section that the basic TO algorithm never causes operations to wait, but instead, restarts them. We also pointed out that even though this is an advantage due to deadlock freedom, it is also a disadvantage, because numerous restarts would have adverse performance implications. The conservative TO algorithms attempt to lower this system overhead by reducing the number of transaction restarts.

Let us first present a technique that is commonly used to reduce the probability of restarts. Remember that a TO scheduler restarts a transaction if a younger conflicting transaction is already scheduled or has been executed. Note that such occurrences increase significantly if, for example, one site is comparatively inactive relative to the others and does not issue transactions for an extended period. In this case its timestamp counter indicates a value that is considerably smaller than the counters of other sites. If the TM at this site then receives a transaction, the operations that are sent to the schedulers at the other sites will almost certainly be rejected, causing the transaction to restart. Furthermore, the same transaction will restart repeatedly until the timestamp counter value at its originating site reaches a level of parity with the counters of other sites.

The foregoing scenario indicates that it is useful to keep the counters at each site synchronized. However, total synchronization is not only costly—since it requires exchange of messages every time a counter changes—but also unnecessary. Instead, each transaction manager can send its remote operations to the transaction managers at the other sites, instead of to the schedulers. The receiving transaction managers can then compare their own counter values with that of the incoming operation. Any manager whose counter value is smaller than the incoming one adjusts its own counter to one more than the incoming one. This ensures that none of the counters in the system run away or lag behind significantly. Of course, if system clocks are used instead of counters, this approximate synchronization may be achieved automatically as long as the clocks are of comparable speeds.

We can now return to our discussion of conservative TO algorithms. The "conservative" nature of these algorithms relates to the way they execute each operation. The basic TO algorithm tries to execute an operation as soon as it is accepted; it is therefore "aggressive" or "progressive." Conservative algorithms, on the other hand, delay each operation until there is an assurance that no operation with a smaller timestamp can arrive at that scheduler. If this condition can be guaranteed, the scheduler will never reject an operation. However, this delay introduces the possibility of deadlocks.

The basic technique that is used in conservative TO algorithms is based on the following idea: the operations of each transaction are buffered until an ordering can be established so that rejections are not possible, and they are executed in that order. We will consider one possible implementation of the conservative TO algorithm. Our discussion follows that of [Herman and Verjus, 1979].

Assume that each scheduler maintains one queue for each transaction manager in the system. The scheduler at site i stores all the operations that it receives from the transaction manager at site j in queue Q_{ij}. Scheduler i has one such queue for each j. When an operation is received from a transaction manager, it is placed in its appropriate queue in increasing timestamp order. The schedulers at each site execute the operations from these queues in increasing timestamp order.

This scheme will reduce the number of restarts, but it will not guarantee that they will be eliminated completely. Consider the case where at site i the queue for site j (Q_{ij}) is empty. The scheduler at site i will choose an operation [say, $R(x)$] with the smallest timestamp and pass it on to the data processor. However, site j may have sent to i an operation [say, $W(x)$] with a smaller timestamp which may still be in transit in the network. When this operation reaches site i, it will be rejected since it violates the TO rule: it wants to access a data item that is currently being accessed (in an incompatible mode) by another operation with a higher timestamp.

It is possible to design an extremely conservative TO algorithm by insisting that the scheduler choose an operation to be sent to the data processor only if there is at least one operation in each queue. This guarantees that every operation that the scheduler receives in the future will have timestamps greater than or equal to those currently in the queues. Of course, if a transaction manager does not have a transaction to process, it needs to send dummy messages periodically to every scheduler in the system, informing them that the operations that it will send in the future will have timestamps greater than that of the dummy message.

The careful reader will realize that the extremely conservative timestamp ordering scheduler actually executes transactions serially at each site. This is very restrictive. One method that has been employed to overcome this restriction is to group transactions into classes. Transaction classes are defined with respect to their read sets and write sets. It is therefore sufficient to determine the class that a transaction belongs to by comparing the transaction's read set and write set, respectively, with the read set and write set of each class. Thus the conservative TO algorithm can be modified so that instead of requiring the existence, at each site, of one queue for each transaction manager, it is only necessary to have one queue for each transaction class. Alternatively, one might mark each queue with the class to which it belongs. With either of these modifications, the conditions for sending an operation to the data processor are changed. It is no longer necessary to wait until there is at least one operation in each queue; it is sufficient to wait until there is at least one operation in each class to which the transaction belongs. This and other weaker conditions that reduce the waiting delay can be defined and are sufficient. A variant of this method is used in the SDD-1 prototype system [Bernstein et al., 1980b].

11.4.3 Multiversion TO Algorithm

Multiversion TO is another attempt at eliminating the restart overhead cost of transactions. Most of the work on multiversion TO has concentrated on centralized databases, so we present only a brief overview. However, we should indicate that multiversion TO algorithm would be a suitable concurrency control mechanism for DBMSs that are designed to support applications which inherently have a notion of versions of database objects (e.g., engineering databases and document databases).

In multiversion TO, the updates do not modify the database; each write operation creates a new version of that data item. Each version is marked by the timestamp of the transaction that creates it. Thus the multiversion TO algorithm trades storage space for time. In doing so, it processes each transaction on a state of the database that it would have seen if the transactions were executed serially in timestamp order.

The existence of versions is transparent to users who issue transactions simply by referring to data items, not to any specific version. The transaction manager assigns a timestamp to each transaction which is also used to keep track of the timestamps of each version. The operations are processed by the schedulers as follows:

1. A $R_i(x)$ is translated into a read on one version of x. This is done by finding a version of x (say, x_v) such that $ts(x_v)$ is the largest timestamp less than $ts(T_i)$. $R_i(x_v)$ is then sent to the data processor.

2. A $W_i(x)$ is translated into $W_i(x_w)$ so that $ts(x_w) = ts(T_i)$ and sent to the data processor if and only if no other transaction with a timestamp greater than $ts(T_i)$ has read the value of a version of x (say, x_r) such that $ts(x_r) > ts(x_w)$. In other words, if the scheduler has already processed a $R_j(x_r)$ such that

$$ts(T_i) < ts(x_r) < ts(T_j)$$

then $W_i(x)$ is rejected.

A scheduler that processes the read and the write requests of transactions according to the rules noted above is guaranteed to generate serializable schedules. To save space, the versions of the database may be purged from time to time. This should be done when the distributed DBMS is certain that it will no longer receive a transaction that needs to access the purged versions.

11.5 OPTIMISTIC CONCURRENCY CONTROL ALGORITHMS

The concurrency control algorithms discussed in Sections 11.3 and 11.4 are pessimistic in nature. In other words, they assume that the conflicts between transactions are quite frequent and do not permit a transaction to access a data item if there is a conflicting transaction that accesses that data item. Thus the execution of any operation of a transaction follows the sequence of phases: validation (V), read (R), computation (C), write (W) (Figure 11.12).[2] Generally, this sequence is valid for an update transaction as well as for each of its operations.

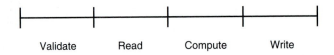

Validate   Read   Compute   Write

Figure 11.12. Phases of Pessimistic Transaction Execution

Optimistic algorithms, on the other hand, delay the validation phase until just before the write phase (Figure 11.13). Thus an operation submitted to an optimistic scheduler is never delayed. The read, compute, and write operations of each transaction are processed freely without updating the actual database. Each transaction initially makes its updates on local copies of data items. The validation phase consists of checking if these updates would maintain the consistency of the database. If the answer is affirmative, the changes are made global (i.e., written into the actual database). Otherwise, the transaction is aborted and has to restart.

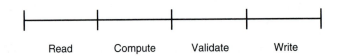

Read   Compute   Validate   Write

Figure 11.13. Phases of Optimistic Transaction Execution

It is possible to design locking-based optimistic concurrency control algorithms (see [Bernstein et al., 1987]). However, the original optimistic proposals ([Kung and Robinson, 1981], [Thomas, 1979]) are based on timestamp ordering. Therefore, we describe only the optimistic approach using timestamps. Our discussion is brief and emphasizes concepts rather than implementation details. The reasons for this are twofold. First, most of the current work on optimistic methods concentrates on centralized rather than distributed DBMSs. Second, optimistic algorithms have

---

[2]We consider only the update transactions in this discussion because they are the ones that cause consistency problems. Read-only actions do not have the computation and write phases. Furthermore, we assume that the write phase includes the commit action.

not been implemented in any commercial or prototype DBMS. Therefore, the information regarding their implementation trade-offs is insufficient. As a matter of fact, the only centralized implementation of optimistic concepts (not the full algorithm) is in IBM's IMS-FASTPATH, which provides primitives that permit the programmer to access the database in an optimistic manner.

The algorithm that we discuss was proposed in [Kung and Robinson, 1981] and was later extended for distributed DBMS [Ceri and Owicki, 1982]. This is not the only extension of the model to distributed databases, however (see, for example, [Sinha et al., 1985]). It differs from pessimistic TO-based algorithms not only by being optimistic but also in its assignment of timestamps. Timestamps are associated only with transactions, not with data items (i.e., there are no read or write timestamps). Furthermore, timestamps are not assigned to transactions at their initiation but at the beginning of their validation step. This is because the timestamps are needed only during the validation phase, and as we will see shortly, their early assignment may cause unnecessary transaction rejections.

Each transaction T_i is subdivided (by the transaction manager at the originating site) into a number of subtransactions, each of which can execute at many sites. Notationally, let us denote by T_{ij} a subtransaction of T_i that executes at site j. Until the validation phase, each local execution follows the sequence depicted in Figure 11.13. At that point a timestamp is assigned to the transaction which is copied to all its subtransactions. The local validation of T_{ij} is performed according to the following rules, which are mutually exclusive.

Rule 1. If all transactions T_k where $ts(T_k) < ts(T_{ij})$ have completed their write phase before T_{ij} has started its read phase (Figure 11.14a),[3] validation succeeds, because transaction executions are in serial order.

Rule 2. If there is any transaction T_k such that $ts(T_k) < ts(T_{ij})$ which completes its write phase while T_{ij} is in its read phase (Figure 11.14b), the validation succeeds if $WS(T_k) \cap RS(T_{ij}) = \emptyset$.

Rule 3. If there is any transaction T_k such that $ts(T_k) < ts(T_{ij})$ which completes its read phase before T_{ij} completes its read phase (Figure 11.14c), the validation succeeds if $WS(T_k) \cap RS(T_{ij}) = \emptyset$, and $WS(T_k) \cap WS(T_{ij}) = \emptyset$.

Rule 1 is obvious; it indicates that the transactions are actually executed serially in their timestamp order. Rule 2 ensures that none of the data items updated by T_k are read by T_{ij} and that T_k finishes writing its updates into the database before T_{ij} starts writing. Thus the updates of T_{ij} will not be overwritten by the updates of T_k. Rule 3 is similar to Rule 2, but does not require that T_k finish writing before T_{ij} starts writing. It simply requires that the updates of T_k not affect the read phase or the write phase of T_{ij}.

---

[3]Following the convention we have adopted, we omit the computation step in this figure and in the subsequent discussion. Thus timestamps are assigned at the end of the read phase.

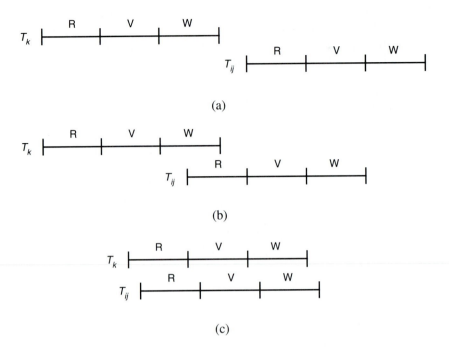

Figure 11.14. Possible Execution Scenarios

Once a transaction is locally validated to ensure that the local database consistency is maintained, it also needs to be globally validated to ensure that the mutual consistency rule is obeyed. Unfortunately, there is no known optimistic method of doing this. A transaction is globally validated if all the transactions that precede it in the serialization order (at that site) terminate (either by committing or aborting). This is a pessimistic method since it performs global validation early and delays a transaction. However, it guarantees that transactions execute in the same order at each site.

An advantage of the optimistic concurrency control algorithms is their potential to allow a higher level of concurrency. It has been shown [Kung and Robinson, 1981] that when transaction conflicts are very rare, the optimistic mechanism performs better than locking. A major problem with optimistic algorithms is the higher storage cost. To validate a transaction, the optimistic mechanism has to store the read and the write sets of several other terminated transactions. Specifically, the read and write sets of terminated transactions that were in progress when transaction T_{ij} arrived at site j need to be stored in order to validate T_{ij}. Obviously, this increases the storage cost.

Another problem is starvation. Consider a situation in which the validation phase of a long transaction fails. In subsequent trials it is still possible that the validation will fail repeatedly. Of course, it is possible to solve this problem by permitting the transaction exclusive access to the database after a specified number of trials. However, this reduces the level of concurrency to a single transaction. The exact "mix" of transactions that would cause an intolerable level of restarts is an issue that remains to be studied.

11.6 DEADLOCK MANAGEMENT

As we indicated before, any locking-based concurrency control algorithm may result in deadlocks, since there is mutual exclusion of access to shared resources (data) and transactions may wait on locks. Furthermore, we have seen that some TO-based algorithms that require the waiting of transactions (e.g., strict TO) may also cause deadlocks. Therefore, the distributed DBMS requires special procedures to handle them.

A deadlock can occur because transactions wait for one another. Informally, a deadlock situation is a set of requests that can never be granted by the concurrency control mechanism.

Example 11.9

> Consider two transactions T_i and T_j that hold write locks on two entities x and y [i.e., $wl_i(x)$ and $wl_j(y)$]. Suppose that T_i now issues a $rl_i(y)$ or a $wl_i(y)$. Since y is currently locked by transaction T_j, T_i will have to wait until T_j releases its write lock on y. However, if during this waiting period, T_j now requests a lock (read or write) on x, there will be a deadlock. This is because, T_i will be blocked waiting for T_j to release its lock on y while T_j will be waiting for T_i to release its lock on x. In this case, the two transactions T_i and T_j will wait indefinitely for each other to release their respective locks.

A deadlock is a permanent phenomenon. If one exists in a system, it will not go away unless outside intervention takes place. This outside interference may come from the user, the system operator, or the software system (the operating system or the distributed DBMS).

A useful tool in analyzing deadlocks is a *wait-for graph* (WFG). A WFG is a directed graph that represents the wait-for relationship among transactions. The nodes of this graph represent the concurrent transactions in the system. An arc $T_i \rightarrow T_j$ exists in the WFG if transaction T_i is waiting for T_j to release a lock on some entity. Figure 11.15 depicts the WFG for Example 11.9.

Using the WFG, it is easier to indicate the condition for the occurrence of a deadlock. A deadlock occurs when the WFG contains a cycle. We should indicate that the formation of the WFG is more complicated in distributed systems, since two transactions that participate in a deadlock condition may be running at different sites. We call this situation a *global deadlock*. In distributed systems, then, it is not sufficient that each local distributed DBMS form a *local wait-for graph* (LWFG) at each site; it is also necessary to form a *global wait-for graph* (GWFG), which is the union of all the LWFGs.

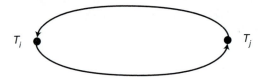

Figure 11.15. A WFG Example

Example 11.10

Consider four transactions T_1, T_2, T_3, and T_4 with the following wait-for relationship among them: $T_1 \rightarrow T_2 \rightarrow T_3 \rightarrow T_4 \rightarrow T_1$. If T_1 and T_2 run at site 1 while T_3 and T_4 run at site 2, the LWFGs for the two sites are shown in Figure 11.16a. Notice that it is not possible to detect a deadlock simply by examining the two LWFGs, because the deadlock is global. The deadlock can easily be detected, however, by examining the GWFG where intersite waiting is shown by dashed lines (Figure 11.16b).

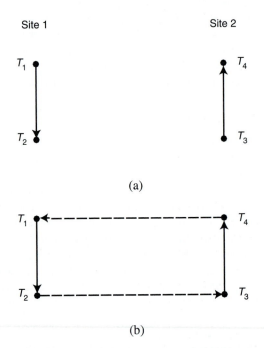

Figure 11.16. Difference between LWFG and GWFG

There are three known methods for handling deadlocks: prevention, avoidance, and detection and resolution.[4]   In the remainder of this section we discuss each approach in more detail.

11.6.1   Deadlock Prevention

Deadlock prevention methods guarantee that deadlocks cannot occur in the first place. Thus the transaction manager checks a transaction when it is first initiated and does not permit it to proceed if it may cause a deadlock. To perform this check, it is required that all of the data items that will be accessed by a transaction be predeclared. The transaction manager then permits a transaction to proceed if all the data items that it will access are available. Otherwise, the transaction is not permitted to proceed. The transaction manager reserves all the data items that are predeclared by a transaction that it allows to proceed.

Unfortunately, such systems are not very suitable for database environments. The fundamental problem is that it is usually difficult to know precisely which data items will be accessed by a transaction. Access to certain data items may depend on conditions that may not be resolved until run time. For example, in the reservation transaction that we developed in Example 10.3, access to CID and CNAME is conditional upon the availability of free seats. To be safe, the system would thus need to consider the maximum set of data items, even if they end up not being accessed. This would certainly reduce concurrency. Furthermore, there is additional overhead in evaluating whether a transaction can proceed safely. On the other hand, such systems require no run-time support, which reduces the overhead. It has the additional advantage that it is not necessary to abort and restart a transaction due to deadlocks. This not only reduces the overhead but also makes such methods suitable for systems that have no provisions for undoing processes.[5]

11.6.2   Deadlock Avoidance

Deadlock avoidance schemes either employ concurrency control techniques that will never result in deadlocks or require that schedulers detect potential deadlock situations in advance and ensure that they will not occur. We consider both of these cases.

The simplest means of avoiding deadlocks is to order the resources and insist that each process request access to these resources in that order. This solution was long ago proposed for operating systems. A revised version has been proposed for database systems as well [Garcia-Molina, 1979]. Accordingly, the lock units in the distributed database are ordered and transactions always request locks in that order. This ordering of lock units may be done either globally or locally at

---

[4]Of course, there is a fourth alternative that the system ignore deadlocks and require either that the application programmer deal with it or that the system be restarted. However, we obviously do not consider this to be a serious alternative.

[5]This is not a significant advantage since most systems have to be able to undo transactions for reliability purposes, as we will see in Chapter 12.

each site. In the latter case, it is also necessary to order the sites and require that transactions which access data items at multiple sites request their locks by visiting the sites in the predefined order.

Another alternative is to make use of transaction timestamps to prioritize transactions and resolve deadlocks by aborting transactions with higher (or lower) priorities. To implement this type of prevention method, the lock manager is modified as follows. If a lock request of a transaction T_i is denied, the lock manager does not automatically force T_i to wait. Instead, it applies a prevention test to the requesting transaction and the transaction that currently holds the lock (say T_j). If the test is passed, T_i is permitted to wait for T_j; otherwise, one transaction or the other is aborted.

Examples of this approach is the WAIT-DIE and WOUND-WAIT algorithms [Rosenkrantz et al., 1978], also used in the MADMAN DBMS [GE, 1976]. These algorithms are based on the assignment of timestamps to transactions. WAIT-DIE is a nonpreemptive algorithm in that if the lock request of T_i is denied because the lock is held by T_j, it never preempts T_j. It follows the following rule:

> **WAIT-DIE Rule.** If T_i **requests a lock on a data item that is already locked by** T_j, T_i **is permitted to wait if and only if** T_i **is older than** T_j. **If** T_i **is younger than** T_j, **then** T_i **is aborted and restarted with the same timestamp.**

A preemptive version of the same idea is the WOUND-WAIT algorithm, which follows the rule:

> **WOUND-WAIT Rule.** If T_i **requests a lock on a data item that is already locked by** T_j, **then** T_i **is permitted to wait if only if it is younger than** T_j; **otherwise,** T_j **is aborted and the lock is granted to** T_i.

The rules are specified from the viewpoint of T_i: T_i waits, T_i dies, and T_i wounds T_j. In fact, the result of wounding and dying are the same: the affected transaction is aborted and restarted. With this perspective, the two rules can be specified as follows:

$$\text{if } ts(T_i) < ts(T_j) \text{ then } T_i \text{ waits else } T_i \text{ dies} \qquad \text{(WAIT-DIE)}$$
$$\text{if } ts(T_i) < ts(T_j) \text{ then } T_j \text{ is wounded else } T_i \text{ waits} \qquad \text{(WOUND-WAIT)}$$

Notice that in both algorithms the younger transaction is aborted. The difference between the two algorithms is whether or not they preempt active transactions. Also note that the WAIT-DIE algorithm prefers younger transactions and kills older ones. Thus an older transaction tends to wait longer and longer as it gets older. By contrast, the WOUND-WAIT rule prefers the older transaction since it never waits for a younger one. One of these methods, or a combination, may be selected in implementing a deadlock prevention algorithm.

Deadlock avoidance methods are more suitable than prevention schemes for database environments. Their fundamental drawback is that they require run-time support for deadlock management, which adds to the run-time overhead of transaction execution.

11.6.3   Deadlock Detection and Resolution

Deadlock detection and resolution is the most popular and best-studied method. Detection is done by studying the GWFG for the formation of cycles. We will discuss means of doing this in considerable detail. Resolution of deadlocks is typically done by the selection of one or more *victim* transaction(s) that will be preempted and aborted in order to break the cycles in the GWFG. Under the assumption that the cost of preempting each member of a set of deadlocked transactions is known, the problem of selecting the minimum total-cost set for breaking the deadlock cycle has been shown to be a difficult (NP-complete) problem [Leung and Lai, 1979]. However, there are some factors that affect this choice [Bernstein et al., 1987]:

1. The amount of effort that has already been invested in the transaction. This effort will be lost if the transaction is aborted.

2. The cost of aborting the transaction. This cost generally depends on the number of updates that the transaction has already performed.

3. The amount of effort it will take to finish executing the transaction. The scheduler wants to avoid aborting a transaction that is almost finished. To do this, it must be able to predict the future behavior of active transactions (e.g., based on the transaction's type).

4. The number of cycles that contain the transaction. Since aborting a transaction breaks all cycles that contain it, it is best to abort transactions that are part of more than one cycle (if such transactions exist).

Now we can return to deadlock detection. We should first indicate that there are three fundamental methods of detecting distributed deadlocks. These are commonly called *centralized, distributed*, and *hierarchical deadlock detection*.

Centralized Deadlock Detection

In the centralized deadlock detection approach, one site is designated as the deadlock detector for the entire system. Periodically, each lock manager transmits its LWFG to the deadlock detector, which then forms the GWFG and looks for cycles in it. Actually, the lock managers need only send changes in their graphs (i.e., the newly created or deleted edges) to the deadlock detector. The length of intervals for transmitting this information is a system design decision: the smaller the interval, the smaller the delays due to undetected deadlocks, but the larger the communication cost.

Centralized deadlock detection has been proposed for distributed INGRES. This method is simple and would be a very natural choice if the concurrency control algorithm were centralized 2PL. However, the issues of vulnerability to failure, and high communication overhead, must also be considered.

Hierarchical Deadlock Detection

An alternative to centralized deadlock detection is the building of a hierarchy of deadlock detectors [Menasce and Muntz, 1979] (see Figure 11.17). Deadlocks that are local to a single site would be detected at that site using the local WFG. Each site also sends its local WFG to the deadlock detector at the next level. Thus, distributed deadlocks involving two or more sites would be detected by a deadlock detector in the next lowest level that has control over these sites. For example, a deadlock at site 1 would be detected by the local deadlock detector (DD) at site 1 (denoted DD_{21}, 2 for level 2, 1 for site 1). If, however, the deadlock involves sites 1 and 2, then DD_{11} detects it. Finally, if the deadlock involves sites 1 and 4, DD_{0x} detects it, where x is either one of 1, 2, 3, or 4.

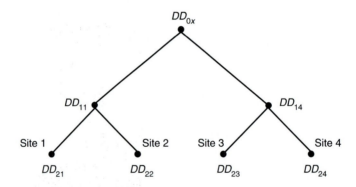

Figure 11.17. Hierarchical Deadlock Detection

The hierarchical deadlock detection method reduces the dependence on the central site, thus reducing the communication cost. It is, however, considerably more complicated to implement and would involve nontrivial modifications to the lock and transaction manager algorithms.

Distributed Deadlock Detection

Distributed deadlock detection algorithms delegate the responsibility of detecting deadlocks to individual sites. Thus, as in the hierarchical deadlock detection, there are local deadlock detectors at each site which communicate their local WFGs with one another (in fact, only the potential deadlock cycles are transmitted). Among the various distributed deadlock detection algorithms, the one implemented in System R* [Obermarck, 1982], [Mohan et al., 1986] seems to be the more widely known and referenced. We therefore briefly outline that method, basing the discussion on [Obermarck, 1982].

The local WFG at each site is formed and is modified as follows:

1. Since each site receives the potential deadlock cycles from other sites, these edges are added to the local WFGs.

2. The edges in the local WFG which show that local transactions are waiting for transactions at other sites are joined with edges in the local WFGs which show that remote transactions are waiting for local ones.

Example 11.11

Consider the example depicted in Figure 11.16. The local WFG for the two sites are modified as shown in Figure 11.18.

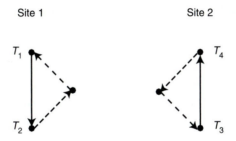

Figure 11.18. Modified LWFGs

Local deadlock detectors look for two things. If there is a cycle that does not include the external edges, there is a local deadlock that can be handled locally. If, on the other hand, there is a cycle involving these external edges, there is a potential distributed deadlock and this cycle information has to be communicated to other deadlock detectors. In the case of Example 11.11, the possibility of such a distributed deadlock is detected by both sites.

A question that needs to be answered at this point is to whom to transmit the information. Obviously, it can be transmitted to all deadlock detectors in the system. In the absence of any more information, this is the only alternative, but it incurs a high overhead. If, however, one knows whether the transaction is ahead or behind in the deadlock cycle, the information can be transmitted forward or backward along the sites in this cycle. The receiving site then modifies its LWFG as discussed above, and checks for deadlocks. Obviously, there is no need to transmit along the deadlock cycle in both the forward and backward directions. In the case of Example 11.11, site 1 would send it to site 2 in both forward and backward transmission along the deadlock cycle.

The distributed deadlock detection algorithms require uniform modification to the lock managers at each site. This uniformity makes them easier to implement. However, there is the potential for excessive message transmission. This happens, for example, in the case of Example 11.11: site 1 sends its potential deadlock information to site 2, and site 2 sends its information to site 1. In this case the deadlock detectors at both sites will detect the deadlock. Besides causing unnecessary message transmission, there is the additional problem that each site may choose a different victim to abort. The algorithm proposed in [Obermarck, 1982] solves the problem by using transaction timestamps as well as the following rule. Let the path that has the potential of causing a distributed deadlock in the local WFG of a site be $T_i \rightarrow \cdots \rightarrow T_j$. A local deadlock detector forwards the cycle information only if $ts(T_i) < ts(T_j)$. This reduces the average number of message transmissions by one-half. In the case of Example 11.11, site 1 has a path $T_1 \rightarrow T_2 \rightarrow T_3$, whereas site 2 has a path $T_3 \rightarrow T_4 \rightarrow T_1$. Therefore, assuming that the subscripts of each transaction denote their timestamp, only site 1 will send information to site 2.

11.7 "RELAXED" CONCURRENCY CONTROL

For most of this chapter, we focused only on distributed concurrency control algorithms that are designed for flat transactions and enforce serializability as the correctness criterion. This is the baseline case. There have been studies that (a) relax serializability in arguing for correctness of concurrent execution, and (b) consider other transaction models, primarily nested ones. We will briefly review these in this section.

11.7.1 Non-Serializable Schedules

Serializability is a fairly simple and elegant concept which can be enforced with acceptable overhead. However, it is considered to be too "strict" for certain applications since it does not consider as correct certain schedules that might be argued as reasonable. We have shown one case when we discussed the ordered shared lock concept. In addition, consider the Reservation transaction of Example 10.10. One can argue that the schedule generated by two concurrent executions of this transaction can be non-serializable, but correct – one may do the Airline reservation first and then do the Hotel reservation while the other one reverses the order – as long as both executions successfully terminate. The question, however, is how one can generalize these intuitive observations. The solution is to observe and exploit the "semantics" of these transactions.

There have been a number of proposals for exploiting transaction semantics. Of particular interest for distributed DBMS is one class that depends on identifying transaction *steps*, which may consist of a single operation or a set of operations, and establishing how transactions can interleave with each other between steps. In [Garcia-Molina, 1983], transactions are classified into classes such that transactions in the same class are *compatible* and can interleave arbitrarily while transactions in different classes are incompatible and have to be synchronized. The synchronization is based on semantic notions, allowing more concurrency than serializability. The use of the concept of transaction classes can be traced back to SDD-1 [Bernstein et al., 1980b].

The concept of compatibility is refined in [Lynch, 1983b] and several levels of compatibility among transactions are defined. These levels are structured hierarchically so that interleavings at higher levels include those at lower levels. Furthermore, [Lynch, 1983b] introduces the concept of *breakpoints* within transactions which represent points at which other transactions can interleave. This is an alternative to the use of compatibility sets.

Another work along these lines uses breakpoints to indicate the interleaving points, but does not require that the interleavings be hierarchical [Farrag and Özsu, 1989]. A transaction is modeled as consisting of a number of steps. Each step consists of a sequence of atomic operations and a breakpoint at the end of these operations. For each breakpoint in a transaction the set of transaction types that are allowed to interleave at that breakpoint is specified. A correctness criterion called *relative consistency* is defined based on the correct interleavings among transactions. Intuitively, a relatively consistent history is equivalent to a history that is stepwise serial (i.e., the operations and breakpoint of each step appear without interleaving), and in which a step (T_{ik}) of transaction T_i interleaves two consecutive steps $(T_{jm}$ and $T_{jm+1})$ of transaction T_j only if transactions of T_i's type are allowed to interleave T_{jm} at its breakpoint. It can be shown that some of the relatively consistent histories are not serializable, but are still "correct" [Farrag and Özsu, 1989].

A unifying framework that combines the approaches of [Lynch, 1983b] and [Farrag and Özsu, 1989] has been proposed in [Agrawal et al., 1994]. A correctness criterion called *semantic relative atomicity* is introduced which provides finer interleavings and more concurrency.

The above mentioned relaxed correctness criteria have formal underpinnings similar to serializability, allowing their formal analysis. However, these have not been extended to distributed DBMS even though this possibility exists. Thus we only provide an overview rather than a detailed study.

11.7.2 Nested Distributed Transactions

We introduced the nested transaction model in the previous chapter. The concurrent execution of nested transactions is interesting, especially since they are good candidates for distributed execution.

Let us consider closed nested transactions [Moss, 1985] first. The concurrency control of nested transactions have generally followed a locking-based approach. The following rules govern the management of the locks and the completion of transaction execution in the case of closed nested transactions:

1. Each subtransaction executes as a transaction and upon completion transfers its lock to its parent transaction.

2. A parent inherits both the locks and the updates of its committed subtransactions.

3. The inherited state will be visible only to descendants of the inheriting parent transaction. However, to access the sate, a descendant must acquire appropriate locks. Lock conflicts are determined as for flat transactions, except that one ignores inherited locks retained by ancestor's of the requesting subtransaction.

4. If a subtransaction aborts, then all locks and updates that the subtransaction and its descendants are discarded. The parent of an aborted subtransaction need not, but may, choose to abort.

From the perspective of ACID properties, closed nested transactions relax durability since the effects of successfully completed subtransactions can be erased if an ancestor transaction aborts. They also relax the isolation property in a limited way since they share their state with other subtransactions within the same nested transaction.

The distributed execution potential of nested transactions is obvious. After all, nested transactions are meant to improve intra-transaction concurrency and one can view each subtransaction as a potential unit of distribution if data are also appropriately distributed.

However, from the perspective of lock management, some care has to be observed. When subtransactions release their locks to their parents, these lock releases cannot be reflected in the lock tables automatically. These subtransaction commit commands do not have the same semantics as given in Algorithms 11.5 and 11.6.

Open nested transactions are even more relaxed than their closed nested counterparts. They have been called "anarchic" forms of nested transactions [Gray and Reuter, 1993]. The open nested transaction model is best exemplified in the saga model [Garcia-Molina and Salem, 1987], [Garcia-Molina et al., 1990] which was discussed in Section 10.3.2.

From the perspective of lock management, open nested transactions are easy to deal with. The locks held by a subtransaction are released as soon as it commits or aborts and this is reflected in the lock tables.

A variant of open nested transactions with precise and formal semantics is the *multilevel transaction* model [Weikum, 1986], [Weikum and Schek, 1984], [Beeri et al., 1988], [Weikum, 1991]. Multilevel transactions "are a variant of open nested transactions in which the subtransactions correspond to operations at different levels of a layered system architecture" [Weikum and Hasse, 1993]. We introduce the concept with an example taken from [Weikum, 1991]. We consider a transaction specification language which allows users to write transactions involving abstract operations so as to be able to exploit application semantics.

Consider two transactions that transfer funds from one bank account to another:

T_1:   Withdraw(o, x) T_2:   Withdraw(o, y)
          Deposit(p, x) Deposit(p, y)

The notation here is that each T_i withdraws x amount from account o and deposits that amount to account p. The semantics of Withdraw is test-and-withdraw to ensure that the account balance is sufficient to meet the withdrawal request. In relational systems, each of these abstract operations will be translated to tuple operations Select (Sel), and Update (Upd) which will, in turn, be translated into page-level Read and Write operations. This results in a layered abstraction of transaction execution as depicted in Figure 11.19 which is taken from [Weikum, 1991].

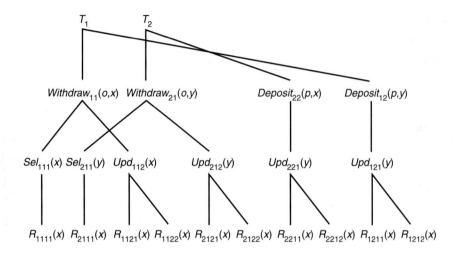

Figure 11.19. Multilevel Transaction Example

The traditional method of dealing with these types of histories is to develop a scheduler that enforces serializability at the lowest level (L_0). This, however, reduces the level of concurrency since it does not take into account application semantics and the granularity of synchronization is too coarse. Abstracting from the lower-level details can provide higher concurrency. For example, the page-level history (L_0) in Figure 11.19 is not serializable with respect to transactions T_1 and T_2, but the tuple-level history L_1 is serializable $(T_2 \rightarrow T_1)$. When one goes up to level L_2, it is possible to make use of the semantics of the abstract operations (i.e., their commutativity) to provide even more concurrency. Therefore, *multilevel serializability* is defined to reason about the serializability of multilevel histories and *multilevel schedulers* are proposed to enforce it [Weikum, 1991].

11.8 CONCLUSION

In this chapter we discussed distributed currency control algorithms that provide the isolation and consistency properties of transactions. The distributed concurrency control mechanism of a distributed DBMS ensures that the consistency of the distributed database is maintained and is therefore one of the fundamental components of a distributed DBMS. This is evidenced by the significant amount of research that has been conducted in this area. In Section 11.9 we point to some of the literature.

Our discussion in this chapter assumed that both the hardware and the software components of the computer systems were totally reliable. Even though this assumption is completely unrealistic, it has served a didactic purpose. It has permitted us to focus only on the concurrency control aspects, leaving to another chapter the features that need to be added to a distributed DBMS to make it reliable in an unreliable environment.

There are a few issues that we have omitted from this chapter. We mention them here for the benefit of the interested reader.

1. *Performance evaluation of concurrency control algorithms.* We have not explicitly included performance analysis results or methodologies. This may be somewhat surprising given the significant number of papers that have appeared in the literature. However, the reasons for this omission are numerous. First, there is no single comprehensive performance study of concurrency control algorithms. The performance studies have developed rather haphazardly and for specific purposes. Therefore, each has made different assumptions and has measured different parameters. It is quite difficult, if not impossible, to make meaningful generalizations that extend beyond the obvious. Second, the analytical methods for conducting these performance analysis studies have not been developed sufficiently.

   It is indicated in [Thomasian, 1996] that the relative performance characteristics of distributed concurrency methods is less understood than their centralized counterparts. Themain reason for this is the complexity of these algorithms. This complexity has resulted in a number of simplifying assumptions such as a fully replicated database, fully interconnected network, network delays represented by simplistic queueing models (M/M/1), etc. [Thomasian, 1996].

2. *Other concurrency control methods.* There is another class of concurrency control algorithms, called "serializability graph testing methods," which we have not mentioned in this chapter. Such mechanisms work by explicitly building a *dependency* (or *serializability*) *graph* and checking it for cycles. The dependency (serializability) graph of a schedule S, denoted $DG(S)$, is a directed graph representing the conflict relations among the transactions in S. The nodes of this graph are the set of transactions in S [i.e., each transaction T_i in S is represented by a node in $DG(S)$]. An arc (T_i, T_j) exists in $DG(S)$ if and only if there is an operation in T_i that conflicts with and precedes another operation in T_j.

Example 11.12

The dependency graph of schedule S_1 discussed in Example 11.6 is given in Figure 11.20.

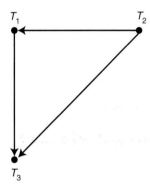

Figure 11.20. Dependency Graph

Schedulers update their dependency graphs whenever one of the following conditions is fulfilled: (1) a new transaction starts in the system, (2) a read or a write operation is received by the scheduler, (3) a transaction terminates, or (4) a transaction aborts.

It is now possible to talk about "correct" concurrency control algorithms based on the dependency graph. Given a schedule S, if its dependency graph $DG(S)$ is acyclic, then S is serializable. In the distributed case we may use a global dependency graph, which can be formed by taking the union of the local dependency graphs and further annotating each transaction by the identifier of the site where it is executed. It is then necessary to show that the global dependency graph is acyclic.

3. *Assumptions about transactions.* In our discussions, we did not make any distinction between read-only transactions and update transactions. It is possible to improve significantly the performance of transactions that only read data items, or of systems with a high ratio of read-only transactions to update transactions. These issues are beyond the scope of this book.

We have also treated read and write locks in an identical fashion. It is possible to differentiate between them and develop concurrency control algorithms that permit "lock conversion," whereby transactions can obtain locks in one mode and then modify their lock modes as they change their requirements. Typically, the conversion is from read locks to write locks.

4. *More "general" algorithms.* There are some indications which suggest that it should be possible to study the two fundamental concurrency control primitives (i.e., locking and timestamp ordering) using a unifying framework. Three major indications are worth mentioning. First, it is possible to develop both pessimistic and optimistic algorithms based on either one of the primitives. Second, a strict TO algorithm performs similarly to a locking algorithm, since it delays the acceptance of a transaction until all older ones are terminated. This does not mean that all schedules which can be generated by a strict TO scheduler would be permitted by a 2PL scheduler. However, this similarity is interesting. Finally, it is possible to develop hybrid algorithms that use both timestamp ordering and locking. Furthermore, it is possible to state precisely rules for their interaction.

One study [Farrag and Özsu, 1985], [Farrag and Özsu, 1987] has resulted in the development of a theoretical framework for the uniform treatment of both of these primitives. Based on this theoretical foundation, it was shown that 2PL and TO algorithms are two endpoints of a range of algorithms that can be generated by a more general concurrency control algorithm. This study, which is only for centralized database systems, is significant not only because it indicates that locking and timestamp ordering are related, but also because it would be interesting to study the nature and characteristics of the algorithms that lie between these two endpoints. In addition, such a uniform framework may be helpful in conducting comprehensive and internally consistent performance studies.

5. *Transaction execution models.* The algorithms that we have described all assume a computational model where the transaction manager at the originating site of a transaction coordinates the execution of each database operation of that transaction. This is called *centralized execution* [Carey and Livny, 1988]. It is also possible to consider a *distributed execution* model where a transaction is decomposed into a set of subtransactions each of which is allocated to one site where the transaction manager coordinates its execution. This is intuitively more attractive because it may permit load balancing across the multiple sites of a distributed database. However, the performance studies indicate that distributed computation performs better only under light load.

11.9   BIBLIOGRAPHIC NOTES

As indicated earlier, distributed concurrency control has been a very popular area of study. [Bernstein and Goodman, 1981] is a comprehensive study of the fundamental primitives which also lays down the rules for building hybrid algorithms. The issues that are addressed in this chapter are discussed in much more detail in [Cellary et al., 1988], [Bernstein et al., 1987], [Papadimitriou, 1986] and [Gray and Reuter, 1993].

Nested transaction models and their specific concurrency control algorithms have been the subjects of some study. Specific results can be found in [Moss, 1985], [Lynch, 1983a], [Lynch and Merritt, 1986], [Fekete et al., 1987a], [Fekete et al., 1987b], [Goldman, 1987], [Beeri et al., 1989], [Fekete et al., 1989] and more recently in [Lynch et al., 1993].

The work on transaction management with semantic knowledge is presented in [Lynch, 1983b], [Garcia-Molina, 1983], and [Farrag and Özsu, 1989]. The processing of read-only transactions is discussed in [Garcia-Molina and Wiederhold, 1982]. Transaction groups [Skarra et al., 1986], [Skarra, 1989] also exploit a correctness criterion called *semantic patterns* that is more relaxed than serializability. Furthermore, work on the ARIES system [Mohan et al., 1993] is also within this class of algorithms. In particular, [Rothermel and Mohan, 1989] discusses ARIES within the context of nested transactions. Epsilon serializability [Ramamritham and Pu, 1995], [Wu et al., 1997] and NT/PV model [Kshemkalyani and Singhal, 1994] are other "relaxed" correctness criteria. An algorithm based on ordering transactions using *serialization numbers* is discussed in [Halici and Dogac, 1989].

There are a number of papers that discuss the results of performance evaluation studies on distributed concurrency control algorithms. These include [Gelenbe and Sevcik, 1978], [Garcia-Molina, 1979], [Potier and LeBlanc, 1980], [Menasce and Nakanishi, 1982a], [Menasce and Nakanishi, 1982b], [Lin, 1981], [Lin and Nolte, 1982], [Lin and Nolte, 1983], [Goodman et al., 1983], [Sevcik, 1983], [Carey and Stonebraker, 1984], [Merrett and Rallis, 1985], [Özsu, 1985a], [Özsu, 1985b], [Koon and Özsu, 1986], [Tsuchiya et al., 1986], [Li, 1987], [Agrawal et al., 1987], [Bhide, 1988], [Carey and Livny, 1988], and [Carey and Livny, 1991]. [Liang and Tripathi, 1996] studies the performance of sagas and Thomasian has conducted a series of performance studies that focus on various aspects of transaction processing in centralized and distributed DBMSs [Thomasian, 1993], [Thomasian, 1998], [Yu et al., 1989]. [Kumar, 1996] focuses on the performance of centralized DBMSs; the performance of distributed concurrency control methods are discussed in [Thomasian, 1996] and [Cellary et al., 1988]. An early but comprehensive review of deadlock management is [Isloor and Marsland, 1980]. Most of the work on distributed deadlock management has been on detection and resolution (see, e.g., [Obermarck, 1982], [Elmagarmid et al., 1988]). Two surveys of the important algorithms are included in [Elmagarmid, 1986] and [Knapp, 1987]. A more recent survey is [Singhal, 1989]. There are two annotated bibliographies on the deadlock problem which do not emphasize the database issues but consider the problem in general: [Newton, 1979], [Zobel, 1983]. The research activity on this topic has slowed down in the last years.

Some of the recent relevant papers are [Yeung and Hung, 1995], [Hofri, 1994], [Lee and Kim, 1995], [Kshemkalyani and Singhal, 1994], [Chen et al., 1996], [Park et al., 1995] and [Makki and Pissinou, 1995].

11.10 EXERCISES

11.1 Which of the following schedules are conflict equivalent? (Ignore the commit (C) and abort (A) commands.)

$$
\begin{aligned}
S_1 &= W_2(x), W_1(x), R_3(x), R_1(x), C_1, W_2(y), R_3(y), R_3(z), C_3, R_2(x), C_2 \\
S_2 &= R_3(z), R_3(y), W_2(y), R_2(z), W_1(x), R_3(x), W_2(x), R_1(x), C_1, C_2, C_3 \\
S_3 &= R_3(z), W_2(x), W_2(y), R_1(x), R_3(x), R_2(z), R_3(y), C_3, W_1(x), C_2, C_1 \\
S_4 &= R_2(z), W_2(x), W_2(y), C_2, W_1(x), R_1(x), A_1, R_3(x), R_3(z), R_3(y), C_3
\end{aligned}
$$

11.2 Which of the above schedules $S_1 - S_4$ are serializable?

11.3 Give a schedule of two complete transactions which is not allowed by a struct 2PL scheduler but is accepted by the basic 2PL scheduler.

*11.4 One says that schedule S is *recoverable* if, whenever transaction T_i reads (some item x) from transaction $T_j (i \neq j)$;in S and C_i occurs in S, then $C_j \prec_S C_i$. T_i "reads x from" T_j in S if

  1. $W_j(x) \prec_S R_i(x)$, and
  2. A_j not $\prec_S R_i(x)$, and
  3. if there is some $W_k(x)$ such that $W_j(x) \prec_S W_k(x) \prec_S R_i(x)$, then $A_k \prec_S R_i(x)$.

Which of the schedules $S_1 - S_4$ given in Exercise 11.1 are recoverable?

**11.5 The distributed 2PL algorithm requires that all transaction managers and lock managers follow the ROWA rule. Assuming unit communication cost between any pair of sites, show (as a graph) the behavior of the total communication cost as a function of the transaction mix (percentage of read-only queries versus the percentage of updates) and the number of sites involved. Assume full replication of data. (Hint: Just show the trend, do not try to derive actual values.)

*11.6 Give the algorithms for the transaction managers and the lock managers for the distributed two-phase locking approach.

**11.7 Modify the centralized 2PL algorithm to handle phantoms. (See Chapter 10 for a definition of phantoms.)

11.8 Timestamp ordering-based concurrency control algorithms depend on either an accurate clock at each site or a global clock that all sites can access (the clock can be a counter). Assume that each site has its own clock which "ticks" every 0.1 second. If all local clocks are resynchronized every 24 hours, what is the maximum drift in seconds per 24 hours permissible at any local site to ensure that a timestamp-based mechanism will successfully synchronize transactions?

**11.9 Incorporate the distributed deadlock strategy described in this chapter
into the distributed 2PL algorithms that you designed in Exercise 11.3.

11.10 Explain the relationship between transaction manager storage requirement
and transaction size (number of operations per transaction) for a transaction
manager using an optimistic timestamp ordering for concurrency control.

*11.11 Give the scheduler and transaction manager algorithms for the distributed
optimistic concurrency controller described in this chapter.

11.12 Recall from the discussion in Section 11.7 that the computational model
that is used in our descriptions in this chapter is a centralized one. How
would the distributed 2PL transaction manager and lock manager algorithms change if a distributed execution model were to be used?

11.13 It is sometimes claimed that serializability is quite a restrictive correctness
criterion. Can you give examples of distributed schedules that are correct
(i.e., maintain the consistency of the local databases as well as their mutual
consistency) but are not serializable?

Chapter 12

DISTRIBUTED DBMS RELIABILITY

We have referred to "reliability" and "availability" of the database a number of times so far without defining these terms precisely. Specifically, we mentioned these terms in conjunction with data replication. It should come as no surprise to the reader that the distribution of the database or the replication of data items is not sufficient to make the distributed DBMS reliable. A number of protocols need to be implemented within the DBMS to exploit this distribution and replication in order to make operations more reliable.

A reliable distributed database management system is one that can continue to process user requests even when the underlying system is unreliable. In other words, even when components of the distributed computing environment fail, a reliable distributed DBMS should be able to continue executing user requests without violating database consistency.

The purpose of this chapter is to discuss the reliability features of a distributed DBMS. From Chapter 10 the reader will recall that the reliability of a distributed DBMS refers to the atomicity and durability properties of transactions. Two specific aspects of reliability protocols that need to be discussed in relation to these properties are the commit and the recovery protocols. In that sense, in this chapter we relax the major assumption of Chapter 11 that the underlying distributed system is fully reliable and does not experience any hardware or software failures. Furthermore, the commit protocols discussed in this chapter constitute the support provided by the distributed DBMS for the execution of commit commands which we have placed in transactions.

It is possible to discuss database reliability in isolation. However, the distributed DBMS is only one component of a distributed computing system. Its reliability is strongly dependent on the reliability of the hardware and software components that make up the distributed environment. Therefore, our discussion in this chapter starts with a general presentation of the reliability issues in distributed computing systems, and then focuses on the reliability aspects of distributed databases.

The organization of this chapter is as follows. As mentioned above, we start with a definition of the fundamental reliability concepts and reliability measures. In Section 12.2 we discuss the reasons for failures in distributed systems as well as an overview of some of the fundamental techniques that are used in designing reliable distributed computing systems. In Section 12.3 we extend the discussion of Section 12.2 to the types of failures in distributed DBMSs. Section 12.4 focuses on the functions of the local recovery manager and provides an overview of reliability measures in centralized DBMS. This discussion forms the foundation for the distributed commit and recovery protocols, which are introduced in Section 12.5. In Sections 12.6 and 12.7 we present detailed protocols for dealing with site failures and network partitioning, respectively. Implementation of these protocols within our architectural model is the topic of Section 12.7.3.

12.1 RELIABILITY CONCEPTS AND MEASURES

Too often, the terms *reliability* and *availability* are used loosely in literature. Even among the researchers in the area of reliable computer systems, there is no consensus on the definitions of these terms. In this section we give precise definitions of a number of concepts that are fundamental to an understanding and study of reliable systems. Our definitions follow those of [Anderson and Lee, 1985] and [Randell et al., 1978]. Nevertheless, we indicate where these definitions might differ from other usage of the terms.

12.1.1 System, State, and Failure

In the context of reliability, *system* refers to a mechanism that consists of a collection of components and interacts with its environment by responding to stimuli from the environment with a recognizable pattern of behavior (Figure 12.1). Each component of a system is itself a system, commonly called a *subsystem*. The environment of a component is the system of which it is a part. The way the components of a system are put together is called the *design* of the system. For example, Figure 4.7 depicts a distributed DBMS with all its components and the design of the DBMS, which indicates the interactions between these components. Note in Figure 4.7 that we have depicted only the software components. The only hardware component that is shown is the disk drive. It is, however, possible and even necessary to define the hardware components if one has to consider the reliability of the entire DBMS.

There are a number of ways of modeling the interaction between the software and the hardware in a computer system. One possible modeling method is to treat the program text as the design of an abstract system whose components are the hardware and software objects that are manipulated during the execution of the program. Another modeling alternative is to specify each software and hardware component explicitly, and let the design represent the way these components interact with one another (similar to Figure 4.7).

An *external state* of a system can be defined as the response that a system gives to an external stimulus. It is therefore possible to talk about a system changing

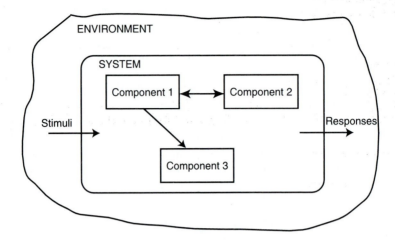

Figure 12.1. Schematic of a System

external states according to repeated stimuli from the environment. We can define the *internal state* of the system similarly. It is convenient to define the internal state as the union of the external states of the components that make up the system. Again, the system changes its internal state in response to stimuli from the environment.

The behavior of the system in providing response to all the possible stimuli from the environment needs to be laid out in an authoritative *specification* of its behavior. The specification indicates the valid behavior of each system state. Such a specification is not only necessary for a successful system design but is also essential to define the following reliability concepts.

Any deviation of a system from the behavior described in the specification is considered a *failure*. For example, in a distributed transaction manager the specification would state that only serializable schedules for the execution of concurrent transactions should be generated. If the transaction manager generates a nonserializable schedule, we say that it has failed.

Each failure obviously needs to be traced back to its cause. Failures in a system can be attributed to deficiencies either in the components that make it up, or in the design, that is, how these components are put together. Each state that a reliable system goes through is valid in the sense that the state fully meets its specification. However, in an unreliable system, it is possible that the system may get to an internal state that may not obey its specification. Further transitions from this state would eventually cause a system failure. Such internal states are called *erroneous states*; the part of the state that is incorrect is called an *error* in the system. Any error in the internal states of the components of a system or in the design of a system is called a *fault* in the system. Thus a fault causes an error that results in a system failure (Figure 12.2).

Figure 12.2. Chain of Events Leading to System Failure

We differentiate between errors (or faults and failures) that are permanent and those that are not permanent. Permanence can apply to a failure, a fault, or an error, although we typically use the term with respect to faults. A *permanent fault*, also commonly called a *hard fault*, is one that reflects an irreversible change in the behavior of the system. Permanent faults cause permanent errors that result in permanent failures. The characteristics of these failures is that recovery from them requires intervention to "repair" the fault. Systems also experience *intermittent* and *transient faults*. In the literature, these two are typically not differentiated; they are jointly called *soft faults*. The dividing line in this differentiation is the repairability of the system that has experienced the fault [Siewiorek and Swarz, 1982]. An intermittent fault refers to a fault that demonstrates itself occasionally due to unstable hardware or varying hardware or software states. A typical example is the faults that systems may demonstrate when the load becomes too heavy. On the other hand, a transient fault describes a fault that results from temporary environmental conditions. A transient fault might occur, for example, due to a sudden increase in the room temperature. The transient fault is therefore the result of environmental conditions that may be impossible to repair. An intermittent fault, on the other hand, can be repaired since the fault can be traced to a component of the system.

Remember that we have also indicated that system failures can be due to design faults. Design faults together with unstable hardware cause intermittent errors which result in system failure. A final source of system failure that may not be attributable to a component fault or a design fault is operator mistakes. These are the sources of a significant number of errors as the statistics included further in this section demonstrate. The relationship between various types of faults and failures is depicted in Figure 12.3.

As indicated previously, there are a number of different definitions of the fundamental reliability terms that we discussed. For example, the terms *fault* and *failure* are used interchangeably in the fault tolerance literature, whereas the terms *failure* and *error* are used interchangeably in the coding theory literature [Elkind, 1982]. Alternatively, a *fault* may be defined as "an erroneous state of hardware or software resulting from failures of components" and an *error* as "a manifestation of a fault within a program or data structure." *Failure* is defined as a "physical change in hardware" [Avizienis, 1977]. These definitions are specific to hardware systems and represent a rather different view as to what causes what. According to these definitions, a failure causes a fault that results in an error.

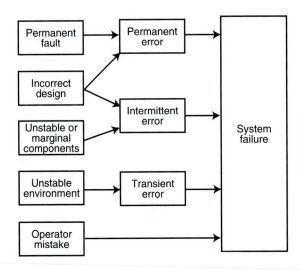

Figure 12.3. Sources of System Failure (Reprinted with permission from THE THEORY AND PRACTICE OF RELIABLE SYSTEM DESIGN, by Daniel P. Siewiorek and Robert S. Swarz, copyright ©Digital Press/Digital Equipment Corporation, 12 Crosby Drive, Bedford, MA 01730.)

12.1.2 Reliability and Availability

Reliability refers to the probability that the system under consideration does not experience any failures in a given time interval. It is typically used to describe systems that cannot be repaired (as in space-based computers), or where the operation of the system is so critical that no downtime for repair can be tolerated.

Formally, the reliability of a system, $R(t)$, is defined as the following conditional probability:

$$R(t) = \Pr\{0 \ \text{failures} \ \text{in} \ \text{time} \ [0,t] \,|\, \text{no failures at } t = 0\}$$

Reliability theory, as it applies to hardware systems, has been developed significantly. Let us therefore illustrate the foregoing formula for hardware components, for which it is customary to assume that failures follow a Poisson distribution. In this case

$$R(t) = \Pr\{0 \ \text{failures} \ \text{in} \ \text{time} \ [0,t]\}$$

Under the same assumptions it is possible to derive that

$$\Pr\{k \text{ failures } \text{in} \text{ time } [0, \ t]\} = \frac{e^{-m(t)}[m(t)]^k}{k!}$$

where $m(t) = \int_0^t z(x) \, dx$. Here $z(t)$ is known as the *hazard function*, which gives the time-dependent failure rate of the specific hardware component under consideration. The probability distribution for $z(t)$ may be different for different electronic components.

The expected (mean) number of failures in time $[0, t]$ can then be computed as

$$E[k] = \sum_{k=0}^{\infty} k \, \frac{e^{-m(t)}[m(t)]^k}{k!} = m(t)$$

and the variance as

$$Var[k] = E[k^2] - (E[k])^2 = m(t)$$

Given these values, $R(t)$ can be written as

$$R(t) = e^{-m(t)}$$

Note that the reliability equation above is written for one component of the system. For a system that consists of n nonredundant components (i.e., they all have to function properly for the system to work) whose failures are independent, the overall system reliability can be written as

$$R_{sys}(t) = \Pi_{i=1}^{n} R_i(t)$$

Availability, $A(t)$, refers to the probability that the system is operational according to its specification at a given point in time t. A number of failures may have occurred prior to time t, but if they have all been repaired, the system is available at time t. It is apparent that availability refers to systems that can be repaired.

If one looks at the limit of availability as time goes to infinity, it refers to the expected percentage of time that the system under consideration is available to perform useful computations. Availability can be used as some measure of "goodness" for those systems that can be repaired and which can be out of service for short periods of time during repair. Reliability and availability of a system are considered to be contradictory objectives [Siewiorek and Swarz, 1982]. It is usually accepted that it is easier to develop highly available systems as opposed to highly reliable systems.

If we assume that failures follow a Poisson distribution with a failure rate λ, and that repair time is exponential with a mean repair time of $1/\mu$, the steady-state availability of a system can be written as

$$A = \frac{\mu}{\lambda + \mu}$$

12.1.3 Mean Time between Failures/Mean Time to Repair

Calculation of the reliability and the availability functions is quite tedious. It is therefore customary to use two single-parameter metrics to model the behavior of systems. The two measures used are *mean time between failures* (MTBF) and *mean time to repair* (MTTR). MTBF is the expected time between subsequent failures in a system with repair.[1]   MTBF can be calculated either from empirical data or from the reliability function as

$$\text{MTBF} = \int_0^\infty R(t)\ dt$$

Since $R(t)$ is related to the system failure rate, there is a direct relationship between MTBF and the failure rate of a system. MTTR is the expected time to repair a failed system. It is related to the repair rate as MTBF is related to the failure rate. Using these two metrics, the steady-state availability of a system with exponential failure and repair rates can be specified as

$$A = \frac{\text{MTBF}}{\text{MTBF} + \text{MTTR}}$$

12.2 FAILURES AND FAULT TOLERANCE IN DISTRIBUTED SYSTEMS

In this section we consider the reasons for failures in distributed systems as well as the basic fault-tolerance techniques that are used to cope with them. This discussion is based on empirical statistics and is not meant to be complete and exhaustive. It is aimed only at providing a general framework for the distributed database reliability issues.

12.2.1 Reasons for Failures

Let us first take a look at soft and hard failures. Soft failures make up more than 90% of all hardware system failures. It is interesting to note that this percentage has not changed significantly since the early days of computing. A 1967 study of the U.S. Air Force indicates that 80% of electronic failures in computers are intermittent [Roth et al., 1967]. A study performed by IBM during the same year concludes that over 90% of all failures are intermittent [Ball and Hardie, 1967]. More recent studies indicate that the occurrence of soft failures is significantly higher than that of hard failures ([Longbottom, 1980], [Gray, 1987]). Gray [1987] also mentions that most of the software failures are transient—and therefore soft—suggesting that a dump and restart may be sufficient to recover without any need to "repair" the software.

Another way of looking at the causes of errors is to investigate various computer system error statistics. A study of the reliability of the IBM/XA operating system indicates that 57% of all system failures are due to hardware, 12% to software, 14% to operations, and 17% to environmental conditions [Mourad and Andres, 1985] (Figure 12.4a). This study was conducted at the Stanford linear accelerator (SLAC). Another study of Tandem computers [Gray, 1985] based on early warning

---

[1]A distinction is sometimes made between MTBF and MTTF (mean time to fail). MTTF is defined as the expected time of the first system failure given a successful startup at time 0. MTBF is then defined only for systems that can be repaired. An approximation for MTBF is given as MTBF = MTTF + MTTR [McConnel and Siewiorek, 1982]. We do not make this distinction in this book.

reports indicates that hardware failures make up 18% of the failures, software is responsible for 25%, maintenance for 25%, operations for 17%, and environment for 14% (Figure 12.4b). Finally, a performance study of the AT&T 5ESS digital switch indicates that as a percentage of total system failures, hardware accounts for 32.3% of failures, software for 44.3%, and operations for 17.5% (Figure 12.4c). The causes of the remaining 5.9% of failures were unknown [Yeager, 1987]. Unfortunately, the environmental causes for failures that cannot be attributable specifically to the 5ESS switch are not included in these figures, so they are not directly comparable to the previous two.

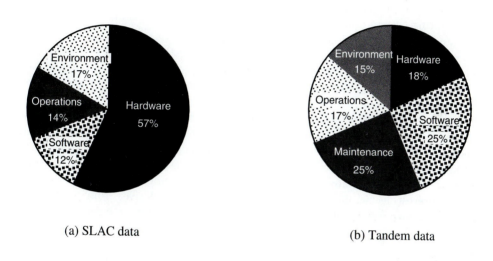

(a) SLAC data

(b) Tandem data

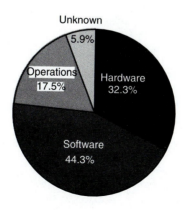

(c) 5ESS switch data

Figure 12.4. Reasons for Computer System Failures

When one investigates hardware causes of failures in more detail, the Tandem data suggest that about 49% of hardware failures are disk failures, 23% are due to communication, 17% to processor failure, 9% to wiring, and 1% to the failure of spares. The latter category is unique to fault tolerant or nonstop computer systems such as Tandem since they use spare modules to achieve fault tolerance. In the case of the 5ESS switch, 32.5% of the hardware failures are due to disk failures, 9.3% are due to electromagnetic interference due to insufficient isolation of wires, and the remaining 58.2% are due to defective components, circuit packs, or cables.

Software failures are more difficult to discuss because there is no agreement on a classification scheme. The Tandem data again suggests that software failures due to communication and database are by far the dominant causes. These are followed by operating system failures, which are then followed by failures in the application code and in the transaction management software.

Software failures are typically caused by "bugs" in the code. The estimates for the number of bugs in software vary considerably. Figures such as 0.25 bug per 1000 instructions to 10 bugs per 1000 instructions have been reported. As stated before, most of the software failures are soft failures. The statistics for software failure are comparable to those we have previously reported on hardware failures. The fundamental reason for the dominance of soft failures in software is the significant amount of design review and code inspection that a typical software project goes through before it gets to the testing stage. Furthermore, most commercial software goes through extensive alpha and beta testing before being released for field use.

An interesting classification for software bugs which derives from physics can also be provided [Gray, 1985]. The classification divides software bugs into Heisenbugs and Bohrbugs. Bohrbugs cause hard faults; they are solid like a Bohr atom and will continue to cause faults at retry. Heisenbugs, on the other hand, behave according to the Heisenberg uncertainty principle in physics, which states that it is not possible to measure both the position and the velocity of an electron accurately and simultaneously. The measurement procedure for one of these will cause a change in the other one. The implication of this principle for software bugs is that the testing process to find a bug may cause sufficient perturbation for the bug to disappear. Thus Heisenbugs cause soft faults and are more challenging to detect. They are sensitive to time of execution, system load, and other similar factors and the system may work on retry.

12.2.2 Basic Fault Tolerance Approaches and Techniques

The two fundamental approaches to constructing a reliable system are fault tolerance and fault prevention. *Fault tolerance* refers to a system design approach which recognizes that faults will occur; it tries to build mechanisms into the system so that the faults can be detected and removed or compensated for before they can result in a system failure. *Fault prevention* techniques, on the other hand, aim at ensuring that the implemented system will not contain any faults. Fault prevention has two aspects. The first is *fault avoidance*, which refers to the techniques used to make sure that faults are not introduced into the system. These techniques involve detailed design methodologies (such as design walkthroughs, design inspections, etc.) and quality control. The second aspect of fault prevention is *fault removal*, which refers to the techniques that are employed to detect any faults that might have remained in the system despite the application of fault avoidance and removes these faults. Typical techniques that are used in this area are extensive testing and validation procedures. Note that these fault removal techniques apply during system implementation prior to field use of the system.

The terms *fault prevention* and *fault avoidance* are used interchangably. Another common name for these approaches is *fault intolerance* [Avizienis, 1976] since they cannot withstand faults that show up during system use. These techniques concentrate on designing systems using high-reliability components and refinement of the packaging techniques followed by extensive testing. Such measures are expected to reduce the occurrence of system failures to a minimum so that the features may then be handled by manual maintenance. Unfortunately, there are a number of environments where manual maintenance and repair is impossible, or the downtime needed for repair would be intolerable. In those environments fault tolerant system designs are the preferred alternative.

It is possible to talk about a third approach to constructing reliable systems. This is *fault detection* [Myers, 1976]. Specification of fault detection as a separate approach may be challenged since detection has to be included in any fault tolerance technique. However, if fault detection techniques are not coupled with fault tolerance features, they issue a warning when a failure occurs but do not provide any means of tolerating the failure. Therefore, it might be appropriate to separate fault detection from strictly fault tolerant approaches.

It is important to note at this point that system failures may be *latent*. A latent failure is one that is detected some time after its occurrence. This period is called *error latency*, and the average error latency time over a number of identical systems is called *mean time to detect* (MTTD). Figure 12.5 depicts the relationship of various reliability measures with the actual occurrences of faults.

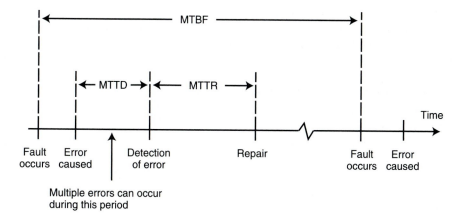

Figure 12.5. Occurrence of Events over Time

The fundamental principle employed in all fault tolerant system designs is that of providing *redundancy* in system components. Redundant components enable the effects of a faulty component to be compensated for. However, redundancy is not sufficient for fault tolerance. The additional and complementary fault tolerance principle is the *modularization* of the design. Each component of the system is implemented as a module with well-defined input and output interfaces with the other components. Modularization enables the isolation of faults within one component. It is therefore an important technique in both hardware and software systems.

These two concepts are utilized in typical systems by means of *fail-stop modules* and *process pairs*. A fail-stop module constantly monitors itself, and when it detects a fault, shuts itself down automatically [Schlichting and Schneider, 1983]. Another name given to such modules is *fail-fast* [Gray, 1985]. The implementation of fail-stop modules in hardware is beyond the scope of our discussion, but in software they can be implemented by defensive programming, where each software module checks its own state during state transitions. A further advantage of fail-stop software modules is a reduction in detection latency [Cristian, 1982].

Process pairs provide fault tolerance by duplicating software modules. The idea is to eliminate single points of failure by implementing each system service as two processes that communicate and cooperate in providing the service. One of these processes is called the *primary* and the other the *backup*. Both the primary and the backup are typically implemented as fail-stop modules that cooperate in providing a service. There are a number of different ways of implementing process pairs, depending on the mode of communication between the primary and the backup. The five common types are *lock-step*, *automatic checkpointing*, *state checkpointing*, *delta checkpointing*, and *persistent* process pairs. A detailed discussion of these alternative implementations is beyond the scope of this chapter. However, a review of them appears in [Gray, 1985]. Additional references are provided in the Bibliographic Notes section at the end of this chapter.

Process pairs require communication between processes. An argument may be made for uniprocessor systems that, for the sake of improved performance, the communication between processes may be implemented by means of shared memory. However, when designing a reliable software environment, it is important to implement an operating system that uses a message-based interprocess communication mechanism. Such an approach contributes to fault isolation since each process executes in its own address space, and an error that one of them might cause will not propagate to the other processes.

Another important related concept is session-oriented communication between processes. Session-oriented communication delegates the responsibility of detecting and handling lost or duplicate messages to the message server of the operating system rather than to the application program. This not only facilitates a simpler application development environment but also enables the operating system to provide a reliable execution environment to application processes.

12.3 FAILURES IN DISTRIBUTED DBMS

Designing a reliable system that can recover from failures requires identifying the types of failures with which the system has to deal. In Section 12.2 we reviewed the major reasons for failures in distributed computer systems. That discussion, together with the termination conditions of transactions, covered in Chapter 10, indicates that a database recovery manager has to deal with four types of failures: transaction failures (aborts), site (system) failures, media (disk) failures, and communication line failures.

12.3.1 Transaction Failures

Transactions can fail for a number of reasons. Failure can be due to an error in the transaction caused by incorrect input data (e.g., Example 10.3) as well as the detection of a present or potential deadlock. Furthermore, some concurrency control algorithms do not permit a transaction to proceed or even to wait if the data that they attempt to access are currently being accessed by another transaction. This might also be considered a failure. The usual approach to take in cases of transaction failure is to *abort* the transaction, thus resetting the database to its state prior to the start of this transaction.

The frequency of transaction failures is not easy to measure. It is indicated that in System R, 3% of the transactions abort abnormally [Gray et al., 1981]. In general, it can be stated that (1) within a single application, the ratio of transactions that abort themselves is rather constant, being a function of the incorrect data, the available semantic data control features, and so on; and (2) the number of transaction aborts by the DBMS due to concurrency control considerations (mainly deadlocks) is dependent on the level of concurrency (i.e., number of concurrent transactions), the interference of the concurrent applications, the granularity of locks, and so on [Härder and Reuter, 1983].

12.3.2 Site (System) Failures

The reasons for system failure constituted the bulk of our discussion in Section 12.2. In short, it can be traced back to a hardware failure (processor, main memory, power supply, etc.) or to a software failure (bug in the operating system or in the DBMS code). The important point from the perspective of this discussion is that a system failure is always assumed to result in the loss of main memory contents. Therefore, any part of the database that was in main memory buffers is lost as a result of a system failure. However, the database that is stored in secondary storage is assumed to be safe and correct. In distributed database terminology, system failures are typically referred to as *site failures*, since they result in the failed site being unreachable from other sites in the distributed system.

We typically differentiate between partial and total failures in a distributed system. *Total failure* refers to the simultaneous failure of all sites in the distributed system; *partial failure* indicates the failure of only some sites while the others remain operational. As indicated in Chapter 1, it is this aspect of distributed systems that makes them more available.

12.3.3 Media Failures

Media failure refers to the failures of the secondary storage devices that store the database. Such failures may be due to operating system errors, as well as to hardware faults such as head crashes or controller failures. The important point from the perspective of DBMS reliability is that all or part of the database that is on the secondary storage is considered to be destroyed and inaccessible.

Duplexing of disk storage and maintaining archival copies of the database are common techniques that deal with this sort of catastrophic problem. Even though the data of Section 12.2 suggest that disk failures are quite common, the techniques described above enable us to assume that media failures do not have an impact more often than once or twice a year [Härder and Reuter, 1983].

Media failures are frequently treated as problems local to one site and therefore not specifically addressed in the reliability mechanisms of distributed DBMSs. We consider techniques for dealing with them in Section 12.4.5 under local recovery management. We then turn our attention to site failures when we consider distributed recovery functions.

12.3.4 Communication Failures

The three types of failures described above are common to both centralized and distributed DBMSs. Communication failures, however, are unique to the distributed case. There are a number of types of communication failures. The most common ones are the errors in the messages, improperly ordered messages, lost (or undeliverable) messages, and line failures. As discussed in Chapter 3, the first two errors are the responsibility of the computer network (specifically, the communication subnet, which consists of the physical, data link, and network layers of the ISO/OSI architectural model); we will not consider them further. Therefore, in our discussions of distributed DBMS reliability, we expect the underlying computer network hardware and software to ensure that two messages sent from a process at some originating site to another process at some destination site are delivered without error and in the order in which they were sent.

Lost or undeliverable messages are typically the consequence of communication line failures or (destination) site failures. If a communication line fails, in addition to losing the message(s) in transit, it may also divide the network into two or more disjoint groups. This is called *network partitioning*. If the network is partitioned, the sites in each partition may continue to operate. In this case, executing transactions that access data stored in multiple partitions becomes a major issue. Maintaining the mutual consistency of the database is a significant problem, especially if the database is replicated across these partitions.

Network partitions point to a unique aspect of failures in distributed computer systems. In centralized systems the system state can be characterized as all-or-nothing: either the system is operational or it is not. Thus the failures are complete: when one occurs, the entire system becomes nonoperational. Obviously, this is not true in distributed systems. As we indicated a number of times before, this is their potential strength. However, it also makes the transaction management algorithms more difficult to design.

If messages cannot be delivered, we will assume that the network does nothing about it. It will not buffer it for delivery to the destination when the service is reestablished and will not inform the sender process that the message cannot be delivered. In short, the message will simply be lost. We make this assumption because it represents the least expectation from the network and places the responsibility of dealing with these failures to the distributed DBMS.

One result of this assumption is that the responsibility of detecting that a message is undeliverable is left to the application program (in this case the distributed DBMS). The detection will be facilitated by the use of timers and a timeout mechanism that keeps track of how long it has been since the sender site has not received a confirmation from the destination site about the receipt of a message. This timeout interval needs to be set to a value greater than that of the maximum round-trip propagation delay of a message in the network. The term for the failure of the communication network to deliver messages and the confirmations within this period is *performance failure*. It needs to be handled within the reliability protocols for distributed DBMSs.

12.4 LOCAL RELIABILITY PROTOCOLS

In this section we discuss the functions performed by the local recovery manager (LRM) that exists at each site. These functions maintain the atomicity and durability properties of local transactions. They relate to the execution of the commands that are passed to the LRM, which are **begin_transaction**, **read**, **write**, **commit**, and **abort**. Later in this section we introduce a new command into the LRM's repertoire that initiates recovery actions after a failure. Note that in this section we discuss the execution of these commands in a centralized environment. The complications introduced in distributed databases are addressed in the upcoming sections.

12.4.1 Architectural Considerations

It is again time to use our architectural model (Figures 4.7 and 10.4) and discuss the specific interface between the LRM and the database buffer manager (BM). Remember that all accesses to the database are via the database buffer manager. The detailed discussion of the algorithms that the buffer manager implements is beyond the scope of this book; we provide a summary later in this subsection. Even

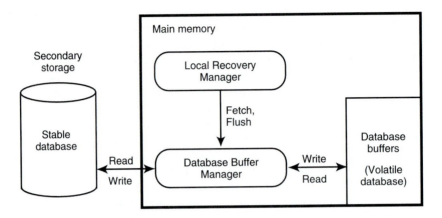

Figure 12.6. Interface Between the Local Recovery Manager and the Buffer Manager

without these details,, we can still specify the interface and its function, as depicted in Figure 12.6.[2]

In this discussion we assume that the database is stored permanently on secondary storage, which in this context is called the *stable storage* [Lampson and Sturgis, 1976]. The stability of this storage medium is due to its robustness to failures. A stable storage device would experience considerably less-frequent failures than would a nonstable storage device. In today's technology, stable storage is typically implemented by means of duplexed magnetic disks which store duplicate copies of data that are always kept mutually consistent. We call the version of the database that is kept on stable storage the *stable database*. The unit of storage and access of the stable database is typically a *page*.

The database buffer manager keeps some of the recently accessed data in main memory buffers. This is done to enhance access performance. Typically, the buffer is divided into pages that are of the same size as the stable database pages. The part of the database that is in the database buffer is called the *volatile database*. It is important to note that the LRM executes the operations on behalf of a transaction only on the volatile database, which, at a later time, is written back to the stable database.

When the LRM wants to read a page of data[3] on behalf of a transaction— strictly speaking, on behalf of some operation of a transaction—it issues a **fetch** command, indicating the page that it wants to read. The buffer manager checks to see if that page is already in the buffer (due to a previous fetch command from

---

[2]This architectural model is similar to that given in [Härder and Reuter, 1983] and [Bernstein et al., 1987].

[3]The LRM's unit of access may be in blocks which have sizes different from a page. However, for simplicity, we assume that the unit of access is the same.

another transaction) and if so, makes it available for that transaction; if not, it reads the page from the stable database into an empty database buffer. If no empty buffers exist, it selects one of the buffer pages to write back to stable storage and reads the requested stable database page into that buffer. There are a number of different algorithms by which the buffer manager may choose the buffer page to be replaced; these are discussed in standard database textbooks.

The buffer manager also provides the interface by which the LRM can actually force it to write back some of the buffer pages. This can be accomplished by means of the **flush** command, which specifies the buffer pages that the LRM wants to be written back. We should indicate that different LRM implementations may or may not use this forced writing. This issue is discussed further in subsequent sections.

As its interface suggests, the buffer manager acts as a conduit for all access to the database via the buffers that it manages. It provides this function by fulfilling three tasks:

1. *Searching* the buffer pool for a given page;

2. If it is not found in the buffer, *allocating* a free buffer page and *loading* the buffer page with a data page that is brought in from secondary storage;

3. If no free buffer pages are available, choosing a buffer page for *replacement*.

Searching is quite straightforward. Typically, the buffer pages are shared among the transactions that execute against the database, so search is global.

Allocation of buffer pages is typically done dynamically. This means that the allocation of buffer pages to processes is performed as processes execute. The buffer manager tries to calculate the number of buffer pages needed to run the process efficiently and attempts to allocate that number of pages. The best known dynamic allocation method is the *working-set algorithm* [Denning, 1968], [Denning, 1980].

A second aspect of allocation is fetching data pages. The most common technique is *demand paging*, where data pages are brought into the buffer as they are referenced. However, a number of operating systems prefetch a group of data pages that are in close physical proximity to the data page referenced. Buffer managers choose this route if they detect sequential access to a file.

In replacing buffer pages, the best known technique is the least recently used (LRU) algorithm that attempts to determine the *logical reference strings* [Effelsberg and Härder, 1984] of processes to buffer pages and to replace the page that has not been referenced for an extended period. The anticipation here is that if a buffer page has not been referenced for a long time, it probably will not be referenced in the near future.

The techniques discussed above are the most common. Other alternatives are discussed in [Effelsberg and Härder, 1984].

Clearly, these functions are similar to those performed by operating system (OS) buffer managers. However, quite frequently, DBMSs bypass OS buffer managers and manage disks and main memory buffers themselves due to a number of problems (see, e.g., [Stonebraker, 1981]). These problems can be listed as follows:

1. In dynamically allocating buffer pages, the OS buffer manager assumes that page references of processes are random and varying over time. Thus the number of buffer pages that are allocated to a process can grow or shrink during its execution. However, it is possible for a DBMS to determine, with significant regularity, its reference pattern to data pages, which allows a more precise calculation of the buffer requirements [Chou, 1985]. In database literature, a number of different algorithms have been proposed such as the hot set model [Sacco and Schkolnick, 1986] and DBMIN [Chou, 1985], [Chou and DeWitt, 1986].

2. Along the same lines, it may not be useful for the OS buffer manager to prefetch data pages when it detects sequential access. Since the DBMS knows its reference pattern, it is in a significantly better position to make that judgment. The reference string is known by the DBMS either as a result of query compilation (e.g., DB2 [Date, 1984]) or during execution "at (or very shortly after) the beginning of its examination of a block" [Stonebraker, 1981] (e.g., INGRES [Stonebraker et al., 1976]).

3. The LRU replacement algorithm, which performs nicely for general-purpose computing, fails to perform adequately in a number of cases. For example, in a nested-loop join, the buffer page that contains one data page of the outer relation is the least recently used if a replacement page is needed to bring in the last data page of the inner relation. However, if the outer relation buffer page is replaced, it will be read in again immediately, causing a buffer fault. Every page reference from then on will result in a buffer fault.

4. The LRU replacement algorithm writes the buffer pages to secondary storage when it needs a new buffer page. This is called *delayed writing*. However, when the DBMS commits a transaction, it expects the log pages about the data items that the transaction has updated to be stored immediately on stable storage (i.e., disk). If the buffer manager keeps these buffer pages around, it may not be possible to guarantee the durability of transactions when failures occur unless certain protocols are followed (we discuss these later). The OS buffer managers are now aware of these protocols.

5. OS buffers are generally mapped to virtual memory, so database buffers would also be in the virtual address space. Therefore, accessing the buffers may not only cause buffer faults to bring in data pages, but may also cause memory faults since the buffer page may not be mapped to a main memory page frame and there may not be any free frames. This phenomenon is commonly called the *double paging problem* [Chou and DeWitt, 1986].

The consequence of these problems is that DBMSs usually manage their own buffer space and treat disks as raw storage devices. This is a duplication of OS services, but is unavoidable with the current DBMS and OS architectures since these two systems do not communicate and collaborate with each other very effectively.

12.4.2 Recovery Information

In this section we assume that only system failures occur. We defer the discussion of techniques for recovering from media failures until later. Since we are dealing with centralized database recovery, communication failures are not applicable.

When a system failure occurs, the volatile database is lost. Therefore, the DBMS has to maintain some information about its state at the time of the failure in order to be able to bring the database to the state that it was in when the failure occurred. We call this information the *recovery information*.

The recovery information that the system maintains is dependent on the method of executing updates. Two possibilities are in-place updating and out-of-place updating. *In-place updating* physically changes the value of the data item in the stable database. As a result, the previous values are lost. *Out-of-place updating*, on the other hand, does not change the value of the data item in the stable database but maintains the new value separately. Of course, periodically, these updated values have to be integrated into the stable database. We should note that the reliability issues are somewhat simpler if in-place updating is not used. However, most DBMSs use it due to its improved performance.

In-Place Update Recovery Information

Since in-place updates cause previous values of the affected data items to be lost, it is necessary to keep enough information about the database state changes to facilitate the recovery of the database to a consistent state following a failure. This information is typically maintained in a database log. Thus each update transaction not only changes the database but is also recorded in the *database log* (Figure 12.7). Before we discuss the contents of the log, let us first see why this information is necessary for the database to recover to a consistent state.

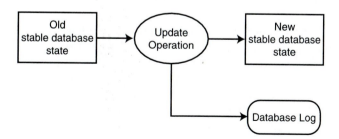

Figure 12.7. Update Operation Execution

Consider the following scenario. The DBMS began executing at time 0 and at time t a system failure occurs. During the period $[0, t]$, two transactions (say, T_1 and T_2) pass through the DBMS, one of which (T_1) has completed (i.e., committed), while the other one has not (see Figure 12.8). The durability property of transactions would require that the effects of T_1 be reflected in the stable database. Similarly, the atomicity property would require that the stable database not contain any of the effects of T_2. However, special precautions need to be taken to ensure this.

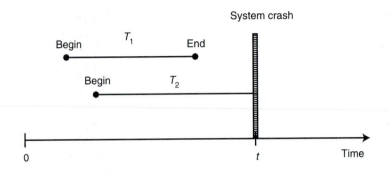

Figure 12.8. Occurrence of a System Failure

Let us assume that the LRM and buffer manager algorithms are such that the buffer pages are written back to the stable database only when the buffer manager needs new buffer space. In other words, the **flush** command is not used by the LRM and the decision to write back the pages into the stable database is taken at the discretion of the buffer manager. In this case it is possible that the volatile database pages that have been updated by T_1 may not have been written back to the stable database at the time of the failure. Therefore, upon recovery, it is important to be able to *redo* the operations of T_1. This requires some information to be stored in the database log about the effects of T_1. Given this information, it is possible to recover the database from its "old" state to the "new" state that reflects the effects of T_1 (Figure 12.9).

Similarly, it is possible that the buffer manager may have had to write into the stable database some of the volatile database pages that have been updated by T_2. Upon recovery from failures it is necessary to *undo* the operations of T_2.[4] Thus the

----

[4]One might think that it could be possible to continue with the operation of T_2 following restart instead of undoing its operations. However, in general it may not be possible for the LRM to determine the point at which the transaction needs to be restarted. Furthermore, the failure may not be a system failure but a transaction failure (i.e., T_2 may actually abort itself) after some of its actions have been reflected in the stable database. Therefore, the possibility of undoing is necessary.

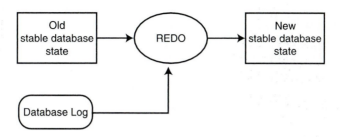

Figure 12.9. REDO Action

recovery information should include sufficient data to permit the undo by taking the "new" database state that reflects partial effects of T_2 and recovers the "old" state that existed at the start of T_2 (Figure 12.10).

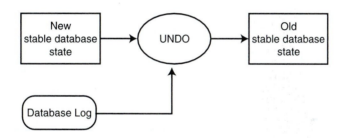

Figure 12.10. UNDO Action

We should indicate that the undo and redo actions are assumed to be idempotent. In other words, their repeated application to a transaction would be equivalent to performing them once. Furthermore, the undo/redo actions form the basis of different methods of executing the commit commands. We discuss this further in Section 12.4.3.

The contents of the log may differ according to the implementation. However, the following minimal information for each transaction is contained in almost all database logs: a begin_transaction record, the value of the data item before the update (called the *before image*), the updated value of the data item (called the *after image*), and a termination record indicating the transaction termination condition (commit, abort). The granularity of the before and after images may be different, as it is possible to log entire pages or some smaller unit. As an alternative to this form of *state logging*, *operational logging*, as in ARIES [Mohan et al., 1993], may be supported where the operations that cause changes to the database are logged rather than the before and after images.

Similar to the volatile database, the log is also maintained in main memory buffers (called *log buffers*) and written back to stable storage (called *stable log*) similar to the database buffer pages (Figure 12.11). The log pages can be written to stable storage in one of two ways. They can be written *synchronously* (more commonly known as *forcing a log*) where the addition of each log record requires that the log be moved from main memory to stable storage. It can also be written *asynchronously*, where the log is moved to stable storage either at periodic intervals or when the buffer fills up. When the log is written synchronously, the execution of the transaction is suspended until the write is complete. This adds some delay to the response-time performance of the transaction. On the other hand, if a failure occurs immediately after a forced write, it is relatively easy to recover to a consistent database state.

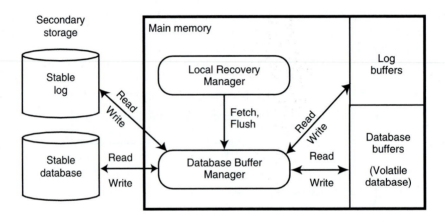

Figure 12.11. Logging Interface

Whether the log is written synchronously or asynchronously, one very important protocol has to be observed in maintaining logs. Consider a case where the updates to the database are written into the stable storage before the log is modified in stable storage to reflect the update. If a failure occurs before the log is written, the database will remain in updated form, but the log will not indicate the update that makes it impossible to recover the database to a consistent and up-to-date state. Therefore, the stable log is always updated prior to the updating of the stable database. This is known as the *write-ahead logging* (*WAL*) protocol [Gray, 1979] and can be precisely specified as follows:

1. Before a stable database is updated (perhaps due to actions of a yet uncommitted transaction), the before images should be stored in the stable log. This facilitates undo.

2. When a transaction commits, the after images have to be stored in the stable log prior to the updating of the stable database. This facilitates redo.

Out-of-Place Update Recovery Information

As we mentioned above, the most common update technique is in-place updating. Therefore, we provide only a brief overview of the other updating techniques and their recovery information. Details can be found in [Verhofstadt, 1978] and the other references given earlier.

Typical techniques for out-of-place updating are *shadowing* ([Astrahan et al., 1979], [Gray, 1979]) and *differential files* [Severence and Lohman, 1976]. Shadowing uses duplicate stable storage pages in executing updates. Thus every time an update is made, the old stable storage page, called the *shadow page*, is left intact and a new page with the updated data item values is written into the stable database. The access path data structures are updated to point to the new page which contains the current data so that subsequent accesses are to this page. The old stable storage page is retained for recovery purposes (to perform undo).

Recovery based on shadow paging is implemented in System R's recovery manager [Gray et al., 1981]. This implementation uses shadowing together with logging.

The differential files approach was discussed in Chapter 6 within the context of integrity enforcement. In general, the method maintains each stable database file as a read-only file. In addition, it maintains a corresponding read-write differential file which stores the changes to that file. Given a logical database file F, let us denote its read-only part as FR and its corresponding differential file as DF. DF consists of two parts: an insertions part, which stores the insertions to F, denoted DF^+, and a corresponding deletions part, denoted DF^-. All updates are treated as the deletion of the old value and the insertion of a new one. Thus each logical file F is considered to be a view defined as $F = (FR \cup DF^+) - DF^-$. Periodically, the differential file needs to be merged with the read-only base file.

Recovery schemes based on this method simply use private differential files for each transaction, which are then merged with the differential files of each file at commit time. Thus recovery from failures can simply be achieved by discarding the private differential files of noncommitted transactions.

There are studies that indicate that the shadowing and differential files approaches may be advantageous in certain environments. One study by [Agrawal and DeWitt, 1985] investigates the performance of recovery mechanisms based on logging, differential files, and shadow paging, integrated with locking and optimistic (using timestamps) concurrency control algorithms. The results indicate that shadowing, together with locking, can be a feasible alternative to the more common log-based recovery integrated with locking if there are only large (in terms of the base-set size) transactions with sequential access patterns. Similarly, differential files integrated with locking can be a feasible alternative if there are medium-sized and large transactions.

12.4.3 Execution of LRM Commands

Recall that there are five commands that form the interface to the LRM. These are the **begin_transaction, read, write, commit**, and **abort** commands. As we indicated in Chapter 10, some DBMSs do not have an explicit commit command.

In this case the end (of transaction) indicator serves as the commit command. For simplicity, we specify commit explicitly.

In this section we introduce a sixth interface command to the LRM: **recover**. The **recover** command is the interface that the operating system has to the LRM. It is used during recovery from system failures when the operating system asks the DBMS to recover the database to the state that existed when the failure occurred.

The execution of some of these commands (specifically, **abort, commit**, and **recover**) is quite dependent on the specific LRM algorithms that are used as well as on the interaction of the LRM with the buffer manager. Others (i.e., **begin_transaction, read**, and **write**) are quite independent of these considerations.

The fundamental design decision in the implementation of the local recovery manager, the buffer manager, and the interaction between the two components is whether or not the buffer manager obeys the local recovery manager's instructions as to when to write the database buffer pages to stable storage. Specifically, two decisions are involved. The first one is whether the buffer manager may write the buffer pages updated by a transaction into stable storage during the execution of that transaction, or it waits for the LRM to instruct it to write them back. We call this the *fix/no-fix* decision. The reasons for the choice of this terminology will become apparent shortly. Note that it is also called the steal/no-steal decision in [Härder and Reuter, 1983]. The second decision is whether the buffer manager will be forced to flush the buffer pages updated by a transaction into the stable storage at the end of that transaction (i.e., the commit point), or the buffer manager flushes them out whenever it needs to according to its buffer management algorithm. We call this the *flush/no-flush* decision. It is called the force/no-force decision in [Härder and Reuter, 1983].

Accordingly, four alternatives can be identified: (1) no-fix/no-flush, (2) no-fix/flush, (3) fix/no-flush, and (4) fix/flush. We will consider each of these in more detail. However, first we present the execution methods of the **begin_transaction, read**, and **write** commands, which are quite independent of these considerations. Where modifications are required in these methods due to different LRM and buffer manager implementation strategies, we will indicate them.

Begin_transaction, Read, and Write Commands

Begin_transaction. This command causes various components of the DBMS to carry out some bookkeeping functions. We will also assume that it causes the LRM to write a begin_transaction record into the log. This is an assumption made for convenience of discussion; in reality, writing of the begin_transaction record may be delayed until the first **write** to improve performance by reducing I/O.

Read. The **read** command specifies a data item. The LRM tries to read the specified data item from the buffer pages that belong to the transaction. If the data item is not in one of these pages, it issues a **fetch** command to the buffer manager in order to make the data available. Upon reading the data, the LRM returns it to the scheduler.

Write. The **write** command specifies the data item and the new value. As with a read command, if the data item is available in the buffers of the transaction, its value is modified in the database buffers (i.e., the volatile database). If it is not in the private buffer pages, a **fetch** command is issued to the buffer manager, and the data is made available and updated. The before image of the data page, as well as its after image, are recorded in the log. The local recovery manager then informs the scheduler that the operation has been completed successfully.

No-fix/No-flush

This type of LRM algorithm is called a redo/undo algorithm in [Bernstein et al., 1987] since it requires, as we will see, performing both the redo and undo operations upon recovery. It is called steal/no-force in [Härder and Reuter, 1983].

Abort. As we indicated before, abort is an indication of transaction failure. Since the buffer manager may have written the updated pages into the stable database, abort will have to undo the actions of the transaction. Therefore, the LRM reads the log records for that specific transaction and replaces the values of the updated data items in the volatile database with their before images. The scheduler is then informed about the successful completion of the abort action. This process is called the *transaction undo* or *partial undo*.

An alternative implementation is the use of an *abort list*, which stores the identifiers of all the transactions that have been aborted. If such a list is used, the abort action is considered to be complete as soon as the transaction's identifier is included in the abort list.

Note that even though the values of the updated data items in the stable database are not restored to their before images, the transaction is considered to be aborted at this point. The buffer manager will write the "corrected" volatile database pages into the stable database at a future time, thereby restoring it to its state prior to that transaction.

Commit. The **commit** command causes an end_of_transaction record to be written into the log by the LRM. Under this scenario, no other action is taken in executing a commit command other than informing the scheduler about the successful completion of the commit action.

An alternative to writing an end_of_transaction record into the log is to add the transaction's identifier to a *commit list*, which is a list of the identifiers of transactions that have committed. In this case the commit action is accepted as complete as soon as the transaction identifier is stored in this list.

Recover. The LRM starts the recovery action by going to the beginning of the log and redoing the operations of each transaction for which both a begin_transaction and an end_of_transaction record is found. This is called *partial redo*. Similarly, it undoes the operations of each transaction for which a begin_transaction record is found in the log without a corresponding end_of_transaction record. This action is called *global undo*, as opposed to the transaction undo discussed above. The difference is that the effects of all incomplete transactions need to be rolled back, not one.

If commit list and abort list implementations are used, the recovery action consists of redoing the operations of all the transactions in the commit list and undoing the operations of all the transactions in the abort list. In the remainder of this chapter we will not make this distinction, but rather will refer to both of these recovery implementations as global undo.

No-fix/Flush

The LRM algorithms that use this strategy are called undo/no-redo in [Bernstein et al., 1987] and steal/force in [Härder and Reuter, 1983].

Abort. The execution of **abort** is identical to the previous case. Upon transaction failure, the LRM initiates a partial undo for that particular transaction.

Commit. The LRM issues a **flush** command to the buffer manager, forcing it to write back all the updated volatile database pages into the stable database. The commit command is then executed either by placing a record in the log or by insertion of the transaction identifier into the commit list as specified for the previous case. When all of this is complete, the LRM informs the scheduler that the commit has been carried out successfully.

Recover. Since all the updated pages are written into the stable database at the commit point, there is no need to perform redo; all the effects of successful transactions will have been reflected in the stable database. Therefore, the recovery action initiated by the LRM consists of a global undo.

Fix/No-flush

In this case the LRM controls the writing of the volatile database pages into stable storage. The key here is not to permit the buffer manager to write any updated volatile database page into the stable database until at least the transaction commit point. This is accomplished by the **fix** command, which is a modified version of the **fetch** command whereby the specified page is fixed in the database buffer and cannot be written back to the stable database by the buffer manager. Thus any **fetch** command to the buffer manager for a write operation is replaced by a **fix** command.[5] Note that this precludes the need for a global undo operation and is therefore called a redo/no-undo algorithm in [Bernstein et al., 1987] and a no-force/no-steal algorithm in [Härder and Reuter, 1983].

Abort. Since the volatile database pages have not been written to the stable database, no special action is necessary. To release the buffer pages that have been fixed by the transaction, however, it is necessary for the LRM to send an **un-fix** command to the buffer manager for all such pages. It is then sufficient to carry

---

[5]Of course, any page that was previously fetched for read but is now being updated also needs to be fixed.

out the abort action either by writing an abort record in the log or by including the transaction in the abort list, informing the scheduler and then forgetting about the transaction.

Commit.   The LRM sends an **unfix** command to the buffer manager for every volatile database page that was previously fixed by that transaction. Note that these pages may now be written back to the stable database at the discretion of the buffer manager. The commit command is then executed either by placing an end_of_transaction record in the log or by inserting the transaction identifier into the commit list as specified for the preceding case. When all of this is complete, the LRM informs the scheduler that the commit has been successfully carried out.

Recover.   As we mentioned above, since the volatile database pages that have been updated by ongoing transactions are not yet written into the stable database, there is no necessity for global undo. The LRM, therefore, initiates a partial redo action to recover those transactions that may have already committed, but whose volatile database pages may not have yet written into the stable database.

Fix/Flush

This is the case where the LRM forces the buffer manager to write the updated volatile database pages into the stable database at precisely the commit point—not before and not after. This strategy is called no-undo/no-redo in [Bernstein et al., 1987] and no-steal/force in [Härder and Reuter, 1983].

Abort.   The execution of **abort** is identical to that of the fix/no-flush case.

Commit.   The LRM sends an **unfix** command to the buffer manager for every volatile database page that was previously fixed by that transaction. It then issues a **flush** command to the buffer manager, forcing it to write back all the unfixed volatile database pages into the stable database.[6]   Finally, the **commit** command is processed by either writing an end_of_transaction record into the log or by including the transaction in the commit list. The important point to note here is that all three of these operations have to be executed as an atomic action. One step that can be taken to achieve this atomicity is to issue only a **flush** command, which serves to unfix the pages as well. This eliminates the need to send two messages from the LRM to the buffer manager, but does not eliminate the requirement for the atomic execution of the flush operation and the writing of the database log. The LRM then informs the scheduler that the **commit** has been carried out successfully. Methods for ensuring this atomicity are beyond the scope of our discussion (see [Bernstein et al., 1987]).

---

[6]Our discussion here gives the impression that two commands (*unfix* and *flush*) need to be sent to the BM by the LRM for each commit action. We have chosen to explain the action in this way only because of pedagogical simplicity. In reality, it is, of course, preferable to implement one command that instructs the BM to both unfix and flush. Using one command would reduce the message overhead between DBMS components.

Recover.   The **recover** command does not need to do anything in this case. This is true since the stable database reflects the effects of all the successful transactions and none of the effects of the uncommitted transactions.

12.4.4 Checkpointing

In most of the LRM implementation strategies, the execution of the recovery action requires searching the entire log. This is a significant overhead because the LRM is trying to find all the transactions that need to be undone and redone. The overhead can be reduced if it is possible to build a wall which signifies that the database at that point is up-to-date and consistent. In that case, the redo has to start from that point on and the undo only has to go back to that point. This process of building the wall is called *checkpointing*.

Checkpointing is achieved in three steps [Gray, 1979]:

1. Write a begin_checkpoint record into the log.

2. Collect the checkpoint data into the stable storage.

3. Write an end_checkpoint record into the log.

The first and the third steps enforce the atomicity of the checkpointing operation. If a system failure occurs during checkpointing, the recovery process will not find an end_checkpoint record and will consider checkpointing not completed.

There are a number of different alternatives for the data that is collected in Step 2, how it is collected, and where it is stored. We will consider one example here, called *transaction-consistent checkpointing* ([Gray, 1979], [Gray et al., 1981]). The checkpointing starts by writing the begin_checkpoint record in the log and stopping the acceptance of any new transactions by the LRM. Once the active transactions are all completed, all the updated volatile database pages are flushed to the stable database followed by the insertion of an end_checkpoint record into the log. In this case, the redo action only needs to start from the end_checkpoint record in the log. The undo action can go the reverse direction, starting from the end of the log and stopping at the end_checkpoint record.

Transaction-consistent checkpointing is not the most efficient algorithm, since a significant delay is experienced by all the transactions. There are alternative checkpointing schemes such as action-consistent checkpoints, fuzzy checkpoints, and others ([Gray, 1979], [Lindsay, 1979]).

12.4.5 Handling Media Failures

As we mentioned before, the previous discussion on centralized recovery considered nonmedia failures, where the database as well as the log stored in the stable storage survive the failure. Media failures may either be quite catastrophic, causing the loss of the stable database or of the stable log, or they can simply result in partial loss of the database or the log (e.g., loss of a track or two).

The methods that have been devised for dealing with this situation are again based on duplexing. To cope with catastrophic media failures, an *archive* copy of both the database and the log is maintained on a different (tertiary) storage medium, which is typically the magnetic tape or CD-ROM. Thus the DBMS deals with three levels of memory hierarchy: the main memory, random access disk storage, and magnetic tape (Figure 12.12). To deal with less catastrophic failures, having duplicate copies of the database and log may be sufficient.

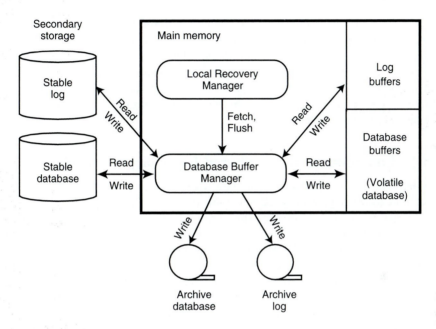

Figure 12.12. Full Memory Hierarchy Managed by LRM and BM

When a media failure occurs, the database is recovered from the archive copy by redoing and undoing the transactions as stored in the archive log. The real question is how the archive database is stored. If we consider the large sizes of current databases, the overhead of writing the entire database to tertiary storage is significant. Two methods that have been proposed for dealing with this are to perform the archiving activity concurrent with normal processing and to archive the database incrementally as changes occur so that each archive version contains only the changes that have occurred since the previous archiving.

12.5 DISTRIBUTED RELIABILITY PROTOCOLS

As with local reliability protocols, the distributed versions aim to maintain the atomicity and durability of distributed transactions that execute over a number of databases. The protocols address the distributed execution of the **begin_transaction, read, write, abort, commit**, and **recover** commands.

At the outset we should indicate that the execution of the **begin_transaction, read,** and **write** commands does not cause any significant problems. **Begin_transaction** is executed in exactly the same manner as in the centralized case by the transaction manager at the originating site of the transaction. The **read** and **write** commands are executed according to the ROWA rule discussed in Chapter 11. At each of these sites, the commands are executed in the manner described in Section 12.4.3. Similarly, abort is executed by undoing its effects.

To facilitate the description of the distributed reliability protocols, we resort to a commonly used abstraction. We assume that at the originating site of a transaction there is a process that executes its operations. This process is called the *coordinator*. The coordinator communicates with *participant* processes at the other sites which assist in the execution of the transaction's operations. Later we will return to our architectural model and discuss how the coordinator and participant processes can be implemented within that framework.

12.5.1 Components of Distributed Reliability Protocols

The reliability techniques in distributed database systems consist of commit, termination, and recovery protocols. Recall from the preceding section that the commit and recovery protocols specify how the commit and the recover commands are executed. Both of these commands need to be executed differently in a distributed DBMS than in a centralized DBMS. Termination protocols are unique to distributed systems. Assume that during the execution of a distributed transaction, one of the sites involved in the execution fails; we would like the other sites to terminate the transaction somehow. The techniques for dealing with this situation are called *termination protocols*. Termination and recovery protocols are two opposite faces of the recovery problem: given a site failure, termination protocols address how the operational sites deal with the failure, whereas recovery protocols deal with the procedure that the process (coordinator or participant) at the failed site has to go through to recover its state once the site is restarted. In the case of network partitioning, the termination protocols take the necessary measures to terminate the active transactions which execute at different partitions, while the recovery protocols address the establishment of mutual consistency of replicated databases following reconnection of the partitions of the network.

The primary requirement of commit protocols is that they maintain the atomicity of distributed transactions. This means that even though the execution of the distributed transaction involves multiple sites, some of which might fail while executing, the effects of the transaction on the distributed database is all-or-nothing. This is called *atomic commitment*. We would prefer the termination protocols to be *nonblocking*. A protocol is nonblocking if it permits a transaction to terminate at the operational sites without waiting for recovery of the failed site. This would significantly improve the response-time performance of transactions. We would also like the distributed recovery protocols to be *independent*. Independent recovery protocols determine how to terminate a transaction that was executing at the time of a failure without having to consult any other site. Existence of such protocols would reduce the number of messages that need to be exchanged during recovery. Note that the existence of independent recovery protocols would imply the existence of nonblocking termination protocols.[7]

12.5.2 Two-Phase Commit Protocol

Two-phase commit (2PC) is a very simple and elegant protocol that ensures the atomic commitment of distributed transactions. It extends the effects of local atomic commit actions to distributed transactions by insisting that all sites involved in the execution of a distributed transaction agree to commit the transaction before its effects are made permanent. There are a number of reasons why such synchronization among sites is necessary. First, depending on the type of concurrency control algorithm that is used, some schedulers may not be ready to terminate a transaction. For example, if a transaction has read a value of a data item that is updated by another transaction that has not yet committed, the associated scheduler may not want to commit the former. Of course, strict concurrency control algorithms that avoid cascading aborts would not permit the updated value of a data item to be read by any other transaction until the updating transaction terminates. This is sometimes called the *recoverability condition* ([Hadzilacos, 1988], [Bernstein et al., 1987]).

Another possible reason why a participant may not agree to commit is due to deadlocks that require a participant to abort the transaction. Note that in this case the participant should be permitted to abort the transaction without being told to do so. This capability is quite important and is called *unilateral abort*.

A brief description of the 2PC protocol that does not consider failures is as follows. Initially, the coordinator writes a begin_commit record in its log, sends a "prepare" message to all participant sites, and enters the WAIT state. When a participant receives a "prepare" message, it checks if it could commit the transaction. If so, the participant writes a ready record in the log, sends a "vote-commit" message to the coordinator, and enters READY state; otherwise, the participant writes an abort record and sends a "vote-abort" message to the coordinator. If the decision of the site is to abort, it can forget about that transaction, since an abort decision serves as a veto (i.e., unilateral abort). After the coordinator has received a reply from every participant, it decides whether to commit or to abort the transaction. If even one participant has registered a negative vote, the coordinator has to abort the transaction globally. So it writes an abort record, sends a "global-abort" message to all participant sites, and enters the ABORT state; otherwise, it writes a commit record, sends a "global-commit" message to all participants, and enters the COMMIT state. The participants either commit or abort the transaction according to the coordinator's instructions and send back an acknowledgment, at which point the coordinator terminates the transaction by writing an end_of_transaction record in the log.

---

[7]The reverse implication is not true, however.

Note the manner in which the coordinator reaches a global termination decision regarding a transaction. Two rules govern this decision, which, together, are called the *global commit rule*:

1. If even one participant votes to abort the transaction, the coordinator has to reach a global abort decision.

2. If all the participants vote to commit the transaction, the coordinator has to reach a global commit decision.

The operation of the 2PC protocol between a coordinator and one participant in the absence of failures is depicted in Figure 12.13, where the circles indicate the states and the dashed lines indicate messages between the coordinator and the participants. The labels on the dashed lines specify the nature of the message.

A few important points about the 2PC protocol that can be observed from Figure 12.13 are as follows. First, 2PC permits a participant to unilaterally abort a transaction until it has decided to register an affirmative vote. Second, once a participant votes to commit or abort a transaction, it cannot change its vote. Third, while a participant is in the READY state, it can move either to abort the transaction or to commit it, depending on the nature of the message from the coordinator. Fourth, the global termination decision is taken by the coordinator according to the global commit rule. Finally, note that the coordinator and participant processes enter certain states where they have to wait for messages from one another. To guarantee that they can exit from these states and terminate, timers are used. Each process sets its timer when it enters a state, and if the expected message is not received before the timer runs out, the process times out and invokes its timeout protocol (which will be discussed later).

There are a number of different communication paradigms that can be employed in implementing a 2PC protocol. The one discussed above and depicted in Figure 12.13 is called a *centralized 2PC* since the communication is only between the coordinator and the participants; the participants do not communicate among themselves. This communication structure, which is the basis of our subsequent discussions in this chapter, is depicted more clearly in Figure 12.14.

Another alternative is *linear 2PC* (also called *nested 2PC* [Gray, 1979]) where participants can communicate with one another. There is an ordering between the sites in the system for the purposes of communication. Let us assume that the ordering among the sites that participate in the execution of a transaction are $1, \ldots, N$, where the coordinator is the first one in the order. The 2PC protocol is implemented by a forward communication from the coordinator (number 1) to N, during which the first phase is completed, and by a backward communication from N to the coordinator, during which the second phase is completed. Thus linear 2PC operates in the following manner.

The coordinator sends the "prepare" message to participant 2. If participant 2 is not ready to commit the transaction, it sends a "vote-abort" message (VA) to participant 3 and the transaction is aborted at this point (unilateral abort by 2).

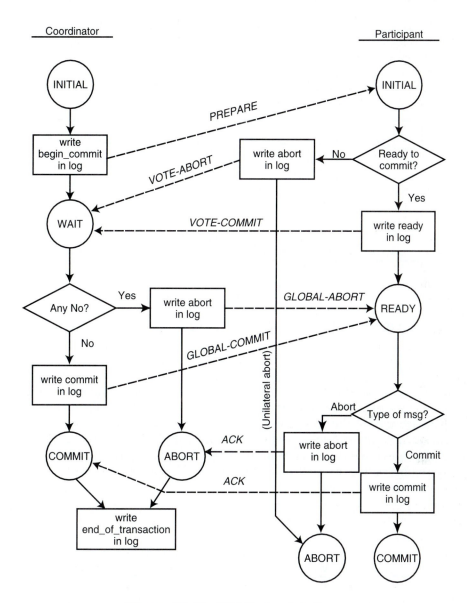

Figure 12.13. 2PC Protocol Actions

If, on the other hand, participant 2 agrees to commit the transaction, it sends a "vote-commit" message (VC) to participant 3 and enters the READY state. This process continues until a "vote-commit" vote reaches participant N. This is the end of the first phase. If N decides to commit, it sends back to $N-1$ "global-

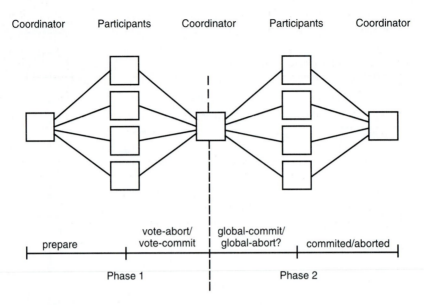

Figure 12.14. Centralized 2PC Communication Structure

commit" (GC); otherwise, it sends a "global-abort" message (GA). Accordingly, the participants enter the appropriate state (COMMIT or ABORT) and propagate the message back to the coordinator.

Linear 2PC, whose communication structure is depicted in Figure 12.15, incurs fewer messages but does not provide any parallelism. Therefore, it suffers from low response-time performance. It may, however, be suitable for networks that do not have broadcasting capability.

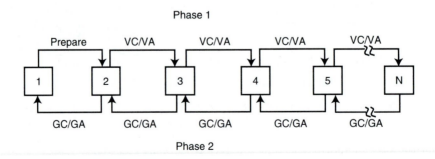

Figure 12.15. Linear 2PC Communication Structure. VC, vote.commit; VA, vote.abort; GC, global.commit; GA, global.abort.

Another popular communication structure for implementation of the 2PC protocol involves communication among all the participants during the first phase of the protocol so that they all independently reach their termination decisions with respect to the specific transaction. This version, called *distributed 2PC*, eliminates the need for the second phase of the protocol since the participants can reach a decision on their own. It operates as follows. The coordinator sends the prepare message to all participants. Each participant then sends its decision to all the other participants (and to the coordinator) by means of either a "vote-commit" or a "vote-abort" message. Each participant waits for messages from all the other participants and makes its termination decision according to the global commit rule. Obviously, there is no need for the second phase of the protocol (someone sending the global abort or global commit decision to the others), since each participant has independently reached that decision at the end of the first phase. The communication structure of distributed commit is depicted in Figure 12.16.

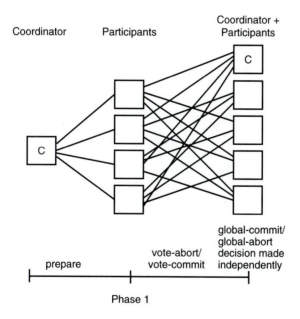

Figure 12.16. Distributed 2PC Communication Structure

One point that needs to be addressed with respect to the last two versions of 2PC implementation is the following. A participant has to know the identity of either the next participant in the linear ordering (in case of linear 2PC) or of all the participants (in case of distributed 2PC). This problem can be solved by attaching the list of participants to the prepare message that is sent by the coordinator. Such an issue does not arise in the case of centralized 2PC since the coordinator clearly knows who the participants are.

The algorithms for the execution of the 2PC protocol by the coordinator and the participants in a centralized communication structure are given in Algorithms 12.1 and 12.2, respectively. The algorithms show the handling of various messages between the coordinator and the participants.

Algorithm 12.1 *2PC-Coordinator*

> **declare-var**
> > *msg* : *Message*
> > *ev* : *Event*
> > *PL* : List of participant {list compiled prior to the start of 2PC protocol}
>
> **begin**
> > WAIT(*ev*)
> > **case of** *ev*   {possible events are *MsgArrival* and *Timeout*}
> > > *MsgArrival*:
> > > **begin**
> > > > Let the arrived message be in *msg*
> > > > **case of** *msg*
> > > > > Commit: {commit command from scheduler}
> > > > > **begin**
> > > > > > write begin_commit record in the log
> > > > > > send "prepare" message to all the participants in *PL*
> > > > > > set timer
> > > > > **end**
> > > > > Vote-Abort: {one participant has voted to abort}
> > > > > **begin**
> > > > > > write abort record in the log
> > > > > > send "global-abort" message to all the participants in *PL*
> > > > > > set timer
> > > > > **end**
> > > > > Vote-Commit:
> > > > > **begin**
> > > > > > update the list of participants who have answered
> > > > > > **if** all the participants have answered **then**
> > > > > > > **begin**   {all must have voted to commit}
> > > > > > > > write commit in the log
> > > > > > > > send "global-commit" to all the participants in *PL*
> > > > > > > > set timer
> > > > > > > **end**
> > > > > **end**

     Ack:
     begin
       update the list of participants who have acknowledged
       if all the participants have acknowledged **then**
        write end_of_transaction in the log
       else
        send global decision to the unanswering participants
       end-if
     end
    end-case
   end
   Timeout:
   begin
     execute the termination protocol   {this will be discussed later}
   end
  end-case
 end. {2PC-Coordinator}

Algorithm 12.2 *2PC-Participant*

 declare-var
  msg : *Message*
  ev : *Event*
 begin
  WAIT(*ev*)
  case of *ev*   {possible events are *MsgArrival* and *Timeout*}
   MsgArrival:
  begin
   Let the arrived message be in *msg*
   case of *msg*
    Prepare:
   begin
     if ready to commit **then**
    begin
      write ready record in the log
      send "vote-commit" message to the coordinator
      set timer
    end

```
              else begin                                    {unilateral abort}
                 write abort record in the log
                 send "vote-abort" message to the coordinator
                 call local data processor to abort the transaction
                 end
              end-if
           end
           Global-abort:
           begin
              write abort record in the log
              call local data processor to abort the transaction
           end
           Global-commit:
           begin
              write commit record in the log
              call local data processor to commit the transaction
           end
        end-case
     end
     Timeout:
     begin
        execute the termination protocol        {this will be discussed later}
     end
  end-case
end. {2PC-Participant}
```

12.5.3 Variations of 2PC

Two variations of 2PC have been proposed to improve its performance. This is accomplished by reducing (1) the number of messages that are transmitted between
the coordinator and the participants, and (2) the number of times logs are written.
These protocols are called *presumed abort* and *presumed commit* [Mohan and Lindsay, 1983], [Mohan et al., 1986]. Presumed abort is a protocol that is optimized to
handle read-only transactions as well as those update transactions, some of whose
processes do not perform any updates to the database while the others do (called
partially read-only). The presumed commit protocol is optimized to handle the
general update transactions. We will discuss briefly both of these variations.

Presumed Abort 2PC Protocol

In the presumed abort 2PC protocol the following assumption is made. Whenever a
prepared participant polls the coordinator about a transaction's outcome and there
is no information in virtual storage about it, the response to the inquiry is to abort
the transaction. This works since, in the case of a commit, the coordinator does
not forget about a transaction until all participants acknowledge, guaranteeing that
they will no longer inquire about this transaction.

When this convention is used, it can be seen that the coordinator can forget about a transaction immediately after it decides to abort it. It can write an abort record and not expect the participants to acknowledge the abort command. The coordinator does not need to write an end_of_transaction record after an abort record.

The abort record does not need to be forced, because if a site fails before receiving the decision and then recovers, the recovery routine will check the log to determine the fate of the transaction. Since the abort record is not forced, the recovery routine may not find any information about the transaction, in which case it will ask the coordinator and will be told to abort it. For the same reason, the abort records do not need to be forced by the participants either.

Since it saves some message transmission between the coordinator and the participants in case of aborted transactions, presumed abort 2PC is expected to be more efficient.

Presumed Commit 2PC Protocol

The presumed abort 2PC protocol improves performance by forgetting about transactions once a decision is reached to abort them. Since most transactions are expected to commit, it is reasonable to expect that it may be similarly possible to improve performance for commits. Hence the presumed commit 2PC protocol.

Presumed commit 2PC is based on the premise that if no information about the transaction exists, it should be considered committed. However, it is not an exact dual of presumed abort 2PC, since an exact dual would require that the coordinator forget about a transaction immediately after it decides to commit it, that commit records (also the ready records of the participants) not be forced, and that commit commands need not be acknowledged. Consider, however, the following scenario. The coordinator sends prepared messages and starts collecting information, but fails before being able to collect all of them and reach a decision. In this case, the participants will wait for a while and then turn the transaction over to their recovery routines. Since there is no information about the transaction, the recovery routines of each participant will commit the transaction. The coordinator, on the other hand, will abort the transaction when it recovers, thus causing inconsistency.

A simple variation of this protocol, however, solves the problem and that variant is called the *presumed commit 2PC*. The coordinator, prior to sending the prepare message, force-writes a collecting record, which contains the names of all the participants involved in executing that transaction. The participant then enters the COLLECTING state. It then sends the prepare message and enters the WAIT state. The participants, when they receive the prepare message, decide what they want to do with the transaction, write an abort record, or write a ready record and respond with either a "vote-abort" or a "vote-commit" message. When the coordinator receives decisions from all the participants, it decides to abort or commit the transaction. If the decision is to abort, the coordinator writes an abort record, enters the ABORT state, and sends a "global-abort" message. If it decides to commit the transaction, it writes a commit record, sends a "global-commit" command, and forgets the transaction. When the participants receive a "global-commit" message, they write a commit record and update the database. If they receive a "global-abort" message, they write an abort record and acknowledge. The participant, upon receiving the abort acknowledgment, writes an end record and forgets about the transaction.

12.6 DEALING WITH SITE FAILURES

In this section we consider the failure of sites in the network. Our aim is to develop nonblocking termination and independent recovery protocols. As we indicated before, the existence of independent recovery protocols would imply the existence of nonblocking recovery protocols. However, our discussion addresses both aspects separately. Also note that in the following discussion we consider only the standard 2PC protocol, not its two variants presented above.

Let us first set the boundaries for the existence of nonblocking termination and independent recovery protocols in the presence of site failures. It can formally be proven that such protocols exist when a single site fails. In the case of multiple site failures, however, the prospects are not as promising. An unfortunate result indicates that it is not possible to design independent recovery protocols (and, therefore, nonblocking termination protocols) when multiple sites fail [Skeen and Stonebraker, 1983]. We first develop termination and recovery protocols for the 2PC algorithm and show that 2PC is inherently blocking. We then proceed to the development of atomic commit protocols which are nonblocking in the case of single site failures.

12.6.1 Termination and Recovery Protocols for 2PC

Termination Protocols

The termination protocols serve the timeouts for both the coordinator and the participant processes. A timeout occurs at a destination site when it cannot get an expected message from a source site within the expected time period. In this section we consider that this is due to the failure of the source site.

The method for handling timeouts depends on the timing of failures as well as on the types of failures. We therefore need to consider failures at various points of 2PC execution. This discussion is facilitated by means of the state transition diagram of the 2PC protocol given in Figure 12.17. Note that the state transition diagram is a simplification of Figure 12.13. The states are denoted by circles and the edges represent the state transitions. The terminal states are depicted by concentric circles. The interpretation of the labels on the edges is as follows: the reason for the state transition, which is a received message, is given at the top, and the message that is sent as a result of state transition is given at the bottom.

Coordinator Timeouts. There are three states in which the coordinator can timeout: WAIT, COMMIT, and ABORT. Timeouts during the last two are handled in the same manner. So we need to consider only two cases:

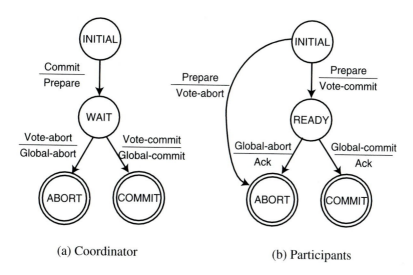

(a) Coordinator   (b) Participants

Figure 12.17. State Transitions in 2PC Protocol

1. *Timeout in the WAIT state.* In the WAIT state, the coordinator is waiting for the local decisions of the participants. The coordinator cannot unilaterally commit the transaction since the global commit rule has not been satisfied. However, it can decide to globally abort the transaction, in which case it writes an abort record in the log and sends a "global-abort" message to all the participants.

2. *Timeout in the COMMIT or ABORT states.* In this case the coordinator is not certain that the commit or abort procedures have been completed by the local recovery managers at all of the participant sites. Thus the coordinator repeatedly sends the "global-commit" or "global-abort" commands to the sites that have not yet responded, and waits for their acknowledgement.

Participant Timeouts.   A participant can time out[8] in two states: INITIAL and READY. Let us examine both of these cases.

1. *Timeout in the INITIAL state.* In this state the participant is waiting for a "prepare" message. The coordinator must have failed in the INITIAL state. The participant can unilaterally abort the transaction following a timeout. If the "prepare" message arrives at this participant at a later

---

[8]In some discussions of the 2PC protocol, it is assumed that the participants do not use timers and do not time out. However, implementing timeout protocols for the participants solves some nasty problems and may speed up the commit process. Therefore, we consider this more general case.

time, this can be handled in one of two possible ways. Either the participant would check its log, find the abort record, and respond with a "vote-abort," or it can simply ignore the "prepare" message. In the latter case the coordinator would time out in the WAIT state and follow the course we have discussed above.

2. *Timeout in the READY state.* In this state the participant has voted to commit the transaction but does not know the global decision of the coordinator. The participant cannot unilaterally make a decision. Since it is in the READY state, it must have voted to commit the transaction. Therefore, it cannot now change its vote and unilaterally abort it. On the other hand, it cannot unilaterally decide to commit it since it is possible that another participant may have voted to abort it. In this case the participant will remain blocked until it can learn from someone (either the coordinator or some other participant) the ultimate fate of the transaction.

Let us consider a centralized communication structure where the participants cannot communicate with one another. In this case the participant that is trying to terminate a transaction has to ask the coordinator for its decision and wait until it receives a response. If the coordinator has failed, the participant will remain blocked. This is undesirable.

If the participants can communicate with each other, a more distributed termination protocol may be developed. The participant that times out can simply ask all the other participants to help it make a decision. Assuming that participant P_i is the one that times out, all the other participants P_j respond in the following manner:

1. P_j is in the INITIAL state. This means that P_j has not yet voted and may not even have received the "prepare" message. It can therefore unilaterally abort the transaction and reply to P_i with a "vote-abort" message.

2. P_j is in the READY state. In this state P_j has voted to commit the transaction but has not received any word about the global decision. Therefore, it cannot help P_i to terminate the transaction.

3. P_j is in the ABORT or COMMIT states. In these states, either P_j has unilaterally decided to abort the transaction, or it has received the coordinator's decision regarding global termination. It can, therefore, send P_i either a "vote-commit" or a "vote-abort" message.

Consider how the participant that times out (P_i) can interpret these responses. The following cases are possible:

1. P_i receives "vote-abort" messages from all P_j. This means that none of the other participants had yet voted, but they have chosen to abort the transaction unilaterally. Under these conditions, P_i can proceed to abort the transaction.

2. P_i receives "vote-abort" messages from some P_j, but some other participants indicate that they are in the READY state. In this case P_i can still go ahead and abort the transaction, since according to the global commit rule, the transaction cannot be committed and will eventually be aborted.

3. P_i receives notification from all P_j that they are in the READY state. In this case none of the participants knows enough about the fate of the transaction to terminate it properly.

4. P_i receives "global-abort" or "global-commit" messages from all P_j. In this case all the other participants have received the coordinator's decision. Therefore, P_i can go ahead and terminate the transaction according to the messages it receives from the other participants. Incidentally, note that it is not possible for some of the P_j to respond with a "global-abort" while others respond with "global-commit" since this cannot be the result of a legitimate execution of the 2PC protocol.

5. P_i receives "global-abort" or "global-commit" from some P_j, whereas others indicate that they are in the READY state. This indicates that some sites have received the coordinator's decision while others are still waiting for it. In this case P_i can proceed as in case 4 above.

These five cases cover all the alternatives that a termination protocol needs to handle. It is not necessary to consider cases where, for example, one participant sends a "vote-abort" message while another one sends "global-commit." This cannot happen in 2PC. During the execution of the 2PC protocol, no process (participant or coordinator) is more than one state transition apart from any other process. For example, if a participant is in the INITIAL state, all other participants are in either the INITIAL or the READY state. Similarly, the coordinator is either in the INITIAL or the WAIT state. Thus all the processes in a 2PC protocol are said to be *synchronous within one state transition* [Skeen, 1981].

Note that in case 3 the participant processes stay blocked, as they cannot terminate a transaction. Under certain circumstances there may be a way to overcome this blocking. If during termination all the participants realize that only the coordinator site has failed, they can elect a new coordinator, which can restart the commit process. There are different ways of electing the coordinator. It is possible either to define a total ordering among all sites and elect the next one in order [Hammer and Shipman, 1980], or to establish a voting procedure among the participants [Garcia-Molina, 1982]. This will not work, however, if both a participant site and the coordinator site fail. In this case it is possible for the participant at the failed site to have received the coordinator's decision and have terminated the transaction accordingly. This decision is unknown to the other participants; thus if they elect a new coordinator and proceed, there is the danger that they may decide to terminate the transaction differently from the participant at the failed site. It is clear that it is not possible to design termination protocols for 2PC that can guarantee nonblocking termination. The 2PC protocol is, therefore, a blocking protocol.

Since we had assumed a centralized communication structure in developing the
2PC algorithms in Algorithms 12.1 and 12.2, we will continue with the same assumption in developing the termination protocols. The portion of code that should
be included in the timeout section of the coordinator and the participant 2PC
algorithms is given in Algorithms 12.3 and 12.4, respectively.

Algorithm 12.3 *2PC-Coordinator-Terminate*

> *Timeout*:
> **begin**
>   **if** in WAIT state **then**
>   **begin**
>   write abort record in the log
>   send "global-abort" message to all the participants
>   **end**
>   **else begin**
>   check for the last log record
>   **if** last log record=abort **then**   {coordinator is in ABORT state}
>   send "global-abort" to all the participants that have not responded
>   **else**   {coordinator is in COMMIT state}
>   send "global-commit" to all the participants that have not responded
>   **end-if**
>   **end**
>   **end-if**
>   set timer
> **end**

Algorithm 12.4 *2PC-Participant-Terminate*

> *Timeout*:
> **begin**
>   **if** in INITIAL state **then**
>   write abort record in the log
>   **else**   {participant is in READY state}
>   send "vote-commit" message to the coordinator
>   reset timer
>   **end-if**
> **end**

Recovery Protocols

In the preceding section we discussed how the 2PC protocol deals with failures from
the perspective of the operational sites. In this section we take the opposite viewpoint: we are interested in investigating protocols that a coordinator or participant
can use to recover their states when their sites fail and then restart. Remember
that we would like these protocols to be independent. However, in general, it is not

possible to design protocols that can guarantee independent recovery while maintaining the atomicity of distributed transactions. This is not surprising given the fact that the termination protocols for 2PC are inherently blocking.

In the following discussion we again use the state transition diagram of Figure 12.17. Additionally, we make two interpretive assumptions: (1) the combined action of writing a record in the log and sending a message is assumed to be atomic, and (2) the state transition occurs after the transmission of the response message. For example, if the coordinator is in the WAIT state, this means that it has successfully written the begin_commit record in its log and has successfully transmitted the "prepare" command. This does not say anything, however, about successful completion of the message transmission. Therefore, the "prepare" message may never get to the participants, due to communication failures, which we discuss separately. The first assumption related to atomicity is, of course, unrealistic. However, it simplifies our discussion of fundamental failure cases. At the end of this section we show that the other cases that arise from the relaxation of this assumption can be handled by a combination of the fundamental failure cases.

Coordinator Site Failures.   The following cases are possible:

1. *The coordinator fails while in the INITIAL state.* This is before the coordinator has initiated the commit procedure. Therefore, it will start the commit process upon recovery.

2. *The coordinator fails while in the WAIT state.* In this case the coordinator has sent the "prepare" command. Upon recovery, the coordinator will restart the commit process for this transaction from the beginning by sending the "prepare" message one more time.

3. *The coordinator fails while in the COMMIT or ABORT states.* In this case the coordinator will have informed the participants of its decision and terminated the transaction. Thus, upon recovery, it does not need to do anything if all the acknowledgments have been received. Otherwise, the termination protocol is involved.

Participant Site Failures.   There are three alternatives to consider:

1. *A participant fails in the INITIAL state.* Upon recovery, the participant should abort the transaction unilaterally. Let us see why this is acceptable. Note that the coordinator will be in the INITIAL or WAIT state with respect to this transaction. If it is in the INITIAL state, it will send a "prepare" message and then move to the WAIT state. Because of the participant site's failure, it will not receive the participant's decision and will time out in that state. We have already discussed how the coordinator would handle timeouts in the WAIT state by globally aborting the transaction.

2. *A participant fails while in the READY state.* In this case the coordinator has been informed of the failed site's affirmative decision about

the transaction before the failure. Upon recovery, the participant at the failed site can treat this as a timeout in the READY state and hand the incomplete transaction over to its termination protocol.

3. *A participant fails while in the ABORT or COMMIT state.* These states represent the termination conditions, so, upon recovery, the participant does not need to take any special action.

Additional Cases. Let us now consider the cases that may arise when we relax the assumption related to the atomicity of the logging and message sending actions. In particular, we assume that a site failure may occur after the coordinator or a participant has written a log record but before it can send a message. For this discussion the reader may wish to refer to Figure 12.13.

1. *The coordinator fails after the begin_commit record is written in the log but before the "prepare" command is sent.* The coordinator would react to this as a failure in the WAIT state (case 2 of the coordinator failures discussed above) and send the "prepare" command upon recovery.

2. *A participant site fails after writing the ready record in the log but before sending the "vote-commit" message.* The failed participant sees this as case 2 of the participant failures discussed before.

3. *A participant site fails after writing the abort record in the log but before sending the "vote-abort" message.* This is the only situation that is not covered by the fundamental cases discussed before. However, the participant does not need to do anything upon recovery in this case. The coordinator is in the WAIT state and will time out. The coordinator termination protocol for this state globally aborts the transaction.

4. *The coordinator fails after logging its final decision record (abort or commit), but before sending its "global-abort" or "global-commit" message to the participants.* The coordinator treats this as its case 3, while the participants treat it as a timeout in the READY state.

5. *A participant fails after it logs an abort or a commit record but before it sends the acknowledgment message to the coordinator.* The participant can treat this as its case 3. The coordinator will handle this by timeout in the COMMIT or ABORT state.

12.6.2 Three-Phase Commit Protocol

The three-phase commit protocol (3PC) [Skeen, 1981] is designed as a nonblocking protocol. We will see in this section that it is indeed nonblocking when failures are restricted to site failures.

Let us first consider the necessary and sufficient conditions for designing nonblocking atomic commitment protocols. A commit protocol that is synchronous within one state transition is nonblocking if and only if its state transition diagram contains neither of the following:

1. No state that is "adjacent" to both a commit and an abort state

2. No noncommittable state that is "adjacent" to a commit state ([Skeen, 1981], [Skeen and Stonebraker, 1983])

The term *adjacent* here means that it is possible to go from one state to the other with a single state transition.

Consider the COMMIT state in the 2PC protocol (see Figure 12.17). If any process is in this state, we know that all the sites have voted to commit the transaction. Such states are called *committable*. There are other states in the 2PC protocol that are *noncommittable*. The one we are interested in is the READY state, which is noncommittable since the existence of a process in this state does not imply that all the processes have voted to commit the transaction.

It is obvious that the WAIT state in the coordinator and the READY state in the participant 2PC protocol violate the nonblocking conditions we have stated above. Therefore, one might be able to make the following modification to the 2PC protocol to satisfy the conditions and turn it into a nonblocking protocol.

We can add another state between the WAIT (and READY) and COMMIT states which serves as a buffer state where the process is ready to commit (if that is the final decision) but has not yet committed. The state transition diagrams for the coordinator and the participant in this protocol are depicted in Figure 12.18. This is called the three-phase commit protocol (3PC) because there are three state transitions from the INITIAL state to a COMMIT state. The execution of the protocol between the coordinator and one participant is depicted in Figure 12.19. Note that this is identical to Figure 12.13 except for the addition of the PRECOMMIT state. Observe that 3PC is also a protocol where all the states are synchronous within one state transition. Therefore, the foregoing conditions for nonblocking 2PC apply to 3PC.

It is possible to design different 3PC algorithms depending on the communication topology. The one given in Figure 12.19 is centralized. It is also straightforward to design a distributed 3PC protocol. A linear 3PC protocol is somewhat more involved, so we leave it as an exercise.

Termination Protocol

As we did in discussing the termination protocols for handling timeouts in the 2PC protocol, let us investigate timeouts at each state of the 3PC protocol.

Coordinator Timeouts. In 3PC, there are four states in which the coordinator can time out: WAIT, PRECOMMIT, COMMIT, or ABORT.

1. *Timeout in the WAIT state.* This is identical to the coordinator timeout in the WAIT state for the 2PC protocol. The coordinator unilaterally decides to abort the transaction. It therefore writes an abort record in the log and sends a "global-abort" message to all the participants that have voted to commit the transaction.

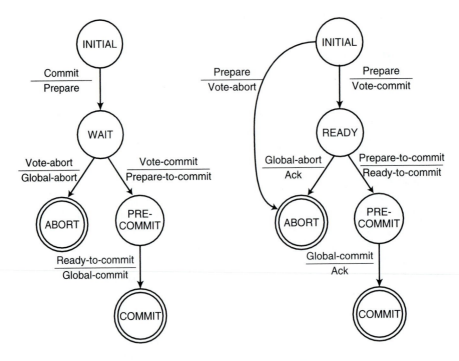

Figure 12.18. State Transitions in 3PC Protocol

2. *Timeout in the PRECOMMIT state.* The coordinator does not know if the nonresponding participants have already moved to the PRECOMMIT state. However, it knows that they are at least in the READY state, which means that they must have voted to commit the transaction. The coordinator can therefore move all participants to PRECOMMIT state by sending a "prepare-to-commit" message go ahead and globally commit the transaction by writing a commit record in the log and sending a "global-commit" message to all the operational participants.

3. *Timeout in the COMMIT (or ABORT) state.* The coordinator does not know whether the participants have actually performed the commit (abort) command. However, they are at least in the PRECOMMIT (READY) state (since the protocol is synchronous within one state transition) and can follow the termination protocol as described in case 2 or case 3 below. Thus the coordinator does not need to take any special action.

Participant Timeouts. A participant can time out in three states: INITIAL, READY, and PRECOMMIT. Let us examine all of these cases.

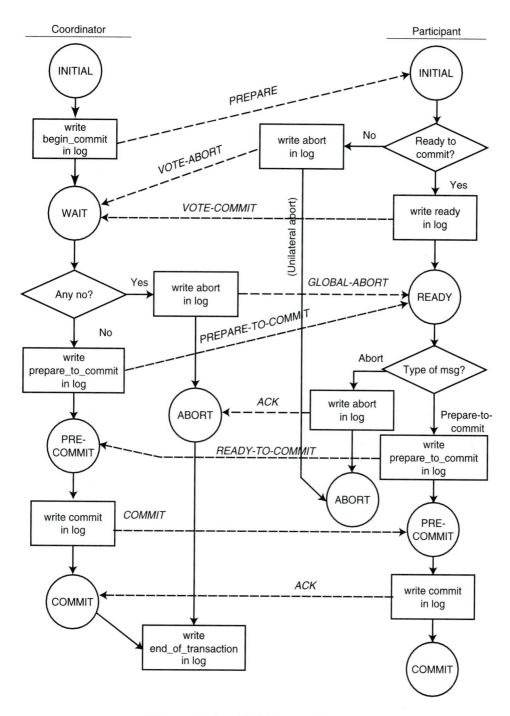

Figure 12.19. 3PC Protocol Actions

1. *Timeout in the INITIAL state.* This can be handled identically to the termination protocol of 2PC.

2. *Timeout in the READY state.* In this state the participant has voted to commit the transaction but does not know the global decision of the coordinator. Since communication with the coordinator is lost, the termination protocol proceeds by electing a new coordinator, as discussed earlier. The new coordinator then terminates the transaction according to a termination protocol that we discuss below.

3. *Timeout in the PRECOMMIT state.* In this state the participant has received the "prepare-to-commit" message and is awaiting the final "global-commit" message from the coordinator. This case is handled identically to case 2 above.

Let us now consider the possible termination protocols that can be adopted in the last two cases. There are various alternatives; let us consider a centralized one [Skeen, 1981]. We know that the new coordinator can be in one of three states: WAIT, PRECOMMIT, COMMIT or ABORT. It sends its own state to all the operational participants, asking them to assume that state. Any participant who has proceeded ahead of the new coordinator (which is possible since it may have already received and processed a message from the old coordinator) simply ignores the new coordinator's message; others make their state transitions and send back the appropriate message. Once the new coordinator gets messages from the participants, it guides the participants toward termination as follows:

1. If the new coordinator is in the WAIT state, it will globally abort the transaction. The participants can be in the INITIAL, READY, ABORT, or PRECOMMIT states. In the first three cases, there is no problem. However, the participants in the PRECOMMIT state are expecting a "global-commit" message, but they get a "global-abort" instead. Their state transition diagram does not indicate any transition from the PRE-COMMIT to the ABORT state. This transition is necessary for the termination protocol, so it should be added to the set of legal transitions that can occur during execution of the termination protocol.

2. If the new coordinator is in the PRECOMMIT state, the participants can be in the READY, PRECOMMIT or COMMIT states. No participant can be in ABORT state. The coordinator will therefore globally commit the transaction and send a "global-commit" message.

3. If the new coordinator is in the ABORT state, at the end of the first message all the participants will have moved into the ABORT state as well.

The new coordinator is not keeping track of participant failures during this process. It simply guides the operational sites toward termination. If some participants fail in the meantime, they will have to terminate the transaction upon recovery according to the methods discussed in the next section. Also, the new coordinator may fail during the process; the termination protocol therefore needs to be reentrant in implementation.

This termination protocol is obviously nonblocking. The operational sites can properly terminate all the ongoing transactions and continue their operations. The proof of correctness of the algorithm is given in [Skeen, 1982a].

Recovery Protocols

There are some minor differences between the recovery protocols of 3PC and those of 2PC. We only indicate those differences.

1. *The coordinator fails while in the WAIT state.* This is the case we discussed at length in the earlier section on termination protocols. The participants have already terminated the transaction. Therefore, upon recovery, the coordinator has to ask around to determine the fate of the transaction.

2. *The coordinator fails while in the PRECOMMIT state.* Again, the termination protocol has guided the operational participants toward termination. Since it is now possible to move from the PRECOMMIT state to the ABORT state during this process, the coordinator has to ask around to determine the fate of the transaction.

3. *A participant fails while in the PRECOMMIT state.* It has to ask around to determine how the other participants have terminated the transaction.

One property of the 3PC protocol becomes obvious from this discussion. When using the 3PC protocol, we are able to terminate transactions without blocking. However, we pay the price that fewer cases of independent recovery are possible. This also results in more messages being exchanged during recovery.

12.7 NETWORK PARTITIONING

In this section we consider how the network partitions can be handled by the atomic commit protocols that we discussed in the preceding section. Network partitions are due to communication line failures and may cause the loss of messages, depending on the implementation of the communication subnet. A partitioning is called a *simple partitioning* if the network is divided into only two components; otherwise, it is called *multiple partitioning*.

The termination protocols for network partitioning address the termination of the transactions that were active in each partition at the time of partitioning. If one can develop nonblocking protocols to terminate these transactions, it is possible for the sites in each partition to reach a termination decision (for a given transaction) which is consistent with the sites in the other partitions. This would imply that the sites in each partition can continue executing transactions despite the partitioning.

Unfortunately, it is not in general possible to find nonblocking termination protocols in the presence of network partitions. Remember that our expectations regarding the reliability of the communication subnet are minimal. If a message cannot be delivered, it is simply lost. In this case it can be proven that no nonblocking atomic commitment protocol exists that is resilient to network partitioning [Skeen and Stonebraker, 1983]. This is quite a negative result since it also means that if network partitioning occurs, we cannot continue normal operations in all partitions, which limits the availability of the entire distributed database system. A positive counter result, however, indicates that it is possible to design nonblocking atomic commit protocols that are resilient to simple partitions. Unfortunately, if multiple partitions occur, it is again not possible to design such protocols [Skeen and Stonebraker, 1983].

In the remainder of this section we discuss a number of protocols that address network partitioning in nonreplicated databases. We did not need to make this distinction in our discussion of site failures in the preceding section, since the termination protocols are identical for both types of database organization. However, the same is not true in the case of network partitioning. Recall from Chapter 11 that in the case of replicated databases, the replica control protocol has to be involved in mapping a read or a write on a logical data item to a read or a write on the physical data item copies. In the presence of network partitioning, the copies may be in different partitions and the replica control protocol has to be concerned with the management of network partitioning. In the presence of network partitioning of nonreplicated databases, on the other hand, the major concern is with the termination of transactions that were active at the time of partitioning. Any new transaction that accesses a data item that is stored in another partition is simply blocked and has to await the repair of the network. Concurrent accesses to the data items within one partition can be handled by the concurrency control algorithm. The significant problem, therefore, is to ensure that the transaction terminates properly. In short, in nonreplicated databases, the network partitioning problem is handled by the commit protocol, and more specifically, by the termination and recovery protocols, whereas in replicated databases it is the responsibility of the replica control protocol. Since replica control protocols have more general objectives than simply managing network partitioning, we defer them to the next section.

The absence of nonblocking protocols that would guarantee atomic commitment of distributed transactions points to an important design decision. We can either permit all the partitions to continue their normal operations and accept the fact that database consistency may be compromised, or we guarantee the consistency of the database by employing strategies that would permit operation in one of the partitions while the sites in the others remain blocked. This decision problem is the premise of a classification of partition handling strategies. We can classify the strategies as *pessimistic* or *optimistic* [Davidson et al., 1985]. Pessimistic strategies emphasize the consistency of the database, and would therefore not permit transactions to execute in a partition if there is no guarantee that the consistency of the database can be maintained. Optimistic approaches, on the other hand, emphasize the availability of the database even if this would cause inconsistencies.

The second dimension is related to the correctness criterion. If serializability is used as the fundamental correctness criterion, such strategies are called *syntactic* since the serializability theory uses only syntactic information. However, if we use a more abstract correctness criterion that is dependent on the semantics of the transactions or the database, the strategies are said to be *semantic*.

Consistent with the correctness criterion that we have adopted in this book (serializability), we consider only syntactic approaches in this section. The following two sections outline various syntactic strategies for nonreplicated databases.

All the known termination protocols that deal with network partitioning in the case of nonreplicated databases are pessimistic. Since the pessimistic approaches emphasize the maintenance of database consistency, the fundamental issue that we need to address is which of the partitions can continue normal operations. We consider two approaches.

12.7.1 Centralized Protocols

Centralized termination protocols are based on the centralized concurrency control algorithms discussed in Chapter 11. Recall that these may be of two types: primary site and primary copy. In the case of primary site concurrency control algorithms, it makes sense to permit the operation of the partition that contains the primary site, since it manages the lock tables.

In the case of primary copy concurrency control algorithms, more than one partition may be operational for different queries. For any given query, only the partition that contains the primary copies of the data items that are in the write set of that transaction can execute that transaction.

Both of these are simple approaches that would work well, but they are dependent on the concurrency control mechanism employed by the distributed database manager. Furthermore, they expect each site to be able to differentiate network partitioning from site failures properly. This is necessary since the participants in the execution of the commit protocol react differently to the different types of failures.

12.7.2 Voting-based Protocols

Voting as a technique for managing concurrent data accesses has been proposed by a number of researchers. A straightforward voting with majority was first proposed in [Thomas, 1979] as a concurrency control method for fully replicated databases. The fundamental idea is that a transaction is executed if a majority of the sites vote to execute it.

The idea of majority voting has been generalized to voting with *quorums*. Quorum-based voting can be used as a replica control method (as we discuss in the next section), as well as a commit method to ensure transaction atomicity in the presence of network partitioning. In the case of nonreplicated databases, this involves the integration of the voting principle with commit protocols. We present next a specific proposal along this line [Skeen, 1982a].

Every site in the system is assigned a vote V_i. Let us assume that the total number of votes in the system is V, and the abort and commit quorums are V_a and V_c, respectively. Then the following rules must be obeyed in the implementation of the commit protocol:

1. $V_a + V_c > V$, where $0 \leq V_a,\ V_c \leq V$.
2. Before a transaction commits, it must obtain a commit quorum V_c.
3. Before a transaction aborts, it must obtain an abort quorum V_a.

The first rule ensures that a transaction cannot be committed and aborted at the same time. The next two rules indicate the votes that a transaction has to obtain before it can terminate one way or the other.

The integration of these rules into the 3PC protocol requires a minor modification of the third phase. For the coordinator to move from the PRECOMMIT state to the COMMIT state, and to send the "global-commit" command, it is necessary for it to have obtained a commit quorum from the participants. This would satisfy rule 2. Note that we do not need to implement rule 3 explicitly. This is due to the fact that a transaction which is in the WAIT or READY state is willing to abort the transaction. Therefore, an abort quorum already exists.

Let us now consider the termination of transactions in the presence of failures. When a network partitioning occurs, the sites in each partition elect a new coordinator, similarly to the 3PC termination protocol in the case of site failures. There is a fundamental difference, however. It is not possible to make the transition from the WAIT or READY state to the ABORT state in one state transition, for a number of reasons. First, more than one coordinator is trying to terminate the transaction. We do not want them to terminate differently or the transaction execution will not be atomic. Therefore, we want the coordinators to obtain an abort quorum explicitly. Second, if the newly elected coordinator fails, it is not known whether a commit or abort quorum was reached. Thus it is necessary that participants make an explicit decision to join either the commit or the abort quorum and not change their votes afterward. Unfortunately, the READY (or WAIT) state does not satisfy these requirements. Thus we introduce another state, PREABORT, between the READY and ABORT states. The transition from the PREABORT state to the ABORT state requires an abort quorum. The state transition diagram is given in Figure 12.20.

With this modification, the termination protocol works as follows. Once a new coordinator is elected, it requests all participants to report their local states. Depending on the responses, it terminates the transaction as follows:

1. If at least one participant is in the COMMIT state, the coordinator decides to commit the transaction and sends a "global-commit" message to all the participants.
2. If at least one participant is in the ABORT state, the coordinator decides to abort the transaction and sends a "global-abort" message to all the participants.

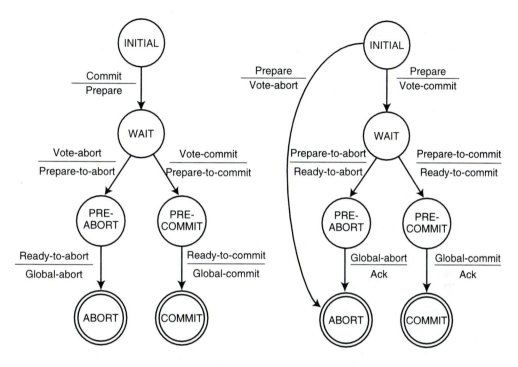

Figure 12.20. State Transitions in Quorum 3PC Protocol

3. If a commit quorum is reached by the votes of participants in the PRE-COMMIT state, the coordinator decides to commit the transaction and sends a "global-commit" message to all the participants.

4. If an abort quorum is reached by the votes of participants in the PRE-ABORT state, the coordinator decides to abort the transaction and sends a "global-abort" message to all the participants.

5. If case 3 does not hold but the sum of the votes of the participants in the PRECOMMIT and READY states are enough to form a commit quorum, the coordinator moves the participants to the PRECOMMIT state by sending a "prepare-to-commit" message. The coordinator then waits for case 3 to hold.

6. Similarly, if case 4 does not hold but the sum of the votes of the participants in the PREABORT and READY states are enough to form an abort quorum, the coordinator moves the participants to the PRE-ABORT state by sending a "prepare-to-abort" message. The coordinator then waits for case 4 to hold.

Two points are important about this quorum-based commit algorithm. First, it is blocking; the coordinator in a partition may not be able to form either an abort or a commit quorum if messages get lost or multiple partitionings occur. This is hardly surprising given the theoretical bounds that we discussed previously. The second point is that the algorithm is general enough to handle site failures as well as network partitioning. Therefore, this modified version of 3PC can provide more resiliency to failures.

The recovery protocol that can be used in conjunction with the above-discussed termination protocol is very simple. When two or more partitions merge, the sites that are part of the new larger partition simply execute the termination protocol. That is, a coordinator is elected to collect votes from all the participants and try to terminate the transaction.

12.7.3 Replication and Replica Control Protocols

As we discussed in Chapter 1, having replicas of data items improves system availability. With careful design, it is possible to ensure that single points of failure are eliminated and the "overall" system availability is maintained even when one more more sites fail. This has been one of the original motivations for replication.

The introduction of replicas also introduces difficulties. As indicated in Chapter 5, if the system workload is predominantly read-only, then it is advantageous to replicate the database – perhaps even replicate it everywhere – since most of the processing becomes local and performance improvements can be achieved by the parallel processing of transactions at different sites (inter-transaction parallelism). This has been a second motivation for replication. However, whenever updates are introduced, the complexity of keeping replicas consistent arises and this is the topic of replication protocols.

Even though the original motivations for replication have been to improve system availability and to improve system performance when reads are predominant, it has become fashionable in recent years to propose replication as an alternative to commit protocols. The argument that is made is that 2PC has a high overhead and, therefore, may not be desirable. Instead, data can be replicated at multiple sites and updated independently even if this leads to inconsistent replicas; inconsistencies can be eliminated later by *lazy replication* protocols which update replicas whenever an access occurs. We discuss these protocols later in this section. It is important to note, however, that replication is not a direct alternative to commit protocols; the two have quite different semantics since commit protocols force the database replicas to have the same value (one-copy equivalence) at the end of the update transaction while lazy replication only promises that they will converge to the same value at some later time.

12.7.4 Strict Replica Control Protocols

What we call *strict replica control protocols* are those that enforce one-copy equivalence as the correctness criterion (Chapter 10). To recall, this correctness criterion requires that all the database copies be mutually consistent at the end of each update transaction. We have already discussed one protocol for enforcing one-copy equivalence: the ROWA protocol which converts a logical read to a read on any one of the replicas, and converts a logical write to a write an **all** the replicas. Thus, when the update transaction commits, all of the replicas have the same value.

ROWA is simple and elegant. However, as we saw during the discussion of commit protocols, it has one significant drawback. Even if one of the replicas is unavailable, then the update transaction cannot be terminated. So, ROWA fails in meeting one of the fundamental goals of replication, namely providing higher availability.

An alternative to ROWA which attempts to address the low availability problem is the Read One Write All Available (ROWA-A) protocol. The general idea is that the write commands are executed on all the available copies and the transaction terminates. The copies that were unavailable at the time will have to "catch up" when they become available.

There have been various versions of this protocol. One that will discuss here is due to [Bernstein and Goodman, 1984], which is also described in [Bernstein et al., 1987], and is generally known as the *available copies protocol*. The coordinator of an update transaction T sends each $W_T(x)$ to all the sites where replicas of x reside and wait for confirmation of execution (or rejection). If it times out before it gets acknowledgement from all the sites, it considers those which have not replied as unavailable and continues with the update on the available sites. The unavailable sites, of course, update their databases to the latest state when they recover. Note, however, that these sites may not even be aware of the existence of T and the update to x that T has made if they had become unavailable before T started.

There are two complications that need to be addressed. The first one is the possibility that the sites that the coordinator thought were unavailable were in fact up and running and may have already updated x but their acknowledgement may not have reached the coordinator before its timer ran out. Second, some of these sites may have been unavailable when T started and may have recovered since then and have started executing transactions. Therefore, the coordinator undertakes a validation procedure before committing:

1. The coordinator checks to see if all the sites it thought were unavailable are still unavailable. It does this by sending an inquiry message to every one of these sites. Those that are available reply. If the coordinator gets a reply from one of these sites, it aborts T since it does not know the state that the previously unavailable site is in: it could have been that the site was available all along and had performed the original $W_T(x)$ but its acknowledgement was delayed (in which case everything is fine), or it could be that it was indeed unavailable when T started but became available later on and perhaps even executed $W_S(x)$ on behalf of another transaction S. In the latter case, continuing with T would make the execution schedule nonserializable.

2. If the coordinator of T does not get any response from any of the sites that it thought were unavailable, then it checks to make sure that all the

sites that were available when $W_T(x)$ executed are still available. If they are, then T can proceed to commit. Naturally, this second step can be integrated into a commit protocol.

The ROWA-A class of protocols are more resilient to failures, including network partitioning, than the simple ROWA protocol. There have been a number of different variants of ROWA which we do not discuss further. Readers can consult [Helal et al., 1997] for further discussion.

Another class of strict replication protocols are those based on voting. The fundamental characteristics of voting were presented in the previous section when we discussed network partitioning in nonreplicated databases. The general ideas hold in replicated case. Fundamentally, each read and write operation has to obtain a sufficient number of votes to be able to commit. These protocols can be pessimistic or optimistic. In what follows we discuss only pessimistic protocols. An optimistic version [Davidson, 1984] compensates transactions to recover if the commit decision cannot be confirmed at completion. This version is suitable wherever compensating transactions are acceptable (see Chapter 10).

The initial voting algorithm was discussed in [Thomas, 1979] and an early suggestion to use quorum-based voting for replica control is due to [Gifford, 1979]. Thomas's algorithm works on fully replicated databases and assigns an equal vote to each site. For any operation of a transaction to execute, it must collect affirmative votes from a majority of the sites. Gifford's algorithm, on the other hand, works with partially replicated databases (as well as with fully replicated ones) and assigns a vote to each copy of a replicated data item. Each operation then has to obtain a *read quorum* (V_r) or a *write quorum* (V_w) to read or write a data item, respectively. If a given data item has a total of V votes, the quorums have to obey the following rules:

1. $V_r + V_w > V$
2. $V_w > V/2$

As the reader may recall from the preceding section, the first rule ensures that a data item is not read and written by two transactions concurrently (avoiding the read-write conflict). The second rule, on the other hand, ensures that two write operations from two transactions cannot occur concurrently on the same data item (avoiding write-write conflict). Thus the two rules ensure that serializability and one-copy equivalence are maintained.

In the case of network partitioning, the quorum-based protocols work well since they basically determine which transactions are going to terminate based on the votes that they can obtain. The vote allocation and threshold rules given above ensure that two transactions that are initiated in two different partitions and access the same data cannot terminate at the same time.

The difficulty with this version of the protocol is that transactions are required to obtain a quorum even to read data. This significantly and unnecessarily slows down read access to the database. We describe below another quorum-based voting protocol [Abbadi et al., 1985] that overcomes this serious performance drawback.

The protocol makes certain assumptions about the underlying communication layer and the occurrence of failures. The assumption about failures is that they are "clean." This means two things:

1. Failures that change the network's topology are detected by all sites instantaneously.

2. Each site has a view of the network consisting of all the sites with which it can communicate.

Based on the presence of a communication network that can ensure these two conditions, the replica control protocol is a simple implementation of the ROWA principle. When the replica control protocol attempts to read or write a data item, it first checks if a majority of the sites are in the same partition as the site at which the protocol is running. If so, it implements the ROWA rule within that partition: it reads any copy of the data item and writes all copies that are in that partition.

Notice that the read or the write operation will execute in only one partition. Therefore, this is a pessimistic protocol that guarantees one-copy serializability. When the partitioning is repaired, the database is recovered by propagating the results of the update to the other partitions.

The fundamental question with respect to implementation of this protocol is whether or not the failure assumptions are realistic. Unfortunately, they are not. Most network failures are not "clean." There is a time delay between the occurrence of a failure and its detection by a site. Because of this delay, it is possible for one site to think that it is in one partition when in fact subsequent failures have placed it in another partition. Furthermore, this delay may be different for various sites. Thus two sites that were in the same partition but are now in different partitions may proceed for a while under the assumption that they are still in the same partition. The violations of these two failure assumptions have significant negative consequences on the replica control protocol and its ability to maintain one-copy serializability.

The suggested solution is to build on top of the physical communication layer another layer of abstraction which hides the "unclean" failure characteristics of the physical communication layer and presents to the replica control protocol a communication service that has "clean" failure properties. This new layer of abstraction provides *virtual partitions* within which the replica control protocol operates. A virtual partition is a group of sites that have agreed on a common view of who is in that partition. Sites join and depart from virtual partitions under the control of this new communication layer, which ensures that the clean failure assumptions hold.

The advantage of this protocol is its simplicity. It does not incur any overhead to maintain a quorum for read accesses. Thus the reads can proceed as fast as they would in a nonpartitioned network. Furthermore, it is general enough so that the replica control protocol does not need to differentiate between site failures and network partitions.

There are many different versions of quorum-based protocols. Some of these are discussed in [Triantafillou and Taylor, 1995], [Paris, 1996], [Tanenbaum and van Renesse, 1988].

12.7.5 Lazy Replication Protocols

Lazy replication protocols do not attempt to perform the Write operations on all copies of the data item within the context of the transaction that updates that data item. Instead, they perform the update on one or more copies and later propagate the changes to all the other copies. A lazy replication scheme can be characterized using four basic parameters [Pacitti et al., 1998]: The *ownership* parameter defines the permissions for updating replica copies. If a replica copy is updatable it is called a *primary* copy, otherwise it is called a *secondary* copy. The node that stores the primary copy of an object is called a *master* for this object, while the nodes that store its secondary copies are called *slaves*. The *propagation* parameter defines *when* the updates to a replica must be propagated towards the nodes storing the other replicas of the same object. The *refreshment* parameter defines the *scheduling* of the refresh transactions. If a refresh transaction is executed as soon as it is received by some node, the strategy is said to be *immediate*. The juxtaposition of the propagation and refreshment parameters determines a specific update propagation strategy. For instance, a *deferred-immediate* update propagation strategy has a deferred propagation and an immediate refreshment. The *configuration* parameter characterizes the nodes and the network.

Based on this characterization, lazy replication protocols can be classified into two groups. The first group consists of lazy replication methods where all replica copies are updatable (*update anywhere*). In this case, there is *group ownership* on the replicas. The common update propagation strategy implemented for this scheme is *deferred-immediate*. A *conflict* happens if two or more nodes update the same replica object. There are several policies for conflict detection and resolution [Goldring, 1995], [Bobrowski, 1996] that can be based on timestamp ordering, node priority and others. The problem with conflict resolution is that during a certain period of time the database may be in an inconsistent state. Conflicts cannot be avoided but its detection may happen earlier by using an immediate propagation.

The second class consists of protocols where there is a single master that is updated (called the *lazy master method*). There are several refreshment strategies for this replication scheme. With *on-demand* refreshment, each time a query is submitted for execution, secondary copies that are read by the query are refreshed by executing all received refresh transactions. Therefore, a delay may be introduced on query response time. When *group* refresh is used, refresh transactions are executed in groups in accordance with the application's freshness requirements. With the *periodic* approach, refreshment is triggered in fixed intervals. At refreshment time, all received refresh transactions are executed. Finaly, with *periodic propagation*, changes performed by update transactions are stored in the master and propagated periodically. Notice that immediate propagation may be used with all refreshment strategies.

12.8 ARCHITECTURAL CONSIDERATIONS

In previous sections we have discussed the atomic commit protocols at an abstract level. Let us now look at how these protocols can be implemented within the framework of our architectural model. This discussion involves specification of the interface between the concurrency control algorithms and the reliability protocols. In that sense, the discussions of this chapter relate to the execution of **commit** and **recover** commands.

Unfortunately, it is quite difficult to specify precisely the execution of these commands. The difficulty is twofold. First, a significantly more detailed model of the architecture than the one we have presented needs to be considered for correct implementation of these commands. Second, the overall scheme of implementation is quite dependent on the recovery procedures that the local recovery manager implements. For example, implementation of the 2PC protocol on top of a LRM that employs a no-fix/no-flush recovery scheme is quite different from its implementation on top of a LRM that employs a fix/flush recovery scheme. The alternatives are simply too numerous. We therefore confine our architectural discussion to three areas: implementation of the coordinator and participant concepts for the commit and replica control protocols within the framework of the transaction manager-scheduler-local recovery manager architecture, the coordinator's access to the database log, and the changes that need to be made in the local recovery manager operations.

One possible implementation of the commit protocols within our architectural model is to perform both the coordinator and participant algorithms within the transaction managers at each site. This provides some uniformity in executing the distributed commit operations. However, it entails unnecessary communication between the participant transaction manager and its scheduler; this is because the scheduler has to decide whether a transaction can be committed or aborted. Therefore, it may be preferable to implement the coordinator as part of the transaction manager and the participant as part of the scheduler. Of course, the replica control protocol is implemented as part of the transaction manager as well. If the scheduler implements a strict concurrency control algorithm (i.e., does not allow cascading aborts), it will be ready automatically to commit the transaction when the prepare message arrives. Proof of this claim is left as an exercise. However, even this alternative of implementing the coordinator and the participant outside the data processor has problems. The first issue is database log management. Recall from Section 12.4 that the database log is maintained by the LRM and the buffer manager. However, implementation of the commit protocol as described here requires the transaction manager and the scheduler to access the log as well. One possible solution to this problem is to maintain a commit log (which could be called the *distributed transaction log* [Bernstein et al., 1987], [Lampson and Sturgis, 1976]) which is accessed by the transaction manager and is separate from the database log that the LRM and buffer manager maintain. The other alternative is to write the commit protocol records into the same database log. This second alternative has a number of advantages. First, only one log is maintained; this simplifies the algorithms that have to be implemented in order to save log records on stable storage. More important, the recovery from failures in a distributed database requires the cooperation of the local recovery manager and the scheduler (i.e., the participant). A single database log can serve as a central repository of recovery information for both these components.

A second problem associated with implementing the coordinator within the transaction manager and the participant as part of the scheduler has to be with integration with the concurrency control protocols. This implementation is based on the schedulers determining whether a transaction can be committed. This is fine for distributed concurrency control algorithms where each site is equipped with a scheduler. However, in centralized protocols such as the centralized 2PL, there is only one scheduler in the system. In this case, the participants may be implemented as part of the local recovery managers, requiring modification to both the algorithms implemented by the LRM and, possibly, to the execution of the 2PC protocol. We leave the details to exercises.

Storing the commit protocol records in the database log maintained by the LRM and the buffer manager requires some changes to the LRM algorithms. This is the third architectural issue we address. Unfortunately, these changes are dependent on the type of algorithm that the LRM uses. In general, however, the LRM algorithms have to be modified to handle separately the prepare command and global commit (or global abort) decisions. Furthermore, upon recovery, the LRM should be modified to read the database log and to inform the scheduler as to the state of each transaction, in order that the recovery procedures discussed before can be followed. Let us take a more detailed look at this function of the LRM.

The LRM first has to determine whether the failed site is the host of the coordinator or of a participant. This information can be stored together with the begin_transaction record. The LRM then has to search for the last record written in the log record during execution of the commit protocol. If it cannot even find a begin_commit record (at the coordinator site) or an abort or commit record (at the participant sites), the transaction has not started to commit. In this case, the LRM can continue with its recovery procedure as we discussed in Section 12.4.3. However, if the commit process has started, the recovery has to be handed over to the coordinator. Therefore, the LRM sends the last log record to the scheduler.

12.9 CONCLUSION

In this chapter we discussed the reliability aspects of distributed transaction management. The studied algorithms (2PC and 3PC) guarantee the atomicity and durability of distributed transactions even when failures occur. One of these algorithms (3PC) can be made nonblocking, which would permit each site to continue its operation without waiting for recovery of the failed site. An unfortunate result that we presented relates to network partitioning. It is not possible to design protocols that guarantee the atomicity of distributed transactions and permit each partition of the distributed system to continue its operation under the assumptions made in this chapter with respect to the functionality of the communication subnet.

The performance of the distributed commit protocols with respect to the overhead they add to the concurrency control algorithms is an interesting issue. Some studies have addressed this issue [Dwork and Skeen, 1983], [Wolfson, 1987].

A final point that should be stressed is the following. We have considered only failures that are attributable to errors. In other words, we assumed that every effort was made to design and implement the systems (hardware and software), but that because of various faults in the components, the design, or the operating environment, they failed to perform properly. Such failures are called *failures of omission*. There is another class of failures, called *failures of commission*, where the systems may not have been designed and implemented so that they would work properly. The difference is that in the execution of the 2PC protocol, for example, if a participant receives a message from the coordinator, it treats this message as correct: the coordinator is operational and is sending the participant a correct message to go ahead and process. The only failure that the participant has to worry about is if the coordinator fails or if its messages get lost. These are failures of omission. If, on the other hand, the messages that a participant receives cannot be trusted, the participant also has to deal with failures of commission. For example, a participant site may pretend to be the coordinator and may send a malicious message. We have not discussed reliability measures that are necessary to cope with these types of failures. The techniques that address failures of commission are typically called *byzantine agreement*.

12.10 BIBLIOGRAPHIC NOTES

There are numerous books on the reliability of computer systems. These include [Anderson and Lee, 1981], [Anderson and Randell, 1979], [Avizienis et al., 1987], [Longbottom, 1980], [Gibbons, 1976], [Pradhan, 1986], [Siewiorek and Swarz, 1982], and [Shrivastava, 1985]. In addition, the survey paper [Randell et al., 1978] addresses the same issues. [Myers, 1976] specifically addresses software reliability. An important software fault tolerance technique that we have not discussed in this chapter is exception handling. This issue is treated in [Cristian, 1982], [Cristian, 1985], and [Cristian, 1987]. [Johnson and Malek, 1988] surveys the existing software tools for reliability measurement.

With respect to our discussion of process pairs, the lock-step process pair approach is implemented in the Stratus/32 systems ([Stratus, 1982], [Kim, 1984]) for hardware processes. An automatic checkpointing process pairs approach is used in the Auras (TM) operating system for Aurogen computers ([Borg et al., 1983], [Gastonian, 1983]). State checkpointing has been used in earlier versions of the Tandem operating systems [Bartlett, 1978], [Bartlett, 1981], which have later utilized the delta checkpointing approach [Borr, 1984]. The latest versions of the Tandem OS utilize persistent process pairs for fault tolerance.

More detailed material on the functions of the local recovery manager discussed in Section 12.4 can be found in [Verhofstadt, 1978], [Härder and Reuter, 1983]. Implementation of the local recovery functions in System R is described in [Gray et al., 1981].

[Kohler, 1981] presents a general discussion of the reliability issues in distributed database systems. [Hadzilacos, 1988] is a formalization of the reliability concept. The reliability aspects of System R* are given in [Traiger et al., 1982], whereas [Hammer and Shipman, 1980] describe the same for the SDD-1 system.

The two-phase commit protocol is first described in [Gray, 1979]. Modifications to it are presented in [Mohan and Lindsay, 1983]. The definition of three-phase commit is due to Skeen [Skeen, 1981], [Skeen, 1982b]. Formal results on the existence of nonblocking termination protocols is due to [Skeen and Stonebraker, 1983].

Replication and replica control protocols have been the subject of significant research in recent years. This work is summarized very well in [Helal et al., 1997]. Replica control protocols that deal with network partitioning are surveyed in [Davidson et al., 1985]. Besides the algorithms we have described here, some notable others are given in [Davidson, 1984], [Eager and Sevcik, 1983], [Herlihy, 1987], [Minoura and Wiederhold, 1982], [Skeen and Wright, 1984], [Wright, 1983]. These algorithms are generally called *static* since the vote assignments and read/write quorums are fixed a priori. An analysis of one such protocol (such analyses are rare) is given in [Kumar and Segev, 1993]. Examples of *dynamic replication protocols* are in [Jajodia and Mutchler, 1987], [Barbara et al., 1986], [Barbara et al., 1989] among others. It is also possible to change the way data are replicated. Such protocols are called *adaptive* and one example is described in [Wolfson, 1987]. An interesting replication algorithm based on economic models is described in [Sidell et al., 1996].

Our discussion of checkpointing has been rather short. Further treatment of the issue can be found in [Bhargava and Lian, 1988], [Dadam and Schlageter, 1980], [Schlageter and Dadam, 1980], [Kuss, 1982], [Ng, 1988], [Ramanathan and Shin, 1988]. Byzantine agreement is surveyed in [Strong and Dolev, 1983] and is discussed in [Babaoglu, 1987], [Pease et al., 1980].

12.11 EXERCISES

12.1 Briefly describe the various implementations of the process pairs concept. Comment on how process pairs may be useful in implementing a fault-tolerant distributed DBMS.

*12.2 Discuss the site failure termination protocol for 2PC using a distributed communication topology.

*12.3 Design a 3PC protocol using the linear communication topology.

*12.4 In our presentation of the centralized 3PC termination protocol, the first step involves sending the coordinator's state to all participants. The participants move to new states according to the coordinator's state. It is possible to design the termination protocol such that the coordinator, instead of sending its own state information to the participants, asks the participants to send their state information to the coordinator. Modify the termination protocol to function in this manner.

**12.5 In Section 12.8 we claimed that a scheduler which implements a strict concurrency control algorithm will always be ready to commit a transaction when it receives the coordinator's "prepare" message. Prove this claim.

**12.6 Assuming that the coordinator is implemented as part of the transaction manager and the participant as part of the scheduler, give the transaction manager, scheduler, and the local recovery manager algorithms for a non-replicated distributed DBMS under the following assumptions.

(a) The scheduler implements a distributed (strict) two-phase locking concurrency control algorithm.

(b) The commit protocol log records are written to a central database log by the LRM when it is called by the scheduler.

(c) The LRM may implement any of the protocols that have been discussed in Section 12.4.3. However, it is modified to support the distributed recovery procedures as we discussed in Section 12.8.

*12.7 Write the detailed algorithms for the no-fix/no-flush local recovery manager.

**12.8 Assume that

(a) The scheduler implements a centralized two-phase locking concurrency control,

(b) The LRM implements no-fix/no-flush protocol. Give detailed algorithms for the transaction manager, scheduler, and local recovery managers.

12.9 Consider data items x and y replicated across the sites as follows:

Site 1	Site 2	Site 3	Site 4
x	x		x
	y	y	y

(a) Assign votes to each site and give the read and write quorum.

(b) Determine the possible ways that the network can partition and for each specify in which group of sites a transaction that updates (reads and writes) x can be terminated and what the termination condition would be.

(c) Repeat **(b)** for y.

**12.10 Give the algorithm of a replica control protocol that implements the quorum-based voting protocol discussed in Section 12.7.2.

Chapter 13

PARALLEL DATABASE SYSTEMS

Distribution usually implies a number of computers connected by a wide area or a local area network. In the previous chapters, we have considered networks of general-purpose computers that can execute both application programs and distributed database management functions. This assumption has facilitated the presentation of generic principles for distributed data management. However, the increasing use of powerful personal computers, workstations and parallel computers in distributed systems has a major impact on distributed database technology.

The integration of workstations in a distributed environment enables a more efficient function distribution in which application programs run on workstations, called *application servers*, while database functions are handled by dedicated computers, called *database servers*. In addition there can be *client servers* to run the user interface. This leads to the present trend in three-tier distributed system architecture, where sites are organized as specialized servers rather than as general-purpose computers.

A parallel computer, or multiprocessor, is itself a distributed system made of a number of nodes (processors and memories) connected by a fast network within a cabinet. Distributed database technology can be naturally revised and extended to implement *parallel database systems*, i.e., database systems on parallel computers [DeWitt and Gray, 1992], [Valduriez, 1992]. Parallel database systems exploit the parallelism in data management [Boral, 1988a] in order to deliver high-performance and high-availability database servers at a much lower price than equivalent mainframe computers.

Research on parallel database systems has been initiated in the context of the relational model, which explains why all commercial products are SQL-based. In this chapter, we present the parallel database system approach as a solution to high-performance and high-availability distributed database management. The objectives are to exhibit the advantages and disadvantages of the various parallel system architectures and to present the generic implementation techniques.

This chapter marks the beginning of the relaxation of the assumptions we made in Chapter 1. here we relax the assumptions about the nature of computers and interconnection between them. In subsequent chapters, we relax others.

This chapter is organized as follows. In Section 13.1, we present the objectives of the database server approach and of the integration of database servers and application servers in a distributed database. In Section 13.5, we make precise the objectives, the functional and architectural aspects of parallel database systems. In particular, we discuss the respective advantages and limitations of the parallel system architectures along several important dimensions including the perspective of both end-users, database administrators and system developers. In Section 13.3, we present the implementation techniques for data placement, data processing, query optimization and load balancing. In Section 13.4, we focus on the problems of parallel query execution for which we provide a complete solution in Section 14.3 in the context of hierarchical architectures.

13.1 DATABASE SERVERS

In this section we introduce the database server approach, which enables distributed applications to access a remote database server. We also discuss their use in distributed databases.

13.1.1 Database Server Approach

Typically, a DBMS runs as a system program on a computer, which is shared by other system and application programs. This traditional approach has several shortcomings. As a result of the recent advances in database theory and technology, the size of the databases and the variety of applications have significantly increased. Nowadays, some databases have several hundred gigabytes or even several terabytes of data. Their management by a general-purpose computer may result in poor utilization of computer resources shared between applications and other complex software programs with different requirements. For example, the DBMS can easily congest the main memory with useless data and saturate the central processor when selecting the relevant data. This approach is inefficient because the general-purpose operating system does not satisfy the particular requirements of database management. This situation stems from the excessive centralization of data and application management functions in the same computer.

A solution to that problem appeared in the early 1970s [Canaday et al., 1974]. The idea is to offload the central processor by isolating the database management functions from the main computer and grouping them in another computer dedicated to their execution. The main computer executing the application programs was termed the *host computer*; the dedicated computer was called the *database machine, database computer*, or *backend computer*. We will use, instead, the more recent terms *application server* for the host computer and *database server* for the dedicated computer. Today, application servers can be anything from a personal computer or workstation to a more general-purpose computer connected to client servers such as personal computers or network computers. Figure 13.1 illustrates a simple view of the database server approach, with application servers connected to one database server via a communication network. This follows the architectural model of Figure 4.7, with the user processor and data processor functions performed by the application server and database server, respectively. The application server manages the application which includes the user interface and the parsing of user queries to be submitted to the database server, and manages the interface and communication with the database server for sending commands and receiving results. The application servers may also run other system and application programs. The database server manages the interface and communication with the application server and performs the database functions.

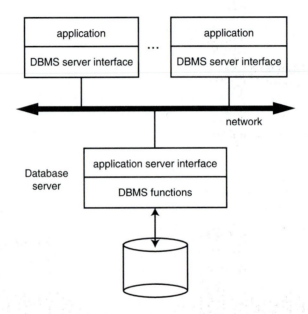

Figure 13.1. Database Server Approach

The database server approach has several potential advantages. First, the single focus on data makes possible the development of specific techniques for increasing data reliability and availability. Second, the overall performance of database management can be significantly enhanced by the tight integration of the database system and a dedicated database operating system. Third, a database server fits naturally in a client-server or distributed environment. Finally, a database server can also exploit recent hardware architectures, such as multiprocessor computers to enhance both performance and data availability.

Although these advantages are significant, they can be offset by the overhead introduced by the additional communication between the application and the data servers. For example, accessing the database server one record at a time may incur a prohibitive communication cost since at least two messages must be exchanged for each record that is useful to the application program. The communication cost can be amortized only if the server interface is sufficiently high level to allow the expression of complex queries involving intensive data processing. The relational model, which favors set-oriented manipulation of data, has therefore been the natural data model supported by the database server approach. As a result, most commercial database servers today are relational.

13.1.2 Database Servers and Distributed Databases

The centralized server approach enables distributed applications to access a single database server efficiently. It is often a cost-effective alternative to distributed databases, whereby all the difficult problems of distributed database management disappear at the local database server level. However, this centralized approach is likely to suffer from the traditional limitations of centralized databases. The addition of new application servers in a local network is technically easy but may require the expansion of the database server's processing power and storage capacity. Furthermore, the access to a single data server from geographically distant application servers is inefficient because communication over a wide area network is relatively slow.

The natural solution to these problems is to combine the database server and distributed database technologies in what could be termed *distributed database server organization*. Figure 13.2 shows a simple example of this organization, in which application servers and database servers are extended with a distributed DBMS component. The distributed database server organization can accommodate a large variety of configurations, each being application dependent. For example, in a geographically distributed distributed database whose sites are connected by a wide area network, each site can consist of a single database server connected by a local network to a cluster of workstations. Any workstation could access the data at any database server through either the local network (local access) or the wide area network (remote access).

The application servers may remain unchanged from the centralized database server approach. In this case a database query is always submitted to the local server, which is in charge of all distributed query processing. An alternative which is illustrated in Figure 13.2 is to have a distributed database interface at the application servers to provide distributed query processing and distributed transaction control. This avoids the systematic access to a single database server in order to retrieve from a remote database server. Although more complex, this solution more efficiently supports configurations where several database servers are connected by a local network.

In the distributed server organization, each database server is fully dedicated to distributed and centralized database management. Therefore, a first solution to improve performance is to implement the DBMS and distributed DBMS modules on top of a distributed database operating system running on a traditional (uniprocessor) computer. Another solution goes one step further and uses a parallel database system.

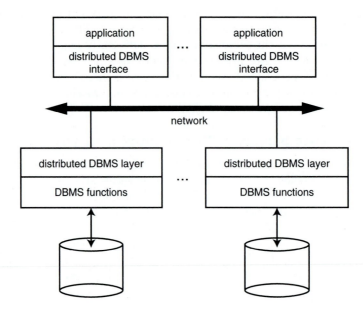

Figure 13.2. Distributed Database Servers

13.2 PARALLEL ARCHITECTURES

In this section we demonstrate the value of parallel systems for efficient database management. We motivate the needs for parallel database systems by reviewing the requirements of very large information systems using current hardware technology. We present the functional and architectural aspects of parallel database systems. In particular, we present and compare the conventional architectures: shared-memory, shared-disk and shared-nothing architectures [Bergsten et al., 1992] and the hybrid exemplified by hierarchical and non-uniform memory access (NUMA) architectures [Graefe, 1993].

13.2.1 Objectives

Parallel processing exploits multiprocessor computers to run application programs by using several processors cooperatively, in order to improve performance. Its prominent use has long been in scientific computing by improving the response time of numerical applications [Kowalik, 1985], [Sharp, 1987]. The recent developments in both general-purpose MIMD parallel computers using standard microprocessors and parallel programming techniques [Osterhaug, 1989] have enabled parallel processing to break into the data processing field.

Parallel database systems combine database management and parallel processing to increase performance and availability. Note that performance was also the objective of the *database machines* (DBMs) in the 70s and 80s [Hsiao, 1983]. The problem faced by conventional database management has long been known as "I/O bottleneck" [Boral and DeWitt, 1983], induced by high disk access time with respect to main memory access time (typically hundreds of thousands times faster). Initially, DBM designers tackled this problem through special-purpose hardware (e.g., by introducing data filtering devices within the disk). However, they failed because of a poor price/performance when compared to the software solution which can easily benefit from hardware progress in silicon technology. A notable exception to these failures is the CAFS-ISP filtering device [Babb, 1979] which is bundled within ICL disk controllers for fast associative search and can be used by the IN-GRES system (when the optimizer decides to do so).

An important result of DBM research, however, is in the general solution to the I/O bottleneck. We can summarize this solution as *increasing the I/O bandwidth through parallelism*. For instance, if we store a database of size D on a single disk with throughput T, the system throughput is bounded by T. On the contrary, if we partition the database across n disks, each with capacity D/n and throughput T' (hopefully equivalent to T), we get an ideal throughput of $n * T'$ which can be better consumed by multiple processors (ideally n). Note that the main memory database system solution [Eich, 1989] which tries to maintain the database in main memory is complementary rather than alternative. In particular, the "memory access bottleneck" can also be tackled using parallelism in a similar way.

Therefore, parallel database system designers strived to develop software-oriented solutions in order to exploit multiprocessor hardware. The objectives of parallel database systems can be achieved by extending distributed database technology, for example, by partitioning the database across multiple (small) disks so that much inter- and intra-query parallelism can be obtained. This can lead to significant improvements in both response time and throughput (number of transactions per second). Motivated by set-oriented processing and application portability, most of the work in this area has focused on supporting SQL. Some relational database products implement this approach, e.g., Teradata's DBC and Tandem's NonStopSQL and the number of such products will increase as the market for general-purpose parallel computers expands. In fact, there are now excellent implementations of existing DBMSs such as INFORMIX and ORACLE on parallel computers.

A parallel database system can be loosely defined as a DBMS implemented on a tightly-coupled multiprocessor. This definition includes many alternatives ranging from the straightforward porting of an existing DBMS, which may require only rewriting the operating system interface routines, to a sophisticated combination of parallel processing and database system functions into a new hardware/software architecture. As always, we have the traditional trade-off between portability (to several platforms) and efficiency. The sophisticated approach is better able to fully exploit the opportunities offered by a multiprocessor at the expense of portability. Interestingly, this gives different advantages to computer manufacturers and software vendors. It is therefore important to characterize the main points in the space of alternative parallel system architectures. In order to do so, we will make precise the parallel database system solution and the necessary functions. This will be useful in comparing the parallel database system architectures.

13.2.2 Functional Aspects

A parallel database system acts as a database server for multiple application servers in the now common client-server organization in computer networks. The parallel database system supports the database functions and the client-server interface, and possibly general-purpose functions. The latter capability distinguishes a parallel database system from a database machine which is fully dedicated to database management and cannot, for instance, run a C program written by a user. To limit the potential communication overhead between client and server, a high-level powerful interface (set-at-a-time rather than record-at-a-time) that encourages data-intensive processing by the server is necessary.

Ideally, a parallel database system should provide the following advantages with a much better price/performance than its mainframe counterparts. To some extent, these advantages are also those of distributed database systems.

1. **High-performance.** This can be obtained through several complementary solutions: database-oriented operating system support, parallelism, optimization, and load balancing. Having the operating system constrained and "aware" of the specific database requirements (e.g., buffer management) simplifies the implementation of low-level database functions and therefore decreases their cost. For instance, the cost of a message can be significantly reduced to a few hundred of instructions by specializing the communication protocol. Parallelism can increase throughput, using inter-query parallelism, and decrease transaction response times, using intra-query parallelism. However, decreasing the response time of a complex query through large-scale parallelism may well increase its total time (by additional communication) and hurt throughput as a side-effect. Therefore, it is crucial to optimize and parallelize queries in order to minimize the overhead of parallelism, e.g., by constraining the degree of parallelism for the query. Load balancing is the ability of the system to divide a given workload equally among all processors. Depending on the multiprocessor architecture, it can be achieved by static physical database design or dynamically at run-time.

2. **High-availability.** Because a parallel database system consists of many similar components, it can exploit data replication to increase database availability. In a highly-parallel system with many small disks, the probability of a disk failure at any time can be higher (than in an equivalent mainframe). Therefore, it is essential that a disk failure does not imbalance the load, e.g., by doubling the load on the available copy. Solutions to this problem require partitioning copies in such a way that they can also be accessed in parallel [Hsiao and DeWitt, 1991].

3. **Extensibility.** In a parallel environment, accommodating increasing database sizes or increasing performance demands (e.g., throughput) should be easier. Extensibility is the ability of smooth expansion of the system by adding processing and storage power to the system. Ideally, the parallel database system should demonstrate two advantages [DeWitt and Gray, 1992]: *linear scaleup* and *linear speedup*. Linear scaleup refers to a sustained performance for a linear increase in both database size and processing and storage power. Linear speedup refers to a linear increase in performance for a constant database size and linear increase in processing and storage power. Furthermore, extending the system should require minimal reorganization of the existing database. Linear scaleup and linear speedup are not appropriate objectives for distributed DBMS.

Assuming a client-server architecture, the functions supported by a parallel database system can be divided into three subsystems much like in a typical RDBMS. The differences, though, have to do with implementation of these functions which must now deal with parallelism, data partitioning and replication, and distributed transactions. Depending on the architecture, a processor can support all (or a subset) of these subsystems. Figure 13.3 shows the architecture using these subsystems named after [Bergsten et al., 1991].

1. **Session Manager.** It plays the role of a transaction monitor (like TUXEDO [Andrade, 1989]), providing support for client interactions with the server. In particular, it performs the connections and disconnections between the client processes and the two other subsystems. Therefore, it initiates and closes user sessions (which may contain multiple transactions). In case of OLTP sessions, the session manager is able to trigger the execution of pre-loaded transaction code within data manager modules.

2. **Request Manager.** It receives client requests related to query compilation and execution. It can access the database directory which holds all meta-information about data and programs. The directory itself should be managed as a database in the server. Depending on the request, it activates the various compilation phases, triggers query execution and returns the results as well as error codes to the client application. Because it supervises transaction execution and commit, it may trigger the recovery procedure in case of transaction failure. To speed up query execution, it may optimize and parallelize the query at compile-time.

3. **Data Manager.** It provides all the low-level functions needed to run compiled queries in parallel, i.e., database operator execution, parallel transaction support, cache management, etc. If the request manager is able to compile dataflow control, then synchronization and communication among data manager modules is possible. Otherwise, transaction control and synchronization must be done by a request manager module.

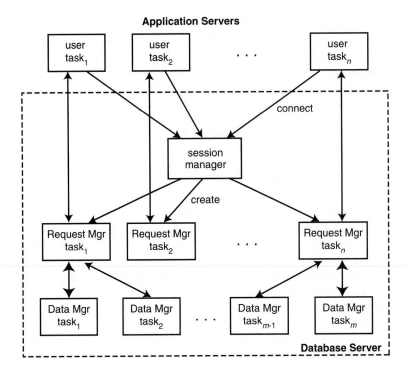

Figure 13.3. General Architecture of a Parallel Database System

13.2.3 Parallel System Architectures

A parallel system represents a compromise in design choices in order to provide the aforementioned advantages with a better cost/performance. One guiding design decision is the way hardware components, i.e., processors, memories, and disks, are interconnected through some fast communication medium. Parallel system architectures range between two extremes, the *shared-memory* and the *shared-nothing* architectures, and a useful intermediate point is the *shared-disk* architecture [Pirahesh et al., 1990]. More recently, hybrid architectures such as *hierarchical* or *NUMA* architectures try to combine the benefits of shared-memory and shared-nothing.

Shared-Memory

In the shared-memory approach (see Figure 13.4), any processor has access to any memory module or disk unit through a fast interconnect (e.g., a high-speed bus or a cross-bar switch). Several new mainframe designs such as the IBM3090, and symmetric multiprocessors such as Sequent and Bull's Escala follow this approach.

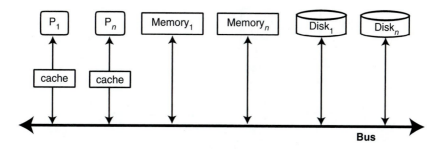

Figure 13.4. Shared-Memory Architecture

Examples of shared-memory parallel database systems include XPRS [Hong, 1992], DBS3 [Bergsten et al., 1991], and Volcano [Graefe, 1990], as well as portings of major commercial DBMSs on shared-memory multiprocessors. In a sense, the implementation of DB2 on an IBM3090 with 6 processors [Cheng et al., 1984] was the first example. Most shared-memory commercial products today can exploit inter-query parallelism to provide high transaction throughput and intra-query parallelism to reduce response time of decision-support queries.

Shared-memory has two strong advantages: simplicity and load balancing. Since meta-information (directory) and control information (e.g., lock table) can be shared by all processors, writing database software is not very different than for single-processor computers. In particular, inter-query parallelism comes for free. Intra-query parallelism requires some parallelization but remains rather simple. Load balancing is excellent since it can be achieved at run-time using the shared-memory.

Shared-memory has three problems: cost, limited extensibility and low availability. High cost is incurred by the interconnect which is fairly complex because of the need to link each processor to each memory module or disk. With faster processors (even with larger caches), conflicting accesses to the shared-memory increase rapidly and degrade performance [Thakkar and Sweiger, 1990]. Therefore, extensibility is limited to tens of processors (20 on a Sequent or Encore). Finally, since the memory space is shared by all processors, a memory fault may affect most processors thereby hurting database availability. A solution is to use duplex memory as in Sequoia systems.

Shared-Disk

In the shared-disk approach (see Figure 13.5), any processor has access to any disk unit through the interconnect but exclusive (non-shared) access to its main memory. Then, each processor can access database pages on the shared disk and copy them into its own cache. To avoid conflicting accesses to the same pages, global locking and protocols for the maintenance of cache coherency are needed [Mohan, 1991].

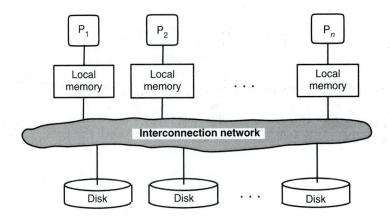

Figure 13.5. Shared-Disk Architecture

Examples of shared-disk parallel database systems include IBM's IMS/VS Data Sharing product and DEC's VAX DBMS and Rdb products. The implementation of ORACLE on DEC's VAXcluster and NCUBE computers is also using the shared-disk approach since it requires minimal extensions of the RDBMS kernel.

Shared-disk has a number of advantages: cost, extensibility, load balancing, availability, and easy migration from uniprocessor systems. The cost of the inter-connect is significantly less than with shared-memory since standard bus technology may be used. Given that each processor has enough cache memory, interference on the shared disk can be minimized. Thus, extensibility can be better (in the hundreds of processors). Since memory faults can be isolated from other processor-memory nodes, availability can be higher. Finally, migrating from a centralized system to shared-disk is relatively straightforward since the data on disk need not be reorganized.

Shared-disk suffers from higher complexity and potential performance problems. It requires distributed database system protocols, such as distributed locking and two-phase commit. As we have discussed in previous chapters, these can be complex. Furthermore, maintaining the coherency of the copies can incur high communication overhead among the nodes. Finally, access to the shared-disk is a potential bottleneck.

Shared-Nothing

In the shared-nothing approach (see Figure 13.6), each processor has exclusive access to its main memory and disk unit(s). Then, each node can be viewed as a local site (with its own database and software) in a distributed database system. Therefore, most solutions designed for distributed databases such as database fragmentation, distributed transaction management and distributed query processing may be reused.

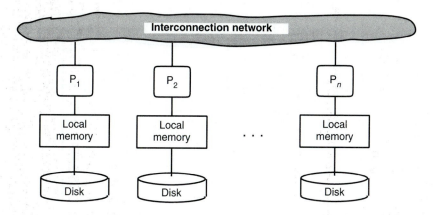

Figure 13.6. Shared-Nothing Architecture

Examples of shared-nothing parallel database systems include the Teradata's DBC and Tandem's NonStopSQL products as well as a number of prototypes such as BUBBA [Boral et al., 1990], EDS [EDS, 1990], GAMMA [DeWitt et al., 1986], GRACE [Fushimi et al., 1986], and PRISMA [Apers et al., 1992].

As demonstrated by the existing products, e.g., [Tandem, 1988], shared-nothing has three main virtues: cost, extensibility, and availability. The cost advantage is the same as for shared-disk. By implementing a distributed database design which favors the smooth incremental growth of the system by the addition of new nodes, extensibility can be better (in the thousands of nodes). For instance, Teradata's DBC can accommodate 1024 processors. With careful partitioning of the data on multiple disks, linear speedup and linear scaleup could be achieved for simple workloads. By replicating data on multiple nodes, high availability can be also achieved.

Shared-nothing is also more complex than shared-memory. Higher complexity is due to the necessary implementation of distributed database functions assuming large numbers of nodes. In addition, load balancing is more difficult to achieve because it relies on the effectiveness of database partitioning for the query workloads. Unlike shared-memory and shared-disk, load balancing is decided based on data location and not the actual load of the system. Furthermore, the addition of new nodes in the system presumably requires reorganizing the database to deal with the load balancing issues.

Hierarchical Architectures

Hierarchical architecture (also called *cluster architecture*), is a combination of shared-nothing and shared-memory. The idea is to build a shared-nothing machine whose nodes are shared-memory. This architecture was first proposed by Bhide [Bhide, 1988], then by Pirahesh [Pirahesh et al., 1990] and Boral [Boral et

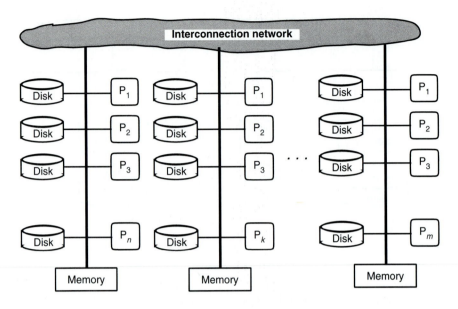

Figure 13.7. Hierarchical Architecture

al., 1990]. A detailed description is proposed by Graefe [Graefe, 1993] and shown in Figure 13.7.

The advantages of such an architecture are evident. It combines flexibility and performance of shared-memory with high extensibility of shared-nothing. In each shared-memory node (SM-node), communication is done efficiently using the shared-memory, thus increasing performance. Finally, load balancing is eased by the shared-memory component of this architecture.

As an evidence, symmetric multiprocessors (SMP), e.g., Sequent, are moving to scalable cluster architectures, while massively parallel processors (MPP), e.g., NCR's Teradata, are evolving to use shared-memory nodes. Another example is Bull's PowerCluster which is a cluster of PowerPC-based SMP nodes.

NUMA Architectures

With the same goal of combining extensibility and flexibility, shared-memory multiprocessors are evolving towards NUMA architectures. The objective is to provide a shared-memory programming model and all its benefits, in a scalable parallel architecture.

Two classes of NUMA architecture have emerged: Cache Coherent NUMA machines (CC-NUMA) [Goodman and Woest, 1988], [Lenoski et al., 1992], which statically divide the main memory among the nodes of the system and Cache Only Memory Architectures (COMA) [Hagersten et al., 1992], [Frank et al., 1993], which

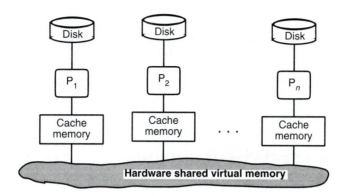

Figure 13.8. Cache Only Memory Architecture (COMA)

convert the per-node memory into a large cache of the shared address space. Thus, the location of a data item is fully decoupled from its physical address and the data item is automatically migrated or replicated in main memory.

Because shared-memory and cache coherency are supported by hardware, remote memory access is very efficient, only several times (typically 4 times) the cost of local access (See Figure 13.8).

NUMA is now based on international standards and off-the-shelf components. For instance, the Data General nuSMP machine and the Sequent NUMA-Q 2000 are using the ANSI/IEEE Standard Scalable Coherent Interface (SCI) [IEEE, 1992] to interconnect multiple Intel Standard High Volume (SHV) server nodes. Each SHV node consists of 4 Pentium Pro processors, up to 4 gigabytes of memory and dual peer PCI/IO subsystems [Intel, 1997], [Data General, 1997c]. Other examples of NUMA computers are Kendal Square Research's KSR1 and Convex's SPP1200 which can scale up to hundreds of processors.

The "strong" argument for NUMA is that it does not require any rewriting of application software. However some rewriting is necessary in the operating system and in the database engine [Bouganim et al., 1999]. In response to the nuSMP announcement from Data General, SCO has provided a NUMA version of Unix called Gemini [Data General, 1997b], Oracle has modified its kernel [Data General, 1997a] in order to optimize the use of 64 Gbytes of main memory allowed by NUMA multiprocessors.

Comparisons

Let us briefly compare these alternative design approaches based on their potential advantages (high-performance, high-availability, and extensibility). It is fair to say that, for a small configuration (e.g., less than 20 processors), shared-memory can provide the highest performance because of better load balancing [Bhide, 1988].

Distributed architectures outperform shared-memory in terms of extensibility. NUMA has good performance until a high number of processors. Some years ago, shared-nothing was the only choice for high-end systems (e.g., requiring more than thousands of transactions-per-second of the TPC-B benchmark [Gray, 1993]). Today, NUMA seems the best choice for medium systems. The advantage of such architecture is the simple (shared-memory) programmation model which eases database tuning. High-end systems may use hierarchical architectures for better extensibility and availability.

13.3 PARALLEL DBMS TECHNIQUES

Implementation of parallel database systems naturally relies on distributed database techniques. Essentially, the transaction management solutions can be reused. However, the critical issues for such architectures are data placement, query parallelism, parallel data processing and parallel query optimization. The solutions to these issues are more involved than in distributed DBMS because the number of nodes may be much higher. In this section, we assume a shared-nothing architecture because it is the most general case and its implementation techniques also apply to other architectures.

13.3.1 Data Placement

Data placement in a parallel database system exhibits similarities with data fragmentation in distributed databases (see Chapters 5 and 8). An obvious similarity is that fragmentation can be used to increase parallelism. In what follows, we use the terms *partitioning* and *partition* instead of horizontal fragmentation and horizontal fragment respectively, in contrast to the alternative strategy, which consists of *clustering* a relation at a single node. In some papers, e.g., [Livny et al., 1987], the term *declustering* is also used to mean partitioning. Vertical fragmentation can also be used to increase parallelism and load balancing much as in distributed databases. Another similarity is that since data is much larger than programs, programs should be executed as much as possible where the data reside [Khoshafian and Valduriez, 1987]. However, there are two important differences with the distributed database approach. First, there is no need to maximize local processing (at each node) since users are not associated with particular nodes. Second, load balancing is much more difficult to achieve in the presence of a large number of nodes. The main problem is to avoid resource contention, which may result in thrashing the entire system (e.g., one node ends up doing all the work while the others remain idle). Since programs are executed where the data resides, data placement is a critical performance issue.

Data placement must be done to maximize system performance, which can be measured by combining the total amount of work done by the system and the response time of individual queries. In Chapter 9 we have seen that maximizing response time (through intra-query parallelism) results in increased total work due to communication overhead. For the same reason, inter-query parallelism results in increased total work. On the other hand, clustering all the data necessary to a program minimizes communication and thus the total work done by the system in executing that program. In terms of data placement, we have the following trade-off: maximizing response time or inter-query parallelism leads to partitioning, whereas minimizing the total amount of work leads to clustering. As we have seen in Chapter 5, this problem is addressed in distributed databases in a rather static manner. The database administrator is in charge of periodically examining fragment reference frequencies, and when necessary, must move and reorganize fragments.

An alternative solution to data placement is *full partitioning*, whereby each relation is horizontally fragmented across *all* the nodes in the system. Full partitioning is used in the DBC/1012, GAMMA, and NonStop SQL. There are three basic strategies for data partitioning: round-robin, hash, and range partitioning (Figure 13.9).

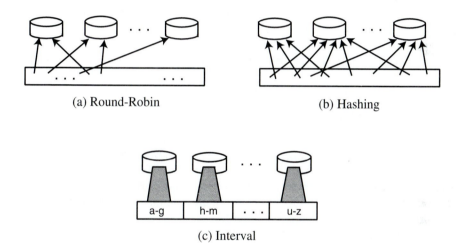

(a) Round-Robin   (b) Hashing

(c) Interval

Figure 13.9. Different Partitioning Schemes

1. *Round-robin partitioning* is the simplest strategy, it ensures uniform data distribution. With n partitions, the ith tuple in insertion order is assigned to partition ($i \bmod n$). This strategy enables the sequential access to a relation to be done in parallel. However, the direct access to individual tuples, based on a predicate, requires accessing the entire relation.

2. *Hash partitioning* applies a hash function to some attribute which yields the partition number. This strategy allows exact-match queries on the selection attribute to be processed by exactly one node and all other queries to be processed by all the nodes in parallel.

3. *Range partitioning* distributes tuples based on the value intervals (ranges) of some attribute. In addition to supporting exact-match queries as with

hashing, it is well-suited for range queries. For instance, a query with a predicate "A between $A1$ and $A2$" may be processed by the only node(s) containing tuples whose A value is in $[A1, A2]$. However, range partitioning can result in high variation in partition size.

In [Livny et al., 1987], the performance of full partitioning is compared to that of clustering the relations on a single disk. The results indicate that for a wide variety of multiuser workloads, partitioning is consistently better. However, clustering may dominate in processing complex queries (e.g., joins). In [Tandem, 1987], the throughput of a system running debit-credit transaction workload [Anon, 1985] in the presence of full partitioning is shown to increase linearly with the number of nodes for up to 32 nodes.

Although full partitioning has obvious performance advantages, high parallel execution might cause a serious performance overhead for complex queries involving joins. For example, in a 1024-node architecture, the worst-case number of messages for a binary join (without select) would be 10,242. Furthermore, full partitioning is not appropriate for small relations that span a few disk blocks. These drawbacks suggest that a compromise between clustering and full partitioning (i.e., *variable partitioning*), needs to be found.

In [Copeland et al., 1988], a solution to data placement by variable partitioning is proposed. The degree of partitioning, in other words, the number of nodes over which a relation is fragmented, is a function of the size and access frequency of the relation. This strategy is much more involved than either clustering or full partitioning because changes in data distribution may result in reorganization. For example, a relation initially placed across eight nodes may have its cardinality doubled by subsequent insertions, in which case it should be placed across 16 nodes.

In a highly parallel system with variable partitioning, periodic reorganizations for load balancing are essential and should be frequent unless the workload is fairly static and experiences only a few updates. Such reorganizations should remain transparent to compiled programs that run on the database server. In particular, programs should not be recompiled because of reorganization. Therefore, the compiled programs should remain independent of data location, which may change rapidly. Such independence can be achieved if the run-time system supports associative access to distributed data. This is different than in a distributed DBMS, where associative access is achieved at compile time by the query processor using the data directory.

One solution to associative access is to have a global index mechanism replicated on each node [Khoshafian and Valduriez, 1987]. The global index indicates the placement of a relation onto a set of nodes. Conceptually, the global index is a two-level index with a major clustering on the relation name and a minor clustering on some attribute of the relation. This global index supports variable partitioning, where each relation has a different degree of partitioning. The index structure can be based on hashing or on a B-tree like organization [Bayer and McCreight, 1972]. In both cases, exact match queries can be processed efficiently with a single node access. However, with hashing, range queries are processed by accessing all the nodes that contain data from the relation queried. Using a B-tree index (usually much larger than a hashed index) enables more efficient processing of range queries, where only the nodes containing data in the specified range are accessed.

Example 13.1

Figure 13.10 provides an example of a global index and a local index for relation EMP(ENO, ENAME, DEPT, TITLE) of the engineering database example we have been using in this book.

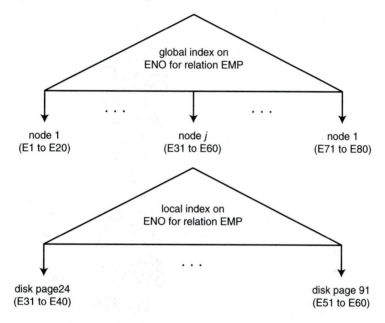

Figure 13.10. Example of Global and Local Indexes

Suppose that we want to locate the elements in relation EMP with ENO value "E50". The first-level index on set name maps the name EMP onto the index on attribute ENO for relation EMP. Then the second-level index further maps the cluster value "E50" onto node number j. A local index within each node is also necessary to map a relation onto a set of disk pages within the node. The local index has two levels, with a major clustering on relation name and a minor clustering on some attribute. The minor clustering attribute for the local index is the *same* as that for the global index. Thus *associative routing* is improved from one node to another based on <relation name, cluster value>. This local index further maps the cluster value "E5" onto page number 91.

[Copeland et al., 1988] provides experimental results for variable partitioning of a workload consisting of a mix of short transactions (debit-credit like) and complex ones. The results indicate that as partitioning is increased, throughput continues to increase for short transactions. However, for complex transactions involving several large joins, further partitioning reduces throughput because of communications overhead.

A serious problem in data placement is dealing with skewed data distributions which may lead to non-uniform partitioning and hurt load balancing. Range partitioning is more sensitive to skew than either round-robin or hash partitioning. A solution is to treat non-uniform partitions appropriately, e.g., by further fragmenting large partitions. The separation between logical and physical nodes is also useful since a logical node may correspond to several physical nodes.

A final complicating factor is data replication for high availability. The simple solution is to maintain two copies of the same data, a primary and a backup copy, on two separate nodes. This is the *mirrored disks* architecture as promoted by Tandem's NonStop SQL system. However, in case of a node failure, the load of the node having the copy may double, thereby hurting load balancing. To avoid this problem, several high-availability data replication strategies have been proposed for parallel database systems [Hsiao and DeWitt, 1991]. An interesting solution is Teradata's interleaved partitioning which partitions the backup copy on a number of nodes (Figure 13.11). In failure mode, the load of the primary copy gets balanced among the backup copy nodes. But if two nodes fail, then the relation cannot be accessed thereby hurting availability. Reconstructing the primary copy from its separate backup copies may be costly. In normal mode, maintaining copy consistency may also be costly.

Node	1	2	3	4
Primary copy	R1	R2	R3	R4
Backup copy		r 1.1	r 1.2	r 1.3
	r 2.3		r 2.1	r 2.2
	r 3.2	r 3.3		r 3.1

Figure 13.11. Example of Interleaved Partitioning

A better solution is Gamma's chained partitioning [Hsiao and DeWitt, 1991] which stores the primary and backup copy on two adjacent nodes (Figure 13.12). The main idea is that the probability that two adjacent nodes fail is much less than the probability that any two nodes fail. In failure mode, the load of the failed node and the backup nodes are balanced among all remaining nodes by using both primary and backup copy nodes. In addition, maintaining copy consistency is cheaper. An open issue remains to perform data placement taking into account data replication. Similar to the fragment allocation in distributed databases, this should be considered an optimization problem.

Node	1	2	3	4
Primary copy	R1	R2	R3	R4
Backup copy	r4	r1	r2	r3

Figure 13.12. Example of Chained Partitioning

13.3.2 Query Parallelism

Inter-query parallelism enables the parallel execution of multiple queries generated by concurrent transactions, in order to increase the transactional throughput. Within a query (*intra-query parallelism*), *inter-operator* and *Intra-operator parallelism* are used to decrease response time. Inter-operator parallelism is obtained by executing in parallel several operators of the query tree on several processors while with intra-operator parallelism, the same operator is executed by many processors, each one working on a subset of the data.

Intra-operator Parallelism

Intra-operator parallelism is based on the decomposition of one operator in a set of independent sub-operators, called *operator instances*. This decomposition is done using static and/or dynamic partitioning of relations. Each operator instance will then process one relation partition also called *bucket*. The operator decomposition frequently benefits from the initial partitioning of the data (e.g., the data is partitioned on the join attribute). To illustrate intra-operator parallelism, let us consider a simple select-join query. The select operator can be directly decomposed into several select operators, each on a different partition and no redistribution is required (Figure 13.13. Note that if the relation is partitioned on the select attribute, partitioning properties can be used to eliminate some select instances. For example, in an exact-match select, only one select instance will be executed if the relation was partitioned by hashing (or range) on the select attribute. For the join operator, it is more complex to decompose the operator. In order to have independent joins, each bucket of the first relation R_i may be joined to the entire relation S. Such a join will be very inefficient (unless if S is very small) because it will imply a broadcast of S on each participating processor. A more efficient way is to use partitioning properties. For example, if R and S are partitioned by hashing on the join attribute and if the join is an equijoin, then we can partition the join into independent joins (see Algorithm 13.3.3 in Section 13.3.3). This is the ideal case which cannot be always used because it depends on the initial partitioning of R and S. In the other cases, one or two operands may be repartitioned [Valduriez and Gardarin, 1984]. Finally, we may notice that the partitioning function (hash, range, round robin) is independent of the local algorithm (e.g., nested loop, hash, sort merge) used to process the join operator (i.e., on each processor). For instance, a hash join using a hash partitioning needs two hash functions. The first one, h_1, is used to partition the two base relations on the join attribute. The second one, h_2, which can be different for each processor, is used to process the join on each processor.

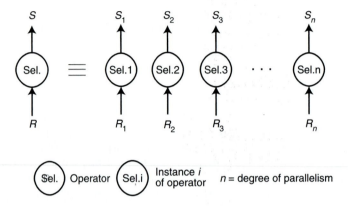

Figure 13.13. Intra-operator Parallelism

Inter-operator Parallelism

Two forms of inter-operator parallelism can be exploited. With *pipeline parallelism*, several operators with a producer-consumer link are executed in parallel. For instance, the select operator in Figure 13.14 will be executed in parallel with the subsequent join operator. The advantage of such execution is that the intermediate result is not materialized, thus saving memory and disk accesses. In the example of Figure 13.14, only S may fit in memory. *Independent parallelism* is achieved when there is no dependency between the operators executed in parallel. For instance, the two select operators of Figure 13.14 can be executed in parallel. This form of parallelism is very attractive because there is no interference between the processors. However, it is only possible for bushy execution (see Section 13.3.4) and may consume more resources [Shekita et al., 1993].

13.3.3 Parallel Data Processing

Partitioned data placement is the basis for the parallel execution of database queries. Given a partitioned data placement, an important issue is the design of parallel algorithms for an efficient processing of database operators (i.e., relational algebra operators) and database queries which combine multiple operators. This issue is difficult because a good trade-off between parallelism and communication cost must be reached. Parallel algorithms for relational algebra operators are the building blocks necessary for parallel query processing.

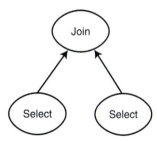

Figure 13.14. Inter-operator Parallelism

Parallel data processing should exploit intra-operator parallelism. As in Chapter 9, we concentrate our presentation of parallel algorithms for database operators on the select and join operators, since all other binary operators (such as union) can be handled very much like join [Bratbersengen, 1984]. The processing of the select operator in a partitioned data placement context is identical to that in a fragmented distributed database. Depending on the select predicate, the operator may be executed at a single node (in the case of an exact match predicate) or in the case of arbitrary complex predicates at all the nodes over which the relation is partitioned. If the global index is organized as a B-tree-like structure (see Figure 13.10), a select operator with a range predicate may be executed only by the nodes storing relevant data.

The parallel processing of join is significantly more involved than that of select. The distributed join algorithms designed for high-speed networks (see Chapter 9) can be applied successfully in a partitioned database context. However, the availability of a global index at run time provides more opportunities for efficient parallel execution. In the following, we introduce three basic parallel join algorithms for partitioned databases: the parallel nested loop (PNL) algorithm, the parallel associative join (PAJ) algorithm, and the parallel hash join (PHJ) algorithm. We describe each using a pseudo-concurrent programming language with three main constructs: **do-in-parallel, send**, and **receive**. **Do-in-parallel** specifies that the following block of actions is executed in parallel. For example,

```
for i from 1 to n do in parallel action A
```

indicates that the action A is to be executed by n nodes in parallel. **Send** and **receive** are the basic communication primitives to transfer data between nodes. **Send** enables data to be sent from one node to one or more nodes. The destination nodes are typically obtained from the global index. **Receive** gets the content of the data sent to a particular node. In what follows we consider the join of two relations R and S that are partitioned over m and n nodes, respectively. For the sake of simplicity, we assume that the m nodes are distinct from the n nodes. A node at which a fragment of R (respectively, S) resides is called an R-node (respectively, S-node).

The parallel nested loop algorithm [Bitton et al., 1983] is the simplest one and the most general. It basically composes the Cartesian product of the relations R and S in parallel. Therefore, arbitrarily complex join predicates may be supported. This algorithm has been introduced in Chapter 9 in the context of Distributed INGRES. It is more precisely described in Algorithm 13.1, where the join result is produced at the S-nodes. The algorithm proceeds in two phases.

Algorithm 13.1 *PNL*
    input: $R_1, R_2, \ldots, R_m$: fragments of relation R;
             $S_1, S_2, \ldots, S_n$: fragments of relation S;
             JP: join predicate
    output:$T_1, T_2, \ldots, T_n$: result fragments
    begin
        for i **from** 1 **to** m **do in parallel**   {send R entirely to each S-node}
          send R_i to each node containing a fragment of S
        end-for
        for j **from** 1 **to** n **do in parallel**   {perform the join at each S-node}
        begin
          $R \leftarrow \bigcup_{i=1}^{m} R_i$ {receive R_i from R-nodes; R is replicated on $S - nodes$}
          $T_j \leftarrow \mathrm{JOIN}(R, S_j, JP)$ {JOIN is a generic function}
        end-for
    end. {PNL}

In the first phase, each fragment of R is sent and replicated at each node containing a fragment of S (there are n such nodes). This phase is done in parallel by m nodes and is efficient if the communication network has a broadcast capability. In this case each fragment of R can be broadcast to n nodes in a single transfer, thereby incurring a total communication cost of m messages. Otherwise, $(m * n)$ messages are necessary.

In the second phase, each S-node j receives relation R entirely, and locally joins R with the fragment S_j. This phase is done in parallel by n nodes. The local join can be done as in a centralized DBMS. Depending on the local join algorithm, join processing may or may not start as soon as data are received. In the first case (e.g., with the nested loop join algorithm), join processing can be done in a pipelined fashion as soon as a tuple of R arrives. In the latter case (e.g., with the sort merge join algorithm), all the data must have been received before the join of the sorted relations begins.

To summarize, the parallel nested loop algorithm can be viewed as replacing the operator $R \bowtie S$ by

$$\bigcup_{i=1}^{n}(R \bowtie S_i)$$

Example 13.2

Figure 13.15 shows the application of the parallel nested loop algorithm with $m = n = 2$.

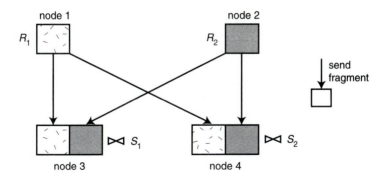

Figure 13.15. Example of Parallel Nested Loop

The parallel associative join algorithm, shown in Algorithm 13.2, applies only in the case of equijoin with one of the operand relations partitioned according to the join attribute. To simplify the description of the algorithm, we assume that the equijoin predicate is on attribute A from R, and B from S. Furthermore, relation S is partitioned according to the hash function h applied to join attribute B, meaning that all the tuples of S that have same value for $h(B)$ are placed at the same node. No knowledge of how R is partitioned is assumed. The application of the parallel associative join algorithm will produce the join result at the nodes where S_i exists (i.e., the S-nodes).

Algorithm 13.2 *PAJ*

    input: $R_1, R_2, \ldots, R_m$: fragments of relation R;
               $S_1, S_2, \ldots, S_n$: fragments of relation S;
               JP: join predicate
    output: $T_1, T_2, \ldots, T_n$: result fragments
    begin   {we assume that JP is $R.A = S.B$ and relation S is fragmented
                                      according to the function $h(B)$}
      for i **from** 1 **to** m **do in parallel** {send R associatively to each S-node}
      begin
            $R_{ij} \leftarrow$ apply $h(A)$ to R_i $(j = 1, \ldots, n)$
            for j **from** 1 **to** n **do**
               send R_{ij} to the node storing S_j
            end-for
      end-for

      for j **from** 1 **to** n **do in parallel**   {perform the join at each S-node}
      begin
            $R_j \leftarrow \bigcup_{i=1}^{m} R_{ij}$ {receive only the useful subset of R}
            $T_j \leftarrow \text{JOIN}(R_j, S_j, JP)$
      end-for
    end. {PAJ}

The algorithm proceeds in two phases. In the first phase, relation R is sent associatively to the S-nodes based on the function h applied to attribute A. This guarantees that a tuple of R with hash value v is sent only to the S-node that contains tuples with hash value v. The first phase is done in parallel by m nodes where R_i's exist. Unlike the parallel nested loop algorithm, the tuples of R get distributed but not replicated across the S-nodes. In the second phase, each S-node j receives in parallel the relevant subset of R, (i.e., R_j), and joins it locally with the fragments S_j. Local join processing can be done as in the parallel nested loop join algorithm.

To summarize, the parallel associative join algorithm replaces the operator $R \bowtie S$ by

$$\bigcup_{i=1}^{n} (R_i \bowtie S_i)$$

Example 13.3

Figure 13.16 shows the application of the parallel associative join algorithm with $m = n = 2$. The squares that are hatched with the same pattern indicate fragments whose tuples match the same hash function.

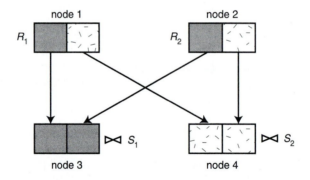

Figure 13.16. Example of Parallel Associative Join

The parallel hash join algorithm, shown in Algorithm 13.3, can be viewed as a generalization of the parallel associative join algorithm. It also applies in the case of equijoin but does not require any particular partitioning of the operand relations. The basic idea is to partition relations R and S into the same number p of mutually exclusive sets (fragments) $R_1, R_2, \ldots, R_p$, and $S_1, S_2, \ldots, S_p$, such that

$$R \bowtie S = \bigcup_{i=1}^{p} (R_i \bowtie S_i)$$

Algorithm 13.3 *PHJ*

> **input:** $R_1, R_2, \ldots, R_m$: fragments of relation R;
> $\quad\quad\quad\;\, S_1, S_2, \ldots, S_n$: fragments of relation S;
> $\quad\quad\quad\;\, JP$: join predicate
> **output:** $T_1, T_2, \ldots, T_n$: result fragments
> **begin**   {we assume that JP is $R.A = S.B$ and h is a hash function
> $\quad\quad\quad\quad\quad\quad\quad\quad\quad\quad\quad$ that returns an element of $[1, p]$}
> $\quad$ **for** i **from** 1 **to** m **do in parallel**   {hash R on the join attribute}
> $\quad$ **begin**
> $\quad\quad$ $R_{ij} \leftarrow$ apply $h(A)$ to R_i $(j = 1, \ldots, p)$
> $\quad\quad$ **for** j **from** 1 **to** p **do**
> $\quad\quad\quad$ send R_{ij} to node j
> $\quad\quad$ **end-for**
> $\quad$ **end-for**
>
> $\quad$ **for** i **from** 1 **to** n **do in parallel**   {hash S on the join attribute}
> $\quad$ **begin**
> $\quad\quad$ $S_{ij} \leftarrow$ apply $h(B)$ to S_i $(j = 1, \ldots, p)$
> $\quad\quad$ **for** j **from** 1 **to** p **do**
> $\quad\quad\quad$ send S_{ij} to node j
> $\quad\quad$ **end-for**
> $\quad$ **end-for**
>
> $\quad$ **for** j **from** 1 **to** p **do in parallel** {perform the join at each S-node}
> $\quad$ **begin**
> $\quad\quad$ $R_j \leftarrow \bigcup_{i=1}^{p} R_{ij}$ $\quad\quad\quad\quad\quad\quad\quad\quad$ {receive from R-nodes}
> $\quad\quad$ $S_j \leftarrow \bigcup_{i=1}^{p} S_{ij}$ $\quad\quad\quad\quad\quad\quad\quad\quad$ {receive from S-nodes}
> $\quad\quad$ $T_j \leftarrow \text{JOIN}(R_j, S_j, JP)$
> $\quad$ **end-for**
> **end.** {PAJ}

As in the parallel associative join algorithm, the partitioning of R and S can be based on the same hash function applied to the join attribute. Each individual join $(R_i \bowtie S_i)$ is done in parallel, and the join result is produced at p nodes. These p nodes may actually be selected at run time based on the load of the system. The main difference with the parallel associative join algorithm is that partitioning of S is necessary and the result is produced at p nodes rather than at n S-nodes.

Example 13.4

Figure 13.17 shows the application of the parallel hash join algorithm with $m = n = 2$. We assumed that the result is produced at nodes 1 and 2. Therefore, an arrow from node 1 to node 1 or node 2 to node 2 indicates a local transfer.

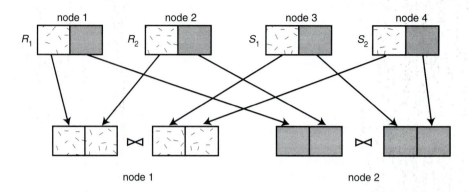

Figure 13.17. Example of Parallel Hash Join

Variations of this algorithm for specific multiprocessor architectures are given in [Valduriez and Gardarin, 1984]. An interesting variation is to divide the algorithm in two phases, a *build* phase and a *probe* phase, in order to pipeline the join result to the subsequent operator [DeWitt and Gerber, 1985]. The build phase hashes R on the join attribute, sends it to the target p nodes which build a hash table for the incoming tuples. The probe phase sends S associatively to the target p nodes which probe the hash table for each incoming tuple. Thus, as soon as the hash tables have been built for R, the S tuples can be sent and processed in pipeline by probing the hash tables.

These parallel join algorithms apply and dominate under different conditions. Join processing is achieved with a degree of parallelism of either n or p. Since each algorithm requires moving at least one of the operand relations, a good indicator of their performance is total cost. To compare these algorithms, we now give a simple analysis of cost, defined in terms of total communication cost, denoted by C_{COM} and processing cost, denoted by C_{PRO}. The total cost of each algorithm is therefore

$$Cost(Alg.) = C_{COM}(Alg.) + C_{PRO}(Alg.)$$

For simplicity, C_{COM} does not include control messages, which are necessary to initiate and terminate local tasks. We denote by $msg(\#tup)$ the cost of transferring a message of $\#tup$ tuples from one node to another. Processing costs (total I/O and CPU cost) will be based on the function $C_{LOC}(m, n)$ which computes the local processing cost for joining two relations of cardinalities m and n. We assume that the local join algorithm is the same for all three parallel join algorithms. Finally, we assume that the amount of work done in parallel is uniformly distributed over all nodes allocated to the operator.

Without broadcasting capability, the parallel nested loop algorithm incurs a cost of $m * n$ messages, where a message contains a fragment of R of size $card(R)/m$. Thus we have

$$C_{COM}(PNL) = m * n * msg\left(\frac{card(R)}{m}\right)$$

Each of the S-nodes must join all of R with its S fragments. Thus we have

$$C_{PRO}(PNL) = n * C_{LOC}(card(R), card(S)/n)$$

The parallel associative join algorithm requires that each R-node partitions a fragment of R into n subsets of size $card(R)/(m * n)$ and sends them to n S-nodes. Thus we have

$$C_{COM}(PAJ) = m * n * msg\left(\frac{card(R)}{m * n}\right) \qquad .$$

and

$$C_{PRO}(PAJ) = n * C_{LOC}(card(R)/n, card(S)/n)$$

The parallel hash join algorithm requires that both relations R and S be partitioned across p nodes in a way similar to the parallel associative join algorithm. Thus we have

$$C_{COM}(PHJ) = m * p * msg\left(\frac{card(R)}{m * p}\right) + n * p * msg\left(\frac{card(S)}{n * p}\right)$$

and

$$C_{PRO}(PHJ) = n * C_{LOC}(card(R)/n, card(S)/n)$$

Let us first assume that $p = n$. In this case the join processing cost for the PAJ and PHJ algorithms is identical. However, it is higher for the PNL algorithm because each S-node must perform the join with R entirely. From the equations above, it is clear that the PAJ algorithm incurs the least communication cost. However, the least communication cost between the PNL and PHJ algorithms depends on the values of relation cardinality and degree of partitioning. If we now choose p so that it is smaller than n, the PHJ algorithm may well incur the least communication cost but at the expense of increased join processing cost. For example, if $p = 1$, the join is processed in a purely centralized way.

In conclusion, the PAJ algorithm is most likely to dominate and should be used when applicable. Otherwise, the choice between the PNL and PHJ algorithms requires estimation of their total cost with the optimal value for p. The choice of a parallel join algorithm can be summarized by the procedure CHOOSE_JA shown in Algorithm 13.4.

Algorithm 13.4 *CHOOSE_JA*

    input: $prof(R)$: profile of relation R;
                $prof(S)$: profile of relation S;
                JP: join predicate
    output:JA: join algorithm
    begin
        if JP is equijoin **then**
            if one relation is partitioned according to the join attribute **then**
                $JA \leftarrow PAJ$
            else if $Cost(PNL) < Cost(PHJ)$ **then**
                $JA \leftarrow PNL$
                else
                    $JA \leftarrow PHJ$
                end-if
            end-if
        else
            $JA \leftarrow PNL$
        end-if
    end. {CHOOSE_JA}

13.3.4 Parallel Query Optimization

Parallel query optimization exhibits similarities with distributed query processing. It should take advantage of both intra-operator parallelism (using the algorithms described above) and inter-operator parallelism. This second objective can be achieved using some of the techniques devised for distributed DBMSs.

Parallel query optimization refers to the process of producing an execution plan for a given query that minimizes an objective cost function. The selected plan is the best one within a set of candidate plans examined by the optimizer, but not necessarily the optimal one among all possible plans. A query optimizer is usually seen as three components: a search space, a cost model, and a search strategy. The *search space* is the set of alternative execution plans to represent the input query. These plans are equivalent, in the sense that they yield the same result but they differ on the execution order of operators and the way these operators are implemented. The *cost model* predicts the cost of a given execution plan. To be accurate, the cost model must have good knowledge about the parallel execution environment. The *search strategy* explores the search space and selects the best plan. It defines which plans are examined and in which order.

Search Space

Execution plans are abstracted, as usual, by means of operator trees, which define the order in which the operators are executed. Operator trees are enriched with *annotations*, which indicate additional execution aspects, such as the algorithm of each operator. An important execution aspect to be reflected by annotations is the fact that two subsequent operators can be executed in *pipeline*. In this case, the second operator can start before the first one is completed. In other words, the second operator starts *consuming* tuples as soon as the first one *produces* them. Pipelined executions do not require temporary relations to be materialized, i.e., a tree node corresponding to an operator executed in pipeline is not *stored*.

Pipeline and store annotations constrain the *scheduling* of execution plans. They split an operator tree into non-overlapping sub-trees, called *phases*. Pipelined operators are executed in the same phase, whereas a storing indication establishes the boundary between one phase and a subsequent phase. Some operators and some algorithms require that one operand be stored. For example, one variation of the parallel hash join algorithm consists of two consecutive phases: build and probe. In the build phase, a hash table is constructed in parallel on the join attribute of the smallest relation. In the probe phase, the largest relation is sequentially scanned and the hash table is consulted for each of its tuples.

Example 13.5

In the left-hand part of Figure 13.18, the temporary relations *Temp1* must be completely produced and the hash table in *Build2* must be finished before *Probe2* can start consuming R_3. The same is true for *Temp2*, *Build3* and *Probe3*. Thus, this tree is executed in four consecutive phases: build R_1's hash table, then probe it with R_2 and build *Temp1*'s hash table, then probe it with R_3 and build *Temp2*'s hash table, then probe it with R_3 and produce the result. In the right-hand part of Figure 13.18, the pipeline annotations are indicated by arrows. This tree can be executed in two phases if enough memory is available to build the hash tables: build the tables for R_1 R_3 and R_4, then execute *Probe1*, *Probe2* and *Probe3* in pipeline.

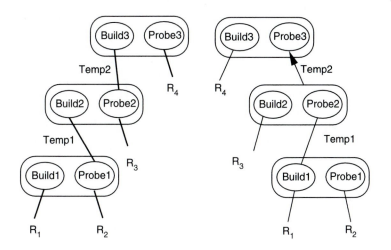

Figure 13.18. Two hash-join trees with a different scheduling.

The set of nodes where a relation is stored is called its *home*. The *home of an operator* is the set of nodes where it is executed and it must be the home of its operands in order for the operator to access its operand. For binary operators such as join, this might imply repartitioning one of the operands. The optimizer might even sometimes find that repartitioning both the operands is of interest. Operator trees bear execution annotations to indicate repartitioning.

Figure 13.19 shows four operator trees, that represent execution plans for a three-way join. An operator tree is a labelled binary tree where the leaf nodes are relations of the input query and each non-leaf node is an operator node (e.g., join, union) whose result is an *intermediate* relation. A join node captures the join between its operands. Execution annotations (e.g., join algorithm) are not shown for simplicity. Directed (respectively undirected) arcs denote that the intermediate relation generated by a tree node is consumed in pipeline (respectively stored) by the subsequent node. Operator trees may be *linear*, i.e. at least one operand of each join node is a base relation or *bushy*.

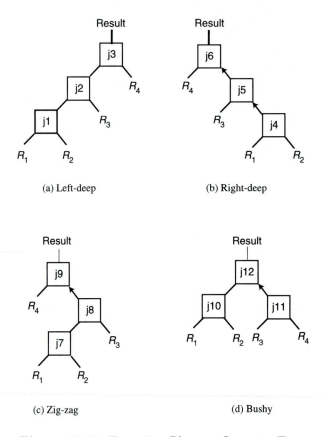

(a) Left-deep   (b) Right-deep

(c) Zig-zag   (d) Bushy

Figure 13.19. Execution Plans as Operator Trees

It is convenient to represent pipelined relations on as right-hand side input of an operator. Thus, right-deep trees express full pipelining while left-deep trees express full materialization of intermediate results. Thus, long right-deep trees are more efficient then corresponding left-deep trees but tend to consume more memory to store left-hand side relations.

Parallel tree formats other than left or right-deep are also interesting. For example, bushy trees (Figure 13.19.(d)) are the only ones to allow independent parallelism. Independent parallelism is useful when the relations are partitioned on disjoint homes. Suppose that the relations in Figure 13.19 are partitioned two (R_1 and R_2) by two (R_3 and R_4) on disjoint homes (resp. h_1 and h_2). Then, joins j_{10} and j_{11} could be independently executed in parallel by the set of nodes that constitutes h_1 and h_2.

When pipeline parallelism is beneficial, *zigzag trees*, which are intermediate formats between left-deep and right-deep trees, can sometimes outperform right-deep trees due to a better use of main memory [Ziane et al., 1993]. A reasonable heuristic is to favor right-deep or zigzag trees when relations are partially fragmented on disjoint homes and intermediate relations are rather large. In this case, bushy trees will usually need more phases and take longer to execute. On the contrary, when intermediate relations are small, pipelining is not very efficient because it is difficult to balance the load between the pipeline stages.

Cost Model

The optimizer cost model is responsible for estimating the cost of a given execution plan. It may be seen as two parts: architecture-dependent and architecture-independent [Lanzelotte et al., 1994]. The architecture-independent part is constituted by the cost functions for operator algorithms, e.g., nested loop for join and sequential access for select. If we ignore concurrency issues, only the cost functions for data repartitioning and memory consumption differ and constitute the architecture-dependent part. Indeed, repartitioning a relation's tuples in a shared-nothing system implies transfers of data across the interconnect, whereas it reduces to hashing in shared-memory systems. Memory consumption in the shared-nothing case is complicated by inter-operator parallelism. In shared-memory systems, all operators read and write data through a global memory, and it is easy to test whether there is enough space to execute them in parallel, i.e., the sum of the memory consumption of individual operators is less than the available memory. In shared-nothing, each processor has its own memory, and it becomes important to know which operators are executed in parallel on the same processor. Thus, for simplicity, it can be assumed that the set of processors (home) assigned to operators to execute do not overlap, i.e., either the intersection of the set of processors is empty or the sets are identical.

To take into account the aspects of parallel execution, we define the cost of a plan [Lanzelotte et al., 1993] as three components: total work (TW), response time (RT), and memory consumption (MC). TW and RT are expressed in *seconds*, and MC in *Kbytes*.

The first two components are used to express a trade-off between response time and throughput. The third component represents the size of memory needed to execute the plan. The cost function is a combination of the first two components, and plans that need more memory than available are discarded. Another approach [Ganguly et al., 1992] consists of using a parameter, specified by the system administrator, by which the maximum throughput is degraded in order to decrease response time. Given a plan p, its cost is computed by a parameterized function $cost_{(W_{RT}, W_{TW})}()$ defined as follows:

$$cost_{(W_{RT}, W_{TW})}(p) = \begin{cases} W_{RT} * RT + W_{TW} * TW & \text{if } MC \text{ of plan } p \text{ does not exceed} \\ & \text{the available memory} \\ \infty & \text{otherwise} \end{cases}$$

where W_{RT} and W_{TW} are weight factors between 0 and 1, such that $W_{RT} + W_{TW} = 1$.

A major difficulty in evaluating the cost is in assigning values to the weight of the first two components. These factors depend on the system state (e.g., load of the system and number of queries submitted to the system), and are ideally determined at run time. This is impossible with static optimization. The total work can be computed by a formula that simply adds all CPU, I/O and communication cost components as in distributed query optimization. The response time is more involved as it must take pipelining into account.

The response time of p, scheduled in phases (each denoted by ph), is computed as follows [Lanzelotte et al., 1994]:

$$RT(p) = \sum_{ph \in p} (max_{Op \in ph}(respTime(Op) + pipe\_delay(Op)) + store\_delay(ph))$$

where Op denotes an operator and $respTime(Op)$ the response time of Op. $pipe\_delay(Op)$ is the waiting period of Op, necessary for the producer to deliver the first result tuples. It is equal to 0 if the input relations of O are stored. $store\_delay(ph)$ is the time necessary to store the output results of phase ph. It is equal to 0 if ph is the last phase, assuming that the result are delivered as soon as they are produced.

To estimate the cost of an execution plan, the cost model uses database statistics and organization information, such as relation cardinalities and partitioning, as with distributed query optimization.

Search Strategy

The search strategy does not need to be different from either centralized or distributed query optimization. However, the search space tends to be much larger because there are more alternative parallel execution plans. Thus, randomized search strategies (see Section 9.1.2) generally outperform deterministic strategies in parallel query optimization.

13.4 PARALLEL EXECUTION PROBLEMS

Parallel query response time can be hurt by several barriers [DeWitt et al., 1992]. This section shows the principal problems introduced by parallel query execution.

13.4.1 Initialization

Before the execution takes place, an initialization step is necessary. This first step is generally sequential. It includes process (or thread) creation and initialization, communication initialization, etc. The duration of this step is proportional to the degree of parallelism and can actually dominate the execution time of low complexity queries. Thus, the degree of parallelism should be fixed according to the query complexity.

In [Wilshut et al., 1992], a formula is given to estimate the maximal speedup reachable during the execution of an operator and to deduce the optimal number of processors. Let us consider the execution of an operator which processes N tuples with n processors. Let c be the average processing time of each tuple and a the initialization time per processor. In the ideal case, the response time of the operator execution is

$$ResponseTime = an + \frac{cN}{n}$$

By derivation, we can obtain the optimal number of processor n_0 to allocate and the maximal speedup S_0 reachable.

$$n_0 = \sqrt{\frac{cN}{a}} \qquad\qquad S_0 = \frac{n_0}{2}$$

In a main memory database system (i.e., no disk accesses during execution) which is the framework of [Wilshut et al., 1992], the initialization time an is important thus limiting the optimal number of processors. In disk-based database systems, relations are read from the disks. Initialization time also limits the optimal number of processors. These equations show that we may not use only intra-operator parallelism (i.e., maximal parallelism degree for each operator) but combine intra and inter-parallelism in order to achieve a better speed-up on each operator.

13.4.2 Interferences and Convoy Effect

A highly parallel execution can be slowed down by *interference*. Interference appears when several processors simultaneously access the same resource, hardware or software.

A typical example of hardware interference is the contention created on the bus of a shared-memory system. When the number of processors is increased, the number of conflicts on the bus increases, thus limiting the extensibility of shared-memory systems. A solution to these interferences is to duplicate shared resources. For instance, disk access interference can be eliminated by adding several disks and partitioning the relations.

Software interference occurs when several processors want to access shared data. To prevent incoherency, mutual exclusion variables are used to protect shared data, thus blocking all but one processor which accesses the shared data. However, shared variables may well become the bottleneck of query execution, creating hot spots and convoy effects [Blasgen et al., 1979]. A typical example of software interference is the access of database internal structures such as indexes. For simplicity, the earlier versions of database systems were protected by a unique mutual exclusion variable. Studies have shown the overhead of such strategy: 45% of the query execution time was consumed by interference between 16 processors.

A general solution to software interference is to partition the data structure. Each global structure may be decomposed in several independent structures protected by a mutual exclusion variable.

13.4.3 Load Balancing

The response time of a set of parallel operators is that of the longest one. Load balancing problems can appear with intra-operator parallelism (variation in partition size), namely *data skew*, and inter-operator parallelism (variation in the complexity of operators). Load balancing is a crucial issue for parallel execution and has been extensively studied. In the rest of this section, we present techniques for intra and inter-operator load balancing.

Intra-Operator Load Balancing

Walton et al. [Walton et al., 1991] classifies the effects of skewed data distribution on a parallel execution. *Attribute value skew (AVS)* is skew inherent in the dataset (e.g.., there are more citizens in Paris than in Rocquencourt) while *tuple placement skew (TPS)* is the skew induced when the data is initially partitioned (on disk) (e.g., with range partitioning). *Selectivity skew (SS)* is induced when there is variation in the selectivity of select predicates on each node. *Redistribution skew (RS)* occurs in the redistribution step between two operators. It is similar to TPS. Finally *join product skew (JPS)* occurs because the join selectivity may vary between nodes. Figure 13.20 illustrates this classification on a query applied to two relations R and S which are poorly partitioned. The boxes are proportional to the size of the corresponding partitions. Such poor partitioning stems from either the data (AVS) or the partitioning function (TPS). Thus, the processing times of the two instances scan1 and scan2 are not equal. The case of the join operator is worse. First, the number of tuples received is different from one instance to another because of poor redistribution of the partitions of R (RS) or variable selectivity according to the partition of R processed (SS). Finally, the uneven size of S partitions (AVS/TPS) yields different processing times for tuples send by the scan operator and the result size is different from one partition to the other due to join selectivity (JPS).

Clearly, it seems difficult to propose a solution based on estimates on the relations involved. Such strategy would require statistics like histogram on join attribute, fragmentation attribute, attributes involved in predicates—potentially on

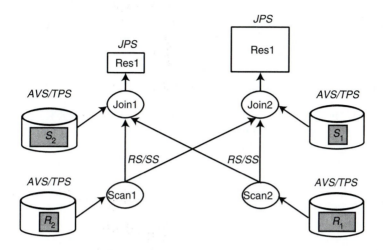

Figure 13.20. Data skew example

all attributes of all relations. Furthermore, a cost model would be necessary to evaluate distribution on intermediate results. A more reasonable strategy is to use a dynamic approach, i.e., redistribute the load dynamically in order to balance the execution.

Several solutions have been proposed to reduce the negative impact from skew. [Kitsuregawa and Ogawa, 1990] presents a robust hash-join algorithm for a specific parallel architecture based on shared-nothing. The idea is to partition each hash bucket in fragments and spread them among the processors (bucket spreading). Then a sophisticated network, the Omega network, is used to redistribute buckets onto the processors. The Omega network contains logic to balance the load during redistribution. [Omiecinski, 1991] proposes a similar approach in a shared-memory parallel system, using the first fit decreasing heuristic to assign buckets to processors. DBS3 [Bergsten et al., 1991], [Dageville et al. 1994] has pioneered the use of an execution model based on relation partitioning (as in shared-nothing) for shared-memory. This model reduces processor interference and shows excellent load balancing for intra-operator parallelism [Bouganim et al., 1996a], [Bouganim et al. 1996b]. [DeWitt et al., 1992] suggests the use of multiple algorithms, each specialized for a different degree of skew, and the use of a small sample of the relations to determine which algorithm is appropriate.

Wolf et al. [Wolf et al., 1993] propose to modify hash join and sort merge join algorithms to insert a scheduling step which is in charge of redistributing the load. Each join is decomposed in a number of join superior to the number of processors and distributed among the processors using estimates on complexity and heuristics like LPT. This strategy is iterated until a "good" load balancing is achieved.

Shatdal et al. [Shatdal and Naughton, 1993] propose to use shared virtual memory (implemented by software) to redistribute dynamically the load. When a processor is idle, it steals work from a random chosen processor using shared virtual memory.

Inter-Operator Load Balancing

In order to obtain a good load balancing at the inter-operator level, it is necessary to choose, for each operator, how many and what processors to assign for its execution. Suppose we have a perfect cost model which allows evaluating the sequential execution time of each operator. We then need to find a way to assign processors to operators in order to obtain the best load balancing.

Metha et al. [Mehta and DeWitt 1995] propose to determine dynamically (just before the execution) the degree of parallelism and the localization of the processors for each operator. The *Rate Match* algorithm uses a cost model in order to match the rate at which tuples are produced and consumed. Six algorithms are then proposed in order to choose the set of processors which will be used for query execution (based on available memory, CPU or disks utilization, etc...)

[Rahm and Marek, 1995] and [Garofalakis and Ioanidis, 1996] propose other algorithms for the choice of the number and localization of processors. They try to distribute efficiently the load in order to maximize the use of several resources using statistics on this usages.

The potential reasons for poor load balancing in shared-nothing are studied in [Wilshut et al., 1995]. First, the degree of parallelism and the allocation of processors to operators, decided in the parallel optimization phase, are based on a possibly inaccurate cost model. Second, the choice of the degree of parallelism is subject to discretization errors because both processors and operators are discrete entities. Finally, the processors associated with the latest operators in a pipeline chain may remain idle a significant time. This is called the pipeline delay problem. These problems stem from the fixed association between data, operators and processors. In the next section, we present an execution model which do not realize any association between processors and operators.

13.5 PARALLEL EXECUTION FOR HIERARCHICAL ARCHITECTURE

In this section we describe a complete solution for query execution on hierarchical architectures, based on [Bouganim et al., 1996c]. In the context of hierarchical systems, load balancing is exacerbated because it must be addressed at two levels, locally among the processors of each shared-memory node and globally among all nodes. None of the approaches presented in Section 13.4.3, can be easily extended to deal with this problem. Load balancing strategies for shared-nothing would experience even more severe problems worsening (e.g., complexity and inaccuracy of the cost model). On the other hand, adapting solutions developed for shared-memory systems would incur high communication overhead.

In this section, we present an execution model, called *Dynamic Processing (DP)* for hierarchical systems which dynamically performs intra- and inter-operator load balancing. The fundamental idea is that the query work is decomposed in self-contained units of sequential processing, each of which can be carried out by any processor. Intuitively, a processor can migrate horizontally and vertically along the query work. The main advantage is to minimize the communication overhead of inter-node load balancing by maximizing intra and inter-operator load balancing within shared-memory nodes.

13.5.1 Problem Formulation

The result of parallel query optimization is a *parallel execution plan* that consists of an operator tree with operator scheduling and allocation of computing resources to operators Figure 13.21 shows a join tree and the corresponding operator tree.

The operator scheduling constraints are:

```
Build1 < Probe1
Build2 > Probe2
Build3 > Probe3
```

The operator scheduling heuristics are:

```
Heuristic1: Build1 < Scan2, Build2 < Scan4, Build3 < Scan3
Heuristic1: Build3 < Scan3
```

Finally, the operator homes are:

```
home (Scan1) = Node A
home (Build1, Probe1, Scan2, Scan3) = Node B
home (Scan4) = Node C
home (Build3, Build2, Probe2, Probe3) = Nodes B and C
```

Given this information, the problem is to produce an execution on a hierarchical architecture which minimizes response time. A necessary condition to minimize response time is to avoid processor idle time. This can be done by using a dynamic load balancing mechanism at two levels: (i) within a SM-node, load balancing is achieved via fast interprocess communication; (ii) between SM-nodes, more expensive message-passing communication is needed. Thus, the problem is to come up with an execution model so that the use of local load balancing is maximized while the use of global load balancing is minimized. Intuitively, parallelizing a query amounts to partition the total work along two dimensions. First, each operator is horizontally partitioned to yield intra-operator parallelism. Second, the query is vertically partitioned into dependent or independent operators to yield inter-operator parallelism. We call *activation* the smallest unit of sequential processing that cannot be further partitioned. The main property of the DP model is to allow any processor to process any activation of its SM-node. Thus, there is no static association between threads and operators. This should yield good load-balancing

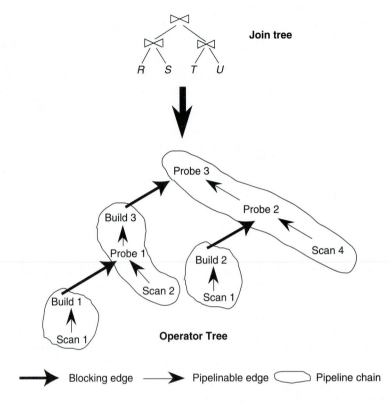

Figure 13.21. A join tree and associated operator tree

for both intra-operator and inter-operator parallelism within a SM-node, and thus, reduce to the minimum the need for global load balancing, i.e., when there is no more work to do in a SM-node. In the rest of this section, we present the basic concepts underlying the DP model and its load balancing strategy which we illustrate with an example.

13.5.2 Basic Concepts

The DP execution model is based on a few concepts: activations, activation queues, fragmentation, and threads. It assumes a modern multithread system. These concepts are simple and their combination provides much flexibility and generality.

Activations

An activation represents a sequential unit of work. Since any activation can be executed by any thread (by any processor), activations must be self-contained and reference all information necessary for their execution: the code to execute and the data to process. Two kinds of activations can be distinguished: trigger activations and data activations. A *trigger activation* is used to start the execution of a leaf operator, i.e., scan. It is represented by an (*Operator, Bucket*) pair which references the scan operator and the base relation bucket to scan. A *data activation* describes a tuple produced in pipeline mode. It is represented by an (*Operator, Tuple, Bucket*) triple which references the operator to process. For a build operator (see Section 13.3.3), the data activation specifies that the tuple must be inserted in the hash table of the bucket and for a probe operator, that the tuple must be probed with the bucket's hash table. Although activations are self-contained, they can only be executed on the SM-node where the associated data (hash tables or base relations) is.

Activation Queues

Moving data activations along pipeline chains is done using *activation queues*, called table queues in [Pirahesh et al., 1990], associated with operators. If the producer and consumer of an activation are on the same SM-node, then the move is done via shared-memory. Otherwise, it requires message-passing. To unify the execution model, queues are used for trigger activations (inputs for scan operators) as well as tuple activations (inputs for build or probe operators).

All threads have unrestricted access to all queues located on their SM-node. Managing a small number of queues (e.g., one for each operator) may yield interference. To reduce interference, one queue is associated with each thread working on an operator. Note that a higher number of queues would likely trade interference for queue management overhead. To further reduce interference without increasing the number of queues, each thread is given priority access to a distinct set of queues, called its primary queues. Thus, a thread always tries to first consume activations in its *primary queues*.

During execution, operator scheduling constraints may imply an operator to be blocked until the end of some other operators (the blocking operators). Therefore, a queue for a blocked operator is also blocked, i.e., its activations cannot be consumed but they can still be produced if the producing operator is not blocked. When all its blocking operators terminate, the blocked queue becomes consumable, i.e., threads can consume its activations. This is illustrated in Figure 13.22 with an execution snapshot for the operator tree of Figure 13.21.

Fragmentation

Let us call *degree of fragmentation* the number of buckets of the building and probing relations. To reduce the negative effects of data skew, the typical solution is to have a degree of fragmentation much higher than the degree of parallelism [Kitsuregawa and Ogawa, 1990], [DeWitt et al., 1992]. If a queue is used for each bucket, a high degree of fragmentation would imply an important queue management overhead [Bouganim et al. 1996b]. Since activations are self-contained, activations of different buckets in the same queue can be mixed, thus reducing the overhead of queue management with a high degree of fragmentation.

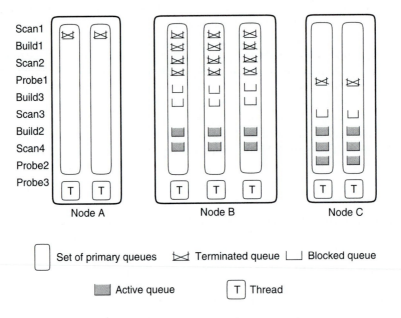

Scan1
Build1
Scan2
Probe1
Build3
Scan3
Build2
Scan4
Probe2
Probe3

Node A   Node B   Node C

☐ Set of primary queues   ⋈ Terminated queue   ⊔ Blocked queue

▨ Active queue   T Thread

Figure 13.22. Snapshot of an execution

Threads

A simple strategy for obtaining good load balancing inside a SM-node is to allocate a number of threads much higher than the number of processors and let the operating system do thread scheduling. However, this strategy incurs high numbers of system calls due to thread scheduling, interference and convoy problems [Pirahesh et al., 1990], [Hong, 1992].

Instead of relying on the operating system for load balancing, it is possible to allocate only one thread per processor per query. This is made possible by the fact that any thread can execute any operator assigned to its SM-node. The advantage of this one-thread-per-processor allocation strategy is to significantly reduce the overhead of interference and synchronization provided that a thread is never blocked. Waiting for some event would cause processor idle time. During the processing of an activation, a thread can be blocked in the following situations:

- the thread cannot insert an activation in a pipeline queue because the queue is full[1];

---

[1]Without any restriction on the queue size, memory consumption may well increase. For instance, consider the concurrent execution of two pipelined operators. If the select strategy favors the producer operator, then it may well end up materializing the entire intermediate result. To avoid this situation, queues have a limited size.

- the use of asynchronous I/O (for multiplexing disk accesses with data processing) can create waiting situations.

This problem can be solved as follows. A thread in a waiting situation suspends its current execution by making a procedure call to find another local activation to process. The advantage is that context saving is done by procedure call, which is much less expensive than operating system based synchronization.

13.5.3 Load Balancing Strategy

Load balancing within a SM-node is obtained by allocating all activation queues in a segment of shared-memory and by allowing all threads to consume activations in any queue. To limit thread interference, a thread will consume as much as possible from its set of primary queues before considering the other queues of the SM-node. Therefore, a thread becomes idle only when there is no more activation of any operator, which means that there is no more work to do on its SM-node which is starving.

When a SM-node starves, we can apply load sharing with another SM-node by acquiring some of its workload [Shatdal and Naughton, 1993]. However, acquiring activations (through message-passing) incurs communication overhead. Furthermore, activation acquisition is not enough since associated data, i.e., hash tables, must also be acquired. Thus, we need a mechanism that can dynamically estimate the benefit of acquiring activations and data.

Let us call "requester" the SM-node which acquires work and "provider" the SM-node which gets off-loaded by providing work to the requester. The problem is to select a queue to acquire activations and decide how much work to acquire. This is a dynamic optimization problem since there is a trade-off between the potential gain of off-loading the provider and the overhead of acquiring activations and data. This trade-off can be expressed by the following conditions: (i) the requester must be able to store in memory the activations and corresponding data; (ii) enough work must be acquired in order to amortize the overhead of acquisition; (iii) acquiring too much work should be avoided; (iv) only probe activations can be acquired since triggered activations require disk accesses and build activations require building hash tables locally; (v) there is no gain to move activations associated with blocked operators which could not be processed anyway. Finally, to respect the decisions of the optimizer, a SM-node cannot execute activations of an operator that it does not own, i.e., the SM-node is not in the operator home.

The amount of load balancing depends on the number of operators that are concurrently executed which provides opportunities for finding some work to share in case of idle times. Increasing the number of concurrent operators can be done by allowing concurrent execution of several pipeline chains or by using non-blocking hash-join algorithms which allow to execute all the operators of the bushy tree concurrently [Wilshut et al., 1995]. On the other hand, executing more operators concurrently can increase memory consumption. Static operator scheduling as provided by the optimizer should avoid memory overflow and solve this tradeoff.

13.5.4   Performance Evaluation

The performance of the DP model is evaluated in [Bouganim et al., 1996c] using an implementation on a 72-processor KSR1 computer. KSR1's shared virtual memory architecture and high number of processors have been organized as a hierarchical parallel system. To experiment with many different queries, large relations and different relation parameters (cardinality, selectivity, skew factor, etc.), the execution of atomic operators has been simulated. Various experiments have been performed at two levels: locally within an SM-node and globally among SM-nodes.

In the shared-memory case, the DP load balancing strategy is compared with synchronous pipelining (SP) and fixed processing (FP). The results are as follows. SP is best for shared-memory but does not work in shared-nothing whereas FP is designed for shared-nothing and also works in shared-memory. FP is always worse because of discretization errors which worsen as the number of processors decreases. The performance of DP is very close to that of SP from 8 to 32 processors and remain close for higher numbers. Both SP and DP strategies show very good speedup, even with highly skewed data.

To assess the performance of the DP global load balancing strategy in a hierarchical system, its performance is compared with that of FP which performs well in shared-nothing. The results are as follows. DP outperforms FP by a factor between 14 and 39% and the communication overhead due to global load balancing is 2 to 4 times smaller. Finally, processor idle time is almost null with DP whereas it is quite significant with FP.

To summarize the performance results, DP performs as well as a dedicated model in shared-memory and can scale up very well to deal with multiple nodes. Considering the current multiprocessor towards hierarchical architectures with database as the main target application, such a model provides two strong advantages: predictable performance across many different configurations and portability of DBMS software.

13.6   CONCLUSION

Parallel database systems strive to exploit modern multiprocessor architectures using software-oriented solutions for data management. Their promises are high-performance, high-availability and extensibility with a much lower price/performance ratio than their mainframe counterparts. Furthermore, parallelism is the only viable solution for supporting very large (Terabyte) databases within a single system. Of course, a distributed DBMS is an answer too with multiple systems.

Although there are successful commercial SQL-based parallel DBMS, a number of open problems hamper the full exploitation of the capabilities of parallel systems. These problems touch on issues ranging from those of parallel processing to distributed database management. The first open issue is to decide which of the various architectures among shared-memory, shared-disk, and shared-nothing and hybrid architectures, is best for database management. For a small configuration (tens of processors), shared-memory can provide the highest performance because of better load balancing. Shared-disk and shared-nothing however outperform shared-memory in terms of availability and extensibility. On the other hand, shared-nothing can scale up to higher numbers of processors. Some years ago, shared-nothing was the only choice for high-end systems (e.g., requiring more than thousands of transactions-per-secon of the TPC-B benchmark [Gray, 1993]). With new hybrid architecture, NUMA seems the best choice for medium systems. The advantage of this architecture is the simple (shared-memory) programming model which eases physical database design and tuning.. High-end systems may use hierarchical architecture for better extensibility and availability. For hierarchical architecture, the question is whether to be extensible and scalable to a limited number of very powerful shared-memory nodes or to a higher number of less powerful nodes. The possibility of using disk arrays makes the question more difficult.

Besides these architectural considerations, the following issues require more work:

1. operating system support for efficient parallel data management with openness to non-database applications as well, e.g., using microkernel operating system technology;

2. benchmarks to stress linear speedup and linear scaleup under mixed workloads including simple and complex transactions as well as batch programs;

3. partitioned data placement techniques to deal with skewed data distributions and data replication so as to achieve load balancing, including in failure mode; and

4. parallel query processing with cost-based optimization and automatic parallelization to deal with mixed workloads of precompiled transactions and complex ad-hoc queries.

13.7 BIBLIOGRAPHIC NOTES

The earlier proposal of the idea of a database server or database machine is given in [Canaday et al., 1974]. A comprehensive survey of database machines is provided in [Graefe, 1993], [Valduriez and Gardarin, 1989], [Ozkarahan, 1986] and [Su, 1988]. Other survey papers are [Boral and Redfield, 1985] and [DeWitt and Hawthorn, 1981]. Experiences and lessons learned from database server applications are discussed in [Taylor, 1987].

Parallel database server architectures are discussed in [Bergsten et al., 1992], [Stonebraker, 1986] and compared using a simple simulation model in [Bhide and Stonebraker, 1988]. NUMA architectures are described in [Lenoski et al., 1992], [Goodman and Woest, 1988]. Its influence on query execution and performance can be found in [Bouganim et al., 1999], [Dageville et al. 1994]. Examples of parallel database prototypes or products are presented in [DeWitt et al., 1986], [Tandem, 1987], [Pirahesh et al., 1990], [Graefe, 1990], [EDS, 1990], [Bergsten et al., 1991], [Hong, 1992] and [Apers et al., 1992]. A good discussion of the issues facing the design of parallel database servers is provided in [Boral, 1988a]. Data placement in a parallel database server is treated in [Livny et al., 1987]. Parallel optimization studies appear in [Shekita et al., 1993], [Ziane et al., 1993], [Lanzelotte et al., 1994] and [Lanzelotte et al., 1994].

Load balancing issues were extensively studied. [Walton et al., 1991] presents a taxonomy of intra-operator load balancing problems, namely, data skew. [DeWitt et al., 1992], [Kitsuregawa and Ogawa, 1990], [Shatdal and Naughton, 1993], [Wolf et al., 1993], [Rahm and Marek, 1995], [Mehta and DeWitt 1995] and [Garofalakis and Ioanidis, 1996] present several aproaches for load balancing in shared-nothing architectures. [Omiecinski, 1991] and [Bouganim et al., 1996a] focus on shared-memory architectures while [Bouganim et al., 1996c] and [Bouganim et al., 1999] are considering load balancing in the hybrid architecure context.

The section on parallel operation processing is based on in [Valduriez and Gardarin, 1984]. The section on parallel query processing is based on [Khoshafian and Valduriez, 1987] and [Khoshafian et al., 1988a]. The section on parallel execution for hierarchical architectures is based on our work reported in [Bouganim et al., 1996c].

13.8 EXERCISES

*13.1 Consider the centralized server organization of Figure 13.1 Also assume that each application server stores a subset of the data directory which is fully stored on the database server. Assume also that the local data directories at different application servers are not necessarily disjoint. What are the implications on data directory management and query processing if the local data directories can be updated by the application servers rather than the database server?

**13.2 Propose an architecture for a parallel shared-memory database server and provide a qualitative comparison with shared-nothing architecture on the basis of expected performance, software complexity (in particular, data placement and query processing), extensibility, and availability.

13.3 Specify the parallel hash join algorithm for the parallel shared-memory database server architecture proposed in Exercise 15.2.

*13.4 Explain the problems associated with clustering and full partitioning in a parallel shared-nothing database server. Propose several solutions and compare them.

13.5 Propose a parallel semijoin algorithm for a parallel shared-nothing database server. How should the parallel join algorithms be extended to exploit this semijoin algorithm?

13.6 Consider the following SQL query:

```
SELECT   ENAME, DUR
FROM     EMP, ASG, PROJ
WHERE    EMP.ENO=ASG.ENO
AND      ASG.PNO=PROJ.PNO
AND      RESP = "Manager"
AND      PNAME = "Instrumentation"
```

Give four possible operator trees: right-deep, left-deep, zigzag and bushy. For each one, discuss the impact on run-time performance.

13.7 Consider a nine way join (ten relations are to be joined), calculate the number of possible right-deep, left-deep and bushy trees, assuming that each relation can be joined with anyone else. What do you conclude about parallel optimization?

**13.8 Propose a data placement strategy for a hierarchical architecture which maximizes *intra-node* parallelism (intra-operator parallelism within a shared-memory node).

**13.9 Consider a multi-user centralized database system. Describe the main change to allow inter-query parallelism from the database system developper point of view. What are the implications for the end-user (data placement, response time, throughput, etc.)

**13.10 Same question for intra-query parallelism on a shared-memory architecture or for a shared-nothing architecture.

Chapter 14

DISTRIBUTED OBJECT DATABASE MANAGEMENT SYSTEMS

In this chapter, we relax another one of the fundamental assumptions we made in Chapter 1 — namely that the system implements the relational data model. Database technology is rapidly evolving toward the support of new applications. Relational databases have proven to be very successful in supporting business data processing applications. However, there is now an important class of applications, commonly referred to as "advanced database applications," that exhibit pressing needs for database management. Examples include computer-aided design (CAD), office information systems (OIS), multimedia information systems, and artificial intelligence (AI). For these applications, object database management systems (object DBMSs) are considered to be more suitable due to the following characteristics [Özsu et al., 1994b]:

1. These advanced applications require explicit storage and manipulation of more abstract data types (e.g., images, design documents) and the ability for the users to define their own application-specific types. Therefore, a rich type system supporting user-defined abstract types is required. Relational systems deal with a single object type, a relation, whose attributes come from simple and fixed data type domains (e.g., numeric, character, string, date). There is no support for explicit definition and manipulation of application-specific types.

2. The relational model structures data in a relatively simple and flat manner. Representing structural application objects in the flat relational model results in the loss of natural structure that may be important to the application. For example, in engineering design applications, it may be preferable to explicitly represent that a vehicle object contains an engine object. Similarly, in a multimedia information system, it is important to note that a hyperdocument object contains a particular video

object and a captioned text object. This "containment" relationship between application objects is not easy to represent in the relational model, but is fairly straightforward in object models by means of *composite objects* and *complex objects*, which we discuss shortly.

3. Relational systems provide a declarative and (arguably) simple language for accessing the data – SQL. Since this is not a computationally complete language, complex database applications have to be written in general programming languages with embedded query statements. This causes the well-known "impedance mismatch" [Copeland and Maier, 1984] problem, which arises because of the differences in the level of abstraction between the relational languages and the programming languages with which they interact. The concepts and types of the query language, typically set-at-a-time, do not match with those of the programming language, which are typically record-at-a-time. In an object system, complex database applications may be written entirely in a single object database programming language [Atkinson and Buneman, 1987]. Of course, this may change as SQL develops toward a computationally complete language.

The main issue in object DBMSs is to provide the above functionality with acceptable performance. It can be argued that the above requirements can be met by relational DBMSs, since one can possibly map them to relational data structures. In a strict sense this is true; however, from a modeling perspective, it makes little sense, since it forces users to map semantically richer and structurally complex objects that they deal with in the application domain to simple structures in representation. This mapping has to be done continually during processing, which is both cumbersome and inefficient. This is the root of what has been referred to as the "impedence mismatch" between the conceptual model and its representation in a database. Impedence mismatch occurs at the programming language level as well. Database query languages are generally set-oriented, while the imperative programming languages in which they are embedded are not. This has resulted in the development of DBMS functions, such as cursor processing, that enable iterating over the sets of data objects retrieved by query languages. As object-oriented programming becomes widespread, there is a possibility of eliminating this impedence mismatch by better integrating programming languages with DBMS languages.

A careful study of the advanced applications mentioned above indicates that they are inherently distributed, and require distributed data management support. This gives rise to distributed object DBMSs, which is the subject of this chapter.

In Section 14.1, we will discuss the fundamental object concepts and issues in developing object models. This discussion is fundamental to the material in the remainder of the chapter. In Section 14.2, we will consider the distribution design of object databases. Section 14.3 is devoted to the discussion of the various distributed object DBMS architectural issues. In Section 14.4, we will discuss the new issues that arise in the management of objects, and in Section 14.5 the focus is on object storage considerations. Sections 14.6 and 14.7 are devoted to fundamental DBMS functions: query processing and transaction management. These issues take interesting twists when considered within the context of this new technology.

14.1 FUNDAMENTAL OBJECT CONCEPTS AND OBJECT MODELS

An object DBMS is a system that uses an "object" as the fundamental modeling and access primitive. Beyond this fairly straightforward statement, what constitutes an object DBMS is a topic of considerable discussion [Atkinson et al., 1989], [Stonebraker et al., 1990a]. Contrary to the relational model, there is no universally accepted and formally specified object model. There are a number of features that are common to most model specifications, but the exact semantics of these features are different in each model. Even the feasibility of defining an object model, in the same sense as the relational model, has been questioned [Maier, 1989]. Some standard object model specifications are emerging as part of language standards (e.g., Object Data Management Group's (ODMG) model [Cattell, 1997] or SQL-3 [Melton, 1998]), but these are not widely adopted. In the remainder of this section, we will review some of the design issues and alternatives in defining an object model.

14.1.1 Object

As indicated above, all object DBMSs are built around the fundamental concept of an *object*. An object represents a real entity in the system that is being modeled. Most simply, it is represented as a pair (OID, state), in which OID is the object identity and the corresponding state is some representation of the current state of the object. Object identity [Khoshafian and Copeland, 1986] is an invariant property of an object which permanently distinguishes it logically and physically from all other objects, regardless of its state. This enables referential object sharing [Khoshafian and Valduriez, 1987], which is the basis for supporting composite and complex (i.e., graph) structures (see Section 14.1.3). In some models, OID equality is the only comparison primitive; for other types of comparisons, the type definer is expected to specify the semantics of comparison. In other models, two objects are said to be *identical* if they have the same OID, and *equal* if they have the same state.

Many object models start to diverge at the definition of the *state*. Some object models define state as either an atomic value or a constructed value (e.g., tuple or set). Let D be the union of the system-defined domains (e.g., domain of integers) and of user-defined abstract data type (ADT) domains (e.g., domain of companies), let I be the domain of identifiers used to name objects, and let A be the domain of attribute names. A *value* is defined as follows:

1. An element of D is a value, called an *atomic value*.

2. $[a_1 : v_1, \ldots, a_n : v_n]$, in which a_i is an element of A and v_i is either a value or an element of I, is called a *tuple value*. $[\ ]$ is known as the tuple constructor.

3. $\{v_1, \ldots, v_n\}$, in which v_i is either a value or an element of I, is called a *set value*. $\{\ \}$ is known as the set constructor.

These models consider object identifiers as values (similar to pointers in programming languages). Set and tuple are data constructors that we consider essential for database applications. Other constructors, such as list or array, could also be added to increase the modeling power.

Example 14.1

Consider the following objects:

$(i_1, 231)$
$(i_2, S70)$
$(i_3, \{i_6, i_{11}\})$
$(i_4, \{1, 3, 5\})$
$(i_5, [LF: i_7, RF: i_8, LR: i_9, RR: i_10])$

Objects i_1 and i_2 are atomic objects and i_3 and i_4 are constructed objects. i_3 is the OID of an object whose state consists of a set. The same is true of i_4. The difference between the two is that the state of i_4 consists of a set of values, while that of i_3 consists of a set of OIDs. Thus, object i_3 references other objects. By considering object identifiers (e.g., i_6) as values in the object model, arbitrarily complex objects may be constructed. Object i_5 has a tuple valued state consisting of four attributes (or instance variables), the values of each being another object.

Contrary to values, objects support a well-defined update operation that changes the object state without changing the object identity. This is analogous to updates in imperative programming languages in which object identity is implemented by main memory pointers. However, object identity is more general than pointers in the sense that it persists following the program termination. Another implication of object identity is that objects may be shared without incurring the problem of data redundancy. We will discuss this further in Section 14.1.3.

Example 14.2

Consider the following objects:

(i_1, Volvo)
$(i_2, [\text{name: John, mycar: } i_1])$
$(i_3, [\text{name: Mary, mycar: } i_1])$

John and Mary share the object denoted by mycar (they both own Volvo cars). Changing the value of object i_1 from "Volvo" to "Chevrolet" is automatically seen by both objects i_2 and i_3.

The above discussion captures the structural aspects of a model – the state is represented as a set of *instance variables* (or *attributes*) which are values. The behavioral aspects of the model are captured in *methods*, which define the allowable operations on these objects and are used to manipulate them. Methods represent the behavioral side of the model because they define the legal behaviors that the object can assume. A classical example is that of an elevator [Jones, 1979]. If the only two methods defined on an elevator object are "up" and "down", they together define the behavior of the elevator object: it can go up or down, but not sideways, for example.

Other object models take a more behavioral approach [Dayal, 1989], [Özsu et al., 1995a]. In these models, there are no instance variables or methods; there are only behaviors, which are applied to objects to achieve a certain result. The behaviors may be implemented either by stored functions or by computed functions, but this distinction is not visible at the user level. Consequently, the "state" of an object is defined by the results returned by the application of these behaviors.

Some object models (e.g., [Özsu et al., 1995a]) eliminate the distinction between values and objects. In uniform models such as these, everything is an object, including system entities and user-defined entities. In these systems there are no (set or tuple) constructors; objects are created by specializing or generalizing other objects. In a sense, these models use the object approach in defining the object model itself, eliminating any extraneous constructs. Consequently, these models are *reflective* [Peters and Özsu, 1993], [Ferber, 1989], [Foote and Robson, 1989], [Cointe, 1987], [Maes, 1987] in that the information about the model is also managed within the model, and this information can be accessed (or reasoned about) through the ordinary access primitives provided by the model.

An important distinction emerges from the foregoing discussion between relational model and object models. Relational databases deal with data values in a uniform fashion. Attribute values are the atoms with which structured values (tuples and relations) may be constructed. In a value-based data model, such as the relational model, data is identified by values. A relation is identified by a name, and a tuple is identified by a key, a combination of values. In object models, by contrast, data is identified by its OID. This distinction is crucial; modeling of relationships among data leads to data redundancy or the introduction of foreign keys in the relational model. The automatic management of foreign keys requires the support of integrity constraints (referential integrity).

Example 14.3

Consider Example 14.2. In the relational model, to achieve the same purpose, one would typically set the value of attribute `mycar` to "Volvo", which would require both tuples to be updated when it changes to "Chevrolet". To reduce redundancy, one can still represent i_1 as a tuple in another relation and reference it from i_1 and i_2 using foreign keys. Recall that this is the basis of 3NF and BCNF normalization. In this case, the elimination of redundancy requires, in the relational model, normalization of relations. However, i_1 may be a structured object whose representation in a normalized relation may be awkward. In this case, we cannot assign it as the value of the `mycar` attribute even if we accept the redundancy, since the relational model requires attribute values to be atomic.

14.1.2   Abstract Data Types

Abstract data types (ADTs) have long been used in programming languages [Guttag, 1977], and more recently in relational databases [Stonebraker et al., 1983b], [Osborn and Heaven, 1986], and [Gardarin and Valduriez, 1989]. In fact, the introduction of abstract data types into relational systems is the basis of the newly emerging object-relational DBMSs [Stonebraker and Brown, 1999]. An *abstract data type* (usually simply called a *type*[1]) is a template for all objects of that type. In this case, we don't make a distinction between primitive system objects (i.e., values), structural (tuple or set) objects, and user-defined objects. An ADT describes the type of data by providing a domain of data with the same structure, as well as operations (also called methods) applicable to elements of that domain. The abstraction capability of ADTs, commonly referred to as *encapsulation*, hides the implementation details of the operations, which can be written in a general-purpose programming language. Thus, each ADT is identifiable to the "outside world" by the properties that it supports. In traditional object models, the properties consist of instance variables that reflect the state of the objects, and methods that define the operations that can be performed on objects of this type. In other models, these properties are abstracted as behaviors. This is similar to the primitive operations (e.g., addition) associated with primitive types (e.g., integer) provided by the programming language. In general, several standard ADT operations, such as conversion for input-output, are mandatory. The user of the ADT only sees the interface data structure and the interface operation names with their associated input and output types.

Example 14.4

> In this chapter we will use an example that demonstrates the power of object models. We will model a car that consists of various parts (engine, bumpers, tires) and will store other information such as make, model, serial number, etc. The type definition of `Car` can be as follows (not using any particular syntax):

```
type Car
   attributes
      engine : Engine
      bumpers : {Bumper}
      tires : [LF: Tire, RF: Tire, LR: Tire, RR: Tire]
      make : Manufacturer
      model : String
      year : Date
      serial_no : String
      capacity : Integer
   methods
      age: Real
```

The type definition specifies that `Car` has eight attributes and one method. Four of the attributes (model, year, serial_no, capacity) are value-based, while

---

[1]We will use these terms interchangeably in the remainder of the text.

the others (engine, bumpers, tires and make) are object-based (i.e., have other objects as their values). Attribute bumpers is set valued (i.e., uses the set constructor), and attribute tires is tuple-valued where the left front (LF), right front (RF), left rear (LR) and right rear (RR) tires are individually identified. Incidentally, we follow a notation where the attributes are lower case and types are capitalized. Thus, **engine** is an attribute and **Engine** is a type in the system.

One more point needs to be made about this example. The method **age** takes the system date, and the **year** attribute value and calculates the date. However, since both of these arguments are internal to the object, they are not shown in the type definition, which is the interface for the user. If there was a method that required the users to provide an external argument, then it would have appeared in the method signature.

The interface data structure of an ADT may be arbitrarily complex or large. For example, **Car** ADT has an operation **age** which takes today's date and the manufacturing date of a car and calculates its age; it may also have more complex operations that, for example, calculate a promotional price based on the time of year. Similarly, a long document with a complex internal structure may be defined as an ADT with operations specific to document manipulation. ADTs provide two major advantages. First, the primitive types provided by the system can easily be extended with user-defined types. Since there are no inherent constraints on the notion of relational domain, such extensibility can be incorporated in the context of the relational model [Osborn and Heaven, 1986]. Second, ADT operations capture parts of the application programs which are more closely associated with data. Therefore, an object model with ADTs allows modeling of both data and operations at the same time. This does not imply, however, that operations are stored with the data. They may be stored in an operation library, similar to the data directory.

14.1.3 Composition (Aggregation)

In the examples we have discussed so far, some of the instance variables have been value-based (i.e., their domains are simple values), such as the **model** and **year** in Example 14.3, while others are object-based, such as the **make** attribute, whose domain is the set of objects that are of type **Manufacturer** In this case, the **Car** type is a *composite type* and its instances are referred to as *composite objects*. Composition is one of the most powerful features of object models. It allows sharing of objects, commonly referred to as *referential sharing*, since objects "refer" to each other by their OIDs as values of object-based attributes.

Example 14.5

Let us revise Example 14.3 as follows. Assume that c_1 is one instance of **Car** type which is defined in Example 14.3. If the following is true:

$(i_2, $ [name: John, mycar: c_1])
$(i_3, $ [name: Mary, mycar: c_1])

then this indicates that John and Mary own the same car.

A restriction on composite objects results in *complex objects*. The difference between a composite and a complex object is that the former allows referential sharing while the latter does not[2]. For example, `Car` type may have an attribute whose domain is type `Tire`. It is not natural for two instances of type `Car`, c_1 and c_2, to refer to the same set of instances of `Tire`, since one would not expect in real life for tires to be used on multiple vehicles at the same time. This distinction between composite and complex objects is not always made, but it is an important one.

The composite object relationship between types can be represented by a *composition (aggregation) graph* (or *composition (aggregation) hierarchy* in the case of complex objects). There is an edge from instance variable I of type T_1 to type T_2 if the domain of I is T_2. The composition graphs give rise to a number of issues that we will discuss in the upcoming sections.

14.1.4 Class

Most of the current object DBMSs do not distinguish between a type and a class. This is a consequence of adopting the type systems of object programming languages such as Smalltalk and C++, which support only the concept of a class. In these systems, a *class* represents both a template for all common objects (i.e., serves as a type) and the grouping of these common objects (i.e., the extent). In this case, the database schema consists of a set of class definitions with the relationships among them (which we will discuss in Section 14.1.6).

Conceptually, however, there is a difference between a type and a class. A type is a template for all objects of that type, whereas a class is a grouping of all object instances of a given type. Some systems make this distinction explicit. In a sense, a type corresponds to a relation schema in relational databases, whereas a class corresponds to a populated relation instance. In other words, a class has an *extent* which is the collection of all objects of the type associated with the class.

14.1.5 Collection

A *collection* is a user-defined grouping of objects. Most conventional systems provide either the class construct or the collection construct. However, it can be argued that both classes and collections are useful, and that they should be supported in an object model [Beeri, 1990]. Collections provide for a clear closure semantics of the query models and facilitate definition of user views.

In systems where both classes and collections are supported, a *collection* is similar to a *class* in that it groups objects, but it differs in the following respects. First, object creation may not occur through a collection; object creation occurs only through classes. This means that collections only form user-defined groupings of existing objects. Second, an object may exist in any number of collections, but

---

[2]This distinction between composite and complex objects is not always made, and the term "composite object" is used to refer to both. Some authors reverse the definition between composite and complex objects. We will use the terms as defined here consistently in this chapter.

is a member of only one class[3]. Third, the management of classes is *implicit*, in that the system automatically maintains classes based on the type lattice, whereas the management of collections is *explicit*, meaning that the user is responsible for their extents. Finally, a class groups the entire extension of a single type (*shallow extent*), along with the extensions of its subtypes (*deep extent*). Therefore, the elements of a class are homogeneous with respect to subtyping and inheritance (see the following section). A collection is heterogeneous in that it can contain objects of types unrelated by subtyping.

14.1.6 Subtyping and Inheritance

Object systems provide extensibility by allowing user-defined types to be defined and managed by the system. This is accomplished in two ways: by the definition of types using type constructors or by the definition of types based on existing primitive types through the process of *subtyping*. Subtyping is based on the *specialization* relationship among types. A type A is a *specialization* of another type B if its interface is a superset of B's interface. Thus, a specialized type is more defined (or more specified) than the type from which it is specialized. A type may be a specialization of a number of types; it is explicitly specified as a *subtype* of a subset of them. Some object models require that a type is specified as a subtype of only one type, in which case the model supports *single subtyping*; others allow *multiple subtyping*, where a type may be specified as a subtype of more than one type. Subtyping and specialization indicate an **is-a** relationship between types. In the above example, A **is-a** B, resulting in *substitutability*: an instance of a subtype (A) can be substituted in place of an instance of any of its *supertypes* (B) in any expression.

Besides enabling extensibility, subtyping also gives rise to a type system that forms the database schema. In many cases, there is a single root of the type system, which is the least specified type. If only single subtyping is allowed, as in Smalltalk [Goldberg and Robson, 1983], the type system is a tree. If multiple subtyping is supported, the type system forms a graph (a semilattice, to be precise). Some systems also define a most specified type, which forms the bottom of a full lattice. It is not necessary, however, for the type system to be rooted at a single type. C++ [Stroustrup, 1986], for example, permits multiple roots, resulting in a type system with multiple graphs. In these graphs/trees, there is an edge from type (class) A to type (class) B if A is a subtype of B.

A type lattice establishes the database schema in object databases. It enables one to model the common properties and differences among types in a concise manner.

Example 14.6

Consider the Car type we defined earlier. A car can be modeled as a special type of Vehicle. Thus, it is possible to define Car as a subtype of Vehicle whose other subtypes may be Motorcycle, Truck, and Bus. In this case, Vehicle would define the common properties of all of these:

---

[3]We ignore subtyping and inheritance for the time being, which raise the possibility for an object to be a member of multiple classes through the deep extent of a class. This topic will be discussed later.

```
type Vehicle as Object
   attributes
      engine : Engine
      make : Manufacturer
      model : String
      year : Date
      serial_no : String
   methods
      age: Real
```

Vehicle is defined as a subtype of Object which we assume is the root of the type lattice. It is defined with five attributes and one method which takes the date of manufacture and today's date (both of which are of system-defined type Date) and returns a real value. Obviously, Vehicle is a generalization of Car that we defined in Example 14.3. Car can now be defined as follows:

```
type Car as Vehicle
   attributes
      bumpers : {Bumper}
      tires : [LF: Tire, RF: Tire, LR: Tire, RR: Tire]
      capacity : Integer
```

Even though Car is defined with only two attributes, its interface is the same as the definition given in Example 14.3. This is because Car **is-a Vehicle**, and therefore "inherits" the attributes and methods of Vehicle.

Declaring a type to be a subtype of another results in *inheritance*. Inheritance allows reuse. A subtype may inherit either the behavior of its subtype, or its implementation, or both. We talk of single inheritance and multiple inheritance based on the subtype relationahip between the types.

14.2 OBJECT DISTRIBUTION DESIGN

Recall from Chapter 5 that the two important aspects of distribution design are fragmentation and allocation. Distribution design in the object world brings new complexities. Conceptually, objects encapsulate methods together with state. In reality, methods are implemented on types and shared by all instance objects of that type. Therefore, the location of objects with respect to their types becomes an issue. For the same reason, partitioning classes is also difficult.

In this section we consider the analogue, in object databases, of the distribution design problem introduced in Chapter 5 by considering fragmentation and allocation within the context of object models. In this discussion we assume an object model that does not distinguish between a class and a type. Distribution design in the object world brings new complexities due to the encapsulation of methods together with object state. This causes problems because methods are implemented on types and shared by all instance objects of that type. Therefore, one has to decide whether fragmentation is performed only on attributes duplicating the methods with each fragment), or whether one can fragment methods as well. The location of objects with respect to their types becomes an issue, as does the type of attributes. As discussed in Section 14.1.3, the domain of some attributes may be other classes. Thus, the fragmentation of classes with respect to such an attribute may have effects on other classes. Finally, if fragmentation is performed with respect to methods as well, it is necessary to distinguish between simple methods and complex methods. Simple methods are those that do not invoke other methods, while complex ones can invoke methods of other classes.

Similar to the relational case, there are three fundamental types of fragmentation: horizontal, vertical, and hybrid [Karlapalem et al., 1994]. In addition to these two fundamental cases, derived horizontal partitioning , associated horizontal partitioning , and path partitioning indexpath partitioning have been defined [Karlapalem and Li, 1995]. Derived horizontal partitioning has similar semantics to its counterpart in relational databases, which we will discuss further in Section 14.2.1. Associated horizontal partitioning, is similar to derived horizontal partitioning except that there is no "predicate clause", like minterm predicate, constraining the object instances. Path partitioning is discussed in Section 14.2.3. In the remainder, for simplicity, we assume a class-based object model which does not distinguish between types and classes.

14.2.1 Horizontal Class Partitioning

There are analogies between horizontal fragmentation of object databases and their relational counterparts. It is possible to identify primary horizontal fragmentation in the object database case identically to the relational case. Derived fragmentation shows some differences, however. In object databases, derived horizontal fragmentation can occur in a number of ways:

1. Partitioning of a class arising from the fragmentation of its subclasses. This occurs when a more specialized class is fragmented, so the results of this fragmentation should be reflected in the more general case. Clearly, care must be taken here, because fragmentation according to one subclass may conflict with those imposed by other subclasses. Because of this dependence, one starts with the fragmentation of the most specialized class and moves up the class lattice, reflecting its effects on the superclasses.

2. The fragmentation of a complex attribute may affect the fragmentation of its containing class.

3. Fragmenation of a class based on a method invocation sequence from one class to another may need to be reflected in the design. This happens in the case of complex methods as defined above.

Let us start the discussion with the simplest case: namely, fragmentation of a class with simple attributes and methods. In this case, primary horizontal partitioning can be performed according to a predicate defined on attributes of the class. Partitioning is easy: given class C for partitioning, we create classes $C_1, \ldots, C_n$, each of which takes the instances of C that satisfy the particular partitioning predicate. If these predicates are mutually exclusive, then classes $C_1, \ldots, C_n$ are disjoint. In this case, it is possible to define $C_1, \ldots, C_n$ as subclasses of C and change C's definition to an *abstract class* – one which does not have an explicit extent (i.e., no instances of its own). Even though this significantly forces the definition of subtyping (since the subclasses are not any more specifically defined than their superclass), it is allowed in many systems.

A complication arises if the partitioning predicates are not mutually exclusive. There are no clean solutions in this case. Some object models allow each object to belong to multiple classes. If this is an option, it can be used to address the problem. Otherwise "overlap classes" need to be defined to hold objects that satisfy multiple predicates.

Example 14.7

Consider the definition of the `Engine` class that is referred to in Example 14.6:

```
Class Engine as Object
   attributes
      no_cylinder : Integer
      capacity : Real
      horsepower: Integer
```

In this simple definition of Engine, all the attributes are simple. Consider the partitioning predicates

$$p_1: \quad \text{horsepower} \leq 150$$
$$p_2: \quad \text{horsepower} > 150$$

In this case, `Engine` can be partitioned into two classes, `Engine1` and `Engine2`, which inherit all of their properties from the `Engine` class, which is redefined as an abstract class. The objects of `Engine` class are distributed to the `Engine1` and `Engine2` classes based on the value of their horsepower attribute value.

This primary horizontal fragmentation of classes is applied to all classes in the system that are subject to fragmentation. At the end of this process, one obtains fragmentation schemes for every class. However, these schemes do not reflect the effect of derived fragmentation as a result of subclass fragmentation (as in the example above). Thus, the next step is to produce a set of derived fragments for each superclass using the set of predicates from the previous step. This essentially requires propogation of fragmentation decisions made in the subclasses to the superclasses. The output from this step is the set of primary fragments created in step two and the set of derived fragments from step three.

The final step is to combine these two sets of fragments in a consistent way. The final horizontal fragments of a class are composed of objects accessed by both applications running only on a class and those running on its subclasses. Therefore, we must determine the most appropriate primary fragment to merge with each derived fragment of every class. Several simple heuristics could be used, such as selecting the smallest or largest primary fragment, or the primary fragment that overlaps the most with the derived fragment. But, although these heuristics are simple and intuitive, they do not capture any quantitiative information about the distributed object database. Therefore, a more precise approach has been developed that is based on an affinity measure between fragments. As a result, fragments are joined with those fragments with which they have the highest affinity.

Let us now consider horizontal partitioning of a class with object-based instance variables (i.e., the domain of some of its instance variables is another class), but all the methods are simple. In this case, the composition relationship between classes comes into effect. In a sense, the composition relationship establishes the owner-member relationship that we discussed in Chapter 5: If class C_1 has an attribute A_1 whose domain is class C_2, then C_1 is the owner and C_2 is the member. Thus, the decomposition of C_2 follows the same principles as derived horizontal partitioning, discussed in Chapter 5.

So far, we have considered fragmentation with respect to attributes only, because the methods were simple. Let us now consider complex methods which require some care. For example, consider the case where all the attributes are simple, but the methods are complex. In this case, fragmentation based on simple attributes can be performed as described above. However, for methods, it is necessary to determine, at compile time, the objects that are accessed by a method invocation. This can be accomplished with static analysis. Clearly, optimal performance will result if invoked methods are contained within the same fragment as the invoking method. Optimization requires locating objects accessed together in the same fragment because this maximizes local relevant access and minimizes local irrelevant accesses.

The most complex case is where a class has complex attributes and complex methods. In this case, the subtyping relationships, aggregation relationships and relationships of method invocations have to be considered. Thus, the fragmentation method is the union of all of the above. One goes through the classes multiple times, generating a number of fragments, and then uses an affinity-based method to merge them.

14.2.2   Vertical Class Partitioning

Vertical fragmentation is considerably more complicated. Given a class C, fragmenting it vertically into $C_1, \ldots, C_m$ produces a number of classes, each of which contains some of the attributes and some of the methods. Thus, each of the fragments is less defined than the original class. Issues that must be addressed include the subtyping relationship between the original class' superclasses and subclasses and the fragment classes, the relationship of the fragment classes among themselves, and the location of the methods. If all the methods are simple, then methods can be partitioned easily. However, when this is not the case, the location of these methods becomes a problem.

Adaptations of the affinity-based relational vertical fragmentation approaches have been developed for object databases [Ezeife and Barker, 1998], [Ezeife and Barker, 1995]. However, the break-up of encapsulation during vertical fragmentation has created significant doubts as to the suitability of vertical fragmentation in object DBMSs. We refer the reader to the above-cited literature for further information.

14.2.3   Path Partitioning

The composition graph presents a representation for composite objects. For many applications, it is necessary to access the complete composite object. Path partitioning is a concept describing the clustering of all the objects forming a composite object into a partition. A path partition consists of grouping the objects of all the domain classes that correspond to all the instance variables in the subtree rooted at the composite object.

A path partition can be represented as a hierarchy of nodes forming a structural index. Each node of the index points to the objects of the domain class of the component object. The index thus contains the references to all the component objects of a composite object, eliminating the need to traverse the class composition hierarchy. The instances of the structural index are a set of OIDs pointing to all the component objects of a composite class. The structural index is an orthogonal structure to the object database schema, in that it groups all the OIDs of component objects of a composite object as a structured index class.

14.2.4   Class Partitioning Algorithms

The main issue in class partitioning is to improve the performance of user queries and applications by reducing the irrelevant data access. Thus, class partitioning is a logical database design technique which restructures the object database schema based on the application semantics. It should be noted that class partitioning is more complicated than relation fragmentation, and is also NP-complete. The algorithms for class partitioning are based on affinity-based and cost-driven approaches.

Affinity-based Approach

As covered in Section 5.3.2, affinity among attributes is used to vertically fragment relations. Similarly, affinity among instance variables and methods, and affinity among multiple methods can be used for horizontal and vertical class partitioning. Ezeife and Barker [1994, 1995] developed horizontal and vertical class partitioning algorithms based on classifying instance variables and methods as being either simple or complex. A complex instance variable is an object-based instance variable and is part of the class composition hierarchy. Malinowski and Chakravarthy [1997] extended the partition evaluator for relational databases to object oriented databases, and the algorithm they propose uses exhaustive enumeration. Karlapalem, et al. [1996a] developed a method induced partitioning scheme, which applies the method semantics and appropriately generates fragments that match the methods data requirements.

Cost-Driven Approach

Though the affinity-based approach provides "intuitively" appealing partitioning schemes, it has been shown [Fung et al., 1997] that these partitioning schemes do not always result in the greatest reduction of disk accesses required to process a set of applications. Therefore, a cost model for the number of disk accesses for processing both queries [Fung et al., 1997] and methods [Fung et al., 1996] on an object oriented database has been developed. Further, an heuristic "hill-climbing" approach which uses both the affinity approach (for initial solution) and the cost-driven approach (for further refinement) has been proposed [Fung et al., 1996]. This work also develops structural join index hierarchies for complex object retrieval, and studies its effectiveness against pointer traversal and other approaches, such as join index hierarchies, multi-index and access support relations (see next section). Each structural join index hierarchy is a materialization of path fragment, and facilitates direct access to a complex object and its component objects.

14.2.5 Allocation

The data allocation problem for object databases involves allocation of both methods and classes. The method allocation problem is tightly coupled to the class allocation problem because of encapsulation. Therefore, allocation of classes will imply allocation of methods to their corresponding home classes. But since applications on object-oriented databases invoke methods, the allocation of methods affects the performance of applications. However, allocation of methods which need to access multiple classes at different sites is a problem which has been not yet been tackled. Four alternatives can be identified [Fang et al., 1994]:

1. **Local behavior – local object.** This is the most straightforward case and is included to form the baseline case. The behavior, the object to which it is to be applied, and the arguments are all co-located. Therefore, no special mechanism is needed to handle this case.

2. **Local behavior – remote object.** This is one of the cases in which the behavior and the object to which it is applied are located at different sites. There are two ways of dealing with this case. One alternative is to move the remote object to the site where the behavior is located. The second is to ship the behavior implementation to the site where the object is located. This is possible if the receiver site can run the code.

3. **Remote behavior – local object.** This case is the reverse of case (2).

4. **Remote function – remote argument.** This case is the reverse of case (1).

Affinity-based algorithms for static allocation of class fragments that use a graph partitioning technique have also been proposed [Bhar and Barker, 1995]. However, these algorithms do not address method allocation and do not consider the interdependency between methods and classes. The issue has been addressed by means of an iterative solution for methods and class allocation [Bellatreche et al., 1998a].

14.2.6 Replication

Replication adds a new dimension to the design problem. Individual objects, classes of objects, or collections of objects (or all) can be units of replication. Undoubtedly, the decision is at least partially object-model dependent. Whether or not type specifications are located at each site can also be considered a replication problem.

14.3 ARCHITECTURAL ISSUES

As indicated in Chapter 4, one way to develop a distributed system is the client/server approach. Most, if not all, of the current object DBMSs are client/server systems. The design issues related to these systems are somewhat more complicated due to the characteristics of object models. Some of the concerns are listed below.

1. Since data and procedures are encapsulated as objects, the unit of communication between the clients and the server is an issue. The unit can be a page, an object, or a group of objects.

2. Closely related to the above issue is the design decision regarding the functions provided by the clients and the server. This is especially important since objects are not simply passive data, and it is necessary to consider the sites where object methods are executed.

3. In relational client/server systems, clients simply pass queries to the server, which executes them and returns the result tables to the client. This is referred to as *function shipping*. In object client/server DBMSs, this may not be the best approach, as the navigation of composite/complex object structures by the application program may dictate that data be moved to the clients (called *data shipping systems*). Since data are shared by many clients, the management of client cache buffers for data consistency becomes a serious concern. Client cache buffer management is closely related to concurrency control, since data that is cached to clients may be shared by multiple clients, and this has to be controlled. Most commercial object DBMSs use locking for concurrency control, so a fundamental architectural issue is the placement of locks, and whether or not the locks are cached to clients.

4. Since objects may be composite or complex, there may be possibilities for prefetching component objects when an object is requested. Relational client/server systems do not usually prefetch data from the server, but this may be a valid alternative in the case of object DBMSs.

These considerations require revisiting some of the issues common to all DBMSs, along with several new ones. We will consider these issues in three sections: those directly related to architectural design — architectural alternatives, buffer management, and cache consistency — are discussed in this section; those related to object management — object identifier management, pointer swizzling, and object migration — are discussed in Section 14.4; and storage management related issues — object clustering and garbage collection — are considered in Section 14.5.

14.3.1 Alternative Client/Server Architectures

Two main types of client/server architectures have been proposed: object servers and page servers. The distinction is partly based on the granularity of data that is shipped between the clients and the servers, and partly on the functionality provided to the clients and servers.

The first alternative is that clients request "objects" from the server, which retrieves them from the database and returns them to the requesting client. These systems are called *object servers* (Figure 14.1). In object servers, the server undertakes most of the DBMS services, with the client providing basically an execution environment for the applications, as well as some level of object management functionality (which will be discussed in Section 14.4). The object management layer is duplicated at both the client and the server in order to allow both to perform object functions. Object manager serves a number of functions. First and foremost, it provides a context for method execution. The replication of the object manager in both the server and the client enables methods to be executed at both the server and the clients. Executing methods in the client may invoke the execution of other methods, which may not have been shipped to the server with the object. The optimization of method executions of this type is an important research problem. Object manager also deals with the implementation of the object identifier (logical, physical, or virtual) and the deletion of objects (either explicit deletion or garbage collection). At the server, it also provides support for object clustering and access methods. Finally, the object managers at the client and the server implement an object cache (in addition to the page cache at the server). Objects are cached at

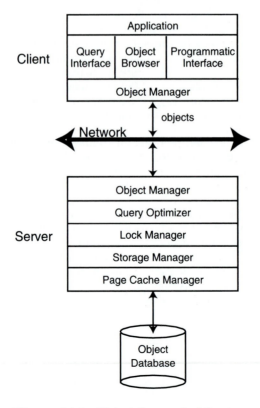

Figure 14.1. Object Server Architecture

the client to improve system performance by localizing accesses. The client goes to the server only if the needed objects are not in its cache. The optimization of user queries and the synchronization of user transactions are all performed in the server, with the client receiving the resulting objects.

It is not necessary for servers in these architectures to send individual objects to the clients; if it is appropriate, they can send groups of objects. If the clients do not send any prefetching hints [Gerlhof and Kemper, 1994] then the groups correspond to contiguous space on a disk page. Otherwise, the groups can contain objects from different pages. Depending upon the group hit rate, the clients can dynamically either increase or decrease the group size [Liskov et al., 1996]. In these systems, one complication needs to be dealt with: clients return updated objects to clients. These objects have to be installed onto their corresponding data pages (called the *home page*). If the corresponding data page does not exist in the server buffer (such as, for example, if the server has already flushed it out), the server must perform an *installation read* to reload the home page for this object.

An alternative organization is a *page server* client/server architecture , in which the unit of transfer between the servers and the clients is a physical unit of data, such as a page or segment, rather than an object (Figure 14.2). Page server architectures split the object processing services between the clients and the servers. In fact, the servers do not deal with objects anymore, acting instead as "value-added" storage managers.

Early performance studies (e.g., [DeWitt et al., 1990]) favored page server architectures over object server architectures. In fact, these results have influenced an entire generation of research into the optimal design of page server-based object DBMSs. However, these results were not conclusive, since they indicated that page server architectures are better when there is a match between a data clustering pattern[4] and the users' access pattern, and that object server architectures are better when the users' data access pattern is not the same as the clustering pattern. These earlier studies were further limited in their consideration of only single client/single server and multiple client/single server environments. There is clearly a need for further study in this area before a final judgment may be reached.

Intuitively, there should be significant performance advantages in having the server understand the "object" concept. One is that the server can apply locking and logging functions to the objects, enabling more clients to access the same page. Of course, this is relevant for small objects less than a page in size.

The second advantage is the potential for savings in the amount of data transmitted to the clients by filtering them at the server, which is possible if the server can perform some of the operations. This is indeed what the relational client/server systems do where the server is responsible for optimizing and executing the entire SQL query passed to it from a client. The situation is not as straightforward in object DBMSs, however, since the applications mix query access with object-by-object navigation. It is generally not a good idea to perform navigation at the server, since doing so would involve continuous interaction between the application and the server, resulting in a remote procedure call (RPC) for each object. In

---

[4]Clustering is an issue we will discuss later in this chapter. Briefly, it refers to how objects are placed on physical disk pages. Because of composite and complex objects, this becomes an important issue in object DBMSs.

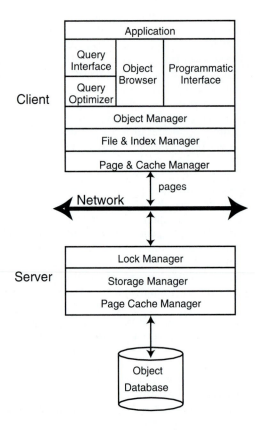

Figure 14.2. Page Server Architecture

fact, the earlier studies were preferential towards page servers, since they mainly considered workloads involving heavy navigation from object to object.

One possibility of dealing with the navigation problem is to ship the user's application code to the server and execute it there as well. This requires significant care, however, since the user code cannot be considered safe and may threaten the safety and reliability of the DBMS. Some systems (e.g., Thor [Liskov et al., 1996]) use a safe language to overcome this problem. Furthermore, since the execution is now divided between the client and the server, data reside in both the server and the client cache, and its consistency becomes a concern. Nevertheless, the "function shipping" approach involving both the clients and the servers in the execution of a query/application must be considered to deal with mixed workloads. The distribution of execution between different machines must also be accommodated as systems move towards peer-to-peer architectures.

Page servers simplify the DBMS code, since both the server and the client maintain page caches, and the representation of an object is the same all the way from the disk to the user interface. Thus, updates to the objects occur only in client caches and these updates are reflected on disk when the page is flushed from the client to the server. Another advantage of page servers is their full exploitation of the client workstation power in executing queries and applications. Thus, there is less chance of the server becoming a bottleneck. The server performs a limited set of functions and can therefore serve a large number of clients. It is possible to design these systems such that the work distribution between the server and the clients can be determined by the query optimizer. Page servers can also exploit operating systems and even hardware functionality to deal with certain problems, such as pointer swizzling (see Section 14.4.2), since the unit of operation is uniformly a page.

Clearly, both of these architectures have important advantages and limitations. Unfortunately, the existing performance studies do not establish clear tradeoffs, even though they provide interesting insights.

Client Buffer Management

The clients can manage either a page buffer, an object buffer, or a dual (i.e., page/object) buffer. If clients have a page buffer, then entire pages are read or written from the server every time a page fault occurs or a page is flushed. Object buffers can read/write individual objects and allow the applications object-by-object access.

Object buffers manage access at a finer granularity and, therefore, can achieve higher levels of concurrency. However, they may experience buffer fragmentation, as the buffer may not be able to accommodate an integral multiple of objects, thereby leaving some unused space. A page buffer does not encounter this problem, but if the data clustering on the disk does not match the application data access pattern, then the pages contain a great deal of unaccessed objects that use up valuable client buffer space. In these situations, buffer utilization of a page buffer will be lower than the buffer utilization of an object buffer.

To realize the benefits of both the page and the object buffers, dual page/object buffers have been proposed [Kemper and Kossman, 1994], [Castro et al., 1997]. In a dual buffer system, the client loads pages into the page buffer. However, when the client flushes out a page, it retains the useful objects from the page by copying the objects into the object buffer. Therefore, the client buffer manager tries to retain well-clustered pages and isolated objects from non-well- clustered pages. The client buffer managers retain the pages and objects across the transaction boundaries (commonly referred to as *inter-transaction caching*). If the clients use a log-based recovery mechanism (see Chapter 12), they also manage an in-memory log buffer in addition to the data buffer. Whereas the data buffers are managed using a variation of the least recently used (LRU) policy, the log buffer typically uses a first-in/first-out buffer replacement policy. As in centralized DBMS buffer management, it is important to decide whether all client transactions at a station should share the cache, or whether each transaction should maintain its own private cache. The recent trend is for systems to have both shared and private buffers [Carey et al., 1994], [Biliris and Panagos, 1995].

Server Buffer Management

The server buffer management issues do not change in object client/server systems, since the servers usually manage a page buffer. We nevertheless discuss the issues here briefly in the interest of completeness. The pages from the page buffer are, in turn, sent to the clients to satisfy their data requests. A grouped object-server constructs its object groups by copying the necessary objects from the relevant server buffer pages, and sends the object group to the clients. In addition to the page level buffer, the servers can also maintain a modified object buffer (MOB) [Ghemawat, 1995]. A MOB stores objects that have been updated and returned by the clients. These updated objects have to be installed onto their corresponding data pages, which may require installation reads as described earlier. Finally, the modified page has to be written back to the disk. A MOB allows the server to amortize its disk I/O costs by batching the installation read and installation write operations.

In a client/server system, since the clients typically absorb most of the data requests (i.e., the system has a high cache hit rate), the server buffer usually behaves more as a staging buffer than a cache. This, in turn, has an impact on the selection of server buffer replacement policies. Since it is desirable to minimize the duplication of data in the client and the server buffers, the *LRU with hate hints* buffer replacement policy can be used by the server [Franklin et al., 1992b]. The server marks the pages that also exist in client caches as *hated*. These pages are evicted first from the server buffer, and then the standard LRU buffer replacement policy is used for the remaining pages.

14.3.2 Cache Consistency

Cache consistency is a problem in any data shipping system that moves data to the clients. So the general framework of the issues discussed here also arise in relational client/server systems. However, the problems arise in unique ways in object DBMSs.

The study of DBMS cache consistency is very tightly coupled with the study of concurrency control, since cached data can be concurrently accessed by multiple clients, and locks can also be cached along with data at the clients. The DBMS cache consistency algorithms can be classified as avoidance-based or detection-based [Franklin et al., 1997]. *Avoidance-based algorithms* prevent the access of stale cache data[5] by ensuring that clients cannot update an object if it is being read by other clients. So they ensure that stale data never exists in client caches. *Detection-based algorithms* allow access of stale cache data, because clients can update objects that are being read by other clients. However, the detection-based algorithms perform a validation step at commit time to satisfy data consistency requirements.

Avoidance-based and detection-based algorithms can, in turn, be classified as *synchronous, asynchronous* or *deferred*, depending upon when they inform the server that a write operation is being performed. In synchronous algorithms, the client sends a lock escalation message at the time it wants to perform a write operation, and it blocks until the server responds. In asynchronous algorithms, the client sends a lock escalation message at the time of its write operation, but does not block waiting for a server response (it optimistically continues). In deferred algorithms,

---

[5]An object in a client cache is considered to be *stale* if that object has already been updated and committed into the database by a different client.

the client optimistically defers informing the server about its write operation until commit time. In deferred mode, the clients group all their lock escalation requests and send them together to the server at commit time. Thus, communication overhead is lower in a deferred cache consistency scheme, in comparison to synchronous and asynchronous algorithms.

The above classification results in a design space of possible algorithms covering six alternatives. Many performance studies have been conducted to assess the strengths and weaknesses of the various algorithms. In general, for data-caching systems, inter-transaction caching of data and locks is accepted as a performance enhancing optimization [Wilkinson and Neimat, 1990], [Franklin and Carey, 1994], because this reduces the number of times a client has to communicate with the server. On the other hand, for most user workloads, invalidation of remote cache copies during updates is preferred over propagation of updated values to the remote client sites [Franklin and Carey, 1994]. Hybrid algorithms that dynamically perform either invalidation or update propagation have been proposed [Franklin and Carey, 1994]. Furthermore, the ability to switch between page and object level locks is generally considered to be better than strictly dealing with page level locks [Carey et al., 1994] because it increases the level of concurrency.

Below, we will discuss each of the alternatives in the design space and comment on their performance characteristics.

- **Avoidance-based synchronous:** Callback-Read Locking (CBL) is the most common synchronous avoidance-based cache consistency algorithm [Franklin and Carey, 1994]. In this algorithm, the clients retain read locks across transactions, but they relinquish write locks at the end of the transaction. The clients send lock requests to the server and they block until the server responds. If the client requests a write lock on a page that is cached at other clients, the server issues callback messages requesting that the remote clients relinquish their read locks on the page. Callback-Read ensures a low abort rate and generally outperforms deferred avoidance-based, synchronous detection-based, and asynchronous detection-based algorithms.

- **Avoidance-based asynchronous:** Asynchronous avoidance-based cache consistency algorithms (AACC) [Özsu et al., 1998] do not have the message blocking overhead present in synchronous algorithms. Clients send lock escalation messages to the server and continue application processing. Normally, optimistic approaches such as this face high abort rates, but it is reduced in avoidance-based algorithms by immediate server actions to invalidate stale cache objects at remote clients as soon as the system becomes aware of the update. Thus, asynchronous algorithms experience lower deadlock abort rates than deferred avoidance-based algorithms, which are discussed next.

- **Avoidance-based deferred:** Optimistic Two-Phase Locking (O2PL) family of cache consistency are deferred avoidance-based algorithms [Franklin and Carey, 1994]. In these algorithms, the clients batch their lock escalation requests and send them to the server at commit time. The server blocks the updating client if other clients are reading the updated objects. As the data contention level increases, O2PL algorithms are susceptible to higher deadlock abort rates than CBL algorithms.

- **Detection-based synchronous:** Caching Two-Phase Locking (C2PL) is a synchronous detection-based cache consistency algorithm [Carey et al., 1991]. In this algorithm, clients contact the server whenever they access a page in their cache to ensure that the page is not stale or being written to by other clients. C2PL's performance is generally worse than CBL and O2PL algorithms, since it does not cache read locks across transactions.

- **Detection-based asynchronous:** No-Wait Locking (NWL) with Notification is an asynchronous detection-based algorithm [Wang and Rowe, 1991]. In this algorithm, the clients send lock escalation requests to the server, but optimistically assume that their requests will be successful. After a client transaction commits, the server propagates the updated pages to all the other clients that have also cached the affected pages. It has been shown that CBL outperforms the NWL algorithm.

- **Detection-based deferred:** Adaptive Optimistic Concurrency Control (AOCC) is a deferred detection-based algorithm. It has been shown [Adya et al., 1995] that AOCC can outperform callback locking algorithms even while encountering a higher abort rate if the client transaction state (data and logs) completely fits into the client cache, and all application processing is strictly performed at the clients (purely data-shipping architecture). Since AOCC uses deferred messages, its messaging overhead is less than CBL. Furthermore, in a purely data-shipping client/server environment, the impact of an aborting client on the performance of other clients is quite minimal. These factors contribute to AOCC's superior performance.

14.4 OBJECT MANAGEMENT

The exact nature of object management functionality is open to discussion. As indicated in Section 14.3.1, this includes tasks such as object identifier management, pointer swizzling, object migration, deletion of objects, method execution, and some storage management tasks at the server. In this section we will discuss some of these problems; those related to storage management are discussed in the next section.

14.4.1 Object Identifier Management

As indicated in Section 14.1, object identifiers (OIDs) are system-generated and used to uniquely identify every object (transient or persistent, system-created or user-created) in the system. Implementing the identity of persistent objects generally differs from implementing transient objects, since only the former must provide global uniqueness. In particular, transient object identity can be implemented more efficiently.

The implementation of persistent object identity has two common solutions, based on either physical or logical identifiers, with their respective advantages and shortcomings. The physical identifier (POID) approach equates the OID with the physical address of the corresponding object. The address can be a disk page address and an offset from the base address in the page. The advantage is that the object can be obtained directly from the OID. The drawback is that all parent objects and indexes must be updated whenever an object is moved to a different page.

The logical identifier (LOID) approach consists of allocating a systemwide unique OID (i.e., a surrogate) per object. Since OIDs are invariant, there is no overhead due to object movement. This is achieved by an OID table associating each OID with the physical object address at the expense of one table look-up per object access. To avoid the overhead of OIDs for small objects that are not referentially shared, both approaches can consider the object value as their identifier. The earlier hierarchical and network database systems used the physical identifier approach. Object-oriented database systems tend to prefer the logical identifier approach, which better supports dynamic environments.

Implementing transient object identity involves the techniques used in programming languages. As for persistent object identity, identifiers can be physical or logical. The physical identifier can be the real or virtual address of the object, depending on whether virtual memory is provided. The physical identifier approach is the most efficient, but requires that objects do not move. The logical identifier approach, promoted by object-oriented programming, treats objects uniformly through an indirection table local to the program execution. This table associates a logical identifier, called an *object oriented pointer* (OOP) in Smalltalk, to the physical identifier of the object. Object movement is provided at the expense of one table look-up per object access.

The dilemma for an object manager is a trade-off between generality and efficiency. The general support of the object model incurs a certain overhead. For example, object identifiers for small objects can make the OID table quite large. By limiting the support of the object model—for example, by not providing object sharing directly, and by relying on higher levels of system (e.g., the compiler of the database language) for that support, more efficiency may be gained. Object identifier management is closely related to object storage techniques, which we will discuss in Section 14.5.

In distributed object DBMSs, it may be more appropriate to use LOIDs, since operations such as reclustering, migration, replication and fragmentation occur frequently. The use of LOIDs raises the following distribution related issues:

- **LOID Generation:** LOIDs must be unique within the scope of the entire distributed domain. It is relatively easy to ensure uniqueness if the LOIDs are generated at a central site. However, a centralized LOID generation scheme is not desirable because of the network latency overhead and the load on the LOID generation site. In multi-server environments, each server site generates LOIDs for the objects stored at that site. The uniqueness of the LOID is ensured by incorporating the server identifier as part of the LOID. Therefore, the LOID consists of both a server identifier part and a sequence number. The sequence number is the logical representation of the disk location of the object. The sequence numbers are unique within a particular server, and are usually not re-used to prevent existing references to the deleted object from pointing to the new object which assumes the same sequence number. During object access time, if the server identifier portion of the LOID is not directly used for object location identification, the object identifier functions as a pure LOID. However, if the server identifier portion of the LOID is used, the LOID functions as a pseudo-LOID.

- **LOID Mapping Location and Data Structures:** The location of the LOID-to-POID mapping information is important. If pure LOIDs are used, and if a client can be directly connected to multiple servers simultaneously, then the LOID-to-POID mapping information must be present at the client. If pseudo-LOIDs are used, the mapping information needs to be present only at the server. The presence of the mapping information at the client is not desirable, because this solution is not scalable (i.e.,the mapping information has to be updated at all the clients which might access the object).

  The LOID-to-POID mapping information is usually stored in hash tables or in B+ trees. There are advantages and disadvantages to both [Eickler et al., 1995]. Hash tables provide fast access, but are not scalable as the database size increases. B+ trees are scalable, but have a logarithmic access time, and require complex concurrency control and recovery strategies.

14.4.2 Pointer Swizzling

In object DBMSs, one can navigate from one object to another using *path expressions* that involve attributes with object-based values (e.g., if c is of type `Car`, then c.engine.manufacturer.name is a path expression[6]). These are basically pointers. Usually on disk, object identifiers are used to represent these pointers. However, in memory, it is desirable to use in-memory pointers for navigating from one object to another. The process of converting a disk version of the pointer to an in-memory version of a pointer is known as "pointer-swizzling". Hardware-based and software-based schemes are two types of pointer-swizzling mechanisms [White and DeWitt, 1994]. In hardware-based schemes, the operating system's page-fault mechanism is used; when a page is brought into memory, all the pointers in it are swizzled, and they point to reserved virtual memory frames. The data pages corresponding to these reserved virtual frames are only loaded into memory when an access is made to these pages. The page access, in turn, generates an operating system page-fault, which must be trapped and processed. In software-based schemes, an object table is used for pointer-swizzling purposes. That is, a pointer is swizzled to point to a location in the object table. There are eager and lazy variations to the software-based schemes, depending upon when exactly the pointer is swizzled. Therefore, every object access has a level of indirection associated with it. The advantage of the hardware-based scheme is that it leads to better performance when repeatedly traversing a particular object hierarchy, due to the absence of a level of indirection for each object access. However, in bad clustering situations where only a few objects per page are accessed, the high overhead of the page-fault handling mechanism makes hardware-based schemes unattractive. Hardware-based schemes also do not prevent client applications from accessing deleted objects on a page. Moreover, in badly clustered situations, hardware-based schemes can exhaust the virtual memory address space, because page frames are aggressively reserved regardless of whether the objects in the page are actually accessed. Finally, since the hardware-based scheme is implicitly page-oriented, it is difficult to provide object-

---

[6]We assume that `Engine` type is defined with at least one attribute, `manufacturer`, whose domain is the extent of type `Manufacturer`. `Manufacturer` type has an attribute called `name`.

level concurrency control, buffer management, data transfer and recovery features. In many cases, it is desirable to manipulate data at the object level rather than the page level.

14.4.3 Object Migration

One aspect of distributed systems is that objects move, from time to time, between sites. This raises a number of issues. First is the unit of migration. In systems where the state is separated from the methods, it is possible to consider moving the object's state without moving the methods. The counterpart of this scenario in purely behavioral systems is the fragmentation of an object according to its behaviors. In either case, the application of methods to an object requires the invocation of remote procedures. This issue was discussed above under object distribution. Even if individual objects are units of migration [Dollimore et al., 1994], their relocation may move them away from their type specifications and one has to decide whether types are duplicated at every site where instances reside or whether the types are accessed remotely when behaviors or methods are applied to objects. Three alternatives can be considered for the migration of classes (types):

1. the source code is moved and recompiled at the destination,

2. the compiled version of a class is migrated just like any other object, or

3. the source code of the class definition is moved, but not its compiled operations, for which a lazy migration strategy is used.

Another issue is that the movements of the objects must be tracked so that they can be found in their new locations. A common way of tracking objects is to leave *surrogates* [Hwang, 1987], [Liskov et al., 1994], or *proxy objects* [Dickman, 1994]. These are place-holder objects left at the previous site of the object, pointing to its new location. Accesses to the proxy objects are directed transparently by the system to the objects themselves at the new sites. The migration of objects can be accomplished based on their current state [Dollimore et al., 1994]. Objects can be in one of four states:

1. Ready: Ready objects are not currently invoked, or have not received a message, but are ready to be invoked to receive a message.

2. Active: Active objects are currently involved in an activity in response to an invocation or a message.

3. Waiting: Waiting objects have invoked (or have sent a message to) another object and are waiting for a response.

4. Suspended: Suspended objects are temporarily unavailable for invocation.

Objects in active or waiting state are not allowed to migrate, since the activity they are currently involved in would be broken. The migration involves two steps:

1. shipping the object from the source to the destination, and

2. creating a proxy at the source, replacing the original object.

Two related issues must also be addressed here. One relates to the maintenance of the system directory. As objects move, the system directory must be updated to reflect the new location. This may be done lazily, whenever a surrogate or proxy object redirects an invocation, rather than eagerly, at the time of the movement. The second issue is that, in a highly dynamic environment where objects move frequently, the surrogate or proxy chains may become quite long. It is useful for the system to transparently compact these chains from time to time. However, the result of compaction must be reflected in the directory, and it may not be possible to accomplish that lazily.

Another important migration issue arises with respect to the movement of composite objects. The shipping of a composite object may involve shipping other objects referenced by the composite object. An alternative method of dealing with this is a method called *object assembly*, which we will consider under query processing in Section 14.6.3.

14.5 DISTRIBUTED OBJECT STORAGE

Among the many issues related to object storage, two are particularly relevant in a distributed system: object clustering and distributed garbage collection . Composite and complex objects provide opportunities, as we mentioned earlier, for clustering data on disk such that the I/O cost of retrieving them is reduced. Garbage collection is a problem that arises in object databases, since they allow reference-based sharing. Thus, object deletion and subsequent storage reclamation requires special care.

Object Clustering

An object model is essentially conceptual, and should provide high physical data independence to increase programmer productivity. The mapping of this conceptual model to a physical storage is a classical database problem. As indicated in Section 14.1, in the case of object DBMSs, two kinds of relationships exist between types: subtyping and composition. By providing a good approximation of object access, these relationships are essential to guide the physical clustering of persistent objects. Object clustering refers to the grouping of objects in physical containers (i.e., disk extents) according to common properties, such as the same value of an attribute or sub-objects of the same object. Thus, fast access to clustered objects can be obtained.

Object clustering is difficult for two reasons. First, it is not orthogonal to object identity implementation (i.e, logical vs. physical OID). Logical OIDs incur more overhead (an indirection table), but enable vertical partitioning of classes. Physical OIDs yield more efficient direct object access, but require each object to contain all inherited attributes. Second, the clustering of complex objects along the composition relationship is more involved because of object sharing (objects with multiple parents).

Given a class graph, there are three basic storage models for object clustering [Valduriez et al., 1986].

1. The *decomposition storage model* (DSM) partitions each object class in binary relations (OID, attribute) and therefore relies on logical OID. The advantage of DSM is simplicity.

2. The *normalized storage model* (NSM) stores each class as a separate relation. It can be used with logical or physical OID. However, only logical OID allows the vertical partitioning of objects along the inheritance relationship [Kim et al., 1987].

3. The *direct storage model* enables multi-class clustering of complex objects based on the composition relationship. This model generalizes the techniques of hierarchical and network databases, and works best with physical OID [Benzaken and Delobel, 1991]. It can capture object access locality and is therefore potentially superior for well-known access patterns. The major difficulty, however, is to recluster an object whose parent has been deleted.

In a distributed system, both DSM and NSM are straightforward, using horizontal partitioning. Goblin [Kersten et al., 1993] implements DSM as a basis for a distributed object DBMS with large main memory. DSM provides flexibility, and its performance disadvantage is compensated by the use of large main memory and caching. Eos [Gruber and Amsaleg, 1993] implements the direct storage model in a distributed single-level store architecture, where each object has a physical, system-wide OID. The Eos grouping mechanism is based on the concept of most relevant composition links and solves the problem of multiparent shared objects. When an object moves to a different node, it gets a new OID. To avoid the indirection of forwarders, references to the object are subsequently changed as part of the garbage collection process without any overhead. The grouping mechanism is dynamic to achieve load balancing and cope with the evolutions of the object graph.

Distributed Garbage Collection

An advantage of object-based systems is that objects can refer to other objects using object identity. As programs modify objects and remove references, a persistent object may become unreachable from the persistent roots of the system when there is no more reference to it. Such an object is "garbage" and should be de-allocated by the garbage collector. In relational DBMSs, there is no need for automatic garbage collection, since object references are supported by join values. However, cascading updates as specified by referential integrity constraints are a simple form of "manual" garbage collection. In more general operating system or programming language contexts, manual garbage collection is typically error-prone. Therefore, the generality of distributed object-based systems calls for automatic distributed garbage collection.

The basic garbage collection algorithms can be categorized as reference counting or tracing-based. In a reference counting system, each object has an associated count of the references to it. Each time a program creates an additional reference that points to an object, the object's count is incremented. When an existing reference to an object is destroyed, the corresponding count is decremented. The memory occupied by an object can be reclaimed when the object's count drops to zero (at which time, the object is garbage).

Tracing-based collectors are divided into *mark and sweep* and *copy-based* algorithms. *Mark and sweep* collectors are two-phase algorithms. The first phase, called the "mark" phase, starts from the root and marks every reachable object (for example, by setting a bit associated to each object). This mark is also called a "color", and the collector is said to color the objects it reaches. The mark bit can be embedded in the objects themselves or in *color maps* that record, for every memory page, the colors of the objects stored in that page. Once all live objects are marked, the memory is examined and unmarked objects are reclaimed. This is the "sweep" phase.

Copy-based collectors divide memory into two disjoint areas called *from-space* and *to-space*. Programs manipulate from-space objects, while the to-space is left empty. Instead of marking and sweeping, copying collectors copy (usually in a depth first manner) the from-space objects reachable from the root into the to-space. Once all live objects have been copied, the collection is over, the contents of the from-space are discarded, and the roles of from- and to-spaces are exchanged. The copying process copies objects linearly in the to-space, which compacts memory.

The basic implementations of mark and sweep and copy-based algorithms are "stop-the-world"; i.e., user programs are suspended during the whole collection cycle. For many applications, however, stop-the-world algorithms cannot be used because of their disruptive behavior. Preserving the response time of user applications requires the use of incremental techniques. Incremental collectors must address problems raised by concurrency. The main difficulty with incremental garbage collection is that, while the collector is tracing the object graph, program activity may change other parts of the object graph. In some cases, the collector may miss tracing some reachable objects, and thus may erroneously reclaim them.

Designing a garbage collection algorithm for object DBMSs is difficult. These systems have several features that pose additional problems for incremental garbage collection, beyond those typically addressed by solutions for non-persistent systems. These problems include the ones raised by the resilience to system failures and the semantics of transactions, and, in particular, by the rollbacks of partially completed transactions, by traditional client-server performance optimizations (such as client caching and flexible management of client buffers), and by the huge volume of data to analyze in order to detect garbage objects. There have been a number of proposals starting with [Butler, 1987]. More recent work has investigated fault-tolerant garbage collection techniques for transactional persistent systems in centralized [Kolodner and Weihl, 1993], [O'Toole et al., 1993] and client-server [Yong et al., 1994], [Amsaleg, 1995], [Amsaleg et al., 1995] architectures.

Distributed garbage collection, however, is even harder than centralized garbage collection. For scalability and efficiency reasons, a garbage collector for a distributed system combines independent per-site collectors with a global inter-site collector. Coordinating local and global collections is difficult because it requires carefully keeping track of reference exchanges between sites. Keeping track of such exchanges is necessary because an object may be referenced from several sites. In addition, an object located at one site may be referenced from live objects at remote sites, but not by any local live object. Such an object must not be reclaimed by the local collector, since it is reachable from the root of a remote site. It is difficult to keep track of inter-site references in a distributed environment where messages can be lost, duplicated or delayed, or where individual sites may crash.

Distributed garbage collectors rely either on distributed reference counting or distributed tracing. Distributed reference counting is problematic for two reasons. First, reference counting cannot collect unreachable cycles of garbage objects (i.e., mutually-referential garbage objects). Second, reference counting is defeated by common message failures; that is, if messages are not delivered reliably in their causal order, then maintaining the reference counting invariant (i.e., equality of the count with the actual number of references) is problematic. However, several algorithms propose distributed garbage collection solutions based on reference counting [Bevan, 1987], [Dickman, 1991]. Each solution makes specific assumptions about the failure model, and is therefore incomplete. A variant of a reference counting collection scheme, called "reference listing" (see [Plainfossé and Shapiro, 1995]), is implemented in Thor [Maheshwari and Liskov, 1994]. This algorithm tolerates server and client failures, but does not address the problem of reclaiming distributed cycles of garbage.

Distributed tracing usually combines independent per-site collectors with a global inter-site collector. The main problem with distributed tracing is synchronizing the distributed (global) garbage detection phase with independent (local) garbage reclamation phases. When local collectors and user programs all operate in parallel, enforcing a global, consistent view of the object graph is impossible, especially in an environment where messages are not received instantaneously, and where communications failures are likely. Therefore, distributed tracing-based garbage collection relies on inconsistent information in order to decide if an object is garbage or not. This inconsistent information makes distributed tracing collector very complex, because the collector tries to accurately track the minimal set of reachable objects to at least eventually reclaim some objects that really are garbage. Ladin and Liskov propose an algorithm that computes, on a central space, the global graph of remote references [Ladin and Liskov, 1992]. Ferreira and Shapiro present an algorithm that can reclaim cycles of garbage that span several disjoint object spaces [Ferreira and Shapiro, 1994]. Finally, Le Fessant et al. present a complete (i.e., both acyclic and cyclic), asynchronous, distributed garbage collector [Fessant et al., 1998].

14.6   OBJECT QUERY PROCESSING

Relational DBMSs have benefitted from the early definition of a precise and formal query model and a set of universally-accepted algebraic primitives. This has not been the case with object DBMSs. The first-generation object DBMSs did not have a declarative query language, and some still do not. It was commonly believed that the application domains that these systems target did not need querying capabilities. This belief no longer holds, and declarative query capability is now accepted as a fundamental feature of object DBMSs [Atkinson et al., 1989], [Stonebraker et al., 1990a].

There is a close relationship between query optimization techniques and the query model and query language. For example, a functional query language lends itself to functional optimization, which is quite different from the algebraic, cost-based optimization techniques used in both relational systems and a number of object-oriented systems. The query model, in turn, is based on the data (or object) model, since the latter defines the access primitives used by the query model. These primitives at least partially determine the power of the query model. The object model issues were discussed in the previous section; we will not dwell long on query model issues here since the focus of this section is on query processing and optimization. For the remainder, we will assume that the user query language is OQL [Cattell, 1997], which is an object-oriented version of the SQL language upon which we have relied heavily in previous chapters. OQL was developed by a consortium of object DBMS vendors (known as the Object Database Group — ODBG), so it serves as a de facto industry standard. Some systems (e.g., O_2 [Deux et al., 1991]) already provide OQL interfaces. As we did earlier, we will take liberties with the language syntax.

Almost all object query processors that have been proposed to date use the optimization techniques that have been developed for relational systems. However, there are a number of issues that make query processing and optimization more difficult in object DBMSs. The more important issues are the following [Özsu and Blakeley, 1994]:

1. Relational query languages operate on very simple type systems consisting of a single type: relation. The closure property of relational languages implies that each relational operator takes one or two relations as operands and generates a relation as a result. In contrast, object systems have richer type systems. The results of object algebra operators are usually sets of objects (or collections), which may be of different types. If the object languages are closed under the algebra operators, these heterogeneous sets of objects can be operands to other operators. This requires the development of elaborate type inferencing schemes to determine which methods can be applied to **all** the objects in such a set. Furthermore, object algebras often operate on semantically different collection types (e.g., set, bag, list), which imposes additional requirements on the type inferencing schemes to determine the type of the results of operations on collections of different types.

2. Relational query optimization depends on knowledge of the physical storage of data (access paths) which is readily available to the query optimizer. The encapsulation of methods with the data upon which they operate in object DBMSs raises at least two important issues. First, determining (or estimating) the cost of executing methods is considerably more difficult than calculating or estimating the cost of accessing an attribute according to an access path. In fact, optimizers have to worry about optimizing method execution, which is not an easy problem because methods may be written using a general-purpose programming language. Second, encapsulation raises issues related to the accessibility of storage information by the query optimizer. Some systems overcome this difficulty by treating the query optimizer as a special application that can break encapsulation and access information directly [Cluet and Delobel, 1992]. Others propose a mechanism whereby objects "reveal" their costs as part of their interface [Graefe and Maier, 1988].

3. Objects can (and usually do) have complex structures whereby the state of an object references another object. Accessing such complex objects involves *path expressions*. The optimization of path expressions is a difficult and central issue in object query languages. We discuss this issue in some detail in this chapter. Furthermore, objects belong to types related through inheritance hierarchies. Optimizing the access to objects through their inheritance hierarchies is also a problem that distinguishes object-oriented from relational query processing.

4. As mentioned earlier, one of the facts of life in object DBMSs is the lack of a universally-accepted object model definition. Even though there is some convergence in the set of basic features that must be supported by any object model (such as object identity, encapsulation of state and behavior, type inheritance, and typed collections), how these features are supported differs among models and systems. As a result, the numerous projects that experiment with object query optimizers follow quite different paths and are, to a certain degree, incompatible, making it quite difficult to amortise on the experiences of others. As this diversity of approaches is likely to prevail for some time, extensible approaches to query optimization that allow experimentation with new ideas as they evolve are important in object query processing. We provide an overview of the various extensibility approaches.

Object query processing and optimization has been the subject of significant research activity. Unfortunately, most of this work has not been extended to distributed object systems. Therefore, in the remainder of this chapter, we will restrict ourselves to a summary of the important issues: object query processing architectures (Section 14.6.1), object query optimization (Section 14.6.2), and query execution strategies (Section 14.6.3).

14.6.1   Object Query Processor Architectures

As indicated in Chapter 7, query optimization can be modeled as an optimization problem whose solution is the choice, based on a *cost function*, of the "optimum" *state*, which corresponds to an algebraic query, in a *state space* (also called *search space*) that represents a family of equivalent algebraic queries. Query processors differ, architecturally, according to how they model these components.

Many existing object DBMS optimizers are either implemented as part of the object manager on top of a storage system, or as client modules in a client/server architecture. In most cases, the above-mentioned components are "hardwired" into the query optimizer. Given that extensibility is a major goal of object DBMSs, one would hope to develop an extensible optimizer that accommodates different search strategies, algebra specifications (with their different transformation rules), and cost functions. Rule-based query optimizers [Freytag, 1987], [Graefe and De-Witt, 1987] provide some amount of extensibility by allowing the definition of new transformation rules. However, they do not allow extensibility in other dimensions. In this section we will discuss some new, promising proposals for extensibility in object DBMSs.

The Open OODB project [Wells et al., 1992] at Texas Instruments concentrates on the definition of an open architectural framework for object DBMSs and description of the design space for these systems. The query module is an example of intra-module extensibility in Open OODB. The query optimizer [Blakeley et al., 1993], built using the Volcano optimizer generator [Graefe and McKenna, 1993], is extensible with respect to algebraic operators, logical transformation rules, execution algorithms, implementation rules (i.e., logical operator-to-execution algorithm mappings), cost estimation functions, and physical property enforcement functions (e.g., presence of objects in memory). The separation between the user query language parsing structures and the operator graph on which the optimizer operates allows the replacement of the user language or optimizer. The separation between algebraic operators and execution algorithms allows exploration with alternative methods for implementing algebraic operators. Code generation is also a well-defined subcomponent of the query module, which facilitates porting the query module to work on top of other object DBMSs. The Open OODB query processor includes a query execution engine containing efficient implementations of scan, indexed scan, hybrid-hash join [Shapiro, 1986], and complex object assembly [Keller et al., 1991], which we discuss later.

The EPOQ project [Mitchell et al., 1993] is another approach to query optimization extensibility, where the search space is divided into *regions*. Each region corresponds to an equivalent family of query expressions that are reachable from each other. The regions are not necessarily mutually exclusive and differ in the queries they manipulate, the control (search) strategies they use, the query transformation rules they incorporate, and the optimization objectives they achieve. For example, one region may cover transformation rules dealing with simple select queries, while another region may deal with transformations for nested queries. Similarly, one region may have the objective of minimizing a cost function, while another region may attempt to transform queries to some desirable form. Each region may be nested to a number of levels, allowing hierarchical searches within a region. Since the regions do not represent equivalence classes, a global control strategy is needed to determine how the query optimizer moves from one region to another.

The TIGUKAT project [Özsu et al., 1995a] uses an object approach to query processing extensibility. TIGUKAT object model is an extensible uniform behavioral model characterized by a purely behavioral semantics and a uniform approach to objects. The model is behavioral in that the only way objects are accessed is by applying behaviors (which replace both the instance variables and the methods available in other object models) to objects. Behaviors are defined on types, and their implementations are modeled as functions. Types and classes are separated, and the concept of an explicitly managed collection is introduced. Queries operate on collections and return collections as a result. Every concept, including types, classes, collections, meta-information, etc., is a first-class object. The uniformity of the object model extends to the query model, treating queries as first-class objects [Peters et al., 1993]. A `Query` type is defined as a subtype of the `Function` type. Thus, queries are specialized kinds of functions that can be compiled and executed. Furthermore, a `Query` type can be specialized based on a classification scheme — for example, as ad hoc and production queries. The inputs and outputs of queries are collections (which are also objects), providing closure.

TIGUKAT query optimizer [Özsu et al., 1995b] follows the same philosophy of representing system concepts as objects and is along the lines of [Lanzelotte and Valduriez, 1991]. The search space, the search strategy and the cost function are modeled as objects. The incorporation of these components into the type system provides extensibility via the basic object principle of subtyping and specialization.

Modeling the building blocks of a cost-based optimizer as objects provides the query optimizer the extensibility inherent in object models. The optimizer basically implements a control strategy that associates a search strategy and cost function to each query.

14.6.2 Query Processing Issues

Query processing methodology in object DBMSs is similar to its relational counterpart, as discussed in Chapters 7-9, but with differences in details as a result of the object model and query model characteristics. In this section we will consider these differences as they apply to algebraic optimization. We will also discuss a particular problem unique to object query models — namely, the execution of path expressions.

Algebraic Optimization

Search Space and Transformation Rules. As discussed in Chapter 8, a major advantage of algebraic optimization is that an algebraic query expression can be transformed using well-defined algebraic properties, such as transitivity, commutativity and distributivity. During the process, one eliminates plans with execution times that are worse than the previously-found minimum.

The transformation rules are very much dependent upon the specific object algebra , since they are defined individually for each object algebra and for their combinations. The lack of a standard object algebra definition is particularly troubling since the community cannot benefit from generalizations of numerous studies. The general considerations for the definition of transformation rules and the manipulation of query expressions is quite similar to relational systems, with one particularly important difference. Relational query expressions are defined on flat relations, whereas object queries are defined on classes (or collections or sets of objects) that have subtyping and composition relationships among them. It is, therefore, possible to use the semantics of these relationships in object query optimizers to achieve some additional transformations.

Consider, for example, three object algebra operators: [Straube and Özsu, 1990a] union (denoted $\cup$), intersection (denoted $\cap$) and parameterized select (denoted $P\sigma_F < Q_1 \ldots Q_k >$), where union and intersection have the usual set-theoretic semantics, and select selects objects from one set P using the sets of objects $Q_1 \ldots Q_k$ as parameters (in a sense, a generalized form of semijoin). The results of these operators are sets of objects as well. The following are some of the transformation rules that can be applied during optimization to get equivalent query expressions (for brevity, we use $QSet$ to denote $Q_1 \ldots Q_k$; $RSet$ is defined similarly):

$$(P\sigma_{F_1} < QSet >)\sigma_{F_2} < RSet > \quad \Leftrightarrow \quad (P\sigma_{F_2} < RSet >)\sigma_{F_1} < QSet >$$
$$(P \cup Q)\sigma_F < RSet > \quad \Leftrightarrow \quad (P\sigma_F < RSet >) \cup (Q\sigma_F < RSet >)$$
$$(P\sigma_{F_1} < QSet >)\sigma_{F_2} < RSet > \quad \Leftrightarrow \quad (P\sigma_{F_1} < QSet >) \cap (P\sigma_{F_2} < RSet >)$$

The first rule captures commutativity of `select`, while the second rule denotes that `select` distributes over `union`. The third rule is an identity which uses the fact that `select` merely restricts its input and returns a subset of its first argument[7].

The first two rules are quite general in that they represent equivalences inherited from set theory. The third is a special transformation rule for a specific object algebra operator defined with a specific semantics. All three, however, are syntactic in nature. Consider the following rules, on the other hand, where C_i denotes the set of objects in the extent of class c_i and C_j^* denotes the deep extent of class c_j (i.e., the set of objects in the extent of c_j, as well as in the extents of all those which are subclasses of c_j):

$$
\begin{aligned}
C_1 \cap C_2 &= \phi \text{ if } c_1 \neq c_2 \\
C_1 \cup C_2^* &= C_2^* \text{ if } c_1 \text{ is a subclass of } c_2 \\
(P\sigma_F < QSet >) \cap R &\overset{c}{\Leftrightarrow} (P\sigma_F < QSet <) \cap (R\sigma_{F'} < QSet >) \\
&\overset{c}{\Leftrightarrow} P \cap (R\sigma_{F'} < QSet >)
\end{aligned}
$$

These transformation rules are semantic in nature, since they depend on the object model and query model specifications. The first rule, for example, is true because the object model restricts each object to belong to only one class. The second rule holds because the query model permits retrieval of objects in the deep extent of the target class. Finally, the third rule relies on type consistency rules [Straube and Özsu, 1990b] for its applicability, as well as a condition (denoted by the c over the $\Leftrightarrow$) that F' is identical to F, except that each occurrence of p is replaced by r.

Since the idea of query transformation is well-known, we will not elaborate on the techniques. The above discussion only demonstrates the general idea and highlights the unique aspects that must be considered in object algebras.

Search Algorithm. As discussed in Chapters 8 and 9, exhaustive search algorithms enumerate the entire search space, applying a cost function to each equivalent expression to determine the least expensive one. An improvement is to use a dynamic programming approach, whereby new expressions are constructed bottom-up using the previously-determined optimal subexpressions [Lee et al., 1988], [Selinger et al., 1979]. The Volcano optimizer generator uses a top-down, dynamic programming approach to search with branch-and-bound pruning [Graefe and McKenna, 1993]. These are called *enumerative algorithms*.

The combinatorial nature of enumerative search algorithms is perhaps more important in object DBMSs than in relational ones. It has been argued that if the number of joins in a query exceeds ten, enumerative search strategies become infeasible [Ioannidis and Wong, 1987]. In applications such as decision support systems which object DBMSs are well-suited to support, it is quite common to find queries of this complexity. Furthermore, as we will address in Section 14.6.2, one method of executing path expressions is to represent them as explicit joins, and then use the well-known join algorithms to optimize them. If this is the case, the number of joins and other operations with join semantics in a query is quite likely to be higher than the empirical threshold of ten.

In these cases, *randomized search algorithms* (which we introduced in Chapters 8 and 9) have been suggested as alternatives to restrict the region of the search space

---

[7]These rules make assumptions about the formulae (F_i), which we will not address in this chapter.

being analyzed. Unfortunately, there has not been any study of randomized search algorithms within the context of object DBMSs. The general strategies are not likely to change, but the tuning of the parameters and the definition of the space of acceptable solutions should be expected to change. It is also interesting to note the surface similarity between randomized search algorithms and the regions approach proposed by Mitchell, et al [1993]. Further studies are required to establish the relationship more firmly. Furthermore, the distributed versions of these algorithms are not available, and their development remains a challenge.

Cost Function. As we have already seen, the arguments to cost functions are based on various information regarding the storage of the data. Typically, the optimizer considers the number of data items (cardinality), the size of each data item, its organization (e.g., whether there are indexes on it or not), etc. This information is readily available to the query optimizer in relational systems (through the system catalog), but may not be in object DBMSs. As indicated earlier, there is a controversy in the research community as to whether the query optimizer should be able to break the encapsulation of objects and look at the data structures used to implement them. If this is permitted, the cost functions can be specified similar to relational systems [Blakeley et al., 1993], [Cluet and Delobel, 1992], [Dogac et al., 1994], [Orenstein et al., 1992]. Otherwise, an alternative specification must be considered.

The cost function can be defined recursively based on the algebraic processing tree. If the internal structure of objects is not visible to the query optimizer, the cost of each node (representing an algebraic operation) has to be defined. One way to define it is to have objects "reveal" their costs as part of their interface [Graefe and Maier, 1988]. A similar approach is provided in the TIGUKAT project [Özsu et al., 1995b]. Since the algebraic operations are behaviors defined on type Collection, the nodes of the algebraic processing tree are behavior applications. There may be various functions that implement each behavior (representing different execution algorithms), in which case the behaviors "reveal" their costs as a function of (a) the execution algorithm and (b) the collection over which they operate. In both cases, a more abstract cost function for behaviors is specified at type definition time from which the query optimizer can calculate the cost of the entire processing tree. The definition of cost functions, especially in the approaches based on the objects revealing their costs, must be investigated further before satisfactory conclusions can be reached.

Parameterization. Compile-time query optimization is a static process in that the optimizer uses the database statistics at the time the query is compiled and optimized in selecting the optimal execution plan. This decision is independent of the execution-time statistics, such as the system load. Furthermore, it does not take into account the changes to the database statistics as a result of updates that may occur between the time the query is optimized and the time it is executed. This is especially a problem in production-type queries which are optimized once (with considerable overhead) and executed a large number of times. It may be an even more serious issue in object DBMSs which may be used as repositories for design prototypes (software or otherwise). These databases are by definition more volatile, resulting in significant changes to the database (which is why dynamic schema evolution is so important in object DBMSs). The query optimization strategy must be able to cope with these changes.

The issue can be handled in one of two ways. One alternative is to determine an optimization/re-optimization interval and re-optimize the query periodically. Even though this is a simple approach, it is based on a fixed time interval whose determination in general would be problematic. A slight variation may be to determine the re-optimization point based on the difference between the actual execution time and the estimated execution time. Consequently, the run-time system will be able to track the actual execution time, and whenever it deviates from the estimated time by more than a fixed threshold, the query will be re-optimized. Again, the determination of this threshold would be a concern, as well as the run-time overhead of tracking query execution.

Another alternative that has been researched [Graefe and Ward, 1989], [Ioannidis et al., 1992] and implemented in ObjectStore [Orenstein et al., 1992] is *parametric query optimization*, which is also called *dynamic plan selection*. In this case, the optimizer maintains multiple execution strategies at compile time and makes a final plan selection at run-time based on various system parameters and the current database statistics. If the optimizer does not have access to all of this data, algebraic optimization can ignore all physical execution characteristics, instead generating a set of "desirable" (however defined) equivalent query expressions which are handed over to the object manager. The object manager can then compare the alternatives (at run time) based on their execution characteristics. However, this approach also has the significant problem of potentially incurring high run-time overhead.

A problem with compile-time parametric optimization (and run-time resolution) is the potential exponential explosion of the dynamic plans as a function of both the complexity of the query and the number of optimization parameters unknown at compile time. This problem, along with the problems of error propagation and inaccuracy of selectivity and cost estimation methods, makes "run-time" query optimization an attractive alternative.

Path Expressions

Most object query languages allow queries whose predicates involve conditions on object access along reference chains. These reference chains are called *path expressions* [Zaniolo, 1983] (sometimes also referred to as *complex predicates* or *implicit joins* [Kim, 1989]). The example path expresion c.engine.manufacturer.name that we used in Section 14.4.2 retrieves the value of the name attribute of the object that is the value of the manufacturer attribute of the object that is the value of the engine attribute of object c, which was defined to be of type Car. It is possible to form path expressions involving attributes as well as methods. Optimizing the computation of path expressions is a problem that has received substantial attention in object-query processing.

Path expressions allow a succinct, high-level notation for expressing navigation through the object composition (aggregation) graph, which enables the formulation of predicates on values deeply nested in the structure of an object. They provide a uniform mechanism for the formulation of queries that involve object composition and inherited member functions. Path expressions may be *single-valued* or *set-valued*, and may appear in a query as part of a predicate, a target to a query (when set-valued), or part of a projection list. A path expression is single-valued if every component of a path expression is single-valued; if at least one component is set-valued, then the whole path expression is set-valued. Techniques to traverse path expressions forward and backward are presented by Jenq et al. [1990].

The problem of optimizing path expressions spans the entire query-compilation process. During or after parsing of a user query, but before algebraic optimization, the query compiler must recognize which path expressions can potentially be optimized. This is typically achieved through *rewriting* techniques, which transform path expressions into equivalent logical algebra expressions [Cluet and Delobel, 1992]. Once path expressions are represented in algebraic form, the query optimizer explores the space of *equivalent algebraic* and execution plans, searching for one of minimal cost [Lanzelotte and Valduriez, 1991], [Blakeley et al., 1993]. Finally, the optimal execution plan may involve algorithms to efficiently compute path expressions, including hash-join [Shapiro, 1986], complex-object assembly [Keller et al., 1991], or indexed scan through path indexes [Maier and Stein, 1986], [Valduriez, 1987], [Kemper and Moerkotte, 1990a], [Kemper and Moerkotte, 1990b].

Rewriting and Algebraic Optimization.   Consider again the path expression c.engine.manufacturer.name. Assume every car instance has a reference to an **Engine** object, each engine has a reference to a **Manufacturer** object, and each manufacturer instance has a **name** field. Also, assume that **Engine** and **Manufacturer** types have a corresponding type extent. The first two links of the above path may involve the retrieval of engine and manufacturer objects from disk. The third path involves only a lookup of a field within a manufacturer object. Therefore, only the first two links present opportunities for query optimization in the computation of that path. An object-query compiler needs a mechanism to distinguish these links in a path representing possible optimizations. This is typically achieved through a *rewriting* phase.

One possibility is to use a type-based rewriting technique, as proposed by Cluet and Delobel [1992]. This approach "unifies" algebraic and type-based rewriting techniques, permits factorization of common subexpressions, and supports heuristics to limit rewriting. Type information is exploited to decompose initial complex arguments of a query into a set of simpler operators, and to rewrite path expressions into joins. Lanzelotte and Valduriez [1991] present a similar attempt to optimizing path expressions within an algebraic framework using an operator called *implicit join*. Rules are defined to transform a series of implicit join operators into an indexed scan using a path index (see below) when it is available.

An alternative operator that has been proposed for optimizing path expressions is *materialize* (Mat) [Blakeley et al., 1993], which represents the computation of each inter-object reference (i.e., path link) explicitly. This enables a query optimizer to express the materialization of multiple components as a group using a single **Mat** operator, or individually using a Mat operator per component. Another way to think of this operator is as a "scope definition," because it brings elements of a path expression into scope so that these elements can be used in later operations or in predicate evaluation. The scoping rules are such that an object component gets into scope either by being scanned (captured using the logical Get operator in the leaves of expressions trees) or by being referenced (captured in the Mat operator). Components remain in scope until a projection discards them. The materialize operator allows a query processor to aggregate all component materializations required for the computation of a query, regardless of whether the components are needed for predicate evaluation or to produce the result of a query. The purpose of the materialize operator is to indicate to the optimizer where path expressions are used and where algebraic transformations can be applied. A number of transformation rules involving Mat are defined.

Path Indexes.   Substantial research on object query optimization has been devoted to the design of index structures to speed up the computation of path expressions [Maier and Stein, 1986], [Bertino and Kim, 1989], [Valduriez, 1987], [Kemper and Moerkotte, 1994].

Computation of path expressions via indexes represents just one class of query-execution algorithms used in object-query optimization. In other words, efficient computation of path expressions through path indexes represents only one collection of implementation choices for algebraic operators, such as materialize and join, used to represent inter-object references. Section 14.6.3 describes a representative collection of query-execution algorithms that promise to provide a major benefit to the efficient execution of object queries. We will defer a discussion of some representative path index techniques to that section. Bertino and Kim [1989] present a more comprehensive survey of index techniques for object query optimization.

14.6.3 Query Execution

The relational DBMSs benefit from the close correspondence between the relational algebra operations and the access primitives of the storage system. Therefore, the generation of the execution plan for a query expression basically concerns the choice and implementation of the most efficient algorithms for executing individual algebra operators and their combinations. In object DBMSs, the issue is more complicated due to the difference in the abstraction levels of behaviorally-defined objects and their storage. Encapsulation of objects, which hides their implementation details, and the storage of methods with objects pose a challenging design problem, which can be stated as follows: "At what point in query processing should the query optimizer access information regarding the storage of objects?" One alternative is to leave this to the object manager [Straube and Özsu, 1995]. Consequently, the query-execution plan is generated from the query expression is obtained at the end of the query-rewrite step by mapping the query expression to a well-defined set of object-manager interface calls. The object-manager interface consists of a set of execution algorithms. This section reviews some of the execution algorithms that are likely to be part of future high-performance object-query execution engines.

A query-execution engine requires three basic classes of algorithms on collections of objects: *collection scan*, *indexed scan*, and *collection matching*. Collection scan is a straightforward algorithm that sequentially accesses all objects in a collection. We will not discuss this algorithm further due to its simplicity. Indexed scan allows efficient access to selected objects in a collection through an index. It is possible to use an object's field or the values returned by some method as a key to an index. Also, it is possible to define indexes on values deeply nested in the structure of an object (i.e., path indexes). In this section we mention a representative sample of path-index proposals. Set-matching algorithms take multiple collections of objects as input and produce aggregate objects related by some criteria. Join, set intersection, and assembly are examples of algorithms in this category.

Path Indexes

As indicated earlier, support for path expressions is a feature that distinguishes object queries from relational ones. Many indexing techniques designed to accelerate the computation of path expressions have been proposed [Maier and Stein, 1986], [Bertino and Kim, 1989] based on the concept of join index [Valduriez, 1987].

One such path indexing technique, developed for the GemStone object DBMS, creates an index on each class traversed by a path [Maier and Stein, 1986]. This technique was also proposed for the Orion object DBMS [Bertino and Kim, 1989]. In addition to indexes on path expressions, it is possible to define indexes on objects across their type inheritance. Kim et al. [1989] provide a thorough discussion of such indexing techniques through inheritance.

Access support relations [Kemper and Moerkotte, 1994] are an alternative general technique to represent and compute path expressions. An access support relation is a data structure that stores selected path expressions. These path expressions are chosen to be the most frequently navigated ones. Studies provide initial evidence that the performance of queries executed using access support relations improves by about two orders of magnitude over queries that do not use access support relations. A system using access support relations must also consider the cost of maintaining them in the presence of updates to the underlying base relations.

Set Matching

As indicated earlier, path expressions are traversals along the composite object composition relationship. We have already seen that a possible way of executing a path expression is to transform it into a join between the source and target sets of objects. A number of different join algorithms have been proposed, such as hybrid-hash join or pointer-based hash join [Shekita and Carey, 1990]. The former uses the divide-and-conquer principle to recursively partition the two operand collections into buckets using a hash function on the join attribute. Each of these buckets may fit entirely in memory. Each pair of buckets is then joined in memory to produce the result. The pointer-based hash join is used when each object in one operand collection (call R) has a pointer to an object in the other operand collection (call S). The algorithm follows three steps, the first one being the partitioning of R in the same way as in the hybrid hash algorithm, except that it is partitioned by OID values rather than by join attribute. The set of objects S is not partitioned. In the second step, each partition R_i of R is joined with S by taking R_i and building a hash table for it in memory. The table is built by hashing each object $r \in R$ on the value of its pointer to its corresponding object in S. As a result, all R objects that reference the same page in S are grouped together in the same hash-table entry. Third, after the hash table for R_i is built, each of its entries is scanned. For each hash entry, the corresponding page in S is read, and all objects in R that reference that page are joined with the corresponding objects in S. These two algorithms are basically centralized algorithms, without any distributed counterparts. So we will not discuss them further.

An alternative method of join execution algorithm, *assembly* [Keller et al., 1991], is a generalization of the pointer-based hash-join algorithm for the case when we need to compute a multi-way join. Assembly has been proposed as an additional object algebra operator. This operation efficiently assembles the fragments of objects' states required for a particular processing step, and returns them as a complex object in memory. It translates the disk representations of complex objects into readily traversable memory representations.

Assembling a complex object rooted at objects of type R containing object components of types S, U, and T, is analogous to computing a four-way join of these sets. There is a difference between assembly and n-way pointer joins in that assembly does not need the entire collection of root objects to be scanned before producing a single result.

Instead of assembling a single complex object at a time, the assembly operator assembles a *window*, of size W, of complex objects simultaneously. As soon as any of these complex objects becomes assembled and passed up the query-execution tree, the assembly operator retrieves another one to work on. Using a window of complex objects increases the pool size of unresolved references and results in more options for optimization of disk accesses. Due to the randomness with which references are resolved, the assembly operator delivers assembled objects in random order up the query execution tree. This behavior is correct in set-oriented query processing, but may not be for other collection types, such as lists.

Example 14.9

> Consider the example given in Figure 14.3, which assembles a set of Car objects. This is similar to the one given from Keller et al. [1991], but adapted to our example. The boxes in the figure represent instances of types indicated at the left, and the edges denote the composition relationships (e.g., there is an attribute of every object of type Car that points to an object of type Engine). Suppose that assembly is using a window of size 2. The assembly operator begins by filling the window with two (since $W = 2$) Car object references from the set (Figure 14.4a). The assembly operator begins by choosing among the current outstanding references, say $C1$. After resolving (fetching) $C1$, two new unresolved references are added to the list (Figure 14.4b). Resolving $C2$ results in two more references added to the list (Figure 14.4c), and so on

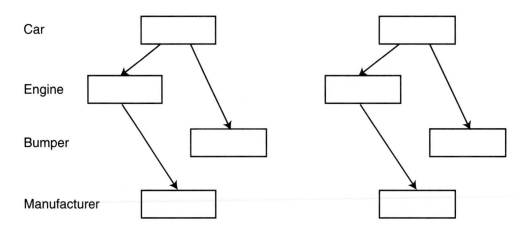

Figure 14.3. Two Assembled Complex Objects

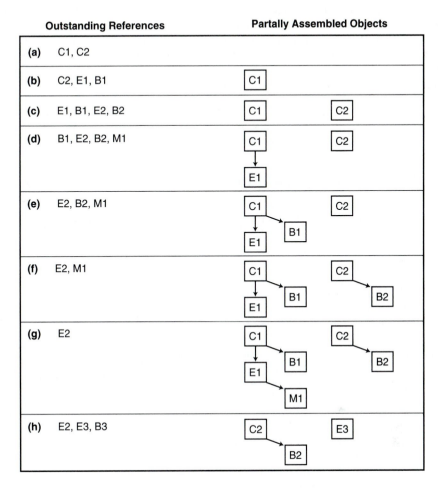

Figure 14.4. An Assembly Example

until the first complex object is assembled (Figure 14.4g). At this point, the assembled object is passed up the query-execution tree, freeing some window space. A new `Car` object reference, $C3$, is added to the list and then resolved, bringing two new references $E3$, $B3$ (Figure 14.4h).

The objective of the assembly algorithm is to simultaneously assemble a window of complex objects. At each point in the algorithm, the outstanding reference that optimizes disk accesses is chosen. There are different orders, or schedules, in which references may be resolved, such as depth-first, breath-first, and elevator. Performance results indicate that elevator outperforms depth-first and breath-first under several data-clustering situations [Keller et al., 1991].

A number of possibilities exist in implementing a distributed version of this operation [Maier et al., 1994]. One strategy involves shipping all data to a central site for processing. This is straightforward to implement, but could be inefficient in general. A second strategy involves doing simple operations (e.g., selections, local assembly) at remote sites, then shipping all data to a central site for final assembly. This strategy also requires fairly simple control, since all communication occurs through the central site. The third strategy is significantly more complicated: perform complex operations (e.g., joins, complete assembly of remote objects) at remote sites, then ship the results to the central site for final assembly. A distributed object DBMS may include all or some of these strategies.

14.7 TRANSACTION MANAGEMENT

Transaction management in *distributed* object DBMSs have not been studied except in relation to the cashing problem discussed earlier. However, transactions on objects raise a number of interesting issues, and their execution in a distributed environment can be quite challenging. This is an area which clearly requires more work. In this section we will discuss, at some length, the particular problems that arise in extending the transaction concept to object DBMSs.

Most object DBMSs maintain page level locks for concurrency control and support the traditional flat transaction model. It has been argued that the traditional flat transaction model would not meet the requirements of the advanced application domains that object data management technology would serve. Some of the considerations are that transactions in these domains are longer in duration, requiring interactions with the user or the application program during their execution. In the case of object systems, transactions do not consist of simple read/write operations, necessitating, instead, synchronization algorithms that deal with complex operations on abstract (and possibly complex) objects. In some application domains, the fundamental transaction synchronization paradigm based on competition among transactions for access to resources must change to one of cooperation among transactions in accomplishing a common task. This is the case, for example, in cooperative work environments.

The more important requirements for transaction management in object DBMSs can be listed as follows [Buchmann et al., 1992], [Kaiser, 1989], [Martin and Pedersen, 1994]:

1. Conventional transaction managers synchronize simple Read and Write operations. However, their counterparts for object DBMSs must be able to deal with *abstract operations*. It may even be possible to improve concurrency by using semantic knowledge about the objects and their abstract operations.

2. Conventional transactions access "flat" objects (e.g., pages, tuples), whereas transactions in object DBMSs require synchronization of access to composite and complex objects. Synchronization of access to such objects requires synchronization of access to the component objects.

3. Some applications supported by object DBMSs have different database access patterns than conventional database applications, where the access is competitive (e.g., two users accessing the same bank account). Instead,

sharing is more cooperative, as in the case of, for example, multiple users accessing and working on the same design document. In this case, user accesses must be synchronized, but users are willing to cooperate rather than compete for access to shared objects.

4. These applications require the support of *long-running activities* spanning hours, days or even weeks (e.g., when working on a design object). Therefore, the transaction mechanism must support the sharing of partial results. Furthermore, to avoid the failure of a partial task jeopardizing a long activity, it is necessary to distinguish between those activities that are essential for the completion of a transaction and those that are not, and to provide for alternative actions in case the primary activity fails.

5. It has been argued that many of these applications would benefit from *active capabilities* for timely response to events and changes in the environment. This new database paradigm requires the monitoring of events and the execution of system-triggered activities within running transactions.

These requirements point to a need to extend the traditional transaction management functions in order to capture application and data semantics, and to a need to relax isolation properties. This, in turn, requires revisiting every aspect of transaction management that we discussed in Chapters 10–12.

14.7.1 Correctness Criteria

In Chapter 11, we introduced serializability as the fundamental correctness criteria for concurrent execution of database transactions. There are a number of different ways in which serializability can be defined, even though we did not elaborate on this point before. These differences are based on how a *conflict* is defined. We will concentrate on three alternatives: *commutativity* [Weihl, 1988], [Weihl, 1989], [Fekete et al., 1989], *invalidation* [Herlihy, 1990], and *recoverability* [Badrinath and Ramamritham, 1987].

Commutativity

Commutativity states that two operations conflict if the results of different serial executions of these operations are not equivalent. The traditional conflict definition discussed in Chapter 11 is a special case. Consider the simple operations $R(x)$ and $W(x)$. If nothing is known about the abstract semantics of the Read and Write operations or the object x upon which they operate, it has to be accepted that a $R(x)$ **following** a $W(x)$ does not retrieve the same value as it would **prior** to the $W(x)$. Therefore, a Write operation always conflicts with other Read or Write operations. The conflict table (or the compatibility matrix) given in Figure 11.5 for Read and Write operations is, in fact, derived from the commutativity relationship between these two operations. This table was called the compatibility matrix in Chapter 11, since two operations that do not conflict are said to be compatible. Since this type of commutativity relies only on syntactic information about operations (i.e., that they are Read and Write), we call this *syntactic commutativity* [Buchmann et al., 1992].

In Figure 11.5, Read and Write operations and Write and Write operations do not commute. Therefore, they conflict, and serializability maintains that either all conflicting operations of transaction T_i precede all conflicting operations of T_k, or vice versa.

If the semantics of the operations are taken into account, however, it may be possible to provide a more relaxed definition of conflict. Specifically, some concurrent executions of Write-Write and Read-Write may be considered non-conflicting. *Semantic commutativity* (e.g., [Weihl, 1988], [Weihl, 1989]) makes use of the semantics of operations and their termination conditions.

Example 14.10

Consider, for example, an abstract data type **set** and three operations defined on it: Insert and Delete, which correspond to a Write, and Member, which tests for membership and corresponds to a Read. Due to the semantics of these operations, two Insert operations on an instance of set type would commute, allowing them to be executed concurrently. The commutativity of Insert with Member and the commutativity of Delete with Member depends upon whether or not they reference the same argument and their results[8].

It is also possible to define commutativity with reference to the database state. In this case, it is usually possible to permit more operations to commute.

Example 14.11

In Example 14.7, we indicated that an Insert and a Member would commute if they do not refer to the same argument. However, if the set already contains the referred element, these two operations would commute even if their arguments are the same.

The question now is how to formalize this intuitive understanding of commutativity of operations on abstract data types based on their semantics. We follow Weihl [1988,1989] in addressing this question.

The conflict relations defined in Weihl [1988] are binary relations between operations that consider both the operation and its result. An operation is now defined as a pair of invocation and response to that invocation; e.g., x: [Insert(3),ok] is a valid invocation of an insert operation on set x that returns that the operation was performed correctly. Two different kinds of commutativity and their corresponding commutativity relation can be defined: *forward commutativity* and *backward commutativity*. Assume two operations P and Q and a state s of an object. Forward commutativity is then defined as follows: For every state s in which P and Q are both defined (individually), $P(Q(s)) = Q(P(s))$ and $P(Q(s))$ is defined (i.e., it is not the null state). The notation used means that if we first apply operation Q to

---

[8]Depending upon the operation, the result may either be a flag that indicates whether the operation was successful (for example, the result of Insert may be "OK") or the value that the operation returns (as in the case of a Read).

	[Insert(i),ok]	[Delete(i),ok]	[Member(i),true]	[Member(i),false]
[Insert(i),ok]	+	-	+	-
[Delete(i),ok]	-	+	+	+
[Member(i),true]	+	-	+	+
[Member(i),false]	-	+	+	+

Figure 14.5. Compatibility Table for Forward Commutativity in Sets

state s and then operation P to that result, we obtain the same result as if we apply first P to state s and then operation Q to the result. Backward commutativity is defined as follows: For every state s in which we know that $P(Q(s))$ is defined (i.e., $Q(s)$ is defined but $P(s)$ may or may not be defined), $P(Q(s)) = Q(P(s))$. Of course, both forward and backward commutativity extend to the case where P and Q are sequences of operations, rather than a single operation.

Example 14.12

The forward and backward compatibility relations for the set ADT are given in Figures 14.5 and 14.6, respectively. In these tables, the Member operation is defined once with a successful execution return code ("true"), and once with an unsuccessful execution code ("false").

It is important to notice the difference in the states over which the operations are defined. In forward commutativity, both operations are defined over the same initial state. Therefore, it makes no difference which operation is applied first, as long as the final result is the same.

	[Insert(i),ok]	[Delete(i),ok]	[Member(i),true]	[Member(i),false]
[Insert(i),ok]	+	-	-	-
[Delete(i),ok]	-	+	-	+
[Member(i),true]	-	-	+	+
[Member(i),false]	-	+	+	+

Figure 14.6. Compatibility Table for Backward Commutativity in Sets

Example 14.13

If the initial state of the set object is {1,2,3}, the first operation on that set object is the pair of invocation-response [Insert(3), ok], and the second operation is [Member(3), true], both operations are defined on {1,2,3}, and the result of applying them in either order is the same. However, if all we know is that the state is {1,2,3} after applying the operation [Insert(3), ok], we cannot say whether the initial state was {1,2} or {1,2,3}. Therefore, for a set object, the operations [Insert(x), ok] and [Member(x), true] do commute forward, but do not commute backwards.

Notice from Figures 14.5 and 14.6 that, for the set object as we defined it, the backward commutativity relation subsumes the forward commutativity relation. However, this is not true for all objects. In general, forward and backward commutativity relations are incomparable.

Example 14.14

This example demonstrates that the forward and backward commutativity relations are incomparable by considering these relations for a bank account abstract data type. The relations are given in Figures 14.7 and 14.8. The operations are self-explanatory, except for Post(i), which posts a given percentage i of interest to the account object. The argument of the operations is amounts of funds.

The incomparability of these two relations causes difficulties in implementing transaction managers that use them. Basically, one or the other must be chosen for enforcement, even though each permits certain operation histories which the other one rejects. Nakajima [1994] extends this work and defines a *general commutativity relation*, which is a superset of both the forward and the backward commutativity relations. If $FC(o)$ and $BC(o)$ are the forward and backward commutativity rela-

	[Withdraw(m),ok]	[Withdraw(m),no]	[Deposit(n),ok]	[Balance,r]	[Post(i),ok]
[Withdraw(m),ok]	-	+	+	-	-
[Withdraw(m),no]	+	+	-	+	+
[Deposit(n),ok]	+	-	+	-	-
[Balance,r]	-	+	-	+	-
[Post(i),ok]	-	+	-	-	-

Figure 14.7. Forward Commutativity Table for a Bank Account Object

	[Withdraw(m),ok]	[Withdraw(m),no]	[Deposit(n),ok]	[Balance,r]	[Post(i),ok]
[Withdraw(m),ok]	+	-	-	-	-
[Withdraw(m),no]	-	+	-	+	+
[Deposit(n),ok]	-	-	+	-	-
[Balance,r]	-	+	-	+	-
[Post(i),ok]	-	+	-	-	-

Figure 14.8. Backward Commutativity Table for a Bank Account Object

tions, respectively, for object o, then the general commutativity relation is defined as $GC(o) = FC(o) \cup BC(o)$. The general commutativity relation for the bank account example is given in Figure 14.9. Even though it seems preferable to use the general commutativity relation, enforcing it is not straightforward.

Invalidation

Invalidation [Herlihy, 1990] defines a conflict between two operations not on the basis of whether they commute or not, but according to whether or not the execution of one invalidates the other. An operation P invalidates another operation Q if there are two histories H_1 and H_2 such that $H_1 \bullet P \bullet H_2$ and $H_1 \bullet H_2 \bullet Q$ are legal, but $H_1 \bullet P \bullet H_2 \bullet Q$ is not. In this context, a *legal history* represents a correct history for the set object and is determined according to its semantics. Accordingly, an *invalidated-by* relation is defined as consisting of all operation pairs (P, Q) such that P invalidates Q. The invalidated-by relation establishes the conflict relation

	[Withdraw(m),ok]	[Withdraw(m),no]	[Deposit(n),ok]	[Balance,r]	[Post(i),ok]
[Withdraw(m),ok]	+	+	+	-	-
[Withdraw(m),no]	+	+	-	+	+
[Deposit(n),ok]	+	-	+	-	-
[Balance,r]	-	+	-	+	-
[Post(i),ok]	-	+	-	-	-

Figure 14.9. General Commutativity Relation for the Bank Account Example

that forms the basis of establishing serializability. Considering the Set example, an Insert cannot be invalidated by any other operation, but a Member can be invalidated by a Delete if their arguments are the same.

Recoverability

Recoverability [Badrinath and Ramamritham, 1987] is another conflict relation that has been defined to determine serializable histories[9]. Intuitively, an operation P is said to be *recoverable with respect to* operation Q if the value returned by P is independent of whether Q executed before P or not. The conflict relation established on the basis of recoverability seems to be identical to that established by invalidation. However, this observation is based on only a few examples, and there is no formal proof of this equivalence. In fact, the absence of a formal theory to reason about these conflict relations is a serious deficiency that must be addressed.

14.7.2 Transaction Models and Object Structures

In Chapter 10, we considered a number of transaction models ranging from flat transactions to workflow systems. In our previous discussion, we did not consider the granularity of database objects upon which these transactions operate (we simply referred to it as a "lock unit"). Now we will consider the alternatives, and, together with the transaction model alternatives, they will provide us with a two-dimensional design space for possible transaction system implementations.

Along the object structure dimension, we identify *simple objects* (e.g., files, pages, records), objects as instances of *abstract data types* (ADTs), *full-fledged objects*, and *active objects* in increasing complexity.

Our previous discussion primarily considered systems that operate on simple objects, mostly physical pages. There are systems that provide for concurrency at the record level, but the overhead is usually high and record operations alone are not atomic, requiring synchronization at the page level as well. The characterizing feature of this class is that the operations on simple objects do not take into account the semantics of the objects. For example, an update of a page is considered a Write on the page, without considering what logical object is stored on the page.

From the perspective of transaction processing, ADTs introduce a need to deal with abstract operations, as we saw in the previous section. Abstract operations lend themselves nicely to the incorporation of their semantics into the definition of the correctness criterion. The execution of transactions on ADTs may require a multi-level mechanism as presented in Chapter 10 [Beeri et al., 1988], [Weikum, 1991]. In such systems, individual transactions represent the highest level of abstraction. The abstract operations constitute a lower level of abstraction, and are further decomposed into simple Reads and Writes at the lowest level. The correctness criterion, whatever it is, must be applied to each level individually.

We make the distinction between objects as instances of abstract data types and full-fledged objects to note that the latter have a complex structure (i.e., con-

---

[9]Recoverability as used in [Badrinath and Ramamritham, 1987] is different from the notion of recoverability as we defined it in Chapter 12 and as found in [Bernstein et al., 1987] and [Hadzilacos, 1988].

tain other objects), and that their types (classes) participate in a subtype (inheritance) lattice[10]. They must be treated separately due to a number of considerations:

1. Running a transaction against a composite object may actually spawn additional transactions on its component objects. This forces an *implicit nesting* [Badrinath and Ramamritham, 1988] on the transaction itself (as opposed to explicit nesting, which we discussed as part of transaction structure in Chapter 10). More importantly, the operations in these nestings are themselves abstract and need to be handled as multilevel transactions [Weikum and Hasse, 1993].

2. Subtyping/inheritance involves the sharing of behavior and/or state among objects. Therefore, the semantics of accessing an object at some level in the lattice must account for this.

We can also distinguish between *passive* and *active* objects. Although the approaches to the management of active objects vary, all proposals are similar in that active objects are capable of responding to events by triggering the execution of actions when certain conditions are satisfied. The events that are to be monitored, the conditions that must be fulfilled, and the actions that are executed in response are typically defined in the form of event-condition-action (ECA) rules [Dayal et al., 1988], [Kotz et al., 1988]. Since events may be detected while executing a transaction on that object, the execution of the corresponding rule may be spawned as a nested transaction. Depending on the manner in which rules are coupled to the original transaction, different nestings may occur [Hsu et al., 1988]. The spawned transaction may execute immediately, it may be deferred to the end of the transaction, or it may execute in a separate transaction. Since additional rules may fire within a rule execution, nestings of arbitrary depth are possible. We will not consider active objects any further.

14.7.3 Transactions Management in Object DBMSs

As indicated above, transaction management in object DBMSs must deal with the composition (aggregation) graph, which shows the composite object structure, and *type (class) lattice*, which represents the **is-a** relationship between objects.

The aggregation graph requires methods for dealing with the synchronization of accesses to objects which have other objects as components. The class (type) lattice requires the transaction manager to take into account schema evolution concerns.

In addition to these structures, object DBMSs store methods together with data. Synchronization of shared access to objects must take into account method executions. In particular, transactions invoke methods which may, in turn, invoke other methods. Thus, even if the transaction model is flat, the execution of these transactions may be dynamically nested.

---

[10]Strictly speaking, abstract data types can have complex structures. However, the transaction work on abstract data types has consistently assumed a "simple" ADT structure. Our reference to "objects as instances of ADTs" should be understood within this context and with this qualification.

All of these factors introduce difficulties in executing transactions. Even the definition of conflicting operations becomes more involved. The conflict definition that we discussed earlier may no longer apply in object DBMSs. The classical conflict definition is based on the (non-)commutativity of operations that access the same object. In object DBMSs, there may be conflicts between operations that access different objects. This is due to the existence of the aggregation graph and the type lattice. Consider an operation O_1 which accesses object x, which has another object y as one of its components (i.e., x is a composite or complex object). There may be another operation O_2 (assume O_1 and O_2 belong to different transactions) which accesses y. According to the classical definition of a conflict, we would not consider O_1 and O_2 to be conflicting, since they access different objects. However, O_1 considers y as part of x and may want to access y while it accesses x, causing a conflict with O_2.

Schemes that are developed for object DBMSs must take these issues into consideration. In the remainder of this section, we will present some of the solutions that have been proposed.

Synchronizing Access to Objects

The inherent nesting in method invocations can be used to develop algorithms based on the well-known nested 2PL and nested timestamp ordering algorithms [Hadzilakos and Hadzilakos, 1991]. In the process, intra-object parallelism may be exploited to improve concurrency. In other words, attributes of an object can be modeled as data elements in the database, whereas the methods are modeled as transactions enabling multiple invocations of an object's methods to be active simultaneously. This can provide more concurrency if special intra-object synchronization protocols can be devised which maintain the compatibility of synchronization decisions at each object.

Consequently, a method execution (modeled as a transaction) on an object consists of *local steps*, which correspond to the execution of local operations together with the results that are returned, and *method steps*, which are the method invocations together with the return values. A local operation is an atomic operation (such as Read, Write, Increment) that affects the object's variables. A method execution defines the partial order among these steps in the usual manner.

One of the fundamental directions of this work is to provide total freedom to objects in how they achieve intra-object synchronization. The only requirement is that they be "correct" executions, which, in this case, means that they should be serializable based on commutativity. As a result of the delegation of intra-object synchronization to individual objects, the concurrency control algorithm concentrates on inter-object synchronization.

An alternative approach based on multigranularity locking is used in Orion [Garza and Kim, 1988] and O_2[11] [Cart and Ferrie, 1990], even though they use different granularity hierarchies.

Multigranularity locking defines a hierarchy of lockable database granules (thus the name "granularity hierarchy") as depicted in Figure 14.10. In relational DBMSs, files correspond to relations and records correspond to tuples. In object DBMSs, the correspondence is with classes and instance objects, respectively.

---

[11]Even though this technique has been proposed for O_2, the commercial implementation of the system uses a straightforward page-level locking scheme.

Database

Areas

Files

Records

Figure 14.10. Multiple Granularities

The advantage of this hierarchy is that it addresses the tradeoff between coarse granularity locking and fine granularity locking. Coarse granularity locking (at the file level and above) has low locking overhead, since a small number of locks are set, but it significantly reduces concurrency. The reverse is true for fine granularity locking.

The main idea behind multigranularity locking is that a transaction that locks at a coarse granularity implicitly locks all the corresponding objects of finer granularities. For example, explicit locking at the file level involves implicit locking of all the records in that file. To achieve this, two more lock types in addition to shared (S) and exclusive (X) are defined: *intention* (or *implicit*) *shared* (IS) and *intention* (or *implicit*) *exclusive* (IX). A transaction that wants to set an S or an IS lock on an object has to first set IS or IX locks on its ancestors (i.e., related objects of coarser granularity). Similarly, a transaction that wants to set an X or an IX lock on an object must set IX locks on all of its ancestors. Intention locks cannot be released on an object if the descendants of that object are currently locked.

One additional complication arises when a transaction wants to read an object at some granularity and modify some of its objects at a finer granularity. In this case, both an S lock and an IX lock must be set on that object. For example, a transaction may read a file and update some records in that file (similarly, a transaction in object DBMSs may want to read the class definition and update some of the instance objects belonging to that class). To deal with these cases, a *shared intention exclusive* (SIX) lock is introduced, which is equivalent to holding an S and an IX lock on that object. The lock compatibility matrix for multigranularity locking is shown in Figure 14.11.

Orion's granularity hierarchy is shown in Figure 14.12. The lock modes that are supported and their compatibilities are exactly those given in Figure 14.11. Instance objects are locked only in S or X mode, while class objects can be locked in all five modes. The interpretation of these locks on class objects is as follows:

- S mode: Class definition is locked in S mode, and all its instances are implicitly locked in S mode. This prevents another transaction from updating the instances.

	S	X	IS	IX	SIX
S	+	-	+	-	-
X	-	-	-	-	-
IS	+	-	+	+	+
IX	-	-	+	+	-
SIX	-	-	+	-	-

Figure 14.11. Compatibility Table for Multigranularity Locking

- X mode: Class definition is locked in X mode, and all its instances are implicitly locked in X mode. Therefore, the class definition and all instances of the class may be read or updated.

- IS mode: Class definition is locked in IS mode, and the instances are to be locked in S mode as necessary.

- IX mode: Class definition is locked in IX mode, and the instances will be locked in either S or X mode as necessary.

- SIX mode: Class definition is locked in S mode, and all the instances are implicitly locked in S mode. Those instances that are to be updated are explicitly locked in X mode as the transaction updates them.

Management of Type Lattice

One of the important requirements of object DBMSs is dynamic schema evaluation. Consequently, systems must deal with transactions that access schema objects (i.e., types, classes, etc.), as well as instance objects. The existence of schema change

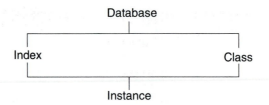

Figure 14.12. Orion's Granularity Hierarchy

operations intermixed with regular queries and transactions, as well as the (multiple) inheritance relationship defined among classes, complicates the picture. First, a query/transaction may not only access instances of a class, but may also access instances of subclasses of that class (i.e., *deep extent*). Second, in a composite object, the domain of an attribute is itself a class. So accessing an attribute of a class may involve accessing the objects in the sublattice rooted at the domain class of that attribute.

One way to deal with these two problems is, again, by using multigranularity locking, as done in Orion. The straightforward extension of multigranularity locking where the accessed class and all its subclasses are locked in the appropriate mode does not work very well. This approach is inefficient when classes close to the root are accessed, since it involves too many locks. The problem may be overcome by introducing *read-lattice* (R) and *write-lattice* (W) lock modes, which not only lock the target class in S or X modes, respectively, but also implicitly lock all subclasses of that class in S and X modes, respectively. However, this solution does not work with multiple inheritance (which is the third problem).

The problem with multiple inheritance is that a class with multiple supertypes may be implicitly locked in incompatible modes by two transactions that place R and W locks on different superclasses. Since the locks on the common class are implicit, there is no way of recognizing that there is already a lock on the class. Thus, it is necessary to check the superclasses of a class that is being locked. Orion handles this by placing *explicit* locks, rather than implicit ones, on subclasses. Consider the type lattice of Figure 14.13, which is simplified from Garza and Kim [1988]. If transaction T_1 sets an IR lock on class A and an R lock on C, it also sets an explicit R lock on E. When another transaction T_2 places an IW lock on F and a W lock on G, it will attempt to place an explicit W lock on E. However, since there is already an R lock on E, this request will be rejected.

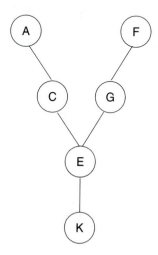

Figure 14.13. An Example Class Lattice

The approach followed by Orion sets explicit locks on subclasses of a class that is being modified. An alternative, which sets locks at a finer granularity, uses ordered sharing, as discussed in Chapter 11 [Agrawal and El-Abbadi, 1994]. In a sense, the algorithm is an extension of Weihl's commutativity-based approach to object DBMSs using a nested transaction model.

Classes are modeled as objects in the system similar to reflective systems that represent schema objects as first-class objects. Consequently, methods can be defined that operate on class objects: $add(m)$ to add method m to the class, $del(m)$ to delete method m from the class, $rep(m)$ to replace the implementation of method m with another one, and $use(m)$ to execute method m. Similarly, atomic operations are defined for accessing attributes of a class. These are identical to the method operations with the appropriate change in semantics to reflect attribute access. The interesting point to note here is that the definition of the $use(a)$ operation for attribute a indicates that the access of a transaction to attribute a within a method execution is through the use operation. This requires that each method explicitly list all the attributes that it accesses. Thus, the following is the sequence of steps that are followed by a transaction, T, in executing a method m:

1. Transaction T issues operation $use(m)$.

2. For each attribute a that is accessed by method m, T issues operation $use(a)$.

3. Transaction T invokes method m.

Commutativity tables are defined for the method and attribute operations. Based on the commutativity tables, ordered sharing lock tables for each atomic operation are determined (see Chapter 11). Specifically, a lock for an atomic operation p has a shared relationship with all the locks associated with operations with which p has a non-conflicting relationship, whereas it has an ordered shared relationship with respect to all the locks associated with operations with which p has a conflicting relation.

Based on these lock tables, a nested 2PL locking algorithm is used with the following considerations:

1. Transactions observe the strict 2PL rule and hold on to their locks until termination.

2. When a transaction aborts, it releases all of its locks.

3. The termination of a transaction awaits the termination of its children (closed nesting semantics). When a transaction commits, its locks are inherited by its parent.

4. *Ordered commitment rule.* Given two transactions T_i and T_j such that T_i is *waiting for* T_j, T_i cannot commit its operations on any object until T_j terminates (commits or aborts). T_i is said to be *waiting-for* T_j if:

   - T_i is not the root of the nested transaction and T_i was granted a lock in ordered shared relationship with respect to a lock held by T_j on an object such that T_j is a descendent of the parent of T_i; or

- T_i is the root of the nested transaction and T_i holds a lock (that it has inherited or it was granted) on an object in ordered shared relationship with respect to a lock held by T_j or its descendants.

Management of Composition (Aggregation) Graph

Studies dealing with the composition graph are more prevalent. The requirement for object DBMSs to model composite objects in an efficient manner has resulted in considerable interest in this problem.

We start the discussion in this section with an overview of Orion's approach to managing the aggregation hierarchy, which is, once more, based on multigranularity locking. Two alternatives are identified. One is, as suggested in the previous section, to lock a composite object and all the classes of the component objects. This is clearly unacceptable, since it involves locking the entire composite object hierarchy, thereby restricting performance significantly. The second alternative is to lock the component object instances within a composite object. In this case, it is necessary to chase all the references and lock all those objects. This is quite cumbersome, since it involves locking so many objects.

The problem is that the multigranularity locking protocol does not recognize the composite object as one lockable unit. To overcome this problem, three new lock modes are introduced: ISO, IXO, and SIXO, corresponding to the IS, IX, and SIX modes, respectively. These lock modes are used for locking component classes of a composite object. The compatibility of these modes is shown in Figure 14.14. The protocol is then as follows: to lock a composite object, the root class is locked in X, IS, IX, or SIX mode, and each of the component classes of the composite object hierarchy is locked in the X, ISO, IXO, and SIXO mode, respectively.

	S	X	IS	IX	SIX	ISO	IXO	SIXO
S	+	-	+	-	-	+	-	-
X	-	-	-	-	-	-	-	-
IS	+	-	+	+	+	+	-	-
IX	-	-	+	+	-	-	-	-
SIX	-	-	+	-	-	-	-	-
ISO	+	-	+	+	-	+	+	+
IXO	-	-	-	-	-	+	+	-
SIXO	N	N	N	N	N	Y	N	N

Figure 14.14. Compatibility Matrix for Composite Objects

The Orion concurrency control algorithms, based on multigranularity locking, enforce serializability. The recovery algorithm used is logging using no-fix/flush, which requires undo but not redo.

An extension of multigranularity locking to deal with aggregation graph is discussed in Herrmann et al. [1990]. The extension has to do with the replacement of a single static lock graph with a hierarchy of graphs associated with each type and query. There is a "general lock graph" which controls the entire process (Figure 14.15). The smallest lockable units are called *basic lockable units* (BLU). A number of BLUs can make up a *homogeneous lockable unit* (HoLU), which consists of data of the same type. Similarly, they can make up a *heterogeneous lockable unit* (HeLU), which is composed of objects of different types. HeLUs can contain other HeLUs or HoLUs, indicating that component objects do not all have to be atomic. Similarly, HoLUs can consist of other HoLUs or HeLUs, as long as they are of the same type. The separation between HoLUs and HeLUs is meant to optimize lock requests. For example, a set of lists of integers is, from the viewpoint of lock managers, treated as a HoLU composed of HoLUs, which, in turn, consist of BLUs. As a result, it is possible to lock the whole set, exactly one of the lists, or even just one integer.

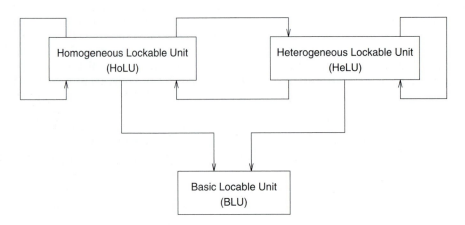

Figure 14.15. General Lock Graph

At type definition time, an object-specific lock graph is created which obeys the general lock graph. As a third component, a query-specific lock graph is generated during query (transaction) analysis. During the execution of the query (transaction), the query-specific lock graph is used to request locks from the lock manager, which uses the object-specific lock graph to make the decision. The lock modes used are the standard ones (i.e., IS, IX, S, X).

Badrinath and Ramamritham [1988] discuss an alternative to dealing with composite object hierarchy based on commutativity. A number of different operations are defined on the aggregation graph:

1. Examine the contents of a vertex (which is a class).

2. Examine an edge (composed-of relationship).

3. Insert a vertex and the associated edge.

4. Delete a vertex and the associated edge.

5. Insert an edge.

Note that some of these operations (1 and 2) correspond to existing object operators, while others (3—5) represent schema operations.

Based on these operations, an *affected-set* can be defined for granularity graphs to form the basis for determining which operations can execute concurrently. The affected-set of a granularity graph consists of the union of:

- *edge-set*, which is the set of pairs (e, a) where e is an edge and a is an operation affecting e and can be one of *insert, delete, examine*

- *vertex-set*, which is the set of pairs (v, a), where v is a vertex and a is an operation affecting v and can be one of *insert, delete, examine*, or *modify*

Using the affected-set generated by two transactions T_i and T_j of an aggregation graph, one may define whether T_i and T_j can execute concurrently or not. Commutativity is used as the basis of the conflict relation. Thus, two transactions T_i and T_j commute on object K if $affected\text{-}set(T_i) \cap_K affected\text{-}set(T_j) = \phi$.

These protocols synchronize on the basis of objects, not operations on objects. It may be possible to improve concurrency by developing techniques that synchronize operation invocations rather than locking entire objects.

Another semantics-based approach is described in Muth et al. [1993]. The distinguishing characteristics of this approach are the following:

1. Access to component objects are permitted without going through a hierarchy of objects (i.e., no multigranularity locking).

2. The semantics of operations are taken into consideration by a priori specification of method commutativities[12].

3. Methods invoked by a transaction can themselves invoke other methods. This results in a (dynamic) nested transaction execution, even if the transaction is syntactically flat.

The transaction model used to support (3) is open nesting, specifically multilevel transactions as described in Chapter 10. The restrictions imposed on the dynamic transaction nesting are:

- All pairs (p, g) of potentially conflicting operations on the same object have the same depth in their invocation trees

- For each pair (f', g') of ancestors of f and g whose depth of invocation trees are the same, f' and g' operate on the same object.

---

[12]The commutativity test employed in this study is state-independent. It takes into account the actual parameters of operations, but not the states. This is in contrast to Weihl's work [Weihl, 1988].

With these restrictions, the algorithm is quite straightforward. A semantic lock is associated with each method, and a commutativity table defines whether or not the various semantic locks are compatible. Transactions acquire these semantic locks before the invocation of methods, and they are released at the end of the execution of a subtransaction (method), exposing their results to others. However, the parents of committed subtransactions have a higher-level semantic lock, which restricts the results of committed subtransactions only to those that commute with the root of the subtransaction. This requires the definition of a semantic conflict test, which operates on the invocation hierarchies using the commutativity tables.

An important complication arises with respect to the two conditions outlined above. It is not reasonable to restrict the applicability of the protocol to only those for which those conditions hold. What has been proposed to resolve the difficulty is to give up some of the openness and convert the locks that were to be released at the end of a subtransaction into *retained locks* held by the parent. A number of conditions under which retained locks can be discarded for additional concurrency.

A very similar, but more restrictive, approach is discussed in Weikum and Hasse [1993]. The multilevel transaction model is used, but restricted to only two levels: the object level and the underlying page level. Therefore, the dynamic nesting that occurs when transactions invoke methods which invoke other methods is not considered. The similarity with the above work is that page level locks are released at the end of the subtransaction, whereas the object level locks (which are semantically richer) are retained until the transaction terminates.

In both of the above approaches [Muth et al., 1993], [Weikum and Hasse, 1993], recovery cannot be performed by page-level state-oriented protocols. Since subtransactions release their locks and make their results visible, compensating transactions must be run to "undo" actions of committed subtransactions.

14.7.4 Transactions as Objects

One important characteristic of relational data model is its lack of a clear update semantics. The model, as it was originally defined, clearly spells out how the data in a relational database is to be retrieved (by means of the relational algebra operators), but does not specify what it really means to update the database. The consequence is that the consistency definitions and the transaction management techniques are orthogonal to the data model. It is possible – and indeed it is common – to apply the same techniques to non-relational DBMSs, or even to non-DBMS storage systems.

The independence of the developed techniques from the data model may be considered an advantage, since the effort can be amortized over a number of different applications. Indeed, the existing transaction management work on object DBMSs have exploited this independence by porting the well-known techniques over to the new system structures. During this porting process, the peculiarities of object DBMSs, such as class (type) lattice structures, composite objects and object groupings (class extents) are considered, but the techniques are essentially the same.

It may be argued that in object DBMSs, it is not only desirable but indeed essential to model update semantics within the object model. The arguments are as follows:

1. In object DBMSs, what is stored are not only data, but operations on data (which are called methods, behaviors, operations in various object models). Queries that access an object database refer to these operations as part of their predicates. In other words, the execution of these queries invokes various operations defined on the classes (types). To guarantee the safety of the query expressions, existing query processing approaches restrict these operations to be side-effect free, in effect disallowing them to update the database. This is a severe restriction that should be relaxed by the incorporation of update semantics into the query safety definitions.

2. As we discussed in Section 14.7.3, transactions in object DBMSs affect the class (type) lattices. Thus, there is a direct relationship between dynamic schema evolution and transaction management. Many of the techniques that we discussed employ locking on this lattice to accommodate these changes. However, locks (even multi-granularity locks) severely restrict concurrency. A definition of what it means to update a database, and a definition of conflicts based on this definition of update semantics, would allow more concurrency.

   It is interesting to note again the relationship between changes to the class (type) lattice and query processing. In the absence of a clear definition of update semantics and its incorporation into the query processing methodology, most of the current query processors assume that the database schema (i.e., the class (type) lattice) is static during the execution of a query.

3. There are a few object models (e.g., OODAPLEX [Dayal, 1989] and TIGUKAT [Özsu et al., 1995a]) that treat all system entities as objects. Following this approach, it is only natural to model transactions as objects. However, since transactions are basically constructs that change the state of the database, their effects on the database must be clearly specified.

   Within this context, it should also be noted that the application domains that require the services of object DBMSs tend to have somewhat different transaction management requirements, both in terms of transaction models and consistency constraints. Modeling transactions as objects enables the application of the well-known object techniques of specialization and subtyping to create various different types of TMSs. This gives the system extensibility.

4. Some of the requirements require rule support and active database capabilities. Rules themselves execute as transactions, which may spawn other transactions. It has been argued that rules should be modeled as objects [Dayal et al., 1988]. If that is the case, then certainly transactions should be modeled as objects too.

As a result of these points, it seems reasonable to argue for an approach to transaction management systems that is quite different from what has been done up to this point. This is a topic of some research potential.

14.8 CONCLUSION

In this chapter we considered the effect of object technology on database management. The thesis of the chapter is that, as database technology moves into new application areas besides business data processing, the requirements change and become more demanding. A richer model (such as the object model) that provides a superset of the functionalities of relational DBMSs is needed. Furthermore, since these new applications are inherently distributed, the object DBMSs must provide distribution support. As this chapter demonstrates, there has been significant amount of work along these lines, but there is much more to do, in particular with respect to providing full distributed DBMS functionality with very good performance.

There is growing commercial interest in a type of DBMS called *object-relational* [Stonebraker and Brown, 1999]. These systems provide a relational view to the users, allowing SQL-based access, but allow the attributes to be structured. In that sense, these are non-normalized relational systems. They are also extensible by enabling the insertion of new data types into the system by means of *data blades*, *cartridges*, or *extenders* (each commercial system uses a different name). However, this extensibility is limited, as it requires significant effort to write a data blade/cartridge/extender, and third-party vendors are currently providing these extensions. We did not discuss object-relational DBMSs in this chapter, since they are a combination of relational and object technologies, and other than a few (but important) implementation issues, there is not much new in terms of principles.

14.9 BIBLIOGRAPHIC NOTES

There are a number of good books on object DBMSs such as [Kemper and Moerkotte, 1994], [Bertino and Martino, 1993], [Cattell, 1994] and [Dogac et al., 1994]. An early collection of readings in object DBMSs is [Zdonik and Maier, 1990]. In addition, object DBMS concepts are discussed in [Kim and Lochovsky, 1989], [Kim, 1994]. There have been a couple of workshops devoted to distribution of object databases. These have appeared as books or proceedings: [Özsu et al., 1994a] and [Bukhres et al., 1995]. [Orfali et al., 1996] is considered the classical book on distributed objects, but the emphasis is mostly on the distributed object platforms (CORBA and COM), not on the fundamental DBMS functionality. We will discuss platforms in the next chapter.

Our discussion of the architectural issues is mostly based on [Özsu et al., 1994a] but largely extended. The object distribution design issues are discussed in significant more detail in [Ezeife and Barker, 1998], [Bellatreche et al., 1998b], and [Bellatreche et al., 1998c]. The query processing and optimization section is based on [Özsu and Blakeley, 1994] and the transaction management issues are from [Özsu, 1994]. Several techniques for distributed garbage collection have been classified in a survey article by Plainfossé and Shapiro [1995]. These sources contain more detail than can be covered in one chapter. Object-relational DBMSs are discussed in detail in [Stonebraker and Brown, 1999] and [Date and Darwen, 1998].

14.10 EXERCISES

14.1 Explain the mechanisms used to support encapsulation in distributed object DBMSs. In particular:

  (a) Describe how the encapsulation is hidden from the end users when both the objects and the methods are distributed.

  (b) How does a distributed object DBMS present a single global schema to end users? How is this different from supporting fragmentation transparency in relational database systems?

14.2 List the new data distribution problems that arise in object DBMSs, that are not present in relational DBMSs, with respect to fragmentation, migration and replication.

**14.3 Partitioning of object databases has the premise of reducing the irrelevant data access for user applications. Develop a cost model to execute queries on unpartitioned object databases, and horizontally or vertically partitioned object databases. Use your cost model to illustrate the scenarios under which partitioning does in fact reduce the irrelevant data access.

14.4 Show the relationship between clustering and partitioning. Illustrate how clustering can deteriorate/improve the performance of queries on a partitioned object database system.

14.5 Why do client-server object DBMSs primarily employ data shipping architecture while relational DBMSs emply function shipping?

14.6 Discuss the strengths and weaknesses of page and object servers with respect to data transfer, buffer management, cache consistency, and pointer swizzling mechanims.

14.7 What is the difference between caching information at the clients and data replication?

*14.8 A new class of applications that object DBMSs support are interactive and deal with large objects (e.g., interactive multimedia systems). Which one of the cache consistency algorithms presented in this chapter are suitable for this class of applications operating across wide area networks?

**14.9 Hardware and software pointer swizzling mechanisms have complementary strengths and weaknesses. Propose a hybrid pointer swizzling mechanism which incorporates the strengths of both.

**14.10 Explain how derived horizontal fragmentation can be exploited to facilitate efficient path queries in distributed object DBMSs. Give examples.

**14.11 Give some heuristics that an object DBMS query optimizer that accepts OQL queries may use to determine how to decompose a query so that parts can be function shipped and other parts have to be executed at the originating client by data shipping.

**14.12 Three alternative ways of performing *distributed* complex object assembly are discussed in this chapter. Give an algorithm for the alternative where complex operations, such as joins and complete assembly of remote objects, are performed at remote sites and the partial results are shipped to the central site for final assembly.

*14.13 Consider the airline reservation example of Chapter 10. Define a Reservation class (type) and give the forward and backward commutativity matrixes for it.

Chapter 15

DATABASE INTEROPERABILITY

Up to this point we have considered technical issues related to (homogeneous) distributed database systems. As we discussed in Chapter 4, these systems are logically integrated and provide a single image of the database, even though they are physically distributed. In this chapter we concentrate on distributed multidatabase systems which provide interoperability among a set of DBMSs. This is only one part of the more general *interoperability* problem. In recent years, new distributed applications have started to pose new requirements regarding the data source(s) they access. In parallel, the management of "legacy systems" and reuse of the data they generate have gained importance. The result has been a renewed consideration of the broader question of information system interoperability. The focus of this chapter is the narrower problem of database interoperability; however, we consider the more general question in the next chapter within the context of the World Wide Web and data management.

Three of the topics addressed in this chapter—global conceptual schema design (Section 15.1), query processing (Section 15.2), and transaction management (Section 15.3)—are the traditional database issues. The presentation of these topics will be based on the related concepts that were developed for distributed DBMSs. Finally, in Section 15.4, we discuss the role of object-orientation in database interoperability. Our primary focus is on data modeling and distributed object computing platforms, and how they can assist with the interoperability problem.

15.1 DATABASE INTEGRATION

Database integration involves the process by which information from participating databases can be conceptually integrated to form a single cohesive definition of a multidatabase. In other words, it is the process of designing the global conceptual schema. Recall from Chapter 4 that not all multidatabase architectures actually require the definition of this integrated view. Thus the discussions in this section are relevant only for those architectures that specify a global conceptual schema.

Recall from Chapter 5 that the design process in multidatabase systems is bottom-up. In other words, the individual databases actually exist, and designing the global conceptual schema involves integrating these component databases into a multidatabase. database integration can occur in two steps (Figure 15.1):

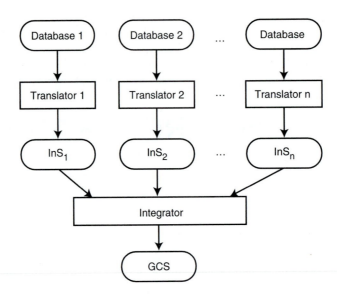

Figure 15.1. Database Integration Process

schema translation (or simply *translation*) and *schema integration*. In the first step, the component database schemas are translated to a common intermediate (InS_1, InS_2, ..., InS_n) canonical representation. The use of a canonical representation facilitates the translation process by reducing the number of translators that need to be written. The choice of the canonical model is important. As a principle, it should be one that is sufficiently expressive to incorporate the concepts available in all the databases that will later be integrated. Most of the recent studies use an object-oriented model for this purpose. This is necessary if one of the component databases that will be integrated is object-oriented. Even when this is not the case, an object model is generally viewed as the most appropriate canonical model. In this section, we will refrain from introducing object-orientation; we will discuss the role of object models and the object-oriented approach to interoperability in Section 15.4. For the time being, we will take a more traditional approach.

Clearly, the translation step is necessary only if the component databases are heterogeneous and each local schema may be defined using a different data model. In recent years, commercial interest has been on the integration of multiple relational databases where this translation step can be bypassed. There is some recent work on the development of system federation, in which systems with similar data models are integrated together (e.g., relational systems are integrated into one conceptual schema and, perhaps, object databases are integrated to another schema) and these integrated schemas are "combined" at a later stage (e.g., AURORA project [Yan, 1997], [Yan et al., 1997]). In this case, the translation step is delayed, providing increased flexibility for applications to access underlying data sources in a manner that is suitable for their needs.

In the second step, each intermediate schema is integrated into a global conceptual schema. In some methodologies, local external schemas are considered for integration rather than local conceptual schemas, since it may not be desirable to incorporate the entire local conceptual schema in the multidatabase.

Example 15.1

To facilitate our discussion of global schema design in multidatabase systems, we will use an example that is an extension of the engineering database we have been using throughout the book. To demonstrate both phases of the database integration process, we introduce some data model heterogeneity into our example.

Consider two organizations, each with their own database definitions. One is the (relational) database example that we have developed in Chapter 2. We repeat that definition in Figure 15.2 for completeness. The underscored attributes are the keys of the associated relations. We have made one modification in the PROJ relation by including attributes LOC and CNAME. LOC is the location of the project, whereas CNAME is the name of the client for whom the project is carried out. The second database also defined similar data, but is specified according to the entity-relationship (E-R) data model [Chen, 1976] as depicted in Figure 15.3.

EMP(<u>ENO</u>, ENAME, TITLE)

PROJ(<u>PNO</u>, PNAME, BUDGET, LOC, CNAME)

ASG(<u>ENO, PNO</u>, RESP, DUR)

PAY(<u>TITLE</u>, SAL)

Figure 15.2. Relational Engineering Database Representation

We assume that the reader is familiar with the entity-relationship data model. Therefore, we will not describe the formalism, except to make the following points regarding the semantics of Figure 15.3. This database is similar to the relational engineering database definition of Figure 15.2, with one significant difference: it also maintain data about the clients for whom the projects are conducted. The rectangular boxes in Figure 15.3 represent the entities modeled in the database, and the diamonds indicate a relationship between the entities to which they are connected. The type of relationship is indicated around the diamonds. For example, the CONTRACTED-BY relation is a many-to-one from the PROJECT entity to the CLIENT entity (e.g., each project has a single client, but each client can have many projects). Similarly, the WORKS-IN relationship indicates a many-to-many relationship between the two connected relations. The attributes of entities and the relationships are shown as elliptical circles.

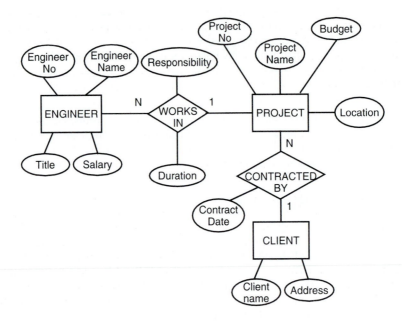

Figure 15.3. Entity-Relationship Database

15.1.1 Schema Translation

Schema translation is the task of mapping from one schema to another. This requires the specification of a target data model for the global conceptual schema definition. Schema translation may not be necessary in a heterogeneous database if it can be accomplished during the integration stage. Combining the translation and integration steps [Brzezinski et al., 1984] provides the integrater with all the information about the entire global database at one time. Obviously, the integrater can make trade-offs between the different local schemas to determine which representation should be given precedence when conflicts arise. This requires that the integrater have knowledge of all the various trade-offs that must be made among several different schemas and their semantics, which may be different.

We will not discuss the specifics of translation between various data models; this can be found in many textbooks. The important point is that equivalences must be established between the concepts of the source model and those of the target model. The following example simply demonstrates the result of translation for the employee/engineering databases.

Example 15.2

Among the two databases, the E-R model is more expressive; therefore we will use it as the canonical model. Translation of relational schemes to an E-R model requires consideration of each relation's role. The first difficulty is the determination of relations that represent entities versus those that represent relationships. This information may be easy to identify if there are specific relations that represent relationships as well as entities. Otherwise, these relationships may be identified from the foreign keys defined for each relation. Once this determination is made, the mapping is straightforward: relations that represent entities are modeled as entities, and relations that represent relationships are modeled as relationships.

A second difficulty relates to the nature of the relationships. Identification of the type of relationship (e.g., many-to-many) and relationship constraints require that semantic information be known about the relational implementation, since these are not intrinsic to the relational model. This typically requires consulting the system directory.

The relational model of the engineering database depicted in Figure 15.2 consists of four relations, three of which (EMP, PROJ and PAY) clearly correspond to entities, whereas one (ASG) corresponds to a relationship. The ENO and PNO attributes of ASG are foreign keys, which indicates that ASG is a relationship between EMP and PROJ. The type of relationship that ASG represents cannot be discerned from the relational schema definition. From our knowledge of the semantics of the database, we know it to be many-to-many. The handling of the PAY relation is more difficult. It can be treated as an entity, in which case it is necessary to establish a relationship between it and one of the other entities, probably EMP. Even though no such relation exists in Figure 15.2, it is possible to create a one-to-many relationship from PAY to EMP. The relationship needs to be one-to-many since each employee can have one salary, but a salary can belong to two employees who happen to have the same title. This is the PAYMENT relation in Figure 15.4a. Another alternative would be to treat salary as an attribute of an engineer entity (Figure 15.4b). This provides a cleaner E-R model but does not explicitly specify the relationship between the employee titles and their salaries.

15.1.2 Schema Integration

Schema integration follows the translation process and generates the global conceptual schema by integrating the intermediate schemas. schema integration is the process of *identifying* the components of a database which are related to one another, *selecting* the best representation for the global conceptual schema, and finally, *integrating* the components of each intermediate schema. Two components can be related as equivalent, one contained in the other, or as disjoint [Sheth et al., 1988a].

Integration methodologies can be classified as binary or *n*ary mechanisms [Batini et al., 1986] (Figure 15.5). Binary integration methodologies involve the manipulation of two schemas at a time. These can occur in a stepwise (ladder) fashion (Figure 15.6a) where intermediate schemas are created for integration with subsequent schemas [Pu, 1988], or in a purely binary fashion (Figure 15.6b), where each schema is integrated with one other, creating an intermediate schema for integration with other intermediate schemas ([Batini and Lenzirini, 1984] and [Dayal and Hwang, 1984]).

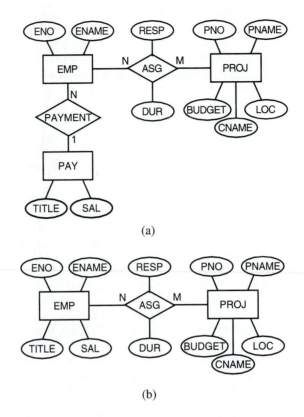

(a)

(b)

Figure 15.4. E-R Equivalent of the Relational Engineering Database

Nary integration mechanisms integrate more than two schemas at each iteration. One-pass integration (Figure 15.7a) occurs when all schemas are integrated at once, producing the global conceptual schema after one iteration. Benefits of this

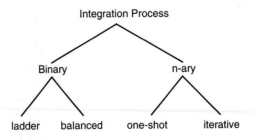

Figure 15.5. Taxonomy of Integration Methodologies

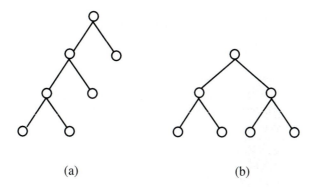

Figure 15.6. Binary Integration Methods

approach include the availability of complete information about all databases at integration time. There is no implied priority for the integration order of schemas, and the trade-offs, such as the best representation for data items or the most understandable structure, can be made between all schemas rather than between a few. Difficulties with this approach include increased complexity and difficulty of automation.

Iterative *n*ary integration (Figure 15.7b) offers more flexibility (typically, more information is available) and is more general (the number of schemas can be varied depending on the integrater's preferences). Binary approaches are a special case of iterative *n*ary. They decrease the potential integration complexity and lead toward automation techniques, since the number of schemas to be considered at each step is more manageable. Integration by an *n*ary process enables the integrater to perform the operations on more than two schemas. For practical reasons, the majority of systems utilize binary methodology, but a number of researchers prefer the one-shot

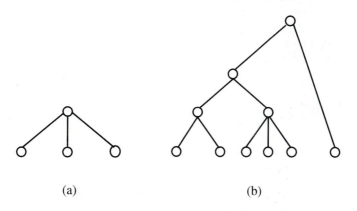

Figure 15.7. *N*ary Integration Methods

approach because complete information is available ([Elmasri et al., 1987] and [Yao et al., 1982b]). Tools have been developed to aid in this integration process (e.g., [Sheth et al., 1988a]).

Schema integration involves two tasks: homogenization and integration ([Yan et al., 1997] and [Yan, 1997]). *Homogenization* involves the determination of structural and semantic "problems" of each component database. These "problems" relate to structural and semantic differences from some norm. The norm could be a particular domain-specific ontology or the schema of another database. The idea is to make sure that component databases are comparable with each other in both structure and semantics once they are homogenized. *Integration* follows homogenization and involves merging the schemas of multiple databases to create a global conceptual schema. It is during this integration step that one of the methods discussed above is applied. We discuss each of these tasks below.

Homogenization

During this phase, both semantic heterogeneity and structural heterogeneity problems are resolved. semantic heterogeneity is a fairly loaded term without a clear definition. It basically refers to the differences among the databases that relate to the meaning, interpretation, and intended use of data [Vermeer, 1997]. Arguably, the more important aspects of semantic heterogeneity reveal themselves as naming conflicts. The fundamental naming problem is that of *synonyms* and *homonyms*. Two identical entities that have different names are synonyms, and two different entities that have identical names are homonyms. For example, ENGINEER in Figure 15.3 and EMP in 15.2 are synonyms; they both refer to an engineer entity. On the other hand, the Budget attribute in the PROJECT entity in Figure 15.3 and the Budget attribute of the PROJ relation in Figure 15.2 may be homonyms if one represents the budget in U.S. dollars and the other in Canadian dollars.

There are a number of alternative methods for dealing with naming conflicts. One is to resolve homonyms by prefixing the terms by the schema or model name [Elmasri et al., 1987]. It is not possible to resolve synonyms in a similar, simple fashion. The approach which is regarded as preferable is to use ontologies. An ontology is specific to a particular application domain and defines the terms, together with the semantics of those terms, that are acceptable in that domain. If every database schema for that domain uses a common ontology, then the naming conflicts are naturally resolved. There is significant effort underway in defining ontologies for various domains, but work is far from being complete.

Example 15.3

In the example that we are considering, integration will be performed on intermediate schemas in E-R notation. The intermediate schemas we will consider are depicted in Figures 15.3 and 15.4(b), which we will refer to as InS_1 and InS_2.

The synonyms between InS_1 and InS_2 are depicted in Figure 15.8, where the corresponding entries on the same row are synonyms (e.g., Salary and SAL). The only homonym is the title attribute that exists in both of the intermediate schemas. In InS_1, the attribute refers to the title of engineers, so its domain is engineering titles, whereas in InS_2 it refers to the titles of

InS_1	InS_2
ENGINEER	EMP
Engineer No	ENO
Engineer Name	ENAME
Salary	SAL
WORKS IN	ASG
Responsibility	RESP
Duration	DUR
PROJECTS	PROJ
Project No	PNO
Project Name	PNAME
Location	LOC

Figure 15.8. Synonyms in the Intermediate Schemas

all employees and therefore has a larger domain. Thus the title attributes in InS_1 and InS_2 form a homonym, since the same attribute name is used to mean two different things.

The naming conflicts in this example will be resolved by renaming entities, attributes, and relationships in the schemas. For simplicity, we will rename the schema of Figure 15.4 to conform to the naming of Figure 15.3. We will rename the homonym TITLE attribute in the manner described above.

Structural conflicts occur in four possible ways: as *type conflicts, dependency conflicts, key conflicts,* or *behavioral conflicts* [Batini et al., 1986]. Type conflicts occur when the same object is represented by an attribute in one schema and by an entity in another. Dependency conflicts occur when different relationship modes (e.g., one-to-one versus many-to-many) are used to represent the same thing in different schemas. Key conflicts occur when different candidate keys are available and different primary keys are selected in different schemas. Behavioral conflicts are implied by the modeling mechanism. For example, deleting the last item from one database may cause the deletion of the containing entity (i.e., deletion of the last employee causes the dissolution of the department).

Example 15.4

We have two structural conflicts in the example we are considering. The first is a type conflict involving clients of projects. In the schema of Figure 15.3, the client of a project is modeled as an entity. In the schema of Figure 15.4, however, the client is included as an attribute of the PROJ entity.

The second structural conflict is a dependency conflict involving the WORKS_IN relationship in Figure 15.3 and the ASG relationship in Figure 15.4. In the former, the relationship is many-to-one from the ENGINEER to the PROJECT, whereas in the latter, the relationship is many-to-many. The resolution of these conflicts is discussed in Example 15.5.

Transformation of entities/attributes/relationships among each another is one way of handling structural conflicts ([Batini and Lenzirini, 1984], [Batini et al., 1986]). One can accomplish these transformations on an instance-by-instance basis. Figure 15.9 depicts the possible atomic transformation scenarios. The dashed lines indicate that a given attribute is an identifier (key) of the associated entity.

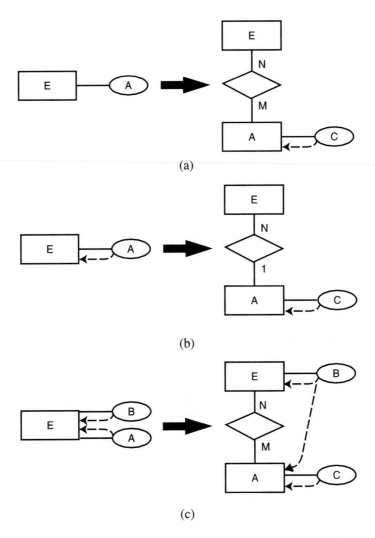

(a)

(b)

(c)

Figure 15.9. Atomic Conformation Alternatives (Adapted from: C. Batini, M. Lenzerini, and S.B. Navathe, Comparison of Methodologies for Database Scheme Integration. *ACM Comp. Surveys*; December 1986; 18(4): 323–364.)

A non-key attribute can be transformed into an entity by creating an intermediate relationship connecting the new entity and a new attribute to represent it.
Figure 15.9a depicts such a transformation of a non-key attribute A of entity E to a
separate entity that is related to E by a many-to-many relationship and is uniquely
identified by a new key attribute, C. Figure 15.9b illustrates a key attribute translation where a key attribute is transformed into an entity that has an identifier
C. C becomes the identifier of both the new entity A and the entity E, because
the relationship between E and A is many-to-one. Figure 15.9c demonstrates the
case where identifier A is only a part of the complete identifier, which requires the
non-standard reference back to the originating entity.

Example 15.5

In the example we are considering, there is one case where such a transformation would be necessary. In Figure 15.4, the attribute CNAME is represented
as an attribute and needs to be converted to an entity using the technique
demonstrated in Figure 15.9a. The result is depicted in Figure 15.10.

Recall that there is a dependency conflict between the two schemas as well.
In this example, we will resolve the conflict by choosing to accept the more
general many-to-many relationship between the ENGINEER and PROJECT
entities. Note that this is a design decision which reflects alternative semantics
of integration, and results in the loss of the more restricting one-to-many
constraint between ENGINEER and PROJECT.

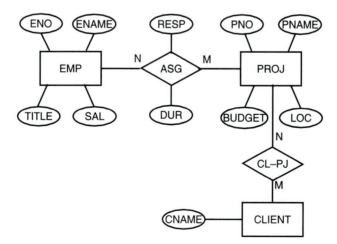

Figure 15.10. Attribute-to-Entity Transformation

The determination of synonyms and homonyms, as well as the identification of structural conflicts, requires specification of the relationship between the intermediate schemas. Two schemas can be related in four possible ways: they can be identical to one another, one can be a subset of the other, some components from one may occur in the other while retaining some unique features, or they could be completely different with no overlap. In the example that we have been considering, InS_2 is a subset of InS_1.

Determination of the type of relationship is essential in global conceptual schema design. For example, equivalence of the schemas is important in determining if two schemas represent the same information, so that the most appropriate schema can be used for the representation [Jajodia et al., 1983]. Unfortunately, the identification of these relationships cannot be done entirely syntactically; the semantics of each schema have to be considered. Recall, for example, our discussion above with respect to the address attribute in two intermediate schemas. To determine whether one attribute is identical to the other requires knowledge about the "meaning" of the information captured by that attribute. A further complication may be that an attribute in one schema may represent the same information as an entity in another one. Unfortunately, the homogenization requires a significant amount of human intervention, since semantic knowledge about all intermediate schemas is required.

Integration

Integration involves the merging of the intermediate schemas and their restructuring. All schemas are merged into a single database schema and then restructured to create the "best" integrated schema. Merging requires that the information contained in the participating schemas be retained in the integrated schema.

Example 15.6

> For this example, the integration step is straightforward. Since InS_2, is a subset of InS_1, we accept InS_1 as the integrated schema. The only complication arises due to the different characteristics of the CONTRACTED_BY relationship in the two schemas. In InS_1, it is many-to-one from the PROJECT entity to the CLIENT entity. However, the same relationship in InS_2 is many-to-many (Figure 15.10), which is more general. This conflict did not manifest itself in the original schema specification, but arose due to the resolution of a type conflict during the confirmation stage. Therefore, merging these two schemas can be accomplished by accepting InS_1 as the result, provided that the CONTRACTED_BY relationship is converted to a many-to-many relationship. The result of the integration is given in Figure 15.11.

Three dimensions of merging and restructuring can be defined: *completeness, minimality,* and *understandability* [Batini et al., 1986]. Merging is *complete* if all the information from all the schemas is integrated into the common schema. To accomplish a complete merging, one may use *subsetting*, a technique that describes one entity in terms of another. The well-known concepts of generalization and specialization are special cases of subsetting. It is possible to devise special operators for this purpose [Motro and Buneman, 1981].

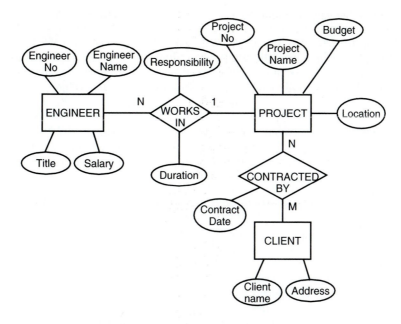

Figure 15.11. Integrated Global Conceptual Schema

A merging is *non-minimal* when redundant relationship information is retained in an integrated schema because of a failure to detect containment where part of one intermediate schema may be included within another intermediate schema. Non-minimal schemas can also result from the translation process, due to the production of an intermediate schema which itself is not minimal.

Understandability is the final dimension for determining the best schema. Once all the elements are merged, the restructuring should facilitate an understandable schema. Unfortunately, quantifying exactly what makes something easily understandable is usually not possible, since the concept itself is highly subjective. It may be necessary to make trade-offs between minimality and understandability, provided that the resulting merged and restructured schema is complete.

15.2 QUERY PROCESSING

Many of the distributed query processing and optimization techniques carry over to multidatabase systems, but there are important differences. Recall from Chapter 7 that we characterized distributed query processing in four steps: query decomposition, data localization, global optimization, and local optimization. This is a generalization of the local query processing steps in centralized DBMSs, which include decomposition, optimization, and execution [Gardarin and Valduriez, 1989]. The nature of multidatabase systems requires slightly different steps.

The first thing to remember in this discussion is the nature of the multi-DBMS. In Chapter 4 (specifically in Figure 4.10), we indicated that the multi-DBMS is a layer of software that runs on top of component DBMSs. Each DBMS has its own query processors, which execute queries according to the three steps listed above.

Query processing in a multidatabase system is more complex than in a distributed DBMS for the following reasons [Sheth and Larson, 1990]:

1. The capability of component DBMSs may be different, which prevents uniform treatment of queries across multiple DBMSs and sites.

2. Similarly, the cost of processing queries may be different on different DBMSs. This increases the complexity of the cost functions that need to be evaluated.

3. There may be difficulties in moving data between DBMSs, since they may differ in their ability to read "moved" data.

4. The local optimization capability of each DBMS may be quite different.

In addition, the autonomy of these systems poses problems [Lu et al., 1993]. Communication autonomy means that a component DBMS may terminate its services at any time. This requires query processing techniques that are tolerant to system unavailability. The question is how the system answers queries where a component system is either unavailable from the beginning or shuts down in the middle of query execution. There has not been much work in this area. Design autonomy may restrict the availability and accuracy of statistical information that is needed for query optimization. The difficulty of determining local cost functions is an issue that we will discuss shortly. The execution autonomy of multidatabase systems makes it difficult to apply some of the query optimization strategies. For example, semijoin-based optimization of distributed joins may be difficult if the source and target relations reside in different component DBMSs, since, in this case, the semijoin execution of a join translates into three queries: one to retrieve the join attribute values of the target relation and to ship it to the source relation's DBMS, the second to perform the join at the source relation, and the third to perform the join at the target relation's DBMS. The problem arises because communication with component DBMSs occurs at a high level of the DBMS API.

In addition to these difficulties, the architecture of a distributed multi-DBMS poses certain challenges. In these systems, there is a multi-DBMS layer at each site (Figure 15.12). Therefore, execution of distributed queries in a distributed multi-DBMS involves cooperation among various local multi-DBMSs.

The architecture depicted in Figure 15.12 points to an additional complexity in distributed multi-DBMSs. In distributed DBMSs, query processors have to deal only with data distribution across multiple sites. In a distributed multi-DBMS environment, on the other hand, data is distributed not only across sites but also across multiple databases, each managed by an autonomous DBMS. Thus, while there are two parties that cooperate in the processing of queries in a distributed DBMSs (the control site and local sites), the number of parties increases to three in the case of a distributed multi-DBMS: the multi-DBMS layer at the control site, which receives the global query; the multi-DBMS layers at the sites, which participate in processing the query; and the component DBMSs, which ultimately optimize and execute the query.

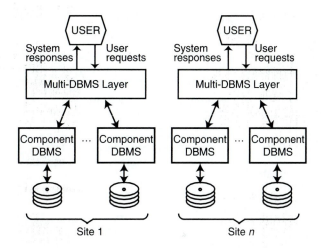

Figure 15.12. Structure of a Distributed Multi-DBMS

15.2.1   Query Processing Layers in Distributed Multi-DBMSs

With this structure in mind, we can now discuss the various steps involved in query processing in distributed multi-DBMSs (Figure 15.13). When a query is received at a site, the first thing that needs to be done is to "split" it into subqueries based on data distribution across multiple sites. At this step, it is only necessary to worry about the placement of data across the sites, rather than its storage across various databases. Therefore, the only information that is required is the typical data allocation information stored in a global directory. The site that receives the query and performs the splitting, called the *control site*, is ultimately responsible for successful completion of the task.

Each subquery is then sent to the site where it is to be processed. The multi-DBMS layer at each site further "fragments" the query for each DBMS that it controls. At this stage, the information within the directory is used. Each subquery is then translated into the language of the respective DBMS. Extensive information about the global query language and the individual languages used by the DBMSs needs to be maintained to facilitate translation. Even though this information can be kept within the directory, it is common to store it as an *auxiliary database* [Landers and Rosenberg, 1982].

The queries submitted to the component DBMSs are processed following decomposition, optimization, and execution steps. The decomposition step involves the simplification of a user query that is specified in some relational calculus and its translation to an equivalent relational algebra query over the conceptual schema. The optimization step involves the reordering of relational algebra operations, as well as determination of the best access paths to data. The resulting schedule is then executed by the run-time support processor.

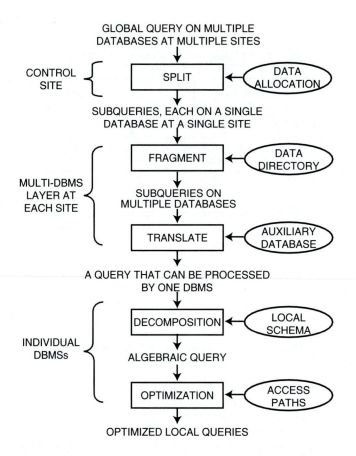

Figure 15.13. Query Processing Steps in Multidatabase Systems

As indicated above, specific translation information is stored in a separate auxiliary database. There is no overriding principle that dictates separation of the global directory from the auxiliary database. In fact, there are prototype heterogeneous systems (such as OMNIBASE [Rusinkiewicz et al., 1988], COSYS [Adiba and Portal, 1978], ADDS [Breitbart and Paolini, 1985], and MRDSM [Wong and Bazek, 1985]) that combine the two pieces of information into one database. We have separated them to highlight their different functionalities and to facilitate the incremental definition of the two databases. This separation serves to emphasize the distinction between distributed databases and distributed multidatabase systems.

The auxiliary database contains information describing how mappings from/to participating schemas and global schema can be performed. It enables conversions between components of the database in different ways. For example, if the global schema represents temperatures in Fahrenheit degrees, but a participating database uses Celsius degrees, the auxiliary database must contain a conversion formula to provide the proper presentation to the global user and the local databases. If the conversion is across types and simple formulas cannot perform the translation, complete mapping tables could be located in the auxiliary database, as illustrated in the age category relations above.

15.2.2   Query Optimization Issues

As indicated earlier, query optimization in multi-DBMSs is similar to that of distributed DBMSs in some respects, but different in others. As with homogeneous distributed DBMSs, query optimization in multi-DBMSs can be either heuristics-based or cost-based. We consider cost-based optimization in most of this section. Two alternative heuristics can be employed in the decomposition of a query into subqueries. The first alternative is to decompose a global query into the smallest possible subqueries, each of which is executed by one component DMBS. Multiple subqueries may be submitted to a given component DMBS; the global query processor collects partial results. This approach has two advantages: decomposition is relatively simple, and there are more opportunities for optimization at the global query optimizer level. The disadvantage, of course, is that the global query processor/optimizer does more work, and there are more messages transmitted to execute the query.

The second alternative heuristic is to decompose the global query into the largest possible subqueries, each of which is executed by one DBMS. Each component DMBS executes only one subquery, the results of which are collected by the global query processor. In this case, the global query processor/optimizer does less work, since inter-site processing is minimized. This results in fewer messages but more sophisticated component interface processors (CIPs). CIPs and the component DMBS optimizers are more involved in processing and optimization. CIPs can exchange messages among themselves, and can store, delete, and operate on temporary files.

If we follow our earlier characterization of cost-based query optimization in terms of search space, search algorithm, and cost functions, the differences are mainly in terms of cost functions. The absence of (or difficulty in obtaining) information about component DBMSs' operations poses problems in defining meaningful global cost function. Why is it necessary to define global cost functions? The main reason is that global queries involve inter-site operations, which require optimization at the multi-DBMS level. Of particular concern, of course, is the optimization of inter-DBMS joins. We consider that problem first, and then consider the issue of defining appropriate cost functions and obtaining information from the component DBMSs.

As discussed in the chapters on query optimization, most commercial cost-based optimizers restrict their search space by eliminating bushy join trees from consideration. Almost all the systems use left linear join orders where the right subtree of a join node is always a leaf node corresponding to a base relation (Figure 15.14a). Consideration of only left linear join trees gives good results in centralized DBMSs for two reasons: it reduces the need to estimate statistics for at least one operand, and indexes can still be exploited for one of the operands. However, in multi-DBMSs, these types of join execution plans are not necessarily the preferred ones,

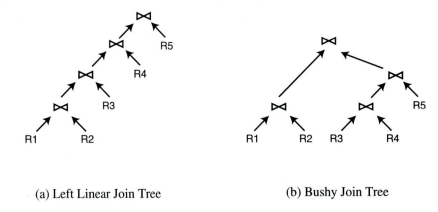

(a) Left Linear Join Tree   (b) Bushy Join Tree

Figure 15.14. Left Linear versus Bushy Join Trees

as they do not allow any parallelism in join execution — an intermediate join has
to wait for the completion of the earlier join operation (See Figure 15.14b). This
is particularly serious if the intermediate join is implemented using a sort-merge
or hash join algorithm since, in this case, the intermediate join cannot even begin
before the earlier one completes [Du et al., 1995]. Strictly speaking, this is also
a problem in tightly coupled distributed DBMSs, but the issue is more serious in
the case of multi-DBMSs, because in the latter systems, we wish to push as much
processing as possible to the component DBMSs.

A way to resolve this problem is to somehow generate bushy join trees and
consider them at the expense of left linear ones. One way to achieve this is to
apply a commercial query optimizer to first generate a left linear join tree, and
then convert it to a bushy one [Du et al., 1995]. In this case, the left linear join
execution plan can be optimal with respect to total time, and the transformation
improves the query response time without severely impacting the total time. Du
et al [1995] propose a hybrid algorithm that concurrently performs a bottom-up
and top-down sweep of the left linear join execution tree, transforming it, step-by-
step, to a bushy one. The algorithm maintains two pointers, called *upper anchor
nodes* (UAN) on the tree. At the beginning, bottom UAN (UAN_B) is set to the
grandparent of the leftmost root node (join 2 in Figure 15.14a), while top UAN
(UAN_T) is set to the root (join 5). For each UAN the algorithm selects a *lower
anchor node* (LAN). This is the node closest to the UAN and whose right child
subtree's response time is within a designer-specified range, relative to that of the
UAN's right child subtree. Intuitively, the LAN is chosen such that its right child
subtree's response time is **close** to the corresponding UAN's right child subtree's
response time. As we will see shortly, this helps in keeping the transformed bushy
tree balanced, which reduces the response time.

At each step, the algorithm picks one of the UAN/LAN pairs (strictly speaking,
it picks the UAN and selects the appropriate LAN, as discussed above), and performs the following translation for the segment between that LAN and UAN pair:

1. The left child of UAN becomes the new UAN of the transformed segment.

2. The LAN remains unchanged, but its right child node is replaced with a new join node of two subtrees, which were the right child subtrees of the input UAN and LAN.

The UAN mode that will be considered in that particular iteration is chosen according to the following heuristic: choose UAN_B if the response time of its left child subtree is smaller than that of UAN_T's subtree; otherwise choose UAN_T. If the response times are the same, choose the one with the more unbalanced child subtree.

At the end of each transformation step, the UAN_B and UAN_T are adjusted. The algorithm terminates when $UAN_B = UAN_T$, since this indicates that no further transformations are possible. The resulting join execution tree will be almost balanced, producing an execution plan whose response time is reduced due to parallel execution of the joins.

The algorithm described above starts with a left linear join execution tree that is generated by a commercial DBMS optimizer. While this is a good starting point, it can be argued that the original linear execution plan may not fully account for the peculiarities of the distributed multidatabase characteristics, such as data replication. A special global query optimization algorithm, developed specifically for the MDBS, can take these into consideration. Evrendilek et al [1997] propose such an algorithm, which generates an initial join execution graph. The algorithm proposes checks for different parenthesizations of this linear join execution order and produces a parenthesized order which is optimal, with respect to response time. The result is an (almost) balanced join execution tree. Performance evaluations indicate that this approach produces better quality plans at the expense of longer optimization time [Evrendilek et al., 1997].

If optimizers are extensible, it is possible to extend a commercial optimizer rather than implementing one from scratch for the MDBS, or revising the output generated by one. This is done in the Garlic system [Haas et al., 1997], where a rule-based optimizer is extended with execution plans that are specific to the multi-database environment. Garlic starts from the rule-based optimizer proposed by Lohman [1988] and extends the rules for new operators to create temporary relations to retrieve locally-stored data. It also creates the `PushDown` operator that pushes a portion of the work to the component DBMSs where they will be executed. The execution plans are represented, as usual, with operator trees, but the operator nodes are annotated with additional information that specifies the source(s) of the operand(s), whether the results are materialized, and so on. The Garlic operator trees are then translated into operators that can be directly executed by the execution engine.

Besides execution space considerations, the definition of a global cost function is a major issue. Global cost function definition, and the associated problem of obtaining cost-related information from component DBMSs, is perhaps the most-studied problem. A number of possible solutions have emerged, which we will discuss below.

The first thing to note is that we are primarily interested in determining the cost of the lower levels of a query execution tree that correspond to the parts of the query executed at component DBMSs. If we assume that all local processing is "pushed down" in the tree, then we can modify it such that the leaves of the tree correspond to subqueries that will be executed at individual component DBMSs. In this case, we are talking about the determination of the costs of these subqueries that are input to the first level (from the bottom) operators. Cost for higher levels of the query execution tree may be calculated recursively, based on the leaf node costs.

Three alternative approaches exist for determining the cost of executing queries at component DBMSs [Zhu and Larson, 1998]:

1. Treat the component DBMS as a black box, run some test queries on them, and from these determine the necessary cost information [Du et al., 1992], [Zhu and Larson, 1998].

2. Use previous knowledge about the component DBMSs, as well as their external characteristics, to subjectively determine the cost information [Zhu and Larson, 1998].

3. Monitor the run-time behavior of component DBMSs and dynamically collect the cost information [Lu et al., 1992].

Among these approaches, the first has attracted the most attention. We will discuss two proposals that follow this approach.

The Pegasus project [Du et al., 1992] addresses this problem by expressing the cost functions logically (e.g., aggregate CPU and I/O costs, selectivity factors), rather than on the basis of physical characteristics (e.g., relation cardinalities, number of pages, number of distinct values for each column). Thus, the cost functions for component DBMSs is expressed as

$$Cost = initialization\ cost + cost\ to\ find\ qualifying\ tuples$$
$$+\ cost\ to\ process\ selected\ tuples$$

The individual terms of this formula will differ for different operators. However, these differences are not difficult to specify a priori. The fundamental difficulty is the determination of the term coefficients in these formulae, which change with different component DBMSs. The approach taken in the Pegasus project is to construct a synthetic database (called a *calibrating database*), run queries against it in isolation, and measure the elapsed time to deduce the coefficients.

A problem that has been noted with this approach is that the calibration database is synthetic, and the results obtained by using it may not apply well to real DBMSs [Zhu and Larson, 1998]. An alternative is proposed in the CORDS project [Zhu and Larson, 1996a], based on running probing queries on component DBMSs to determine cost information. Probing queries can, in fact, be used to gather a number of cost information factors. For example, probing queries can be issued to retrieve data from component DBMSs to construct and update the multidatabase catalog. Statistical probing queries can be issued that, for example, count the number of tuples of a relation. Finally, performance measuring probing queries can be issued to measure the elapsed time for determining cost function coefficients.

A special case of probing queries are sample queries. In this case [Zhu and Larson, 1998], queries are classified according to a number of criteria, and sample queries from each class are issued and measured to derive component cost information. Query classification can be performed according to query characteristics (e.g., unary operation queries, two-way join queries), characteristics of the underlying component DBMSs (e.g., the access methods that it supports). The global cost function is similar to the Pegasus cost function in that it consists of three components: initialization cost, cost of retrieving a tuple, and cost of processing a tuple. The difference is in the way the parameters of this function are determined. Instead of using a calibrating database, sample queries are executed and costs are measured. The global cost equation is treated as a regression equation, and the regression coefficients are calculated [Zhu and Larson, 1996b] using the measured costs of sample queries. The regression coefficients are the cost function parameters.

15.3 TRANSACTION MANAGEMENT

Among all database interoperability problems, transaction management has probably been studied the most extensively. The challenge is to permit concurrent global updates to the component databases without violating their autonomy. In general, it is not possible to provide the same semantics as (homogeneous) distributed DBMSs without violating some autonomy.

Execution autonomy implies that the global transaction management functions are performed independent of the component transaction execution functions. In other words, the individual component DBMSs (more specifically, their transaction managers) are not modified to accommodate global updates. Design autonomy has the additional implication that the transaction managers of each DBMS may employ different concurrency control and commit protocols.

In this section, we describe the specific problems and review the existing work in the literature. First we discuss a transaction and computation model, and then we present an extension to the serializability theory that accommodates multidatabase systems.

15.3.1 Transaction and Computation Model

Let us first elaborate on the architectural aspects of multidatabase transaction processing. As described in Chapter 4 (specifically in Figure 4.10), the MDBS architecture involves a number of DBMSs, each with its own transaction manager (called *local transaction managers* or LTMs) and a multi-DBMS layer on top. The transaction manager of the multi-DBMS layer is called the *global transaction manager* (GTM) since it manages the execution of global transactions. Further, in a distributed multi-DBMS, the architecture of Figure 4.10 exists at each site. Thus our architectural model can be further abstracted, as in Figure 15.15, for the purposes of distributed transaction management.

In a multidatabase system, there are two types of transaction: *local* transactions, which are submitted to each DBMS, and *global* transactions, which are submitted to the multi-DBMS layer. Local transactions execute on a single database, whereas global transactions access multiple databases. A global transaction is divided into a set of *global subtransactions*, each of which executes on one database. For a global transaction GT_i, its global subtransaction, which executes on database j, will be denoted as GST_{ij}. For a distributed transaction GT_i (which, by definition, must be global), the global subtransaction that executes at site k is denoted as GST_i^k.

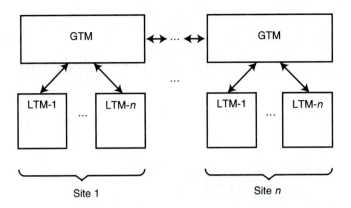

Figure 15.15. Distributed Multi-DBMS Transaction Management

Example 15.7

Consider the two databases that we designed in Section 15.1 (Figures 15.2 and 15.3). In this example, we ignore distribution for simplicity and without loss of generality. Let us denote the relational engineering database as 1, and the E-R engineering database as 2, and assume that these databases reside at the same site. Assume that a global transaction updates the salary of "J. Doe" by 15%. Let us denote this transaction as GT_1. First note that GT_1 may be specified on the global conceptual schema (if one is defined) which is specified in Example 14.11 (Figure 15.11). This global transaction will be subdivided into two subtransactions, as specified below, each executing on one of the databases. For the relational DBMS, we use an embedded SQL notation to specify the transaction; for the E-R DBMS, we use a straightforward algorithmic notation.

GST_{11}:   EXEC SQL   SELECT TITLE INTO $temp1$
                              FROM EMP
                              WHERE ENAME = "J. Doe"

          if $temp1$ is empty   then
             abort
          else begin
             EXEC SQL   UPDATE PAY
                              SET SAL = SAL * 1.15
                              WHERE ENAME = "J. Doe"

          commit
          endif

GST_{12}:   read(ENGINEER.Salary) into *temp*
             where ENGINEER.Name = "J.Doe"
          if *temp* is empty then
             abort
          else begin
             ENGINEER.Salary ← *temp* ∗ 1.15
             write(ENGINEER.Salary)
             commit
          end

There could be other transactions that may have been submitted directly to the component DBMSs. For example, the following local transactions LT_1 and LT_2 update, respectively, the salaries of all electrical engineers in database 1 by 50% and the budgets of maintenance projects by $50,000 in database 3.

LT_1:   EXEC SQL   UPDATE PAY
                     SET SAL = SAL ∗ 1.5
                     WHERE TITLE = "Elect. Eng."
          Commit
LT_2:   read(PROJECT.Budget) into *temp*
             where PROJECT.Name = "Maintenance"
          PROJECT.Budget ← *temp* + 50000
          write(PROJECT.Budget)
          Commit

The execution of these transactions on the architectural model of Figure 15.15 is depicted in Figure 15.16.

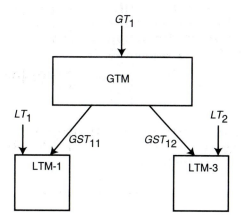

Figure 15.16. Transaction Execution Model Example

15.3.2 Multidatabase Concurrency Control

There have been many proposals for ensuring consistency of concurrently executing transactions in a multidatabase environment. Recall from Chapters 10 and 11 that concurrency control algorithms maintain the consistency and isolation properties of transactions. Given the autonomy of the component DBMSs, it is not easy to maintain these properties. A number of rather strict conditions must be satisfied, which we will discuss shortly.

Concurrency control algorithms synchronize concurrent transactions by ordering their conflicting operations such that a serialization order can be maintained among transactions. Recall from Chapter 11 that two transactions conflict if they each have one operation that accesses the same data item, and one of these operations is a write (causing read-write or write-write conflict). It is not easy for the GTM to determine conflicts in a multi-DBMS. Two global transactions that are handled by the GTM may not appear to conflict at all. However, the existence of local transactions may cause conflicts at the component databases among transactions. *Indirect conflicts* of this type cannot be detected by the GTM and are a source of significant difficulty in multi-DBMSs.

Example 15.8

Consider data items x_1, x_2 stored at component database 1 of a multi-DBMS. For this example, we do no need to consider data at other component databases. Consider two global transactions:

$$
\begin{array}{ll}
GT_1: & Read(x_1) \\
       & \text{Update } x_1 \\
       & Write(x_1) \\
       & \text{Commit}
\end{array}
$$

$$
\begin{array}{ll}
GT_2: & Read(x_2) \\
       & \text{Update } x_2 \\
       & Write(x_2) \\
       & \text{Commit}
\end{array}
$$

These two transactions execute at site 1 and do not conflict. Thus, GTM may release both of them to DBMS-1. However, there may be a local transaction executing at this site unknown to GTM:

$$
\begin{array}{ll}
LT: & Read(x_1) \\
    & Read(x_2) \\
    & x_2 \leftarrow f(x_1) \text{ [Update } x_2 \text{ based on } x_1] \\
    & Write(x_2) \\
    & \text{Commit}
\end{array}
$$

LT introduces a conflict between GT_1 and GT_2, which is not known to the GTM.

A series of conditions have been defined that specify when global transactions can safely update a multidatabase system ([Gligor and Popescu–Zeletin, 1986] and [Gligor and Luckenbaugh, 1984]). These conditions are helpful in determining the minimal functionality required of the various transaction managers.

The first condition for providing global concurrency control is to have the individual database managers guarantee local synchronization atomicity. This means that the local transaction managers are simply responsible for the correct execution of the transactions on their respective databases. If serializability is the correctness criterion used, each local transaction manager is responsible for maintaining that its schedule is serializable and recoverable. These schedules are made up of global subtransactions as well as local ones. Whether this condition can be enforced in an interoperable DBMS environment is questionable. As discussed in Chapter 10, many commercial systems allow less than serializable schedules. It may not be possible to enforce this requirement on all component DBMSs. Furthermore, the multi-DBMS has to deal with component DBMSs with different levels of transaction consistency enforcement.

The second condition requires that each LTM maintain the relative execution order of the subtransactions determined by the GTM. The global transaction manager, then, is responsible for coordinating the submission of the global subtransactions to the local transaction managers and coordinating their execution. If serializability is the correctness criterion used, the global transaction manager is responsible for the serializability of the global transaction execution schedules. Furthermore, the GTM is responsible for dealing with global deadlocks that occur among global transactions. Obviously, if the GTM awaits the result of one subtransaction before submitting the next, this ordering can be maintained. Whether this is possible without serializing transaction execution is a topic of much debate. There are methods that force component DBMSs to maintain the relative order. We discuss these in the next section.

In a distributed multi-DBMS, the global transaction manager is also responsible for the coordination of the distributed execution of global transactions. This involves a different execution paradigm than the one used in distributed DBMSs. In the latter, the transaction manager at the site where the transaction is submitted (called the *coordinating transaction manager*) can communicate directly with schedulers at its site and other sites. In distributed multi-DBMSs, however, this is not possible for two reasons. First, component DBMSs do not necessarily know how to communicate in a distributed environment. The earlier discussion on the functionality of the local transaction managers, together with our architectural discussions in Chapter 4, indicate that each component DBMS only knows how to communicate with an application program that executes on the same machine as itself. Second, global transaction managers usually have difficulty in scheduling transactions across multiple sites, so it may not be feasible for them to get even more involved with transaction scheduling across multiple DBMSs at one site. This would mean that a global transaction manager would send a global subtransaction to another global transaction manager at another site and expect it to coordinate the execution of the global subtransaction. The global transaction manager at the other site may then further decompose the transaction into global subtransactions, depending on the organization of the local databases at its site. The condition that governs the execution of global transactions states that a global transaction should have only one global subtransaction executing at any one site.

Example 15.9

Consider the following transaction, which, among other things, accesses two data items x and y stored at site 2.

$$GT_1: \quad \text{read}(x)$$
$$\vdots$$
$$\text{write}(x)$$
$$\vdots$$
$$\text{read}(y)$$
$$\vdots$$
$$\text{write}(y)$$
$$\text{commit}$$

Since GT_1 accesses, among others, two data items that are stored in site 2, it may be tempting (but incorrect, as we will demonstrate) for the coordinating global transaction manager to split it into the following two global subtransactions to be submitted to the global transaction manager of site 2:

$$GST_{11}^2: \quad \text{read}(x)$$
$$\vdots$$
$$\text{write}(x)$$
$$\text{commit}$$

and

$$GST_{12}^2: \quad \text{read}(y)$$
$$\vdots$$
$$\text{write}(y)$$
$$\text{commit}$$

Now consider a local transaction LT_1 that conflicts with either GST_{11}^2 or GST_{12}^2 (e.g., reading x or y). Then serializability of the global transaction GT_1 and the local transaction LT_1 would require that either $GT_1 \prec LT_1$ or $LT_1 \prec GT_1$. In terms of the subtransactions, this would mean that $GST_{11}^2 \prec GST_{12}^2 \prec LT_1$ or $LT_1 \prec GST_{11}^2 \prec GST_{12}^2$. However, it is possible to have an execution schedule, as, for example, $GST_{11}^2 \prec LT_1 \prec GST_{12}^2$. Certainly, this schedule is not serializable with respect to the local and global transactions.

The above discussion and example assume an execution model in which the multi-DBMS layer communicates with the component DBMSs by means of a high-level interface. This has been called the *service request* approach [Breitbart et al., 1992a]. It has also been suggested that some component DBMSs may expose an interface that allows the GTM to submit transaction operations (e.g., read, write, commit, abort) one by one. If component DBMSs open up their interfaces like this, the GTM can have finer control on transaction execution.

How can one deal with concurrency control, given these rather difficult conditions? There have been numerous proposals; in fact, too numerous for us to review here. Some of these solutions are interesting, however, so we will discuss them briefly. A good survey of other solutions is given in [Breitbart et al., 1992a].

One approach has been to revise the set of acceptable solutions. Consider the schedule in Example 15.9. The careful reader will have noticed that the schedule $GST_{11}^2 \prec LT_1 \prec GST_{12}^2$ may not necessarily be wrong, even though it is not serializable. For example, if LT_1 conflicts with GT_1 by reading x, and if GST_{12}^2 never accesses x, the database would be consistent at the end of the execution schedule above, even though it may not be serializable. This is actually a known property of serializability theory: serializable schedules are only a subset of the correct execution schedules. Thus serializability is quite conservative in the schedules it allows. In multidatabase systems this becomes even more significant. A corollary of the third condition that we discussed above is that a global subtransaction of a distributed transaction should not be split further by the global transaction manager at the site to which it is submitted.

Example 15.10

Consider the same transaction GT_1 that we considered in Example 14.13, but this time assume that x and y are stored in different databases at the same site (say, site 2). GT_1 can be split into a number of global subtransactions, one of which is submitted to the global transaction manager at site 2 as follows:

$$GST_1^2: \quad \text{read}(x, y)$$
$$\vdots$$
$$\text{write}(x)$$
$$\text{write}(y)$$
$$\text{commit}$$

Since x and y are in different databases, the global transaction manager itself may split GST_1^2 into GST_{11}^2 and GST_{12}^2 as defined in Example 14.13. Again notice that, if there is a local transaction LT_i that conflicts with either of these subtransactions, we would have a schedule that is not serializable but is correct.

This restriction is quite severe in multidatabase systems, since it makes it very difficult to find a computation model for executing transactions. Again considering the example above, where x and y are stored in different databases, to maintain serializability, the global transaction manager at site 2 has to hold exclusive access rights to data items at one local database (say, x) long after the transaction that accesses the data item (in this case, GST_{11}^2) may have completed.

This realization has caused some researchers to argue that serializability theory, as it is defined for distributed database systems, is unsuitable for distributed multidatabase systems [Du et al., 1989]. The outcome is a modification of the serializability theory such that the resulting class of schedules is a superset of the serializable schedules ([Du and Elmagarmid, 1989], [Breitbart and Silberschatz, 1988], [Barker and Özsu, 1990], [Mehrotra et al., 1991], and [Mehrotra et al., 1992]).

There are other solutions that do not relax serializability. These solutions can be classified as those that assume that the component DBMSs are black boxes (i.e., design and execution autonomy is fully respected) and those that assume some knowledge about the operations of the component DBMSs.

One interesting solution that falls into the first category is the ticketing approach ([Georgakopoulos, 1990], [Georgakopoulos et al., 1991]). This approach addresses the problems of indirect conflicts by converting them into direct conflicts. Each site has a special data item, called a *ticket*. Each global subtransaction reads the ticket at the site where it executes, increments it, and writes it into the database. Any potential indirect conflicts between global subtransactions may be exposed in this way, since every global transaction has to read and write the ticket, inducing conflicts among them. Thus, GTM can serialize the transactions in a particular order. The important question then becomes the enforcement of GTM's serialization order at the component DBMSs. Since component DBMSs are autonomous, they can reorder global subtransactions without the GTM being able to dictate an order. This was demonstrated in Example 15.9. The ticketing approach solves this problem, since each global subtransaction increments the ticket value. Thus, the ticket value read indicates the serialization order of the global subtransaction at that site.

The above algorithms consider the component DBMSs as black boxes, without assuming anything about the way they perform concurrency control. There have been many other proposals (e.g., [Breitbart et al., 1991], [Salem et al., 1989]). We do not discuss these further, as it is not clear that, in a multi-DBMS environment, it is possible to make assumptions about component DBMSs. Some of these assumptions seem reasonable, since they relate, for example, to the nature of the schedules generated by LTMs. However, given that commercial DBMSs permit less-than-serializable executions, as discussed in Chapter 10, even these reasonable-looking assumptions are questionable. In the final analysis, we may need more relaxed transaction models, such as workflows, to address multidatabase concurrency control problems.

15.3.3 Multidatabase Recovery

Recovery protocols, as discussed in Chapter 12, deal with the atomicity and durability properties of transactions. The fundamental issue in this context is the implementation of atomic commitment protocols to ensure transaction atomicity. The autonomy of component DBMSs poses difficulties in this regard as well. We highlight the important issues in this section.

The most important consideration in the development of atomic commitment protocols for multi-DBMSs is whether or not the component DBMSs export a prepared-to-commit interface. If they do, the 2PC protocols discussed in Chapter 12 can be implemented. The remaining problems have to do with the differences in 2PC implementations across systems. There are standards, but, as is common, there are a number of them (e.g., LU6.2, OSI TP, RDA), and it will take additional effort to resolve the differences among them. In the end, however, advantages of interoperability will probably encourage vendors to provide a prepared-to-commit interface.

There have been a number of proposals to deal with those cases where the component DBMSs do not have a prepared-to-commit interface. This condition is common, since non-distributed DBMSs do not need to implement a 2PC protocol, thus removing the need to have this interface. The solutions in this case fall into two general groups. One approach is to somehow modify the global subtransactions before they are submitted to component DBMSs, so that they perform a "callback" to the GTM when they reach the Commit command [Wolski and Veijelainen, 1990], [Barker, 1990]. The GTM can then use this callback as the "vote-commit" message to proceed with 2PC actions. The second approach is to redo the global subtransaction that has not committed [Mehrotra et al., 1992]. The hope is that eventually the transaction will succeed. The third approach is to use compensating transactions to semantically undo the effects of the global subtransactions that have committed [Breitbart et al., 1992a]. As discussed in previous chapters, compensation works only in certain circumstances.

15.4 OBJECT ORIENTATION AND INTEROPERABILITY

Object orientation is expected to play a significant role in addressing some of the model and architectural issues in database interoperability. The modeling issues are relevant if the interoperability framework includes object DBMSs as well as relational ones. In this case, the global conceptual schema has to be object-oriented, since that is the most general model. We do not discuss this aspect of object-orientation in this chapter.

Two characteristics of object models are particularly important in addressing interoperability concerns. The first is encapsulation, which allows the differences in interfaces and implementations of component DBMSs to be hidden. In Section 15.1.1 we referred to this as schema translation. However, when object-orientation is brought to bear, "translator" does not accurately capture the role of this piece of software. A more appropriate term that has been proposed is *wrapper*, since the component DBMS is "wrapped" and its internal operations are hidden from other system components. We will discuss wrappers further in the next chapter when we discuss interoperability concerns related to World Wide Web data repositories. For the time being, it is sufficient to understand that wrappers encapsulate the data sources and provide a completely uniform interface to the outside world.

Example 15.11

> Consider two component DBMSs, one relational and the other an old network model-based one. We don't need to know how network model DBMSs work, except to note that they represent relationships between entities using labeled directed edges (similar to Entity-Relationship model), and the database access is by means of navigation along these edges. The relational DBMS provides an SQL interface, but the network DBMS only provides navigational primitives. The encapsulation property of object models enables the translation of the underlying database schemas to an object-oriented one. The wrappers also encapsulate the routines that translate the user query language (let's assume SQL) to the languages of the component DBMSs (Figure 15.17).

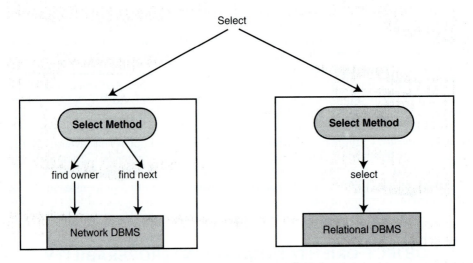

Figure 15.17. Encapsulation of Heterogeneous DBMSs

Another property of object-orientation that is useful for managing database interoperability is *specialization/generalization*, which is modeled by subtyping and supertyping, as discussed in Chapter 14. This allows for the creation of types which abstract the similarities of entities stored in different databases.

Example 15.12

Consider two `Employee` entities defined differently in two component databases. Assume that the definition in the first database assigns attributes `ENUM` and `SALARY`, and the second assigns attributes `ENUM` and `ADDRESS`. In the integrated (object-oriented) schema, these two entities could be modeled as subtypes of a more general `EMP` entity which abstracts the commonalities between the entity definitions (Figure 15.18).

In addition to these modeling advantages, there are a number of distributed object computing platforms whose main purpose is to facilitate the development of open systems by allowing applications to easily communicate with each other. Two such platforms are the Object Management Architecture (OMA) from Object Management Group (OMG) [Siegel, 1996] and Component Object Model (COM), Distributed Component Object Model (DCOM) and Object Linking and Embedding (OLE) environment from Microsoft [Brockschmidt, 1995]. These platforms take the view that interoperability among information systems requires an environment that supports a common way to design each software piece (which is commonly referred to as *componentization*) whereby there are certain functions that can be expected of each component. The platforms provide an infrastructure that supports communication between components and between application programs and components, and incorporate services that are commonly needed by all distributed

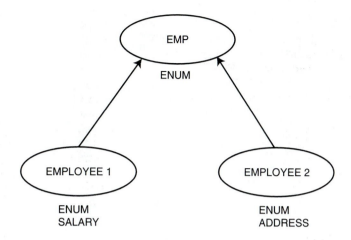

Figure 15.18. Abstraction of Heterogeneous Entities

applications. The various platforms differ in how they accomplish these goals, and in the remainder, we discuss the two competing environments. We will present the fundamentals of each of these platforms and discuss how they can be used for DBMS interoperability.

15.4.1 Object Management Architecture

The Object Management Architecture (OMA) is an environment defined by the Object Management Group (OMG), which is a consortium of industry vendors committed to an object-oriented approach to building distributed systems. OMG puts forth standards and allows vendors to develop products that meet those standards. OMA defines a common object model, a common model of interaction by means of object invocations, and a set of common object services and facilities (Figure 15.19). OMA modules consist of the application objects; the Common Object Request Broker (CORBA), which directs requests and responses between objects; a set of common object services (COSS), which are the basic functions required for object management (e.g., naming, transactions, life cycle management); and a set of common facilities, which are generic object-oriented tools for various applications. Common facilities are divided into horizontal ones that are used by all applications (e.g., user interface, class browser) and vertical ones that are developed specifically for vertical market segments (e.g., healthcare, finance, telecommunications).

OMA's object model is a generic one that provides objects, values, operations, types, classes and subtype/supertype relationship among types. An object is an abstraction with a state and a set of operations. The operations have well-defined signatures, and the operations together with the signatures form the interface of each object. Each object and operation has a type. This is very similar to the object model that we described in Chapter 14. The communication between objects is by means of sending requests, whereby a request is an operation call with one or more

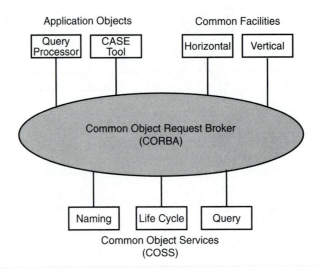

Figure 15.19. CORBA Architecture

parameters, any of which may identify an object (multi-targeting). The arguments and results are passed by value.

Common Object Request Broker--CORBA

CORBA (Figure 15.20) is the key communication mechanism of OMA, in which objects communicate with each other via an Object Request Broker (ORB) that provides brokering services between clients and servers. Brokering involves target object location, message delivery, and method binding. Clients send a request to the ORB asking for certain services to be performed by whichever server can fulfill those needs. ORB finds the server, passes it the message from the client, and receives the result, which it then passes to the client.

The ORB performs the following functions, which we will describe in some detail below:

- Request dispatch to determine the identity of a method to be calle.

- Parameter encoding to convey local representation of parameter values.

- Delivery of request and result messages to the proper objects (which may be at different sites).

- Synchronization of the requesters with the responses of the requests.

- Activation and deactivation of persistent objects.

- Exception handling to report various failures to requesters and servers.

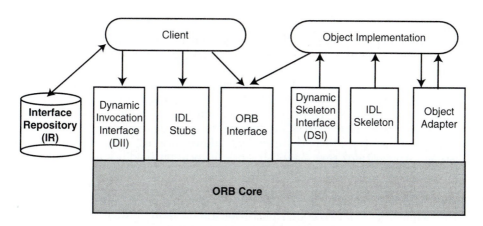

Figure 15.20. CORBA Architecture

- Security mechanisms to assure the secure conveyance of messages among objects.

The basic communication between two CORBA objects is accomplished by the ORB core. OMG does not place any restriction on how ORBs are implemented. In most ORB implementations, existing IPC (Inter-Process Communication) methods, such as Unix socket libraries, shared memory and multithreaded libraries, are used to achieve actual communication among clients, servers and the ORB. Yet ORB can be as simple as a library that supports communication among objects and their clients which are co-resident in the same process space.

To make a request, the client needs to know the operations that it is going to request of an object. In other words, it needs to know the interface of the object that will respond to the request. From here, the client can determine the reference of the target object which will service the request. This can be obtained either from the ORB as the reference of an existing object that is generally created by an object factory, or by using the Naming Services – one of the COSS modules. The target object reference, together with the requested operations, constitutes the request.

The interfaces are defined by means of the Interface Definition Language (IDL). IDL is a host language-independent, declarative language, not a programming language. It forces interfaces to be defined separately from object implementations. Objects can be constructed using different programming languages and still communicate with one another. IDL enables a particular object implementation to introduce itself to potential clients by "advertising" its interface. The IDL interface specifications are compiled to declarations in the programmer's own language. Language mappings determine how IDL features are mapped to facilities of a given programming language. There are standardized language mappings for C, C++, Smalltalk, Ada and Java. IDL language mappings are those in which the abstractions and concepts specified in CORBA meet the "real world" of implementation.

IDL compilers generate client-side *stubs* and server-side *skeletons*. These are interface-specific code segments that cooperate to effectively exchange requests and results. A stub is a mechanism that effectively creates and issues requests on the client's behalf. A skeleton is a mechanism that delivers requests to CORBA object implementation. Communicating through stubs and skeletons is known as *static invocation*, since the linkage between the client and the server is established at compile time. An alternative is to use *dynamic invocation* through the Dynamic Invocation Interface (DII) at the client side, and the Dynamic Skeleton Interface (DSI) at the server side. DII allows clients to send requests to servers without the compile-time generation of stubs; DSI allows servers to be written without skeletons. Applications that establish static invocation bindings at compile time execute faster and are easier to program, since the programming interface is similar to ordinary object-oriented programs – a method is invoked on an identified object. Furthermore, static invocation permits static type checking, and the code is self-documenting. However, dynamic invocation is more flexible, leading to code genericity, and it allows runtime addition of CORBA objects and classes, which are needed for various tools, such as schema browsers.

For either of these modes, but particularly for dynamic invocation, the client application must have a way to know the types of interfaces supported by the server objects. The CORBA Interface Repository (IR) allows the IDL type system to be accessed and written programmatically at run time. IR is itself a CORBA object that has a standard interface. Using this interface, an application can traverse the entire hierarchy of IDL information.

Object implementations access most of the services provided by the ORB via object adapters (OA), each of which is an interface to the ORB allowing ORB to locate, activate, and invoke operations on an ORB object. The OA is a "glue" between CORBA object implementation and the ORB itself. It is an object that adapts the interface of another object to the interface expected by a caller. It uses delegation to allow a caller to invoke requests on an object even though the caller does not know the object's true interface. Until recently, only the Basic Object Adapter (BOA) was defined and had to be provided by all commercial ORBs. BOA is designed to be used with most of the object implementations and provides for generation and interpretation of object references, method invocation, registration, activation and deactivation of object implementations, selection of proper object implementation for a given object reference, and authentication. Recently OMG released a standard as an alternative to BOA. This standard, called the Persistent Object Adapter (POA), provides ORB portability. Some CORBA products have already started include POA as part of their basic system offering. There are expectations that, in the future, OMG will publish another standard for object DBMSs. Since object DBMSs provide some "ORB-like" services, such as object reference generation and management, this adapter will be tuned to integrate object DBMSs with ORB distribution and communication. Library object adapters will be tuned for implementations resident in the client's process space.

Earlier versions of CORBA (prior to Version 2.0) suffered from a lack of interoperability among various CORBA products, caused by the fact that earlier CORBA specification did not mandate any particular data formats or protocols for ORB communications. CORBA 2.0 specifies an interoperability architecture based on the *General Inter-ORB Protocol* (GIOP), which specifies transfer syntax and a standard set of message formats for ORB interoperation over any connection-oriented transport. CORBA 2.0 also mandates the *Internet Inter-ORB Protocol* (IIOP), which is an implementation of GIOP over TCP/IP transport. With IIOP, ORBs can interoperate with one another over the Internet.

Common Object Services

Object Services provide the main functions for implementing basic object functionality using ORB. Each object service has a well-defined interface definition and functional semantics that are orthogonal to other services. This orthogonality allows objects to use several object services at the same time without any confusion.

The set of services will eventually include naming, lifecycle, transaction, trader, security, event, concurrency, query, persistence, relationships, collections, time, properties, externalization, licensing, and change management. These services are at different phases of development. At the time of writing this chapter, standards (and, in most cases, products) are available for the first six listed above. For others, requests for proposals have been released, but no standards have yet been established.

The provision of these services, and their use by other CORBA objects, provide "plug-and-play" reusability to these objects. As an example, a client can move any object that supports Lifecycle Services by using the standard interface. If the object does not support the standard Lifecycle Services, then the user needs to know "move semantics" for the object and its corresponding interface.

Common Facilities

Common facilities consist of components that provide services for the development of application objects in a CORBA environment. Two classes of facilities have been identified. Horizontal facilities consist of those facilities that are used by all (or many) application objects. Examples of these facilities include user interfaces, systems management, and task management. Vertical facilities, on the other hand, are specialized components for selected application domains, such as health care, transportation, manufacturing, electronic commerce, and telecommunications.

15.4.2 CORBA and Database Interoperability

As an object-oriented distributed computing platform, OMA, and in particular CORBA, can be helpful for database interoperability. The fundamental contribution is in terms of managing heterogeneity and, to a lesser extent, managing autonomy. As discussed earlier, heterogeneity in a distributed system can occur at the hardware and operating system (which we can jointly call platform) level, communication level, DBMS level and semantic level. CORBA deals mainly with platform and communication heterogeneities. It also addresses DBMS heterogeneity by means of IDL interface definitions. However, the real problem of managing multiple DBMSs in the sense of a multidatabase system introduced earlier requires the development of a global layer that includes the global-level DBMS functionality. One issue with which CORBA cannot be helpful is semantic heterogeneity.

Using CORBA as the infrastructure affects the upper layers of a multidatabase system, since CORBA and COSS together provide basic database functionality to manage distributed objects. The most important database-related services included in COSS are Transaction Services, Backup and Recovery Services, Concurrency Services, and Query Services. If these services are available in the ORB implementation used, it is possible to develop the global layers of a multidatabase system on CORBA mainly by implementing the standard interfaces of these services for the involved objects. For example, by using a Transaction Service, implementing a global transaction manager occurs by implementing the interfaces defined in the Transaction Service specification for the involved DBMSs.

In this section, we discuss the design issues that must be resolved to use CORBA for database interoperability. This discussion is based, to a large extent, on the experiences with the MIND project ([Dogac et al., 1996a], [Dogac et al., 1996b], [Dogac et al., 1998b]).

A fundamental design issue is the granularity of the CORBA objects. In registering a DBMS to CORBA, a row in a relational DBMS, an object or a group of objects in an object DBMS, or a whole DBMS can be an individual CORBA object. The advantage of fine granularity objects is the finer control they permit. However, in this case, all the DBMS functionalities to process (e.g., querying and transactional control) and manage these objects have to be supported by the global system level (i.e., the multidatabase system). If, on the other hand, a whole DBMS is registered as a CORBA object, the functionality needed to process the entities is left to that DBMS.

Another consideration regarding granularity has to do with the capabilities of the particular ORB being used. In the case of ORBs that provide BOA, each insertion and deletion of classes necessitates recompiling of the IDL code and rebuilding the server. Thus, if the object granularity is fine, these ORBs incur significant overhead. A possible solution to this problem is to use DII. This prevents recompilation of the code and rebuilding of the server, but suffers the run-time performance overhead discussed earlier.

A second design issue is the definition of interfaces to the CORBA objects. Most commercial DBMSs support the basic transaction and query primitives, either through their Call Level Interface (CLI) library routines or their XA Interface library routines. This property makes it possible to define a generic database object interface through CORBA IDL to represent all the underlying DBMSs. CORBA allows multiple implementations of an interface. Hence it is possible to encapsulate each of the local DBMSs by providing a different implementation of the generic database object.

Another issue is the association mode between a client request and server method. CORBA provides three alternatives for this: one interface to one implementation, one interface to one of many implementations, and one interface to multiple implementations. If there exists only one implementation of an interface (i.e., there is only one component DBMS that implements that interface), all of the requests should be directed to a server that supports this single implementation. If there is more than one implementation of an interface (i.e., there are more than one DBMSs that can fulfill the request), ORB can direct the requests to a server that supports any one of the existing implementations. In both cases, implementations handle all operations defined in the interface, and after implementation selection, ORB always uses the same implementation for requests to a particular object. If each implementation of an interface does not handle all of the operations defined in the interface—that is, if each implementation provides only a part of the interface—

the third method is used for associating a client request with a server method. In this case, ORB directs the requests to a server that supports an implementation of the interface that handles the invoked operation. The choice of the alternative is dependent both on the data location and the nature of the database access requests. If the requested data is contained in one database, then it is usually sufficient to use the second alternative and choose the DBMS that manages that data, since DBMSs registered to CORBA provide basic transaction management and query primitives for all the operations the interface definition specifies. If the request involves data from multiple databases, then the third alternative needs to be chosen.

CORBA defines three call communication modes between a client and a server – namely, synchronous, deferred synchronous, and one-way. Synchronous mode is blocked communication, where the client waits for the completion of the requested operation. Synchronous mode can be restrictive for clients who issue operations that can be executed in parallel with multiple objects. In deferred synchronous mode, the client continues its execution after server selection and keeps polling the server to get the results until the operation is completed. In one-way operation, a client sends a request without any intention of getting a reply. CORBA does not support asynchronous mode, since the only method of communication is via a request. This implies that if a client is to receive asynchronous messages, it should also act as a server that implements an object that can receive requests. In other words, asynchronous mode of operation can be achieved between two CORBA objects by sending one-way requests to each other. The only disadvantage of this peer-to-peer approach is the increased complexity of the client code. For objects of a multidatabase system, synchronous call mode is generally sufficient. Deferred synchronous mode or the peer-to-peer approach should be used when parallel execution is necessary. For example, in order to provide parallelism in query execution, the global query manager of a multidatabase should not wait for the query to complete after submitting it to a component DBMS.

When registering objects to CORBA, it is necessary to specify an activation policy for the implementation of each kind of object. This policy identifies how each implementation gets started. An implementation may support shared, unshared, server-per-method or persistent activation policies. While a server that uses a shared activation policy can support more than one object, a server that uses an unshared activation policy can support only one object at a time for an implementation. In the server-per-method activation policy, a new server is used for each method invocation. the persistent activation policy is similar to the shared activation policy, except that the server is never started automatically. Some of the objects in a multidatabase system need to be concurrently active. This can be achieved either by using threads on a server that uses a shared activation policy or by using separate servers activated in the unshared mode for each object. Otherwise, since a server can only give service for one object at a time, client requests to other client requests to the objects owned by the same server should wait for the current request to complete. Further, if the server keeps transient data for the object throughout its life cycle, all requests to an object must be serviced by the same server. For example, if a global transaction manager is activated in shared mode, it would be necessary to preserve the transaction contexts in different threads. However, if the global transaction manager is activated in unshared mode, the same functionality can be obtained with a simpler implementation at the cost of having one process for each active transaction.

15.4.3 Distributed Component Object Model

An alternative to CORBA infrastructure is the Distributed Component Object Model/Object Linking and Embedding (DCOM/OLE) environment from Microsoft. DCOM is similar in functionality to CORBA ORB, while OLE is the complete environment for componentization. DCOM/OLE is a single vendor proposal and, therefore, its contents are somewhat fluid and changing. DCOM's root is Microsoft's Component Object Model (COM). The transition from COM to DCOM is conceptually simple. We will discus COM first and then present DCOM extensions.

COM object model is quite different than CORBA's; COM objects are really not "objects" in the sense defined in Chapter 14. The main differences with CORBA object model are the following:

- A COM (or OLE) object is one which supports one or more interfaces as defined by its class. Thus, there could be multiple interfaces to an object. All objects support one interface called IUnknown.

- COM objects have no identifiers.

- There is no inheritance defined among object classes. The relationship among them is defined by means of containment/delegation and aggregation.

- COM objects do not have state; applications obtain a pointer to interfaces that point to the methods that implement them.

- There are two definition languages: Interface Definition Language (IDL) for defining interface, and Object Definition Language (ODL) for describing object types.

All COM objects have the following characteristics:

1. They are identified by a Globally Unique Identifier (GUID). GUID is not an object identifier in the classical sense.

2. They must register with the Window's registry. This registration is then used by COM library functions to locate, start and stop the components.

3. They must publish and implement a set of interfaces. COM also defines a set of interfaces that must be supported by all COM objects, in addition to the particular interfaces they support in the context of the application in which they intend to participate.

COM objects exist in two forms: DLLs and EXEs. Regardless of the form it is in, a COM object must meet all the standards prescribed by the COM component architecture. DLLs must reside on the same platform as the client, they are often referred to as "local servers." EXE objects can be accessed via networks; they are often referred to as the "remote servers."

Clients access COM objects by means of the interface defined for each object. This is accomplished by indirection through an *Interface Function Table*, each of whose entries points to an interface implementation inside the COM object (Figure 15.21). There is one Interface Function Table per each interface that the object

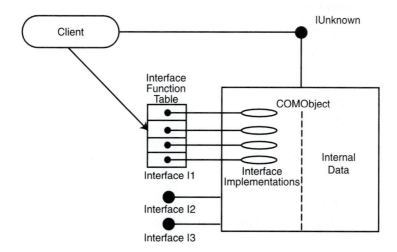

Figure 15.21. COM Objects and Interfaces

supports. The client obtains a pointer to the Interface Function Table that corresponds to the particular interface that it wishes to access, and invokes the interface functions contained therein. This method isolates clients from interface implementations.

The `IUnknown` interface has three methods: `QueryInterface`, by which the client can interrogate the COM objects as to whether it supports a particular interface, and `AddRef` and `Release` methods, which are for reference counting to be used for garbage collection.

DCOM is "COM with a longer wire." The move from COM to DCOM is straightforward, because most COM library functions support distributed and networked components. Further, Windows provides the code needed to locate and communicate with components over a network. This facility allows clients to locate components across the network either transparently or by requesting a component residing on a particular machine.

"Remoting" a component requires no change to the implementation of this component or the clients that access it; the communication is handled via Windows' registry and networking facilities. These facilities provide us with the elegant "longer wire" feel of COM/DCOM's way of building distributed software.

OLE adds componentization by encapsulating a COM object together with a class factory for object creation. In this sense, OLE objects are almost identical to COM objects. As discussed earlier, true reusability of "objects" requires a complete componentization framework. OLE provides this in the Microsoft environment.

An OLE server (also referred to as a COM server) performs a number of functions. It encapsulates a COM object and a class factory. In addition to the COM object interfaces that it supports, it provides an `IClassFactory` interface to interact with the class factory. The functions that the server performs are the following: (a) it implements a class factory interface, (b) it registers the classes that it supports (there is an OLE registry for this purpose), (c) it initializes the COM library, (d) it verifies that the library version is compatible with the object version, (e) it implements a method for terminating itself when no clients are active, and (f) it terminates the use of the library when it is no longer needed.

COM/OLE is supported by the COM/OLE library, an API that provides component management services that are useful for all clients and components. This library guarantees that the most important and tedious operations are done in the same way for all components. Indeed, COM is a way of designing and building systems that can be used on any platform and with any language. However, Microsoft Windows so far provides the most support for COM programming in the form of the COM library. In the future, there may be ports of the environment to non-Windows environments.

15.4.4   COM/OLE and Database Interoperability

Database interoperability in the COM/OLE environment is provided by OLE DB [Blakeley, 1996]. OLE DB extends the OLE environment to data repositories. It defines a uniform interface for all data repositories in the form of *rowsets*. In other words, all OLE DB data providers expose their data as rowsets, which are tabular representations of their data. COM objects that deal with repositories, therefore, communicate in terms of rowsets.

A rowset object (Figure 15.22) serves the function of a wrapper in providing a uniform interface. In its basic form, a rowset object has three interfaces in addition to `IUnknown`: `IRowset` provides methods for sequential iteration over the rows of a rowset, `IColumnsInfo` provides information about the columns of the rowset, and `IAccessor` permits the definition of column bindings to client program variables. More elaborate OLE DB interfaces are defined for more inserting, deleting, and

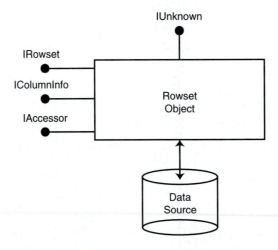

Figure 15.22. Rowset Object Abstraction

updating rows in a rowset, as well as more sophisticated ways of accessing a rowset (e.g., direct access, scrolling).

Using OLE DB, many of the design decisions discussed within the context of CORBA and database interoperability are made automatically for the system designer. There are commercial OLE DB providers for many of the relational DBMSs, which can be used to put together an interoperability framework for relational DBMSs. Similar providers are supposed to be available for object DBMSs as well.

15.5 CONCLUSION

In this chapter we have surveyed the issues and some of the work performed to date in the area of distributed multidatabase systems. The emphasis in this discussion has been on highlighting the major research areas.

Fundamental to any other work in the area is a determination of the need for a global conceptual schema and its meaning. The existence or lack of the GCS reflects upon the user view of the multidatabase, as well as the manner in which some of the issues are handled. If a GCS is to exist, its design is a problem that needs to be tackled. Even though the issues are well understood, automated tools are hard to design. A fully automated design tool is probably not a realistic expectation. Currently, no such tool exists. However, an automated interactive tool to assist the designer in the translation and integration process would be useful.

Query processing is fairly well understood. There are significant differences between the multidatabase environment and the distributed DBMS. Query optimization in multi-DBMSs is hampered by the lack of knowledge about the workings of the query optimizers in component DBMSs. The research to date has come up with a number of proposals. The efficacy of these proposals has only been tested in restricted environments. The key problem that remains is, arguably, the definition of accurate global cost models. Part of the issue is the estimation of component DBMS costs. These are likely to remain inaccurate, causing the global cost function to be inaccurate. Thus, static, cost-based optimization may be problematic, requiring a hybrid approach involving run-time, dynamic optimization (e.g., [Dogac et al., 1996c], [Dogac et al., 1997]) and static optimization. Another query optimization question is the scalability of the solutions as the number of component DBMSs increases.

Transaction management has been studied extensively over the last decade. So many solutions have been proposed that the real challenge now is sorting out the landscape and determining which solutions are feasible. Despite numerous proposals, the autonomy of the component DBMSs poses significant challenges. The realistic solutions to this problem are likely to involve good engineering, as real scientific breakthroughs are unlikely. In particular, the proposed solutions seem to be getting more and more esoteric.

Object-orientation to deal with database interoperability is perhaps the new major direction occupying the researchers. Finding scalable solutions that do not force unnecessary difficulties is a key concern. As we saw in Chapter 14, many of the traditional database problems take on additional difficulties in object DBMSs. The challenge is to find flexible interoperability frameworks that bring in the additional complexities only when they are warranted.

Another major issue that requires attention is the role of distributed object computing platforms in database interoperability. There are many projects that experiment with these platforms, but the performance of these systems are unknown. There are anecdotal claims about the performance overhead of these platforms, but we do not know of any published performance results that are based on solid scientific experimentation. A related issue is the possibility of building open systems using these platforms. In particular, the OMA framework provides a number of services (e.g., query service, transaction service, naming service) which can be used to develop an open and interoperable DBMS. This has not yet been tried, and therefor, we do not know what the performance problems of such a system might be. There is much work that remains to be done in this regard.

Finally, we should note that we did not discuss in this chapter other interoperability frameworks, such as ODBC and KDBS. There is extensive literature on these topics for interested readers.

15.6 BIBLIOGRAPHIC NOTES

Interest in heterogeneous database systems has a long history. There are some good tutorial papers on the topic ([Sheth and Larson, 1990], [Litwin, 1988], [Gligor and Luckenbaugh, 1984], [Hsiao and Kamel, 1989], [Litwin et al., 1990] and [Bright and Hurson, 1992]). There is also a new book devoted to this topic [Elmagarmid et al., 1999].

A large number of prototype multidatabase implementations exist. Some of the more interesting ones are SIRIUS-DELTA ([Litwin et al., 1982] and [Ferrier and Stangret, 1982]), Multibase ([Smith et al., 1981], [Landers and Rosenberg, 1982], and [Dayal and Hwang, 1984]), MERMAID [Templeton et al., 1987], DDTS [Dwyer and Larson, 1987], ADDS [Breitbart and Tieman, 1985], OMNIBASE [Rusinkiewicz et al., 1988], [Rusinkiewicz et al., 1989], InterBase [Elmagarmid and Du, 1990] and AURORA ([Yan, 1997], [Yan et al., 1997]).

As already indicated, most of the early work concentrated on global schema design, specifically on data translation. A good review of some of the earlier work on translation can be found in [Han and Fisher, 1983], [Schneiderman and Thomas, 1982] and [Larson, 1983]. The entire topic of schema integration is covered in [Batini et al., 1986], which also forms the basis of the presentation in Section 15.1. We should indicate that some of the definitions provided in that paper (which are also included in our discussion) are not universally accepted. This controversy over terminology (as well as methodology) reflects the unsettled nature of the topic and makes it quite difficult to compare discussions in the literature. [Sheth, 1987] discusses a methodology for building multidatabase systems consisting of heterogeneous and autonomous databases. [Sheth et al., 1988a] describes a tool developed for integrating schemas in an extended E-R model.

Many of the papers that describe systems also address multidatabase query processing issues (e.g., [Brill et al., 1984], [Dayal and Hwang, 1984], and [Landers and Rosenberg, 1982]). A detailed discussion of multidatabase query processing can be found in Chapter 4 of [Yu and Meng, 1998]. A brief overview of query optimization issues can be found in [Meng et al., 1993].

A very nice overview of transaction processing issues in multi-DBMSs is [Breit-bart et al., 1992a]. The issue is also treated in chapters of [Elmagarmid, 1992], [Kim, 1994] and [Elmagarmid et al., 1999]. In addition to the papers referred to in Section 15.3, some early work (e.g., [Motro and Buneman, 1981]) treated the multidatabase layer as a "superview" (see Chapter 6 for a discussion of views). Thus the update problem in multidatabase systems reduces to the update problem of views. The superview approach is also used for schema integration [Motro, 1987]. [Pu, 1988] defines "superdatabases" as hierarchical structures whose leaves consist of individual databases. The global transactions are managed by the super-DBMS at the lowest level that covers the individual databases affected. This approach assumes that a super-DBMS at one level is aware of all the local transactions submitted to its constituent DBMSs. Concurrency control proposals are given in [Alonso et al., 1987], [Breitbart et al., 1987], [Sugihara, 1987], [Elmagarmid and Helal, 1986], [Du and Elmagarmid, 1989], and [Barker and Özsu, 1990].

The object-oriented approach to interoperability is fairly new. A survey of the issues is provided in [Pitoura et al., 1995] and [Bukhres and Elmagarmid, 1996]. The latter includes chapters describing a number of systems. [Kent, 1994] also provides a summary of the major concerns. [Brodie, 1994], [Brodie and Stonebraker, 1995] address the legacy system problem as it arises in interoperable information systems. Both [Dogac et al., 1994] and [Dogac et al., 1998a] contain chapters devoted to this topic.

Distributed object platforms are described in a number of books and papers. Section 15.4 is based on, and derived extensively from, [Dogac et al., 1998b], [Yan et al., 1997] and [Özsu et al., 1994b]. A very nice discussion of distributed object platforms is given in [Orfali et al., 1996]. [Siegel, 1996] gives an in-depth treatment of OMG's OMA, and [Brockschmidt, 1995] provides the same treatment for COM/OLE. A comparison of the two platforms can be found in `http://www.bell-labs.com/user/emerald/dcom_corba/Paper.html`.

15.7 EXERCISES

15.1 Distributed database systems and distributed multidatabase systems represent two different approaches to systems design. Find three real-life applications for which each of these approaches would be more appropriate. Discuss the features of these applications that make them more favorable for one approach or the other.

15.2 Some architectural models favor the definition of a global conceptual schema, whereas others do not. What do you think? Justify your selection with detailed technical arguments.

*15.3 Give an algorithm to convert a relational schema to an entity-relationship one.

**15.4 Consider the two databases given in Figures 15.23 and 15.24 and described below. Design a global conceptual schema as a union of the two databases by first translating them into the E-R model. Use the methodology discussed in Section 15.1.

DIRECTOR(<u>NAME</u>, PHONE_NO, ADDRESS)
LICENSES(<u>LIC_NO</u>, CITY, DATE, ISSUES, COST, DEPT, CONTACT)
RACER(NAME, ADDRESS, MEM_NUM)
SPONSOR(<u>SP_NAME</u>, CONTACT)
RACE(<u>R_NO</u>, LIC_NO, DIR, MAL_WIN, FRM_WIN, SP_NAME)

Figure 15.23. Road Race Database

Figure 15.23 describes a relational race database used by organizers of road races and Figure 15.24 describes an entity-relationship database used by a shoe manufacturer. The semantics of each of these database schemas is discussed below. Figure 15.23 describes a relational road race database with the following semantics:

DIRECTOR is a relation that defines race directors who organize races; we assume that each race director has a unique name (to be used as the key), a phone number, and an address.

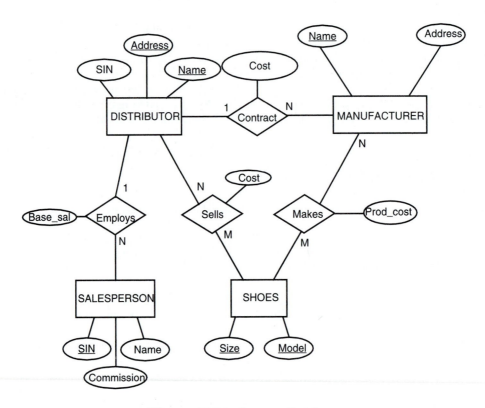

Figure 15.24. Sponsor Database

LICENSES is required because all races require a governmental license, which is issued by a CONTACT in a department who is the ISSUER, possibly contained within another government department DEPT; each license has a unique LIC_NO (the key), which is issued for use in a specific CITY on a specific DATE with a certain COST.

RACER is a relation that describes people who participate in a race. Each person is identified by NAME, which is not sufficient to identify them uniquely, so a compound key formed with the ADDRESS is required. Finally, each racer may have a MEM_NUM to identify him or her as a member of the racing fraternity, but not all competitors have membership numbers.

SPONSOR indicates which sponsor is funding a given race. Typically, one sponsor funds a number of races through a specific person (CONTACT), and a number of races may have different sponsors.

RACE uniquely identifies a single race which has a license number (LIC_NO) and race number (R_NO) (to be used as a key, since a race may be planned without acquiring a license yet); each race has a winner in the male and female groups (MAL_WIN and FEM_WIN) and a race director (DIR).

Figure 15.24 illustrates an entity-relationship schema used by the sponsor's database system with the following semantics:

SHOES are produced by sponsors of a certain MODEL and SIZE, which forms the key to the entity.

MANUFACTURER is identified uniquely by NAME and resides at a certain ADDRESS.

DISTRIBUTOR is a person that has a NAME and ADDRESS (which are necessary to form the key) and a SIN number for tax purposes.

SALESPERSON is a person (entity) who has a NAME, earns a COMMISSION, and is uniquely identified by his or her SIN number (the key).

Makes is a relationship that has a certain fixed production cost (PROD_COST). It indicates that a number of different shoes are made by a manufacturer, and that different manufacturers produce the same shoe.

Sells is a relationship that indicates the wholesale COST to a distributor of shoes. It indicates that each distributor sells more than one type of shoe, and that each type of shoe is sold by more than one distributor.

Contract is a relationship whereby a distributor purchases, for a COST, exclusive rights to represent a manufacturer. Note that this does not preclude the distributor from selling different manufacturers' shoes.

Employs indicates that each distributor hires a number of salespeople to sell the shoes; each earns a BASE_SALARY.

**15.5 Logic (first-order logic, to be precise) has been suggested as a uniform formalism for schema translation and integration. Discuss how logic can be useful for this purpose.

**15.6 Can any type of global optimization be performed on global queries in a multidatabase system? Discuss and formally specify the conditions under which such optimization would be possible.

*15.7 Consider three prototype multidatabase systems (e.g., MULTIBASE, SIRIUS, ADDS, MERMAID) and discuss their query processing strategies with respect to their functionalities.

**15.8 Can every transaction be subdivided into a set of subtransactions, such that the third condition specified by Gligor and Popescu-Zeletin will be satisfied? (See Section 14.3.1 for a definition of the condition.) Formally specify the conditions under which such splitting may be possible.

**15.9 As stated in Section 15.3, recovery poses an especially difficult problem in concurrent updates of multidatabase systems. A fundamental difficulty is with the definition of the commit point of global transactions.

> **(a)** How would you define the commit point of a global transaction in a multidatabase system?

> **(b)** What type of computational model that specifies the execution of global transactions between the global transaction manager and the local ones can be developed to support this definition?

15.10 State an algorithm to detect global deadlocks in a multidatabase system without violating the autonomy of the component DBMSs.

Chapter 16

CURRENT ISSUES

In this chapter, we discuss four topics that are of growing importance in distributed database management. The topics are data warehousing (Section 16.2), the World Wide Web (WWW, or Web for short) and its effect on distributed data management (Section 16.3), push-based technologies for data dissemination (Section 16.4), and mobile database management (Section 16.5). In this introduction, we will justify the choice of these topics before going into the details.

In previous chapters, we pointed several times to the changes in the technologies underlying distributed DBMSs. One of the changes we highlighted was the emergence of broadband networks, and we discussed the effects of these networks on the architecture and query processing/optimization routines of distributed DBMSs. Another major change is the expanding use and reach of the Internet, the proliferation of *intranets* and the ongoing advances in the World Wide Web. This has fueled the development of a wide range of data intensive applications and information dissemination systems. In such an environment, providing integrated access to multiple, distributed databases and other heterogeneous data sources has more than ever been the focus of the database community. One of these data-intensive applications is decision support systems. Over the years, companies have built *operational* databases to support their day-to-day operations with On-Line Transaction Processing (OLTP) applications. OLTP applications, such as airline reservation or banking systems, are transaction-oriented and update-intensive. They need extensive data control and availability, high multiuser throughput and predictable, fast response times. The users are clerical. Operational databases are medium to large (up to several gigabytes). In effect, distributed databases have been used to provide integrated access to multiple operational databases.

Decision support applications have been termed *On-line Analytical Processing* (OLAP) [Codd, 1995] to better reflect their different requirements. OLAP applications, such as trend analysis or forecasting, need to analyze historical, summarized data coming from operational databases. They use complex queries over potentially very large tables and are read-intensive. Because of their strategic nature, response time is important. The users are managers or analysts. Performing OLAP queries directly over distributed operational databases raises two problems. First, it hurts the OLTP applications' performance by competing for local resources. Second, the overall response time of the OLAP queries can be very poor because large quantities of data must be transferred over the network. Furthermore, most OLAP applications do not need the most current versions of the data, and thus do not need direct access to operational data. The now-popular solution to this problem is *data warehousing* [Inmon, 1992] which extracts and summarizes data from the operational databases in a separate database, dedicated to OLAP. Data warehousing is often considered an alternative to distributed databases, but we will see in Section 16.2 that these are complementary technologies.

With the ongoing advance in Web technology, everyone today can publish information on the Web independently at any time. The flexibility and autonomy of producing and sharing information on Web is impressive. On the other hand, one has to learn to deal with the rapid increase of volume and diversity of online information and the constant changes of information sources in number, content, and location. The diversity of applications that are deployed on the Web require different data delivery modes and protocols in different frequencies [Liu et al., 1998]. The design space of data delivery alternatives can be characterized in a number of ways. We examine these alternatives in some detail in Section 16.1. Two important points in this design space are *pull-based* systems, where clients access data servers to retrieve the required data, and *push-based* systems, where the servers "deliver" data to clients without waiting to be asked.

The typical method of accessing data on the Web is pull-based. The Web was initially designed to provide a distributed hypertext system on the Internet. It has had great and widespread success, due primarily to its graphical interface and its browsers—for example, Internet Explorer and Netscape, which make navigation through distributed documents easy. Since its inception the Web interface has been made increasingly multimedia and interactive. The Web has become a truly global network, now linking hundreds of thousands of servers. Organizations are extensively using the Web in intranets, which are private networks of Web servers, for various applications such as information publishing, workflow, groupware and accessing information systems.

Web technology remains document-oriented and provides information retrieval engines to search distributed documents. However, the database industry has developed gateways to interface Web documents with databases. As a result, the number of heterogeneous data sources that can be accessed from a Web browser is gigantic. Thus, providing integrated access to multiple, distributed data sources on the Web has become a major technical challenge. Distributed database and data warehouse technologies are useful here, but need to be significantly extended to deal with several issues. One is the very wide heterogeneity of the data sources and their computing capabilities, ranging from highly structured databases to unstructured files with semistructured documents as an interesting intermediate point. Another issue is the need to scale up to high numbers of distributed data sources that can be dynamically added or dropped. We consider the relationship between Web technology and distributed data management in Section 16.3.

Push-based technologies, on the other hand, are being proposed in response to communication asymmetry exhibited by many applications, such as news delivery, software distribution, and traffic information systems [Franklin and Zdonik, 1997]. Communication asymmetry refers to the fact that the communication from the clients to the server is more restricted than the communication from the server to the clients. In these environments, it may make more sense to "push" data from the servers without waiting for the clients to "pull" them. There is significant commercial interest in push-based information delivery, including announcements by major Web browser vendors about plans to incorporate push into their products. We discuss the issues in designing these systems in Section 16.4.

In addition to the proliferation of broadband networks and the Internet, a third major technological change affecting distributed data management is the emergence of mobile networks. In this context, we are not referring to satellite-based systems, but to digital cellular networks. These networks have quite interesting characteristics which require reconsideration of major data management algorithms and protocols. We consider these issues in Section 16.5.

16.1 DATA DELIVERY ALTERNATIVES

We characterize the data delivery alternatives along three orthogonal dimensions: delivery modes, frequency and communication methods. The entire design space is depicted in Figure 16.1, which is a combination of characterizations proposed in [Franklin and Zdonik, 1997] and [Liu et al., 1998]. In the remainder, we discuss the design alternatives along the axes, but not every possible alternative system architecture.

The alternative delivery modes are pull-only, push-only and hybrid. In the *pull-only* mode of data delivery, the transfer of data from servers to clients is initiated by a client pull. When a client request is received at a server, the server responds by locating the requested information. The main characteristic of pull-based delivery is that the arrival of new data items or updates to existing data items are carried out at

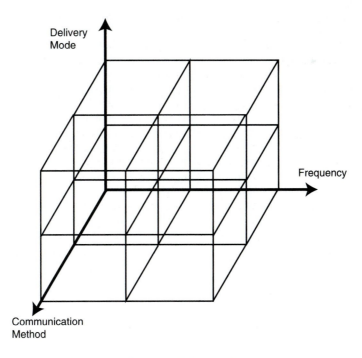

Figure 16.1. Data Delivery Alternatives

a server without notification to clients unless clients explicitly poll the server. Also, in pull-based mode, servers must be interrupted continuously to deal with requests from clients. Furthermore, the information that clients can obtain from a server is limited to when and what clients know to ask for. Conventional DBMSs (including relational and object-oriented ones) offer primarily pull-based data delivery.

In the *push-only* mode of data delivery, the transfer of data from servers to clients is initiated by a server push in the absence of any specific request from clients. The main difficulty of the push-based approach is in deciding which data would be of common interest, and when to send them to clients (periodically, irregularly, or conditionally). Thus, the usefulness of server push depends heavily upon the accuracy of a server to predict the needs of clients. In push-based mode, servers disseminate information to either an unbounded set of clients (random broadcast) who can listen to a medium or selective set of clients (multicast), who belong to some categories of recipients that may receive the data.

The hybrid mode of data delivery combines the client-pull and server-push mechanisms. The continual query approach described in [Liu et al., 1996] presents one possible way of combining the pull and push modes: namely, the transfer of information from servers to clients is first initiated by a client pull, and the subsequent transfer of updated information to clients is initiated by a server push.

The hybrid mode represented by the continual queries approach can be seen as a specialization of push-only mode. The main difference between hybrid mode and push-only mode is the initiation of the first data delivery. More concretely, in a hybrid mode, clients receive the information that matches their profiles from servers continuously. In addition to new data items and updates, previously existing data that matches the profile of a client who initially pulled the server are delivered to the client immediately after the initial pull.

There are three typical frequency measurements that can be used to classify the regularity of data delivery. They are *periodic, conditional*, and *ad-hoc* or *irregular*.

In periodic delivery, data are sent from the server to clients at regular intervals. The intervals can be defined by system default or by clients using their profiles. Both pull and push can be performed in periodic fashion. Periodic delivery is carried out on a regular and pre-specified repeating schedule. A client request for IBM's stock price every week is an example of a periodic pull. An example of periodic push is when an application can send out stock price listing on a regular basis, say every morning. Periodic push is particularly useful for situations in which clients might not be available at all times, or might be unable to react to what has been sent, such as in the mobile setting where clients can become disconnected.

In conditional delivery, data are sent from servers whenever certain conditions installed by clients in their profiles are satisfied. Such conditions can be as simple as a given time span or as complicated as event-condition-action rules. Conditional delivery is mostly used in the hybrid or push-only delivery systems. Using conditional push, data are sent out according to a pre-specified condition, rather than any particular repeating schedule. An application that sends out stock prices only when they change is an example of conditional push. An application that sends out a balance statement only when the total balance is 5% below the pre-defined balance threshold is an example of hybrid conditional push. Conditional push assumes that changes are critical to the clients, and that clients are always listening and need to respond to what is being sent. Hybrid conditional push further assumes that missing some update information is not crucial to the clients.

Ad-hoc delivery is irregular and is performed mostly in a pure pull-based system. Data are pulled from servers to clients in an ad-hoc fashion whenever clients request it. In contrast, periodic pull arises when a client uses polling to obtain data from servers based on a regular period (schedule).

The third component of the design space of information delivery alternatives is the communication method. These methods determine the various ways in which servers and clients communicate for delivering information to clients. The alternatives are *unicast* and *one-to-many*. In unicast, the communication from a server to a client is one-to-one: the server sends data to one client using a particular delivery mode with some frequency. In one-to-many, as the name implies, the server sends data to a number of clients. Note that we are not referring here to a specific protocol; one-to-many communication may use a multicast or broadcast protocol.

We should note that this characterization is subject to considerable debate. It is not clear that every point in the design space is meaningful. Furthermore, specification of alternatives such as conditional **and** periodic (which may make sense) is difficult. However, it serves as a first-order characterization of the complexity of emerging distributed data management systems.

16.2 DATA WAREHOUSING

Data warehousing refers to a collection of technologies aimed at improving decision making. A data warehouse can be defined as a subject-oriented collection of data integrated from various operational databases. Information is classified by subjects of interest to business analysts, such as customers, products and accounts. Data warehouses are reminiscent of older mainframe-based reporting systems. However, they are based on open systems and relational databases. Furthermore, a data warehouse can be directly accessed by end-users on powerful workstations via sophisticated, graphical analysis tools, thus eliminating the need to rely on skilled application programmers.

Warehouse information is historical in nature, reflecting OLTP transactions that have occurred in the previous months or years. Thus, to facilitate access and analysis, warehouse data are typically summarized and aggregated in a multidimensional fashion. OLAP operations manipulate the data along the multiple dimensions, for instance to increase or decrease the level of aggregation. Warehouse data are generally read-only.

In the rest of this section, we present the various architectures for data warehousing, the OLAP multidimensional data model and the OLAP servers. We conclude with open issues.

16.2.1 Architectures

Figure 16.2 illustrates a simplified architecture of a data warehouse, with its various elements. One or more source databases, containing operational data updated by OLTP applications, are integrated in a single target database, or data warehouse. The target database is accessed through queries by desktop applications such as query and analysis, reporting and data mining tools. Popular desktop applications for data analysis are spreadsheet programs.

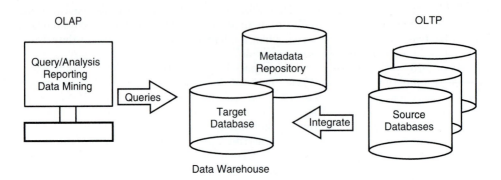

OLAP   OLTP

Figure 16.2. Architecture of a Data Warehouse

The metadata repository is a separate database that keeps track of the data currently stored in the data warehouse. Typical metadata include descriptions of target tables with their source definitions. The metadata repository is useful to isolate the data warehouse from changes in the schema of source databases. For instance, when a change occurs in a source database schema, the data warehouse administrator can simply update the repository, and the change is automatically propagated to the target database and the OLAP applications.

The integration of multiple source databases in a data warehouse raises several issues. At design time, an integrated schema must be defined. Schema integration in a data warehouse is similar to schema integration in multidatabase systems (see Chapter 15), and must deal with semantic conflicts across distinct, autonomous source databases. Schema integration in data warehousing typically assumes that each source database provides a relational interface. Thus schema integration can be done by defining relational views over the source tables [Roussopoulos, 1998].

Populating the data warehouse relies on data extraction, cleaning and loading utilities [Chaudhuri and Dayal, 1997]. Data extraction is implemented using gateways supporting standard interfaces, such as Open Database Connectivity (ODBC). Data are also usually cleaned to reduce inconsistencies, like missing entries or invalid values. After extraction and cleaning, data are loaded in the data warehouse, with additional processing like summarization and aggregation. Loading data essentially means materializing the relational views of the integrated schema. Furthermore, data in the data warehouse are organized for efficient query processing with various kinds of indices.

After it is populated, the data warehouse must be refreshed from time to time to reflect updates to the source databases. Refreshing is usually done periodically, for instance daily or weekly. It can also be done immediately after every update for OLAP applications that need to see current data. To avoid populating entire tables, only updates to the source data should be propagated to the data warehouse. This is done using asynchronous replication techniques that perform incremental maintenance of replicas from primary copies.

There are many ways to build data warehouses in an organization. Two extreme approaches are centralized and decentralized [Eckerson, 1994]. But they can

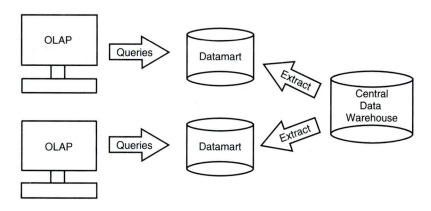

Figure 16.3. Centralized Data Warehouse

be combined in various ways. The centralized approach is illustrated in Figure 16.3. It loads all the operational databases of the organization into a central data warehouse. Functional groups, such as departments, can then extract subsets of data and load them in smaller functional warehouses called *datamarts*. The advantage of this approach is that it ensures consistency of decision-support data across the organization. However, it is very hard to create a global enterprise model for the central data warehouse and ensure that all functional groups use it.

The decentralized approach is illustrated in Figure 16.4. The data warehouse here is virtual and provides the OLAP applications with a global view of the data, using a global data dictionary managed by a data warehouse gateway. Global queries are decomposed into local queries sent to the operational DBMSs, and the results are integrated by the data warehouse gateway. This is a direct application of distributed database technology with one global schema [Hull and Zhou, 1996].

16.2.2 OLAP Data Model

The OLAP data model is *multidimensional*. The data is represented by a multi-dimensional array of *numeric measures*, such as sales or revenue, which is useful for analysis. The dimensions uniquely determine the measure. In a sales data warehouse, for instance, interesting dimensions may include time of sale, location and product (Figure 16.5). Each dimension can be represented by one or more attributes. For instance, the time dimension which is of particular interest to OLAP applications can have attributes date, week, month, quarter and year. The attributes of a dimension are often organized as a hierarchy like year $\rightarrow$ quarter $\rightarrow$ month $\rightarrow$ week or industry $\rightarrow$ category $\rightarrow$ product.

OLAP operations enable end users, such as business analysts, to manipulate multidimensional data with a powerful spreadsheet style interface. Most of these operations deal with aggregation. Aggregation of a measure along a subset of the dimensions is done by *pivoting* (reorienting) the multidimensional view of the data.

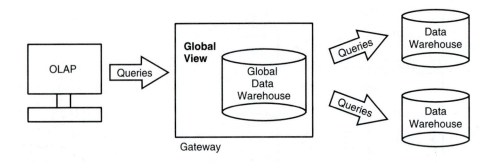

Figure 16.4. Decentralized Data Warehouse

For example, let us consider the three-dimensional array in Figure 16.5. Pivoting that array along the location and time dimensions would produce a two-dimensional array in which each point (x, y) gives the aggregated sales for location x at time y.

Aggregation of a measure at different levels of a dimension hierarchy is supported by *roll-up* and *drill-down* operators. Roll-up increases the level of aggregation by moving up the dimension hierarchy. For example, we can roll-up along the time dimension to aggregate sales per year. Drill-down is the inverse of roll-up, and is useful to increase the level of detail. Another popular operator is *slice-and-dice*, which corresponds to select-project on a subset of the dimensions. Other operators deal with ranking and computed attributes.

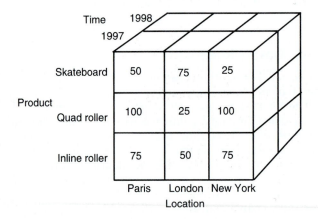

Figure 16.5. Multidimensional Data

Most OLAP queries can be expressed in SQL using aggregation (SUM, AVG, etc.) and grouping (GROUP BY). However, some queries cannot be directly expressed and require significant extensions. This is the case for queries which involve ranking (e.g., select the top ten cities ranked by sales).

16.2.3 OLAP Servers

There are two main approaches to implementing data warehouse servers [Colliat, 1996]. *Multidimensional OLAP* (MOLAP) servers directly support OLAP operations on multidimensional data structures, whereas *Relational OLAP* (ROLAP) servers extend relational databases to support OLAP operations.

MOLAP servers store the data in a multidimensional data structure that is dedicated to OLAP operations. The data structure typically has two-levels to deal with large data sets that do not fit in main memory. With such a data structure, OLAP operations can be processed very efficiently in memory [Finkelstein, 1995]. However, changing the multidimensional array, e.g., by adding another dimension, requires a complete reconstruction of the array. Furthermore, MOLAP servers do not scale up to very large databases because the core index must fit in memory. A final problem is that there is no standard multidimensional data model, and MOLAP servers are substantially different in addressing the requirements of OLAP.

ROLAP servers are extended relational DBMS or intermediate servers in front of relational DBMS that store the data in relations. A multidimensional array is represented by two kinds of relations. The *fact table* relates the dimensions to the measures with a relation whose primary key is the set of dimension identifiers. For example, the multidimensional array in Figure 16.5 yields the fact table (location-id, time-id, product-id, sales) with the key $location - id, time - id, product - id$. Each dimension is represented by a *dimension table* whose key is the dimension identifier. For example, the time dimension yields the relation (time-id, date, week, month, quarter, year).

OLAP operations are mapped into complex SQL queries on the fact and dimension tables, which may involve many join, aggregate and group-by operators. Therefore, efficient access methods and query processing are necessary to deal with large relations. Indices on the fact and dimension tables are important. Furthermore, join indices [Valduriez, 1987] and their recent extensions, such as bit-mapped join indices [O'Neil and Graefe, 1995] and variant indices [O'Neil and Quass, 1997] are very efficient for directly relating the values of attributes in a dimension table with the matching tuples in the fact table. Like indices, *materialized views* are useful to precompute summary data and aggregates. The major issues are the efficient updating of materialized views using incremental techniques and the transformation of user queries in terms of materialized views [Blakeley et al., 1986]. Another complementary solution for efficient OLAP processing is parallelism (see Chapter 13). In fact, a major application of parallel database systems is data warehousing. Compared to MOLAP servers, ROLAP servers have many advantages, such as a standard data model, and scale up to very large databases. However, the mapping of OLAP queries to SQL is hard to make efficient. For small to medium-size data warehouses, MOLAP servers are likely to be more efficient.

16.2.4   Research Issues

Because data warehousing has been a fast growing market for software products and services, the practice has been and still is preceding research. All the leading software vendors, in particular relational DBMS vendors, are offering data warehouse systems. However, most of the current products present severe limitations in terms of flexibility, efficiency and scalability. To overcome these limitations, important research issues must be addressed.

Data quality is becoming a major issue as more and more strategic decisions rely on the data warehouse. Typical data quality parameters are data accessibility, interpretability, usefulness, believability and validation. To improve data quality, data warehouse design and evolution should incorporate formal models of information quality. The DWQ project in Europe [Sellis et al., 1997] addresses this problem by developing a "semantic foundation to allow the designers of data warehouse to link the choice of deeper models, richer data structures and rigorous implementation techniques to quality-of-service factors in a systematic manner." It does so by developing advanced data warehouse components with a reasoning capability based on description logic.

Data warehouse management is also getting difficult with the deployment of decentralized datamarts as an alternative to the centralized data warehouse approach. For operational reasons, these datamarts are fairly autonomous, and tend to grow and duplicate information without global consistency control within the organization. Besides the data quality issues mentioned above, architectural issues should be addressed to avoid uncontrolled data duplication and yield flexibility and scalability. This requires a better combination of data warehouse and distributed database technologies.

Materialized view maintenance in a data warehouse is significantly more difficult than in DBMS [Widom, 1995], [Quass and Widom, 1997]. Views stored in the data warehouse tend to be more complicated than conventional views, with aggregated and summarized information [Dar et al., 1996a], [Gupta et al., 1995], [Griffin and Libkin, 1995]. Thus, it is not always possible to express view definitions in SQL. Furthermore, views may be based on histories of source data and thus should include temporal capabilities. Finally, there might be multiple views of the same data—for instance, to support different kinds of analysis. Therefore, more research is needed to design view languages for data warehouses and to revisit view maintenance algorithms accordingly.

The problems of physical design and query optimization must also be revisited. New kinds of indices, buffer management strategies, cost models and query transformations should be devised by considering the special requirements of data warehouses, in particular, read-only queries with aggregation.

Data integration, including data extraction, cleaning, loading and refreshing, still presents serious challenges. In addition to schema inconsistencies traditionally studied in heterogeneous data integration, data cleaning should emphasize data inconsistencies. Another problem is *change detection*, which detects and propagates the changes in the source data to the data warehouse. Data sources can be classified according to their ability for change detection [Widom, 1995]. *Cooperative sources* provide trigger capabilities which ease the programming of automatic notifications of changes. *Logged sources* maintain a log from which changes can be extracted. *Queryable sources* can be queried by the data warehouse. Finally, *snapshot sources* can only be copied off-line. The WHIPS data warehousing project at Stanford

[Hammer et al., 1995a], [Labio et al., 1997] addresses the problem of automatic change detection and incremental data integration in the data warehouse.

Another problem related to data integration is improving the freshness of warehouse data. Replication techniques have been used successfully for refreshing the data warehouse periodically [Helal et al., 1997]. But for some applications, such as on-line financial analysis, very high freshness is crucial and traditional replication solutions do not work [Gray et al. 1996]. Asynchronous replication techniques that support near real-time constraints [Pacitti et al., 1998] are necessary here.

16.3 WORLD WIDE WEB

The world-wide, frontier-free dimension of the Web, combined with its portability and ease of use, makes it a major enabling element of the future information society. The Web has grown exponentially and the number and diversity of users (individuals, enterprises, governments, etc.) and applications (education, on-line publication, electronic commerce, etc.) are growing continuously. It has become something that no organization, public or private, which expects to develop and to grow can afford to ignore.

The development has been so rapid that many technical problems have become acute, in particular, security and information access. Searching for relevant information is becoming increasingly difficult; existing tools, for example, search engines such as Alta Vista and Yahoo, support primitive searching of documents and cannot exploit data structures. Nor can they be used to provide fast access to many data sources of data, in particular, within intranets.

Therefore, the Web provides many avenues of research in distributed databases[1] which we will discuss. In the rest of this section, we briefly present the architecture of the Web and introduce its standard protocols. We then describe architectures that support database access and information integration on the Web. We also define semistructured data which are proliferating on the Web. We end with short presentations of research projects and open issues.

16.3.1 Architecture and Protocols

The Web architecture is client-server, with its simple standard communication protocol HTTP (HyperText Transfer Protocol) implemented on top of TCP/IP, the ubiquitous Internet protocol. With HTTP, any client browser can request a document on a Web server using its *uniform resource locator* (URL). The entry point to a Web site is its *home page*, identified by a URL. For example, the URL of the World Wide Web consortium (W3C), which is responsible for defining the Web standards, is `http://www.w3c.org`[2]. The home page refers to other documents' URLs, thus providing for hypertext navigation. HTTP is efficient in allowing high numbers of independent, stateless connections. The counterpart is that it does not maintain any context between client and server, which makes it hard to support sessions.

---

[1]Some researchers like to see the Web as a gigantic distributed database.

[2]All information regarding Web standards is available at that site.

HTML (HyperText Markup Language) is the standard page description language for the Web. It allows users to describe the content of a page (text, sound, image, etc.) with markups for displaying. HTML should be used only to mark up information according to its meaning, regardless of how it will be displayed by the browser. Conceptually, HTML and HTTP are independent of platforms and protocols, thereby solving the problem of portability of client graphical interfaces. However, HTML is quite permissive, and this has been exploited by Web browsers to include proprietary markups for displaying. As a result, some HTML documents cannot be properly displayed by various browsers. To provide browser independence, an extended version of HTML called XML (eXtended Markup Language) has been defined by the W3C. XML is a subset of SGML (Standard Generalized Markup Language) and provides a clean separation between content structure and presentation. With XML, one can encode structure information in documents much more precisely than with HTML. Besides its exploitation for better displaying by Web browsers, XML-encoded information can also be used for searching in more sophisticated SQL-like ways. XML is already having a major impact as a standard for data access.

HTTP enables access to *static* Web pages, i.e., pages already stored in files in the Web server. However, Web applications that access a DBMS or some other file server must create *dynamic* Web pages. The CGI (Common Gateway Interface) protocol makes this possible by enabling a Web server to call an executable program specified in the URL. A typical example of this kind of program is one that performs SQL access. The output produced by the program is returned to the Web server and is used to construct the dynamic Web page.

16.3.2 Database Access

With the Web, the client is highly portable and is sometimes called "universal client". This yields a new form of client/server architecture called *three-tier client/server* (Figure 16.6). With traditional (two-tier) client/server architectures, the server runs the database programs, and the client runs the application programs and the graphical interface. The problems with this architecture are now well understood. As the number of application programs increases, the clients get "fatter" and require more storage and computing power. Furthermore, propagating changes to application programs on many heterogeneous clients may be difficult.

With the three-tier client/server architecture, an application server is introduced to run application programs. The client is a Web browser dedicated to the graphical interfaces. Application logic that may be needed at the client, e.g., to check data entry, can be supported through *applets*, which are small application programs

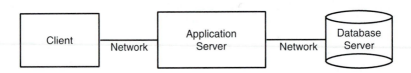

Figure 16.6. Three-Tier Client/Server Architecture

downloaded from the application server. Applets are typically programmed in Java, a secure programming language, and run in a restricted address space (the "sandbox") which prevents disk access. As a side effect, the client does not need as much computing power as before. The concept of a *Network Computer* (NC), essentially a PC without a hard disk, has been proposed by Oracle as a cheaper alternative to the PC. It is very likely that PC and NC will complement each other in performing different tasks.

The three-tier architecture can naturally generalize to n-tier with various application servers. Figure 16.7 illustrates this generalization to enable database access from a Web server, as most DBMS do. The Web browser communicates with the Web server using HTTP. The database gateway is a CGI program that performs the mapping between HTML inputs and query strings, and between result tuples and HTML report forms. Nguyen and Srinivasan [1996] propose a general-purpose cross language variable substitution to achieve this in the DB2 WWW Connection system. The database gateway is called by the Web server using the URL and associated inputs (for the query), and sends the corresponding query to the database server. After the query has been executed, it transforms the result tuples into dynamic HTML pages. Thus, the application developer can use both HTML for creating query forms and reports, and the database language (SQL) for querying.

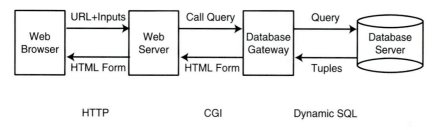

Figure 16.7. Database Access from a Web Browser

16.3.3 Semistructured Data

The Web is usually regarded as an interconnected collection of unstructured documents. However, a large number of structured data sources are now becoming available on the Web using database gateways. These sources include both free and commercial databases on product information, stock market information, real estate, automobiles, and entertainment. The interface to such sources is typically a collection of *fill-out forms*. The query answer usually takes the form of an HTML document that is very structured, and can be parsed and converted into a set of tuples or more complex data types. There are other structured information sources that are available online but not on the Web, such as name servers, bibliographic sources, and university- and company-wide information systems, and they too provide query interfaces.

Consequently, the data available on the Internet is structured in many different ways. The two extremes are fully unstructured data, such as raw text and image, and fully structured data, such as relational or object databases. But most data, such as HTML and SGML data, are somewhere in between, and have thus been termed *semistructured* [Abiteboul, 1997], [Suciu, 1997]. Semistructured data differ from structured data in many important ways. The structure may be irregular because of data heterogeneity, implicit as in SGML, or partial. The schema may be very large, rapidly evolving or completely ignored in queries for Information Retrieval (IR) or browsing.

Semistructured data are typically modeled as a labeled graph whose nodes are labeled structured objects or atomic values, and whose edges are references. Data in the labeled graph are self-describing and have no schema. Let us illustrate such labeled graphs with the well-known Object Exchange Model (OEM) [Papakonstantinou et al., 1995]. An OEM object consists of

1. a label which is the name of the object class

2. a type which is either atomic (integer, string, etc.) or set

3. a value which is either atomic or a set of objects

4. an optional object identifier

Figure 16.8 shows an OEM object with the label "Highlights98", whose value is a set of the major sport events in 1998, like the Roland Garros tennis tournament in Paris and the soccer World Cup in France. As the example suggests, it is very easy to integrate heterogeneous data, since they are self-describing. However, type information is embedded in the objects and is difficult to extract. To describe the structure of semistructured objects, graph schemas [Buneman, 1997] and data guides [Goldman 1997] have been proposed.

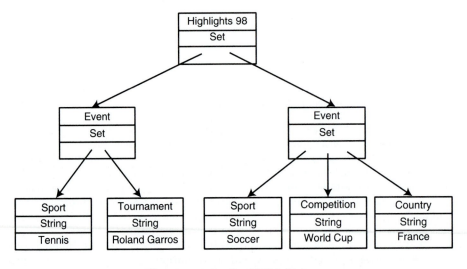

Figure 16.8. An OEM Object

Research on semistructured data is only beginning. Traditional database techniques rely heavily on the database schema, and are therefore not suited for semistructured data. New (or extensions of existing) database languages, techniques and architectures are necessary.

16.3.4 Architectures for Information Integration

Integrating information from data sources over the Internet requires creating some form of integrated view to allow for distributed querying. The context of the Internet raises a number of issues for information integration that are far more difficult than those of multidatabase systems. First, the number of data sources may be very high, thereby making view integration and conflict resolution a problem. Second, the space of data sources is very dynamic, so adding or dropping a data source should be done with minimal impact on the integrated view. Third, the data sources may have different computing capabilities, ranging from full-featured DBMS to simple files. This is unlike multidatabase systems or data warehousing, which assume data sources with an SQL interface. Finally, data sources may be unstructured or semistructured, thus providing virtually no information for view integration.

To address these problems, the database research community has revisited the multidatabase architecture with data source *wrappers* and *mediators* (Figure 16.9).

- For each data source, a wrapper exports some information about its source schema, data, and query processing capabilities [Cluet et al., 1998].

- A mediator centralizes the information provided by the wrappers in a unified view of all available data (stored in the global data dictionary), decomposes the user query in smaller queries (executable by the wrappers), gathers the partial results and computes the answer to the user query.

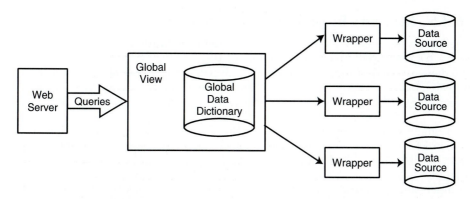

Figure 16.9. Mediator-Wrapper Architecture

There is no consensus on how wrappers describe their sources' capabilities, nor on how much of this information is exposed to the mediator. But the mediator-wrapper model itself is a widely adopted abstraction for the information integration problem. The mediator-wrapper architecture differs fundamentally from a data warehouse in that integrated data is not materialized. Thus, it is rather complementary, since a mediator can be used as a source database for a data warehouse.

The mediator-wrapper architecture has several advantages. First, the specialized components of the architecture allow the various concerns of different kinds of users to be handled separately. Second, mediators typically specialize in a related set of data sources with "similar" data, and thus export schemas and semantics related to a particular domain. The specialization of the components leads to a flexible and extensible distributed system. Figure 16.10 illustrates a hierarchy of specialized mediators, with one IR mediator for various search engines, one DB mediator for heterogeneous databases, and an IR/DB mediator that provides IR and database query capabilities.

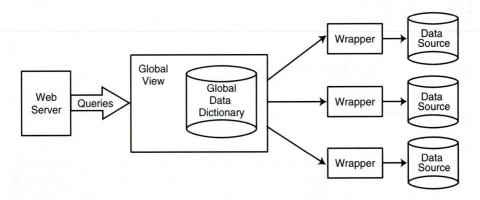

Figure 16.10. Hierarchy of Mediators

16.3.5 Research Projects and Open Issues

There have been many research projects on data integration in the context of the Web. We only briefly mention a sample of them that have been well prototyped and demonstrated: Tsimmis at Stanford University (USA), Garlic at IBM Almaden Research Laboratories (USA), Information Manifold and Strudel at AT&T Research Laboratories (USA), and Disco at Inria (France). We conclude with some open issues.

Tsimmis [Hammer et al., 1995b] (The Stanford-IBM Manager of Multiple Information Sources) is a DARPA-funded joint project of the Stanford database group and the IBM Almaden database group for integrating semistructured Web data. Tsimmis follows the mediator-wrapper architecture, allowing for hierarchies of wrappers and mediators. The components communicate using the OEM semistructured data model and an associated query language called MSL (Mediator Specification Language). MSL statements are Datalog-like logical rules that can deal with objects. Tsimmis stresses the automatic generation of wrappers and mediators using a context-free grammar that facilitates the description of query capabilities. Tsimmis focuses on the optimization of select-project queries, with little attention to joins, which are considered unlikely in the Web context.

Garlic [Haas et al., 1997], [Tork Roth and Schwarz, 1997] is an information integration project of the IBM Almaden database group. Garlic assumes that the query capabilities of the sources are unknown to the mediator, and finding an execution plan amounts to negotiating with the sources as to how much of a plan they can handle. The Garlic strategy may lead to unnecessary network traffic between the mediator and the wrappers, but it is powerful enough to deal with virtually every kind of conjunctive query.

Garlic provides an object-oriented view of the data sources, modeling all collections of similar items in class interfaces. For each interface, there may be more than one implementation, each of which corresponds to some subset of that collection, located in some data source. The wrappers, too, are objects: their methods correspond to supported operators. Query planning is done by invocating the wrapper methods and deducing from the return result how much the wrapper can handle. Garlic deals with conjunctive queries only.

The Information Manifold (IM) project [Levy et al., 1996] at AT&T Research provides uniform access to large heterogeneous collections of data sources over the Web. IM provides a mechanism to describe declaratively the contents and query capabilities of available data sources. IM has several innovative features. First, it provides a practical mechanism to describe declaratively the contents and query capabilities of data sources. In particular, the contents of the sources are described as queries over a set of relations and classes. Thus, it is possible to model the fine-grained distinctions between the contents of different sources, and it is easy to add and delete sources. Modeling the query capabilities of data sources is crucial in order to interact with many existing sources. Second, IM employs an efficient algorithm that uses the source descriptions to create query plans that can access several data sources to answer a query. The algorithm prunes the sources that are accessed to answer the query, and considers the capabilities of the different sources. The query planning algorithm is a variation on algorithms for rewriting queries using views. In addition, IM is able to reason about sources that are known to be *complete* [Levy, 1996] and with probabilistic information about the sources [Florescu et al., 1997]. [Ullman, 1997] provides a detailed comparison of IM and Tsimmis.

Strudel [Fernandez et al., 1998] is another subsequent information integration project at AT&T Research focusing on semistructured data. The Strudel system applies concepts from database management systems to the process of building Web sites. Strudel's key idea involves separating the management of the site's data, the creation and management of the site's structure, and the visual presentation of the site's pages. First, the site builder creates a uniform model of all data available at the site. Second, the builder uses this model to declaratively define the Web site's structure by applying a "site-definition query" to the underlying data. Third, the builder specifies the visual presentation of pages in Strudel's HTML-template language. The data model underlying Strudel is a semistructured model of labeled directed graphs.

Disco [Tomasic et al., 1997], [Tomasic et al., 1998] (Distributed Information Search Components) is a data integration project at Inria, Rocquencourt. Disco's architecture is based on the three-tier architecture, extended with several novel features. Disco mediators and wrappers operate independently: a mediator accesses a wrapper simply through a URL-like description of the wrapper. This feature means that wrappers can easily be shared among multiple mediators. Each Disco wrapper exports its capabilities using a grammar-like description of the operations that the wrapper supports. Disco mediators automatically adapt to the capabilities of wrappers by using an elegant distinction between the preliminary execution plan (which does not consider wrapper capabilities at all) and the final execution plan, which accounts for wrapper capabilities [Kapitskaia et al., 1997]. In addition, wrappers optionally export *cost statistics* and *cost equations* that describe the size of the data in the underlying sources and the cost of accessing the sources [Naacke et al., 1998]. Disco mediators use this cost information to perform sophisticated cost-based query optimization.

Disco mediator query processing can continue to function when some data sources are unavailable. During query processing, unavailable data sources are detected. Query processing continues with the available data sources by saving the partial results of these sources. When the unavailable data sources become available, their results are integrated with the saved results to produce the answer to the query. Additional research has focused on an extension to this idea, such that the saved partial results can be examined by applications through the use of secondary queries, called *parachute queries* [Bonnet, 1998].

As the projects described above suggest, research on information integration on the Internet is very challenging and is only beginning. These projects have improved our understanding of information integration from heterogeneous distributed data sources. But much more work is needed to ease the deployment of mediators and wrappers in various application domains. Besides dealing with semistructured data, there are important issues, such as mixing IR and database capabilities, dealing with data source failures, updating either integrated or source data, and improving the overall data quality.

16.4 PUSH-BASED TECHNOLOGIES

The push-based approach to data delivery and dissemination is a response to some of the problems inherent in pull-based systems. One of these problems is that users need to know a priori where and when to look for data. When data volatility is high, users must hunt for new data frequently, wasting time and effort [Franklin and Zdonik, 1998]. A second problem is the mismatch between the asymmetric nature of some applications (we listed some of these in the introduction) and the symmetric communications infrastructure on applications such as the Internet. There are, of course, asymmetric communication media, such as the cable TV network and satellite-based systems, but an increasing amount of data communication is being done over the Internet, for which this problem exists.

A number of different types of asymmetry can be identified [Franklin and Zdonik, 1997], each having an impact on the data delivery mechanism. The first, and most obvious, is network asymmetry, where the network bandwidth is different in the upstream (from clients to server) than the downstream (from server to clients) channels. This type of asymmetry is exhibited in mobile networks, satellite-based systems, cable TV networks, and even telephone networks with the emerging ADSL technologies.

A second type of asymmetry arises in distributed information systems, due to the imbalance between the number of clients and the number of servers. Typically, the number of clients is larger than the number of servers, but if this ratio becomes too high, it causes delays and difficulties in data delivery. Server overload is a well-known problem (thus the nickname of the WWW as the World Wide Wait).

The third type of asymmetry is the result of differences in the amount of data transmitted between servers and clients. For example, traditional Web search engines transmit only a few keywords upstream, but the downstream transmission of the research results may involve significant amounts of data.

Data volatility is the source of a fourth type of asymmetry. If the data and services that clients wish to access change frequently (data may be updated, or new services may be provided), there will be an asymmetry in the "control" of data flow, since the servers will mostly control the action.

In environments which exhibit one or more of these asymmetries, pull-based data delivery may not yield good results. The alternative is to resort to push-based techniques, which resolve the problems faced by pull-based systems in meeting the requirements of these environments.

A fundamental difficulty with the push-based approach is that the control of data delivery is transferred from the clients to the servers. Clients no longer request data when they need it; data are delivered to them when the server transmits them. This raises a number of issues. The first is the generation of a data transmission schedule that meets clients' needs. A second, related problem is managing client caches so that the average wait time to access data is minimized. Finally, there is the problem of propagating data updates to all the clients. We investigate these problems within the context of a particular push-based approach called "broadcast disks" [Acharya et al., 1995], [Acharya, 1998].

16.4.1 Delivery Schedule Generation

Data delivery schedule generation arises as a problem in push-based systems because clients no longer pull the data they need whenever they need them. Thus, the servers have to determine when to push which data to the clients. A straightforward method is to broadcast the data when it becomes available. At steady-state, this amounts to transmitting data continuously and repeatedly at fixed intervals. This approach is similar to a disk which spins at a fixed rate, from which clients read the relevant data as they pass by[3] – hence the name "broadcast disk." When each data item is broadcast at the same, fixed interval, it is referred to as a flat disk. Figure 16.11a depicts a flat disk schedule, where data items A, B and C are broadcast in the order A-B-C.

If the applications access data items at fixed intervals, then the flat disk is the optimal approach. If application access to data is not uniform, then flat disks do not perform well. It is preferable to transmit pages that are more in demand (*hot pages*) more frequently than those which are demanded less frequently (*cold pages*). There are two alternative schedules in this case: skewed and multi-disk. In skewed broadcast (Figure 16.11b), the subsequent broadcasts of each hot page are spaced randomly in the schedule. In the example of Figure 16.11b, this results in the

---

[3]Note that all the clients "hear" the same data page at the same time.

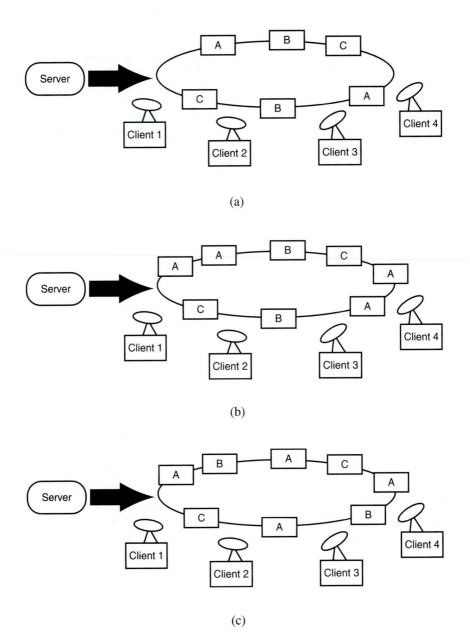

(a)

(b)

(c)

Figure 16.11. Alternative Broadcast Disk Schedules

schedule A-A-B-C, since A is the hot page and is transmitted twice as frequently as B and C. In the multi-disk approach (Figure 16.11c), hot pages are broadcast more frequently, but at regular intervals; that is, the inter-arrival time of each page is fixed. This is similar to placing data on multiple disks with varying speeds – hence the name. Studies indicate that the multi-disk approach gives the best performance in cases where application access to data is non-uniform [Acharya et al., 1995].

The question now is how to generate a multi-disk schedule. The input to a schedule generation algorithm is the applications' (clients') access pattern to data. Determining this is not easy. One possibility is for the clients to post their access profiles – similar to what happens in a publish/subscribe-based system. Given this information, the schedule generation problem can be formulated as a mathematical optimization problem that allocates bandwidth to different data items, such that the expected delay for a data item is minimized. We leave the formulation as an exercise for the readers, and instead describe an heuristic algorithm proposed in [Acharya et al., 1995] and [Acharya, 1998].

The algorithm generates a periodic schedule, in which the inter-arrival times of subsequent transmissions of a data item are fixed. With these constraints, the algorithm allocates as much of the bandwidth as possible in order not to waste any resources. The steps of the algorithm are as follows:

1. Order the data items from hottest to coldest.

2. Partition the data items into ranges of items, such that the items in each range have similar application access profiles[4]. The number of ranges is denoted by *num_ranges*.

3. Choose the relative broadcast frequency for each range as integers (rel_freq_i, where i is the range).

4. Divide each range into smaller elements, called *chunks* (C_{ij} is the j-th chunk of range i). Determine the number of chunks into which range i is divided as $num\_chunk_i = max\_chunks/rel\_freq_i$, where max_chunks is the least common multiple of $rel\_freq_i, \forall i$.

5. Create the broadcast schedule by interleaving the chunks of each range using the following procedure:

> **for** i **from** 0 **to** $max\_chunks - 1$ **by** 1 **do**
> > **for** j **from** 1 **to** max_ranges **by** 1 **do**
> > > Broadcast chunk $C_{j,(i \bmod num\_chunks_j)}$
> > **end-for**
> **end-for**

Example 16.1

We demonstrate the algorithm using an example taken from [Acharya et al., 1995], [Acharya, 1998]. Consider 11 data items $D_1, \ldots, D_{11}$, where D_1 is the hottest and D_{11} is the coldest. Assume that data item D_1 has one access

---

[4]Each range corresponds to a disk of a particular speed.

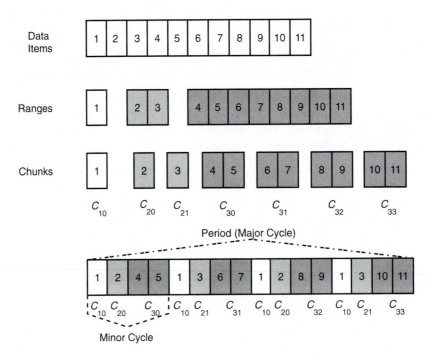

Figure 16.12. Example Broadcast Schedule (From [Acharya et al., 1995])

pattern, items D_2 and D_3 have another access pattern, and items $D_4, \ldots, D_{11}$ have a third. Thus, we have three ranges (Figure 16.12). Let us assume that, based on the access profiles, it is decided to transmit range 1 twice as frequently as range 2, which should be transmitted twice as frequently as range 3. Thus, $rel\_freq_1 = 4, rel\_freq_2 = 2, rel\_freq_3 = 1$.

In the fourth step of the algorithm, these ranges are subdivided into chunks. The least common multiple of rel_freq's is 4, from which we obtain $num\_chunk_1 = 4/4 = 1, num\_chunk_2 = 4/2 = 2, num\_chunk_3 = 4/1 = 4$. Step 5 of the algorithm creates a periodic broadcast schedule in which each period (or major cycle) consists of four sub-periods (or minor cycles), where each minor cycle contains one data item from a different chunk. Thus, the inter-arrival time for each data item is fixed. The resulting schedule is depicted in Figure 16.12.

16.4.2 Client Cache Management

The broadcast schedule is determined by the server based on the access profiles of many clients. Thus, the schedule represents a compromise between the access patterns of many clients. Furthermore, the server may give higher priority to the requests of some clients over others. Since the bandwidth is fixed, improving the delay for one client inevitably causes a degradation in the delay for another client. Client profiles may also change over time, causing schedules that were once optimal to cease being optimal after a while. Thus, it is important for clients to manage their caches so as to keep as many of the needed data items as possible in their caches.

There is a difference between pull-based and push-based systems in the cache management algorithms that are employed. These differences are exhibited in both the demand-driven cache replacement policies and the prefetching mechanisms. We discuss both in the remainder.

If traditional caching policies (such as LRU) are used, then each client caches its hottest pages. However, this may not be optimal. Consider a case where D_i is the hottest data item. This means that D_i will be broadcast more frequently than other items. Thus, even if D_i is not in its cache, the client is not likely to wait for it for too long. On the other hand, a cold data item D_j is broadcast much less frequently, and the client would be well-advised to keep D_j in its cache in order to reduce the delay in accessing it. This points to an important issue: cache replacement algorithms in this environment must take into account the cost of replacing a page[5]. This cost is different for each client, since a client's hot page may be different from the global hot page. Thus, the caching algorithm should cache, at each client, those pages that are hot locally but cold globally. These are the ones that are likely to be accessed by a client but are not broadcast frequently, making them expensive to get from the broadcast.

An idealized algorithm for page replacement is one which determines the page with the smallest ratio between its probability of access and its frequency of broadcast. This algorithm, called PIX [Acharya et al., 1995], calculates the "cost" of replacing a page (where cost is a function of both the access probability and the frequency of broadcast) and replaces the least costly one. PIX is an idealized algorithm because it cannot be implemented without a perfect knowledge of the access probabilities. Even if it were implemented, its run-time overhead would be very high, as it requires the calculation of this ratio for each cache-resident page every time a page is replaced.

An implementable approximation of PIX, called LIX, is described in [Acharya et al., 1995]. LIX maintains a number of linked lists of cached pages, one per range (or disk) that is involved in the broadcast schedule. When a page is brought into the cache, it is always inserted into the chain that corresponds to the range (disk) to which the page belongs. LIX can flush out a page from any of the linked lists to open up space for the incoming page. Thus, the sizes of the linked lists dynamically change as pages come in and out of the cache. As in the well-known LRU algorithm, LIX orders the pages in each chain, such that the pages that are most recently accessed are at the top of the chain, and those that have been least recently used are at the bottom. To control this action, the algorithm maintains two variables for each cached page: (a) Pr_i, which is the probability of access of page P_i, and (b) LT_i, the time of the most recent access to page P_i. The operation of the algorithm is as follows:

---

[5]We assume that each data item is equivalent to a page in size. This simplifies the description of the issues.

1. When a page P_i is brought into cache and inserted into a chain,

$$Pr_i = 0$$
$$LT_i = CurrentTime$$

2. When P_i is accessed again, it is moved to the top of its own chain and the following calculations are made:

$$Pr_i = HF/(CurrentTime - LT_i) + (1 - HF) * LT_i$$
$$LT_i = CurrentTime$$

HF is called the history factor and is a constant that weighs the most recent access with respect to the running probability estimate.

3. If a new page needs to be flushed out to open up space, a *lix* value is calculated for the pages at the bottom of each chain and the page with the lowest *lix* value is flushed out. The *lix* value is calculated as follows:

$$lix_i = Pr_i/rel\_freq_i$$

where rel_freq_i is the relative broadcast frequency of the range (disk) to which that page P_i belongs.

Performance studies demonstrate that a page replacement algorithm, such as LIX, is superior to the traditional algorithms, such as LRU, in terms of the average response time to access data items [Acharya et al., 1995].

A natural issue to consider next is prefetching and its impact on the average response time. Prefetching in the broadcast disk environment is cheap; the client gets the data anyway, so would be well-advised to grab it. As in the case of the page replacement algorithm, the prefetching algorithms in a broadcast disk system are also cost-based, taking into account the cost of accessing a page in determining which page to prefetch. This can be done by determining the "worth" of each page when it is broadcast, and if its worth is higher than that of any page currently in the cache, a prefetch (and a consequent page flush-out) is performed. This value for a page P_i can be computed as $pt = Pr_i * tr$, where tr is the time remaining before P_i's next broadcast. This is the basis of the PT algorithm [Acharya et al., 1996a].

The pt value of a page is dynamic, since one of its components (tr) changes with each clock tick. pt is highest at time t_i, when it is broadcast. From there on, it steadily reduces until the next broadcast at time t_j, when it shoots up again. The result is a sawtooth-shaped pt curve. This points to a fundamental difference between the demand-based page replacement algorithm PIX and the prefetching algorithm PT. When PIX is used as a prefetcher, the cache will fill up with the pages with the highest PIX values, and since these are static, prefetching will stop when the cache is full. In contrast, since pt values of pages change with every tick, the contents of the cache will continually change.

PT is also an idealized algorithm and is impractical to implement, since it requires that the *pt* values of *all* cached pages be computed at every clock tick – clearly not an acceptable overhead. The solution is to follow the example of LIX and divide the cached pages into ranges, such that each range has the same access probability. This ensures that there is only one candidate victim for replacement for each range, thus reducing the number of *pt* values that must be calculated. This approximation of PT, which is called APT, maintains a doubly-linked circular list for the pages in each range. Furthermore, for each range, it maintains a pointer (*PRV*) to the page with the smallest *tr*; i.e., the page that is that range's potential replacement victim. When a page must be flushed out, APT calculates the *pt* values for only the *PRV* pages in each of the ranges and chooses the one with the smallest value. The freed-up page is allocated to the range into which the new prefetched page is to enter.

As expected, prefetching can provide significant performance improvements over demand-based caching. In this case, experiments reveal a 10-30% improvement in favor of APT over LIX [Acharya et al., 1996a]. In push-based environments, a fundamental problem with prefetching—namely, the additional load it places on system resources—does not exist, since prefetching is controlled locally by each client according to his/her own access profile.

16.4.3 Propagating Updates

Updating a database means adding, deleting, or modifying data. In a push-based system, these roughly correspond to adding and deleting pages from the broadcast schedule, or modifying page contents. Adding a new page to the schedule is, perhaps, the least problematic, since the server can compute the new broadcast schedule and inform the clients of the changes. Deletions and modifications are more problematic.

Some of the difficulties arise from the fact that a push-based system, as we have described it in this section, is a data shipping system in which the server broadcasts data and the clients cache them. Thus, the issues that we discussed in Chapter 14 regarding client cache management apply here as well. One of those problems, to remind ourselves, is notifying clients of deletions and modifications. In the case of deletions, an invalidation approach is applicable where the server informs the clients that the pages they have in their caches are no longer valid and should be flushed. In the case of data modification, the server may either invalidate the modified pages in clients' buffers or propagate the changes and ask the clients to apply these changes to the pages in their buffers.

In the case of data modification, there are additional problems related to the consistency of the data. The issue was discussed in Chapters 10–12 within the context of regular database transaction processing. In push-based systems, a number of differences arise. One difference is, again, the result of the data shipping nature of the system: how does an update that originates in one client get propagated to other clients? This particular issue was also discussed in Chapter 14 within the context of client cache management. A second problem is the consistency constraint that is used and its possible effect on the propagation of updates. A number of possible consistency models can be identified [Acharya et al., 1996b]:

- *Latest value*: Clients are required to access the most recent value of a data item.

- *Quasi-caching*: Clients can access data items which deviate from the latest value according to a tolerance that is defined individually for each client [Alonso et al., 1990]. This tolerance may be temporal or value-based, or it may be defined otherwise.

- *Periodic*: Data values change at periodic intervals (e.g., at the beginning of minor or major cycles in the broadcast schedule).

- *Serializability*: Clients' data access schedules are required to result in a serializable schedule.

- *Opportunistic*: Clients access whichever version of the data they can find.

It is clear that some of the consistency models will affect the broadcast schedule and the way in which caches are utilized. For example, if *latest value* is the accepted consistency definition, then either clients should not cache any data and wait for the server to broadcast updates immediately, or an algorithm must be devised which would allow the clients to cache data, but allow them to "back-up" if the values they have read are not the latest values (perhaps determined by timestamping both the server notifications and the client-cached data).

The problem of propagating updates in a push-based system is not well understood. There is only one study at this time [Acharya et al., 1996b] that has analyzed the problem in a relatively restricted setting, where all the updates are collected at the server and clients do not have any opportunity to communicate with the server (they just listen to the broadcast). Clearly, more studies are required in this area.

16.5 MOBILE DATABASES

In Chapter 3 we discussed wireless networks and their characteristics (Section 3.5, to be precise). In this section we discuss some of the issues that arise in building DBMSs over such networks. Since the discussion in Section 3.5 is far removed from this one, we start with a summary of our discussion in that section.

A wireless network consists of a "wireline" (fixed) backbone network on which a number of control stations are located. Each control station coordinates the communication from a mobile computer [also called *mobile station* (MS) or *mobile unit* (MU)] in its respective cell to another mobile computer in the same cell, or in another cell, or to a stationary computer on the wireline network. This is depicted in Figure 16.13 (which is the same as Figure 3.13).

In such an environment, data can reside on either the fixed network or the mobile stations. In this section, we are fairly flexible in our definition of a mobile database—we use the term to refer to any arrangement in which the database access is performed by mobile stations over a wireless link.

There can be a number of different types of mobile stations. One type involves fairly simple computers with limited capabilities. In this case, data are located in computers on the wireline network, with the mobile stations "downloading" data as they need them. This scenario is realistic for some applications, and is currently the most common. However, the distributed data management problem

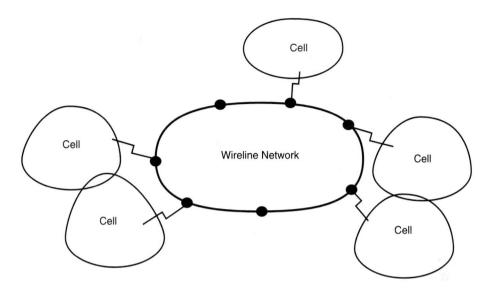

Figure 16.13. Cellular Networks

is not significantly affected by mobility because data resides primarily on wireline computers. More interesting is the environment in which the mobile stations are more powerful and store native data that may need to be shared by others — the so-called "walkstation" case [Imielinski and Badrinath, 1994]. It is this latter class of devices, which can hold data and process them, that raises the interesting questions.

Mobile computing environments are characterized by three issues [Forman and Zahorjan, 1994]: communication characteristics, mobility and portability. Communication is conducted over wireless networks which are prone to disconnections, noise, echo, and low bandwidth. Mobility of some of the equipment on the network causes static data in stationary networks to become dynamic and volatile in wireless networks. Mobility raises issues such as address migration, maintenance of directories and difficulty in locating stations. Finally, portability places restrictions on the type of equipment that can be used in these environments. For example, easy portability and the desire for long operation between battery recharges usually restrict the type and size of storage that can be used.

These characteristics of mobile environments can be expanded [Alonso and Korth, 1993], [Dunham and Helal, 1995], [Imielinski and Badrinath, 1994], [Pitoura and Samaras, 1998] as follows:

1. The wireless networks have restricted bandwidth. They can be either wireless cellular networks, which have a bandwidth in the order of 10 Kbps, or they can be wireless local area networks with a bandwidth of 10 Mbps. The former can cover larger geographic areas, while the latter is restricted to smaller areas, typically within a building.

2. The power supplies (i.e., batteries) in mobile stations have limited life-times. Even with the new advances in battery technology, the typical lifetime of a battery is only a few hours, which is reduced further with increased computation and disk operations. This problem is not likely to disappear in the near future, since battery power is expected to increase by only 30% over the next five years.

3. Because of power restrictions, mobile stations are not available as widely as stationary ones. They are usually powered off when they are not in use. For the same reason, the amount of computation that can be performed on mobile stations is restricted.

4. As the name suggests, mobile stations move in these systems. This requires additional system functionality to track them, in particular if they store data shared by others. The mobility also necessitates the management of heterogeneity of the base stations, since they can have quite varying capabilities. Finally, station mobility causes constant change in the topology of the underlying network.

These issues raise interesting questions for the design of distributed DBMSs, since they cause significant changes to the infrastructure upon which such systems are built: almost all the DBMS functions are affected to varying degrees. In the remainder, we highlight these issues.

16.5.1 Directory Management

Directory management is very much linked to distribution design. The problem here is the "optimum" distribution of data across the nodes of the wireline (stationary) network, as well as data that can reside on the walkstations. As discussed in Chapter 5, this is a problem in stationary networks, and it becomes more difficult in mobile environments due to the mobility of the walkstations (which move resident data) and other mobile stations. The typical optimality measures take into account who is trying to access data from where, and distribution algorithms attempt to place some or all of that data in close proximity to the access points. These measures and the related design arguments must be revisited in mobile environments.

The fundamental question is how to locate a mobile station which may hold the required data. Two solutions have been discussed in the literature [Imielinski and Badrinath, 1994]. In one solution, each mobile station has a "home" base station which keeps track of its location by receiving notifications of its movements. Thus, any other station (say, station A) which wishes to find this mobile station (say, station B) contacts B's home base, where it learns the current location. This method, which is currently used in cellular networks, is simple, but may cause significant access latency if the mobile station is far from its home base. The second solution is based on restricted broadcast within the area of the (mobile or stationary) station which wishes to access the mobile station in question. In this scheme, station A, which wishes to establish access, first broadcasts an inquiry message to the base stations in its own neighborhood to see if B is in that area. If this does not yield a positive result, then A contacts B's home base. A number of other alternatives are possible, of course, even though they are not mentioned in the literature. For example, if a mobile station knows its itinerary, the directory information can be updated in advance to improve the chances of success in the second algorithm. Another alternative may be for mobile stations to leave behind their new addresses as they move, allowing them to be tracked (similar to the object migration techniques discussed in Section 14.4.3). This, coupled with the caching of location information at the accessing stations, may reduce the directory search latency at the expense of movement tracking.

A second directory management problem is finding the optimum location of data when the accessing unit is moving. If data exists at multiple sites, the locations where data access occurs when the accessing station is moving becomes important. This is related to query optimization, which we discuss in Section 16.5.4; however, an important component of the problem is directory management, since the data must be located first.

16.5.2   Caching

Many of the applications of mobile information systems (e.g., traffic monitoring and advice, sales and customer tracking) involve caching data at the mobile station for a period of time. As indicated above, the limited power supply at the mobile stations also restricts the amount of processing that is performed at the mobile stations, requiring the computation to be done on stationary stations and the resulting data to be sent to the mobile stations. This is a typical example of a query shipping system. More powerful mobile stations may also participate in data shipping, where an entire DBMS resides at the mobile station. As such, issues related to the management of the caches at mobile stations arise. A thorough discussion of caching issues such as fetching, coherency and replacement can be found in the literature [Pitoura and Samaras, 1998].

In the mobile environment, caching granularity becomes a crucial issue. Trade-offs between page and object caching were discussed in Chapter 14. Both of these issues can create severe performance problems due to the limited bandwidth of wireless computing. Semantic caching has been proposed as a solution to overcome some of these performance problems associated with traditional granularities [Dar et al., 1996b] [Keller and Basu, 1996]. With semantic caching, the granularity of cached data is the result of a query. The contents are defined based upon a predicate indicating the selection criteria. The benefits of semantic caching to mobile computing are the reduced network traffic and reduced space requirements for caching at the mobile station. In addition, semantic caching easily supports replacement strategies based on location. As the mobile unit moves, data associated with certain remote locations (see the discussion of location dependent data below) may become obsolete and need to be replaced. Semantic caching supports this type of cache management strategy. In addition, semantic caching may prove to be beneficial in supporting disconnected operation. This is due to both the reduced space requirements for the cache and an increased hit ratio because of the semantic similarity of the client's queries.

Cache coherency of the mobile station cache has been studied extensively. Updates at the server may either be propagated to the mobile stations, or mobile station caches may be invalidated. Simulation studies have shown the effectiveness of both types at reducing the uplink traffic on the wireless link [Cai et al., 1997].

16.5.3   Broadcast Data

Broadcasting data from base stations to mobile ones can improve the performance of mobile applications. All the issues we discussed in the previous section on push-based technologies apply in this case as well. One particular constraint is that, since the mobile stations power off frequently to conserve energy, it is necessary to either have a very regular broadcast schedule (so that they can "wake up" at the right time to receive relevant data) or have the data be self-indexed [Barbara and Imielinski, 1994], [Imielinski et. al., 1994].

Due to the mobility of the mobile stations, the content of any data to be broadcast should be dynamic and adaptive. One approach proposes cooperation between the clients and servers [Datta et al., 1997]. A performance metric called *tuning time* was used to evaluate how long a client must listen to a channel. Periodic broadcast performed best at high loads, while an a periodic approach was best at a lower workload. The air-cache approach dynamically changes the content of the broadcast disk based on the access frequency of the data [Stathatos et al., 1997]. Changes in access frequency change the content of the data that is broadcast. The mobility factor again complicates this issue. As the mobile station moves from cell to cell, the client's need for data moves with him/her. Thus, the content of the data broadcast should adapt to this movement. As the user moves from one cell, the data needed only by that user should be dropped from the content of the data broadcast in the old cell. Also, it should be added to the data broadcast in the new cell.

16.5.4   Query Processing and Optimization

Query processing is one of the DBMS functions affected most by the mobility of the environment. The effects are both in terms of the queries that are posed and the optimization techniques that can be used.

Queries in this environment can be "location dependent." For example, the query "What are the names and addresses of French restaurants in this city?" returns different results depending on which city the mobile station is located in. Location dependence may be more sophisticated, involving the tracking of moving objects. For example, if a user asks the query "Where is a branch of XYZ bank within 1 kilometer of where I am?" while driving a car, the system has to track the movement of the car in order to answer the query. There are cases in which it is even necessary to track the movement of multiple objects. There is some work in this area [Sistla et al., 1997], [Li et. al., 1997], but it is still a largely unresolved problem.

In traditional DBMSs, only the characteristics of the processing node are taken into consideration for managing data, not its physical location. The traditional approach thus promotes "location transparency". The need to support location dependent queries, however, changes this requirement in the mobile computing arena. Location Dependent Data (LDD) are data whose values are determined by its location [Dunham and Kumar, 1998]. For example, data about local TV stations' affiliation with national networks will vary from city to city. LDD can be used to answer location dependent queries. With this approach, the same query stated in different locales will obtain different results because the data values themselves are different. These multiple "correct" values of data produce a new type of data replication based on location called spatial replication. Different spatial replicas of the same data object may have different values because they are associated with different locations. LDD complicates caching functions. Cached data can become stale not because of the update of the data at the server, but because the mobile unit has moved into a new region where the cached data is not valid.

Location dependent queries can be processed by augmenting each query with location information, by assuming that queries are not modified but that location dependent data are used, or by a combination of these two approaches. Regardless of the approach used, when a query is requested, it must be bound to a location and a set of data values. Since the mobile unit is moving, the query could be bound to different locations: the location of the mobile unit when the query was requested, the location of the mobile unit when the query terminates, a projected location of the mobile unit based on its current movement, or a location as specifically indicated in the query.

With respect to query optimization, the mobility of access stations makes it difficult to determine communication costs between the accessing station and the station where the data resides. Furthermore, if the requested data is stored on one of the walkstations, then both network nodes may be in motion. The low bandwidth and, more importantly, the variability of the bandwidth between the wireless part and the backbone, complicate the picture further.

In a centralized database environment, query optimization usually involves determining the best approach, among a set of alternatives, to process a query which minimizes I/O cost. In a distributed environment, the dominant cost is usually viewed to be that of network traffic. While I/O and network costs are still important, in a mobile computing environment the mobility and dynamic state of the mobile unit complicate optimization even further. The contents of the cache may change dynamically. As the mobile unit moves, data may or may not become available via a broadcast disk. The best location from which to access data on a database server in the fixed network may change as the mobile unit moves. Thus, in the mobile computing environment, the plans and costs associated with various plans change based on the movement. Static optimization strategies are not appropriate. Dynamic strategies which adapt to the changing environment are required.

16.5.5 Transaction Management

The disconnection of stations for possibly long periods of time and bandwith limitations require a serious reevaluation of transaction model and transaction processing techniques. Typical concurrency control techniques rely on locking. Since wireless networks are more failure-prone than their stationary counterparts, locking may not be a good solution. Locks on data items at a failed station may be held for a long time, blocking the termination of a transaction. If that transaction holds locks at other sites, this would reduce the availability of data. It is necessary to consider different consistency criteria, as well as algorithms and techniques to enforce them. For the same reason, atomic commitment protocols such as 2PC may not be suitable, since the disconnection of one station may seriously reduce the availability of the database system. Therefore, it has been suggested that longer transaction models, coupled with data replication and lazy replication schemes, may be more suitable for the wireless environment.

There have been many proposals to model mobile transactions (e.g., [Chrysan-this, 1993], [Pitoura and Bhargava, 1995], [Walborn and Chrysanthis, 1995], [Yeo and Zaslavsky, 1994], [Dunham and Helal, 1997]) with different notions of a mobile transaction. The most common view seems to be a database transaction which is requested from a mobile station. Most of these approaches view a mobile trans-action as consisting of subtransactions which have some flexibility in consistency and commit processing. Certainly a relaxation of the ACID properties is deemed necessary due to the anticipated high rate of disconnection. This disconnection and the associated limited battery power of the mobile units reflect themselves in a temporary suspension or failure of the mobile transactions. The management of these transactions may be static at the mobile unit or the database server, or may move from base station to base station as the mobile unit moves.

16.6   BIBLIOGRAPHIC NOTES

data warehouse has been, and still is, the subject of many books, research papers and trade articles. One of the earlier books is [Inmon, 1992]. OLAP was first defined by E. Codd [Codd, 1995]. Excellent surveys are presented in [Chaudhuri and Dayal, 1997] and [Eckerson, 1994]. The paper by [Widom, 1995] gives a good overview of the research problems. A comparison between MOLAP and ROLAP servers can be found in [Colliat, 1996]. The pioneering paper on materialized view maintenance is [Blakeley et al., 1986]. Papers addressing materialized view maintenance in the context of data warehouse are [Gupta et al., 1995], [Griffin and Libkin, 1995], [Dar et al., 1996a], [Sellis et al., 1997], [Roussopoulos, 1998]. The book by [Helal et al., 1997] presents the state of the art in data replication. Asynchronous replication techniques that support near real-time constraints are proposed in [Gray et al. 1996], [Pacitti et al., 1998]. data warehousing research projects include the WHIPS project at Stanford [Hammer et al., 1995a] and the DWQ project in Europe [Sellis et al., 1997].

All information on the Web and associated products and services is obviously available on the Web itself. Information on standard protocols such as HTTP, HTML and XML is available at the W3C site : http://www.w3c.org. Interfacing the Web with databases through CGI is described in [Nguyen and Srinivasan, 1996]. Semistructured data are surveyed in [Abiteboul, 1997], [Suciu, 1997]. Research prototypes for information integration include Tsimmis at Stanford [Hammer et al., 1995b], Garlic at IBM Almaden Research [Haas et al., 1997], Information Manifold [Levy et al., 1996] and Strudel [Fernandez et al., 1998] at AT&T Research, and Disco [Tomasic et al., 1998] at Inria.

Push-based systems have recently been the topics of significant research and commercial activity. Broadcast-based data delivery systems are not new and have been studied in the context of broadcast networks [Ammar and Wong, 1987], [Wong, 1988] and mobile networks [Imielinski and Badrinath, 1994]. Our focus in this chapter has been the "broadcast disks" project carried out at Brown University and the University of Maryland. Most of this work is in the Ph.D. thesis of Swarup Acharya [Acharya, 1998]. Other related references were cited in Section 16.4. Further information on the project can be obtained at http://www.cs.umd.edu/projects/bdisk/.

Mobile data management issues were quite popular in the early 1990's, but interest seems to have cooled off. This is both interesting and unfortunate, since the wireless communication environment has started to explode. Digital cellular networks now have almost complete coverage in Europe and are growing significantly in other parts of the world, including North America. Portable computer modems now have connections to digital and analog cellular phones, and stand-alone mobile modems have started to appear. The need for data management over these environments is likely to increase in the future and there is considerable room for research.

There are two books on mobile databases [Imielinski and Korth, 1996], [Pitoura and Samaras, 1998] and three overview papers [Alonso and Korth, 1993], [Imielinski and Badrinath, 1994], [Dunham and Helal, 1995]. There are also special journals and conferences organized by ACM and IEEE, which are devoted to mobile computing, but their scope is more general than data management.

BIBLIOGRAPHY

[ANSI, 1992] American National Standard for Information Systems. *Database Language SQL*. ANSI X3.135-1992, November 1992.

[ATM, 1996] ATM Forum. *ATM Traffic Management Specification, Version 4.0*, Upper Saddle River, NJ: Prentice--Hall, 1996.

[Abbadi et al., 1985] A. E. Abbadi, D. Skeen, and F. Cristian. An Efficient, Fault--Tolerant Protocol for Replicated Data Management. In *Proc. 4th ACM SIGACT--SIGMOD Symp. on Principles of Database Systems*, March 1985, pp. 215--229.

[Abiteboul, 1997] S. Abiteboul. Querying Semi-Structured Data. In *Proc. 6th Int. Conf. on Database Theory*, Vol. 1186 of Lecture Notes in Computer Science, Springer-Verlag, January 1997, pp. 1--18.

[Abramson, 1973] N. Abramson. The ALOHA System. In N. Abramson and F. F. Kuo (eds.), *Computer Communication Networks*; Englewood Cliffs, N.J.: Prentice-Hall, 1973.

[Acharya, 1998] S. Acharya. *Broadcast Disks: Dissemination-based Data Management for Asymmetric Communication Environments*. Ph.D. thesis, Providence, R.I.: Brown University, May 1998.

[Acharya et al., 1995] S. Acharya, M. Franklin, and S. Zdonik. Broadcast Disks: Data Management for Asymmetric Communications Environment. In *Proc. ACM SIGMOD Int. Conf. on Management of Data*, May 1995, pp. 199--210.

[Acharya et al., 1996a] S. Acharya, M. Franklin, and S. Zdonik. Prefetching from a Broadcast Disk. In *Proc. 12th Int. Conf. on Data Engineering*, February 1986, pp. 276--287

[Acharya et al., 1996b] S. Acharya, M. Franklin, and S. Zdonik. Disseminating Updates on Broadcast Disks. In *Proc. 22nd Int. Conf. on Very Large Data Bases*, September 1996, pp. 354--365.

[Adiba, 1981] M. Adiba. Derived Relations: A Unified Mechanism for Views, Snapshots and Distributed Data. In *Proc. 7th Int. Conf. on Very Large Data Bases*, September 1981, pp. 293--305.

[Adiba and Lindsay, 1980] M. Adiba and B. Lindsay. Database Snapshots. In *Proc. 6th Int. Conf. on Very Large Data Bases*, October 1980, pp. 86--91.

605

[Adiba and Portal, 1978] M. Adiba and D. Portal. A Cooperation System for Heterogeneous Data Base Management Systems. *Inf. Syst.* (1978), 3: 209--215.

[Adiba et al., 1978] M. Adiba, J. C. Chupin, R. Demolombe, G. Gardarin, and J. Le Bihan. Issues in Distributed Data Base Management Systems: A Technical Overview. In *Proc. 4th Int. Conf. on Very Large Data Bases*, September 1978, pp. 89--110.

[Adya et al., 1995] A. Adya, R. Gruber, B. Liskov, and U. Maheshwari. Efficient Optimistic Concurrency Control Using Loosely Synchronized Clocks. In *Proc. ACM SIGMOD Int. Conf. on Management of Data*, June 1995, pp. 23--34.

[Agrawal and DeWitt, 1985] R. Agrawal and D. J. DeWitt. Integrated Concurrency Control and Recovery Mechanisms. *ACM Trans. Database Syst.*, (December 1985), 10(4): 529--564.

[Agrawal and El-Abbadi, 1990] D. Agrawal and A. El-Abbadi. Locks with Constrained Sharing. In *Proc. ACM SIGACT-SIGMOD Symp. on Principles of Database Systems*, April 1990, pp. 85--93.

[Agrawal and El-Abbadi, 1994] D. Agrawal and A. El-Abbadi. A Nonrestrictive Concurrency Control Protocol for Object-Oriented Databases. *Distributed and Parallel Databases* (January 1994), 2(1):7--31.

[Agrawal et al., 1987] R. Agrawal, M. Carey and M. Livny. Concurrency Control Performance Modeling: Alternatives and Implications. *ACM Trans. Database Syst.* (December 1987), 12(4): 609--654.

[Agrawal et al., 1994] D. Agrawal, J. L. Bruno, A. El-Abbadi, and V. Krishnasawamy. Relative Serializability: An Approach for Relaxing the Atomicity of Transactions. In *Proc. ACM SIGACT-SIGMOD Symp. on Principles of Database Systems*, May 1994, pp. 139--149.

[Alonso and Korth, 1993] R. Alonso and H. F. Korth. Database System Issues in Nomadic Computing. In *Proc. ACM SIGMOD Int. Conf. on Management of Data*, May 1993, pp. 388--392.

[Alonso et al., 1987] R. Alonso, H. Garcia--Molina, and K. Salem. Concurrency Control and Recovery for Global Procedures in Federated Database Systems. *IEEE Quart. Bull. Database Eng.* (September 1987), 10(3): 5--11.

[Alonso et al., 1990] R. Alonso, D. Barbara, and H. Garcia-Molina. Data Caching Issues in an Information Retrieval System. *ACM Trans. Database Syst.* (September 1990), 15(3):359--384.

[Alsberg and Day, 1976] P. A. Alsberg and J. D. Day. A Principle for Resilient Sharing of Distributed Resources. In *Proc. 2nd Int. Conf. on Software Engineering*, 1976, pp. 562--570.

[Ammar and Wong, 1987] M. Ammar and J. Wong. On the Optimality of Cyclic Transmission in Teletext Systems. *IEEE Trans. Comm.* (January 1987), 35(1):68--73.

[Amsaleg, 1995] L. Amsaleg. *Conception et réalisation d'un glaneur de cellules adapté aux SGBDO client-serveur.* PhD thesis, Université Paris 6 Pierre et Marie Curie, Paris, France, June 1995.

[Amsaleg et al., 1995] L. Amsaleg, M. Franklin, and O. Gruber. Efficient Incremental Garbage Collection for Client-Server Object Database Systems. In *Proc. 21th Int. Conf. on Very Large Data Bases*, September 1995, pp. 42--53.

[Anderson and Lee, 1981] T. Anderson and P. A. Lee. *Fault Tolerance: Principles and Practice*. Englewood Cliffs, N.J.: Prentice-Hall, 1981.

[Anderson and Lee, 1985] T. Anderson and P. A. Lee. Software Fault Tolerance Terminology Proposals. In [Shrivastava, 1985], pp. 6--13.

[Anderson and Randell, 1979] T. Anderson and B. Randell (eds.). *Computing Systems Reliability*. Cambridge: Cambridge University Press, 1979.

[Andrade, 1989] J. Andrade, M. Carges, and K. Kovach. Building a Transaction Processing System on UNIX System. In *Proc. Unix Transaction Processing Workshop*, May 1989.

[Anon, 1985] Anon. A Measure of Transaction Processing Power. *Datamation* (April 1985), 31(7): 112--118.

[Apers, 1981] P. M. G. Apers. Redundant Allocation of Relations in a Communication Network. In *Proc. 5th Berkeley Workshop on Distributed Data Management and Computer Networks*, 1981, pp. 245--258.

[Apers et al., 1983] P. M. G. Apers, A. R. Hevner, and S. B. Yao. Optimization Algorithms for Distributed Queries. *IEEE Trans. Software Eng.* (1983), 9(1): 57--68.

[Apers et al., 1992] P. Apers, C. van den Berg, J. Flokstra, P. Grefen, M. Kersten, A. Wilschut. Prisma/DB: a Parallel Main-Memory Relational DBMS. *IEEE Trans. Data and Knowl. Eng.*, (1992), 4: 541-554.

[Armstrong, 1974] W. W. Armstrong. Dependency Structures of Data Base Relationships. In *Proc. Information Processing '74*, 1974, pp. 580--583.

[Astrahan et al., 1979] M.M. Astrahan, M.W. Blasgen, D.D. Chamberlin, K.P. Eswaran, J.N. Gray, P.P. Griffiths, W.F. King, R.A. Lorie, P.R. McJones, J.W. Mehl, G.R. Putzolu, I.L. Traiger, B.W. Wade, and V. Watson. System R: A Relational Database Management System. *ACM Trans. on Database Syst.* (June 1976), 1(2):97--137.

[Atkinson and Buneman, 1987] M. P. Atkinson and O. P. Buneman. Types and Persistence In Database Programming Languages. *ACM Comput. Surv.* (June 1987), 19(2): 105--190.

[Atkinson et al., 1989] , M. Atkinson, F. Bancilhon, D.J. DeWitt, K. Dittrich, D. Maier, and S. Zdonik. The Object-Oriented Database System Manifesto. In *Proc. 1st Int. Conf. on Deductive and Object-Oriented Databases*, December 1989, pp. 40--57.

[Avizienis, 1976] A. Avizienis. Fault-Tolerant Systems. *IEEE Trans. Comput.* (December 1976), C-25(12): 1304--1312.

[Avizienis, 1977] A. Avizienis. Fault-Tolerant Computing: Progress, Problems, and Prospects. In *Proc. Information Processing '77*, 1977, pp. 405--420.

[Avizienis et al., 1987] A. Avizienis, H. Kopetz, and J. C. Laprie (eds.). *The Evolution of Fault-Tolerant Computing*. Vienna: Springer--Verlag, 1987.

[Babaoglu, 1987] Ö. Babaoglu. On the Reliability of Consensus-Based Fault-Tolerant Distributed Computing Systems. *ACM Trans. Comput. Syst.* (November 1987), 5(3): 394--416.

[Babb, 1979] E. Babb. Implementing a Relational Database by Means of Specialized Hardware. *ACM Trans. Database Syst.*, (March 1979), 4(1): 1--29.

[Badrinath and Ramamritham, 1987] B. R. Badrinath and K. Ramamritham. Semantics-Based Concurrency Control: Beyond Commutativity. In *Proc. 3th Int. Conf. on Data Engineering*, February 1987, pp. 304--311.

[Badrinath and Ramamritham, 1988] B. R. Badrinath and K. Ramamritham. Synchronizing Transactions on Objects. *IEEE Trans. Comput.* (May 1988), C-37(5): 541--547.

[Ball and Hardie, 1967] M. O. Ball and F. Hardie. *Effects and Detection of Intermittent Failures in Digital Systems*. Internal Report 67-825-2137. IBM, 1967. Cited in [Siewiorek and Swarz, 1982].

[Balter et al., 1982] R. Balter, P. Berard, and P. Decitre. Why Control of Concurrency Level in Distributed Systems Is More Important Than Deadlock Management. In *Proc. ACM SIGACT--SIGOPS Symp. on Principles of Distributed Computing*, August 1982, pp. 183--193.

[Bancilhon and Spyratos, 1981] F. Bancilhon and N. Spyratos. Update Semantics of Relational Views. *ACM Trans. Database Syst.* (December 1981), 6(4): 557--575.

[Barbara and Imielinski, 1994] D. Barbara and T. Imielinski. Sleepers and Workaholics: Caching Strategies in Mobile Environments. In *Proc. ACM SIGMOD Int. Conf. on Management of Data*, May 1994, pp. 1--12.

[Barbara et al., 1986] D. Barbara, H. Garcia-Molina, and A. Spauster. Policies for Dynamic Vote Reassignment. In *Proc. IEEE Int. Conf. on Distributed Computing Systems*, May 1986, pp. 37--44.

[Barbara et al., 1989] D. Barbara, H. Garcia Molina, and A. Spauster. Increasing Availability Under Mutual Exclusion Constraints with Dynamic Voting Reassignment. *ACM Trans. Computer Syst.* (November 1989), 7(4): 394--426.

[Barker, 1990] K. Barker. *Transaction Management in Multidatabase Systems*, Ph.D. thesis, Edmonton, Canada: Department of Computing Science, University of Alberta, 1990.

[Barker and Özsu, 1988] K. Barker and M. T. Özsu. *A Survey of Issues in Distributed Heterogeneous Database Systems*. Technical Report TR88-9, Edmonton, Canada: Department of Computing Science, University of Alberta, 1988.

[Barker and Özsu, 1990] K. Barker and M. T. Özsu. Concurrent Transaction Execution in Multidatabase Systems. In *Proc. COMPSAC'90*, October 1990, pp. 224--233.

[Bartlett, 1978] J. Bartlett. A NonStop Operating System. In *Proc. 11th Hawaii Int. Conf. on System Sciences*, 1978, pp. 103--117.

[Bartlett, 1981] J. Bartlett. A NonStop Kernel. In *Proc. 8th ACM Symp. on Operating System Principles*, December 1981, pp. 22--29.

[Batini and Lenzirini, 1984] C. Batini and M. Lenzirini. A Methodology for Data Schema Integration in Entity-Relationship Model. *IEEE Trans. Software Eng.* (November 1984), SE-10(6): 650--654.

[Batini et al., 1986] C. Batini, M. Lenzirini, and S. B. Navathe. A Comparative Analysis of Methodologies for Database Schema Integration. *ACM Comput. Surv.* (December 1986), 18(4): 323--364.

[Bayer and McCreight, 1972] R. Bayer and E. McCreight. Organization and Maintenance of Large Ordered Indexes. *Acta Inf.* (1972), 1: 173--189.

[Beeri, 1990] C. Beeri. A Formal Approach to Object-Oriented Databases. *Data & Knowledge Eng.* (1990), 5: 353--382.

[Beeri et al., 1988] C. Beeri, H.-J. Schek, and G. Weikum. Multi-Level Transaction Management, Theoretical Art or Practical Need? In J.W. Schmidt, S. Ceri, and M. Missikof, editors, *Advances in Database Technology--EDBT'88*, Volume 303 of *Lecture Notes in Computer Science*, New York: Springer-Verlag, 1988: pp. 134--154.

[Beeri et al., 1989] C. Beeri, P. A. Bernstein, and N. Goodman. A Model for Concurrency in Nested Transaction Systems. *J. ACM* (April 1989), 36(2): 230--269.

[Bell and Grimson, 1992] D. Bell and J. Grimson. *Distributed Database Systems*. Reading, Mass.: Addison-Wesley, 1992.

[Bellatreche et al., 1998a] L. Bellatreche, K. Karlapalem, and Q. Li. Complex Methods and Class Allocation in Distributed Object Oriented Database Systems, Technical Report, HKUST98-yy, Department of Computer Science, Hong Kong Univeristy of Science and Technology, March 1998.

[Bellatreche et al., 1998b] L. Bellatreche, K. Karlapalem, and Q. Li. Algorithms and Support for Horizontal Class Partitioning in Object-Oriented Databases. *Distributed and Parallel Databases*, in press.

[Bellatreche et al., 1998c] L. Bellatreche, K. Karlapalem, and Q. Li. A Framework for Class Partitioning in Object Oriented Databases. *Distributed and Parallel Databases*, in press.

[Berenson et al., 1995] H. Berenson, P. Bernstein, J. Gray, J. Melton, E. O'Neil, and P. O'Neil. A Critique of ANSI SQL Isolation Levels. In *Proc. ACM SIGMOD Int. Conf. on Management of Data*, May 1995, pp. 1--10.

[Bergsten et al., 1991] B. Bergsten, M. Couprie, P. Valduriez. Prototyping DBS3, a Shared-Memory Parallel Database System. In *Proc. Int. Conf. on Parallel and Distributed Information Systems*, December 1991, pp. 226-234.

[Bergsten et al., 1992] B. Bergsten, M. Couprie, P. Valduriez. Overview of Parallel Architectures for Databases. *The Computer Journal* (1993) 36(8): 734-739.

[Berners-Lee et al., 1994] T. Berners-Lee, R. Cailliau, A. Luotonen, J. F. Nielsen, and A. Secret. The World-Wide Web. *Commun. ACM* (August 1994), 37(8): 76--82.

[Bernstein and Blaustein, 1982] P. Bernstein and B. Blaustein. Fast Methods for Testing Quantified Relational Calculus Assertions. In *Proc. ACM SIGMOD Int. Conf. on Management of Data*, June 1982, pp. 39--50.

[Bernstein and Chiu, 1981] P. A. Bernstein and D. M. Chiu. Using Semi-joins to Solve Relational Queries. *J. ACM* (January 1981), 28(1): 25--40.

[Bernstein and Goodman, 1981] P. A. Bernstein and N. Goodman. Concurrency Control in Distributed Database Systems. *ACM Comput. Surv.* (June 1981), 13(2): 185--222.

[Bernstein and Goodman, 1984] P. A. Bernstein and N. Goodman. An Algorithm for Concurrency Control and Recovery in Replicated Distributed Databases. *ACM Trans. Database Syst.* (December 1984), 9(4): 596--615.

[Bernstein and Goodman, 1985] P. A. Bernstein and N. Goodman. Serializability Theory for Replicated Databases. *J. Comput. Syst. Sci.* (December 1985), 31(3): 355--374.

[Bernstein and Newcomer, 1997] P. A. Bernstein and E. Newcomer. *Principles of Transaction Processing for the Systems Professional*. San Mateo, Calif.: Morgan Kaufmann, 1997.

[Bernstein et al., 1980a] P. Bernstein, B. Blaustein, and E. M. Clarke. Fast Maintenance of Semantic Integrity Assertions Using Redundant Aggregate Data. In *Proc. 6th Int. Conf. on Very Large Data Bases*, October 1980, pp. 126--136.

[Bernstein et al., 1980b] P. Bernstein, P.A. Shipman, and J. B. Rothnie. Concurrency Control in a System for Distributed Databases (SDD-1). *ACM Trans. Database Syst.* (March 1980), 5(1): 18--51.

[Bernstein et al., 1981] P. A. Bernstein, N. Goodman, E. Wong, C. L. Reeve, and J. B. Rothnie, Jr. Query Processing in a System for Distributed Databases (SDD-1). *ACM Trans. Database Syst.* (December 1981), 6(4): 602--625.

[Bernstein et al., 1987] P. A. Bernstein, V. Hadzilacos, and N. Goodman. *Concurrency Control and Recovery in Database Systems*. Reading, Mass.: Addison-Wesley, 1987.

[Bertino and Kim, 1989] E. Bertino and W. Kim. Indexing Techniques for Queries on Nested Objects. *IEEE Trans. Knowledge and Data Eng.* (June 1989), 1(2): 196--214.

[Bertino and Martino, 1993] E. Bertino and L. Martino. *Object-Oriented Database Systems*. Reading, Mass.: Addison-Wesley, 1993.

[Bevan, 1987] D. I. Bevan. Distributed Garbage Collection Using Reference Counting. In J. de Bakker, L. Nijman, and P. Treleaven, editors, *Parallel Architectures and Languages Europe*, Lecture Notes in Computer Science, Eindhoven, The Netherlands: Springer-Verlag, June 1987, pp. 117--187.

[Bhar and Barker, 1995] S. Bhar and K. Barker. Static Allocation in Distributed Object-base Systems: A Graphical Approach. In *Proc. 6th Int. Conf. on Information Systems and Data Management*, November 1995, pp. 92--114.

[Bhargava, 1987] B. Bhargava (ed.). *Concurrency Control and Reliability in Distributed Systems*. New York: Van Nostrand Reinhold, 1987.

[Bhargava and Lian, 1988] B. Bhargava and S.-R. Lian. Independent Checkpointing and Concurrent Rollback for Recovery in Distributed Systems: An Optimistic Approach. In *Proc. 7th Symp. on Reliable Distributed Systems*, October 1988, pp. 3--12.

[Bhide, 1988] A. Bhide. An Analysis of Three Transaction Processing Architectures. *Proc. ACM SIGMOD Int. Conf. on Management of Data*, June 1988, pp. 339--350.

[Bhide and Stonebraker, 1988] A. Bhide and M. Stonebraker. A Performance Comparison of Two Architectures for Fast Transaction Processing. In *Proc. 4th Int. Conf. on Data Engineering*, February 1988, pp. 536--545.

[Biliris and Panagos, 1995] A. Biliris and E. Panagos. A High Performance Configurable Storage Manager. In *Proc. 11th Int. Conf. on Data Engineering*, March 1995, pp. 35--43.

[Bitton et al., 1983] D. Bitton, H. Boral, D. J. DeWitt, and W. K. Wilkinson. Parallel Algorithms for the Execution of Relational Database Operations. *ACM Trans. Database Syst.* (September 1983), 8(3): 324--353.

[Blakeley, 1996] J. Blakeley. Data Access for the Masses Through OLE DB. In *Proc. ACM SIGMOD Int. Conf. on Management of Data*, June 1966, pp. 161--172.

[Blakeley et al., 1986] J. A. Blakeley, P.-A. Larson, and F. W. Tompa. Efficiently Updating Materialized Views. *Proc. ACM SIGMOD Int. Conf. on Management of Data*, May 1986, pp. 61--71.

[Blakeley et al., 1993] J. Blakeley, W. McKenna, and G. Graefe. Experiences Building the Open OODB Query Optimizer. In *Proc. ACM SIGMOD Int. Conf. on Management of Data*, May 1993, pp. 287--296.

[Blasgen et al., 1979] M. Blasgen, J. Gray, M. Mitoma, and T. Price. The Convoy Phenomenon. *ACM Oper. Syst. Rev.* (1979), 13(2): 20--25.

[Blaustein, 1981] B. Blaustein. *Enforcing Database Assertions: Techniques and Applications.* Ph.D. thesis, Cambridge, Mass.: Harvard University, August 1981.

[Bobrowski, 1996] S. Bobrowski. *Oracle 7 Server Concepts, Release 7.3*, Redwood City, Calif.: Oracle Corp., 1996.

[Bochmann, 1983] G. von Bochmann. *Concepts for Distributed Systems Design.* Berlin: Springer-Verlag, 1983.

[Bonnet, 1998] P. Bonnet and A. Tomasic. Partial Answers for Unavailable Data Sources. In *Proc. Workshop on Flexible Query-Answering Systems (FQAS'98)*, Department of Computer Science, Roskilde University, Preprint -- Final version to appear in Lecture Notes in Artificial Intelligence (Springer Verlag), 1998, pp. 43--54.

[Boral, 1988a] H. Boral. Parallelism and Data Management. In *Proc. 3rd Int. Conf. on Data and Knowledge Bases*, June 1988, pp. 362--373.

[Boral and DeWitt, 1983] H. Boral and D.J. DeWitt. Database Machines: An Idea Whose Time Has Passed? A Critique of the Future of Database Machines. In *Proc. 3rd Int. Workshop on Database Machines*, September 1983, pp. 166--187.

[Boral and Redfield, 1985] H. Boral and S. Redfield. Database Machine Morphology. In *Proc. 11th Int. Conf. on Very Large Data Bases*, August 1985, pp. 59--71.

[Boral et al., 1990] H. Boral, W. Alexander, L. Clay, G. Copeland, S. Danforth, M. Franklin, B. Hart, M. Smith, and P. Valduriez. Prototyping Bubba, A Highly Parallel Database System. *IEEE Trans. Knowledge and Data Eng.* (March 1990), 2(1): 4--24.

[Borg et al., 1983] A. Borg, J. Baumbach, and S. Glazer. A Message System Supporting Fault Tolerance. In *Proc. 9th ACM Symp. on Operating System Principles*, Bretton Woods, N.H., October 1983, pp. 90--99.

[Borr, 1984] A. Borr. Robustness to Crash in a Distributed Database: A Non Shared-Memory Multiprocessor Approach. In *Proc. 10th Int. Conf. on Very Large Data Bases*, August 1984, pp. 445--453.

[Borr, 1988] A. Borr. High Performance SQL through Low-Level System Integration. In *Proc. ACM SIGMOD Int. Conf. on Management of Data*, June 1988, pp. 342--349.

[Boudec, 1992] J-Y. Le Boudec. The Asynchronous Transfer Mode: A Tutorial. *Computer Networks and ISDN Systems* (1992), 24: 279--309.

[Bouganim et al., 1996a] L. Bouganim, B. Dageville, P. Valduriez. Adaptative Parallel Query Execution in DBS3. In *Advances in Database Technology--EDBT'96*, Berlin: Springer-Verlag, 1996, pp. 481--484

[Bouganim et al. 1996b] L. Bouganim, B. Dageville, D. Florescu. Skew Handling in the DBS3 Parallel Database System. In *Proc. International Conference on ACPC*, 1996.

[Bouganim et al., 1996c] L. Bouganim, D. Florescu, P. Valduriez. Dynamic Load Balancing in Hierarchical Parallel Database Systems. In *Proc. 22th Int. Conf. on Very Large Data Bases*, September 1996, pp. 436--447.

[Bouganim et al., 1999] L. Bouganim, D. Florescu, P. Valduriez. Multi-Join Query Execution with Skew in NUMA Multiprocessors. *Distributed and Parallel Databases* (1999), 7(1): in press.

[Bratbersengen, 1984] K. Bratbergsengen. Hashing Methods and Relational Algebra Operations. In *Proc. 10th Int. Conf. on Very Large Data Bases*, August 1984, pp. 323--333.

[Breitbart and Paolini, 1985] Y. Breitbart and P. Paolini. The Multidatabase Session Chairmen's Report. In F. A. Schreiber and W. Litwin (eds.), *Distributed Data Sharing Systems*, Amsterdam: North-Holland, 1985, pp. 3--6.

[Breitbart and Silberschatz, 1988] Y. Breitbart and A. Silberschatz. Multidatabase Update Issues, In *Proc. ACM SIGMOD Int. Conf. on Management of Data*, June 1988, pp. 135--142.

[Breitbart and Tieman, 1985] Y. Breitbart and L. Tieman. ADDS: Heterogeneous Distributed Database System. In F. A. Schreiber and W. Litwin (eds.), *Distributed Data Sharing Systems*, Amsterdam: North-Holland, 1985, pp. 7--24.

[Breitbart et al., 1987] Y. Breitbart, A. Silberschatz, and G. Thompson. An Update Mechanism for Multidatabase Systems. *IEEE Quart. Bull. Database Eng.* (September 1987), 10(3): 12--18.

[Breitbart et al., 1991] Y. Breitbart, D. Georgakopoulos, M. Rusinkiewicz, and A. Silberschatz. On Rigorous Transaction Scheduling. *IEEE Trans. Software Eng.* (September 1991), 17(9): 954--960.

[Breitbart et al., 1992a] Y. Breitbart, H. Garcia-Molina, and A. Silberschatz. Overview of Multidatabase Transaction Management. *VLDB Journal* (October 1992), 1(2): 181--293.

[Bright and Hurson, 1992] M. Bright and A. Hurson. A Taxonomy and Current Issues in Multidatabase Systems. *Computer* (March 1992), 25(3): 50--60.

[Brill et al., 1984] D. Brill, M. Templeton, and C. Yu. Distributed Query Processing Strategies in MERMAID: A Front-end to Data Management Systems. In *Proc. First Int. Conf. on Data Engineering*, 1984, pp. 211--218.

[Brockschmidt, 1995] K. Brockschmidt. *Inside OLE, 2nd edition*. Redmond, Wash.: Microsoft Press, 1995.

[Brodie, 1994] M. L. Brodie. The Promise of Distributed Computing and the Challenges of Legacy Information Systems. In [Dogac et al., 1994], pp. 251--269.

[Brodie and Schmidt, 1982] M. K. Brodie and J. W. Schmidt. Final Report of the ANSI/X3/SPARC DBS-SG Relational Database Task Group. *ACM SIGMOD Rec.* (July 1982), 12(4): i1--i62.

[Brodie and Stonebraker, 1995] M. Brodie and M. Stonebraker. *Migrating Legacy Systems: Gateways, Interfaces, and the Incremental Approach*, San Francisco: Morgan Kaufmann, 1995.

[Brzezinski et al., 1984] Z. Brzezinski, J. Getta, J. Rybnik, and W. Stepniewski. Unibase: An Integrated Access to Database. In *Proc. 10th Int. Conf. on Very Large Data Bases*, August 1984, pp. 388--400.

[Bucci and Golinelli, 1977] G. Bucci and S. Golinelli. A Distributed Strategy for Resource Allocation in Information Networks. In *Proc. Int. Computing Symp.*, 1977, pp. 345--356.

[Buchmann et al., 1992] A. Buchmann, M.T. Özsu, M. Hornick, D. Georgakopoulos, and F.A. Manola. A Transaction Model for Active Distributed Object Systems. In [Elmagarmid, 1982], pp. 123--158.

[Bukhres and Elmagarmid, 1996] *Object-Oriented Multidatabase Systems*, Englewood Cliffs, NJ: Prentice-Hall, 1996.

[Bukhres et al., 1995] O. Bukhres, M.T. Özsu and M.C. Shan (eds.). *Proc. Int. Workshop on Research Issues in Data Eng.*, IEEE CS Press, 1995.

[Buneman, 1997] P. Buneman, S. Davidson, M. Fernandez and D. Suciu. Adding Structure to Unstructured Data. In *Proc. 6th Int. Conf. on Database Theory*, Vol. 1186 of Lecture Notes in Computer Science, Springer-Verlag, January 1997, pp. 336-350.

[Butler, 1987] M. Butler. Storage Reclamation in Object Oriented Database Systems. In *Proc. of the ACM SIGMOD Int. Conf. on Management of Data*, May 1987, pp. 410--425.

[Bux et al., 1983] W. Bux, F. Closs, K. Kummerle, H. Keller, and H. Mueller. Architecture and Design of a Reliable Token-Ring Network. *IEEE J. Sel. Areas Commun.* (November 1983), SAC-1(5): 756--765.

[CCA, 1980] Computer Corporation of America. *A Component Architecture for Database Management Systems.* NBS-GCR-81-340, June 1980.

[CCA, 1982] Computer Corporation of America. *An Architecture for Database Management Standards.* NBS Special Publication 500--86, January 1982.

[Cai et al., 1997] J. Cai, K-L. Tan, and B. C. Ooi. On Incremental Cache Coherency Schemes in Mobile Computing Environments. In *Proc. 13th IEEE Int. Conf. on Data Eng.*, 1997, pages 114--123.

[Canaday et al., 1974] R. H. Canaday, R. D. Harrisson, E. L. Ivie, J. L. Rydery, and L. A. Wehr. A Back-End Computer for Data Base Management. *Commun. ACM* (October 1974), 17(10): 575--582.

[Cardenas, 1987] A. F. Cardenas. Heterogeneous Distributed Database Management: HD--DBMS. *Proc. IEEE* (May 1987), 75(5): 588--600.

[Carey and Livny, 1988] M. J. Carey and M. Livny. Distributed Concurrency Control Performance: A Study of Algorithms, Distribution and Replication. In *Proc. 14th Int. Conf. on Very Large Data Bases*, August 1988, pp. 13--25.

[Carey and Livny, 1991] M. J. Carey and M. Livny. Conflict Detection Tradeoffs for Replicated Data. *ACM Trans. Database Syst.* (December 1991), 16(4): 703--746.

[Carey and Stonebraker, 1984] M. Carey and M. Stonebraker. The Performance of Concurrency Control Algorithms for Database Management Systems. In *Proc. 10th Int. Conf. on Very Large Data Bases*, August 1984, pp. 107--118.

[Carey et al., 1991] M. J. Carey, M. Franklin, M. Livny, and E. Shekita. Data Caching Tradeoffs in Client-Server DBMS Architectures, In *Proc. ACM SIGMOD Int. Conf. on Management of Data*, May 1991, pp. 357--366.

[Carey et al., 1994] M. Carey, M. Franklin, and M. Zaharioudakis. Adaptive, Fine-Grained Sharing in a Client-Server OODBMS: A Callback-Based Approach. *ACM Trans. Database Syst.* (December 1997), 22(4): 570--627.

[Carey et al., 1994] M. J. Carey, D. J. DeWitt, M. J. Franklin, N. E. Hall, M. L. McAuliffe, J. F. Naughton, D. T. Schuh, M. H. Solomon, C. K. Tan, O. G. Tsatalos, S. J. White, M. J. Zwilling. Shoring Up Persistent Applications. In *Proc. ACM SIGMOD Int. Conf. on Management of Data*, June 1994, pp. 383--394.

[Cart and Ferrie, 1990] M. Cart and J. Ferrie. Integrating Concurrency Control Into an Object-Oriented Database System. In *Advances in Database Technology --- EDBT'90*, Berlin: Springer-Verlag, 1990, pp. 363--377.

[Casey, 1972] R. G. Casey. Allocation of Copies of a File in an Information Network. In *Proc. Spring Joint Computer Conf.*, 1972, pp. 617--625.

[Castro et al., 1997] M. Castro, A. Adya, B. Liskov, and A. Myers. HAC: Hybrid Adaptive Caching for Distributed Storage Systems. In *Proc. ACM Symp. on Operating System Principles*, 1997, pp. 102--115.

[Cattell, 1994] R.G.G. Cattell. *Object Data Management, 2nd edition*. Reading, Mass.: Addison-Wesley, 1994.

[Cattell, 1997] R. Cattell. *The Object Database Standard: ODMG-2.0*, San Francisco, Calif.: Morgan Kaufmann, 1997.

[Cellary et al., 1988] W. Cellary, E. Gelenbe and T. Morzy. *Concurrency Control in Distributed Database Systems*. Amsterdam: North--Holland, 1988.

[Ceri and Navathe, 1983] S. Ceri and S. B. Navathe. A Methodology for the Distribution Design of Databases. In *Digest of Papers--COMPCON*, 1983, pp. 426--431.

[Ceri and Owicki, 1982] S. Ceri and S. Owicki. On the Use of Optimistic Methods for Concurrency Control in Distributed Databases. In *Proc. 6th Berkeley Workshop on Distributed Data Management and Computer Networks*, February 1982, pp. 117--130.

[Ceri and Pelagatti, 1982] S. Ceri and G. Pelagatti. A Solution Method for the Nonadditive Resource Allocation Problem in Distributed System Design. *Inf. Process. Lett.* (October 1982), 15(4): 174--178.

[Ceri and Pelagatti, 1983] S. Ceri and G. Pelagatti. Correctness of Query Execution Strategies in Distributed Databases. *ACM Trans. Database Syst.* (December 1983), 8(4): 577--607.

[Ceri and Pelagatti, 1984] S. Ceri and G. Pelagatti. *Distributed Databases: Principles and Systems*. New York: McGraw-Hill, 1984.

[Ceri and Pernici, 1985] S. Ceri and B. Pernici. DATAID--D: Methodology for Distributed Database Design. In A. Albano, V. de Antonellis, and A. di Leva (eds.), *Computer-Aided Database Design*, Amsterdam: North-Holland, 1985: pp. 157--183.

[Ceri et al., 1982a] S. Ceri, M. Negri, and G. Pelagatti. Horizontal Data Partitioning in Database Design. In *Proc. ACM SIGMOD Int. Conf. on Management of Data*, June 1982, pp. 128--136.

[Ceri et al., 1982b] S. Ceri, G. Martella, and G. Pelagatti. Optimal File Allocation in a Computer Network: A Solution Method Based on the Knapsack Problem. *Comput. Networks* (1982), 6: pp. 345--357.

[Ceri et al., 1983] S. Ceri, S. Navathe, and G. Wiederhold. Distribution Design of Logical Database Schemes. *IEEE Trans. Software Eng.* (July 1983), SE-9(4): 487--503.

[Ceri et al., 1986] S. Ceri, G. Gottlob, and G. Pelagatti. Taxonomy and Formal Properties of Distributed Joins. *Inf. Syst.* (1986), 11(1): 25--40.

[Ceri et al., 1987] S. Ceri, B. Pernici, and G. Wiederhold. Distributed Database Design Methodologies. *Proc. IEEE* (May 1987), 75(5): 533--546.

[Chamberlin et al., 1975] D. Chamberlin, J. Gray, and I. Traiger. Views, Authorization and Locking in a Relational Database System. In *Proc. National Computer Conf.*, 1975, pp. 425--430.

[Chang and Cheng, 1980] S. K. Chang and W. H. Cheng. A Methodology for Structured Database Decomposition. *IEEE Trans. Software Eng.* (March 1980), SE-6(2): 205--218.

[Chang and Liu, 1982] S. K. Chang and A. C. Liu. File Allocation in a Distributed Database. *Int. J. Comput. Inf. Sci.* (1982), 11(5): 325--340.

[Chaudhuri and Dayal, 1997] S. Chaudhuri and U. Dayal. An Overview of Data Warehousing and OLAP Technology. *ACM SIGMOD Record*, (March 1997), 26(1): 65--74.

[Chen, 1976] P. P. S. Chen. The Entity-Relationship Model: Towards a Unified View of Data. *ACM Trans. Database Syst.* (March 1976), 1(1): 9--36.

[Chen et al., 1996] S. Chen, Y. Deng, P. Attie, and W. Sun. Optimal Deadlock Detection in Distributed Systems Based on Locally Constructed Wait-For Graphs. In *Proc. IEEE Int. Conf. Dist. Comp. Sys.*,May 1996, pp. 613--619.

[Cheng et al., 1984] J.M. Cheng et al., IBM Database 2 Performance : Design, Implementation and Tuning. *IBM Systems Journal* (MOIS 1984) 23(2): 189--210.

[Chiu and Ho, 1980] D. M. Chiu and Y. C. Ho. A Methodology for Interpreting Tree Queries into Optimal Semi-join Expressions. In *Proc. ACM SIGMOD Int. Conf. on Management of Data*, May 1980, pp. 169--178.

[Chou, 1985] H. T. Chou. *Buffer Management of Database Systems*. Ph.D. dissertation, Madison, Wis.: Department of Computer Science, University of Wisconsin, 1985.

[Chou and DeWitt, 1986] H. T. Chou and D. J. DeWitt. An Evaluation of Buffer Management Strategies for Relational Database Systems. *Algorithmica* (1986), 1(3): 311--336.

[Chrysanthis, 1993] P. K. Chrysanthis. Transaction Processing in Mobile Computing Environment. In *Proc. IEEE Workshop on Advances in Parallel and Distributed Systems*, October 1993, pages 77--82.

[Chu, 1969] W. W. Chu. Optimal File Allocation in a Multiple Computer System. *IEEE Trans. Comput.* (October 1969), C-18(10): 885--889.

[Chu, 1973] W. W. Chu. Optimal File Allocation in a Computer Network. In N. Abramson and F. F. Kuo (eds.), *Computer Communication Networks*, Englewood Cliffs, N.J.: Prentice-Hall, 1973, pp. 82--94.

[Chu, 1976] W. W. Chu. Performance of File Directory Systems for Data Bases in Star and Distributed Networks. In *Proc. National Computer Conf.*, 1976, pp. 577--587.

[Chu and Nahouraii, 1975] W. W. Chu and E. E. Nahouraii. File Directory Design Considerations for Distributed Databases. In *Proc. First Int. Conf. on Very Large Data Bases*, September 1975, pp. 543--545.

[Civelek et al., 1988] F.N. Civelek, A. Dogac, and S. Spaccapietra. An Expert System Approach to View Definition and Integration. In *Proc. 7th Int'l. Conf. on Entity-Relationship Approach*, November 1988, pp. 229--249.

[Cluet and Delobel, 1992] S. Cluet and C. Delobel. A General Framework for the Optimization of Object-Oriented Queries. In *Proc. ACM SIGMOD Int. Conf. on Management of Data*, June1992, pp. 383--392.

[Cluet et al., 1998] S. Cluet, C. Delobel, J. Simeon and K. Smaga. Your Mediators Need Data Conversion! In *Proc. ACM-SIGMOD Int. Conf. on Management of Data*, June 1997, pp. 177--188.

[Codd, 1970] E. F. Codd. A Relational Model for Large Shared Data Banks. *Commun. ACM* (October 1970), 13(6): 377--387.

[Codd, 1972] E. F. Codd. Relational Completeness of Data Base Sublanguages. In R. Rustin (ed.), *Data Base Systems*, Englewood Cliffs, N.J.: Prentice--Hall, 1972, pp. 65--98.

[Codd, 1974] E. F. Codd. Recent Investigations in Relational Data Base Systems. In *Information Processing '74*, 1974, pp. 1017--1021.

[Codd, 1979] E. F. Codd. Extending the Database Relational Model to Capture More Meaning. *ACM Trans. Database Syst.* (December 1979), 4(4): 397--434.

[Codd, 1982] E. F. Codd. Relational Databases: A Practical Foundation for Productivity, *Commun. ACM* (February 1982), 25(2): 109--117.

[Codd, 1995] E. Codd. Twelve Rules for On-Line Analytical Processing. *Computerworld*, April 13 1995.

[Cointe, 1987] P. Cointe. Metaclasses are First Class: The ObjVlisp Model. In *Proc. Int. Conf. on OOPSLA*, October 1987, pp. 156--167.

[Colliat, 1996] G. Colliat. Relational and Multidimensional Database Systems. *ACM SIGMOD Rec.*, (September 1996), 25(3): 64--69.

[Copeland and Maier, 1984] G. Copeland and D. Maier. Making SmallTalk a Database System. In *Proc. ACM SIGMOD Int. Conf. on Management of Data*, June 1984, pp. 316--325.

[Copeland et al., 1988] G. Copeland, W. Alexander, E. Bougherty, and T. Keller. Data Placement in Bubba. In *Proc. ACM SIGMOD Int. Conf. on Management of Data*, May 1988, pp. 99--108.

[Cristian, 1982] F. Cristian. Exception Handling and Software Fault Tolerance. *IEEE Trans. Comput.* (June 1982), C-31(6): 531--540.

[Cristian, 1985] F. Cristian. A Rigorous Approach to Fault--Tolerant Programming. *IEEE Trans. Software Eng.* (January 1985), SE-11(1): 23--31.

[Cristian, 1987] F. Cristian. *Exception Handling*. Technical Report RJ 5724, San Jose, Calif., IBM Almaden Research Laboratory, 1987.

[DAFTG, 1986] Database Architecture Framework Task Group. Reference Model for DBMS Standardization. *ACM SIGMOD Rec.* (March 1986), 15(1): 19--58.

[D'Oliviera, 1977] C. R. D'Oliviera. *An Analysis of Computer Decentralization.* Technical Memo TM-90, Cambridge, Mass.: Laboratory for Computer Science, Massachusetts Institute of Technology, 1977.

[Dadam and Schlageter, 1980] P. Dadam and G. Schlageter. Recovery in Distributed Databases Based on Non-synchronized Local Checkpoints. In *Information Processing '80*, 1980, pp. 457--462.

[Dageville et al. 1994] B. Dageville, P. Casadessus, P. Borla-Salamet. The Impact of the KSR1 AllCache Architecture on the Behavior of the DBS3 Parallel DBMS. In *Proc. International Conf. on Parallel Architectures and Language*, 1994.

[Dahlin et al., 1994] M. Dahlin, R. Wang, T. Anderson, and D. Patterson. Cooperative Caching: Using Remote Client Memory to Improve File System Performance. In *Proc. 1st USENIX Symp. on Operating Syst. Design and Imp.*, November 1994, pp. 267--280.

[Dar et al., 1996a] S. Dar, H. Jagadish, A. Levy and D. Srivastava. Answering Queries with Aggregation using Views. In *Proc. 22nd Int. Conf. on Very Large Data Bases*, September 1996, pp. 318--329.

[Dar et al., 1996b] S. Dar, M. J. Franklin, B. T. Jonsson, D. Srivatava, and M. Tan,. Semantic Data Caching and Replacement. In *Proc. 22nd Int. Conf. on Very Large Data Bases*, September 1996, pp. 318--329.

[Data General, 1997a] Data General Corporation. Data General and Oracle to Optimize Oracle Universal Server for ccNUMA System. Can be retrieved at *http://www.dg.com/news/press_releases/11_4_96.html*

[Data General, 1997b] Data General Corporation. The NUMA Invasion. Can be retrieved at *http://www.dg.com/newdocs1/ccnuma/iw1_6_97.html*

[Data General, 1997c] Data General Corporation. Standard High Volume Servers: The New Building Block. Can be retrieved at *http://www.dg.com/newdocs1/ccnuma/index.html#a*

[Date, 1983] C. J. Date. *An Introduction to Database Systems,* Volume 2. Reading, Mass.: Addison-Wesley, 1983.

[Date, 1984] C. J. Date. *Guide to DB2.* Reading, Mass.: Addison-Wesley, 1984.

[Date, 1986] C. J. Date. *An Introduction to Database Systems,* Volume 1 (4th edition). Reading, Mass.: Addison-Wesley, 1986.

[Date, 1987] C. J. Date. *A Guide to the SQL Standard.* Reading, Mass.: Addison-Wesley, 1987.

[Date and Darwen, 1998] C.J. Date and H. Darwen. *Foundation for Object/Relational Databases--The Third Manifesto*, Reading, Mass.: Addison-Wesley, 1998.

[Datta et al., 1997] A. Datta, A. Celik, J. Kim, D. E. VanderMeer, and and Vijay Kumar. Adaptive Broadcast Protocols to Support Power Conservant Retrieval by Mobile Users. In *Proc. 13th IEEE Int. Conf. on Data Engineering,*1997, pages 124--133.

[Davenport, 1981] R. A. Davenport. Design of Distributed Data Base Systems. *Comput. J.* (1981), 24(1): 31--41.

[Davidson, 1984] S. B. Davidson. Optimism and Consistency in Partitioned Distributed Database Systems. *ACM Trans. Database Syst.* (September 1984), 9(3): 456--481.

[Davidson et al., 1985] S. B. Davidson, H. Garcia--Molina, and D. Skeen. Consistency in Partitioned Networks. *ACM Comput. Surv.* (September 1985), 17(3): 341--370.

[Dawson, 1980] J. L. Dawson. A User Demand Model for Distributed Database Design. In *Digest of Papers--COMPCON*, 1980, pp. 211--216.

[Dayal, 1989] U. Dayal. Queries and Views in an Object-Oriented Data Model. In *Proc. 2nd Int. Workshop on Database Programming Languages*, June 1989, pp. 80--102.

[Dayal and Bernstein, 1978] U. Dayal and P. Bernstein. On the Updatability of Relational Views. In *Proc. 4th Int. Conf. on Very Large Data Bases*, September 1978, pp. 368--377.

[Dayal and Hwang, 1984] U. Dayal and H. Hwang. View Definition and Generalization for Database Integration in MULTIBASE: A System for Heterogeneous Distributed Database. *IEEE Trans. Software Eng.* (November 1984), SE-10(6): 628--644.

[Dayal et al., 1988] U. Dayal, A. Buchmann, and D. McCarthy. Rules Are Objects Too: A Knowledge Model for an Active Object-Oriented Database System. In *Advances in Object-Oriented Database Systems. Proc. of the 2nd Int. Workshop on Object-Oriented Database Systems*, 1988, pp. 129--143.

[Dayal et al., 1991] U. Dayal, M. Hsu, and R. Ladin. A Transactional Model for Long-Running Activities. In *Proc. 17th Int. Conf. on Very Large Databases*, 1991, pp. 113--122.

[DeWitt and Gerber, 1985] D. J. DeWitt and R. Gerber. Multi Processor Hash-Based Join Algorithms. In *Proc. 11th Int. Conf. on Very Large Data Bases*, August 1985, pp. 151--164.

[DeWitt and Gray, 1992] D. J. DeWitt and J. Gray. Parallel Database Systems: The Future of High Performance Database Systems. *Commun. ACM* (June 1992), 35(6): 85--98.

[DeWitt and Hawthorn, 1981] D. J. DeWitt, P. B. Hawthorn. A Performance Evaluation of Database Machine Architectures. In *Proc. 7th Int. Conf. on Very Large Data Bases*, September 1981, pp. 199--213.

[DeWitt et al., 1986] D. J. DeWitt, R. H. Gerber, G. Graek, M. L. Heytens, K. B. Kumar, and M. Muralikrishna. GAMMA: A High Performance Dataflow Database Machine. In *Proc. 12th Int. Conf. on Very Large Data Bases*, August 1986, pp. 228--237.

[DeWitt et al., 1990] D. J. DeWitt, P. Futtersack, D. Maier, and F. Velez. A Study of Three Alternative Workstation-Server Architectures for Object-Oriented Database Systems. In *Proc. 16th Int. Conf. on Very Large Data Bases*, August 1990, pp. 107--121.

[DeWitt et al., 1992] D.J. DeWitt, J.F. Naughton, D.A. Schneider, S. Seshadri . Practical Skew Handling in Parallel Joins. In *Proc. 22th Int. Conf. on Very Large Data Bases*, August 1992, pp. 27--40.

[Denning, 1968] P. J. Denning. The Working Set Model for Program Behavior. *Commun. ACM* (May 1968), 11(5): 323--333.

[Denning, 1980] P. J. Denning. Working Sets: Past and Present. *IEEE Trans. Software Eng.* (January 1980), SE-6(1): 64--84.

[Deux et al., 1991] O. Deux et al., The O₂ system. *Commun. of the ACM* (October 1991), 34(10): 34--48.

[Dickman, 1991] P. Dickman. *Distributed Object Management in a Non-Small Graph of Autonomous Networks With Few Failures.* PhD thesis, University of Cambridge, England, September 1991.

[Dickman, 1994] P. Dickman. The Bellerophon Project: A Scalable Object-Support Architecture Suitable for a Large OODBMS? In [Özsu et al., 1994a], pp. 287--299.

[Diffie and Hellman, 1976] W. Diffie and M. E. Hellman. New Directions in Cryptography. *IEEE Trans. Inf. Theory* (November 1976), IT--22(6): 644--654.

[Dogac and Ozkarahan, 1980] A. Dogac and E. A. Ozkarahan. A Generalized DBMS Implementation on a Database Machine. In *Proc. ACM SIGMOD Int. Conf. on Management of Data*, May 1980, pp. 133--143.

[Dogac et al., 1994] A. Dogac, M.T. Özsu, A. Biliris, and T. Sellis (eds.). *Advances in Object-Oriented Database Systems*, Berlin: Springer-Verlag, 1994.

[Dogac et al., 1996a] A. Dogac, C. Dengi, E. Kilic, G. Ozhan, F. Ozcan, S. Nural, C. Evrendilek, U. Halici, B. Arpinar, P. Koksal, N. Kesim, S. Mancuhan. A Multidatabase System Implementation on CORBA. In *Proc. 6th Int. Workshop on Res. Issues in Data Eng.*, February 1996, pp. 2--11.

[Dogac et al., 1996b] A. Dogac, U. Halici, E. Kilic, G. Ozhan, F. Ozcan, S. Nural, C. Dengi, S. Mancuhan, B. Arpinar, P. Koksal, C. Evrendilek. METU Interoperable Database System -- Demo Description. In *Proc. ACM SIGMOD Int. Conf. on Management of Data*, June 1996, pp. 552.

[Dogac et al., 1996c] F. Ozcan, S. Nural, P. Koksal, C. Evrendilek, A. Dogac. Dynamic Query Optimization on a Distributed Object Management Platform, In *Proc. 5th Int. Conf. on Information and Knowledge Management*, November 1996, pp. 117--124.

[Dogac et al., 1997] F. Ozcan, S. Nural, P. Koksal, C. Evrendilek, A. Dogac. Dynamic Query Optimization in Multidatabases. *IEEE Quar. Bull. Data Eng.* (September 1997), 20(3): 38--45.

[Dogac et al., 1998a] A. Dogac, L. Kalinichenko, M.T. Özsu, and A. Sheth (eds.). *Advances in Workflow Systems and Interoperability*, Berlin: Springer-Verlag, 1998.

[Dogac et al., 1998b] A. Dogac, C. Dengi, and M. T. Özsu. Distributed Object Computing Platforms. *Commun. ACM* (September 1998), 41(9): 95--103.

[Dollimore et al., 1994] J. Dollimore, C. Nascimento, and W. Xu. Fine-Grained Object Migration. In [Özsu et al., 1994a], pp. 182--186.

[Dowdy and Foster, 1982] L. W. Dowdy and D. V. Foster. Comparative Models of the File Assignment Problem. *ACM Comput. Surv.* (June 1982), 14(2): 287--313.

[Du and Elmagarmid, 1989] W. Du and A. Elmagarmid. Quasi-serializability: A Correctness Criterion for Global Concurrency Control in InterBase. In *Proc. 15th Int. Conf. on Very Large Data Bases*, August 1989, pp. 347--355.

[Du et al., 1989] W. Du, A. Elmagarmid, Y. Leu, and S. Ostermann. Effects of Local Autonomy on Global Concurrency Control in Heterogeneous Distributed Database Systems. In *Proc. Int. Conf. on Data and Knowledge Management for Manufacturing and Engineering*, 1989, pp. 113--120.

[Du et al., 1992] W. Du, R. Krishnamurthy, M.C. Shan. Query Optimization in a Heterogeneous DBMS. In *Proc. 18th Int. Conf. on Very Large Data Bases*, August 1992, pp. 277--291.

[Du et al., 1995] W. Du, M.C. Shan and U. Dayal. Reducing Multidatabase Query Response Time by Tree Balancing. In *Proc. ACM SIGMOD Int. Conf. on Management of Data*, May 1995, pp. 293--303.

[Dunham and Helal, 1995] M. H. Dunham and A. Helal. Mobile Computing and Databases: Anything New? *ACM SIGMOD Rec.* (December 1995), 24(4): 5--9.

[Dunham and Helal, 1997] M. H. Dunham, A. Helal, and S. Balakrishnan. A Mobile Transaction Model That Captures Both the Data and Movement Behavior, *ACM/Baltzer Journal on Special Topics in Mobile Networks and Applications* (1997), 2: 149--162.

[Dunham and Kumar, 1998] M. H. Dunham and V. Kumar. Location Dependent Data and its Management in Mobile Databases. In *Proc. Mobility in Databases and Distributed Systems Workshop at DEXA '98*, August 1998, pp. 414--419.

[Dwork and Skeen, 1983] C. Dwork and D. Skeen. The Inherent Cost of Nonblocking Commitment. In *Proc. 2nd ACM SIGACT--SIGOPS Symp. on Principles of Distributed Systems*, August 1983, pp. 1--11.

[Dwyer and Larson, 1987] P. Dwyer and J. L. Larson. Some Experiences with a Distributed Database Testbed System. *Proc. IEEE* (May 1987), 75(5): 633--648.

[Dwyer et al., 1986] P. Dwyer; K. Kasravi and M. Pham *A Heterogeneous Distributed Database Management System (DDTS/RAM)*. Report CSC-86-7:8216, Golden Valley, Minn.: Honeywell Corporate Research Center, 1986.

[EDS, 1990] European Declarative System (EDS) Database Group. EDS-Collaborating for a High-Performance Parallel Relational Database. In *Proc. ESPRIT Conf.*, November 1990, pp. 274--295.

[Eager and Sevcik, 1983] D. L. Eager and K. C. Sevcik. Achieving Robustness in Distributed Database Systems. *ACM Trans. Database Syst.* (September 1983), 8(3): 354--381.

[Eckerson, 1994] W. Eckerson. Data Warehouses: Product Requirements, Architectures and Implementation Strategies. In *Open Information Systems*, Patricia Seybold, 9(8), August 1994.

[Effelsberg and Härder, 1984] W. Effelsberg and T. Härder. Principles of Database Buffer Management. *ACM Trans. Database Syst.* (December 1984), 9(4): 560--595.

[Eich, 1989] M.H. Eich, Main Memory Database Research Directions. In *Int. Workshop on Database Machines*, June 1989, pp. 251-268.

[Eickler et al., 1995] A. Eickler, C. Gerlhof, and D. Kossmann. A Performance Evaluation of OID Mapping Techniques. In *Proc. 21st Int. Conf. on Very Large Data Bases*, September 1995, pp. 18--29.

[Eisner and Severance, 1976] M. J. Eisner and D. G. Severance. Mathematical Techniques for Efficient Record Segmentation in Large Shared Databases. *J. ACM* (October 1976), 23(4): 619--635.

[Elkind, 1982] S. A. Elkind. Reliability and Availability Techniques. In [Siewiorek and Swarz, 1982], pp. 63--181.

[Elmagarmid, 1986] A. K. Elmagarmid. A Survey of Distributed Deadlock Detection Algorithms. *ACM SIGMOD Rec.* (September 1986), 15(3): 37--45.

[Elmagarmid, 1990] A. Elmagarmid, Y. Leu, W. Litwin, and M. Rusinkiewicz. A Multidatabase Transaction Model for InterBase. In *Proc. 16th Int. Conf. on Very Large Databases*, 1990, pp. 507--518.

[Elmagarmid, 1992] A.K. Elmagarmid (ed.). *Transaction Models for Advanced Database Applications*. San Mateo, Calif.: Morgan Kaufmann, 1992.

[Elmagarmid and Du, 1990] A. K. Elmagarmid and W. Du. A Paradigm for Concurrency Control in Heterogeneous Database Systems. In *Proc. 6th Int. Conf. on Data Engineering*, February 1990, pp. 347--355.

[Elmagarmid and Helal, 1986] A. K. Elmagarmid and A. A. Helal. *Heterogeneous Database Systems*. Technical Report TR-86-004, University Park, Pa.: Program of Computer Engineering, Pennsylvania State University, 1986.

[Elmagarmid et al., 1988] A. K. Elmagarmid, N. Soundararajan, and M. T. Liu. A Distributed Deadlock Detection and Resolution Algorithm and Its Correctness Proof. *IEEE Trans. Software Eng.* (October 1988), 14(10): 1443--1452.

[Elmagarmid et al., 1999] A. Elmagarmid, M. Rusinkiewicz, and A. Sheth (eds.). *Management of Heterogeneous and Autonomous Database Systems*, San Francisco: Morgan Kaufmann, 1999.

[Elmasri and Navathe, 1994] R. Elmasri and S. B. Navathe. *Fundamentals of Database Systems, 2nd edition*. Menlo Park, Calif.: Benjamin-Cummings, 1994.

[Elmasri et al., 1987] R. Elmasri, J. Larson, and S. B. Navathe. *Integration Algorithms for Database and Logical Database Design*. Technical Report, Golden Valley, Minn.: Honeywell Corporate Research Center, 1987.

[Enderton, 1972] H. B. Enderton. *A Mathematical Introduction to Logic*. New York: Academic Press, 1972.

[Epstein and Stonebraker, 1980] R. Epstein and M. Stonebraker. Analysis of Distributed Data Base Processing Strategies. In *Proc. 5th Int. Conf. on Very Large Data Bases*, October 1980, pp. 92--101.

[Epstein et al., 1978] R. Epstein, M. Stonebraker, and E. Wong. Query Processing in a Distributed Relational Database System. In *Proc. ACM SIGMOD Int. Conf. on Management of Data*, May 1978, pp. 169--180.

[Eswaran, 1974] K. P. Eswaran. Placement of Records in a File and File Allocation in a Computer Network. In *Information Processing '74*, 1974, pp. 304--307.

[Eswaran et al., 1976] K. P. Eswaran, J. N. Gray, R. A. Lorie, and I. L. Traiger. The Notions of Consistency and Predicate Locks in a Database System. *Commun. ACM* (November 1976), 19(11): 624--633.

[Evrendilek et al., 1997] C. Evrendilek, A. Dogac, S. Nural, and F. Ozcan. Multidatabase Query Optimization. *Distributed and Parallel Database* (1997), 5(1): 77--114.

[Ezeife and Barker, 1995] C. I. Ezeife and K. Barker. A Comprehensive Approach to Horizontal Class Fragmentation in a Distributed Object Based System. *Distributed and Parallel Databases* (July 1995), 3(3): 247--272.

[Ezeife and Barker, 1998] C. I. Ezeife and K. Barker. Distributed Object Based Design: Vertical Fragmentation of Classes. *Distributed and Parallel Databases* (October 1998), 6(4): 327--360.

[Fagin, 1977] R. Fagin. Multivalued Dependencies and a New Normal Form for Relational Databases. *ACM Trans. Database Syst.* (September 1977), 2(3): 262--278.

[Fagin, 1978] R. Fagin. On an Authorization Mechanism. *ACM Trans. Database Syst.* (December 1978), 3(4): 310--320.

[Fagin, 1979] R. Fagin. Normal Forms and Relational Database Operators. In *Proc. ACM SIGMOD Int. Conf. on Management of Data*, May 1979, pp. 153--160.

[Fagin and Vardi, 1984] R. Fagin and M. Y. Vardi. *The Theory of Data Dependencies: A Survey*. Research Report RJ 4321 (47149), San Jose, Calif.: IBM Research Laboratory, June 1984.

[Fang et al., 1994] D. Fang, J. Hammer, and D. McLeod. An Approach to Behavior Sharing in Federated Database Systems. In [Özsu et al., 1994a], pp. 334--346.

[Farrag, 1986] A. Farrag. *Concurrency and Consistency in Database Systems*. Ph.D. thesis, Edmonton, Canada: Department of Computing Science, University of Alberta, 1986.

[Farrag and Özsu, 1985] A. A. Farrag and M. T. Özsu. A General Concurrency Control for Database Systems. In *Proc. National Computer Conf.*, New York, July 1985, pp. 567--573.

[Farrag and Özsu, 1987] A. A. Farrag and M. T. Özsu. Towards a General Concurrency Control Algorithm for Database Systems. *IEEE Trans. Software Eng.* (October 1987), 13(10): 1073--1079.

[Farrag and Özsu, 1989] A. A. Farrag and M. T. Özsu. Using Semantic Knowledge of Transactions to Increase Concurrency. *ACM Trans. on Database Syst.* (December 1989), 14(4): 503--525.

[Fekete et al., 1987a] A. Fekete, N. Lynch, M. Merritt, and W. Weihl. *Nested Transactions and Read/Write Locking*. Technical Memo MIT/LCS/TM--324, Cambridge, Mass.: Massachusetts Institute of Technology, April 1987.

[Fekete et al., 1987b] A. Fekete, N. Lynch, M. Merritt, and W. Weihl. *Nested Transactions, Conflict-Based Locking, and Dynamic Atomicity*. Technical Memo MIT/LCS/TM--340, Cambridge, Mass.: Massachusetts Institute of Technology, September 1987.

[Fekete et al., 1989] A. Fekete, N. Lynch, M. Merritt, and W. Weihl. *Commutativity-Based Locking for Nested Transactions*. Technical Memo MIT/LCS/TM-370b, Cambridge, Mass.: Massachusetts Institute of Technology, October 1989.

[Ferber, 1989] J. Ferber. Computational Reflection in Class Based Object-Oriented Languages. In *Proc. Int. Conf. on OOPSLA*, October 1989, pp. 317--326.

[Fernandez et al., 1981] E. B. Fernandez, R. C. Summers, and C. Wood. *Database Security and Integrity*. Reading, Mass.: Addison-Wesley, 1981.

[Fernandez et al., 1998] M. Fernandez, D. Florescu, J. Kang, A. Levy and D. Suciu. Catching the Boat with Strudel: A Web-site Management System. In *Proc. ACM-SIGMOD Int. Conf. on the Management of Data*, June 1998, pp. 549--552.

[Ferreira and Shapiro, 1994] P. Ferreira and M. Shapiro. Garbage Collection and DSM Consistency. In *Proc. of the First Symposium on Operating Systems Design and Implementation*, November 1994, pp. 229--241.

[Ferrier and Stangret, 1982] A. Ferrier and C. Stangret. Heterogeneity in the Distributed Data Management System SIRIUS-DELTA. In *Proc. 8th Int. Conf. on Very Large Data Bases*, September 1982, pp. 45--53.

[Fessant et al., 1998] F. Le Fessant, I. Piumarta, and M. Shapiro. An Implementation of Complete, Asynchronous, Distributed Garbage Collection. In *Proc. ACM SIGPLAN Conf. on Programming Language Design and Implementation*, June 1998, pp. 152--161.

[Finkelstein, 1995] R. Finkelstein. Multidimensional Databases : Where Relational Fears to Tread. *Database Programming & Design* (April 1995).

[Fisher and Hochbaum, 1980] M. K. Fisher and D. S. Hochbaum. Database Location in Computer Networks. *J. ACM* (October 1980), 27(4): 718--735.

[Fisher et al., 1980] P. S. Fisher, P. Hollist, and J. Slonim. A Design Methodology for Distributed Data Bases. In *Digest of Papers--COMPCON*, 1980, pp. 199--202.

[Florentin, 1974] J. J. Florentin. Consistency Auditing of Databases. *Comput. J.* (1974), 17(1): 52--58.

[Florescu et al., 1997] D. Florescu, D. Koller and A. Levy. Using Probabilistic Information in Data Integration. In *Proc. 23rd Int. Conf. on Very Large Data Bases*, September 1997, pp. 216--225.

[Foote and Robson, 1989] B. Foote and R. E. Johnson. Reflective Facilities in Smalltalk-80. In *Proc. Int. Conf. on OOPSLA*, October 1989, pp. 327--335.

[Forman and Zahorjan, 1994] G. H. Forman and J. Zahorjan. The Challenges of Mobile Computing. *Computer* (April 1994), 27(4): 38--47.

[Foster and Browne, 1976] D. Foster and J. C. Browne. File Assignment in Memory Hierarchies. In E. Gelenbe (ed.), *Modelling and Performance Evaluation of Computer Systems*, Amsterdam: North-Holland, 1976: pp. 119--127.

[Frank et al., 1993] S. Frank, H. Burkhardt, J. Rothnie. The KSR1: Bridging the Gap Between Shared-Memory and MPPs. In *Digest of Papers--COMPCON*, February 1993, pp. 285--294.

[Franklin and Carey, 1994] M. J. Franklin and M. J. Carey. Client-Server Caching Revisited. In [Özsu et al., 1994a], pp. 57--78.

[Franklin and Zdonik, 1997] M. Franklin and S. Zdonik. A Framework for Scalable Dissemination-Based Systems. In *Proc. Int. Conf. on OOPSLA*, October 1997, pp. 94--105.

[Franklin and Zdonik, 1998] M. Franklin and S. Zdonik. "Data In Your Face": Push Technology in Perspective. In *Proc. ACM SIGMOD Int. Conf. on Management of Data*, June 1998, pp. 516--519.

[Franklin et al., 1992b] M. J. Franklin, M. Carey, and M. Livny. Global Memory Management in Client-Server DBMS Architectures. In *Proc. 18th Int. Conf. on Very Large Data Bases*, August 1992, pp. 596--609.

[Franklin et al., 1996] M. J. Franklin, B. T. Jonsson, D. Kossman. Performance Tradeoffs for Client-Server Query Processing. In *Proc. ACM SIGMOD Int. Conf. on Management of Data*, June 1996, pp. 149--160.

[Franklin et al., 1997] M. Franklin, M. Livny, and M. Carey. Transactional Client-Server Cache Consistency: Alternatives and Performance. *ACM Trans. Database Syst.* (September 1997), 22(3): 315--367.

[Freeley et al., 1995] M. Freeley, W. Morgan, F. Pighin, et al. Implementing Global Memory Management in a Workstation Cluster. In *Proc. 15th ACM Symp. on Operating Syst. Principles*, December 1995, pp. 201--212.

[Freytag, 1987] J. C. Freytag. A Rule-Based View of Query Optimization. In *Proc. ACM SIGMOD Int. Conf. on Management of Data*, May 1987, pp. 173--180.

[Freytag et al., 1994] J. C. Freytag, D. Maier, and G. Vossen. *Query Processing for Advanced Database Systems*, San Mateo, Calif.: Morgan Kaufmann, 1994.

[Fung et al., 1996] C. W. Fung, K. Karlaplem, and Q. Li. An Analytical Approach Towards Evaluating Method Induced Vertical Partitioning Algorithms. Technical Report, HKUST96-33, Department of Computer Science, Hong Kong University of Science and Technology, August 1996.

[Fung et al., 1997] C. W. Fung, K. Karlapalem, and Q. Li. Cost-Driven Evaluation of Vertical Class Partitioning in Object-Oriented Databases. In *Proc. 5th Int. Conf. on Database Systems for Advanced Applications*, April 1997, pp. 11--20.

[Fushimi et al., 1986] S. Fushimi, M. Kitsuregawa and H. Tanaka. An Overview of the System Software of a Parallel Relational Database Machine GRACE. In *Proc. 12th Int. Conf. on Very Large Data Bases*, August 1986, pp. 209--219.

[GE, 1976] General Electric Research and Development Center. *MADMAN User Manual*. Schenectady, N.Y.: General Electric Company, 1976.

[Gallaire et al., 1984] H. Gallaire, J. Minker, and J.-M. Nicolas. Logic and Databases: A Deductive Approach. *ACM Comput. Surv.* (June 1984), 16(2): 153--186.

[Ganguly et al., 1992] S. Ganguly, W. Hasan, and R. Krishnamurty. Query Optimization for Parallel Execution. In *Proc. ACM SIGMOD Int. Conf. on Management of Data*, June 1992, pp. 9--18.

[Garcia-Molina, 1979] H. Garcia--Molina. *Performance of Update Algorithms for Replicated Data in a Distributed Database*. Ph.D. thesis, Stanford, Calif.: Department of Computer Science, Stanford University, 1979.

[Garcia-Molina, 1982] H. Garcia--Molina. Elections in Distributed Computing Systems. *IEEE Trans. Comput.* (January 1982), C-31(1): 48--59.

[Garcia-Molina, 1983] H. Garcia--Molina. Using Semantic Knowledge for Transaction Processing in a Distributed Database. *ACM Trans. Database Syst.* (June 1983), 8(2): 186--213.

[Garcia-Molina and Salem, 1987] H. Garcia-Molina and K. Salem. Sagas. In *Proc. ACM SIGMOD Int. Conf. on Management of Data*, 1987, pp. 249--259.

[Garcia-Molina and Wiederhold, 1982] H. Garcia--Molina and G. Wiederhold. Read--Only Transactions in a Distributed Database. *ACM Trans. Database Syst.* (June 1982), 7(2): 209--234.

[Garcia-Molina et al., 1990] H. Garcia-Molina, D. Gawlick, J. Klein, K. Kleissner, and K. Salem. Coordinating Multi-Transaction Activities. Technical Report CS-TR-247-90, Department of Computer Science, Princeton University, February 1990.

[Gardarin and Valduriez, 1989] G. Gardarin and P. Valduriez. *Relational Databases and Knowledge Bases*. Reading, Mass.: Addison--Wesley, 1989.

[Garofalakis and Ioanidis, 1996] M. N. Garofalakis, Y. E. Ioannidis. Multi-dimensional Resource Scheduling for Parallel Queries. In *Proc. ACM SIGMOD Int. Conf. on Management of Data*, June 1996, pp. 365--376.

[Garrett, 1996] M. W. Garrett. A Service Architecture for ATM: From Applications to Scheduling. *IEEE Network Magazine* (May 1996).

[Garza and Kim, 1988] J. F. Garza and W. Kim. Transaction Management in an Object-Oriented Database System. In *Proc. ACM SIGMOD Int. Conf. on Management of Data*, June 1988, pp. 37--45.

[Gastonian, 1983] R. Gastonian. The Auragen System 4000. *IEEE Quart. Bull. Database Eng.* (June 1983), 6(2).

[Gavish and Pirkul, 1986] B. Gavish and H. Pirkul. Computer and Database Location in Distributed Computer Systems. *IEEE Trans. Comput.* (July 1986), C-35(7): 583--590.

[Gelenbe and Gardy, 1982] E. Gelenbe and D. Gardy. The Size of Projections of Relations Satisfying a Functional Dependency. In *Proc. 8th Int. Conf. on Very Large Data Bases*, September 1982, pp. 325--333.

[Gelenbe and Sevcik, 1978] E. Gelenbe and K. Sevcik. Analysis of Update Synchronization for Multiple Copy Databases. In *Proc. 3rd Berkeley Workshop on Distributed Data Management and Computer Networks*, August 1978, pp. 69--88.

[Georgakopoulos, 1990] D. Georgakopoulos. *Transaction Management in Multidatabase Systems*. PhD thesis, Department of Computer Science, University of Houston, 1990.

[Georgakopoulos et al., 1991] D. Georgakopoulos, M. Rusinkiewicz, and A. Sheth. On Serializability of Multidatabase Transactions Through Forced Local Conflicts. In *Proc. 7th Int. Conf. on Data Engineering*, April 1991, pp. 314--323.

[Georgakopoulos et al., 1995] D. Georgakopoulos, M. Hornick and A. Sheth. An Overview of Workflow Management: From Process Modeling to Workflow Automation Infrastructure. *Distributed and Parallel Databases* (1995), 3: 119--153.

[Gerlhof and Kemper, 1994] C. Gerlhof and A. Kemper. A Multi-Threaded Architecture for Prefetching in Object Bases. In M. Jarke, J. A. Bubenko Jr., and K. G. Jeffery (editors): *Advances in Database Technology--EDBT'94, Lecture Notes in Computer Science, Vol. 779*, Berlin: Springer, 1994, pp. 351--364.

[Ghemawat, 1995] S. Ghemawat. *The Modified Object Buffer: A Storage Management Technique for Object-Oriented Databases*. Ph.D. dissertation, Cambridge, Mass.: Massachusetts Institute of Technology, 1995.

[Gibbons, 1976] T. Gibbons. *Integrity and Recovery in Computer Systems*. Manchester, England, NCC Publications, 1976.

[Gifford, 1979] D. K. Gifford. Weighted Voting for Replicated Data. In *Proc. 7th ACM Symp. on Operating System Principles*, December 1979, pp. 150--159.

[Gligor and Luckenbaugh, 1984] V. D. Gligor and G. L. Luckenbaugh. Interconnecting Heterogeneous Database Management Systems. *Computer* (January 1984), 17(1): 33--43.

[Gligor and Popescu--Zeletin, 1986] V. Gligor and R. Popescu--Zeletin. Transaction Management in Distributed Heterogeneous Database Management Systems. *Inf. Syst.* (1986), 11(4): 287--297.

[Goldberg and Robson, 1983] A. Goldberg and D. Robson. *SmallTalk-80: The Language and Its Implementation*. Reading, Mass.: Addison--Wesley, 1983.

[Goldman, 1987] K. J. Goldman. *Data Replication in Nested Transaction Systems*. Technical Report MIT/LCS/TR-390, Cambridge, Mass.: Massachusetts Institute of Technology, May 1987.

[Goldman 1997] R. Goldman and J. Widom. DataGuides : Enabling Query Formulation and Optimization in Semistructured Databases. In *Proc. 23rd Int. Conf. on Very Large Data Bases*, September 1997, pp.436--445.

[Goldring, 1995] R. Goldring. Things Every Update Replication Customer Should Know. In *Proc. ACM SIGMOD Int. Conf. on Management of Data*, May 1995, pp. 439--440.

[Goodman, 1991] D. J. Goodman. Trends in Cellular and Cordless Communications. *IEEE Communications Magazine* (June 1991), 29(6):31--40.

[Goodman and Woest, 1988] J. R. Goodman, P. J. Woest. The Wisconsin Multicube: A New Large-Scale Cache-Coherent Multiprocessor. Technical Report TR766, University of Wisconsin-Madison, April 1988.

[Goodman et al., 1983] N. Goodman, R. Suri, and Y. C. Tay. A Simple Analytic Model for Performance of Exclusive Locking in Database Systems. In *Proc. 2nd ACM SIGACT--SIGMOD Symp. on Principles of Database Systems*, March 1983, pp. 203--215.

[Graefe, 1990] G. Graefe. Encapsulation of Parallelism in the Volcano Query Processing Systems. In *Proc. ACM SIGMOD Int. Conf. on Management of Data*, May 1990, pp. 102--111.

[Graefe, 1993] G. Graefe. Query Evaluation Techniques for Large Databases. *ACM Comp. Surv.* (June 1993), 25(2): 73--170.

[Graefe and DeWitt, 1987] G. Graefe and D. DeWitt. The EXODUS Optimizer Generator. In *Proc. ACM SIGMOD Int. Conf. on Management of Data*, May 1987, pp. 160--172.

[Graefe and Maier, 1988] G. Graefe and D. Maier. Query optimization in Object-Oriented Database Systems: The REVELATION Project. Technical Report CS/E 88-025, Oregon Graduate Center, 1988.

[Graefe and McKenna, 1993] G. Graefe and W. McKenna. The Volcano Optimizer Generator. In *Proc. 9th Int. Conf. on Data Engineering*, April 1993, pp. 209--218.

[Graefe and Ward, 1989] G. Graefe and K. Ward. Dynamic Query Evaluation Plans. In *Proc. ACM SIGMOD Int. Conf. on Management of Data*, 1989, pp. 358--366.

[Grant, 1984] J. Grant. Constraint Preserving and Lossless Database Transformations. *Inf. Syst.* (1984), 9(2): 139--146.

[Grapa and Belford, 1977] E. Grapa and G. G. Belford. Some Theorems to Aid in Solving the File Allocation Problem. *Commun. ACM* (November 1977), 20(11): 878--882.

[Gray, 1979] J. N. Gray. Notes on Data Base Operating Systems. In R. Bayer, R. M. Graham, and G. Seegmüller (eds.), *Operating Systems: An Advanced Course*, New York: Springer-Verlag, 1979, pp. 393--481.

[Gray, 1981] J. Gray. The Transaction Concept: Virtues and Limitations. In *Proc. 7th Int. Conf. on Very Large Data Bases*, September 1981, pp. 144--154.

[Gray, 1985] J. Gray. *Why Do Computers Stop and What Can Be Done About It*. Technical Report 85-7, Cupertino, Calif.: Tandem Computers, 1985.

[Gray, 1987] J. Gray. *Why Do Computers Stop and What Can Be Done About It*. Tutorial Notes, CIPS (Canadian Information Processing Society) Edmonton '87 Conf., Edmonton, Canada, November 1987.

[Gray, 1989] J. Gray. *Transparency in its Place--The Case Against Transparent Access to Geographically Distributed Data*. Technical Report TR89.1, Cupertino, Calif.: Tandem Computers Inc., 1989.

[Gray, 1993] J. Gray (editor). *The Benchmark Handbook for Database and Transaction Processing Systems*. 2nd edition. San Francisco, Calif.: Morgan Kaufmann, 1993.

[Gray and Reuter, 1993] J. Gray and A. Reuter. *Transaction Processing: Concepts and Techniques*. San Mateo, Calif.: Morgan Kaufmann, 1993.

[Gray et al., 1976] J. N. Gray, R. A. Lorie, G. R. Putzolu, and I. L. Traiger. Granularity of Locks and Degrees of Consistency in a Shared Data Base. In G. M. Nijssen (ed.), *Modelling in Data Base Management Systems*, Amsterdam: North-Holland, 1976, pp. 365--394.

[Gray et al., 1981] J. N. Gray, P. McJones, M. Blasgen, B. Lindsay, R. Lorie, T. Price, F. Putzolu, and I. Traiger. The Recovery Manager of the System R Database Manager. *ACM Comput. Surv.* (June 1981), 13(2): 223--242.

[Gray et al. 1996] J. Gray, P. Helland, P. O'Neil, and D. Shasha. The danger of replication and a solution. *ACM SIGMOD Int. Conf on Management of Data*, June 1996, pp. 173--182.

[Griffin and Libkin, 1995] T. Griffin and L. Libkin. Incremental Maintenance of Views with Duplicates. In *Proc. ACM SIGMOD Int. Conf. on Management Data.*, May 1995, pp. 328--339.

[Griffiths and Wade, 1976] P. P. Griffiths and B. W. Wade. An Authorization Mechanism for a Relational Database System. *ACM Trans. Database Syst.* (September 1976), 1(3): 242--255.

[Gupta et al., 1995] A. Gupta, V. Harinarayan, and D. Quass. Aggregate Query Processing in Data Warehouses. In *Proc. 21st Int. Conf. on Very Large Data Bases*, August 1995, pp. 358--369.

[Guttag, 1977] J. Guttag. Abstract Data Types and the Development of Data Structures. *Commun. ACM* (June 1977), 20(6): 396--404.

[Haas et al., 1997] L. Haas, D. Kossmann, E. Wimmers and J. Yang. Optimizing Queries across Diverse Data Sources. In *Proc. 23rd Int. Conf. on Very Large Data Bases*, September 1997, pp. 276--285.

[Hadzilacos, 1988] V. Hadzilacos. A Theory of Reliability in Database Systems. *J. ACM* (January 1988), 35(1): 121--145.

[Hadzilakos and Hadzilakos, 1991] T. Hadzilacos and V. Hadzilacos. Transaction Synchroniation in Object Bases. *Journal of Computer and System Sciences* (August 1991), 43(1):2--24.

[Haessig and Jenny, 1980] K. Haessig and C. J. Jenny. *An Algorithm for Allocating Computational Objects in Distributed Computing Systems*. Research Report RZ 1016, Zurich: IBM Research Laboratory, June 1980.

[Hagersten et al., 1992] E. Hagersten, E. Landin, S Haridi. Ddm - a Cache-Only Memory Architecture. *Computer* (September 1992), 25(9): pp.44--54.

[Halici and Dogac, 1989] U. Halici and A. Dogac. Concurrency Control in Distributed Databases through Time Intervals and Short-Term Locks. *IEEE Trans. Software Eng.* (August 1989), 15(8): 994--995.

[Halsall, 1988] F. Halsall. *Data Communications, Computer Networks and OSI* (2nd edition). Wokingham, Berkshire, England: Addison--Wesley, 1988.

[Hammer and Niamir, 1979] M. Hammer and B. Niamir. A Heuristic Approach to Attribute Partitioning. In *Proc. ACM SIGMOD Int. Conf. on Management of Data*, May 1979, pp. 93--101.

[Hammer and Shipman, 1980] M. Hammer and D. W. Shipman. Reliability Mechanisms for SDD-1: A System for Distributed Databases. *ACM Trans. Database Syst.* (December 1980), 5(4): 431--466.

[Hammer et al., 1995a] J. Hammer, H. Garcia-Molina, J. Widom, W. Labio and Y. Zhuge. The Stanford Data Warehousing Project. In *IEEE Quart. Bull. Data Eng.* (June 1995), 18(2): 41--48.

[Hammer et al., 1995b] J. Hammer, H. Garcia-Molina, K. Ireland, Y. Papakonstantinou, J. Ullman, and J. Widom. Information Translation, Mediation, and Mosaic-Based Browsing in the TSIMMIS System. In *Proc. ACM SIGMOD Int. Conf. on Management Data.*, May 1995, pp. 483.

[Han and Fisher, 1983] M. J. Han and P. S. Fisher. The Problems of Data Structure and Application Software Conversion in a Heterogeneous Environment. In P. S. Fisher, J. Slonim, and E. A. Unger (eds.), *Advances in Distributed Processing Management,* Volume 2, Chichester, West Sussex, England: Wiley, 1983, pp. 145--178.

[Härder and Reuter, 1983] T. Härder and A. Reuter. Principles of Transaction-Oriented Database Recovery. *ACM Comput. Surv.* (December 1983), 15(4): 287--317.

[Heimbigner and McLeod, 1985] D. Heimbigner and D. McLeod. A Federated Architecture for Information Management. *ACM Trans. Office Inf. Syst.* (July 1985), 3(3): 253--278.

[Helal et al., 1997] A. A. Helal, A. A. Heddaya, and B. B. Bhargava. *Replication Techniques in Distributed Systems*, Boston, MA: Kluwer Academic Publishers, 1997.

[Herlihy, 1987] M. Herlihy. Concurrency versus Availability: Atomicity Mechanisms for Replicated Data. *ACM Trans. Comput. Syst.* (August 1987), 5(3): 249--274.

[Herlihy, 1990] M. Herlihy. Apologizing versus Asking Permission: Optimistic Concurrency Control for Abstract Data Types. *ACM Trans. on Database Syst.* (March 1990), 15(1):96--124.

[Herman and Verjus, 1979] D. Herman and J. P. Verjus. An Algorithm for Maintaining the Consistency of Multiple Copies. In *Proc. First Int. Conf. on Distributed Computing Systems*, 1979, pp. 625--631.

[Herrmann et al., 1990] U. Herrmann, P. Dadam, K Küspert, E.A. Roman, and G. Schlageter. A Lock Technique for Disjoint and Non-Disjoint Complex Objects. In *Advances in Database Technology--EDBT'90*, Berlin: Springer-Verlag, 1990, pp. 219--237.

[Hevner and Schneider, 1980] A. R. Hevner and G. M. Schneider. An Integrated Design System for Distributed Database Networks. In *Digest of Papers--COMPCON*, 1980, pp. 459--465.

[Hevner and Yao, 1979] A. R. Hevner and S. B. Yao. Query Processing in Distributed Database Systems. *IEEE Trans. Software Eng.* (March 1979), 5(3): 177--182.

[Hoffer, 1975] J. A. Hoffer. *A Clustering Approach to the Generation of Subfiles for the Design of a Computer Data Base*. Ph.D. dissertation, Ithaca, N.Y.: Department of Operations Research, Cornell University, January 1975.

[Hoffer and Severance, 1975] H. A. Hoffer and D. G. Severance. The Use of Cluster Analysis in Physical Data Base Design. In *Proc. First Int. Conf. on Very Large Data Bases*, September 1975, pp. 69--86.

[Hoffman, 1977] J. L. Hoffman. *Model Methods for Computer Security and Privacy*, Englewood Cliffs, N.J.: Prentice-Hall, 1977.

[Hofri, 1994] M. Hofri. On Timeout for Global Deadlock Detection in Decentralized Database Systems. *Inf. Proc. Letters* (1994), 51(6): 295--302.

[Holtzman and Goodman, 1993] J. M. Holtzman and D. J. Goodman (editors). *Wireless Communications: Future Directions*, Boston, Mass., Kluwer, 1993.

[Hong, 1992] W. Hong. Exploiting Inter-Operation Parallelism in XPRS. In *Proc. ACM SIGMOD Int. Conf. on Management of Data*, June 1992, pp. 19--28.

[Hsiao, 1983] D. Hsiao (ed.). Advanced Database Machine Architectures. Englewood Cliffs, N.J.: Prentice-Hall, 1983.

[Hsiao and DeWitt, 1991] H.-I. Hsiao, D. De Witt. A Performance Study of three High-Availability Data Replication Strategies. In *Proc. Int. Conf. on Parallel and Distributed Information Systems*, December 1991, pp. 18-28.

[Hsiao and Kamel, 1989] D. Hsiao and M. Kamel. Heterogeneous Databases: Proliferations, Issues and Solutions. *IEEE Trans. on Knowledge and Data Eng.* (1989), 1(1): 45--62.

[Hsu, 1993] M. Hsu (ed.). *Special Issue on Workflow and Extended Transaction Systems*, *IEEE Quart. Bull. Data Eng.*, (June 1993), 16.

[Hsu et al., 1988] M. Hsu, R. Ladin, and D. McCarthy. An Execution Model for Active Database Management Systems. In *Proc. 3rd Int. Conf. on Data and Knowledge Bases: Improving Usability and Responsiveness*, June 1988, pp. 171--179.

[Hull and Zhou, 1996] R. Hull and G. Zhou. A Framework for Supporting Data Integration using the Materialized and Virtual Approaches. In *Proc. ACM-SIGMOD, Int. Conf. on the Management of Data*, June 1996, pp. 481--492.

[Hunt and Rosenkrantz, 1979] H. B. Hunt and D. J. Rosenkrantz. The Complexity of Testing Predicate Locks. In *Proc. ACM SIGMOD Int. Conf. on Management of Data*, May 1979, pp. 127--133.

[Hwang, 1987] D. J. Hwang. *Constructing a Highly-Available Location Service for a Distributed Environment*. Technical Report MIT/LCS/TR-410, Cambridge, Mass.: Massachusetts Institute of Technology, 1987.

[IEEE, 1992] IEEE Computer Society. IEEE Standard for Scalable Coherent Interface (SCI). *IEEE Std 1596.*, New York, August 1992.

[ISO, 1983] International Standards Organization. *Information Processing Systems--Open Systems Interconnection--Basic Reference Model*. ISO 7498, 1983.

[Ibaraki and Kameda, 1984] T. Ibaraki and T. Kameda. On the Optimal Nesting Order for Computing N-Relation Joins. *ACM Trans. Database Syst.* (September 1984), 9(3): 482--502.

[Imielinski and Badrinath, 1994] T. Imielinski and B.R. Badrinath. Data Management Issues in Mobile Computing. *Commun. ACM* (October 1994), 37(10):18--28.

[Imielinski and Korth, 1996] T. Imielinski and H. Korth (eds.). *Mobile Computing*, Boston, Mass., Kluwer, 1996.

[Imielinski et. al., 1994] T. Imielinski, S. Viswanathan, and B. R. Badrinath. Energy Efficient Indexing on Air. In *Proc. ACM SIGMOD Int. Conf. on Management of Data*, June 1994, pp. 25--36.

[Inmon, 1992] W. Inmon. *Building the Data Warehouse*. John Wiley and Sons, 1992.

[Intel, 1997] Intel Corporation. Standard High Volume Servers: Changing the Rules for Business Computing. Can be retrieved at
http://www.intel.com/procs/servers/feature/shv/

[Ioannidis, 1996] Y. Ioannidis. Query Optimization. In A. Tucker (ed.), *The Computer Science and Engineering Handbook*, CRC Press, 1996, pp. 1038--1054.

[Ioannidis and Wong, 1987] Y.E. Ioannidis and E. Wong. Query optimization by simulated annealing. In *Proc. ACM SIGMOD Int. Conf. on Management of Data*, June 1987, pp. 9-22.

[Ioannidis et al., 1992] Y. Ioannidis, R. Ng, K. Shim, and T. Sellis. Parametric Query Optimization. In *Proc. 18th Int. Conf. on Very Large Data Bases*, 1992, pp. 103--114.

[Irani and Khabbaz, 1982] K. B. Irani and N. G. Khabbaz. A Methodology for the Design of Communication Networks and the Distribution of Data in Distributed Computer Systems. *IEEE Trans. Comput.* (May 1982), C-31(5): 419--434.

[Isloor and Marsland, 1980] S. S. Isloor and T. A. Marsland. The Deadlock Problem: An Overview. *Computer* (September 1980), 13(9): 58--78.

[Jacobs et al., 1978] I. M. Jacobs, R. Binder, and E. V. Hoversten. General Purpose Packet Satellite Networks. *Proc. IEEE* (1978), 6(11): 1448--1467.

[Jajodia and Mutchler, 1987] S. Jajodia and D. Mutchler. Dynamic Voting. In *Proc. ACM SIGMOD Int. Conf. on Management of Data*, May 1987, pp. 227--238.

[Jajodia et al., 1983] S. Jajodia, P. A. Ng, and F. N. Springsteel. The Problem of Equivalence for Entity-Relationship Diagrams. *IEEE Trans. Software Eng.* (September 1983), SE-9(5): 617--629.

[Jarke and Koch, 1984] M. Jarke and J. Koch. Query Optimization in Database Systems. *ACM Comput. Surv.* (June 1984), 16(2): 111--152.

[Jenq et al., 1990] B. Jenq, D. Woelk, W. Kom, and W.-L. Lee. Query Processing in Distributed ORION. In *Advances in Database Technology --- EDBT'90*, Berlin: Springer-Verlag, 1990, pp. 169--187.

[Johnson and Malek, 1988] A. M. Johnson, Jr., and M. Malek. Survey of Software Tools for Evaluating Reliability, Availability and Serviceability. *ACM Comput. Surv.* (December 1988), 20(4): 227--269.

[Jones, 1979] A. K. Jones. The Object Model: A Conceptual Tool for Structuring Software. In R. Bayer, R. M. Graham, G. Seegmüller (eds.), *Operating Systems: An Advanced Course*, New York: Springer-Verlag, 1979: 7--16.

[Kaiser, 1989] G.E. Kaiser. Transactions for concurrent object-oriented programming systems. In *Proc. ACM SIGPLAN Workshop on Object-Based Concurrent Programming*, 1989, pp. 136--138.

[Kambayashi et al., 1982] Y. Kambayashi, M. Yoshikawa, and S. Yajima. Query Processing for Distributed Databases Using Generalized Semi--joins. In *Proc. ACM SIGMOD Int. Conf. on Management of Data*, June 1982, pp. 151--160.

[Kangassalo, 1983] H. Kangassalo. *On the Selection of the Approach for the Development of the Reference Model for DBMS Standards*. ISO/TC 97/SC 5/WG 5 Document N104, 1983.

[Kapitskaia et al., 1997] O. Kapitskaia, A. Tomasic and P. Valduriez. Dealing with Discrepancies in Wrapper Functionality. INRIA Research Report RR-3138, 1997.

[Karlapalem and Li, 1995] K. Karlapalem and Qing Li. Partitioning Schemes for Object Oriented Databases. In [Bukhres et al., 1995], pp. 42--49.

[Karlapalem and Navathe, 1994] K. Karlapalem and S. B. Navathe. Materialization of Redesigned Distributed Relational Databases. Technical Report HKUST-CS94-14. Hong Kong University of Science and Technology, Department of Computer Science, 1994.

[Karlapalem et al., 1994] K. Karlapalem, S. B. Navathe, and M. A. Morsi. Issues in Distribution Design of Object-Oriented Databases. In [Özsu et al., 1994a], pp.148--164.

[Karlapalem et al., 1996b] K. Karlapalem, S. B. Navathe, and M. Ammar. Optimal Redesign Policies to Support Dynamic Processing of Applications on a Distributed Relational Database System. *Inf. Syst.* (1996), 21(4): 353--367.

[Kazerouni and Karlapalem, 1997] L. Kazerouni and K. Karlapalem. Stepwise Redesign of Distributed Relational Databases. Technical Report HKUST-CS97-12. Hong Kong University of Science and Technology, Department of Computer Science, 1997.

[Keller, 1982] A. M. Keller. Update to Relational Databases through Views Involving Joins. In *Proc. 2nd Int. Conf. on Databases: Improving Usability and Responsiveness*, June 1982, pp. 363--384.

[Keller and Basu, 1996] A. M. Keller and J. Basu. A Predicate-based Caching Scheme for Client-server Database Architectures. *The VLDB Journal* (January 1996), 5(1): 35--47.

[Keller et al., 1991] T. Keller, G. Graefe, and D. Maier. Efficient Assembly of Complex Objects. In *Proc. ACM SIGMOD Int. Conf. on Management of Data*, May 1991, pp. 148--157.

[Kemper and Kossman, 1994] A. Kemper and D. Kossmann. Dual-Buffering Strategies in Object Bases. In *Proc. 20th Int. Conf. on Very Large Data Bases*, 1994, pp. 427--438.

[Kemper and Moerkotte, 1990a] A. Kemper and G. Moerkotte. Access Support in Object Bases. In *Proc. ACM SIGMOD Int. Conf. on Management of Data*, May 1990, pp. 364--374.

[Kemper and Moerkotte, 1990b] A. Kemper and G. Moerkotte. Advanced Query Processing in Object Bases Using Access Support Relations. In *Proc. 16th Int. Conf. on Very Large Databases* August 1990, pp. 290--301.

[Kemper and Moerkotte, 1994] A. Kemper and G. Moerkotte. Physical Object Management. In [Kim, 1994], pp. 175--202.

[Kent, 1994] W. Kent. Object-Orientation and Interoperability. In [Dogac et al., 1994], pp. 287--305.

[Kerschberg et al., 1982] L. Kerschberg, P. D. Ting, and S. B. Yao. Query Optimization in Star Computer Networks. *ACM Trans. Database Syst.* (December 1982), 7(4): 678--711.

[Khoshafian and Copeland, 1986] S. Khoshafian and G. Copeland. Object Identity. In *Proc. Int. Conf. on OOPSLA*, September 1986, pp. 406--416.

[Khoshafian and Valduriez, 1987] S. Khoshafian and P. Valduriez. Sharing Persistence and Object-Orientation: A Database Perspective. In *Int. Workshop on Database Programming Languages*, September 1987, pp. 181--205.

[Khoshafian et al., 1988a] S. Khoshafian, P. Valduriez, and G. Copeland. Parallel Query Processing of Complex Objects. In *Proc. 4th Int. Conf. on Data Engineering*, February 1988, pp, 202--209.

[Kim, 1984] W. Kim. Highly Available Systems for Database Applications. *ACM Comput. Surv.* (March 1984), 16(1): 71--98.

[Kim, 1989] W. Kim. A Model of Queries for Object-Oriented Databases. In *Proc. 15th Int. Conf. on Very Large Data Bases*, August 1989, pp. 423--432.

[Kim, 1994] W. Kim (ed). *Modern Database Management -- Object-Oriented and Multi-database Technologies*. Reading, Mass.: Addison-Wesley/ACM Press, 1994.

[Kim and Lochovsky, 1989] W. Kim and F. Lochovsky (ed.). *Object-Oriented Concepts, Databases, and Applications*. Reading, Mass.: Addison-Wesley, 1989.

[Kim et al., 1985] W. Kim, D. S. Reiner, and D. S. Batory (eds.). *Query Processing in Database Systems*. New York: Springer-Verlag, 1985.

[Kim et al., 1987] W. Kim, J. Banerjee, H. Chou, J. Garza, and D. Woelk. Composite Objects Support in an Object-Oriented Database System. In *Proc. Int. Conf. on OOPSLA*, October 1987, pp. 118--125.

[Kitsuregawa and Ogawa, 1990] M. Kitsuregawa, Y. Ogawa. Bucket Spreading Parallel Hash: A New, Robust, Parallel Hash Join Method for Data Skew in the Super Database Computer. In *Proc. 16th Int. Conf. on Very Large Data Bases*, August 1990, pp. 210--221.

[Knapp, 1987] E. Knapp. Deadlock Detection in Distributed Databases. *ACM Comput. Surv.* (December 1987), 19(4): 303--328.

[Kohler, 1981] W. H. Kohler. A Survey of Techniques for Synchronization and Recovery in Decentralized Computer Systems. *ACM Comput. Surv.* (June 1981), 13(2): 149--183.

[Kollias and Hatzopoulos, 1981] J. G. Kollias and M. Hatzopoulos. Criteria to Aid in Solving the Problem of Allocating Copies of a File in a Computer Network. *Comput. J.* (1981) 24(1): 29--30.

[Kolodner and Weihl, 1993] E. Kolodner and W. Weihl. Atomic Incremental Garbage Collection and Recovery for Large Stable Heap. In *Proc. of the ACM SIGMOD Int. Conf. on Management of Data*, June 1993, pp. 177--185.

[Koon and Özsu, 1986] T. M. Koon and M. T. Özsu. Performance Comparison of Resilient Concurrency Control Algorithms for Distributed Databases. In *Proc. 2nd Int. Conf. on Data Engineering*, February 1986, pp. 565--573.

[Korth and Silberschatz, 1986] H. Korth and A. Silberschatz. *Database System Concepts*. New York: McGraw-Hill, 1986.

[Korth et al., 1990] H.F. Korth, E. Levy, and A. Silberschatz. Compensating Transactions: A New Recovery Paradigm. In *Proc. 16th Int. Conf. on Very Large Databases*, August 1990, pp. 95--106.

[Kotz et al., 1988] A.M. Kotz, K.R. Dittrich, and J.A. Mulle. Supporting Semantic Rules by a Generalized Event/Trigger Mechanism. In *Advances in Database Technology--EDBT'88*, Berlin: Springer-Verlag, 1988, pp. 76--91.

[Kowalik, 1985] J.S. Kowalik (ed.). Parallel MIMD Computation : the HEP Supercomputer and its applications. MIT Press, Cambridge, Mass., 1985.

[Krishnamurthy et al., 1986] R. Krishnamurthy, H. Boral, and C. Zaniolo. Optimization of Non-recursive Queries. In *Proc. 11th Int. Conf. on Very Large Data Bases*, August 1986, pp. 128--137.

[Kshemkalyani and Singhal, 1994] A. Kshemkalyani and M. Singhal. On Characterization and Correctness of Distributed Deadlocks. *Journal of Parallel and Dist. Comp.* (July 1994), No 22, pp. 44--59.

[Kumar, 1996] V. Kumar (ed.). *Performance of Concurrency Control Mechanisms in Centralized Database Systems*. Englewood Cliffs, NJ: Prentice-Hall, 1996.

[Kumar and Segev, 1993] A. Kumar and A. Segev. Cost and Availability Tradeoffs in Replicated Data Concurrency Control. *ACM Trans. Database Syst.* (March 1993), 18(1): 102--131.

[Kung and Papadimitriou, 1979] H. T. Kung and C. H. Papadimitriou. An Optimality Theory of Concurrency Control for Databases. In *Proc. ACM SIGMOD Int. Conf. on Management of Data*, May 1979, pp. 116--125.

[Kung and Robinson, 1981] H. T. Kung and J. T. Robinson. On Optimistic Methods for Concurrency Control. *ACM Trans. Database Syst.* (June 1981), 6(2): 213--226.

[Kuss, 1982] H. Kuss. On Totally Ordering Checkpoint in Distributed Data Bases. In *Proc. ACM SIGMOD Int. Conf. on Management of Data*, June 1982, 174--174.

[LaChimia, 1984] J. LaChimia. Query Decomposition in a Distributed Database System Using Satellite Communications. In *Proc. 3rd Seminar on Distributed Data Sharing Systems*, 1984, pp. 105--118.

[Labio et al., 1997] W. Labio, Y. Zhuge, J. Wiener, H. Gupta, H. Garcia-Molina, J. Widom. The WHIPS Prototype for Data Warehouse Creation and Maintenance. In *Proc. ACM SIGMOD Int. Conf. on Management of Data*, May 1997, pp. 557--559.

[Lacroix and Pirotte, 1977] M. Lacroix and A. Pirotte. Domain-Oriented Relational Languages. In *Proc. 3rd Int. Conf. on Very Large Data Bases*, October 1977, pp. 370--378.

[Ladin and Liskov, 1992] R. Ladin and B. Liskov. Garbage Collection of a Distributed Heap. In *Proc. Int. Conf. on Distributed Computing Systems*, June 1992, pp. 708--715.

[Lam and Yu, 1980] K. Lam and C. T. Yu. An Approximation Algorithm for a File Allocation Problem in a Hierarchical Distributed System. In *Proc. ACM SIGMOD Int. Conf. on Management of Data*, May 1980, pp. 125--132.

[Lampson and Sturgis, 1976] B. Lampson and H. Sturgis. *Crash Recovery in Distributed Data Storage System*. Technical Report, Palo Alto, Calif.: Xerox Palo Alto Research Center, 1976.

[Landers and Rosenberg, 1982] T. Landers and R. L. Rosenberg. An Overview of MULTIBASE. In H.-J. Schneider (ed.), *Distributed Data Bases*; Amsterdam: North-Holland, 1982, pp. 153--184.

[Lanzelotte and Valduriez, 1991] R. Lanzelotte, P. Valduriez. Extending the Search Strategy in a Query Optimizer. In *Proc. 17th Int. Conf. on Very Large Data Bases*, September 1991, pp. 363-373.

[Lanzelotte et al., 1993] R. Lanzelotte, P. Valduriez, and M. Zaït. On the Effectiveness of Optimization Search Strategies for Parallel Execution Spaces. In *Proc. 19th Int. Conf. on Very Large Data Bases*, September 1993, pp. 493--504.

[Lanzelotte et al., 1994] R. Lanzelotte, P. Valduriez, M. Zaït, and M. Ziane. Industrial-Strength Parallel Query Optimization: issues and lessons. *Inf. Syst.* (1994), 19(4): 311-330.

[Larson, 1983] J. Larson. Bridging the Gap between Network and Relational Database Management Systems. *Computer* (September 1983), 16(9): 82--92.

[Lee and Kim, 1995] S. Lee and J. Kim. An Efficient Distributed Deadlock Detection Algorithm. In *Proc. IEEE Int. Conf. Dist. Comp. Syst.*, May 1995, pp. 169--178.

[Lee et al., 1988] M. Lee, J. C. Freytag, and G. Lohman. Implementing an Interpreter for Functional Rules in a Query Optimizer. In *Proc. 14th Int. Conf. on Very Large Databases*, August-September 1988, pp. 218--229.

[Lenoski et al., 1992] D. Lenoski, J. Laudon, K. Gharachorloo, W. D. Weber, A. Gupta, J. Henessy, M. Horowitz, M. S. Lam. The Stanford Dash Multiprocessor. *Computer* (March 1992), 25(3) : pp. 63--79.

[Leung and Lai, 1979] J. Y. Leung and E. K. Lai. On Minimum Cost Recovery From System Deadlock. *IEEE Trans. Comput.* (September 1979), 28(9): 671--677.

[Levin and Morgan, 1975] K. D. Levin and H. L. Morgan. Optimizing Distributed Data Bases: A Framework for Research. In *Proc. National Computer Conf.*, 1975, pp. 473--478.

[Levy, 1996] A. Levy. Obtaining Complete Answers from Incomplete Databases. In *Proc. 22nd Int. Conf. on Very Large Data Bases*, September 1996, pp. 402-412.

[Levy et al., 1996] A. Levy, A. Rajaraman and J. Ordille. Querying Heterogeneous Information Sources Using Source Descriptions In *Proc. 22nd Int. Conf. on Very Large Data Bases*, September 1996, pp. 251--262.

[Li, 1987] V. O. K. Li. Performance Models of Timestamp-Ordering Concurrency Control Algorithms in Distributed Databases. *IEEE Trans. Comput.* (September 1987), C-36(9): 1041--1051.

[Liang and Tripathi, 1996] D. Liang and S. K. Tripathi. Performance Analysis of Long-Lived Transaction Processing Systems with Rollbacks and Aborts. *IEEE Trans. Knowledge and Data Eng.* (October 1996), 8(5): 802--815.

[Li et. al., 1997] J. Z. Li, M.T. Özsu, and D. Szafron. Modeling of Moving Objects in a Video Database. In *Proc. IEEE Int. Conf. Multimedia Computing and Systems*, June 1997, pp. 336--343.

[Lin, 1981] W. K. Lin. Performance Evaluation of Two Concurrency Control Mechanisms in a Distributed Database System. In *Proc. ACM SIGMOD Int. Conf. on Management of Data*, April 1981, pp. 84--92.

[Lin and Nolte, 1982] W. K. Lin and J. Nolte. Performance of Two Phase Locking. In *Proc. 6th Berkeley Workshop on Distributed Data Management and Computer Networks*, February 1982, pp. 131--160.

[Lin and Nolte, 1983] W. K. Lin and J. Nolte. Basic Timestamp, Multiple Version Timestamp, and Two-Phase Locking. In *Proc. 9th Int. Conf. on Very Large Data Bases*, October--November 1983, pp. 109--119.

[Lindsay, 1979] B. Lindsay. *Notes on Distributed Databases*. Technical Report RJ 2517, San Jose, Calif.: IBM San Jose Research Laboratory, 1979.

[Liskov et al., 1994] B. Liskov, M. Day, and L. Shirira. Distributed Object Management in Thor. In [Özsu et al., 1994a], pp. 79--91.

[Liskov et al., 1996] B. Liskov, A. Adya, M. Castro, M. Day, S. Ghemawat, R. Gruber, U. Maheshwari, A. Myers, and L. Shrira. Safe and Efficient Sharing of Persistent Objects in Thor. In *ACM SIGMOD Int. Conf. on Management of Data*, May 1996, pp. 318--329.

[Litwin, 1988] W. Litwin. From Database Systems to Multidatabase Systems: Why and How. In *Proc. British National Conference on Databases*, Cambridge: Cambridge University Press, 1988, pp. 161--188.

[Litwin and Abdellatif, 1986] W. Litwin and A. Abdellatif. Multidatabase Interoperability. *Computer* (December 1986), 19(12): 10--18.

[Litwin and Abdellatif, 1987] W. Litwin and A. Abdellatif. An Overview of the Multidatabase Manipulation Language -- MDL. *Proc. IEEE.* (May 1987), 75(5): 621--631.

[Litwin et al., 1982] W. Litwin, J. Baudenant, C. Esculier, A. Ferrier, A. M. Glorieux, J. La Chimia, K. Kabbaj, C. Moulinoux, P. Rolin, and C. Stangret. SIRIUS Systems for Distributed Data Management. In H.-J. Schneider (ed.), *Distributed Data Bases*, Amsterdam: North-Holland, 1982, pp. 311--366.

[Litwin et al., 1990] W. Litwin, L. Mark, and N. Roussolopulos. Interoperability of Multiple Autonomous Databases. *ACM Comp. Surveys* (September 1990), 22(3): 267--293.

[Liu et al., 1996] L. Liu, C. Pu, R. Barga, and T. Zhou. Differential Evaluation of Continual Queries. In *Proc. IEEE Int. Conf. Dist. Comp. Syst.*, May 1996, pp. 458--465.

[Liu et al., 1998] L. Liu, L.L. Yan, and M.T. Özsu. Interoperability in Large-Scale Distributed Information Delivery Systems. In [Dogac et al., 1998a], pp. 246--280.

[Livny et al., 1987] M. Livny, S. Khoshafian and H. Boral. Multi-disk Management. In *Proc. ACM SIGMETRICS Conf. on Measurement and Modeling of Computer Systems*, 1987, pp. 69--77.

[Locke, 1982] P. W. Locke. A Guide to DBMS Standardization Activities. *Comput. & Stand.* (1982), 1: 169--187.

[Lohman and Mackert, 1986] G. Lohman and L. F. Mackert. R* Optimizer Validation and Performance Evaluation for Distributed Queries. In *Proc. 11th Int. Conf. on Very Large Data Bases*, August 1986, pp. 149--159.

[Lohman et al., 1985] G. Lohman, C. Mohan, L. Haas, D. Daniels, B. Lindsay, P. Selinger, and P. Wilms. Query Processing in R*. In [Kim et al., 1985], pp. 31--47.

[Longbottom, 1980] R. Longbottom. *Computer System Reliability.* Chichester, England: Wiley, 1980.

[Lu and Carey, 1985] H. Lu and M. J. Carey. Some Experimental Results on Distributed Join Algorithms in a Local Network. In *Proc. 10th Int. Conf. on Very Large Data Bases*, August 1985, pp. 292--304.

[Lu et al., 1992] H. Lu, B. Ooi and C. Goh. On Global Multidatabase Query Optimization. *ACM SIGMOD Rec.* (December 1992), 21(4): 6--11.

[Lu et al., 1993] H. Lu, B. Ooi and C. Goh. Multidatabase Query Optimization: Issues and Solutions. In *Proc. 3rd Int. Workshop on Res. Issues in Data Eng.*, April 1993, pp. 137--143.

[Lynch, 1983a] N. Lynch. Concurrency Control for Resilient Nested Transactions. In *Proc. 2nd ACM SIGACT--SIGMOD Symp. on Principles of Database Systems*, March 1983, pp. 166--181.

[Lynch, 1983b] N. Lynch. Multilevel Atomicity: A New Correctness Criterion for Database Concurrency Control. *ACM Trans. Database Syst.* (December 1983), 8(4): 484--502.

[Lynch and Merritt, 1986] N. Lynch and M. Merritt. *Introduction to the Theory of Nested Transactions*. Technical Report MIT/LCS/TR-367, Cambridge, Mass.: Massachusetts Institute of Technology, July 1986.

[Lynch et al., 1993] N. Lynch, M. Merritt, W. E. Weihl, and A. Fekete. *Atomic Transactions in Concurrent Distributed Systems*. San Mateo: Calif.: Morgan Kaufmann, 1993.

[Mackert and Lohman, 1986] L. F. Mackert and G. Lohman. R* Optimizer Validation and Performance Evaluation for Local Queries. In *Proc. ACM SIGMOD Int. Conf. on Management of Data*, May 1986, pp. 84--95.

[Maes, 1987] P. Maes. Concepts and Experiments in Computational Reflection. In *Proc. Int. Conf. on OOPSLA*, October 1987, pp. 147--155.

[Maheshwari and Liskov, 1994] U. Maheshwari and B. Liskov. Fault-Tolerant Distributed Garbage Collection in a Client-Server Object-Oriented Database. In *Proc. 3rd Int. Conf. on Parallel and Distributed Information Systems*, September 1994, pp. 239--248.

[Mahmoud and Riordon, 1976] S. A. Mahmoud and J. S. Riordon. Optimal Allocation of Resources in Distributed Information Networks. *ACM Trans. Database Syst.* (March 1976), 1(1): 66--78.

[Maier, 1989] D. Maier. *Why Isn't There an Object-Oriented Data Model?* Technical Report CS/E 89-002, Portland, Oregon: Oregon Graduate Center, 1989.

[Maier and Stein, 1986] D. Maier and J. Stein. Indexing in an Object-Oriented DBMS. In *Proc. Int. Workshop on Object-Oriented Database Systems*, September 1986, pp. 171--182.

[Maier et al., 1994] D. Maier, G. Graefe, L. Shapiro, S. Daniels, T. Keller, and B. Vance. Issues in Distributed Object Assembly. In [Özsu et al., 1994a], pp. 165--181.

[Makki and Pissinou, 1995] K. Makki and N. Pissinou. Detection and Resolution Algorithm for Deadlocks in Distributed Database Systems. In *Proc. ACM Int. Conf. on Information and Knowledge Management*, November 1995, pp. 411--416.

[Martin, 1985] J. Martin. *Fourth Generation Languages*. Englewood Cliffs, N.J.: Prentice-Hall, 1985.

[Martin and Pedersen, 1994] B. Martin and C.H. Pedersen. Long-lived concurrent activities. In [Özsu et al., 1994a], pp. 188--211.

[McConnel and Siewiorek, 1982] S. McConnel and D. P. Siewiorek. Evaluation Criteria. In [Siewiorek and Swarz, 1982], pp. 201--302.

[McCormick et al., 1972] W. T. McCormick, P. J. Schweitzer, and T. W. White. Problem Decomposition and Data Reorganization by a Clustering Technique. *Oper. Res.* (1972), 20(5): 993--1009.

[Medina-Mora et al., 1993] R. Medina-Mora, H.K.T. Wong, and P. Flores. Action Workflow as the Enterprise Integration Technology. *IEEE Quart. Bull. Database Eng.* (1993), 16(2):49--52.

[Mehrotra et al., 1991] S. Mehrotra, R. Rastogi, H. F. Korth, and A. Silberschatz. Non-Serializable Executions in Heterogeneous Distributed Database Systems. In *Proc. 1st Int. Conf. on Parallel and Distributed Information Systems*, December 1991, pp. 245--252.

[Mehrotra et al., 1992] S. Mehrotra, R. Rastogi, Y. Breitbart, H. F. Korth, and A. Silberschatz. Ensuring Transaction Atomicity in Multidatabase Systems. In *Proc. 11th ACM Symp. on Principles of Database Systems*, May 1992, pp. 164--175.

[Mehta and DeWitt 1995] M. Metha, D. DeWitt. Managing Intra-operator Parallelism in Parallel Database Systems. *Proc. 21st Int. Conf. on Very Large Data Bases*, September 1995.

[Melton, 1998] J. Melton. *Object-Oriented SQL*. San Francisco: Morgan Kaufmann, in press.

[Menasce and Muntz, 1979] D. A. Menasce and R. R. Muntz. Locking and Deadlock Detection in Distributed Databases. *IEEE Trans. Software Eng.* (May 1979), SE-5(3): 195--202.

[Menasce and Nakanishi, 1982a] D. A. Menasce and T. Nakanishi. Optimistic versus Pessimistic Concurrency Control Mechanisms in Database Management Systems. *Inf. Syst.* (1982), 7(1): 13--27.

[Menasce and Nakanishi, 1982b] D. A. Menasce and T. Nakanishi. Performance Evaluation of a Two-Phase Commit Based Protocol for DDBS. In *Proc. First ACM SIGACT--SIGMOD Symp. on Principles of Database Systems*, 1982, pp. 247--255.

[Meng et al., 1993] W. Meng, C. Yu, W. Kim, G. Wang, T. Phan, and S. Dao. Construction of Relational Front-End for Object-Oriented Database Systems. In *Proc. IEEE Int. Conf. on Data Eng.*, April 1993, pp. 476--483.

[Merrett and Rallis, 1985] T. H. Merrett and N. Rallis. An Analytic Evaluation of Concurrency Control Algorithms. In *Proc. CIPS (Canadian Information Processing Society) Congress '85*, June 1985, pp. 435--439.

[Minoura and Wiederhold, 1982] T. Minoura and G. Wiederhold. Resilient Extended True-Copy Token Scheme for a Distributed Database System. *IEEE Trans. Software Eng.* (May 1982), SE-8(3): 173--189.

[Mitchell et al., 1993] G. Mitchell, U. Dayal, and S. Zdonik. Control of an Extensible Query Optimizer: A Planning-Based Approach. In *Proc. 19th Int. Conf. on Very Large Databases*, August 1993, pp. 517--528.

[Mohan, 1979] C. Mohan. *Data Base Design in the Distributed Environment*. Working Paper WP-7902, Austin, Tex.: Department of Computer Sciences, University of Texas at Austin, May 1979.

[Mohan, 1991] C. Mohan and I. Narang. Efficient Locking and Caching of Data in the Multi-system Shared Disks Transaction Environment. IBM Research Report RJ 8301, August 1991.

[Mohan and Lindsay, 1983] C. Mohan and B. Lindsay. Efficient Commit Protocols for the Tree of Processes Model of Distributed Transactions. In *Proc. 2nd ACM SIGACT--SIGMOD Symp. on Principles of Distributed Computing*, March 1983, pp. 76--88.

[Mohan and Yeh, 1978] C. Mohan and R. T. Yeh. Distributed Data Base Systems: A Framework for Data Base Design. In *Distributed Data Bases, Infotech State-of-the-Art Report*, London: Infotech, 1978.

[Mohan et al., 1986] C. Mohan, B. Lindsay, and R. Obermarck. Transaction Management in the R* Distributed Database Management System. *ACM Trans. Database Syst.* (December 1986), 11(4): 378--396.

[Mohan et al., 1993] C. Mohan, D. Haderle, B. Lindsay, H. Pirahesh and P. Schwarz. ARIES: A Transaction Recovery Method Supporting Fine-Granularity Locking and Partial Rollbacks Using Write-Ahead Logging. *ACM Trans. Database Syst.* (March 1992), 17(1): 94--162.

[Morgan and Levin, 1977] H. L. Morgan and K. D. Levin. Optimal Program and Data Location in Computer Networks. *Commun. ACM* (May 1977), 20(5): 315--322.

[Moss, 1985] E. Moss. *Nested Transactions*. Cambridge, Mass.: MIT Press, 1985.

[Motro, 1987] A. Motro. Superviews: Virtual Integration of Multiple Databases. *IEEE Trans. Software Eng.* (July 1987), SE-13(7): 785--798.

[Motro and Buneman, 1981] A. Motro and P. Buneman. Constructing Superviews. In *Proc. ACM SIGMOD Int. Conf. on Management of Data*, April 1981, pp. 56--64.

[Mourad and Andres, 1985] S. Mourad and D. Andres. The Reliability of the IBM/XA Operating System. In *Proc. 15th Annual Int. Symp. on Fault-Tolerant Computing Systems*, 1985, pp. 93--98.

[Muro et al., 1983] S. Muro, T. Ibaraki, H. Miyajima, and T. Hasegawa. File Redundancy Issues in Distributed Database Systems. In *Proc. 9th Int. Conf. on Very Large Data Bases*, October-November 1983, pp. 275--277.

[Muro et al., 1985] S. Muro, T. Ibaraki, H. Miyajima and T. Hasegawa. Evaluation of File Redundancy in Distributed Database Systems. *IEEE Trans. Software Eng.* (February 1985), SE-11(2): 199--205.

[Muth et al., 1993] P. Muth, T.C. Rakow, G. Weikum, P. Brössler, and C. Hasse. Semantic Concurrency Control in Object-Oriented Database Systems. In *Proc. 9th Int. Conf. on Data Engineering*, 1993, pp. 233--242.

[Myers, 1976] G. J. Myers. *Software Reliability: Principles and Practices*. New York: Wiley, 1976.

[NBS, 1977] U. S. Department of Commerce/National Bureau of Standards. *Data Encryption Standard*. Federal Information Processing Standards Publication 46, January 1977.

[Naacke et al., 1998] H. Naacke, G. Gardarin and A. Tomasic. An Extensible Cost Model for Heterogeneous Data Sources. In *Proc. 14th IEEE Int. Conf. on Data Engineering*, February 1998, pp. 351--360.

[Nakajima, 1994] T. Nakajima. Commutativity Based Concurrency Control for Multiversion Objects. In [Özsu et al., 1994a], pp. 231--247.

[Navathe et al., 1984] S. Navathe, S. Ceri, G. Wiederhold, and J. Dou. Vertical Partitioning of Algorithms for Database Design. *ACM Trans. Database Syst.* (December 1984), 9(4): 680--710.

[Newman, 1994] P. Newman. ATM Local Area Networks. *IEEE Communications Magazine* (March 1994) 32(3): 86--98.

[Newton, 1979] G. Newton. Deadlock Prevention, Detection and Resolution: An Annotated Bibliography. *ACM Oper. Syst. Rev.* (April 1979), 13(2): 33--44.

[Ng, 1988] P. Ng. A Commit Protocol for Checkpointing Transactions. In *Proc. 7th. Symp. on Reliable Distributed Systems*, October 1988, pp. 22--31.

[Nguyen and Srinivasan, 1996] T. Nguyen and V. Srinivasan. Accessing Relational Databases from the World Wide Web. In *Proc. ACM-SIGMOD, Int. Conf. on the Management of Data*, June 1996, pp. 529--540.

[Niamir, 1978] B. Niamir. *Attribute Partitioning in a Self--Adaptive Relational Database System*. Technical Report 192, Cambridge, Mass.: Laboratory for Computer Science, Massachusetts Institute of Technology, 1978.

[Nicolas, 1982] J. M. Nicolas. Logic for Improving Integrity Checking in Relational Data Bases. *Acta Inf.* (1982), 18: 227--253.

[Nodine and Zdonik, 1990] M. Nodine and S. Zdonik. Cooperative Transaction Hierarchies: A Transaction Model to Support Design Applications. In *Proc. 16th Int. Conf. on Very Large Databases*, 1990, pp. 83--94.

[O'Neil and Graefe, 1995] P. O'Neil and G. Graefe. Multi-Table Joins through Bitmapped Join Indices. *ACM SIGMOD Record*, (September 1995), 24(3): pp. 8--11.

[O'Neil and Quass, 1997] P. O'Neil and D. Quass. Improved Query Performance with Variant Indexes. In *Proc. ACM SIGMOD, Int. Conf. on the Management of Data*, May 1997, pp. 38--49.

[O'Toole et al., 1993] J. O'Toole, S. Nettles, and D. Gifford. Concurrent Compacting Garbage Collection of a Persistent Heap. In *Proc. 14th ACM Symp. Operating Syst. Principles*, December 1993, pp. 161--174.

[Obermarck, 1982] R. Obermarck. Deadlock Detection for All Resource Classes. *ACM Trans. Database Syst.* (June 1982), 7(2): 187--208.

[Omiecinski, 1991] E. Omiecinski. Performance Analysis of a Load Balancing Hash-Join Algorithm for a Shared-Memory Multiprocessor. *Proc. 17th Int. Conf. on Very Large Data Bases* September 1991, pp. 375--385.

[Orenstein et al., 1992] J. Orenstein, S. Haradvala, B. Margulies, and D. Sakahara. Query Processing in the ObjectStore Database System. In *Proc. ACM SIGMOD Int. Conf. on Management of Data*, 1992, pp. 403--412.

[Orfali et al., 1996] R. Orfali, D. Harkey and J. Edwards. *The Essential Distributed Objects Survival Guide*. New York: Wiley, 1996.

[Osborn and Heaven, 1986] S. L. Osborn and T. E. Heaven. The Design of a Relational Database System with Abstract Data Types for Domains. *ACM Trans. Database Syst.* (September 1986), 11(3): 357--373.

[Osterhaug, 1989] A. Osterhaug. *Guide to Parallel Programming on Sequent Computer Systems*. Englewood Cliffs, N. J.: Prentice-Hall, 1989.

[Ozkarahan, 1986] E. A. Ozkarahan. *Database Machines and Database Management*. Englewood Cliffs, N. J.: Prentice-Hall, 1986.

[Özsoyoglu and Zhou, 1987] Z. M. Özsoyoglu and N. Zhou. Distributed Query Processing in Broadcasting Local Area Networks. In *Proc. 20th Hawaii Int. Conf. on System Sciences*, January 1987, pp. 419--429.

[Özsu, 1985a] M. T. Özsu. Performance Comparison of Distributed vs Centralized Locking Algorithms in Distributed Database Systems. In *Proc. 5th Int. Conf. on Distributed Computing Systems*, May 1985, pp. 254--261.

[Özsu, 1985b] M. T. Özsu. Modeling and Analysis of Distributed Concurrency Control Algorithms Using an Extended Petri Net Formalism. *IEEE Trans. Software Eng.* (October 1985), SE-11(10): 1225--1240.

[Özsu, 1994] M. T. Özsu. Transaction Models and Transaction Management in OODBMSs. In [Dogac et al., 1994], pp. 147--184.

[Özsu and Barker, 1990] M.T. Özsu and K. Barker. Architectural Classification and Transaction Execution Models of Multidatabase Systems. In *Proc. Int. Conf. on Computing and Information*, May 1990, pp. 275--279.

[Özsu and Blakeley, 1994] M. T. Özsu and J. Blakeley. Query Processing in Object-Oriented Database Systems. In W. Kim, editor, *Modern Database Management -- Object-Oriented and Multidatabase Technologies*, Addison-Wesley/ACM Press, 1994, pp. 146--174.

[Özsu and Valduriez, 1991] M. T. Özsu and P. Valduriez. Distributed Database Systems: Where Are We Now? *Computer* (August 1991), 24(8): 68--78.

[Özsu and Valduriez, 1994] M. T. Özsu and P. Valduriez. Distributed Data Management: Unsolved Problems and New Issues. In T. Casavant and M. Singhal (eds.), *Readings in Distributed Computing Systems*, Los Alamitos, Calif.: IEEE/CS Press, 1994, pp. 512--544.

[Özsu and Valduriez, 1997] M. T. Özsu and P. Valduriez. Distributed and Parallel Database Systems. In A. Tucker (ed.), *Handbook of Computer Science and Engineering*, Boca Raton, Flo.: CRC Press, 1997, pp. 1093--1111.

[Özsu et al., 1994a] M.T. Özsu, U. Dayal, and P. Valduriez (eds.). *Distributed Object Management*. San Mateo, Calif.: Morgan-Kaufmann, 1994.

[Özsu et al., 1994b] M.T. Özsu, U. Dayal, and P. Valduriez. An Introduction to Distributed Object Management. In [Özsu et al., 1994a], pp. 1--24.

[Özsu et al., 1995a] M.T. Özsu, R.J. Peters, D. Szafron, B. Irani, A. Munoz, and A. Lipka. TIGUKAT: A Uniform Behavioral Objectbase Management System. *VLDB Journal* (August 1995), 4: 445--492.

[Özsu et al., 1995b] M. T. Özsu, A. Munoz and D. Szafron. An Extensible Query Optimizer for an Objectbase Management System. In *Proc. 4th Int. Conf. on Information and Knowledge Management*, November 1995, pp. 188--196.

[Özsu et al., 1998] M. T. Özsu, K. Voruganti, and R. Unrau. An Asynchronous Avoidance-Based Cache Consistency Algorithm for Client Caching DBMSs. In *Proc. 24th Int. Conf. on Very Large Data Bases*, September 1998, pp. 440--451.

[Pacitti et al., 1998] E. Pacitti, E. Simon, and R. de Melo. Improving Data Freshness in Lazy Master Schemes. In *Proc. 17th Int. Conf. on Distributed Computing Systems*, May 1998, pp. 164--171.

[Page and Popek, 1985] T. W. Page and G. J. Popek. Distributed Data Management in Local Area Networks. In *Proc. ACM SIGACT--SIGMOD Symp. on Principles of Database Systems*, March 1985, pp. 135--142.

[Papadimitriou, 1979] C. H. Papadimitriou. Serializability of Concurrent Database Updates. *J. ACM* (October 1979), 26(4): 631--653.

[Papadimitriou, 1986] C. H. Papadimitriou. *The Theory of Concurrency Control*. Rockville, Md.: Computer Science Press, 1986.

[Papakonstantinou et al., 1995] Y. Papakonstantinou, H. Garcia-Molina and J. Widom. Object Exchange across Heterogeneous Information Sources. In *Proc. 11th Int. Conf. on Data Engineering*, March 1995, pp. 251--260.

[Paris, 1996] J. F. Paris. Voting with Witnesses: A Consistency Scheme for Replicated Files. In *Proc. 6th Int. Conf. on Distributed Computing Systems*, May 1986, pp. 606--612.

[Park et al., 1995] Y. Park, P. Scheuermann, and H. Tang. A Distributed Deadlock Detection and Resolution Algorithm Based on a Hybrid Wait-For Graph and Probe Generation Scheme. In *Proc. ACM Int. Conf. Information and Knowledge Management*, November 1995, pp. 378--86.

[Pease et al., 1980] M. Pease, R. Shostak, and L. Lamport. Reaching Agreement in the Presence of Faults. *J. ACM* (April 1980), 27(2): 228--234.

[Peters and Özsu, 1993] R. J. Peters and M.T.Özsu. Reflection in a Uniform Behavioral Object Model. In *Proc. 12th Int. Conf. on Entity-Relationship Approach*, December 1993, pp. 37--49.

[Peters et al., 1993] R. J. Peters, A. Lipka, M. T. Özsu, and D. Szafron. An Extensible Query Model and its Languages for a Uniform Behavioral Object Management System. In *Proc. 2nd International Conference on Information and Knowledge Management*, November 1993, pp. 403--412.

[Piatetsky and Connell, 1984] G. Piatetsky--Shapiro and C. Connell. Accurate Estimation of the Number of Tuples Satisfying a Condition. In *Proc. ACM SIGMOD Int. Conf. on Management of Data*, June 1984, pp. 256--276.

[Pirahesh et al., 1990] H. Pirahesh, C. Mohan, J. M. Cheng, T. S. Liu, and P. G. Selinger. Parallelism in RDBMS : Architectural Issues and Design. In *Proc. 2nd Int. Symp. on Databases in Distributed and Parallel Systems*, July 1990, pp. 4--29.

[Pitoura and Bhargava, 1995] E. Pitoura and B. Bhargava. Maintaining Consistency of Data in Mobile Distributed Environments. In *Proc. 15th Int. Conf. on Distributed Computing Systems*, May/June 1995, pp. 404--413.

[Pitoura and Samaras, 1998] E. Pitoura and G. Samaras. *Data Management for Mobile Computing*, Norwell, Mass.: Kluwer Academic, 1998.

[Pitoura et al., 1995] E. Pitoura, O. Bukhres, and A. Elmagarmid. Object-Orientation in Multidatabase Systems. *ACM Comput. Surv.* (June 1995), 27(2): 141--195.

[Plainfossé and Shapiro, 1995] D. Plainfossé and M. Shapiro. A Survey of Distributed Garbage Collection Techniques. In *Proc. Int. Workshop on Memory Management*, September 1995, pp. 211--249.

[Pongpinigpinyo, 1996] S. Pongpinigpinyo. *Distributed Query Processing Using Two Stage Simulated Annealing*. Ph.D. dissertation, Hobart, Australia: Department of Computer Science, University of Tasmania, June 1996.

[Potier and LeBlanc, 1980] D. Potier and P. LeBlanc. Analysis of Locking Policies in Database Management Systems. *Commun. ACM* (October 1980), 23(10): 584--593.

[Pradhan, 1986] D. K. Pradhan (ed.) *Fault-Tolerant Computing: Theory and Techniques*, Volume 2. Englewood Cliffs, N.J.: Prentice-Hall, 1986.

[Pu, 1988] C. Pu. Superdatabases for Composition of Heterogeneous Databases. In *Proc. 4th Int. Conf. on Data Engineering*, February 1988, pp. 548--555.

[Quass and Widom, 1997] D. Quass and J. Widom. On-Line Warehouse View Maintenance for Batch Updates. In *Proc. ACM SIGMOD Int. Conf. on Management of Data*, May 1997, pp. 393--404.

[Rahimi, 1987] S. Rahimi. *Reference Architecture for Distributed Database Management Systems*. Tutorial Notes, *3rd Int. Conf. on Data Engineering*, 1987.

[Rahm and Marek, 1995] E. Rahm and R. Marek. Dynamic Multi-Resource Load Balancing in Parallel Database Systems. In *Proc. 21st Int. Conf. on Very Large Data Bases*, September 1995, pp. 395--406.

[Ramamoorthy and Wah, 1983] C. V. Ramamoorthy and B. W. Wah. The Isomorphism of Simple File Allocation. *IEEE Trans. Comput.* (March 1983), C-23(3): 221--231.

[Ramamritham and Pu, 1995] K. Ramamritham and C. Pu. A Formal Characterization of Epsilon Serializability. *IEEE Trans. Knowledge and Data Eng.* (December 1995), 7(6): 997--1007.

[Ramanathan and Shin, 1988] P. Ramanathan and K. G. Shin. Checkpointing and Rollback Recovery in a Distributed System Using Common Time Base. In *Proc. 7th Symp. on Reliable Distributed Systems*, October 1988, pp. 13--21.

[Randell et al., 1978] B. Randell, P. A. Lee and P. C. Treleaven. Reliability Issues in Computing System Design. *ACM Comput. Surv.* (June 1978), 10(2): 123--165.

[Rappaport et al., 1996] T. S. Rappaport, J. H. Reed, and B. D. Woerner. Position Location Using Wireless Communications on Highways of the Future. *IEEE Communications Magazine* (October 1996), 34(10): 33--41.

[Rivera-Vega et al., 1990] P.I. Rivera-Vega, R. Varadarajan, and S. B. Navathe. Scheduling Data Redistribution in Distributed Databases In *Proc. Int. Conf. on Data Eng.*, 1990, pp. 166--173.

[Rivest et al., 1978] R. L. Rivest, A. Shamir, and L. Adelman. A Method for Obtaining Digital Signatures and Public-Key Cryptosystems. *Commun. ACM* (February 1978), 21(2): 120--126.

[Rosenkrantz and Hunt, 1980] D. J. Rosenkrantz and H. B. Hunt. Processing Conjunctive Predicates and Queries. In *Proc. 6th Int. Conf. on Very Large Data Bases*, October 1980, pp. 64--72.

[Rosenkrantz et al., 1978] D. J. Rosenkrantz, R. E. Stearns, and P. M. Lewis. System Level Concurrency Control for Distributed Database Systems. *ACM Trans. Database Syst.* (June 1978), 3(2): 178--198.

[Rothermel and Mohan, 1989] K. Rothermel and C. Mohan. ARIES/NT: A Recovery Method based on Write-Ahead Logging for Nested Transactions. In *Proc. 15th Int. Conf. on Very Large Data Bases*, August 1989, pp. 337--346.

[Roth et al., 1967] J. P. Roth, W. G. Bouricius, E. C. Carter, and P. R. Schneider. *Phase II of an Architectural Study for a Self-Repairing Computer*. Report SAMSO-TR-67-106, El Segundo, Calif.: U. S. Air Force Space and Missile Division, 1967. Cited in [Siewiorek and Swarz, 1982].

[Rothnie and Goodman, 1977] J. B. Rothnie and N. Goodman. A Survey of Research and Development in Distributed Database Management. In *Proc. 3rd Int. Conf. on Very Large Data Bases*, 1977, pp. 48--62.

[Roussopoulos, 1998] N. Roussopoulos. Materialized Views and Data Warehouse. *ACM SIGMOD Record*, (March 1998), 27(1), pp. 21--26.

[Rusinkiewicz et al., 1988] M. Rusinkiewicz, R. Elmasri, B. Czejdo, D. Georgakopulos, G. Karabatis, A. Jamoussi, K. Loa, Y. Li, J. Gilbert, and R. Musgrove. *Query Processing in OMNIBASE -- A Loosely Coupled Multi--Database System*. Technical Report UH-CS-88-05, Houston, Tex.: Department of Computer Science, University of Houston, February 1988.

[Rusinkiewicz et al., 1989] M. Rusinkiewicz, R. Elmasri, B. Czejdo, D. Georgakopulos, G. Karabatis, A. Jamoussi, K. Loa, and Y. Li. Query Processing in a Heterogeneous Multi-database Environment. In *Proc. First Annual Symp. Parallel and Distributed Computing*, 1989, pp. 162--169.

[SPARC, 1975] ANSI/X3/SPARC Study Group on Data Base Management Systems. Interim Report. *ACM FDT Bull.* (1975), 7(2).

[Sacca and Wiederhold, 1985] D. Sacca and G. Wiederhold. Database Partitioning in a Cluster of Processors. *ACM Trans. Database Syst.* (October 1985), 10(1): 29--56.

[Sacco and Schkolnick, 1986] G. M. Sacco and M. Schkolnick. Buffer Management in Relational Database Systems. *ACM Trans. Database Syst.* (December 1986), 11(4): 473--498.

[Sacco and Yao, 1982] M. S. Sacco and S. B. Yao. Query Optimization in Distributed Data Base Systems. In M.C. Yovits (ed.), *Advances in Computers*, Volume 21, New York: Academic Press, 1982, pp. 225--273.

[Salem et al., 1989] K. Salem, H. Garcia-Molina, and R. Alonso. Altruistic Locking: A Strategy for Coping with Long Lived Transactions. In D. Gawlick, M. Haynie, and A. Reuter (eds.), *High Performance Transaction Systems*, Lecture Notes in Computer Science, Vol. 359. Berlin: Springer-Verlag, pp. 175--199.

[Schlageter and Dadam, 1980] G. Schlageter and P. Dadam. Reconstruction of Consistent Global States in Distributed Databases. In C. Delobel and W. Litwin (eds.), *Distributed Data Bases*, Amsterdam: North-Holland, 1980, pp. 191--200.

[Schlichting and Schneider, 1983] R. D. Schlichting and F. B. Schneider. Fail--Stop Processors: An Approach to Designing Fault--Tolerant Computing Systems. *ACM Trans. Comp. Syst.* (August 1983), 1(3): 222--238.

[Schmidt, 1977] J. W. Schmidt. Some High Level Language Constructs for Data of Type Relation. *ACM Trans. Database Syst.* (September 1977), 2(3): 247--261.

[Schneiderman and Thomas, 1982] B. Schneiderman and G. Thomas. Automatic Database System Conversion: Schema Revision, Data Translation and Source--to--Source Program Transformation. In *Proc. National Computer Conf.*, 1982, pp. 579--587.

[Schreiber, 1977] F. Schreiber. A Framework for Distributed Database Systems. In *Proc. Int. Computing Symposium*, 1977, pp. 475--482.

[Selinger and Adiba, 1980] P. G. Selinger and M. Adiba. Access Path Selection in Distributed Data Base Management Systems. In *Proc. First Int. Conf. on Data Bases*, 1980, pp. 204--215.

[Selinger et al., 1979] P. G. Selinger, M. M. Astrahan, D. D. Chamberlin, R. A. Lorie and T. G. Price. Access Path Selection in a Relational Database Management System. In *Proc. ACM SIGMOD Int. Conf. on Management of Data*, May 1979, pp. 23--34.

[Sellis et al., 1997] T. Sellis, P. Vassiliadis, S. Ligoudistianos, C. Quix, M. Jeusfeld, E. Franconi, U. Sattler, D. Calvanese, G. De Giacomo, M. Lenzerini, D. Nardi, R. Rosati, E. Simon, M. Matulovic, W. Nutt. Data Warehouse Quality Requirements and Framework. DWQ ESPRIT Long Term Research Project, Deliverable D1.1, National Technical University of Athens, July 1997.

[Sevcik, 1983] K. C. Sevcik. Comparison of Concurrency Control Methods Using Analytic Models. In *Information Processing '83*, 1983, pp. 847--858.

[Severence and Lohman, 1976] D. G. Severence and G. M. Lohman. Differential Files: Their Application to the Maintenance of Large Databases. *ACM Trans. Database Syst.* (September 1976), 1(3): 256--261.

[Shapiro, 1986] L. Shapiro. Join Processing in Database Systems with Large Main Memories. *ACM Trans. Database Syst.* (September 1986), 11(3): 239--264.

[Sharp, 1987] J.A. Sharp. *An Introduction to Distributed and Parallel Processing*. Blackwell Scientific Publications, Oxford, England, 1987.

[Shasha and Wang, 1991] D. Shasha and T.-L. Wang. Optimizing Equijoin Queries in Distributed Databases Where Relations are Hash Partitioned. *ACM Trans. Database Syst.* (June 1991), 16(2): 279--308.

[Shatdal and Naughton, 1993] A. Shatdal and J. F. Naughton. Using Shared Virtual Memory for Parallel Join Processing. In *Proc. ACM SIGMOD Int. Conf. on Management of Data*, May 1993, pp. 119--128.

[Shaw and Zdonik, 1989] G. Shaw and S. Zdonik. An Object-Oriented Query Algebra. *IEEE Quart. Bull. Database Eng.* (September 1989), 12(3): 29--36.

[Shekita and Carey, 1990] E. J. Shekita and M. J. Carey. A Performance Evaluation of Pointer-Based Joins. In *Proc. ACM SIGMOD Int. Conf. on Management of Data*, May 1990, pp. 300--311.

[Shekita et al., 1993] E. J. Shekita H. C. Young, and K. L. Tan. Multi-Join Optimization for Symmetric Multiprocessor. *Proc. 19th Int. Conf. on Very Large Data Bases*, August 1993, pp. 479--492.

[Sherman, 1985] K. Sherman. *Data Communications: A User's Guide* (2nd edition). Reston, Va.: Reston Publishing Co., 1986.

[Sheth, 1987] A. Sheth. Building Federated Database Systems. *IEEE Dist. Comput. Tech. Commun. Newsl.* (November 1988), 10(2): 50--58.

[Sheth and Larson, 1990] A. Sheth and J. Larson. Federated Databases: Architectures and Integration. *ACM Comput. Surv.*, Special Issue on Heterogeneous Databases, 1990.

[Sheth et al., 1988a] A. Sheth, J. Larson, A. Cornellio, and S. Navathe. A Tool for Integrating Conceptual Schemas and User Views. In *Proc. 4th Int. Conf. on Data Engineering*, February 1988, pp. 176--183.

[Sheth et al., 1988b] A. Sheth, J. Larson, E. Watkins. TAILOR, A Tool for Updating Views. In *Advances in Database Technology -- EDBT'88*, Berlin: Springer-Verlag, 1988, pp. 190--213.

[Shrivastava, 1985] S. K. Shrivastava (ed.). *Reliable Computer Systems*. Berlin: Springer-Verlag, 1985.

[Sidell et al., 1996] J. Sidell, P. M. Aoki, A. Sah, C. Staelin, M. Stonebraker, and A. Yu. Data Replication in Mariposa. In *Proc. 12th Int. Conf. on Data Eng.*, February-March 1996, pp. 485--494.

[Siegel, 1987] M. D. Siegel. *A Survey of Heterogeneous Database Systems*. BUCS Technical Report 87-011, Boston, Mass.: Boston University, October 1987.

[Siegel, 1996] J. Siegel (editor). *CORBA Fundamentals and Programming*. New York: Wiley, 1996.

[Siewiorek and Swarz, 1982] D. P. Siewiorek and R. S. Swarz. *The Theory and Practice of Reliable System Design*. Bedford, Mass.: Digital Press, 1982.

[Simon and Valduriez, 1984] E. Simon and P. Valduriez. Design and Implementation of an Extendible Integrity Subsystem. In *Proc. ACM SIGMOD Int. Conf. on Management of Data*, June 1984, pp. 9--17.

[Simon and Valduriez, 1986] E. Simon and P. Valduriez. Integrity Control in Distributed Database Systems. In *Proc. 19th Hawaii Int. Conf. on System Sciences*, January 1986, pp. 622--632.

[Simon and Valduriez, 1987] E. Simon and P. Valduriez. *Design and Analysis of a Relational Integrity Subsystem*. Technical Report DB-015-87, Austin, Tex.: Microelectronics and Computer Corporation, January 1987.

[Singhal, 1989] M. Singhal. Deadlock Detection in Distributed Systems. *Computer* (November 1989), 22(11): 37-48.

[Sinha et al., 1985] M. K. Sinha, P. D. Nanadikar and S. L. Mehndiratta. Timestamp Based Certification Schemes for Transactions in Distributed Database Systems. In *Proc. ACM SIGMOD Int. Conf. on Management of Data*, May 1985, pp. 402--411.

[Sistla et al., 1997] A.P. Sistla, O. Wolfson, S. Chamberlain, and S. Dao. Modeling and Querying Moving Objects. In *Proc. 13th Int. Conf. on Data Engineering*, February 1997, pp. 422--432.

[Skarra, 1989] A. Skarra. Concurrency Control for Cooperating Transactions in an Object-Oriented Database. *Proc. ACM SIGPLAN Workshop on Object-Based Concurrent Programming*, 1989, pp. 145--147.

[Skarra et al., 1986] A.H. Skarra, S.B. Zdonik, and S.P. Reiss. An object server for an object-oriented database system. In *Proc. of the 1st Int. Workshop on Object-Oriented Database Systems*, September 1986, pp. 196--204.

[Skeen, 1981] D. Skeen. Nonblocking Commit Protocols. *Proc. ACM SIGMOD Int. Conf. on Management of Data*, April--May 1981, pp. 133--142.

[Skeen, 1982a] D. Skeen. A Quorum-Based Commit Protocol. In *Proc. 6th Berkeley Workshop on Distributed Data Management and Computer Networks*, February 1982, pp. 69--80.

[Skeen, 1982b] D. Skeen. *Crash Recovery in a Distributed Database Management System*. Ph.D. thesis, Berkeley, Calif.: Department of Electrical Engineering and Computer Science, University of California at Berkeley, 1982.

[Skeen and Stonebraker, 1983] D. Skeen and M. Stonebraker. A Formal Model of Crash Recovery in a Distributed System. *IEEE Trans. Software Eng.* (May 1983), SE-9(3): 219--228.

[Skeen and Wright, 1984] D. Skeen and D. Wright. Increasing Availability in Partitioned Networks. In *Proc. 3rd ACM SIGACT--SIGMOD Symp. on Principles of Database Systems*, April 1984, pp. 290--299.

[Smith and Chang, 1975] J. M. Smith and P. Y. Chang. Optimizing the Performance of a Relational Algebra Database Interface. *Commun. ACM* (1975), 18(10): 568--579.

[Smith et al., 1981] J. M. Smith, P. A. Bernstein, U. Dayal, N. Goodman, T. Landers, K. Lin, and E. Wong. MULTIBASE: Integrating Heterogeneous Distributed Database Systems. In *Proc. National Computer Conf.*, May 1981, pp. 487--499.

[Stallings, 1984] W. Stallings. *Local Networks: An Introduction*. New York: Macmillan, 1984.

[Stallings, 1988] W. Stallings. *Data and Computer Communications* (2nd edition). New York: Macmillan, 1988.

[Stathatos et al., 1997] K. Stathatos, N. Roussopoulos, and J. S. Baras. Adaptive Data Broadcast in Hybrid Networks. In *Proc. 23rd Int. Conf. on Very Large Data Bases*, August 1997, pp. 326--335 .

[Stearns et al., 1976] R. E. Stearns, P. M. Lewis, II and D. J. Rosenkrantz. Concurrency Controls for Database Systems. In *Proc. 17th Symp. on Foundations of Computer Science*, 1976, pp. 19--32.

[Steel, 1982] T. B. Steel, Jr. International Standardization and Distributed Data Bases. In H.-J. Schneider (ed.), *Distributed Data Bases*, Amsterdam: North-Holland, 1982, pp. 1--7.

[Stoll, 1963] R. R. Stoll. *Set Theory and Logic*. San Fransisco, Calif.: W.H. Freeman, 1963.

[Stonebraker, 1975] M. Stonebraker. Implementation of Integrity Constraints and Views by Query Modification. In *Proc. ACM SIGMOD Int. Conf. on Management of Data*, May 1975, pp. 65--78.

[Stonebraker, 1981] M. Stonebraker. Operating System Support for Database Management. *Commun. ACM* (July 1981), 24(7): 412--418.

[Stonebraker, 1986] M. Stonebraker. The Case for Shared Nothing. *IEEE Q. Bull. Database Eng.* (March 1986), 9(1): 4--9.

[Stonebraker and Brown, 1999] M. Stonebraker and P. Brown. *Object-Relational DBMSs, 2nd edition*, San Fransisco, CA: Morgan Kaufmann, 1999.

[Stonebraker and Neuhold, 1977] M. Stonebraker and E. Neuhold. A Distributed Database Version of INGRES. In *Proc. 2nd Berkeley Workshop on Distributed Data Management and Computer Networks*, May 1977, pp. 9--36.

[Stonebraker et al., 1976] M. Stonebraker, P. Kreps, W. Wong, and G. Held. The Design and Implementation of INGRES. *ACM Trans. Database Syst.* (September 1976), 1(3): 198--222.

[Stonebraker et al., 1983b] M. Stonebraker, B. Rubenstein and A. Guttman. Application of Abstract Data Types and Abstract Indices to CAD Databases. In *Proc. Annual Meeting Database Week*, May 1983, pp. 107--115. Also in M. Stonebraker (ed.). *The INGRES Papers: Anatomy of a Relational Database System*. Reading, Mass.: Addison-Wesley, 1986, pp. 317--333.

[Stonebraker et al., 1990a] M. Stonebraker, L.A. Rowe, B. Lindsay, J. Gray, M. Carey, M. Brodie, P. Bernstein, and D. Beech. Third-Generation Data Base System Manifesto. *ACM SIGMOD Record* (September 1990), 19(3): 31--44.

[Stratus, 1982] Stratus Computers. *Stratus/32 System Overview*. Natick, Mass: Stratus, 1982.

[Straube and Özsu, 1990a] D.D. Straube and M.T. Özsu. Queries and Query Processing in Object-Oriented Database Systems. *ACM Trans. Inf. Syst.* (October 1990), 8(4):387--430.

[Straube and Özsu, 1990b] D.D. Straube and M.T. Özsu. Type Consistency of Queries in an Object-Oriented Database, In *Proc. Joint ACM OOPSLA/ECOOP '90 Conference on Object-Oriented Programming: Systems, Languages and Applications*, October 1990, pp. 224--233.

[Straube and Özsu, 1995] D.D. Straube and M.T. Özsu. Query Optimization and Execution Plan Generation in Object-Oriented Database Systems. *IEEE Trans. Knowledge and Data Eng.* (April 1995), 7(2): 210--227.

[Strong and Dolev, 1983] H. R. Strong and D. Dolev. Byzantine Agreement. In *Digest of Papers --- COMPCON*, San Francisco, Calif., March 1983, pp. 77--81.

[Stroustrup, 1986] B. Stroustrup. *The C++ Programming Language*. Reading, Mass.: Addison--Wesley, 1986.

[Su, 1988] S. Y. W. Su. *Database Computers: Principles, Architectures and Techniques*. New York: McGraw-Hill, 1988.

[Suciu, 1997] D. Suciu. Management of Semistructured Data. *ACM SIGMOD Record* (December 1997), 26(4): 4--7.

[Sugihara, 1987] K. Sugihara. Concurrency Control Based on Cycle Detection. In *Proc. 3rd Int. Conf. on Data Engineering*, February 1987, pp. 267--274.

[Swami, 1989] A. Swami. Optimization of Large Join Queries: combining heuristics and combinatorial techniques. In *Proc. ACM SIGMOD Int. Conf. on Management of Data*, June 1989, pp. 367--376.

[Tandem, 1987] The Tandem Database Group. NonStop SQL -- A Distributed High-Performance, High-Availability Implementation of SQL. In *Proc. Int. Workshop on High Performance Transaction Systems*, September 1987. pp. 60--104.

[Tandem, 1988] The Tandem Performance Group. A Benchmark of NonStop SQL on the Debit Credit Transaction. In *Proc. ACM SIGMOD Int. Conf. on Management of Data*, June 1988, pp. 337--341.

[Tanenbaum, 1997] A. S. Tanenbaum. *Computer Networks* (3rd edition). Englewood Cliffs, N.J.: Prentice-Hall, 1997.

[Tanenbaum and van Renesse, 1985] A. S. Tanenbaum and R. van Renesse. Distributed Operating Systems. *ACM Comput. Surv.* (December 1985), 17(4): 419--470.

[Tanenbaum and van Renesse, 1988] A. S. Tanenbaum and R. van Renesse. Voting with Ghosts. In *Proc. 8th Int. Conf. on Distributed Computing Systems*, June 1988, pp. 456-461.

[Taylor, 1987] R. W. Taylor. Data Server Architectures: Experiences and Lessons. In *Proc. CIPS (Canadian Information Processing Society) Edmonton '87 Conf.*, 1987, pp. 334--342.

[Taylor and Frank, 1976] R. W. Taylor and R. L. Frank. CODASYL Data-Base Management Systems. *ACM Comput. Surv.* (March 1976), 8(1): 67--103.

[Templeton et al., 1987] M. Templeton, D. Brill, S. K. Dao, E. Lund, P. Ward, A. L. P. Chen, and R. MacGregor. Mermaid -- A Front-End to Distributed Heterogeneous Databases. *Proc. IEEE* (May 1987), 75(5): 695--708.

[Thakkar and Sweiger, 1990] S. S. Thakkar and M. Sweiger. Performance of an OLTP Application on Symmetry Multiprocessor System. In *Proc. 17th Int. Symposium on Computer Architecture*, May 1990, pp. 228--238.

[Thomas, 1979] R. H. Thomas. A Majority Consensus Approach to Concurrency Control for Multiple Copy Databases. *ACM Trans. Database Syst.* (June 1979), 4(2): 180--209.

[Thomasian, 1993] A. Thomasian. Two-Phase Locking and its Thrashing Behavior. *ACM Trnas. Database Syst.* (December 1993), 18(4): 579--625.

[Thomasian, 1996] A. Thomasian. *Database Concurrency Control: Methods, Performance, and Analysis*, Boston, MA: Kluwer Academic Publishers, 1996.

[Thomasian, 1998] A. Thomasian. Distributed Optimistic Concurrency Control Methods for High Performance Transaction Processing. *IEEE Trans. Data and Knowl. Eng.* (January/February 1998), 10(1): 173--189.

[Tomasic et al., 1997] A. Tomasic, R. Amouroux, P. Bonnet, O. Kapitskaia, H. Naacke and L. Raschid. The Distributed Information Search Component (DISCO) and the World-Wide Web -- Prototype Demonstration. In *Proc. ACM SIGMOD Int. Conf. on Management of Data*, May 1997, pp. 546--548.

[Tomasic et al., 1998] A. Tomasic, L. Raschid, and P. Valduriez. Scaling Access to Distributed Heterogeneous Data Sources with Disco. In *IEEE Trans. Knowl. and Data Eng.* (1998), in press.

[Tork Roth and Schwarz, 1997] M. Tork Roth and P. Schwarz. Don't Scrap It, Wrap It! A Wrapper Architecture for Legacy Data Sources. In *Proc. 23rd Int. Conf. on Very Large Data Bases*, September 1997, pp. 266--275.

[Traiger et al., 1982] I. L. Traiger, J. Gray, C. A. Galtieri, and B. G. Lindsay. Transactions and Recovery in Distributed Database Systems. *ACM Trans. Database Syst.* (September 1982), 7(3): 323--342.

[Triantafillou and Taylor, 1995] P. Triantafillou and D. J. Taylor. The Location-Based Paradigm for Replication: Achieving Efficiency and Availability in Distributed Systems. *IEEE Trans. Software Eng.* (January 1995), 21(1): 1--18.

[Tsichritzis and Klug, 1978] D. Tsichritzis and A. Klug. The ANSI/X3/SPARC DBMS Framework Report of the Study Group on Database Management Systems. *Inf. Syst.* (1978), 1: 173--191.

[Tsichritzis and Lochovsky, 1976] D. C. Tsichritzis and F. H. Lochovsky. Hierarchical Data-Base Management: A Survey. *ACM Comput. Surv.* (March 1976), 8(1): 105--123.

[Tsichritzis and Lochovsky, 1977] D. C. Tsichritzis and F. H. Lochovsky. *Data Base Management Systems.* New York: Academic Press, 1977.

[Tsichritzis and Lochovsky, 1981] D. C. Tsichritzis and F. H. Lochovsky. *Data Models.* Englewood Cliffs, N.J.: Prentice-Hall, 1981.

[Tsuchiya et al., 1986] M. Tsuchiya, M. P. Mariani, and J. D. Brom. Distributed Database Management Model and Validation. *IEEE Trans. Software Eng.* (April 1986), SE-12(4): 511--520.

[Ullman, 1982] J. D. Ullman. *Principles of Database Systems* (2nd edition). Rockville, Md.: Computer Science Press, 1982.

[Ullman, 1988] J. D. Ullman. *Principles of Database and Knowledge Base Systems*, Volume 1. Rockville, Md.: Computer Science Press, 1988.

[Ullman, 1997] J. Ullman. Information Integration using Logical Views. In *Proc. 6th Int. Conf. on Database Theory*, Vol. 1186 of Lecture Notes in Computer Science, Springer-Verlag, January 1997, pp. 19--40.

[Valduriez, 1982] P. Valduriez. Semi-Join Algorithms for Distributed Database Machines. In J.-J. Schneider (ed.), *Distributed Data Bases*, Amsterdam: North-Holland, 1982, pp. 23--37.

[Valduriez, 1986] P. Valduriez. Optimization of Complex Queries Using Join Indices. *IEEE Q. Bull. Database Eng.* (December 1986), 9(4): 10--16.

[Valduriez, 1987] P. Valduriez. Join Indices. *ACM Trans. Database Syst.* (June 1987), 12(2): 218--246.

[Valduriez, 1992] P. Valduriez. Parallel Database Systems: Open Problems and New Issues. *Distributed and Parallel Databases* (1993), 1: 137-165.

[Valduriez and Boral, 1986] P. Valduriez and H. Boral. Evaluation of Recursive Queries Using Join Indices. In *Proc. First Int. Conf. on Expert Database Systems*, 1986, pp. 197--208.

[Valduriez and Gardarin, 1984] P. Valduriez and G. Gardarin. Join and Semi-join Algorithms for a Multi Processor Database Machine. *ACM Trans. Database Syst.* (March 1984), 9(1): 133--161.

[Valduriez and Gardarin, 1989] P. Valduriez and G. Gardarin. *Analysis and Comparison of Relational Database Systems.* Reading, Mass.: Addison-Wesley, 1989.

[Valduriez et al., 1986] P. Valduriez, S. Khoshafian, and G. Copeland. Implementation Techniques of Complex Objects. In *Proc. 11th Int. Conf. on Very Large Databases*, August 1986, pp. 101--109.

[Varadarajan et al., 1989] R. Varadarajan, P.I. Rivera-Vega, and S. B. Navathe. Data Redistribution Scheduling in Fully Connected Networks. In *Proc. 27th Annual Allerton Conf. on Communication, Control, and Computing*, September 1989.

[Verhofstadt, 1978] J. S. Verhofstadt. Recovery Techniques for Database Systems. *ACM Comput. Surv.* (June 1978), 10(2): 168--195.

[Vermeer, 1997] M. Vermeer. *Semantic Interoperability for Legacy Databases*, Ph.D. thesis, Enschede, Netherlands: Department of Computer Science, University of Twente, 1997.

[Wah and Lien, 1985] B. W. Wah and Y. N. Lien. Design of Distributed Databases on Local Computer Systems. *IEEE Trans. Software Eng.* (July 1985), SE-11(7): 609--619.

[Walborn and Chrysanthis, 1995] D. G. Walborn, and P. Chrysanthis. Supporting Semantics Based Transaction Processing in Mobile Database Applications. In *Proc. 14th IEEE Symp. on Reliable Distributed Systems*, September 1995, pp. 31--40.

[Walton et al., 1991] C.B. Walton, A.G. Dale, and R.M. Jenevin. A taxonomy and Performance Model of Data Skew Effects in Parallel Joins. *Proc. 17th Int. Conf. on Very Large Data Bases*, September 1991, pp. 537--548.

[Wang and Rowe, 1991] Y. Wang and L. Rowe. Cache Consistency and Concurrency Control in a Client/Server DBMS Architecture. In *Proc. ACM SIGMOD Int. Conf. on Management of Data*, May 1991, pp. 367--376.

[Weihl, 1988] W. Weihl. Commutativity-Based Concurrency Control for Abstract Data Types. *IEEE Trans. Comput.* (December 1988), C-37(12): 1488--1505.

[Weihl, 1989] W. Weihl. Local Atomicity Properties: Modular Concurrency Control for Abstract Data Types. *ACM Trans. Prog. Lang. Syst.* (April 1989), 11(2): 249--281.

[Weikum, 1986] G. Weikum. Pros and Cons of Operating System Transactions for Data Base Systems. In *Proc. Fall Joint Computer Conf.*,1986, pp. 1219--1225.

[Weikum, 1991] G. Weikum. Principles and Realization Strategies of Multilevel Transaction Management. *ACM Trans. on Database Syst.* (March 1991), 16(1):132--180.

[Weikum and Hasse, 1993] G. Weikum and C. Hasse. Multi-Level Transaction Management for Complex Objects: Implementation, Performance, Parallelism. *The VLDB Journal* (October 1993), 2(4):407--454.

[Weikum and Schek, 1984] G. Weikum and H.-J. Schek. Architectural Issues of Transaction Management in Layered Systems. In *Proc. 10th Int. Conf. on Very Large Databases*, 1984, pp. 454--465.

[Wells et al., 1992] D. Wells, J. Blakeley, and C. Thompson. Architecture of an Open Object-Oriented Database Management System. *Computer* (October 1992), 25(10): 74--82.

[White and DeWitt, 1994] S. White and D. DeWitt. QuickStore: A High Performance Mapped Object Store. In *Proc. 18th Int. Conf. on Very Large Data Bases*, August 1992, pp. 419--431.

[Widom, 1995] J. Widom. Research Problems in Data Warehousing. In *Proc. 4th Int. Conf. on Information and Knowledge Management*, November 1995, pp. 25--30.

[Wiederhold, 1982] G. Wiederhold. *Database Design* (2nd edition). New York: McGraw-Hill, 1982.

[Wilkinson and Neimat, 1990] K. Wilkinson and M. Neimat. Maintaining Consistency of Client-Cached Data. In *Proc. 16th Int. Conf. on Very Large Data Bases*, August 1990, pp. 122--133.

[Williams et al., 1982] R. Williams, D. Daniels, L. Haas, G. Lapis, B. Lindsay, P. Ng, R. Obermarck, P. Selinger, A. Walker, P. Wilms, and R. Yost. R*: An Overview of the Architecture. In *Proc. 2nd Int. Conf. on Databases*, June 1982, pp. 1--28.

[Wilms and Lindsay, 1981] P. F. Wilms and B. G. Lindsay. *A Database Authorization Mechanism Supporting Individual and Group Authorization*. Research Report RJ 3137, San Jose, Calif.: IBM Research Laboratory, May 1981.

[Wilshut et al., 1992] A. N. Wilshut and P.G Apers. Parallelism in a Main-Memory System: The Performance of PRISMA/DB. In *Proc. 22th Int. Conf. on Very Large Data Bases*, August 1992, pp. 23--27.

[Wilshut et al., 1995] A. N. Wilshut, J. Flokstra, and P.G Apers. Parallel Evaluation of Multi-join Queries. *Proc. ACM SIGMOD Int. Conf. on Management of Data*, May 1995, pp. 115--126.

[Wilson and Navathe, 1986] B. Wilson and S. Navathe. An Analytical Framework for the Redesign of Distributed Databases. In *Proc. 6th Advanced Database Symposium*, 1986, pp. 77--83.

[Wolf et al., 1979] J. L. Wolf, M. T. Liu, B. W. Weide and D. P. Tsay. Design of a Distributed Fault-Tolerant Loop Network. In *Proc. 9th Int. Symp. on Fault-Tolerant Computing Systems*, 1979, pp. 17--23.

[Wolf et al., 1993] J. L. Wolf, D.M. Dias, S. Yu and J. Turek. Algorithms for Parallelizing Relational Database Joins in the Presence of Data Skew. Research Report RC19236 (83710), Yorktown Heights, NY: IBM Research Division (Watson Research Center), October 1993.

[Wolfson, 1987] O. Wolfson. The Overhead of Locking (and Commit) Protocols in Distributed Databases. *ACM Trans. Database Syst.* (September 1987), 12(3): 453--471.

[Wolski and Veijelainen, 1990] A. Wolski and J. Veijalainen: 2PC Agent Method: Achieving Serializability in Presence of Failures in a Heterogeneous Multidatabase. In *Proc. 1st Int. Conf. on Databases, Parallel Architectures and Their Applications*, 1990, pp. 268--287.

[Wong, 1977] E. Wong. Retrieving Dispersed Data from SDD-1. In *Proc. 2nd Berkeley Workshop on Distributed Data Management and Computer Networks*, 1977, pp. 217--235.

[Wong, 1988] J. Wong. Broadcast Delivery. *Proc. IEEE* (1988), 76(12): 1566--1577.

[Wong and Bazek, 1985] K. K. Wong and P. Bazek. MRDSM: A Relational Multidatabase Management System. In F. A. Schreiber and W. Litwin (eds.), *Distributed Data Sharing Systems*, Amsterdam: North-Holland, 1985, pp. 77--85.

[Wong and Youssefi, 1976] E. Wong and K. Youssefi. Decomposition: A Strategy for Query Processing. *ACM Trans. Database Syst.* (September 1976), 1(3): 223--241.

[Wright, 1983] D. D. Wright. *Managing Distributed Databases in Partitioned Networks*. Technical Report TR83-572, Ithaca, N.Y.: Department of Computer Science, Cornell University, September 1983.

[Wu et al., 1997] K-L. Wu, P.S. Yu, and C. Pu. Divergence Control Algorithms for Epsilon Serializability. *IEEE Trans. Knowledge and Data Eng.* (March-April 1997), 9(2): 262--274.

[Yan, 1997] L. L. Yan. Towards Efficient and Scalable Mediation: The AURORA Approach. In *Proc. IBM CASCON Conference*, November 1997, pp. 15--29.

[Yan et al., 1997] L.L. Yan, M.T. Özsu, L. Liu. Accessing Heterogeneous Data Through Homogenization and Integration Mediators. In *Proc. 2nd Int. Conf. on Cooperative Information Systems* (CoopIS'97), June 1997, pp. 130--139.

[Yao et al., 1982a] S. B. Yao, S. B. Navathe, and J-L. Weldon. An Integrated Approach to Database Design. In *Data Base Design Techniques I: Requirements and Logical Structures*, Lecture Notes in Computer Science 132, New York: Springer-Verlag, 1982, pp. 1--30.

[Yao et al., 1982b] S. B. Yao, V. Waddle and B. Housel. View Modeling and Integration Using the Functional Data Model. *IEEE Trans. Software Eng.* (November 1982), SE-8(6): 544--554.

[Yeager, 1987] D. A. Yeager. 5ESS^{TM} Switch Performance Metrics. In *Proc. Int. Conf. on Communications, Volume 1*, June 1987, pp. 46--52.

[Yeo and Zaslavsky, 1994] L.H. Yeo and A. Zaslavsky. Submission of Transactions from Mobile Workstations in a Cooperative Multidatabase Processing Environment. In *Proc. 14th Int. Conf. on Distributed Computing Systems*, 1994, pp. 372--379.

[Yeung and Hung, 1995] C. Yeung and S. Hung. A New Deadlock Detection Algorithm for Distributed Real-Time Database Systems. In *Proc. 14th Int. Symp. Reliable Distributed Systems*, September 1995, pp. 146--153.

[Yong et al., 1994] V. Yong, J. Naughton, and J. Yu. Storage Reclamation and Reorganization in Client-Server Persistent Object Stores. In *Proc. 10th Int. Conf. on Data Engineering*, Houston, February 1994, pp. 120--133.

[Yormark, 1977] B. Yormark. The ANSI/SPARC/DBMS Architecture. In D. A. Jardine (ed.), *ANSI/SPARC DBMS Model*,Amsterdam: North-Holland, 1977, pp. 1--21.

[Yoshida et al., 1985] M. Yoshida, K. Mizumachi, A. Wakino, I. Oyake, and Y. Matsushita. Time and Cost Evaluation Schemes of Multiple Copies of Data in Distributed Database Systems. *IEEE Trans. Software Eng.* (September 1985), SE-11(9): 954--958.

[Yu and Chang, 1984] C. T. Yu and C. C. Chang. Distributed Query Processing. *ACM Comput. Surveys* (December 1984), 16(4): 399--433.

[Yu and Meng, 1998] C. Yu and W. Meng. *Principles of Query Processing for Advanced Database Applictions*, San Francisco: Morgan Kaufmann, 1998.

[Yu et al., 1989] P. S. Yu, D. Cornell, D. M. Dias, and A. Thomasian. Performance Comparison of the IO Shipping and Database Call Shipping Schemes in Multi-system Partitioned Database Systems. *Performance Evaluation* (1989), 10: 15--33.

[Zaniolo, 1983] C. Zaniolo. The Database Language GEM. In *Proc. ACM SIGMOD Int. Conf. on Management of Data*, May 1983, pp. 207--218.

[Zdonik and Maier, 1990] S. Zdonik and D. Maier (eds.). *Readings in Object-Oriented Database Systems*. San Mateo, Calif.: Morgan Kaufmann, 1990.

[Zhu and Larson, 1996a] Q. Zhu and P.A. Larson. Developing Regression Cost Models for Multidatabase Systems. In *Proc. 4th Int. Conf. on Parallel and Distributed Information Systems (PDIS)*, December 1996, pp.220--231.

[Zhu and Larson, 1996b] Q. Zhu and P.A. Larson. Global Query Processing and Optimization in the CORDS Multidatabase System. In *Proc. 9th Int. Conf. on Parallel and Distributed Computing Systems (PDCS)*, September 1996, pp. 640--647.

[Zhu and Larson, 1998] Q. Zhu and P.A. Larson. Solving Local Cost Estimation Problem for Global Query Optimization in Multidatabase Systems. *Distributed and Parallel Databases* (October 1998), 6(4): 373--420.

[Zhu and Larson, 1998] Q. Zhu and P.A. Larson. A Query Sampling Method of Estimating Local Cost Parameters in a Multidatabase System. In *Proc. 10th International Conference on Data Engineering*, February 1994, pp. 144--153.

[Ziane et al., 1993] M. Ziane, M. Zaït, and P. Borla-Salamet. Parallel Query Processing with Zigzag Trees. *The VLDB Journal* (July 1993), 2(3): 277--301.

[Zloof, 1977] M. M. Zloof. Query-by-Example: A Data Base Language. *IBM Syst. J.* (1977), 16(4): 324--343.

[Zobel, 1983] D. D. Zobel. The Deadlock Problem: A Classifying Bibliography. *ACM Oper. Syst. Rev.* (October 1983), 17(2): 6--15.

SUBJECT INDEX